COMPUTER GRAPHICS

Volume 19 • Number 3 • July 1985
A quarterly report of ACM SIGGRAPH
Production Editor John C. Beatty

SIGGRAPH '85 Conference Proceedings
July 22-26, 1985, San Francisco, California
Edited by Brian A. Barsky

Sponsored by the Association for Computing Machinery's
Special Interest Group on Computer Graphics

The Association for Computing Machinery, Inc.
11 West 42nd Street
New York, New York 10036

ISBN 0-89791-166-0

SIGGRAPH '85 is sponsored by the Association for Computing Machinery's Special Interest Group on Computer Graphics in cooperation with IEEE Technical Committee on Computer Graphics and Eurographics.

Additional copies may be ordered prepaid from:
ACM Order Department
P.O. Box 64145
Baltimore, MD 21264
ACM Order Number: 428850

Price:
Members: $30.00
All Others: $40.00

Manufactured By K Graphics, Inc.

Printed in the U.S.A.

Contents

Preface 7
Conference Committee 9
Exhibitors 11

Wednesday, 24 July 1985

9:00-10:30 **Opening Session**

ACM / SIGGRAPH '85 Welcome
Pat Cole, Robert L. Heilman

ACM / SIGGRAPH Report

1985 ACM / SIGGRAPH Awards 13

10:45-12:15 **Reflectance Models**
Chair: Norman I. Badler

Anisotropic Reflection Models 15
James T. Kajiya

Continuous Tone Representation of Three-Dimensional Objects Taking Account of Shadows and Interreflection 23
Tomoyuki Nishita, Eihachiro Nakamae

The Hemi-Cube: a Radiosity Solution for Complex Environments 31
Michael F. Cohen, Donald P. Greenberg

1:45- 3:15 **Rendering Techniques**
Chair: Henry Fuchs

Compositing 3-D Rendered Images 41
Tom Duff

Bounding Ellipsoids for Ray-Fractal Intersection 45
Christian Bouville

Efficient Alias-Free Rendering Using Bit-Masks and Look-Up Tables 53
Greg Abram, Lee Westover, Turner Whitted

3:30- 5:00 **Sampling and Filtering**
Chair: Franklin C. Crow

Statistically Optimized Sampling for Distributed Ray Tracing 61
Mark E. Lee, Richard A. Redner, Samuel P. Uselton

Antialiasing Through Stochastic Sampling 69
Mark A. Z. Dippé, Erling Henry Wold

Integrated Analytic Spatial and Temporal Antialiasing for Polyhedra in 4-Space 79
Charles W. Grant

A Two-and-a-Half-D Motion-Blur Algorithm 85
Nelson L. Max, Douglas M. Lerner

Thursday, 25 July 1985

9:00-10:30 **Hardware**
Chair: J. Nick England

Fast Image Generation of Constructive Solid Geometry Using a Cellular Array Processor ... 95
Hiroyuki Sato, Mitsuo Ishii, Keiji Sato, Morio Ikesaka, Hiroaki Ishihata, Masanori Kakimoto, Katsuhiko Hirota, Kouichi Inoue

The Drawing Prism: A Versatile Graphic Input Device ... 103
Richard Greene

Fast Spheres, Shadows, Textures, Transparencies, and Image Enhancements in Pixel-Planes ... 111
Henry Fuchs, Jack Goldfeather, Jeff P. Hultquist, Susan Spach, John D. Austin, Frederick P. Brooks, Jr., John G. Eyles, John Poulton

10:45-12:15 **Geometric Modeling**
Chair: A. Robin Forrest

Bintrees, CSG Trees, and Time ... 121
Hanan Samet, Markku Tamminen

Geometric Modeling of Solid Objects by Using a Face Adjacency Graph Representation ... 131
Silvia Ansaldi, Leila De Floriani, Bianca Falcidieno

A Unified Approach to Interference Problems Using a Triangle Processor ... 141
Fujio Yamaguchi

1:45- 3:15 **Curves and Surfaces**
Chair: Jeffrey Lane

Techniques for Conic Splines ... 151
Vaughan Pratt

Blend Surfaces for Set Theoretic Volume Modeling Systems ... 161
Alan E. Middleditch, Kenneth H. Sears

On Ray Tracing Parametric Surfaces ... 171
Daniel L. Toth

3:30- 5:00 **User Interface Management Systems**
Chair: R. Daniel Bergeron

There's More to Menu Systems than Meets the Screen ... 181
Henry Lieberman

Input/Output Linkage in a User Interface Management System ... 191
Dan R. Olsen, Jr., Elizabeth P. Dempsey, Roy Rogge

Squeak: a Language for Communicating with Mice ... 199
Luca Cardelli, Rob Pike

The University of Alberta User Interface Management System ... 205
Mark Green

Friday, 26 July 1985

9:00-10:30 **Input and Drawing Techniques**
Chair: Marceli Wein

Issues and Techniques in Touch-Sensitive Tablet Input 215
William Buxton, Ralph Hill, Peter Rowley

An Automatic Beautifier for Drawings and Illustrations 225
Theo Pavlidis, Christopher J. Van Wyk

Juno, a Constraint-Based Graphics System 235
Greg Nelson

10:45-12:15 **Animation**
Chair: Edwin E. Catmull

Animating Rotation with Quaternion Curves 245
Ken Shoemake

Parametric Keyframe Interpolation Incorporating Kinetic Adjustment and Phrasing Control 255
Scott N. Steketee, Norman I. Badler

Computational Modeling for the Computer Animation of Legged Figures 263
Michael Girard, Anthony A. Maciejewski

1:45- 3:15 **Texture and Patterns**
Chair: James T. Kajiya

Construction of Fractal Objects with Iterated Function Systems 271
Stephen Demko, Laurie Hodges, Bruce Naylor

Solid Texturing of Complex Surfaces 279
Darwyn R. Peachey

An Image Synthesizer 287
Ken Perlin

3:30- 5:00 **Natural Phenomena**
Chair: Alain Fournier

Visual Simulation of Clouds 297
Geoffrey Y. Gardner

Modeling the Mighty Maple 305
Jules Bloomenthal

Approximate and Probabilistic Algorithms for Shading and Rendering Structured Particle Systems 313
William T. Reeves, Ricki Blau

Panels

Wednesday, 24 July 1985

10:45-12:15 **Perspective - Computer Graphics in Europe and Japan** 323
Chairs: Jose Encarnacao, Tosiyasu L. Kunii
Moderator: Bertram Herzog
Panelists: Frank Lillehagen, Xavier Nicolas, Yukari Shirota, Wolfgang Strasser, Shunichiro Tsurumi, Takao Wachi

1:45- 3:15 **Issues at the Interface: an Historical Trace of Prompting, Concurrency, Signification and Ease of Use** 324
Chair: Robert M. Dunn
Panelists: Sara Bly, Richard Guedj, William J. Poduska, William Lasser

3:30- 5:00 **Sizing the Market: Where Do All Those Numbers Come From?** 324
Chair: Carl Machover
Panelists: Charles Foundyller, Robert H. Katzive, Neil Kleinman, Christopher M. Saleh, Beth Tucker

Thursday, 25 July 1985

9:00-10:30 **Animated Computer Graphics in Television Broadcasting** 325
Chairs: Christine Barton, Carl Rosendahl
Panelists: Robert Brandel, Larry Elin, Susan Rugtiv, Douglas Towey

10:45-12:15 **Font Formats** 325
Chair: Charles Bigelow
Panelists: Philippe Coueignoux, John Hobby, Peter Karow, Vaughn Pratt, Luis Trabb-Pardo, John Warnock

1:45- 3:15 **Aesthetics of Computer Graphics** 326
Chair: Mihai Nadin
Panelists: Charles Csuri, Frank Dietrich, Thomas Linehan, Hiroshi Kawano

3:30- 5:00 **The Creation of New Kinds of Interactive Environments in Art, Education, and Entertainment** 326
Chair: Stephen Wilson
Panelists: David Backer, Myron Krueger, Peter Richards, Sonia Sheridan, David Ucko

Friday, 26 July 1985

9:00-10:30 **Real-Time Simulation in the Real World** 327
Chair: Zsuzsanna Molnar
Panelists: Pieter Buning, Peter Doenges, Robert Langridge, Tom Lasinski, Randy Smith

10:45-12:15 **Fundamental Algorithms: Retrospect and Prospect** 327
Chair: Rae A. Earnshaw
Panelists: James H. Clark, A. Robin Forrest, Robert D. Parslow, David F. Rogers

1:45- 3:15 **Computer Graphics Technology** 328
Chair: John Staudhammer
Panelists: Dean Bailey, Steven Dines, Louis J. Doctor, Karl Guttag, Jack L. Hancock, Klaus W. Lindenberg, Edmund Y. Sun

3:30- 5:00 **Solid Modeling With Hardware** 328
Chair: Pierre J. Malraison
Panelists: Gershon Kedem, Greg Lee, Donald Meagher

Author Index 331
Image Credits 332

Preface

Welcome to SIGGRAPH'85 – the Twelfth Annual Conference on Computer Graphics and Interactive Techniques. The conference is being held 22-26 July 1985 in San Francisco, California. These proceedings contain full papers corresponding to the oral presentations given in the technical program of the conference and are being published as a special issue of *Computer Graphics*. This year's technical program is of the utmost quality thanks to an unprecedented number of submissions. A total of 175 papers were submitted, a jump of approximately 50% over previous years. Of these, only 35 articles were accepted – a mere 20% of the submissions. The task of paper selection was performed by the Technical Program Committee.

The reviewing process began when papers were submitted in response to a call for participation. Immediately after the submission deadline, the papers were divided among the Technical Program Committee. Each paper was allocated to one committee member; a special effort was made to give each committee member a set of papers whose subject areas closely matched his area of expertise. Although this resulted in an uneven distribution, the members with a large number of papers all agreed to handle the additional workload. This procedure resulted in an improved reviewing process.

To enhance the reliability of this step, I solicited the help of two committee members, Norm Badler and Ed Catmull, in dividing up the papers. As a still further check on the process, each committee member was sent a complete list of all submitted papers so that he would be aware of submissions that were not allocated to him. This enabled each member to request a copy of any paper that was particularly appropriate to his area of expertise and to provide additional input on it.

Each committee member is a senior reviewer and was responsible both for reviewing each paper as well as for sending it to at least two other reviewers (usually outside the committee) for additional comments. Another new idea this year was the insistence that at least two of the reviewers be from institutions different from that of the committee member.

After assembling all the reviews, the Technical Program Committee met to select the papers on March 8 and 9. Due to the unexpected volume of submissions, the meeting had been extended to two days from the one day session that was originally planned. At the meeting, each paper was discussed, taking into account the reviews and any other information available to the committee. After two days of discussion, a technical program of 35 papers emerged which aptly portrays a snapshot of the best results in this rapidly maturing field.

The already tremendous task of paper selection was exacerbated by the huge number of submissions; consequently, the committee members and the reviewers that they selected must be commended for their extensive efforts. Their comments provide valuable feedback for improvement of both the accepted and rejected papers. The composition of the Technical Program Committee and a complete list of the reviewers appear in the next section.

I would like to express my appreciation to John Beatty and Bob Kushner, the production editor and printer, respectively, for these proceedings. The quality of the appearance of this document is due to them. Finally, I am grateful to my secretary, Lindy Foster, who did a superb job of keeping all the administrative details under control.

Brian A. Barsky
Technical Program Chairman
Editor

Conference Committee

CONFERENCE CO-CHAIRS

Pat Cole
Hewlett-Packard

Robert L. Heilman
Gould Inc.

CONFERENCE COMMITTEE CHAIRS

Karl Anderson, *Merchandise*
Independent

Michael Bailey, *Courses*
Purdue University

Brian A. Barsky, *Technical Program*
University of California at Berkeley

Susan Brennan, *Conference Editor*
Hewlett-Packard Labs

Robert L. Cook, *Film and Video Show*
Lucasfilm Ltd.

Louise R. Etra, *Art Show*
Independent

John E. French, Jr., *User Groups*
Exxon Production Research Co.

Cheryl Landman, *Publicity*
Seiko Instruments

Andy Goodrich, *Volunteer Coordinator*
Ramtek

Gaye L. Graves, *Speaker Slide Coordinator*
NASA/Ames Research Center

Randy Nickel, *Exhibits*
Independent

Bertram Herzog, *Panels*
Herzog Associates, Inc.

Gregory MacNicol, *Slide Sets*
Digital Design

Adele Newton, *Registration*
University of Waterloo

Elaine L. Sonderegger, *Treasurer*
Independent

TECHNICAL PROGRAM COMMITTEE

Russell J. Athay (Evans and Sutherland Computer Corp.)
Norman I. Badler (University of Pennsylvania)
Brian A. Barsky, *Chair* (University of California, Berkeley)
John C. Beatty (University of Waterloo)
R. Daniel Bergeron (University of New Hampshire)
Edwin E. Catmull (Lucasfilm Ltd.)
Franklin C. Crow (Xerox PARC)
Nick England (Adage, Inc.)
David C. Evans (Evans and Sutherland Computer Corp.)
James D. Foley (George Washington University)
A. Robin Forrest (University of East Anglia)
Alain Fournier (University of Toronto)
Henry Fuchs (University of North Carolina, Chapel Hill)
James T. Kajiya (California Institute of Technology)
Jeffrey M. Lane (Daisy Systems Corp.)
James C. Michener (Apollo Computer, Inc.)
Richard F. Riesenfeld (University of Utah)
Marceli Wein (National Research Council of Canada)

TECHNICAL PROGRAM REVIEWERS

John Amanatides
Norman Angerhofer
Peter R. Atherton
Ron Baecker
R.E. Barnhill
Al Barr
Richard Bartels
Ronen Barzel
Jürgen Bettels
Gary Bishop
Terry Bleser
Jim Blinn
Sara Bly
Chuck Bohling
Kellogg S. Booth
I.C. Braid
Bruce Brown
Maxine Brown
Jean Brouwers
Bob Burton
Bill Buxton
Tom Calvert
Ingrid Carlbom
Loren Carpenter
Steve Carson
Ed Catmull
Richard Cheng
Hank Christiansen
Alan Cline
Jim Cobb
Elaine Cohen
Ephraim Cohen
Rob Cook
William Cowan
M.G. Cox
Andy Davidson
Robert Demb
Patty Denbrook
A. de Pennington
Persi Diaconis
Mark Dippé
David Dobkin
Brian Donahue
Steve Duepner
Tom Duff
Rae Earnshaw
Glenn Entis
Steve Feiner
Tom Ferrin
Russ Fish
Eugene Fiume
R. Franke
Wm. Randolph Franklin
Don Fussell
Bob Futrelle
Steven Gabriel
Morven Gentleman
Ziv Gigus
Andrew S. Glassner
Sakunthala Gnanamgari
Ron Goldman
Julian Gomez
David Gorgen
Tamar Granor
Mark Green
Don Greenberg
Leo J. Guibas
Pat Hanrahan
Paul Heckbert
Randy Heiland
Michael Herman
Terry Higgins
A. Hlady
Dave Hurley
Dave Kasik
George Kedem
Gershon Kedem
Ashok Khosla
Victor Klassen
I. Michele Klucewicz
Lew Knapp
Doris Kochanek
Hal Lane
Sam Leffler
Paul MacDougal
Robert Magedson
Nadia Magnenat-Thalmann
Robert Marchot
Aaron Marcus
Rudi Mathon
Gary W. Meyer
Jim Miller
Don P. Mitchell
Jeff Mock
Fanya Montalvo
Delfin Montuno
Henry P. Moreton
Tim Mueller
David Myers
Emily Nagle
Sanjai Narain
Bruce Naylor
Martin Newell
Peter Nishimoto
Connie O'Dell
Dan Olsen
Alan W. Paeth
Theo J. Pavlidis
Ken Perlin
J. W. Peterson
Rob Pike
Mike Pique
Steve Platt
Tom Porter
Mike Potel
Michael Potmesil
John W. Poulton
Dick Puk

(TECHNICAL PROGRAM REVIEWERS, continued)

Marc Raibert
Michael Rarick
Bill Reeves
James Rhyne
Henry Rich
Alan Roberts
Gary Rogers
George Rogers
David S. H. Rosenthal
Randy Rost
M.A. Sabin
David Salesin
Kestudis Salkauskas
Peter Schoeler
Timothy Schreiner
Tom Sederberg
Chuck Seum
Kim L. Shelley
Stephen Shelley
Ken Shoemake
Alvy Ray Smith
Randy Smith
Dick Sonderegger
Elaine Sonderegger
Norman Soong
Richard Sowar
Rick Speer
Maureen Stone
David Sturman
Mike Sweeney
Peter Tanner
James Templeman
Daniel Thalmann
Bill Thibeault
Spencer W. Thomas
Ken Turkowski
Samuel P. Uselton
Tim Van Hook
Mitch Wade
Colin Ware
Van Warren
Jack Washam
Kevin Weiler
Richard Weinberg
J. Turner Whitted
Mary Whitton
Meredith Whyles
Jane Wilhelms
Lance Williams
Larry Yaeger
Morten Zachrisen
David Zeltzer

PANEL ADVISORY COMMITTEE

Mike Bailey (Purdue University)
Del Coates (San Jose State University)
Michael Dearing (University of Wisconsin)
Robert Ellis (G.E./Calma)
James E. George (Mesa Graphics)
David Luther (Visual Intelligence Corporation)
Carl Machover (Machover Associates, Inc.)
Zuzsanna Molnar (Silicon Graphics, Inc.)
Richard L. Phillips (University of Michigan)
Craig Reynolds (Symbolics Graphics Division)
Jane Veeder (Independent)

CONFERENCE PLANNING COMMITTEE

John C. Beatty (University of Waterloo)

Kellogg S. Booth (University of Waterloo)

Ingrid Carlbom (Schlumberger-Doll Research)

Pat Cole (Hewlett-Packard)

Kathy Eastman-Hinrichs (Tektronix, Inc.)

Raymond L. Elliott (Los Alamos National Laboratory)

Robert A. Ellis, *Chair* (Calma Company)

Ellen Gore (ISSCO)

Robert L. Heilman (Gould Inc.)

Richard Mueller (Control Data Corporation)

Richard A. Weinberg (Fifth Generation Graphics)

PROFESSIONAL SUPPORT

ACM Liaison
Jim Adams
Roberta Bukar

Art Show Administration
Rachel Carpenter

Aural/Visual Management
Video Research Consultants
David Balch
Mark Fausner
Jody Gillerman
Johnie Horn
Doris Kochanek
Phil Morton
Sally Rosenthal
Harland Snodgrass
Marilyn Wulff

Conference Coordinator
Dixie A. Quinlin

Conference Management
Smith Bucklin and Associates, Inc.
John Fetters
Ellen Frisbie
Shiela Hoffmeyer
Joy Lee
Cindy Stark

Courses Executive Assistant
Martha Schlegel
Purdue University

Decorator/Drayage
Bob Borsz
Betty Fuller
Ken Gallagher
Barby Patronski
John Patronski

Exhibition Management
Robert T. Kenworthy, Inc.
Robert T. Kenworthy
Hank Cronan
Barbara Voss

Film and Video Show Administration
Craig Good
Lucasfilm Ltd.

Graphic Design
Light FX
Richard Winn Taylor II
Lorraine Schweizer

Technical Program Administration
Lindy Foster
University of California, Berkeley

Exhibitors

Abekas Video Systems, Inc.
Abel Graphix
Adage, Inc.
Addison-Wesley Publishing
Advanced Color Technology, Inc.
Advanced Electronics Design, Inc. (AED)
Advanced Technology Center
Alias Research Corporation
AMF Logic Sciences, Inc.
Amtron Corporation
Analog Technology Corporation
Ann Arbor Terminals, Inc.
Antics Enterprises Inc.
Apollo Computer
Artronics/3M
AT&T Information Systems, Computer Systems Division
Auscom, Inc.
Autodesk, Inc.
Autographix, Inc.
AVL
AV Video (Montage Publishing)
Aztek, Inc.
Barco Industries, Inc.
Benson, Inc.
Robert Bosch Corporation, Video Equipment Division
Cadmus Computer Systems
CalComp
Calos Inc.
CASE Technology, Inc.
Ceegen Corporation
CELCO (Constantine Engineering Laboratories Co.)
Chartpak
Chorus Data Systems, Inc.
Chromatics Inc.
COHU Inc., Electronics Division
Commodore Business Machines
Computer-Aided Engineering
Computer Graphics Laboratories, Inc.
Computer Graphics Today
Computer Graphics World
Conrac Division, Conrac Corporation
Cray Research, Inc.
Crown Zellerbach, Electrographic Papers Division
CSP Inc.
Cubicomp Corporation
C. V. F. Computer Video Film
Daikin Industries Ltd.
Dalim
Datacube, Inc.
Datagraphic Systems
Dataplotting Services Inc.
dB Time
Design Technology
DICOMED Corporation
Digital Engineering, Inc.
Digital Equipment Corporation
Dubner Computer Systems, Inc.
Dunn Instruments
DYNAIR Electronics, Inc.
EAG Group
EDN Magazine
Eastman Kodak Company
EIKONIX Corporation
Electrohome Limited
Electronic Business
Electronic Cottage, Inc.
Elographics, Inc.
Enertronics Research, Inc.
Equitable Life Leasing Corporation
Evans & Sutherland Computer Corporation
Ferranti International Controls
Floating Point Systems, Inc.
Focus Graphics, Inc.
Frontier Technologies Corporation
FTG Data Systems
General Electric Company
General Parametrics Corporation
Genigraphics
GIXI Inc.
Gould Imaging & Graphics Division
Government Data Systems
Grafpoint
Graphic Controls Corporation
Graphic Devices, Inc.
GraphOn Corporation
GTCO Corporation
Gulton Industries Inc., Graphic Instruments Division
Hardcopy Magazine
Hewlett-Packard Company
Hitachi America Ltd.
Houston Instrument
Human Designed Systems, Inc.
Ibis Systems
ID Systems Corporation
IEEE Computer Society
Ikegami Electronics (U.S.A.), Inc.
Imaging Technology Incorporated
ImagiTex, Inc.
Imtec Equipment Inc.
I. N. A.
Inflight Services
Information Now
Inmos Corporation
Inovion Corporation
Intecolor, An Intelligent Systems Company
Interactive Machines, Inc.
International Imaging Systems
Iris Graphics, Inc.
Island Graphics Corporation
ISSCO
ITF (Images Transfert France)
C. Itoh Electronics, Inc.
Jupiter Systems, Inc.
JVC (Victor Company of Japan)
King Concept Corporation
Kloss Video Corporation
KMS Advanced Produc.., Inc.
KMW Systems Corporation

Kontron Electronics
Kurta Corporation
Laserus Productions, Inc.
Lexidata Corporation
Lucasfilm Ltd. (Pixar)
Lundy Electronics & Systems, Inc.
Lyon Lamb VAS, Inc
Machine Design
MASSCOMP
Matrix Instruments, Inc.
Matrox Electronic Systems Ltd.
McDonnell Douglas Corporation
MCI/Quantel (Micro Consultants, Inc.)
Measurement Systems Inc.
Megatek Corporation
MegaVision Inc.
Mercury Computer Systems, Inc.
Metheus Corporation
MicroTouch Systems, Inc.
Mini-Micro Systems
Minolta Corporation/Industrial Meter Division
Mitsubishi International Corporation
Mitsui & Co. (U.S.A.), Inc.
Moniterm Corporation
Monitronix Corporation
Multesoft
Multiwire Division
NEC Electronics, Inc.
New England Technology Group
New GEA Corporation
Nicolet's Computer Graphics Division
Nippon Gakki Co., Ltd.
N.I.S.E., Inc.
Nova Graphics International
Number Nine Computer Corp.
Numonics Corporation
OCLI
Omnicomp Graphics Corporation
Oxberry Div. of Richmark Camera Service, Inc.
Panasonic Industrial Company/Computer Components Division
Panasonic Industrial Company/PIC Communications Division
Parallax Graphics
Perceptics Corporation
Peritek Corporation
Perspective Technologies
Polaroid Corporation
Polhemus Navigation Sciences Division
Precision Visuals, Inc.
PrintaColor Corporation
Printronix, Inc.
PRIOR Data Sciences Ltd.
PRIVAC, Inc.
QMS, Inc. (Quality Micro Systems, Inc.)
Quintar Corporation
Qume Corporation
Ramtek Corporation
Raster Technologies, Inc.
Recognition Concepts, Inc.
Ridge Computers
Saber Technology Corporation
SAS Institue Inc.
Schoeller Technical Papers, Inc.
Scriptel Corporation
Seiko Instruments U.S.A., Inc.
Selanar Corporation
Silicon Graphics, Inc.
SlideTek Incorporated
Sogitec Audio Visual
Springer-Verlag New York Assn.
SPSS Inc.
Stereographics Corporation
Summagraphics Corporation
Sun Microsystems, Inc.
Symbolics Inc.
Systems Research Laboratories, Inc.
Talaris Systems Inc.
Tandberg Data, Inc.
TAT Graphics Group, Inc.
Tektronix, Inc.
Television Equipment Associates, Inc.
Telex Communications, Inc.
TELMAT
Template Division, Megatek Corporation
Texas Instruments
Texas Memory Systems, Inc.
3M/Artronics
Time Arts Inc.
TriCom, Inc.
Ultratek
Unicad, Inc.
UNIRAS, Inc.
Universal Data Systems
Universal Technical Graphics/Graphic Resources
Vectrix Corporation
VersaCad
Versatec, Inc., A Xerox Company
Verticom Inc.
Via Video, Inc.
Video Monitors Inc.
Visiquest Corporation
Visual Engineering
Visual Intelligence Corporation
VLSI Design
VMI-Vermont Microsystems, Inc.
West End Film
Western Graphtec, Inc.
Westward Technology Inc.
Winsted Corporation
Xtar Electronics, Inc.

ACM/SIGGRAPH Awards

Steven A. Coons Award for Outstanding Creative Contributions to Computer Graphics

Dr. Pierre Bézier

SIGGRAPH is pleased and honored to present the 1985 Coons Award for Computer Graphics to Pierre Bézier. In the field of computer aided design and computer graphics, Dr. Bézier has been a pioneer whose stature can only be compared with Coons's. As a contemporary of Coons's, he enjoyed a relationship with him based on mutual affection, admiration, and deep respect.

Coons and Bézier were the two great pioneers in Computer Aided Design. Coons specialized in interpolation schemes (the Coons Patch), and Bézier specialized in approximation schemes. His Bézier curves and surfaces became an example and inspiration for further work.

Bézier's work is significant for several reasons: (1) He was one of the very first in CAD to come to grips with the problem of specifying the shape of a free-form curve or surface. No one else had a method that guaranteed an absence of undulations or other undesirable surprises in form. His approximation methods have fundamental advantages for free-form shape specification, and the study of those advantages inspired a large and important body of subsequent work. (2) As a director of Renault he was able to affect and influence Renault in a way that made it a world leader in computer aided design. Therefore he is not only a leader in terms of theory and new algorithms, he is also a leader in terms of influencing the "real world." (3) He wrote a book on numerical control which has become a standard reference for anyone working in the field of free-form curves and surfaces. (4) His work inspired people to discover a connection between raster graphics and free-form surfaces. (5) He was a professor at the Ecole des Artes et Metiers in Paris, where he also participated in training students in this new subject matter as well as writing scholarly articles. This role was carried out simultaneously with being a director of Renault in Paris. (6) He has maintained a position of visibility and leadership in the world community of computer graphics and CAD/CAM. References to his work are ubiquitous in graphics books and classes. Indeed, implementing some of his schemes is a routine lab exercise given in graphics classes throughout the world. (7) In addition to his professional identities as a director, a scientist, an engineer, and a professor, he is also a bona fide designer who profoundly understands the issues of style, form, and function so important for the development of user-friendly systems. It is this additional gift that made his results so important.

Computer Graphics Achievement Award

Dr. Loren Carpenter

Loren Carpenter is a pioneer in the design of algorithms for generating raster computer graphics; his recent images approach photographic realism. He received his Master's degree from the University of Washington in 1976, and worked for the Boeing

Company from 1966 through 1980. He is now a senior scientist in the Computer Graphics Group at Lucasfilm.

His early work concerned hidden surfaces, most notably joint work with Jeffrey Lane on adaptively subdividing parametrically defined surfaces into approximating polygons.

In 1980, simultaneously with (but independently of) Alain Fournier and Don Fussell, he applied Benoit Mandelbrot's ideas of fractals to generate images of complex natural terrain by recursively subdividing triangles from a small data base. His beautiful computer animated film "Vol Libre" popularized fractals and inspired much further work in computer imagery.

More recently, Carpenter has invented the "A-buffer," an enhanced version of the standard Z-buffer with which he produced antialiased images by accounting for sub-pixel areas. Jointly with Rob Cook and Tom Porter, he proposed a method of "distributed ray tracing" that simultaneously solved most of the outstanding problems in computer graphics realism: motion blur, shadow penumbras, glossy and translucent surfaces, and depth-of-field effects. Both of these algorithms have been used at Lucasfilm to produce animated sequences; Carpenter is currently consulting on the design of high-performance hardware implementations of them.

Anisotropic Reflection Models

James T. Kajiya
California Institute of Technology
Pasadena, Ca. 91125

KEYWORDS: computer graphics, raster graphics, lighting models, surface mapping, texture mapping, frame mapping.

CR CATEGORIES: I.3.3, I.3.5, I.3.7

ABSTRACT. We present a new set of lighting models derived from the equations of electromagnetism. These models describe the reflection and refraction of light from surfaces which exhibit anisotropy—surfaces with preferred directions. The model allows a new mapping technique, which we call ***frame mapping***. We also discuss the general relationship between geometric models, surface mapping of all types, and lighting models in the context of rendering images with extreme complexity.

§1 Introduction

A thread that runs throughout computer graphics is the quest for detail. Nature presents a nearly infinite complexity and richness of form over an enormous range of scales. In image synthesis it is our task to make convincing pictures of such natural phenomena: thus how to represent this range of scales becomes a central problem.

This paper explores the idea that along with geometric models and surface mapping, we include the use of custom lighting models to capture model complexity.

§2 Anisotropic Lighting Models

It is surprising how many surface materials in the natural world exhibit anisotropy. For example, cloth is a weave of threads. Each thread scatters light narrowly in the direction of the thread and widely in the perpendicular direction. For the same reason, hair and fur should be rendered via an anisotropic lighting model. Another example is brushed or burnished metal, as well as metal surfaces which have been treated with various chemical finishes, anodizing, alodyning, etc. These are basically surfaces with microfeatures in particular directions. Because these features have a characteristic direction their scattering profiles exhibit anisotropy.

In this paper, we will develop the basic lighting models for reflection from dielectric anisotropic surfaces. We do this more or less directly from Maxwell's basic equations of electromagnetism. For conducting surfaces the treatment may be adapted by setting the index of refraction ratio to infinity, simplifiying the ensuing integral.

Although this work develops a method of calculating a reflection model for a general surface, it is not strictly necessary to do so. It is relatively straightforward to generalize a parametric model such as the Phong or Torrance-Sparrow model to the anisotropic case. But calculating the scattering cross sections of surfaces given their actual micro-features is needed to perform the level-of-detail hierarchy calculations in section 5. Thus if one is interested in just any surface that exhibits anisotropy, a Phong-like model is sufficient. On the other hand, if one is interested in a particular surface, the treatment below is called for.

2.1 Related work

Phong(1973) introduced to computer graphics the first lighting model which went beyond the diffuse Lambert shading model, introducing highlights. Blinn (1977,1978) introduced and adapted to a form suitable for computer graphics the lighting models of Torrance and Sparrow (1967) and Trowbridge and Reitz (1975). These models used a geometrical optics model for light reflection from surfaces and were effective in simulating the reflection from surfaces with microscopic roughness. Cook and Torrance (1981) adapted models from the above sources as well as using a model based on Beckmann(1963) which is concerned with scattering of electromagnetic radiation from rough surfaces. Beckmann's models do not make the geometrical optics assumptions. Wavelength dependence was an innovation of their work.

Catmull (1975) introduced the notion of color mapping onto surfaces. Shortly thereafter, Blinn(1977) generalized the notion of surface mapping to include the case of perturbation of surface normals as well as mapping arbitrary parameters in the lighting models he introduced. In this way he was able to render images with macroscopic as well as microscopic roughness.

We also mention an image brought to our attention by one of the reviewers. In it Tomohiro Ohira has used an anisotropic reflection model.

2.2 Paper organization

Since much of what follows is a development from a simple case, we urge the reader to review the appendix describing how light reflects from a smooth plane surface. This appendix presents a review of all the equations relevant to the model we pursue.

The case for a general surface model, following Beckmann, is treated in section 3. We show how these equations can be used in a rendering algorithm to generate custom lighting models. Section 4 discusses how parameters in the model may be mapped and how this extends Blinn's well known technique. Section 5 treats in a general way the overall relationship between lighting models, surface mapping, and model geometry. It suggests a strategy for rendering complex images. Section 6 presents results of the new model. Section 7 discusses further work. The appendix reviews light reflection from a smooth surface.

§3 Reflection from a rough surface

In this section we rederive Beckmann's (1963) general formula for scattering from a rough surface in a form more suitable for computer graphics. We then present the new lighting model for anisotropic surfaces. The notation for this section is developed in the appendix.

3.1 Kirchhoff approximation

The Kirchhoff approximation for reflection from a rough surface approximates the field at any point of the surface by the field which would occur if we replaced the surface by its tangent plane. See figure 1.

If the surface is of low curvature in relation to the wavelength of light then the approximation is valid. Specifically, Brekhovskikh (Beckmann 1963 p.29) gives the criterion

$$4\pi r_c \cos(k_1, n) \gg \lambda.$$

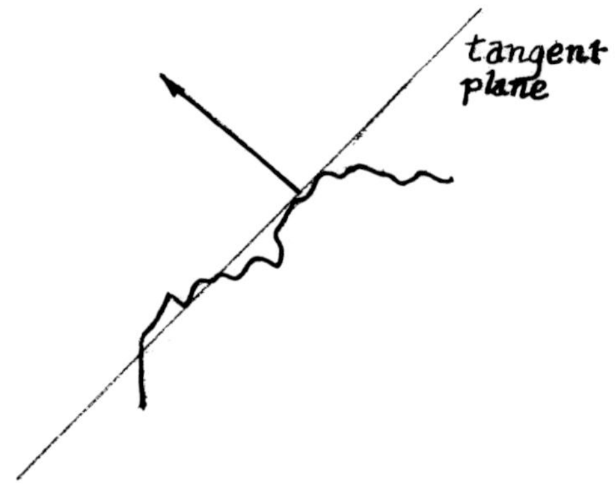

Figure 1. The Kirchhoff approximation

Where r_c is the radius of curvature of the surface, $\cos(k_1, n)$ is the cosine of the angle of incidence, and λ is the wavelength of our wave.

For lighting model calculations we assume that the incident field is always a plane wave ψ_1 with wave vector k_1. Thus for the field at the boundary we make the approximation

$$\psi|_S = (1+R)\exp(ik_1 \cdot s) \qquad (1)$$

$$\left.\frac{\partial \psi}{\partial n}\right|_s = (1-R)\exp(ik_1 \cdot s) ik_1 \cdot n \qquad (2)$$

That is, the field at the boundary $\psi\ |_S$ is simply the sum of the incident field ψ_1 and the reflected field $R\psi_1$ calculated by the Fresnel formula.

When equations (A1),(1), and (2) are substituted into equation (A7) we have a formula suitable for computing a lighting model from a specified surface microstructure.

$$\psi(x) = -\frac{i\exp(i|k||r_0|)}{4\pi|r_0|}\int_S n \cdot [R(k_1 - k_2) - (k_1 + k_2)] \times \exp(i(k_1 - k_2)\cdot s)dS. \qquad (3)$$

Following Beckmann, we calculate the reflection coefficient rather than the reflected field by normalizing by $\psi_0(x)$ the field of a smooth, perfectly conducting plane in the specular direction for the same angle of incidence and same distance. In this case, the mirror equation implies $n_0 \cdot (k_1 + k_2) = 0$ and $n_0 \cdot (k_1 - k_2) = 2n_0 \cdot k_1$. Because the surface is smooth s lies in the plane $z = 0$ and $n_0 \cdot (k_1 - k_2) = 0$. The assumption of perfect conductivity implies $R = 1$. Thus

$$\psi_0(x) = -\frac{i|k|\exp(i|k||r_0|)}{2\pi|r_0|} n_0 \cdot k_1 A \qquad (4)$$

Where A is the area of the surface we integrate over. Dividing equation (4) into (3) obtains the reflection coefficient formula:

$$\rho(x) = \frac{1}{2n_0 \cdot k_1 A}\int_S n \cdot [R(k_1 - k_2) - (k_1 + k_2)] \times \exp(i(k_1 - k_2)\cdot s)dS. \qquad (5)$$

Note that the reflection coefficient is not just a function of x, but also a function of the incidence and emittance vectors k_1, k_2, as well as the normal n. The integral is over the entire surface, but since only the first few fresnel zones are required in practice a very small surface element will suffice. The above derivation is essentially Beckmann's general solution for a surface rough in both dimensions but we have expressed it in vector form.

3.2 Using the lighting model

Using the equation we can compute a lighting model which gives the average field power scattered from an arbitrary surface. To use equation 5 there are two things to be specified. First, we must specify the micro-surface displacement function. Second, we must calculate the integral.

Specifying the surface may be done is several ways. One way is to expand the height function into a set of Fourier coefficients. These coefficients may be specified as a $1/f^{\alpha}$ function to give fractal behavior. A second way is to use bump maps from a higher scale level. Once a bump map perturbs surfaces on a scale less than a pixel it should be included in the lighting model.

Calculating the integral should be via an asymptotic expansion using the method of stationary phase. Note that the wave vectors k_1 and k_2 are very large compared with an area to integrate over. Now, the factor and integrand outside the exponential can have this large magnitude cancelled from them, so that unit vectors may be considered. The exponential term, however, is rapidly varying. Using stationary phase, this integral is easily approximated.

To calculate the integral each time a reflection coefficient is required is prohibitvely expensive. By computing the model off line this cost may be virtually eliminated. We do this by storing the lighting model reflection function in a table, linearly interpolating the values. An index i, j into the table corresponds to a pair of small cells of solid angle for the incidence and emittance directions. We store the square of the reflectance function $S_{ij} = \rho(x, k_1, k_2)$ at each cell, where k_1 and k_2 lie in the i and j cell correpondingly. The procedure is as follows:

Perform the first 3 steps offline.

1. Divide a hemisphere centered about the surface element into a number of discrete cells (say 5 by 20 cells equally divided in lattitude and longitude).

2. For each pair of cells calculate ρ by the integral in equation (5) using the microsurface of interest.

3. The incoherent scattering function for each of the cells is calculated by $S_{ij} = |\rho|^2$ and stored away.

4. Now, when calculating the lighting model for a particular ray or pixel, use the incidence and emittance vectors, ***with respect to the surface frame***, to (linearly) interpolate the sampled specular reflectance function S_{ij}.

Note that in step 4, we do not use the absolute incidence and emittance vectors. Rather, because of anisotropy, the vectors are specified in terms of the surface frame (normal, tangent, and binormal). We discuss this further in the following section. It should also be noted that, although the offline steps may be quite time consuming for every lighting model we compute, the time critical step, step 4, is simply a table lookup and linear interpolation.

§4 Frame mapping

Blinn in (Blinn 1977 and 1978) introduced an extension of Catmull's idea of surface color mapping to mapping more general parameters of a lighting model onto a surface. In this way he obtained an ability to vary the specularity and reflectivity of surfaces as well as the much celebrated ability to map apparent bumps and wrinkles onto the surface through the mapping of surface normals. The above lighting model allows us to apply Blinn's idea to the mapping of surface frame bundles.

A ***frame bundle*** for a surface is simply a local coordinate system given by the tangent, binormal, and normal to the surface. Both the tangent and binormal lie in the tangent plane to the surface. For isotropic surfaces they have no intrinsic physical significance—any othonormal set of vectors lying in the plane can serve as a frame. For anisotropic surfaces, however, we take the tangent of the surface to orient along a reference direction, e.g. the "grain" of the surface.

The idea behind frame mapping is simply to perturb the entire frame bundle—not just the normal vector—at each point on the surface. This allows a mapping of the directionality of surface features in nature, e.g. hair, cloth, etc.

Suppose we are attempting to render a surface element. For isotropic lighting models with fixed incidence and emittance vectors, the only significant geometric features about the surface element are its position in space x_0 and its normal n_0. For anisotropic lighting models the entire frame is significant because there is a preferred direction for the surface.

The rendering of an isotropic surface with frame mapping proceeds as follows: first calculate the frame of the surface element. Then for each point x_0 on the surface look up an orthogonal matrix $M(x_0) = [t\,b\,n]$ which transforms the plain surface frame to a mapped surface frame. The columns of this matrix are simply the perturbed tangent vector t, binormal vector b, and normal vector n expressed in the coordinate system of the plain surface frame.

There are nine quantities in an orthogonal matrix but orthogonality requires that the columns form an orthonormal set. Because there are six such pairwise equations, there are

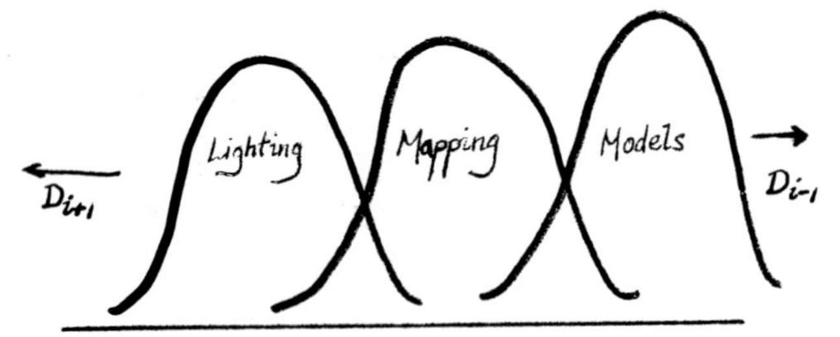

Figure 2. Hierarchy of detail

only three independent quantities. These quantities may be specified by, say, Euler angles. In what follows, its easier to use two orthonormal vectors. Two unit magnitude constraints and an inner product constraint reduce the number of independent parameters of a pair of orthonormal vectors to three.

On mapping a frame bundle, fixing the tangent and normal vectors determines the binormal. Frame mapping may be specified by the tangent and normal maps. Thus the two vectors we choose above are the normal and tangent vectors.

To map frames, we calculate the binormal by cross products. We then map the plain surface frame by multiplying by the constructed orthogonal matrix. This perturbed frame is then used to determine the incidence and emittance direction cosines used in the anisotropic lighting model. We note that the idea of frame mapping works with any anisotropic model: the general anisotropic model above as well as a parametric Phong-like model.

As an example, suppose we have calculated the scattering cross-section of a thread. Since cloth is a cross weave of threads, we set up the frame map to correspond to map the tangent of the surface to the direction of the threads according to the pattern of the weave.

§5 A hierarchy of scale

One of the striking features of images approaching the complexity of nature, is the wide range of scales represented in them. It has been suggested that the natural strategy is to use a succession of a number of geometric models, each capturing a different level of detail (Crow 1975).

We suggest that within each level of detail D_i we have three natural scales shown in figure 4.

The largest scale within D_i is the geometric model, which is the traditional scale manipulated in computer graphics. Geometric features participate in the full range of graphics manipulations: they require visibility computations, they cast shadows, etc. The next range of scale in D_i is surface mapping. In this range, the details which would be geometric at D_{i+1} are collected into surface perturbations.

The final range of scale contains the smallest detail. This is the realm of lighting models. At D_i the lighting model is derived from the surface map and lighting model of D_{i+1}.

Thus the hierarchy of detail would use several levels of geometric models, surface maps and custom lighting models for each range of scales. At any level of detail D_i, the surface maps capture geometry at a finer scale D_{i+1}. They should be derived as in (Blinn 1978). We calculate the custom lighting model for D_i using the surface map of D_{i+1} by using equation (5). The custom lighting models then capture the detail in maps at the next finer scale.

It is clear that surface maps cannot handle arbitrarily fine surface detail, for they tend to alias. Blinn has suggested filtering the surface perturbation as an expedient, but has left the antialiasing of normal maps as an open problem. Lighting models are the natural way to anti-alias normal maps.

There are a number of notable exceptions to the hierarchy of scales model outlined above. Some models use only very simple smooth surfaces. Indeed, the common practice in computer graphics is to use surfaces of this type. For this case, only geometry is necessary. No surface maps are needed and a simple, fixed lighting model is only required. Another set of exceptions to the hierarchy of scales model are the few cases in which lighting models are used directly. For example a method for rendering point light sources (Gabriel 1975), uses a trivial geometry but complex lighting models. In a real sense, the volume density ray tracing technique (Kajiya 1984) uses no geometry at all, just the calculation of a rather complex lighting model. Blinn's atmospheric model paper (Blinn 1982) is also all lighting model with very little geometry.

§6 Results

Figures 5 and 6 illustrate the anisotropic models plus the frame mapping technique in the ray tracing context. Figure 5 shows four spheres resting on a plane. The leftmost pair of spheres are simply color mapped with a stripe pattern. The right most pair are frame mapped. The tangent of the surface points in orthogonal directions on alternating stripes. Because of this, the highlights follow the stripes on one set and are transversal to the stripes on the other set. Only the tangents are mapped in this example, the normal remaining unperturbed.

Figure 6 shows a single sphere resting on a plane. The plane frame map transforms both tangent and normal fields. The anisotropic model is one for a thread. We map the surface with a cloth weave pattern which not only maps the direction of the thread but also models the threads crossing above and below each other.

Both these images were computed via ray tracing, they are 512 by 512 pixel images adaptively subsampled to a 4 by 4 subpixel grid. We have filtered the subsampled image with a simple box filter which is responsible for the moire. These images each consumed 12 hours of IBM4341 CPU time.

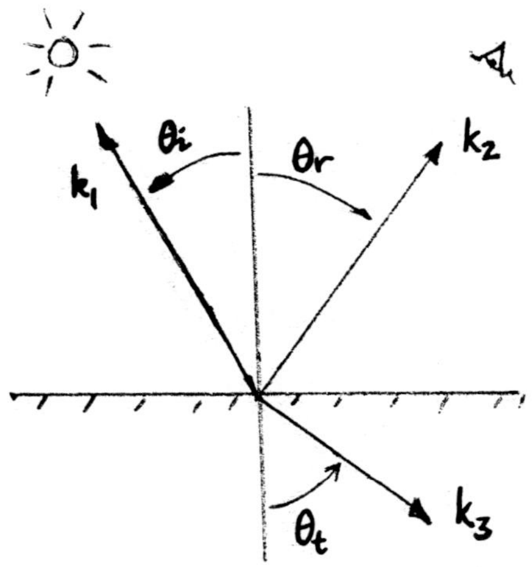

Figure 3. Reflection from a dielectric surface.

§7 Further work

It may be attractive to characterize the surface statistically. We can then compute statistical lighting models by computing the mean of the reflection coefficient intensity $\langle|\rho|^2\rangle$. This will give us a lighting model in the more conventional sense. However, for anisotropic surfaces, the ensuing integrals are extremely complex. Aside from the complexity of evaluating the integral, the ensuing complexity of the analytic formulation would make numerical evaluation of the function quite costly. Thus, precomputing tables which are then evaluated may be necessary anyway.

Appendix. Reflection from a smooth plane surface

This appendix is a brief review of the electromagnetic theory we use in this paper. This section is intended to recall and introduce notation for someone already acquainted with this subject. The reader interested in treatments of this material in full detail are encouraged to consult Jackson(1975) and Born and Wolf(1980). Knowledge of the above is essential to reading this appendix.

Plane wave solutions

Maxwell's equations in the absence of matter reduces to the wave equation which decouples the E and B fields and their spatial components:

$$\frac{1}{c}\frac{\partial\psi}{\partial t} + \Delta\psi = 0$$

Where ψ is any single component of the E or B vector. The solutions to this equation that we will be most interested in are the ***plane wave*** solutions:

$$U = \exp(i(\omega ct - kx))$$

Where c is the speed of light, ω is the frequency of the wave, and k is the wave vector—a 3-vector whose direction is the direction of propagation of the wave and whose magnitude is the reciprocal of the wavelength.

We first consider some kinematic constraints of a plane wave reflecting from an interface between two dielectric media, see figure 1.

At each point, the spatial and time variation of each of the components of the fields are unique. Specifically, at the boundary the spatial variation of the reflected, incident, and transmitted wave must match. This gives rise to the equation:

$$(k_1 \cdot x)_{z=0} = (k_2 \cdot x)_{z=0} = (k_3 \cdot x)_{z=0}$$

Where k_1, k_2, k_3 are the wave vectors of the incident, reflected, and transmitted waves. In many graphics papers k_1 and k_2 are known as L and E. When measuring the angle from the normal we get:

$$|k_1|\sin\theta_i = |k_2|\sin\theta_r = |k_3|\sin\theta_t.$$

Since the magnitudes of the wave vectors are

$$|k_1| = |k_2| = \frac{\omega}{c}\sqrt{\mu_1\epsilon_1}$$
$$|k_3| = \frac{\omega}{c}\sqrt{\mu_2\epsilon_2}$$

Where μ_i, ϵ_i are the magnetic permeability and dielectric constant of the two media. Thus $\sqrt{\mu_i\epsilon_i} = \eta_i$ are the indices of refraction of the media.

From the first these equations we obtain the Mirror Equation. That is, the angle of reflection equals the angle of incidence, $\theta_i = \theta_r$. From the second of these equations we obtain Snell's law, $\eta_1 \sin\theta_i = \eta_2 \sin\theta_t$.

The Fresnel formulae

A second set of kinematic constraints arise from the continuity of the tangential component of the E vector and the normal component of the B vector. These give rise to the Fresnel formulae. We skip the derivation of these equations which may be found in Jackson(1975) and Born and Wolf(1980). The importance of the Fresnel formulae is that they fix the reflection and transmission coefficients for a smooth interface between two dielectrics.

$$R_\perp = \frac{\eta_1\cos\theta_i - \eta_2\cos\theta_t}{\eta_1\cos\theta_i + \eta_2\cos\theta_t}$$
$$R_\parallel = \frac{\eta_2\cos\theta_i - \eta_1\cos\theta_t}{\eta_1\cos\theta_t + \eta_2\cos\theta_i}$$
$$T_\perp = \frac{2\eta_1\cos\theta_i}{\eta_1\cos\theta_i + \eta_2\cos\theta_t}$$
$$T_\parallel = \frac{2\eta_1\cos\theta_i}{\eta_2\cos\theta_i + \eta_1\cos\theta_t}$$

Where $R_\perp, R_\parallel, T_\perp, T_\parallel$ are the reflection and transmission coefficients for waves polarized in directions perpendicular and parallel to the surface.

Now, for unpolarized light, the reflection and transmission coefficients coefficients are simply the average of the two polarized coeffients. This is because unpolarized light is composed of rapidly fluctuating random polarizations whose time average is half for each of the polarizations (Born and Wolf 1980). Thus the unpolarized reflection and transmission coefficients are:

$$R = \frac{\cos^2\theta_i - \cos^2\theta_t}{\cos^2\theta_i + \cos^2\theta_t + \left(\frac{\eta_1^2+\eta_2^2}{\eta_1\eta_2}\right)\cos\theta_i\cos\theta_t} \qquad (A1)$$

$$T = \frac{\eta_1\cos\theta_i(\eta_1+\eta_2)(\cos\theta_i+\cos\theta_t)}{\cos\theta_i\cos\theta_t(\eta_1^2+\eta_2^2)+\eta_1\eta_2(\cos^2\theta_i+\cos^2\theta_t)} \qquad (A2)$$

Note that R is really a function of the angles of incidence and emittance, it should properly be written as $R(\theta_i, \theta_r)$. Note also that the reflection coefficents should be squared for incoherent illumination—because the power rather than the energy is what contributes to the total brightness of an image.

It somewhat curious that these formulae have been noted many times (Blinn 1978, Cook 1981), but have largely been ignored in Computer graphics. Their effect is quite significant. They say for example, that at normal incidence the reflection from a window is far less than the reflection from a grazing angle.

Scalar Diffraction Theory

The Kirchhoff diffraction integral is obtained from the scalar wave equation. It describes the value of any component of the E or B field, call it ψ, at a point in space x given that we know the field at an emitting surface S.

$$\psi(x) = -\frac{1}{4\pi}\int_S \psi\frac{\partial\varsigma}{\partial n} - \varsigma\frac{\partial\psi}{\partial n}\,dS. \qquad (A3)$$

Where $\frac{\partial}{\partial n}$ is the normal derivative for the emitting surface, ς is the converging spherical wave Green's function centered about the point x. We have

$$\varsigma = \frac{\exp(i|k||r|)}{|r|}$$
$$\frac{\partial\varsigma}{\partial n} = \frac{\exp(i|k||r|)}{|r|}\left[i|k| - \frac{1}{|r|}\right]\cos(n, r) \qquad (A4)$$

Note that $|k_2| = |k_1| = |k| = \frac{2\pi}{\lambda}$ is the wave number of the incident and scattered waves. And since $|r| \gg \lambda$ we ignore the term containing $1/|r|$ to give the equation

$$\frac{\partial\varsigma}{\partial n} = \frac{\exp(i|k||r|)}{|r|}i|k|\cos(n, r) \qquad (A5)$$

With this integral, once we know the value of the field and its normal derivative at all points of the surface of interest, will allow us calculate the scattered field. Now usually we will be interested in the scattered field in a *direction* given by the wave vector k_2, that is, we are interested in the field at points which are very far away compared to the wavelength

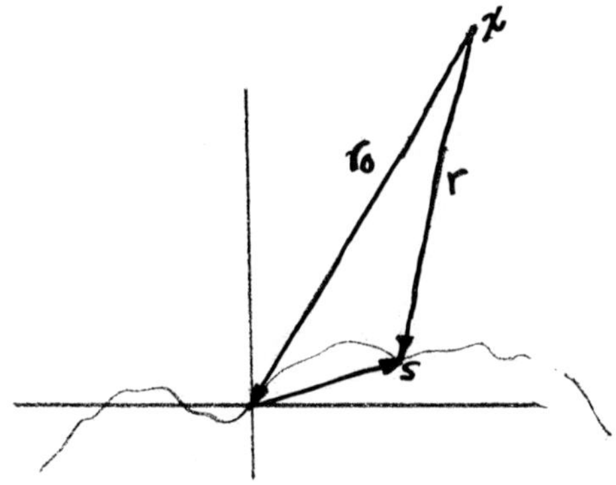

Figure 4. Scattering geometry

light and dimensions of the microstructure of the surface for which we are computing a lighting model. For this we use the Fraunhofer approximation to the Kirchhoff integral. The vector pointing from x to the surface point s we're integrating over is $r = x - s$. Let r_0 be the vector from the point x to the center of the region of scattering, see figure 2. Then,

$$r = r_0 + s$$

and

$$|r|^2 = |r_0|^2 + |s|^2 + 2|r_0||s|\cos(r_0, s).$$

But, since $|r_0| \gg |s|$ we can take square roots to obtain

$$|r| \approx |r_0| + |s|\cos(r_0, s).$$

Now, the vector r_0 and the wave vector k_2 point in opposite directions

$$\frac{k_2}{|k|} = -\frac{r_0}{|r_0|},$$

so $\cos(r_0, s) = -\cos(k_2, s)$ and we can use the cosine formula for the inner product to obtain

$$|r| \approx |r_0| - \frac{k_2 \cdot s}{|k|} \qquad (A6)$$

Substituting equations (A4),(A5), and (A6) into the Kirchhoff integral (A3) gives:

$$\psi(x) = -\frac{\exp(i|k||r_0|)}{4\pi|r_0|}\int_S\left[n\cdot k_2 i\psi - \frac{\partial\psi}{\partial n}\right] \times \exp(-ik_2\cdot s)\,dS. \qquad (A7)$$

This is the equation for computing a lighting model once we know the field at the surface of interest.

§8 References

P. Beckmann and A. Spizzichino (1963) *The scattering of electromagnetic waves from rough surfaces* Pergamon, Oxford.

J. Blinn (1977) "Models of light reflection for computer synthesized pictures", *Computer Graphics* v.11,2, pp.192-198.

J. Blinn (1978) "Simulation of wrinkled surfaces" *Computer Graphics* v.12,3, August 1978.

J. Blinn(1978) "Computer Display of Curved Surfaces", *Ph.D. thesis* University of Utah.

J. Blinn(1982) "Light reflection functions for simulation of clouds and dusty surfaces" *Computer Graphics* v.16,3, pp.21-29.

M. Born and E. Wolf(1980) *Principles of Optics* Pergamon, Oxford.

E. Catmull(1975) "Computer display of curved surfaces", *IEEE Conf. on Computer Graphics, Pattern Recognition and Data structures*May 1975, pp.11-17.

R. Cook and K. Torrance(1981) "A reflectance model for computer graphics" *Computer Graphics* v.13,3, pp.307-316.

F. Crow(1982) "A more flexible image generation environment" *Computer Graphics* v.16,3, pp.9-18.

S. Gabriel(1975), The Evans and Sutherland Lufthansa Flight simulator, *private communication.*

J. Jackson(1975) *Classical Electrodynamics* Wiley, New York.

J. Kajiya(1984) "Ray tracing volume densities", *Computer Graphics, v. 19,3.*

B. Phong(1973) "Illumination for computer generated pictures", Comm. ACM v.18,6 June 1975, pp.311-317.

K. Torrance and E. Sparrow(1967) "Theory for off-specular reflection from roughened surfaces", *J. Opt. Soc. Am.* v.57,9. Sept 1967, pp. 1105-1114.

T. Trowbridge and K. Reitz(1975) "Average irregularity representation for a roughened surface for ray reflection", *J. Opt. Soc. Am.* 65,5. May 1975,. pp.531-536.

Figure 5.

Figure 6.

Continuous Tone Representation of Three-Dimensional Objects Taking Account of Shadows and Interreflection

Tomoyuki Nishita and Eihachiro Nakamae

Fukuyama University
Higashimura, Fukuyama
729-02, Japan

Hiroshima University
Saijocho, Higashihiroshima
724, Japan

Abstract

The effect of shadows and interreflection created by room obstructions is an important factor in the continuous tone representation of interiors. For indirect illumination, in most cases a uniform ambient light has been considered, even though the interreflection gives very complex effects with the shaded images.

The proposed method for indirect lighting with shadows results in the following advanced points:
1) The indirect illuminance caused by the surfaces of objects such as ceilings, floors, walls, desks, bookcases etc. gives added realism to images.
2) The proposed method is suitable for every type of light source such as point sources, linear sources, and area sources.

CR Categories and Subject Descriptors: I.3.7 [Computer Graphics]: Three-Dimensional Graphics and Realism; I.3.3 [Computer Graphics]: Picture/Image Generation

General Terms: Algorithms

Additional Key Words and Phrases: Shading, interreflection of light, diffuse reflections, area light source, shadows, penumbrae

1. INTRODUCTION

Continuous tone representation of three-dimensional objects is a useful tool for CAD of buildings, machines and various lighting problems. The degree of realism of the shaded image of a three-dimensional scene depends remarkably on the successful simulation of shadowing and shading effects. In order to display three-dimensional objects that look more realistic, researchers have developed techniques for simulating the properties of objects such as reflection, refraction, and transparency (e.g., Ref.[1,2,3]). In most computer-generated pictures, however, ambient light has been treated in a perfunctory way; i.e., a constant rough estimate is used. Particularly when displaying the interior of a room, indirect illumination caused by interreflection is very significant; this component usually forms about 30 percent of the total illuminance and the ambient light is not uniform.

In the traditional lighting design methods for handling interreflection (e.g.,[4,5]), it is assumed that the light sources are point sources, the room is rectangular and empty(i.e., the room is defined by six rectangles and every surface can be seen from every other surface). It is also assumed that the distribution of illuminance is uniform on each surface.

Recently, Jepsen et al. [6] developed a calculation method of interreflection taking into account shadows. This method is, however, only available for the interreflection between two parallel(or perpendicular) surfaces with uniform illumination. Goral et al. [7] also proposed modeling the interaction of light with color bleeding, but only discussed this in an empty room.

The shading method proposed in this paper is applicable to an arbitrary shaped room; it calculates shadows caused by obstructions such as desks, bookcases in the room, and it allows direct and indirect illumination from various types of light sources. Color bleeding is not considered.

Direct illuminance calculation for various types of light sources such as point sources, linear sources, area sources, and polyhedron sources is performed using the method of Ref.[8,9]. Area light sources illuminating a computer room are calculated as an example in order to show the effect of interreflection.

2. PREPARATION AND OUTLINE OF PROCEDURE

We assume the following for this discussion.
1) The algorithm described here applies to objects composed of several convex polyhedra. The normal of a face consisting of a polyhedron is an outward-pointing vector.
2) All surfaces of polyhedra are perfect diffuse

surfaces(i.e., Lambertian reflecting surfaces).

3) The types of light sources handled here are point light sources, linear light sources, area light sources and polyhedron light sources. Except for point sources, the distribution characteristics of sources are Lambertian distribution. The shape of area sources and polyhedron sources are convex.

4) The calculation of direct illuminance and interreflection illuminance is applied to diffuse reflection not to transparency and specular reflection.

The fundamental ideas of the algorithm are as follows:

1) If the calculation of shadows on surfaces is executed by using the point by point method, it takes considerable computation time. In order to save time, the shadow areas(penumbrae and umbrae) are predetected before scanning for hidden surface removal. The shadows are determined in the following manner. First, shadow volumes for penumbrae and umbrae formed by a convex polyhedron and a light source are obtained; these shadow volumes are named penumbra volumes and umbra volumes, respectively[8,9]. Then, the penumbrae (or umbrae) on each face are obtained as the intersection areas of penumbra(or umbra) volumes and the face. We give a brief description of shading calculations for area(or polyhedron) light sources in Appendix.

2) The interreflection of light is obtained by the following method. The faces in a room, such as walls and objects, are subdivided into pieces (elements) called subfaces(or zones). The interreflection of light at the vertices of each subsurface is calculated before scanning for shading and each point on the screen is obtained by interpolation.

The outline of the procedure is as follows:

(1) Input of three-dimensional objects.
(2) Subdivision of faces into subsurfaces.
(3) Classification of faces of each polyhedron for shading. Faces are classified into three classes; faces receiving light from the whole region of the source, faces receiving light from a part of the source, and faces receiving no light from the source.
(4) Obtaining penumbra volumes and umbra volumes.
(5) Calculation of penumbrae and umbrae on each face.
(6) Calculation of interreflection of light.
(7) Determining priority of visibility for a given viewpoint.
(8) Hidden surface removal and calculation of direct illuminance at each point on a screen(see Ref.[10,11] for hidden surface removal and anti-aliasing).

3. CALCULATION OF INTERREFLECTION OF LIGHT

3.1 Traditional Calculation Method of Interreflection of Light

In illumination engineering, calculation methods for interreflection already have been developed for an empty room. In the traditional methods mentioned before, the surfaces of the room are subdivided into some subsurfaces such as rectangles. This subdivision is similar to mesh generation in finite element analysis. The total illumination(direct and indirect) are obtained by solving the matrix equation.

The traditional methods ignoring the shadow effect are as follows: Let's consider the interreflection between the two faces S_i and S_j (see Fig. 1). The equation of interreflection is given by

$$E_i = E_{0i} + \int_{A_j} \rho_j e_0(i,j) E_j dA_j \quad , \qquad (1)$$

where E_{0i} = direct(initial) illuminance at P_i,
E_i = final illuminance at P_i,
E_j = final illuminance at P_j,
ρ_j = reflectance at P_j,
A_j = area of S_j,
$e_0(i,j)$=radiative exchange factor
r_{ij} = distance between P_i and P_j
θ_i(or θ_j)= the angle between normal of S_i(or S_j) and line segment P_iP_j

The second term in equation (1) indicates the indirect illuminance component.

It is difficult to solve the above integral equation, therefore, some solving methods such as Fourier Series analysis[6] are used. In this paper, the equation is solved by employing a finite approximation. That is, an enclosure is subdivided into subsurfaces which are rectangular planes.

If a room consists of n subsurfaces, the illuminance is given by

$$E_i = E_{0i} + \sum_{j=1}^{n} \int_{A_j} \rho_j e_0(i,j) E_j dA_j \ . \qquad (2)$$

If illuminance and reflectance are uniform over the entire extent of subsurfaces, E_i is expressed by multiplying $1/A_i$,

$$E_i = E_{0i} + \sum_{j=1}^{n} \rho_j F_{ij} E_j \ , \qquad (3)$$

where

$$F_{ij} = 1/(A_i) \int_{A_j} \int_{A_i} \cos\theta_i \cos\theta_j / (\pi r_{ij}^2) dA_i dA_j$$

(F_{ij} is called Form Factor)

A_i = area of S_i

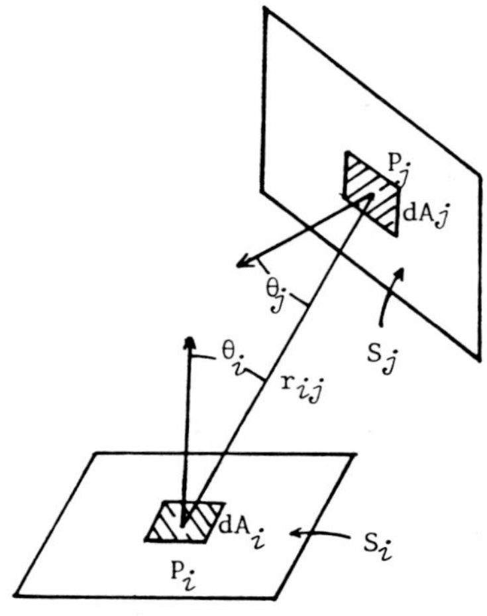

Fig.1 Interreflection between two faces.

and when $\cos\theta_i \leqq 0$ or $\cos\theta_j \leqq 0$, $F_{ij}=0$. Let $d_{ij}=\rho_j F_{ij}$, illuminance can be obtained by solving the following simultaneous equation of n unknowns.

$$\begin{bmatrix} E_1 \\ E_2 \\ E_3 \\ \cdot \\ E_n \end{bmatrix} = \begin{bmatrix} 1-d_{11} & -d_{12} & -d_{13} & \cdot & -d_{1n} \\ -d_{21} & 1-d_{22} & -d_{23} & \cdot & -d_{2n} \\ -d_{31} & -d_{32} & 1-d_{33} & \cdot & -d_{3n} \\ \cdot & \cdot & \cdot & \cdot & \cdot \\ -d_{n1} & -d_{n2} & -d_{n3} & \cdot & 1-d_{nn} \end{bmatrix}^{-1} \begin{bmatrix} E_{01} \\ E_{02} \\ E_{03} \\ \cdot \\ E_{0n} \end{bmatrix} \quad (4)$$

In equation (4) introduced by the traditional method, we assume that the number of subsurfaces is n, the direct illuminances E_{0i} (i=1,2,.., n) are described by the column vector E_0, the illuminances E_i(i = 1,2,...,n) are described by the column vector E and D is coefficients matrix. The illuminance of each subsurface is obtained by

$$E = D^{-1}E_0 \; . \quad (5)$$

The algorithm proposed here accounts not only for the shadows caused by room obstructions such as desks, bookcases but also for the interreflection between these objects. Therefore, we modify the coefficients matrix D in order to calculate shadow effects, and increase the order n of D(D is n × n matrix) because of the following two reasons.

1) Subdividing of not only faces of a room, but also the faces of objects in the room in order to account for reflection from faces of objects in the room.
2) The illuminance distribution is complicated due to shadows.

3.2 Calculation of interreflection taking into account shadows

In order to calculate shadows, a test to determine whether or not objects exist between every pair of subsurfaces is required. Due to the complexity of this test, it is executed only for the four corner points of every subsurface. That is, the shadow test is done between every corner point. Following this method, the illuminance at the corner points of each subsurface is calculated, and the illuminance of each subsurface is assumed to be an average of the illuminance at its four corner points.

Even though n in equation (5) was the number of subsurfaces, n is now assumed to be the number of points. That is, both shadow calculation and illuminance calculation are done at corner points of subsurfaces. We define shadow function v_{ij} for adding shadow influence between corner points P_i and P_j, weighting coefficients w_j for illuminance calculation at P_j, and α_{ij} is given by $v_{ij}w_jd_{ij}$ (i.e., $\alpha_{ij}=v_{ij}w_j\rho_jF_{ij}$; d_{ij} is the element of the coefficient matrix, ρ_j =reflectance, F_{ij}=form factor). The shadow function v_{ij}(v is step function) and the weighting coefficient, w_j, are given by

$$v_{ij} = \begin{cases} 1: \text{ if no objects between } P_i \text{ and } P_j; \\ 0: \text{ if blocked;} \end{cases}$$

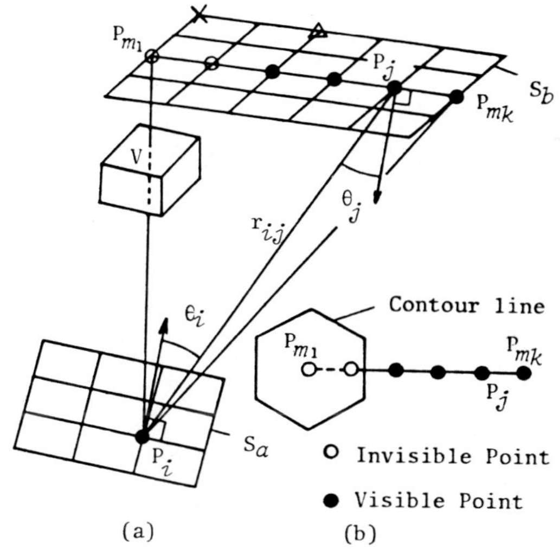

Fig.2 Calculation of shadow function.

$$w_j = \begin{cases} 1/4: P_j \text{ is a corner point of polygon(e.g., "x" in Fig. 2)} \\ 1/2: P_j \text{ is a point on the edge on polygon (e.g., "}\Delta\text{" in Fig. 2)} \\ 1 \;\; : \text{else.} \end{cases}$$

The subsurfaces are usually very small, then form factor F_{ij} in equation (3) can be approximated as follows:

First, we define the function F(S,P) which means the perpendicular distance between a face S and a point P(X,Y,Z). Let the coefficients of the plane of S be (a,b,c,d) where (a,b,c) are the coefficients of the outward pointing normal to the plane of S.

$$F(S,P) = aX + bY + cZ + d \; . \quad (6)$$

We assume that P_i exists on face S_a, P_j exists on face S_b and the area of subsurface including P_j is A_j. Then the following relations are held: $\cos\theta_i=F(S_a,P_j)/r_{ij}$, $\cos\theta_j=F(S_b,P_i)/r_{ij}$. Therefore, F_{ij} is given by

$$F_{ij}=F(S_a,P_j)F(S_b,P_i)/(\pi r_{ij}^4)A_j \; . \quad (7)$$

Let's explain how to obtain the shadow functions. The calculation of shadow functions v_{ij} are complex. If v_{ij} are calculated by the point by point method, we need much time.

A line segment $P_{ml}P_{mk}$ consisting of P_j(j=ml,...,mk) on a face of a polyhedron, S_b, is handled as a linear light source. As shown in Fig.2, the shadow function for a point P_i on a face of another polyhedron, S_a, is obtained by the following steps:

1) Set V_{ij}(j=ml,....,mk) to 1.
2) Remove polyhedra behind S_a and S_b.
3) Remove the polyhedra not intersecting the triangle $P_iP_{ml}P_{mk}$ by using the bounding boxes of the triangle and the polyhedra.

4) Obtain the polyhedra intersecting the plane of the triangle $P_i P_{ml} P_{mk}$.
5) Extract contour lines(silhouette contours) of the polyhedra viewed from P_i, calculate the intersection between these contour lines and the segment $P_{ml} P_{mk}$.
6) Search the sections(i.e., invisible parts) of $P_{ml} P_{mk}$ enclosed by these contour lines when viewed from P_i, and set v_{ij} =0 at every point in these sections(Fig. 2-b shows the contour line of a convex polyhedron and the line segment $P_{ml} P_{mk}$ when viewed from calculation point P_i)

3.3 Calculation of interreflection for a large number of subsurfaces

Equation (5) can be solved by using Gauss Seidel iteration. However, in this method when the number of unknowns, n , is large(e.g., more than 1000), enormous memory capacity(i.e., $n \times n$) is required for the coefficient matrix D. In order to avoid preparing D in the main memory, equation (5) is approximated as follows.

We assume that matrix A consist of α_{ij}(i.e., A=I-D, I=unit matrix) and E_k is the illuminance of the k-th order reflection. E_k is obtained by

$$E_k = AE_{k-1} (k=1,2,...), \qquad (8)$$

where E_0 is direct illuminance. The total illuminance is obtained by summing up every order of the components of illuminance. The values of the higher-order components can be neglected. If we use the equation including the terms up to the K-th order of illuminance, the total illuminance is given by

$$E = \sum_{k=1}^{K} E_k \qquad (9)$$

Once the calculation of direct illuminance E_0, E_1, E_2,.., and E_k are calculated, then the total illuminance is obtained by the summation of these values. By using this calculation method, matrix A is not necessarily stored in the main memory(A is stored in disk) because each of row vectors of A is called from the disk when equation (8) is calculated. Therefore, only three column vectors, E, E_k and E_{k-1}, are required in the main memory.

3.4 Subdivision into subsurfaces

The ceilings, walls, floors and faces of objects within a room are subdivided into subsurfaces. If we take into account all faces of objects in the room for interreflection, the number of subsurfaces become too large, so small faces having low reflectance are ignored.

Let the size of a face to be subdivided be $W_u \times W_v$, and the desired width of a subsurface be W. The width of mesh, w_u and w_v, are obtained by

$$w_u=W_u/[W_u/W+0.5], \quad w_v=W_v/[W_v/W+0.5], \qquad (10)$$

where the symbol [ ] means truncation. Basically the shape of a face to be subdivided is a rectangle or a parallelogram. For other shapes of faces, the minimum rectangle surrounding the face is subdivided and the reflectance at the mesh points outside the original shape of the face are set at zero (points marked "×" in Fig.3-a). Note that the weighting coefficients inner original shape is set as the ratio of the original shapes area in four subsurfaces including the calculation point(e.g., P_1, P_2, P_3 and P_4 in Fig. 3-a are 0.25, 0.5, 1.0 and 0.6, respectively).

Considering the practical case of the interior of a room, there are doors and windows on the walls. The distributions of their reflectance are different. In order to take into account these effects, different reflectance values are given for the mesh points inside these special areas(e.g., points marked "." in Fig. 3-b). To save memory, only point numbers with changing reflectance values are memorized using a run length encoding method.

3.5 Illuminance at each point on a screen

The illuminance calculation at each point on a scan line is described. Here, we only discuss the indirect component(see Appendix for direct component).

If each subsurface were displayed as a constant intensity, the intensity at the boundaries of the subsurfaces would change stepwise. For smooth shading, indirect illuminance at inner points of the subsurface is obtained by using the linear interpolation in the object space. As shown in Fig. 4-a, let the corner points be $P_{i,j}$, $P_{i+1,j}$, $P_{i+1,j+1}$, $P_{i,j+1}$, and the indirect illuminance at these points $E_{i,j}$, $E_{i+1,j}$, $E_{i+1,j+1}$, $E_{i,j+1}$, respectively. The indirect illuminance at an inner point P is given by

$$E = (1-\alpha)(1-\beta)E_{i,j} + (1-\alpha)\beta E_{i+1,j} + (1-\beta)\alpha E_{i,j+1} + \alpha\beta E_{i+1,j+1}, \qquad (11)$$

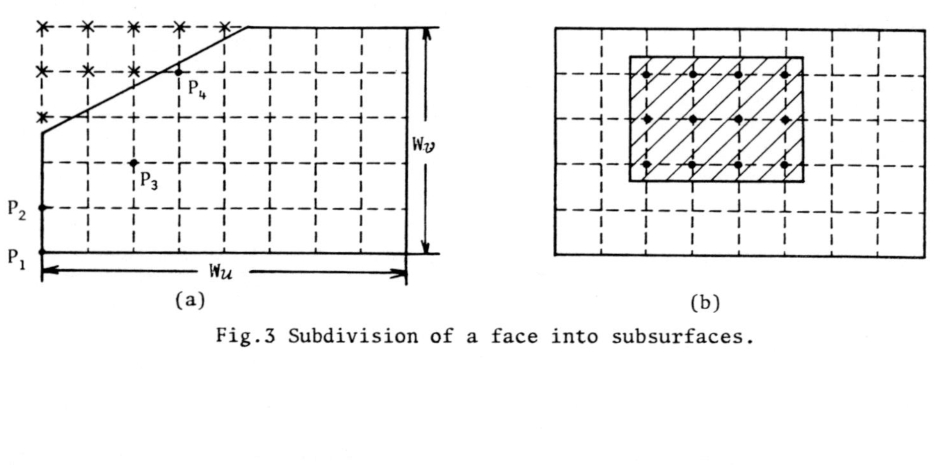

(a) (b)

Fig.3 Subdivision of a face into subsurfaces.

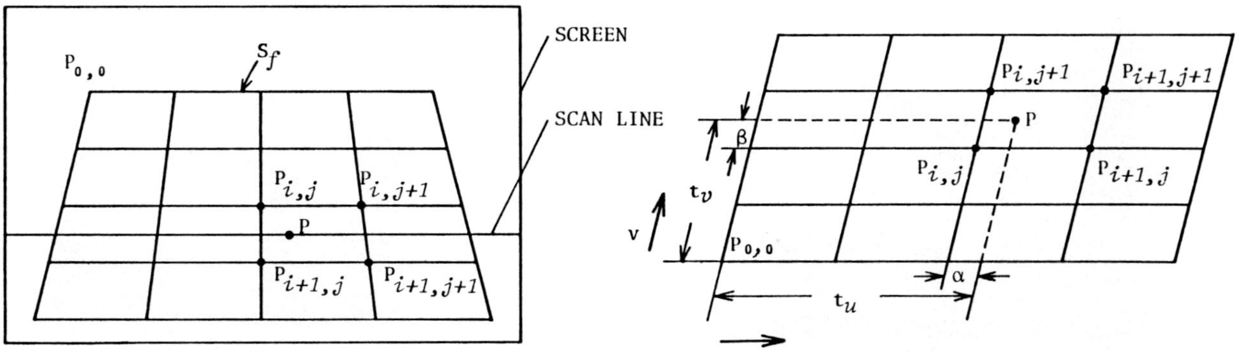

(a) A point P on a screen (b) A point P on 3-D space

Fig.4 Illuminance calculation on a screen.

where weighting factors α and β are obtained by the following.

As shown in Fig. 4-b, we assume that u and v are vectors which indicate i-direction and j-direction of mesh of S_f, and their magnitude are w_u^{-1} and w_v^{-1}, respectively.

Subsurface (i,j) containing P is determined by

$$i=[t_u],\ j=[t_v]\ , \qquad (12)$$

where $\quad t_u=(P-P_{0,0})\cdot u \ ,\ t_v=(P-P_{0,0})\cdot v$

Thus α and β are obtained by

$$\alpha=t_u-[t_u],\ \beta=t_v-[t_v]. \qquad (13)$$

4. EXAMPLES

Fig. 5 shows a computer room illuminated by area light sources; these examples are made in this room. Pictures (a) and (b) are the room illuminated by the light only from the windows; the windows are usually assumed as area sources. (c) and (d) show night scenes illuminated by two ceiling lamps (rectangle sources).

Pictures (a) and (c) are calculated only for direct illuminance, and (b) and (d) are calculated for direct and indirect illuminance; in all these cases, shadow effects are included.

Picture (e) shows the illuminance distributions of the night scene. The upper left side shows the direct and indirect illuminance, the upper right side only shows the direct illuminance; both of them take into account the shadow effect. While the lower left one shows the direct and indirect illuminance but does not consider the shadow effect. The lower right one only shows the indirect illuminance taking account of shadows; in other words, it shows the difference between the upper left and the upper right.

As shown in picture (e), even though there is no direct illumination on the ceiling, the ceiling is bright due to the indirect illumination, and it shows that the indirect component is not uniform due to obstructions within the room. In these examples, the order of reflection, K, is four, because the illuminance distributions for K=4 and K=5 are almost the same, but some differences exist between 3 and 4. The number of subsurfaces, 980, was chosen in the same way.

These examples make clear that accounting for indirect illumination and shadows(especially penumbrae) is an indispensable condition for generating realistic images.

5. CONCLUSION

This paper described a representation method for three-dimensional objects taking account interreflection and shadows.

The following conclusions can be stated from the results.

(1) It requires a terrible amount of computation time to calculate the interreflection at every point, thus faces are subdivided into subsurfaces. The calculation of interreflection is done on subsurfaces before shading at each point on the screen.

(2) Predetermination of the boundaries of penumbrae and umbrae for direct illumination also can be applied to the calculation of indirect illuminance, including shadows, at each subsurface.

(3) Shading effects between subsurfaces belonging to different faces is calculated at the corner points of subsurfaces. This calculation is done efficiently by handling the series of corner points existing on the same line as a linear source.

(4) When direct illuminance including penumbra and interreflection is calculated precisely, the realism of half-tone representation is much improved.

(5) The algorithm can handle direct and indirect illumination for all types of light sources such as point sources, linear sources, area sources, and polyhedron sources. The proposed algorithm thus can be expected to work well for realistic lighting designs.

ACKNOWLEDGEMENTS

We gratefully appreciate the many helpful comments from Laurin Herr of Pacific Interface.

(a)

(b)

(c)

(d)

(e)

Fig.5 Examples.
(a) and (b) show the room illuminated by the light from a window.
(c) and (d) show night scenes illuminated by two rectangular sources.
(a) and (c) are considered only about direct illumination.
(e) shows the illuminance distribution: upper left; direct+indirect, upper right; direct only, lower left; direct+indirect(no shadows), lower right; indirect only.

Appendix: Shading for finite size light sources

The case of an area light source is discussed here because shading methods for other types of light sources is similar.

(1) Shadow boundaries on faces

In deciding whether or not one convex polyhedron casts its shadow(umbra and penumbra) on another polyhedron, we use the shadow volumes which are formed by polyhedra and light sources; the fundamental idea of shadow volumes was introduced by Crow[12].

The umbra volume and the penumbra volume for an area source are determined by the following method:

We consider a shadow volume U_ℓ which is formed by a convex polyhedron V and one vertex Q_ℓ of a source(as shown in Fig. 6). Then, a penumbra volume is defined as the minimum convex volume surrounding all U_ℓ $(\ell=1,2,..,m)$, and an umbra volume is defined as the intersection of $U_\ell(\ell=1,2,..,m)$.

The same method of application for the area source mentioned above determines umbra and penumbra volumes for linear and polyhedron sources.

The shadow boundary on a face is obtained by the intersection region of the penumbra(or umbra) volume and the face.

(2) Illuminance Calculation

Here we assume that the light sources are composed of uniformly bright surfaces. The illuminance for area light sources can be calculated by the contour integration method for the boundary of the source. As shown in Fig. 7, if the area source has m vertices and an intensity of L, the illuminance at a point P on a face S_f is given by

$$E = L/2 \sum_{\ell=1}^{m} \beta_\ell \cos\delta_\ell , \qquad (14)$$

where β_ℓ is the angle between PQ_ℓ and $PQ_{\ell+1}$, δ_ℓ is the angle between the face S_f and the triangle $PQ_\ell Q_{\ell+1}$. The illuminance calculation for polyhedron sources can be obtained by the contour integration method for the contour line of the source when viewed from the calculating point.

For umbrae, the direct illuminance calculation is simplified. Where we consider the shadows from many polyhedra, if the point P is included in at least one umbra, then the direct illuminance at P is zero.

On the other hand, the direct illuminance calculation in the penumbra is more complex. A penumbra area is the region in which the light from the source is partially interrupted by several polyhedra. Therefore, the illuminance at the point P must be calculated by obtaining the visible parts of the light source viewed from P.

The illuminance in the penumbra caused by several polyhedra interrupting light from an area (or polyhedron) source can be calculated by the following method:

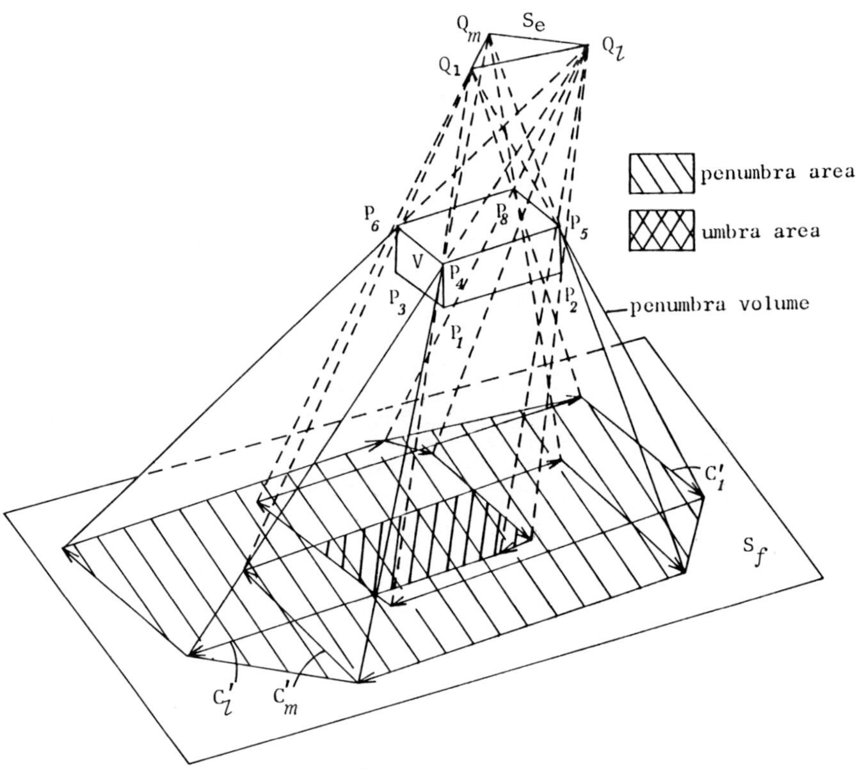

Fig.6 Regions of umbra and penumbra for an area source.

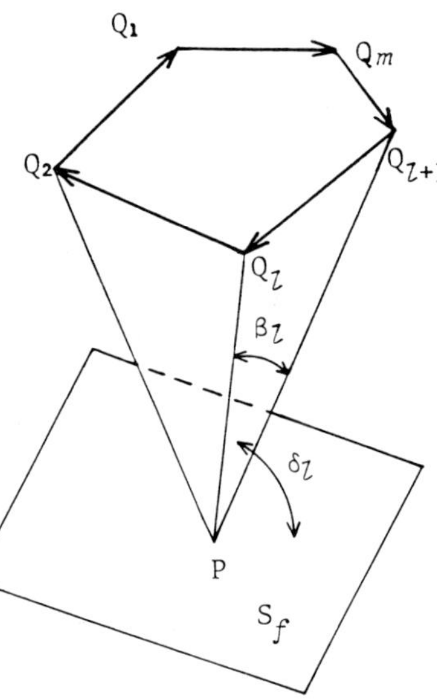

Fig.7 Illuminance calculation for an area source.

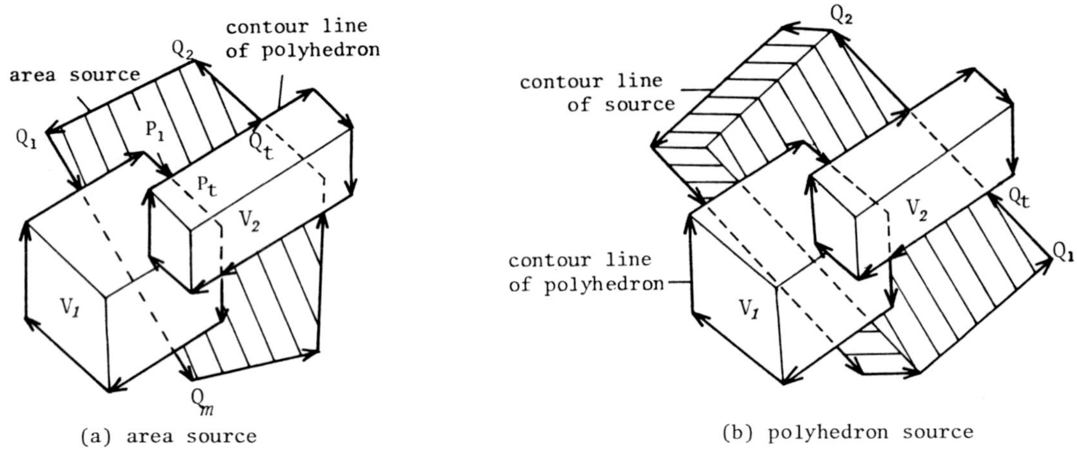

Fig.8 Illuminance calculation in penumbra by using the contour integration method.

The illuminance at P is obtained by summing up the integrated values in the following integrations because it is equal to the integration of the closed region (shaded regions in Fig. 8); integration of the visible segments (e.g., Q_tQ_2 in Fig. 8-a, Q_1Q_t in Fig. 8-b) of the contour line of the source in a counter-clockwise direction, and integration of the segments which exist within the contour line of the source and outside the contour lines of another polyhedra (e.g., P_1P_t in Fig. 8-a), in a clockwise direction.

References

[1] Bui-Tuong,Phong: Illumination for Computer-Generated Pictures, Comm. ACM, Vol.18, No.6 (1975) pp.311-317.

[2] Cook, R.L. and Torrance, K.E.: A Reflectance Model for Computer Graphics, ACM Trans. on Graphics, Vol.1, No.1(1982) pp.7-24.

[3] Blinn, J.F. and Newell, M.E.: Texture and Reflection in Computer Generated Images, Comm. ACM, Vol.19, No. 10(1976) pp.542-546.

[4] Illuminating Engineering Society of North America, IES LIGHTING HANDBOOK Reference Volume(1981).

[5] Takahashi, Ishino et al.: Computer Method for Predetermining Illuminance in an Interior Lighting Installation, Journal of Illuminating Institute of Japan(Japanese), Vol.54, No.12 (1970) pp.697-707.

[6] Jensen, P. and Lewin, I.: The Effect of Room Obstructions on the Calculation of Inter-reflected Components, IES Tech. Conf. Priprint No. 29(1982).

[7] Goral, C.M., Torrance,K.E., Greenberg,D.P. and Battaile, B.: Modeling the Interaction of Light Between Diffuse Surfaces, Computer Graphics, Vol.18,No.3(1984) pp.213-222.

[8] Nishita, T., Okamura,I. and Nakamae,E.: Shading Models for Point and Linear Sources, submitted for publication(TOG) (1983).

[9] Nishita, T. and Nakamae, E.: Half-Tone Representation of 3-D Objects Illuminated by Area Sources or Polyhedron Sources, Proceedings of The IEEE Computer Society's International Computer Software and Applications Conference (COMPSAC)(1983) pp.237-241.

[10] Nishita, T. and Nakamae,E. : An Algorithm for Half-tone Representation of Three-Dimensional Objects, Information Processing in Japan, Vol.14 (1974) pp.93-99.

[11] Nishiata, T. and Nakamae, E.: Half-Tone Representation of 3-D Objects with Smooth Edges by Using a Multi-Scanning Method,Transactions of Information Processing Society of Japan (Japanese), Vol. 25, No.5(1984) pp.703-711.

[12] Crow, F.C.: Shadow Algorithms for Computer Graphics, Computer Graphics, Vol.11, No.2(1977) pp.242-247.

THE HEMI-CUBE
A RADIOSITY SOLUTION FOR COMPLEX ENVIRONMENTS

Michael F. Cohen and Donald P. Greenberg
Cornell University
Ithaca, N. Y. 14853

ABSTRACT

This paper presents a comprehensive method to calculate object to object diffuse reflections within complex environments containing hidden surfaces and shadows. In essence, each object in the environment is treated as a secondary light source. The method provides an accurate representation of the "diffuse" and "ambient" terms found in typical image synthesis algorithms. The phenomena of "color bleeding" from one surface to another, shading within shadow envelopes, and penumbras along shadow boundaries are accurately reproduced. Additional advantages result because computations are independent of viewer position. This allows the efficient rendering of multiple views of the same scene for dynamic sequences. Light sources can be modulated and object reflectivities can be changed, with minimal extra computation. The procedures extend the radiosity method beyond the bounds previously imposed.

CR Categories and Subject Descriptors: I.3.7 [Computer Graphics]: Three-Dimensional Graphics and Realism; I.3.3 [Computer Graphics]: Picture/Image Generation

General Terms: Algorithms

Additional Keywords and Phrases: Radiosity, diffuse reflections, hidden surface, form-factors, depth buffer.

INTRODUCTION

The representation of a realistic image of both actual and imagined scenes has been the goal of artists and scholars for centuries. The invention of the camera allowed the photographer to mechanically record the light passing through a lens and focused onto a piece of film, thus producing a realistic image. Today, within the field of computer graphics, one aspect of current research has been the attempt to produce realistic images of non-existent scenes. This is accomplished by simulating the distribution of light energy given a geometric and physical description of the environment. One major difficulty has been the correct simulation of the global illumination effects.

Light leaving an object surface originates from the surface by direct emission, as from a light source, or by the reflection or transmission of incident light. The incident light on a surface can arrive directly from a light source (along a direct line of sight) or indirectly by generally complex intermediate reflections and transmissions from other surfaces within the environment. Previously these secondary light "sources" have been ignored in computer graphics image generation algorithms. The summation of these sources have usually been approximated by an added constant term, referred to as the ambient component. [9] Some aspect of the global illumination has been achieved by the addition of a specular component found in ray tracing algorithms [13]. In essence, rays are traced only in the mirror reflection or transmission directions, point sampling the environment at the specific surface intersections. Ray tracing with cones [1] or distributed ray tracing [2] extends this procedure by gathering light from more than one point per ray, but can not accurately model the global environmental lighting effects.

The majority of surfaces in a real environment are "diffuse" reflectors, i.e., an incident beam of light is reflected or scattered in all directions within the entire hemisphere above the reflecting surface. A special case of diffuse reflection is the so-called "ideal" diffuse or "Lambertian" reflection. In this case, the incident light is reflected from a surface with equal intensity in all directions. Ideal diffuse reflection is assumed in this paper. Specular reflections, from mirror-like surfaces, which account for a much smaller proportion of the reflected light energy, are not considered.

Thermal engineers have previously developed methods to determine the exchange of radiant energy between surfaces. [10] [11] Methods have been developed to determine the energy exchange within enclosures. The application of one such method, known as the radiosity method to computer graphics, was outlined in a paper by Goral. [5]

This paper extends the use of the radiosity method, to a broader class of problems. In particular, complex environments with occluded surfaces are allowed. In addition, very efficient procedures to render an image from the radiosity data are discussed and illustrated with examples.

RADIOSITY

The radiosity method describes an equilibrium energy balance within an enclosure. The essential features are summarized here for completeness. [5] It is assumed that all emission and reflection processes are ideal diffuse. Thus, after reflection from a surface, the past history or direction of a ray is lost.

The light leaving a surface (its radiosity) consists of self-emitted light and reflected or transmitted incident light. The amount of light arriving at a surface requires a complete specification of the geometric relationships among all reflecting and transmitting surfaces, as well as the light leaving every other surface. This relationship is given by:

$$\text{Radiosity}_i = \text{Emission}_i + \text{Reflectivity}_i \int_{env} \text{Radiosity}_j \, \text{Form-factor}_{ij} \qquad (1)$$

Radiosity (B): The total rate of energy leaving a surface. Sum of emitted and reflected energy. (energy/unit time/unit area)

Emission (E): The rate of energy (light) emitted from a surface. (energy/unit time/unit area)

Reflectivity (P): The fraction of incident light which is reflected back into the environment. (unitless)

Form-factor (F): The fraction of the energy leaving one surface which lands on another surface. (unitless)

This equation states that the amount of energy (or light) leaving a particular surface is equal to the self-emitted light plus the reflected light. The reflected light is equal to the light leaving every other surface multiplied by both the fraction of that light which reaches the surface in question, and the reflectivity of the receiving surface. The sum of the reflected light from a given surface plus the light emitted directly from the surface is termed its radiosity. (Figure 1)

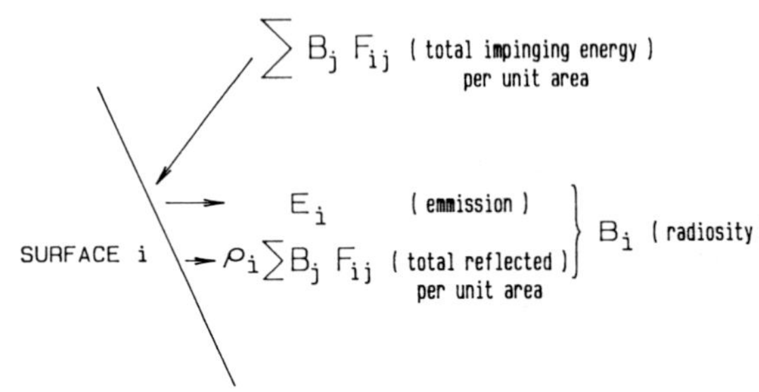

RADIOSITY RELATIONSHIPS

Figure 1

If the environment is subdivided into discrete surface elements or "patches", for which a constant radiosity is assumed, a set of simultaneous equations can be generated to describe the interaction of light energy within the environment. [5]

These equations take the form: (2)

$$\begin{bmatrix} 1-\rho_1F_{11} & -\rho_1F_{12} & \cdots & -\rho_1F_{1N} \\ -\rho_2F_{21} & 1-\rho_2F_{2N} & \cdots & -\rho_2F_{2N} \\ \cdot & \cdot & & \cdot \\ \cdot & \cdot & & \cdot \\ -\rho_NF_{N1} & -\rho_NF_{N2} & \cdots & 1-\rho_NF_{NN} \end{bmatrix} \begin{bmatrix} B_1 \\ B_2 \\ \cdot \\ \cdot \\ B_N \end{bmatrix} = \begin{bmatrix} E_1 \\ E_2 \\ \cdot \\ \cdot \\ E_N \end{bmatrix}$$

The color of an object is determined by its reflectivity (or emission in the case of a light source) at each wavelength of the visible spectrum. The reflectivity and emission terms in the above equations are, therefore, valid for a particular wavelength or band of wavelengths. It is necessary to form and solve the above matrix for each band of interest in order to determine the full radiosity of each patch. For the current discussion, it is sufficient to state that each point or patch is assumed to have a single constant radiosity B, even though this radiosity may be a set of three or more values to represent the radiosity at the different bands of interest. It is important to note that the form-factors are solely a function of geometry and are thus independent of any color considerations.

The FORM-FACTOR

The form-factor specifies the fraction of the energy leaving one surface which lands on another. By definition the sum of all the form-factors from a particular point or patch is equal to unity. Previous derivations do not account for occluding surfaces, and have therefore not reproduced shadows and penumbras.

The geometric terms in the form-factor derivation are illustrated in Figure 2. For non-occluded environments the form-factor for one differential area to another is given by:

$$F_{dAi\ dAj} = \frac{\cos\phi_i \cos\phi_j}{\pi r^2} \qquad (3)$$

By integrating over area j , the form-factor from a finite area (or patch) to a differential area can be expressed:

$$F_{dAi\ Aj} = \int_{A_j} \frac{\cos\phi_i \cos\phi_j}{\pi r^2}\, dA_j \qquad (4)$$

The form-factor between finite surfaces (patches) is defined as the area average and is thus:

$$F_{Ai\ Aj} = \frac{1}{Ai} \int_{Ai}\int_{Aj} \frac{\cos\phi_i \cos\phi_j}{\pi r^2}\, dAj\, dAi \qquad (5)$$

This expression for the form-factor does not account for the possibility of occluding objects hiding all or part of one patch from another. There is, therefore, a missing term within the integrand if hidden surfaces are to be accounted for.

$$F_{Ai\ Aj} = \frac{1}{Ai} \int_{Ai}\int_{Aj} \frac{\cos\phi_i \cos\phi_j}{\pi r^2}\, HID\, dAj\, dAi \qquad (6)$$

The function (HID) takes on a value of one or zero depending on whether differential area i can "see" differential area j. The HID function has the effect of producing the projection of area j visible from differential area i. It is the solution for this double area integral (6), which must be found to solve for radiosities in any non-convex environment.

In the past this double area integral has proven difficult to solve analytically for general applications. Form-factors between specific shapes and orientations, such as parallel rectanglar plates or circular disks, have been solved and tabulated [10]. An area integral, which is a double integral itself, can be transformed via Stoke's theorem into a single contour integral which can then be evaluated [5] [11]. For non-occluded environments the double area integral can be transformed into a double contour integral. A more general approach is needed to handle complex geometries.

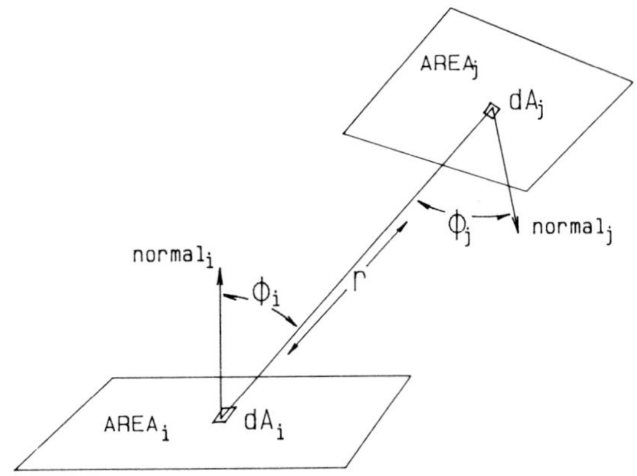

FORM-FACTOR GEOMETRY

Figure 2

Numerical techniques can provide a more efficient means to compute form-factors for general complex environments. Starting from a geometric analog to the analytic derivation, a numerical method is outlined to approximate the patch to patch form-factors which includes the hidden surface effects.

If the distance between the two patches is large compared to their size, and they are not partially occluded from one another, it can be seen that the integrand of the inner integral remains almost constant. In that case the effect of the outer integral is simply a multiplication by one and finding a solution to the inner integral will provide a good approximation for the form-factor. If the patches are close together relative to their size, or there is partial occlusion, the patches can be subdivided into smaller patches and the single integral equation approximation can still be used.

The form-factor from patch to patch is approximated with the differential area to finite area equation (4) by using the center point of patch i to represent the average position of patch i. Each patch has as its "view" of the environment, the hemisphere surrounding its normal.

A geometric analog for the form-factor integral was developed by Nusselt [10] and has been used to obtain form-factors by both photography and planimetry. (Figure 3). For a finite area, the form-factor is equivalent to the fraction of the circle (which is the base of the hemisphere) covered by projecting the area onto the hemisphere and then orthographically down onto the circle.

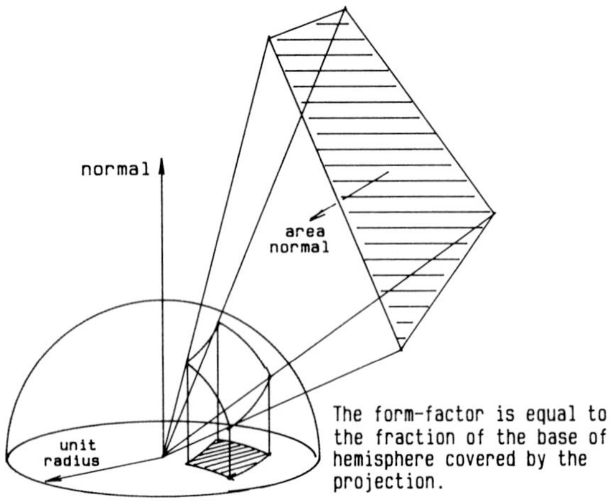

The projection onto the hemisphere accounts for the 1/r term as well as the cosine of the angle between the normal of the projecting patch and the r vector. The orthographic projection onto the circle has the effect of multiplying by the cosine of the angle between the "r" vector and the normal of the receiving patch. The PI in the denominator accounts for the area of a circle with unit radius.

NUSSELT ANALOG

Figure 3

This hemisphere can be broken into small delta solid angles, each representing a delta form-factor. The delta form-factor is equal to the fraction of the hemisphere subtended by the delta solid angle multiplied by the cosine of the angle from the normal. The form-factor to a patch is equal to the sum of the delta form-factors covered when projecting the patch onto the hemisphere. If all the patches in the environment are projected onto the hemisphere, removing the more distant areas in the case of an overlap, the final projection and summations would provide the form-factors to all patches from the patch represented at the center of the hemisphere. This procedure would then intrinsically include the effects of hidden surfaces.

In order to perform the summation of delta form-factors for each patch one would like a convenient means for discretizing the surface of the hemisphere. An evaluation can then be made as to which patch projects onto that discrete area. Difficulty in creating equal sized elements on a sphere as well as creating a set of linear coordinates to uniquely describe locations on its surface makes this approach impractical.

THE HEMI-CUBE

An efficient algorithm to compute form factors in general complex environments is described below.

From the definition of the form-factor it can be seen that any two patches in the environment, which when projected onto the hemisphere occupy the same area and location, will have the same form-factor value. This is also true for projections onto any other surrounding surface. (Figure 4)

Instead of projecting onto a sphere, an imaginary cube is constructed around the center of the receiving patch. (Figure 5) The environment is transformed to set the patch's center at the origin with the patch's normal coinciding with the positive Z axis. In this orientation the hemisphere described above is replaced by the upper half of the surface of the cube, the lower half being below the "horizon" of the patch. One full face, facing in the Z direction and four half-faces, facing in the +X -X +Y and -Y directions replace the hemisphere. These faces are divided into square "pixels" at a given resolution, generally between 50 x 50 and 100 x 100, and the environment is then projected onto the five planar surfaces. (Figure 6) Each full face of the cube covers exactly a 90 degree frustum as viewed from the center of the cube. This creates clipping planes of Z = X , Z = -X , Z = Y, and Z = -Y , allowing for simple comparisons to determine which side of a clipping plane any point lies. Every other patch in the environment is clipped to the frustum using a Sutherland-Hodgman type polygon clipper [8] streamlined to handle 90 degree frustums.

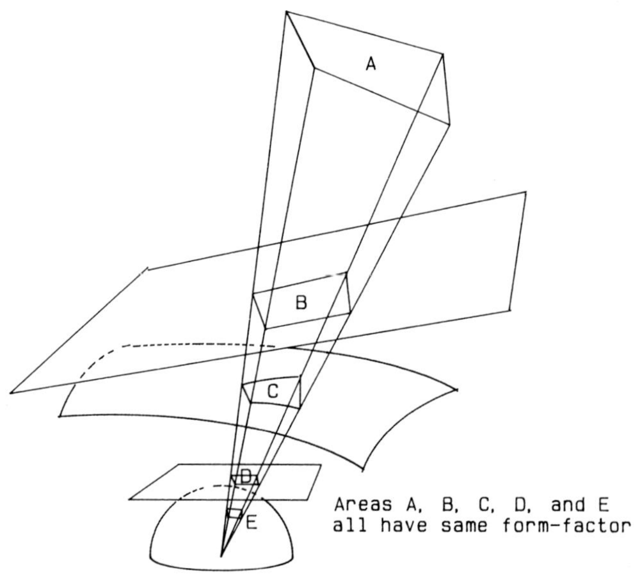

AREAS WITH IDENTICAL FORM-FACTOR

Figure 4

If two patches project onto the same pixel on the cube, a depth determination is made as to which patch is "seen" in that particular direction by comparing distances to each patch and selecting the nearer one. This depth buffer type hidden surface algorithm is well known in computer graphics. [3] However, rather than maintaining intensity information, an item buffer is maintained of which patch is seen at each pixel on the cube. [12]

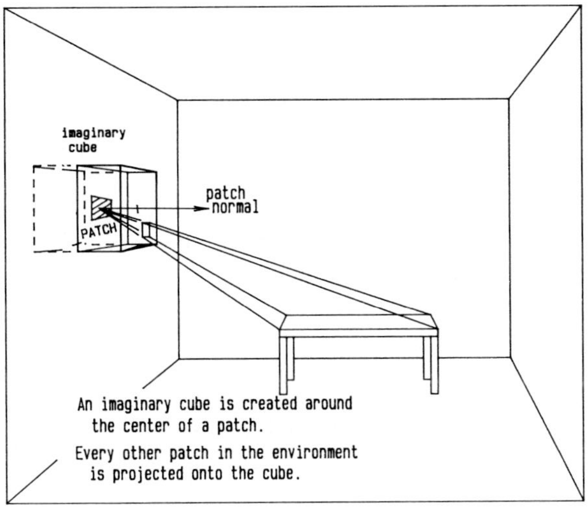

PROJECTION OF THE ENVIRONMENT ONTO THE HEMI-CUBE

Figure 5

After determining which patch(j) is visible at each pixel on the hemi-cube, a summation of the delta form-factors for each pixel occupied by patch(j) determines the form-factor from patch (i) at the center of the cube to patch(j). This summation is performed for each patch(j) and a complete row of N form-factors is found.

At this point the hemi-cube is positioned around the center of another patch and the process is repeated for each patch in the environment. The result is a complete set of form-factors for complex environments containing occluded surfaces.

$$F_{ij} = \sum_{q=1}^{R} \Delta F_q \tag{7}$$

ΔF_q = Delta form-factor associated with pixel_q on hemi-cube

R = Number of hemi-cube pixels covered by projection of patch onto the hemi-cube

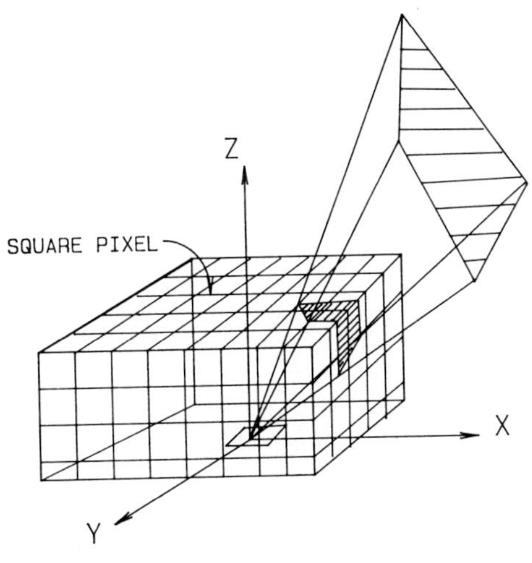

THE HEMI-CUBE

Figure 6

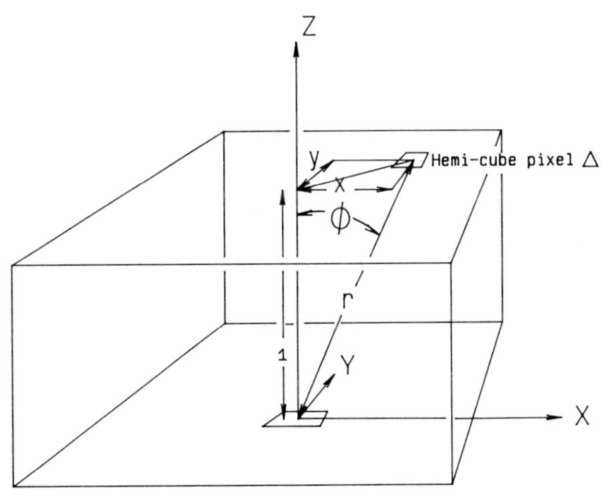

TOP OF HEMI-CUBE

$$r = \sqrt{x^2 + y^2 + 1}$$

$$\cos \phi_i = \cos \phi_j$$

$$\cos \phi = \frac{1}{\sqrt{x^2 + y^2 + 1}}$$

$$\Delta\text{Form-factor} = \frac{\cos \phi_i \cos \phi_j}{\pi r^2} \Delta A$$

$$= \frac{1}{\pi (x^2 + y^2 + 1)^2} \Delta A$$

DERIVATION OF DELTA FORM-FACTORS

Figure 7a

DELTA FORM FACTORS

The contribution of each pixel on the cube's surface to the form-factor value varies and is dependent on the pixel location and orientation. (Figure 7)

A specific delta form-factor value for each pixel on the cube is found from equation (3) for the differential area to differential area form-factor and stored in a lookup table. This table need only contain values for one eighth of the top face and one quarter of one side face due to symmetry.

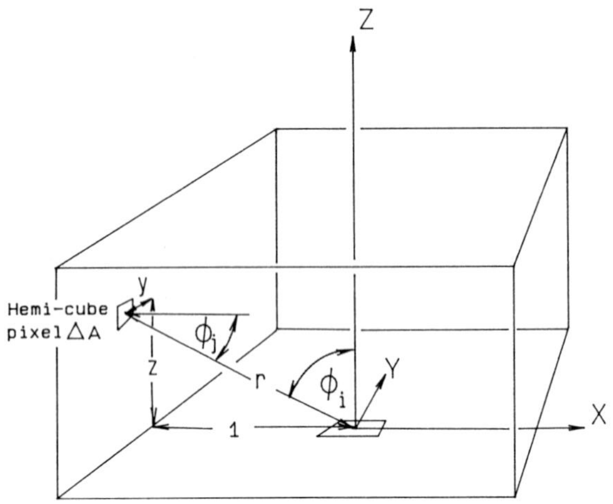

SIDE OF HEMI-CUBE

$$r = \sqrt{y^2 + z^2 + 1}$$

$$\cos \phi_i = \frac{z}{\sqrt{y^2 + z^2 + 1}}$$

$$\cos \phi_j = \frac{1}{\sqrt{y^2 + z^2 + 1}}$$

$$\Delta \text{Form-factor} = \frac{\cos \phi_i \cos \phi_j}{\pi r^2} \Delta A$$

$$= \frac{z}{\pi (y^2 + z^2 + 1)^2} \Delta A$$

DERIVATION OF DELTA FORM-FACTORS

Figure 7b

THE ENERGY BALANCE SOLUTION

The solution for the series of simultaneous equations can be performed with any standard equation solver. However, a Gauss-Siedel iterative approach has a number of advantages. [6] The matrix is well suited to this technique due to the fact that it is diagonally dominant (the sum of the absolute values of each row is less than the main diagonal term). This is always true since, by definition, the sum of any row of form-factors is equal to unity. In the matrix to be solved, each form factor term is multiplied by its surface reflectivity, which is also less than unity. Thus the summation of the absolute values of all terms in any row exclusive of the main diagonal term is also less than one. The main diagonal term is equal to one minus its own form-factor. Since any polygonal (or convex) patch cannot see itself, its own form-factor is equal to zero. Therefore, the main diagonal term is always equal to one, the matrix is strictly diagonally dominant, and guaranteed to converge rapidly to a solution.

An initial guess for the radiosities, which must be supplied for the first iteration, is simply the emission of each patch (only the primary light sources have any initial radiosity). During each iteration each radiosity is solved for, using the previously found values of the other radiosities. Iterations continue until no radiosity value changes by more than a preselected small percentage. The iterative process converges very rapidly, generally in six to eight iterations, and a solution is found in a fraction of the time needed for standard elimination techniques.

Additional computational savings are made by compressing the null entries from the matrix. Zero valued form-factors will occur when one patch cannot "see" another due to occluding surfaces, if they belong to the same polygon, or face away from each other. Zeros will also occur in the matrix if reflectivities are equal to zero.

The matrix is formed and solved for the radiosities from the computed form-factors for each color band of interest. This is generally performed for three channels (red, green, blue) but could be done on a wavelength basis if desired.

RENDERING

To render an image the discretized radiosity information is used to create a continuous shading across a given surface (or polygon). A number of shading schemes have been devised in the past [5], however, most of these take place in image space and are axis dependent. An object space smoothing algorithm is desired in order to be able to render sequences of different views such that the same point in space would retain the same intensity values.

The adopted method uses a bilinear interpolation within each patch. This bilinear variation of radiosities insures first order continuity at patch edges. In order to perform the interpolation, radiosity values must be transferred from the patches themselves to each vertex of the patches. (Figure 8a)

For each polygon, the radiosities of patch vertices which are interior to the polygon containing the patch are computed as the average of radiosities of the surrounding patches. Exterior vertex radiosities are extrapolated values from the adjacent interior vertex radiosities through an average of the adjacent patch radiosities. Finally, the resulting vertex radiosities are used for the bilinear interpolation within each patch. (Figure 8b)

The radiosity solution is independent of view position and direction. To render an image on a raster display device, the eye position as well as the viewing direction and frustum angle must be specified. A transformation matrix sets the eye and view direction within the environment. A depth-buffer/item-buffer algorithm determines which patch is seen at each pixel of the screen.

Finding the intersection between a line from the eye through a pixel, and the plane of the patch which occupies the pixel provides a location within the patch. In order to perform the bilinear interpolation within the patch, this x,y,z position is converted to parametric (u,v) coordinates within the patch.

With this information bilinear interpolation of the three radiosity values are made and the pixel displayed.

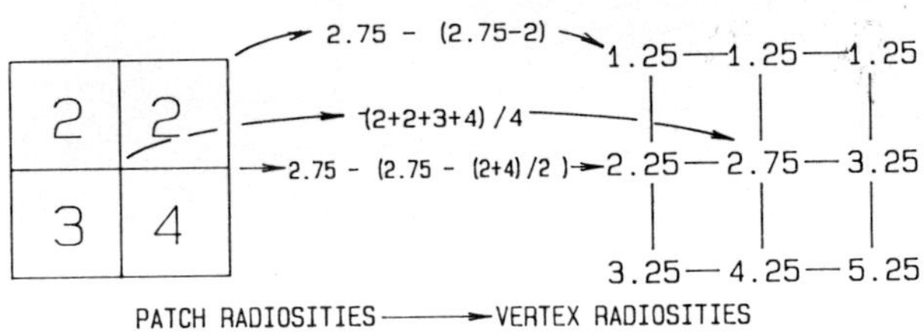

VERTEX RADIOSITIES

Figure 8a

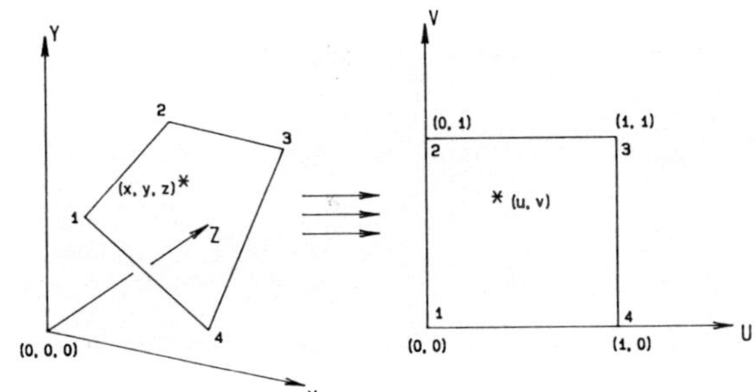

$$B_{(u,v)} = (1-u)(1-v)B_1 + (1-u)\,v\,B_2 + u\,v\,B_3 + u\,(1-v)\,B_4$$

BILINEAR INTERPOLATION OF PIXEL RADIOSITY FROM VERTEX RADIOSITIES

Figure 8b

PROGRAM SUMMARY (Figure 9)

Input: The environment geometry is input from a file containing polygon descriptions and the associated vertex coordinates. Associated with each polygon are reflectivity and emission values for each color band and a parameter for subdividing the polygon into patches.

Form-factors: After the patches are defined, the hemi-cube is set around the center of each patch and a row of form-factors is determined from that patch to all others through their projections onto the cube. A file containing the matrix of form-factors is created.

Radiosity solution: For each color band a matrix is constructed using the form-factors and the appropriate set of reflectivities. The corresponding emission values are then used to solve for patch radiosities. A file containing the radiosities for each color band is written.

Rendering: An eye position, view direction, and frustum angle are specified from which an image is rendered. For each pixel, the location of the ray-patch intersection is computed. The color(s) are found through a bilinear interpolation of the vertex color values and then displayed.

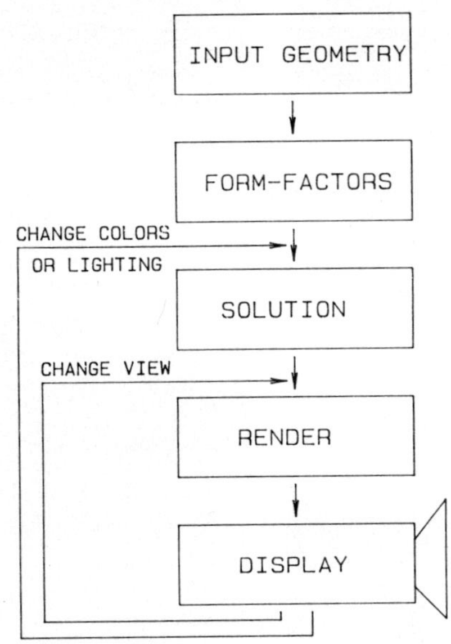

PROGRAM FLOW

Figure 9

SIMULATION VS REALITY

An experimental setup was devised to test the accuracy of computer simulations. A physical model of the simple environment simulated in figure 10 was constructed of wood and cardboard. The light and painted surfaces were made as diffuse as possible. Radiometric measurements were made at locations on the model and compared with the calculated values. A visual side-by-side comparison was made by a group of experimental subjects. Great lengths were taken to control the test conditions for both methods of comparisons. The results from both tests provide conclusive validation of the radiosity method. Details and illustrations of the experimental setup and the results are contained in an article by Meyer et. al. [7].

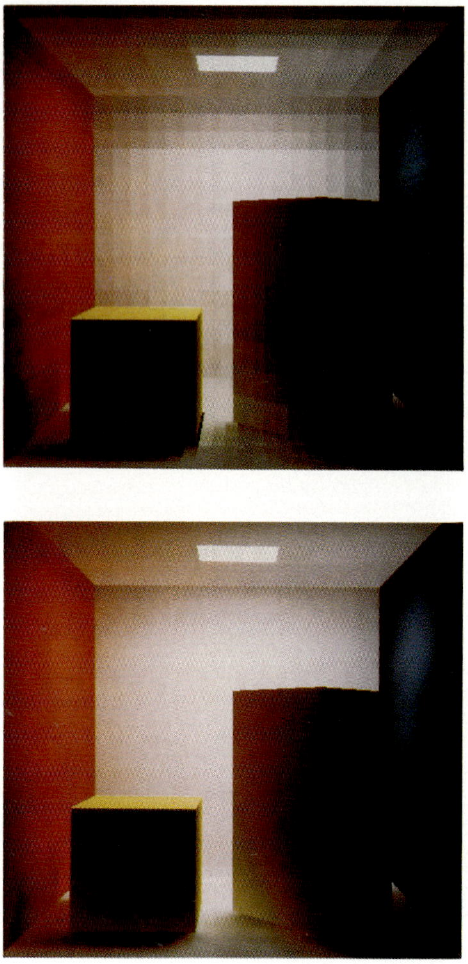

Figure 10

The environment simulated above, although simple in geometry displays a variety of shading characteristics. The patch radiosities are displayed on the top as constantly shaded and on the bottom after the bilinear interpolation for pixel radiosities.

Note:

(1) The distinct color bleeding onto the white and yellow boxes.

(2) The red shadow to the left of the yellow box. The majority of the light which reaches the shaded area arrives indirectly from the red wall, thus the red shadow.

(3) The variation of light intensity on the walls due to the diffuse light source.

No. of Patches: 2370

Form-factor computation: 337 Min.

Solution of matrices: 18 Min.

Rendering and display: 14 Min.

(A)

(B)

(C)

Figure 11

*All computation was performed on a VAX 11/780. The images were displayed on a Grinnell 512 x 480 frame buffer.

The images of figure 11 demonstrate the computational savings achieved when rendering multiple images of the same environment.

No. of patches: 1740	Image A	Image B	Image C
Form-factor comp.:	180 Min.	0 Min.	0 Min.
Matrix solution:	10 Min.	10 Min.	0 Min.
Rendering:	16 Min.	16 Min.	16 Min.
TOTAL:	208 Min.	26 Min.	16 Min.

By changing only the viewing parameters, only the rendering portion of the computation was repeated to produce Image C, thus the savings in total time.

CONCLUSION

The extension of the radiosity solution to environments with occluded surfaces allows the simulation of complex scenes. All surfaces are treated as light sources and thus the global illumination effects are correctly modeled. The influence of occluded surfaces is contained within the solution for the form-factors, and thus shadows and shadow boundaries are properly reproduced.

It should be emphasized that the object space intensity computations are performed independent of the view position and direction. Thus, each phase of the procedure is independent of the modules which follow it. The independence of the algorithm steps permits rendering of dynamic sequences with little additional computation. The rendering can be repeated from different viewpoints without recomputing form-factors or radiosities. If the geometry of the environment remains static, the information to render changes in the lighting conditions is already contained in the form-factors. Thus lights can be turned on/off and object colors can be changed simply by resolving the matrices. The iterative solution converges rapidly, typically in six to eight interations, regardless of the size of the matrix. The entire process need be repeated only with changes in geometry.

The extension of the radiosity method to occluded environments permits the rendering of complex scenes, and thus should have great relevance to computer generated imagery. The computational expense is minimal compared to ray-tracing algorithms especially when rendering dynamic sequences within a static geometry.

A number of issues must be addressed in order to make the radiosity method both general and efficient. Since the accuracy/fineness of the numerical integration of the form-factor depends partially upon the area projected onto the hemi-cube, problems can occur due to aliasing for small projections. In general, objects whose projection onto the hemi-cube is small have little effect. However, for very bright patches such as light sources, the effect of the inaccuracy can have a substantial deleterious effect.

Generalizations must be made to accomodate curved surfaces. Polygonal approximation that would allow use of the same algorithms may suffice for the form-factor computations. However, the exact surface description should be used during rendering.

Since the size of the radiosity computation grows with the square of the number of patches, methods of approximation must be developed to keep the computation manageable as the complexity of the environment increases. Small variations in intensity across a patch have little effect on the overall global illumination. Rather than continue the subdivision of the patches to discern small radiosity variations, more detailed intensity information within a patch can be derived from a coarse patch radiosity solution. In this way the number of patches, and thus the computation time, can be kept to a minimum while allowing complex environments to be rendered. Texture mapping falls into the same category, and can be handled by treating a textured patch's effect on the environment as one average intensity during the radiosity solution.

Provisions must be made to incorporate specular and transparent surfaces into the rendering process or, better yet, into the initial radiosity formulation.

The radiosity method offers a fundamentally new approach to image synthesis by beginning from basic principles of conservation of energy. The radiosity method has been shown to be able to render complex environments. Radiosity should play a major role in future realistic image synthesis systems.

ACKNOWLEDGEMENTS

This research was conducted at the Cornell University Program of Computer Graphics and was supported by the National Science Foundation grant DCR8203979. As with all of the research efforts at CUPCG, this paper is the result of a team effort. Thanks must go to Cindy Goral and Professor Kenneth Torrance for their groundwork introducing radiosity to the computer graphics community. Thanks to David Immel, Philip Brock, and Channing Verbeck for help in software development, to Jutta Joesch, Lisa Maynes, and James Ferwerda for editing the text. Also to Gary Meyer and Holly Rushmeier for conduting experiments to verify the radiosity algorithms, to Janet Brown in preparing the text, and to Emil Ghinger for photography. Thank you, reviewers, for your helpful comments.

REFERENCES

[1] Amanatides, John. Ray Tracing with Cones. ACM Computer Graphics (Proceedings 1985), pp. 129-135.

[2] Cook, Robert. Distributed Ray Tracing. ACM Computer Graphics (Proceedings 1984), pp. 137-145.

[3] Foley, J. D. and Van Dam, A. Fundamentals of Computer Graphics. Addison-Wesley Publishing Co., 1982.

[4] Goral, Cindy M., Torrance, Kenneth E., Greenberg, Donald P., Battaile, Bennett, Modeling the Interaction of Light Between Diffuse Surfaces, ACM Computer Graphics (Proceedings 1984), pp. 213-222.

[5] Gouraud, Henri, Computer Display of Curved Surfaces, Ph.D. Dissertation, University of Utah, 1971.

[6] Hornbeck, Robert W., Numerical Methods. Quantum Publishers, 1975, pp. 101-106.

[7] Meyer, Gary W., Rushmeier, Holly E., Cohen, Michael F., Greenberg, Donald P., Torrance, Kenneth E., Assessing the Realism of Computer Graphics Images, submitted for publication, 1985.

[8] Newman, William M. and Sproull, Robert F., Principles of Interactive Computer Graphics, McGraw Hill, 1979.

[9] Phong, Bui Tuong, Illumination for Computer Generated Images, Ph.D. Dissertation, University of Utah, 1973.

[10] Siegel, Robert and Howell, John R., Thermal Radiation Heat Transfer, Hemisphere Publishing Corp., 1978.

[11] Sparrow, E. M. and Cess R. D., Radiation Heat Transfer, Hemisphere Publishing Corp., 1978.

[12] Weghorst, Hank, Hooper, Gary, and Greenberg, Donald P., Improved Computational Methods for Ray Tracing, ACM Transactions on Graphics, Jan, 1984, pp. 52-69.

[13] Whitted, Turner, An Improved Illumination Model for Shaded Display, Communications of the ACM, June, 1980.

Compositing 3-D Rendered Images

Tom Duff

Room 2C-425
AT&T Bell Laboratories
600 Mountain Avenue
Murray Hill, NJ 07974

ABSTRACT

The complexity of anti-aliased 3-D rendering systems can be controlled by using a tool-building approach like that of the UNIX(TM) text-processing tools. Such an approach requires a simple picture representation amenable to anti-aliasing that all rendering programs can produce, a compositing algorithm for that representation and a command language to piece together scenes. This paper advocates a representation that combines Porter and Duff's compositing algebra with a Z-buffer to provide simple anti-aliased 3-D compositing.

CR Categories and Subject Descriptors: I.3.3 [Picture and Image Generation] Display algorithms, Viewing algorithms, I.3.5 [Computational Geometry and Object Modelling] Curve, surface, solid and object representations, I.3.7 [Three-Dimensional Graphics and Realism] Visible line/surface algorithms

General Terms: Algorithms

Additional Keywords and Phrases: image synthesis, 3-D rendering, hidden-surface elimination, anti-aliasing, Z-buffer, compositing

1. Introduction

3-D rendering programs capable of dealing with detailed scenes are usually large and complex. For example, the version of REYES [1] used at Lucasfilm to create "The Adventures of André & Wally B." [12] is a 40,000 line C program. There are at most two people who understand it in its entirety.

There are several approaches to controlling this complexity. The NYIT Computer Graphics Laboratory has a set of special-purpose rendering programs that all use Z-buffer algorithms (see below) [4]. Each can initialize its Z-buffer with the results produced by the others and add objects to a scene. Thus, to produce a scene containing quadric surfaces, fractal terrain and polyhedra, three simple programs, each rendering one surface type can replace a combined quadric surface/fractal terrain/polyhedron rendering program.

Frank Crow at Ohio State University built a system that combines the output of heterogeneous rendering programs using a list-priority algorithm [3]. [15] describes a rendering test-bed that reduces objects on-the-fly to polygons, slices the polygons into spans the height of scan lines or smaller, and combines the spans using a Z-buffer (usually). The compositing algebra described in [10] is used at Lucasfilm to combine the output of many rendering tools (including REYES).

Their method is a list-priority algorithm with the list ordering worked out manually. A similar algorithm is used at most motion picture special effects houses, running on optical printers instead of digital computers [7].

All these systems have drawbacks. Z-buffer methods are hard to anti-alias, because their data representation is point-sampled (but note chapter 7 of [2]). The Lucasfilm and Ohio State systems require that all surfaces be linearly separable [9]. Even when it is possible to separate a scene by dicing it with cutting planes [5], the primitives in the diced scene may be more complex than in the original. It may even be impossible to find separating planes for scenes containing surfaces that intersect in non-planar curves.

Whitted and Weimer's approach requires that the various rendering sub-methods be connected by a complex polygon-span data structure. Considerable understanding of the system's internals is required to add new features. Anti-aliasing is difficult, but easier than with other Z-buffer style methods.

A similar complexity problem obtains with many document preparation systems and "integrated application environments." Emacs [6] is a text-editor with 450 commands, and more coming every day. Lotus 1-2-3 is a desk calculator with a 250 page instruction manual. The UNIX text processing tools [8] avoid this syndrome by cutting the text processing problem into many small sub-problems, with a small program to handle each piece. Because all the programs read and write a simple common data representation (ASCII character streams with end-of-line marked by a newline character) they can be wired together for particular applications by a simple command language. We would like to apply this philosophy to the problem of anti-aliased 3-D rendering. To do that, we need a simple picture representation that all our rendering programs can produce, a compositing algorithm for that representation and a command language with which to piece together scenes.

2. The rgbαz Representation

The **rgbαz** representation is a straightforward combination of the **rgbα** representation in [10] and a Z-buffer [2]. The hidden-surface algorithms for these representations are based on binary operators that combine a pair of images f and b pixel-by-pixel to produce a composite image $c = f$ **op** b. Applying the operator to a sequence of images in an appropriate order will produce the final image of the visible surfaces.

The Z-buffer operator f **zmin** b operates on a color value **rgb** and a depth coordinate **z** stored at each pixel in the frame buffer. The composite image has $\mathbf{rgb}_c = (\textbf{if } \mathbf{z}_f < \mathbf{z}_b \textbf{ then } \mathbf{rgb}_f \textbf{ else } \mathbf{rgb}_b)$, and $\mathbf{z}_c = \min(\mathbf{z}_f, \mathbf{z}_b)$ at each pixel. [13] categorizes this algorithm, along with the ray-tracing approach advocated by [14], as "brute-force image space" methods (although ray-tracing is usually done in object space), dismissing both as impractical. Ironically, they are the two most popular hidden surface algorithms in use today.

The **rgbα** compositing operator f **over** b operates on pixels containing an **rgb** value and a value α between 0 and 1, which may be thought of as the fraction of the pixel that the object covers. Each component of **rgb** is between 0 and α (see [10] for details).

The operator **over** computes $\mathbf{rgb}_c = \mathbf{rgb}_f + (1-\alpha_f)\mathbf{rgb}_b$ and $\alpha_c = \alpha_f + (1-\alpha_f)\alpha_b$ at each pixel. The foreground $\mathbf{rgb}_f$ is unattenuated at each pixel, and $\mathbf{rgb}_b$ shows through more as α_f decreases. When $\alpha_f = 1$, $c = f$ and when $\alpha_f = 0$, $c = b$, since each component of $\mathbf{rgb}_f$ must be 0 when $\alpha_f = 0$. Using **over** with more than two elements requires knowledge of their front-to-back order, so that the operator can be applied to elements or previous composites that are adjacent in depth.

f **over** *b* is inherently anti-aliased (really area-sampled) if, as is usually the case, α_f and α_b are uncorrelated. It can make mistakes when, for example, two elements share an edge. The only apparent way to solve this problem is to store an unbounded amount of information inside each pixel. [1] is an example of such a method, but it runs slowly and is difficult to implement correctly.

zmin is commutative and associative; that is, the order in which objects are composed is irrelevant. Because the method is point-sampled, anti-aliasing is difficult. **over** trades commutativity for anti-aliasing. It doesn't care whether elements are composited front-to-back or back-to-front or some recursive combination of the two, but they must be adjacent in depth when they are combined.

The **rgbαz** algorithm's compositing operator **comp** combines the action of **zmin** and **over**. Each pixel contains **rgb** and α along with the **z** value at each corner. Corners that are not covered have **z** set to a value (called $+\infty$) larger than any legitimate **z** value. Since each **z** value is used in 4 pixels, we keep the upper left-hand corner **z** with its pixel and get the other values from adjacent pixels. (This means that we must store an extra column off-screen at the right, and a row off the bottom, whose **rgb** and α we never use.)

f **comp** *b* is computed by first comparing $\mathbf{z}_f$ to $\mathbf{z}_b$ at each corner of the pixel. There are $2^4 = 16$ possible outcomes. If the comparisons are not the same at all four corners, we say the pixel is *confused*. Along each pixel edge at whose ends the **z**'s compare differently, we linearly interpolate the **z**'s and find the point at which they are equal. Figure 1 shows how to divide the pixel in each case to compute the fraction β on which *f* is in front. Then $\mathbf{rgb\alpha}_c = \beta(f\ \mathbf{over}\ b) + (1-\beta)(b\ \mathbf{over}\ f)$, and $\mathbf{z}_c = \min(\mathbf{z}_f, \mathbf{z}_b)$.

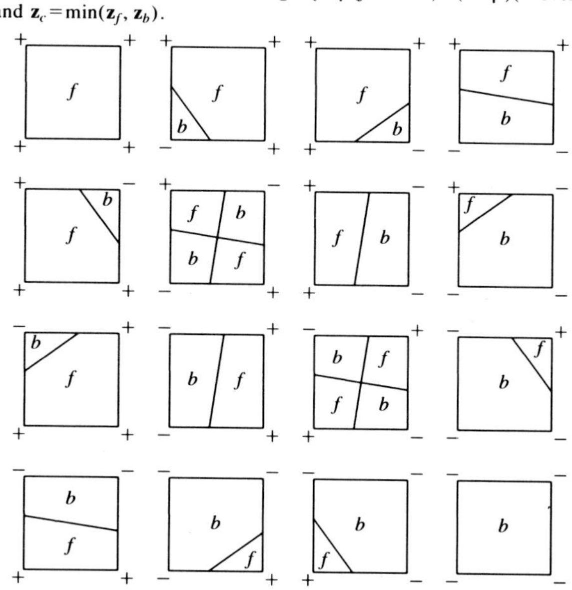

Figure 1 – The 16 Cases

Each square represents a pixel. The corners are marked with the sign of $\mathbf{z}_b - \mathbf{z}_f$. The label in each pixel fragment indicates which picture is visible in it. β is the total area of the fragments labeled *f*.

If $\mathbf{z}_f$ or $\mathbf{z}_b$ is $+\infty$ at some corner, we must pick an appropriate value to use as a surrogate in the comparisons and interpolations above. Currently, we circle the pixel clockwise and anticlockwise from the uncovered corner looking for two legitimate **z**'s and use their average.

Note that **comp** is commutative, since if we interchange *f* and *b*, β is replaced by $1-\beta$. For unconfused pixels, the result's **rgbα** is just *f* **over** *b* or *b* **over** *f*, as appropriate, and therefore the operation is associative in the unconfused case. This is almost good enough to let us combine pictures in any order. Since linearly separable objects have no confused pixels, **comp** performs just as well on them as **over**. For confused pixels associativity breaks down and mistakes can occur. For objects that legitimately intersect, the algorithm effectively computes a sub-pixel resolution polygonal curve that will be close to the intersection curve of the original objects and correctly mattes the objects together along the approximate curve. If an element *q* is between *p* and *r*, the pixels of *p* **comp** *r* can be confused with those of *q*, so elements cannot be composited in completely arbitrary order. Fortunately, the errors are usually small, so a cavalier attitude to compositing order is at least partially justified. If these errors are a problem, a group of elements can be composited all at once by sorting their pixels on their **z** coordinates and applying **comp** on adjacent elements. Then confusion-induced errors will only arise among elements whose confusion is intrinsic.

The **comp** algorithm may also encounter errors caused by the point-sampled **z** coordinates. In particular, small objects may be lost if they fall between the pixels. Furthermore, pixels are combined by area-sampling rather than convolution with a higher-order filter, which can introduce slightly scalloped intersection edges. **comp** shares with **over** the problem that errors can occur when its operands are not uncorrelated, as can happen in pixels crossed by many edges.

3. Examples

I have written a small set of programs to test these ideas. *3matte* executes the **comp** algorithm on a set of input pictures, producing an **rgbαz** output picture. *Quad* draws an anti-aliased rendition of a single quadric surface (figure 2), given the equation of its quadratic form. Using *3matte* to combine the output of multiple *quad* runs generates more complex surfaces, like the knobby-kneed robot of figure 3.

The *quad-3matte* combination is hardly a practical quadric-surface rendering system. It does show that with powerful compositing methods high quality renderings of significant objects can be produced using minimal tools.

Terrain generates anti-aliased perspective views of terrain from National Cartographic Information Center digital terrain data. Figure 4 is a view of central New Jersey, with the elevations exaggerated by a factor of 20. *Bg* generates background cards given the colors at the top and bottom of the screen. Figure 5 shows a small covey of flying saucers over New Jersey with a sky-colored background.

Figure 5 shows the sort of error that can be made when confused pixels are treated naively. Where a saucer passes behind the the right-most foreground hill the silhouette of the hill is a little too dark near the peak.

Programs that do certain kinds of 2- and 3-dimensional image processing can operate on **rgbαz** pictures. For example, *hrot* rotates the hue of a picture, leaving alone its saturation and value [11]. The middle flying saucer of figure 5 was generated in the same colors as the one on the left, and had its hue rotated 30 degrees. *Fog* is a program that makes foggy images by mixing its input image with a fog color in an amount that depends on the **z** coordinates of the pixels. Figure 6 is the result of applying a purple haze to figure 5. The shadow-generation algorithm of [16] works on **rgbαz** pictures and could be enhanced to take advantage of the increased information available in the **rgbαz** representation.

These programs are all small and simple to write. *3matte* is 270 lines of C, *quad* is 428 lines, *terrain* is 339 lines, *bg* is 58 lines, *hrot* is 76 lines, and *fog* is 73 lines, for a total of 1244 lines.

Figure 5 is a frame from a short animated sequence produced using these programs. The sequence was 227 frames long, and took 34 hours and 26 minutes to compute (total wall-clock time, half on each of 2 VAX 11/750s, one with a floating-point accelerator and one without), or roughly 9 minutes per frame. Profiling the programs revealed that roughly 80% of their time was spent encoding and decoding the run-length encoded disk files in which the elements were stored. Not counting picture I/O, the time per frame was about 1.8 minutes. An extremely large frame buffer could eliminate picture I/O altogether.

4. Conclusions

The UNIX text-processing environment demonstrates that a suite of small programs acting on a common data representation, and bound together by a powerful command language, can be more powerful than a large integrated application program that tries to cover all eventualities. We believe that the same principle applies to image synthesis.

Experimentation is encouraged in an environment where little changes don't involve digging into, and possibly breaking, a huge monolithic program. New methods are easier to try out, and the consequences of failure are localized.

The **rgbαz** representation is easily produced by almost any rendering program and has a simple, fast anti-aliased compositing operation whose output is of high enough quality for all but the most exacting applications. The representation is the basis for a 3-D image synthesis toolkit. We expect that as we build more image synthesis and processing tools a rich 3-D graphics environment will emerge.

Acknowledgements

Don Mitchell designed the robot of figure 3. Rob Pike gave the paper a good critical reading.

References

[1] Loren Carpenter, "The A-buffer, an Antialiased Hidden Surface Method," *Computer Graphics*, Vol. 18, No. 3 (1984), pp. 103-108

[2] Edwin Catmull, *A Subdivision Algorithm for Computer Display of Curved Surfaces*, Ph.D. dissertation, Department of Computer Science, University of Utah, Salt Lake City, December 1974

[3] Frank Crow, "A More Flexible Image Generation Environment," *Computer Graphics*, Vol. 16, No. 3 (1982), pp. 9-18

[4] Tom Duff, *The Soid and Roid Manual*, NYIT Computer Graphics Laboratory internal memorandum, 1980

[5] Henry Fuchs, Zvi M. Kedem and Bruce F. Naylor, "On Visible Surface Generation By A Priori Tree Structures," *Computer Graphics*, Vol. 14, No. 3 (1980), pp 124-133

[6] James Gosling *UNIX Emacs*, CMU internal memorandum, August, 1982

[7] L. Bernard Happé, *Basic Motion Picture Technology*, Hastings House, New York, 1975

[8] Brian Kernighan and Rob Pike, *The UNIX Programming Environment*, Prentice-Hall, Englewood Cliffs NJ, 1984

[9] Martin E. Newell, "The Utilization of Procedure Models in Digital Image Synthesis," *University of Utah Computer Science Department*, UTEC-CSc-76-218, Summer 1975

[10] Thomas Porter and Tom Duff, "Compositing Digital Images," *Computer Graphics*, Vol 18, No. 3 (1984), pp. 253-259

[11] Alvy Ray Smith, "Color Gamut Transform Pairs," *Computer Graphics*, Vol 12, No. 3 (1978), pp 12-19

[12] Alvy Ray Smith, Loren Carpenter, Ed Catmull, Rob Cook, Tom Duff, Craig Good, John Lasseter, Eben Ostby, William Reeves, and David Salesin, "The Adventures of André & Wally B.," created by the Lucasfilm Computer Graphics Project. July 1984.

[13] Ivan Sutherland, Robert Sproull and R. A. Schumaker, "A Characterization of Ten Hidden Surface Algorithms," *Computing Surveys*, Vol. 6, No. 1 (1974), pp. 1-55

[14] Turner Whitted, "An Improved Illumination Model for Shaded Display," *Comm. ACM*, Vol. 23, No. 6 (June 1980), 343-349

[15] Turner Whitted and David Weimer, "A Software Test-Bed for the Development of 3-D Raster Graphics Systems," *Computer Graphics*, Vol. 15, No. 3 (1981), pp. 271-277

[16] Lance Williams, "Casting Curved Shadows on Curved Surfaces," *Computer Graphics*, Vol. 12, No. 3 (1978), pp. 270-274

Figure 2 — Ellipsoid rendered by *quad*

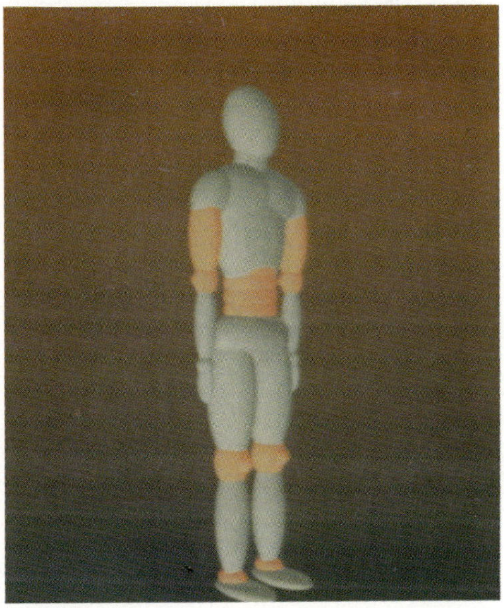

Figure 3 — Robot rendered by *quad*, *bg* and *3matte*

Figure 4 — New Jersey rendered by *terrain*

Figure 6 — Fog added to previous picture using *fog*

Figure 5 — Flying Saucers over New Jersey, rendered by *quad*, *bg*, *terrain* and *3matte*

BOUNDING ELLIPSOIDS FOR RAY-FRACTAL INTERSECTION

Christian BOUVILLE

Centre Commun d'Études de

Télévision et de Télécommunications

France

ABSTRACT. Recently published papers have shown that, with appropriate intersection algorithms, the rendering of many procedural objects is possible with all the advantages offered by the ray-tracing techniques. In the case of stochastic surfaces, the intersection can be computed by a recursive subdivision technique. The efficiency of this algorithm depends essentially on the bounding volume whose size and shape are directly related to the stochastic characteristics of these surfaces. After a brief review of the rendering of stochastic surfaces and the bounding volume selection problem, two types of bounding volume are studied, describing how their intersection with a ray can be computed and how their size can be derived from the stochastic characteristics. The efficiency then, of these bounding volumes are compared.

1.0 INTRODUCTION

Ray-tracing picture synthesis has seen some important developments over the last few years and appreciable improvements have been made to some critical problems ([1], [2], [3], [4]). This method has thus lost something of its original simplicity but the results confirm the superiority of this approach for very high quality picture generation. Its major drawback still lies in the processing time that remains long compared to other methods. In most cases, ray-surface intersection computing time has crucial effects on the overall computing time especially in the case of procedurally defined objects such as stochastic surfaces. Efficient rendering algorithms may pose difficult problems if one wishes to depart from the scenes composed of spheres and parallelipipeds that we usually see in ray-tracing.

There have been a number of intersting works on this subject including ([6], [7], [4]) J. Kajiya's algorithm for the Ray-tracing of stochastic surfaces [6]. In addition to the gain in computing time, the main advantage of this algorithm is to avoid the computation and storage of all the polygons that make up the surface. This advantage may be extremely important if this algorithm is to be implemented with special purpose multiprocessor hardware [4].

The intersection computation in Kajiya's algorithm is based on the recursive subdivision principle. The efficiency of such algorithms depends essentially on the adequacy of the bounding volume that should be as tight as possible to make the algorithm converge in few iterations, but should also be simple enough to have fast intersection computations. In his paper, Kajiya uses triangular prisms as boundary volume and this volume has proved to be non-optimal with regard to the criteria given above. This inadequacy is particularly evident when the stochastic surface is defined by several initial triangles. The algorithm described below is an attempt to solve this problem showing that more appropriate bounding volumes can be used when the « fractal dimension » H is greater then 0.5, which covers most applications.

2.0 THE BACKGROUND TO THE RENDERING OF STOCHASTIC SURFACES

2.1 Stochastic Surfaces Generation

Stochastic surfaces generation is based on recursive subdivision algorithms applied to certain types of surface [5]. In the following, we shall consider the subdivision of triangles, applying recursively the process described below:

1. first compute the middle of each edge.
2. add to these points a displacement in a fixed direction P. The length of this displacement is a sample of a gaussian variable whose variance V_i is proportionnal to the square of the edge length.
3. store the four new triangles defined by the new points and the vertices of the previous triangle.

As the dimension of the triangles are roughly divided by two at each subdivision, we now have [5]:

$$V_i = k^2 \; 2^{-2iH}$$

where i is the iteration level, k is a scale factor and H is the « fractal dimension ». If n is the maximum level of iteration, each edge of the initial triangle will be subdivided into 2^n segments and the initial triangle itself will be subdivided into 2^{2n} triangles. In actual fact, this process generates a quadtree with nodes corresponding to triangles and levels corresponding to levels of iteration. In the following, Kajiya's terminology will be used: triangles to be evolved (corresponding to intermediate nodes) will be called facets and triangles corresponding to leaves will be called primitive facets.

2.2 Intersecting a Stochastic Surface

To avoid intersecting each ray with all the primitive facets, Kajiya devised an algorithm that takes advantage of the very particular generation process of stochastic surfaces. In this algorithm, it is necessary to determine a bounding volume or extent that must enclose a fully evolved facet at any iteration level. At each iteration, the algorithm updates an active list containing all the facets whose extent has been intersected. In our implementation of the algorithm, the facets are sorted in order of increasing distance from the origin of the ray. The algorithm then runs through the following loop until the first facet is primitive:

1. extract the first facet from the active list and subdivide it. This will produce four new facets.
2. compute the intersection of the ray with the extent of the new facets. If no intersection is detected, start again.
3. insert the intersected facets in the active list. If a new facet is primitive, remove the following facets from the active list.

In this algorithm, the primitive facets are not necessarily the triangles obtained at a given maximum level of iteration. In actual fact, a facet may be considered as primitive if the size of its extent or the angle from which it is seen from the origin of the ray is sufficiently small.

3.0 SELECTING A BOUNDING VOLUME

3.1 Selection Criteria

The selection of a bounding volume must satisfy two inconsistent requirements. On the one hand, the bounding volume must enclose the surface tightly to ensure a rapid convergence of the algorithm. On the other hand, this volume must be simple enough to have fast intersection computations. At a certain level of complexity, the selection of a tighter extent will obviously become much more complex for a trifling gain, or even a loss in performance. Although it may sometimes be difficult to estimate, this level can be considered as optimal.

The bounding volume problem is quite general in ray-tracing but it takes on a particularly critical importance for this type of algorithm where intersection computations may be numerous before finding a solution for a single ray. Moreover, the case of stochastic surfaces differs from other objects owing to their very nature: for a given bouding volume, the probability of wrong intersection results is non-zero and this probability increases as the extent becomes tighter. The selection of a boundary volume therefore implies good theoretical knowledge of the stochastic propertie of the surface.

The main shortcoming of the « cheese-cake » extent lies in this point [6]. As a matter of fact, this volume is a triangular prism centered on the triangle to be evolved (Fig. 1). Since the variance of displacement decreases as we approach the vertices of the triangle, the extent becomes too broad in these regions.

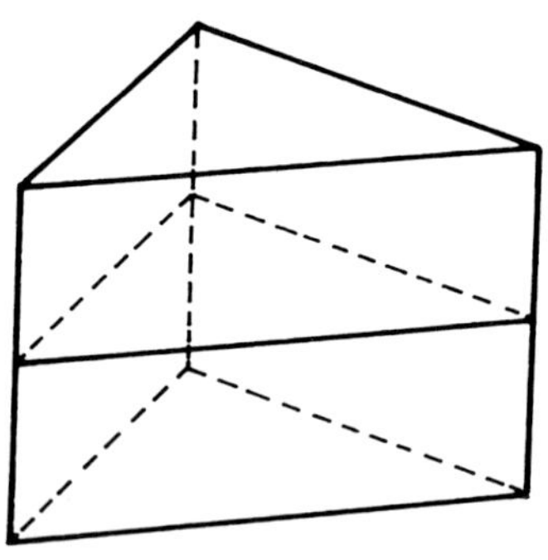

Fig. 1 « Cheese-cake » extent.

To palliate this drawback, several types of boundary volume have been tested. However, only the most efficient will be analyzed below.

As emphasized by B. Mandelbrot [8], the characteristics of stochastic surfaces described in [5] are different from those of fractal surfaces and consequently the theoretical analysis of fractal surfaces cannot be strictly applied to stochastic surfaces. The stochastic properties of these surfaces have thus been analyzed in the case of the subdivision of triangles and the main points are detailed in appendix A and B. In conclusion, we shall see that the sizing of extents is simple when H is greater than 0.5, which covers most cases.

3.2 Ellipsoids as Bounding Volume

3.2.1 Defining and Intersecting the Ellipsoid

This type of extent has already been suggested by Kajiya. The major difficulties with this extent lie in the positioning and sizing of the ellipsoid. As the variance of displacements is zero at the vertices of the triangle, these vertices should be on the ellipsoid surface. Moreover, as all the displacements have the same direction P, one of the main axes should be oriented in this direction. Direct computation of the equation of such an ellipsoid in the ray coordinate system is generally difficult and unnecessary (by « ray coordinate system » we mean the coordinate system in which the ray equation is expressed). Instead, we shall proceed as described in [9] by transforming the ray equation so that the intersection computations will be performed in a more adequate coordinate system. This coordinate system will be called local coordinate system to keep Roth's terminology.

In our case, the objective is obviously to transform the ellipsoid into a sphere centered at the origin and of unit radius. In this local coordinate system, the triangle will be equilateral and contained in the xOy plane. To obtain this result, three transformations called T1, T2 and T3 will be consecutively applied to the ray equation. T1 will change the ray coordinate system into an intermediate coordinate system in which the origin is a vertex B of the triangle, the x axis lies along BC and the axis is perpendicular to the triangle plane (Fig. 2).

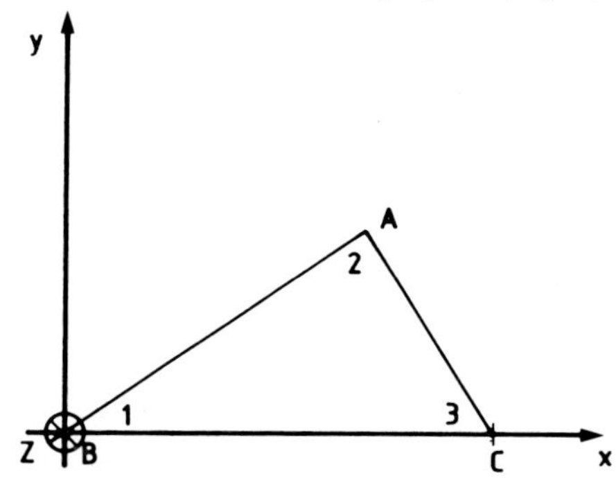

Fig. 2 — Intermediate coordinate system.

After applying T2, the triangle will become equilateral so that the circle passing through its vertices will be centered at its centroid (it can be shown that in the intermediate coordinate system, the corresponding ellipsoid is also centered at the centroid). The origin of this coordinate system will be the centroid and the xOy plane will remain the triangle plane. Eventually, after the change of coordinate system defined by T3, the direction of P will become parallel to the z axis with a scale factor along this axis so that the fully evolved surface is contained in a sphere of unit radius centered at the origin. The matrices of T1, T2 and T3 will be determined below.

3.2.2 Transformation T1

This transformation is a composition of a rotation and a translation. With respect to the ray coordinate system, the unit vectors of the intermediate coordinate system can be expressed as follows:

$$U = BC/|BC|$$
$$W = U*(BA/|BA|)$$
$$V = U*W$$

Where |BC| denotes length of BC and * denotes cross-product (Fig. 2).

With respect to the intermediate coordinate system, the translation vector has coordinates:

$$T_x = (B.U)$$
$$T_y = (B.V)$$
$$T_z = (B.W)$$

where (B.U) denotes the dot-product of B and U.

Composing the rotation and translation, we obtain:

$$T1 = \begin{bmatrix} U_x & V_x & W_x & 0 \\ U_y & V_y & W_y & 0 \\ U_z & V_z & W_z & 0 \\ T_x & T_y & T_z & 1 \end{bmatrix}$$

3.2.3 Transformation T2

The objective of T2 is to transform the ellipse passing through the vertices of the triangle and centered at its centroid into a circle of unit radius making the triangle equilateral. Thus, only the x and y coordinate will be affected by this transformation. In fact, this transformation is a combination of three elementary transformations that we shall examine below.

The pupose of the first step is to make the length of BA and BC both equal to $\sqrt{3}$ (Fig. 3). The corresponding transformation matrix is:

$$L1 = \begin{bmatrix} S_{1x} & 0 & 0 & 0 \\ 0 & S_{1y} & 0 & 0 \\ 0 & 0 & 1 & 0 \\ 0 & 0 & 0 & 1 \end{bmatrix}$$

where $S_{1x} = \sqrt{3}/X_c$

$S_{1y} = [3(1 - X_A^2/X_C^2)]^{1/2}/Y_A$

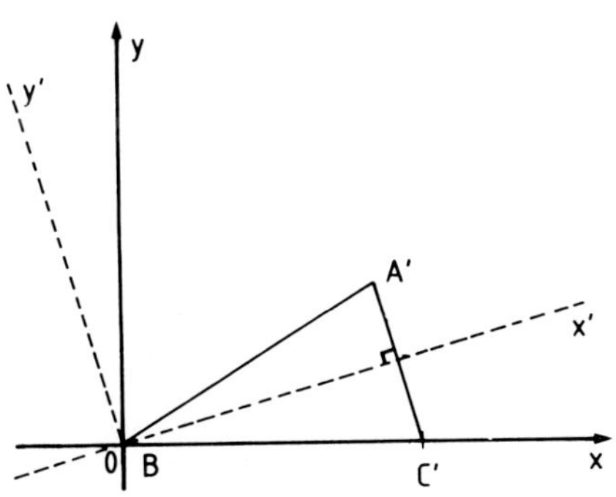

Fig. 3

The second step consists of a rotation around the z axis to make the x axis perpendicular to AC (Fig. 3). The corresponding rotation matrix is:

$$L2 = \begin{bmatrix} R_x & -R_y & 0 & 0 \\ R_y & R_x & 0 & 0 \\ 0 & 0 & 1 & 0 \\ 0 & 0 & 0 & 1 \end{bmatrix}$$

where $R_x = [(1 + X_A/X_C)/2]^{1/2}$

$R_y = [(1 - X_A/X_C)/2]^{1/2}$

In the third step, the following transformations will be applied simultaneously (Fig. 4):

1. a scale factor in y to make $|AC|$ equal to $\sqrt{3}$.
2. a scale factor in x to make the altitude of AC equal to 3/2.
3. a translation to place the origin of the new coordinate system at the centroid of the triangle.

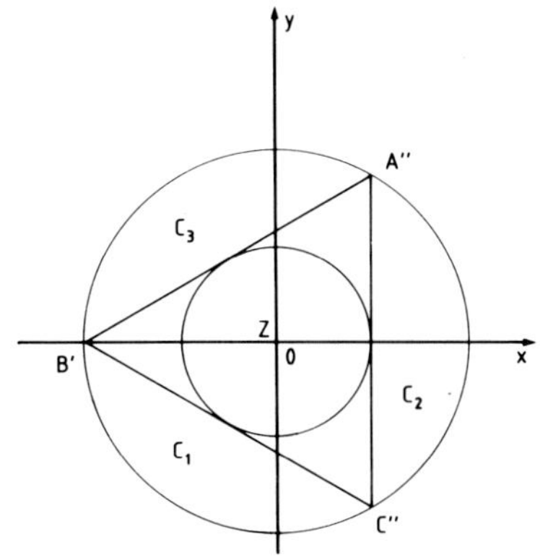

Fig. 4

The corresponding transformation matrix will be:

$$L3 = \begin{bmatrix} S_{2x} & 0 & 0 & 0 \\ 0 & S_{2y} & 0 & 0 \\ 0 & 0 & 1 & 0 \\ -1 & 0 & 0 & 1 \end{bmatrix}$$

where $S_{2y} = [2(1 - X_A/X_C)]^{-1/2}$

$S_{2x} = \sqrt{3}\,[2(1 + X_A/X_C)]^{-1/2}$

The combination of these three transformations leads to the matrix of T2:

$$L1 * L2 * L3 = T2 = \begin{bmatrix} A_{11} & A_{21} & 0 & 0 \\ A_{12} & A_{22} & 0 & 0 \\ 0 & 0 & 1 & 0 \\ -1 & 0 & 0 & 1 \end{bmatrix}$$

where $A_{11} = 3/(2X_C)$

$A_{12} = 3(1 - X_A/X_C)/(2Y_A)$

$A_{21} = -\sqrt{3}/(2X_C)$

$A_{22} = \sqrt{3}(1 + X_A/X_C)/(2Y_A)$

3.2.4 Transformation T3

Let D be the vector of direction P whose length is equal to the normalization factor of the displacements d_M, that is:

$$D = d_M\, P$$

The factor d_M is such that the extent encloses the volume with a sufficiently small overflow probability. The computation of d_M will be examined in the next section. The object of T3 is to make D equal to the unit vector of the z axis. Let D_x, D_y and D_z be the coordinates of D after applying T1 and T2. The inverse transformation of T3 is thus defined by the matrix:

$$(T3)^{-1} = \begin{bmatrix} 1 & 0 & 0 & 0 \\ 0 & 1 & 0 & 0 \\ D_x & D_y & D_z & 0 \\ 0 & 0 & 0 & 1 \end{bmatrix}$$

Inverting this matrix, we obtain:

$$T3 = \begin{bmatrix} 1 & 0 & 0 & 0 \\ 0 & 1 & 0 & 0 \\ C_x & C_y & C_z & 0 \\ 0 & 0 & 0 & 1 \end{bmatrix}$$

where
$$C_x = -D_x/D_z$$
$$C_y = -D_y/D_z$$
$$C_z = 1/D_z$$

3.2.5 Sizing the Extent

In the transformations defined above, the only term reflecting the stochastic nature of the enclosed object is the normalization factor d_M. The determination of d_M must take three factors into account:

1. the stochastic properties of the surface. The main points are to locate the regions where the variance of displacements is maximum and to compute this variance.
2. the shape of the extent characterized by a geometrical shape factor.
3. the allowed probability for the surface to extend beyond its bounding volume, also called overflow probability.

The main stochactic characteristics of the surface described in section 2.1 has been studied and an abstract of these computations can be found in appendix A. Let us simply recall the most interesting results. First, when $H>0.5$, the variance is maximum at the middle of each edge of the triangle. This maximum variance is:

$$V_M = k\, 2^{-2iH} \qquad (1)$$

where the iteration level at which the triangle has been obtained is $i-1$.

Let us now consider the variance along the median of the triangle. Still with $H>0.5$, the variance has a local minimum near the centroid and a local maximum at the middle of the median. This local maximum has the value:

$$V'_M = k\, 2^{-2iH}\, (2^{-2iH} + 1/2)$$

The geometrical shape factor reflects the fact that, in the local coordinate system, the region of maximum overflow probability does not coincide with the region of maximum available height above the triangle plane (namely the centroid). To determine the region of maximum overflow probability, let us consider the circle resulting from the intersection (in the local coordinate system) of the spherical extent with a plane perpendicular to the median at a given point (Fig. 4). The radius of this circle is 1 when this point is the centroid, $\sqrt{15}/4$ when it is the middle of the median and $\sqrt{3}/2$ when the plane contains the edge of the triangle. Comparing these values with those of variance at the same points, it is clear that the regions of maximum overflow probability are located on the edges of the triangle.

Let us now consider the variance profile along one edge of the triangle. This variance profile has been computed in appendix B and this curve is represented in Fig. 5 for various values of H.

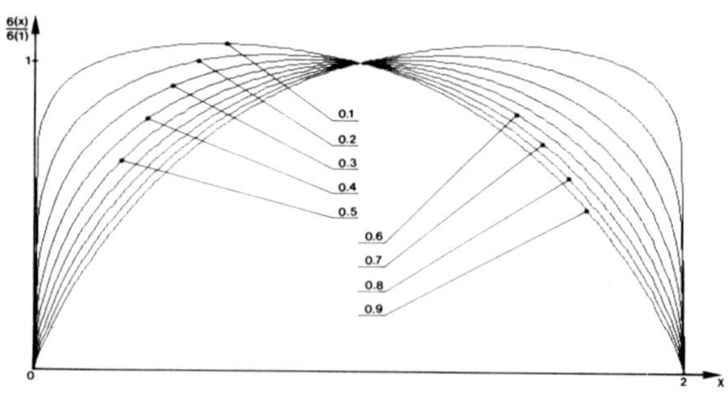

Fig. 5 — Variance profiles.

In this figure, the edge has been scaled to have a length equal to 2 and the variance has been normalized to its value at the middle of the edge. Note that for $H>0.5$, all these curves are contained within a semi circle with the edge as its diameter. For $H = 0.5$, the variance profile is identical to this semi-circle. Therefore, this circle can be seen as a scaled section of the extent and the points of maximum overflow probability are located at the middle of each edge. Thus, using equation (1), we have:

$$d_M = 2\alpha k 2^{-iH} / \sqrt{3}$$

where α is a function of the maximum overflow probability p_M. As the displacements have gaussian distribution, we have:

$$p_M = 1 - \Theta(\alpha)$$

For example, if $p_M = 10^{-5}$, $\alpha = 3.123$ and if $p_M = 10^{-6}$, $\alpha = 3.46$. In fact, as the number of primitive facets is finite and as the displacements are pseudo-random variables, there exists an α for which $p_M = 0$.

When $H>0.5$, the geometrical shape factor is constant ($\sqrt{3}/2$), which greatly simplifies the extent sizing computations. When $H<0.5$, it can be shown from the equations derived in appendix A that points of maximum variance are located within the triangle and therefore, the geometrical shape factor is not constant. In actual fact, when we consider the variance profile for small values of H, it appears that the cheese-cake extent would be more appropriate in this case.

3.3 Bounding Volume with Spherical Triangles

3.3.1 Definition

From the previous section, it appears that, in the local coordinate system, the sphere is well-suited to the surface in the z direction but leaves large voids in the x and y directions, namely the portions of sphere identified by C_1, C_2 and C_3 in Fig. 4. These areas can be removed by intersecting the sphere (in the Boolean sense) with a prism, namely:

$$V = S \cap P$$

where S is the spherical extent and P is the half-space delimited by the three planes parallel to the z axis, each containing one edge of the triangle. The resulting volume V is delimited vertically by two spherical triangles whose vertices are the same as the plane triangle, and laterally by three disks of radius $\sqrt{3}/2$.

The sizing of this bounding volume is identical to that indicated for a sphere since the volume P is independent of the surface.

3.3.2 Intersecting the Extent

The volumes S and P always have two intersections with a ray except when the ray intersects one edge of P. The ray equation can be expressed as follows:

$$M = tU + 0$$

where U is the direction vector, 0 is the origin of the ray and M is a point on the ray. If U is a unit vector, t is the distance between M and 0.

Let us call the values of t corresponding to the intersections of the ray with S and P respectively (t_{s1}, t_{s2}) and (t_{p1}, t_{p2}). To compute the nearest intersection with V, the ray segments (t_{s1}, t_{s2}) and (t_{p1}, t_{p2}) can be combined as described in [9]. First, the ray intersects V if the two segments overlap that is:

$$\min(t_{s1}, t_{s2}) < \max(t_{p1}, t_{p2}) \text{ and } \max(t_{s1}, t_{s2}) > \min(t_{p1}, t_{p2})$$

When this condition is verified, the nearest intersection is given by:

$$t = \max[\min(t_{s1}, t_{s2}), \min(t_{p1}, t_{p2})]$$

3.4 Results

The algorithm described above has been implemeted in Fortran-77 on a Vax 11/750 for the rendering of stochastic surfaces with shadowing. The pictures represented in Fig. 9 and 10 have been produced using this algorithm. Both pictures have been generated with four original triangles and a resolution of 1024 x 1024 x 24.

The efficiency of the bounding volumes described above has been tested on two pictures at a resolution of 100 x 100. The first one has the same original database triangles as the picture in Fig. 9 and the second one has only one original triangle. For each picture and for each type of bounding volume, Table 1 shows the maximum number of iterations, the average number of iterations and the CPU time. The coefficient α of equation (2) is identical for the first two bounding volumes but it is lower for the triangular prism to take account of the fact that, at an equal value of α, the triangular prism is less tight and, that there is, therefore, less probability of wrong intersections. To make the comparison as fair as possible, α has been adjusted so that the total number of detected intersections is the same for the three bounding volumes.

The results of Table 1 clearly show the better efficiency of the bounding volumes defined with ellipsoids. Compared to the simple ellipsoid, the extent defined with spherical triangles significantly decreases the maximum number of iterations with a gain of 30 % in CPU time. When the number of original triangles is increased, the results remain satisfactory for the ellipsoidal bounding volumes but the triangular prism yields poor efficiency owing to the large increase in iterations when the intersection is located near the common boundary of adjacent triangles.

A tighter bounding volume can be defined by intersecting the sphere with a triangular prism of half-heigth equal to $\sqrt{3}/2$ in the local coordinate system. This bounding volume has not been analyzed here because it yields slightly inferior results in CPU time compared to the spherical triangle. However, this observation allows us to estimate that the spherical triangle extent is almost optimal with regard to the criterion stated above.

Table 1

	Ellipsoid		Sph. Triangles		Trian. Prism	
	1 tri.	4 tri.	1 tri.	4 tri.	1 tri.	4 tri.
Max. Iteration	58	75	40	55	62	105
Aver. Iteration	21	29	14	22	33	42
C.P.U time (Min)	14	33	10	23	20	47

4.0 CONCLUSION

The interest of this algorithm is not limited to the rendering stochastic surfaces. As pointed out by Kajiya, it can also be applied to the visualisation of height fields. Moreover, the bounding volume technique can be used in many other applications.

In spite of the improvements brought about by the bounding volumes described above, the computing time remains long. However, there are various ways of decreasing the computing time at the expense of slight picture impairment. For example, the maximum level of iteration can be limited to 4 or 5 for the shadow computations. The resultant loss of detail in the shadow outline is often unnoticeable. Moreover, it is possible to stop the stochastic surfaces generation process at a certain level and then to use the stochastic texture generation process described in [10].

Computing time can be significantly decreased by the use of special purpose hardware based on the parallel processing technique and fast matrix multipliers. Research in this direction is in progress at the C.C.E.T.T. [4] but, at the creation stage, the production of animated scenes demands a faster generation technique such as the Z-buffer approach. The picture generation system under study will thus incorporate the ray-tracing technique for high quality picture generation and the Z-buffer technique for fast shaded picture generation allowing visual interaction and real time playback of animated sequences.

APPENDIX A

STOCHASTIC CHARACTERISTICS COMPUTATIONS

Given the symmetry of the geometrical elements in the local coordinate system, knowledge of the variance on a median of the triangle is sufficient to solve our problem. The objectif will be to compute the variance at a point $S_{1\,n+1}$ corresponding the middle of one edge of the triangle $T_{1\,n}$ obtained at iteration level n (Fig. 6).

$T_{1\,n}$ is the inner triangle obtained after subdivision of $T_{1\,n-1}$ whose vertices are $S_{1\,n-1}$, $S_{2\,n-1}$ and $S_{3\,n-1}$, $T_{1\,n-1}$ being the inner triangle obtained after subdivision of $T_{1\,n-2}$ and so forth.

The coordinates of S_{in} are random variables but their mean values define points located on a median of the initial triangle. As n increases, the average of $S_{1\,n}$ approaches the centroid.

In the following analysis, points directly obtained after subdivision will be called S_{ji}, and S^*_{ji} will be the same point after adding the displacement. Thus, we have:

$$S^*_{1\,n+1} = S_{1\,n+1} + 2^{-(n+1)H} B_1(n+1) \qquad (1)$$

where $B_1(n+1) = b_1(n+1)P$

and $b(n+1)$ is a gaussian random variable with zero mean-value and unit variance. In should be remembered that P is the displacement direction vector.

Moreover,

$$S_{1\,n+1} = (S^*_{2\,n} + S^*_{3\,n})/2 \qquad (2)$$

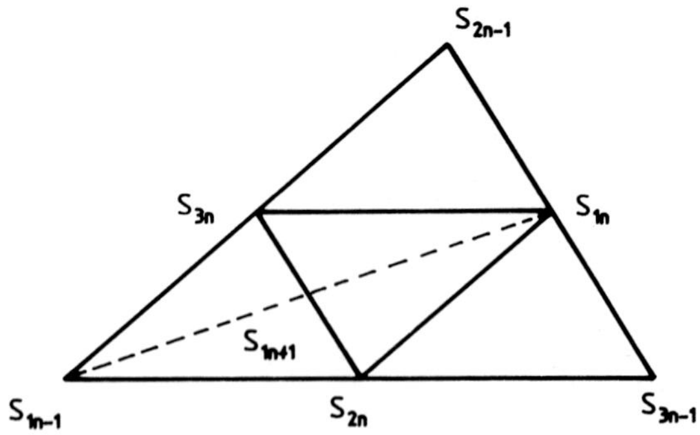

Fig. 6

Let us replace S^*_{2n} and S^*_{3n} in (2) by:

$$S^*_{2n} = (S^*_{1\,n-1} + S^*_{3\,n-1})/2 + 2^{-nH}\, B_2(n)$$

$$S^*_{3n} = (S^*_{1\,n-1} + S^*_{2\,n-1})/2 + 2^{-nH}\, B_3(n)$$

and: $S_{1n} = (S^*_{3\,n-1} + S^*_{2\,n-1})/2$

We then obtain:

$$S_{1\,n+1} = (S_{1\,n-1} + S_{1n})/2 + [B_2(n) + B_3(n)]\, 2^{-nH}/2 + B_1(n-1) 2^{-(n-1)H}/2 \qquad (3)$$

Using the same substitution for the iteration levels n through $n - i + 1$, we would obtain:

$$S_{1\,n+1} = V_i S_{1\,n-i} + V_{i-1}\, S_{n-i-1}/2 + \sum_{j=0}^{i} R_{n-j}\, 2^{-(n-j)H} + V_{i-1}\, B_1(n-i-1) 2^{-(n-i-1)H} \qquad (4)$$

where:

$$R_{n-j} = V_{j-1}\, [B_2(n-j) + B_3(n-j)]/2 + V_{j-2}\, B_1(n-j)/2 \qquad (5)$$

and the V_j are defined recursively by:

$$V_j = (V_{j-1} + V_{j-2})/2 \text{ with } V_{-2} = 0 \text{ and } V_{-1} = 1 \qquad (6)$$

With $i = n - 1$ in (4), iteration levels n through 1 will be taken into account and the equation (4) becomes:

$$S = M + B$$

where M and B are the mean value and the random component respectively. They are defined as follows:

$$M = V_{n-1}\, S_{11} + V_{n-2}\, S_{10}/2 \qquad (7)$$

$$B = \sum_{j=0}^{n-1} R_{n-j}\, 2^{-(n-j)H} \qquad (8)$$

Note that in (4), $B_1(n-i-1) = B_1(0) = 0$ since S_{10} is a vertex of the initial triangle. Note also that $S_{10}\, S_{11}$ is a median of the initial triangle and that M lies on this median. As n increases, V_n approaches 2/3 (see below) and therefore M approaches the centroid.

It could be shown that the V_i have the value:

$$V_i = \frac{2}{3}[1 - (-1/2)^{i+2}] \qquad (9)$$

Since the displacements R_{n-j} are statistically independent, the variance of $S^*_{1\,n+1}$ can easily be derived from equation (4):

$$\mathrm{Var}(S^*_{1\,n+1}) = \sigma^2_{n+1} = 2^{-2(n+1)H} + \frac{1}{2}\sum_{j=0}^{n-1} (V^2_{j-1} + V^2_{j-2}/2)\, 2^{-2(n-j)H} \qquad (10)$$

Using (9), we would obtain:

$$\sigma^2_{n+1} = 2^{-2(n+1)H} + \frac{2^{-2nH} - 1}{3(1 - 2^{2H})} + \frac{2(2^{-2nH} - 2^{-2n})}{3\,(4 - 2^{2H})} \qquad (11)$$

From equation (10), it can be shown that $\sigma^2_{n+1} - \sigma^2_n$ is always negative when $H>0.5$. Consequently, the variance of S^*_{1n} is a decreasing function of n and S_{11} is the point of maximum variance on the median. Furthermore, as S_{11} approaches the centroid as n increases, the variance has a local minimum in this region. Generalizing this result, we can state that the variance at the vertices of inner triangles decreases as we subdivide.

On the other hand, as the displacements at S_{31}, S_{11} and S_{21} (see Fig. 7) are statistically independent, the variance on the edges of triangle $S_{31}\, S_{11}\, S_{21}$ is less than the variance on the edges of $S_{10}\, S_{20}\, S_{30}$. Moreover, it is shown in appendix B that the variance on an edge of the original triangle decreases as we approache the vertices when $H>0.5$. Consequently, the variance is maximum at the middle of each edge of the original triangle.

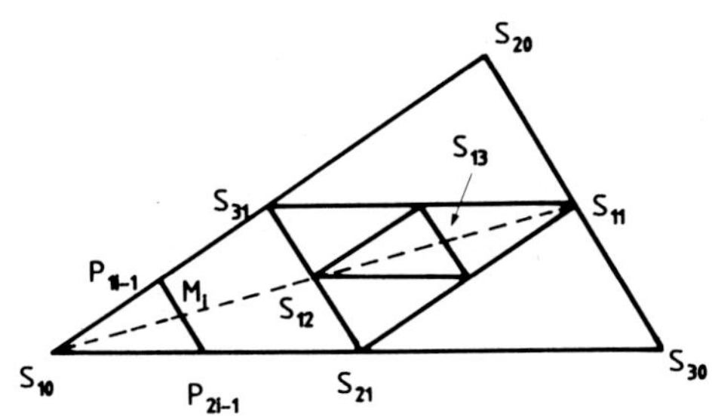

Fig. 7

APPENDIX B
VARIANCE PROFILE ALONG AN EDGE

The variance profile along an edge is a continuous function deduced from the variance values at particular points. If m is the maximum number of iterations, the recursive subdivision process will produce $2^m - 1$ points P(i). These points will be numbered from 0 to 2^m (P(0) and P(2^m) being the segment ends) so that the $\overline{P(i)}$ are uniformly distributed along the segment (Fig. 8), $\overline{P(i)}$ being the average of P(i).

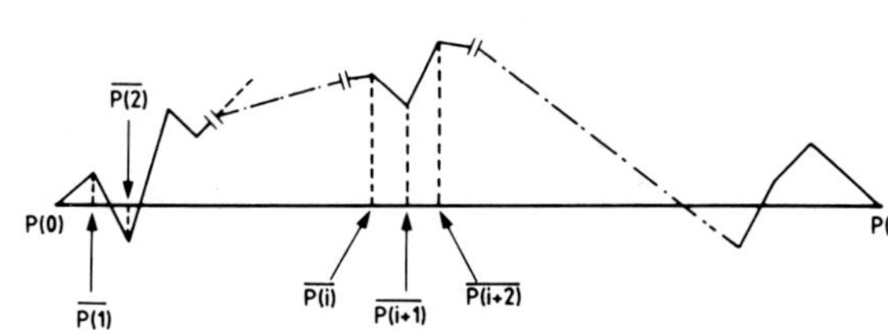

Fig. 8

Let us consider the subdivision process stopped at the j iteration level and let P(i) and P(i') be two adjacent points where P(i) has been obtained at iteration level j and P(i') at iteration level ℓ with $\ell < j$. Thus we have:

$i = k2^{m-j}$ and $i' = k'2^{m-l}$ where k' amd k' are odd integers

As P(i) and P(i') are adjacent, we have:

$$i' = (k-1)2^{m-j} = i - 2^{m-j}$$

Let us now, expand P(i) in terms of P(i'), P(i'') and the displacements, P(i'') being the point adjacent to P(i') at iteration level ℓ. Therefore:

$$i'' = (k'+1)2^{m-l} = i' + 2^{m-l}$$

Here, P(i') is on the left of P(i) but the result remains valid in the opposite case.

P(i) has been generated at iteration level j by the subdivision of the segment $P(i-2^{m-j})\ P(i+2^{m-j})$. Hence:

$$P(i) = [P(i-2^{m-j}) + P(i+2^{m-j})]/2 + B_j(i) \qquad (12)$$

where $B_j(i)$ is the displacement vector.

Similarly at iteration level j–p, we have:

$$P(i-r_{p-1}2^{m-j}) = \left(P(i-2^{m-j}) + P(i+r_p 2^{m-j})\right)/2 \qquad (12')$$
$$+ B_{j-p}\ (i+r_{p-1}\ 2^{m-j})$$

where $0 < p < j-l-1$ and $r_p = 2^{p+l} - 1$

Note that $i + r_{j-l-1}\ 2^{m-j} = i''$

Replacing $P(i + 2^{m-j})$ in (17) by its expression according to (12') with p=j–1 and so forth for all the $P(i+r_p\ 2^{m-j})$ until p=j–1–l, we obtain:

$$P(i) = P(i-2^{m-j})(1/2 + 1/4 + ... + (1/2)^{j-l})$$
$$+ P(i+r_{j-l-1}\ 2^{m-j})\ 2^{-(j-l)} + \sum_{q=0}^{j-l-1} B_{j-q}\ (i+r_{q-1}\ 2^{m-j})/2^q$$

or:

$$P(i) = P(i')\ (1 - 2^{-(j-l)}) + P(i'')2^{-(j-l)}$$
$$+ \sum_{q=0}^{j-l-1} B_{j-q}\ (i+r_{q-1}\ 2^{m-j})/2^q \qquad (13)$$

If l=0, then i'=0, k'=0 and $i''=2^m$, P(i') and P(i'') are the segment ends. In this case, k=1 and P(i) is the nearest point from P(0) at iteration level j and P(i) approaches P(0) as j augments.

The variance at point P(i) can easily be deduced from (13) since all the B_{j-q} are statistically independent and have the same direction P. As the variance of the length of B_{j-q} is $2^{-2(j-q)H}$, the variance at point $P(2^{m-j})$ is given by:

$$Vr(2^{m-j}) = \sum_{q=0}^{j-1} 2^{-2(j-q)H-2q} \qquad (14)$$

or:

$$Vr(2^{m-j}) = 2^{-2jH}\ (2^{2(H-1)j} - 1)/(2^{2(H-1)} - 1)$$

with $1 \leqslant j \leqslant m$

If the segment is scaled to have a length equal to 2, the quantity $x=2^{-j+1}$ can be considered as the distance between P(i) and P(0) (it should be remembered that the P(i) for i=0 through 2^m are equally spaced). Therefore, the variance profile can be expressed as:

$$\sigma^2(x) = (x/2)^{2H}\left((x/2)^{-2(H-1)} - 1\right)/(2^{2(H-1)} - 1)$$

with $0 \leqslant x \leqslant 1$

The profile on the other half-segment can be obtained by replacing x by 2–x in the above equation.

As $\sigma(1) = 2^{-2H}$ vve have :

$$\sigma^2(x)/\sigma^2(1) = x^{2H}\left((x/2)^{-2(H-1)} - 1\right)/(2^{2(H-1)} - 1)$$

This equation has been derived from the variance values at particular points. Applying equation (13) for iteration level l and so forth until iteration level 0 is reached, the variance at any point on the edge can be computed and it can be shown that the variance profile is identical to the variance curve only when H=0.5. For other values of H, the variance at other points is less than or equal to the value obtained from the variance profile equation (see the example of fig. 11) when H = 0.5. Therefore, the variance profile is adequate for bounding volume determination.

This variance profile has been represented in Fig. 5 for various values of H. Note that this curve is a semi-circle of unit radius when H=0.5 and that all the curves are contained in this semi-circle when H>0.5.

The above expression is indeterminate if H=1 but the variance profile for H=1 can be easily derived from (14). The curve equation is then:

$$\sigma(x)/2^{-2} = x^2\ [l - \log(x)]$$

REFERENCES

[1] « Ray-tracing session 1 and 1 », SIGGRAPH 84, Comp. Graphics, 18, 3, (Jul. 84), p. 119-174.

[2] WEGHORST H., G. HOOPER, D.P. GREENBERG « Improved Computational Methods for Ray-Tracing », A.C.M. Trans. on Graphics, 3, 1, p. 52-69.

[3] HALL R.A., D.P. GREENBERG, « A Testbed for Realistic Image Synthesis » I.E.E.E. Comp. Graphics and Appl. 3, 10, p. 10-20.

[4] BOUVILLE C., J.L. DUBOIS, I. MARCHAL « Generating High Quality Pictures », Comp. Graphics Forum, Special Issue on Raster Graphics (to be published).

[5] FOURNIER A., D. FUSSELL, L. CARPENTIER « Computer Rendering of Stochastic Model » Comm. of the A.C.M., 25, 6, p. 371-384.

[6] KAJIYA J.T. « New Techniques for Ray-Tracing Procedurally Defined Objects », A.C.M. Trans. on Graphics, 2, 3, p. 161-181.

[7] Van Vijk J.J. « Ray-Tracing Objects Defined by Sweeping a Sphere », Proc. Eurographics 84, p. 161-181.

[8] MANDELBROT B. « Comment on Computer Rendering of Fractal Stochastic Models », Comm. A.C.M., 25, 3, p. 581-583.

[9] ROTH S.D. « Ray-Casting for Modelling Solids », Comp. Graphics and Image Processing, 18, 2, p. 109-144.

[10] HARUYAMA S., A.B. BARSKY « Using Stochastic Modeling for Texture Generation » I.E.E.E. Comp. Graphics and Applications 4, 3, p. 7-19.

Fig 9

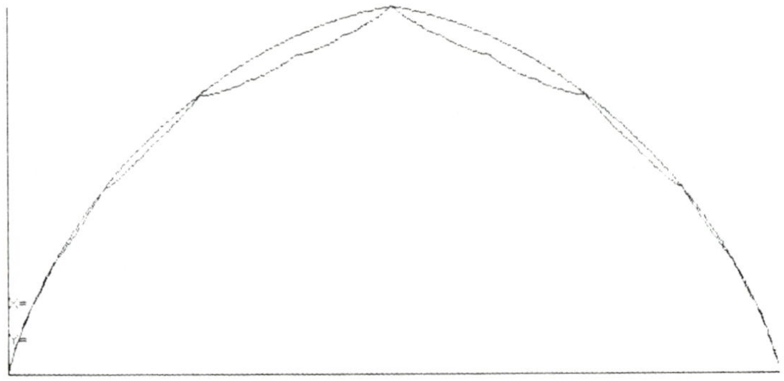

Fig 11 Variance profile (upper curve) and variance curve (lower curve) for H = 0.8.

Fig. 10

Efficient Alias-free Rendering using Bit-masks and Look-up Tables

Greg Abram and Lee Westover

The University of North Carolina at Chapel Hill

Turner Whitted

Numerical Design Ltd.

Abstract

We demonstrate an efficient method of rendering alias-free synthetic images using precomputed convolution integrals. The method is based on the observation that a visible polygon fragment's contribution to an image is solely a function of its position and shape, and that within a reasonable level of accuracy, a limited number of shapes represent the majority of cases encountered in images commonly rendered.

The convolution integral is precomputed for all pixels affected by the polygon fragment and is stored in a table. Completely visible fragments which are either triangular or trapezoidal produce two indices into the table. Most other fragments which are represented as differences of simple fragments. The remaining cases are characterized by a bit-mask for which each bit has a corresponding set of look up tables.

The basic technique has been applied to several fundamentally different rendering algorithms. In addition, we illustrate a version of the newly introduced non-uniform sampling technique implemented in the same program, but with different table values.

CR CATEGORIES AND SUBJECT DESCRIPTORS: I.3.3 [**Computer Graphics**]: Picture/Image Generation - Display algorithms;

GENERAL TERMS: Algorithms

ADDITIONAL KEY WORDS AND PHRASES: anti-aliasing, image synthesis

1. Preface

The superior quality of computer generated images produced through anti-aliasing rendering procedures has virtually eliminated any argument of whether anti-aliasing is worthwhile. Furthermore, a survey of the literature would lead one to believe that the same technique has never been implemented twice - that for every display system there is a unique approach to anti-aliasing.

The technique described here is an extension of two algorithms devised by Catmull [3, 4]. Catmull's original algorithm was implemented as part of a scan line ordered polygon renderer. Similarly, this algorithm was implemented as part of a scan-line ordered rendering system.

We have found that the procedure is applicable to several fundamentally different visible surface algorithms including a polygon clipper algorithm [1] and an A-Buffer [2]. We have attempted to extend it to the Pixel-Planes algorithm [10] without success.

2. Previous Work

The least painful manner of reducing aliases in computer generated images is to increase the effective resolution and filter prior to resampling at the display resolution. As Crow points out [7] this approach can produce arbitrarily good results with an arbitrarily large amount of computation. As a practical matter, effective resolutions of 4-8 times the display resolution produce images without noticeable artifacts except for pathological cases such as textures rendered in perspective. To eliminate artifacts in all cases requires a mechanism for finding visible portions of surface elements and accounting for the contribution of all of these elements to the final image samples.

Catmull's original scan line algorithm [3] included both of these features, but it computed intensity contributions by "area sampling." Area sampling divides the image plane into abutting square regions, each of which surround an image sample. The algorithm clips all polygons to the boundary of each sample square and computes samples as the polygon shade multiplied by the area of the polygon within the sample square. If polygons overlap within a sample square, then they are clipped against each other to produce visible fragments. From the signal processing viewpoint, this amounts the use of a filter whose cutoff frequency is too high for ideal anti-aliasing. The resulting images, however, were much better than would have been produced with no filtering at all. The frequency of the low pass filter can be reduced by using overlapping sample squares, but the filter shape is still not optimal.

More recently, the use of bit-masks to approximate sample square coverage has been used with good results [2, 9, 14].

Feibush, Levoy, and Cook [8] devised a method which will accommodate an arbitrary filter function. In their algorithm, polygons are clipped to the region under the filter kernel for which the kernel is not zero. Filtering is accomplished by a good discrete approximation of a convolution integral. The algorithm is slow, but the results are excellent.

A later algorithm by Catmull [4] combines elements of his earlier scan-line area sampling method with the filtering scheme of Feibush, Levoy, and Cook. His approach treats each pixel independently while the algorithm described in this paper treats each polygon fragment independently. His algorithm supports motion blur whereas ours does not.

Our algorithm combines the simplicity of Catmull's original method with the effectiveness of the Feibush, Levoy, and Cook technique. The technique originated in a scan-line ordered rendering system that demanded efficiency, but needed the ability to use arbitrarily good filter responses for some applications.

3. The Algorithm

One normally thinks of filtering as a process of convolving the filter function with all elements that fall under the filter kernel (figure 1) when the kernel is centered over a display sample:

$$I(x,y) = \sum_{i=1}^{n} \int\int h(x-u, y-v)\ I(polygon_i)\ du\ dv$$

where n is the number of polygons covered by the filter kernel. The process can be turned "inside out" by convolving a single surface fragment with filter kernels centered over all pixels to which the fragment can contribute intensity as shown in figure 2. This yields a contribution to each nearby pixel from the polygon fragment:

$$Intensity_1 \mathrel{+}= \int\int h(x_1-u, y_1-v) I(fragment)\,du\,dv$$

$$Intensity_2 \mathrel{+}= \int\int h(x_2-u, y_2-v) I(fragment)\,du\,dv$$

$$Intensity_n \mathrel{+}= \int\int h(x_m-u, y_m-v) I(fragment)\,du\,dv$$

where m is the number of sample squares affected by the fragment. This assumes, of course, that only visible fragments are considered. Image samples in this case act as accumulators whose final intensity value is reached when all fragments which contribute to it have been processed.

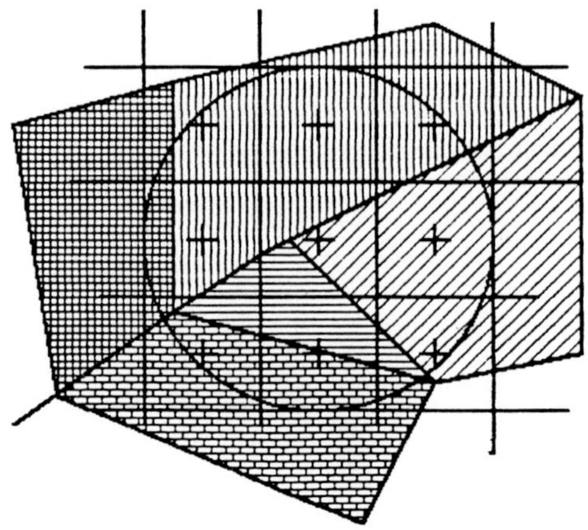

Figure 1. Convolution over all polygons contributing to the center pixel.

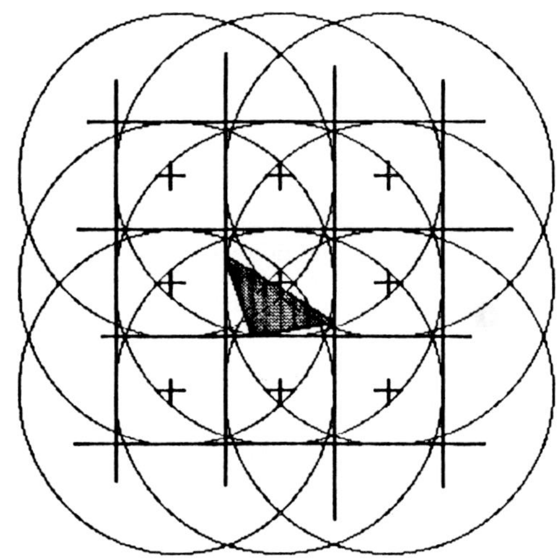

Figure 2. Convolutions for all pixels affected by one fragment.

For large polygon fragments of arbitrary shape, this approach is essentially useless since the convolution operation is prohibitively expensive. However, algorithms which clip polygons to the boundary of a sample square [3], produce fragments which fall into one of seven categories:

1) no fragment in the sample square,
2) fragment completely covers the sample square,
3) a trapezoidal fragment which splits the sample square along opposite edges,
4) a triangular fragment that splits the sample square along adjacent edges,
5) a pentagonal fragment that is the complement of case 4),

6) an odd shaped fragment that lies within the sample square that can be described by the difference of two or more type 3, 4, or 5 fragments, and
7) an odd shaped fragment that lies within the sample square but cannot be easily defined in terms of simpler cases.

For cases 1 and 2, the convolution can be precomputed and stored trivially. For cases 3 and 4 we select approximations to the actual fragments that intersect the sample square boundary at a several discrete positions. We chose 8 discrete positions because of previous experience with supersampling [18]. With 8 intersection positions along each of two edges, there are 64 possible triangular fragment approximations and the same number of trapezoidal fragment approximations.

Intensity for case 5 is computed by looking up the contribution for its complementary triangle and subtracting it from the contribution for a completely covered sample square.

If we assume that intensity is a constant over each fragment, then we can precompute the result of convolving unit intensity over the fragment with filter kernels centered over any number of nearby pixels. The fragment intensity is then multiplied by this precomputed value to determine its contribution to each nearby pixel. The number of table values required is then

$$(1+64+64)*N$$

where N is the number of nearby pixels affected by each fragment. In any event, the table size is small and the expense of precomputing convolution integrals has no bearing on the time needed to generate an anti-aliased image.

The constant intensity assumption can be relaxed slightly if an intensity value is computed for each vertex of a polygon fragment and is then interpolated across a fragment. Using an interpolant that is expressed as the sum of a basis function times each intensity value, contribution tables are generated by convolving the filter kernel with the basis function. This alternative requires more tables, more table accesses, and more arithmetic. We have not attempted this approach because fragments produced by clipping against sample square boundaries are too small to show significant variations in intensity across the fragment.

Figure 3 shows nine polygon fragments with different shapes and positions within a sample square. Figure 4 shows the contribution of each fragment to a 3x3 cluster of pixels centered about the sample square containing the fragment. If area sampling had been used instead, only the center pixel of each cluster would have any contribution.

4. Odd Shaped Fragments

Contributions from odd shaped fragments whose vertices all lie on the sample square boundary (case 6) can be calculated by adding and subtracting contributions from simple components.

For other odd shaped fragments (case 7) we resort to a bit-mask to define coverage and associate a table value with each non-zero bit of the mask for the sake of efficiency. Previous experience [2] has shown that this approach is reasonable. Accuracy of the intensity computed this way is purely a function of bit mask resolution. Using a high resolution bit-mask increases the size of the intensity table but does not affect execution speed. As we shall see, using bit masks of low resolution (i.e. 64 bits per pixel) forces an adjustment to the table values for the simple fragments.

For images containing a high percentage of sample squares that do not fit one of the five simple cases, an efficient technique is needed to recognize case 6. In the current implementation edges of a fragment within a sample square are tested to determine if they coincide with the sample square boundary. Edges are ignored if they do coincide with the boundary and retained if they

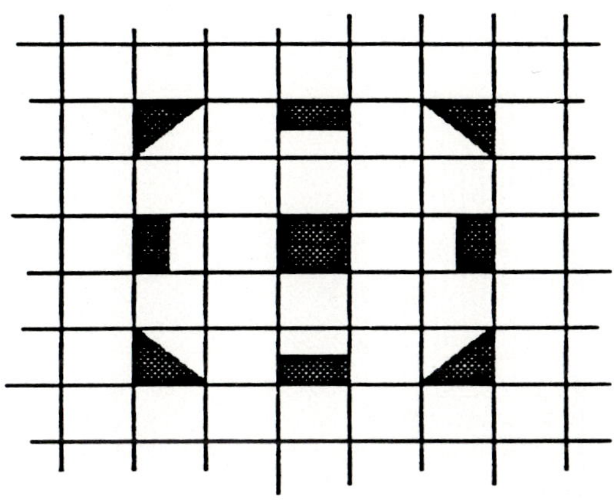

Figure 3. Nine different simple fragments.

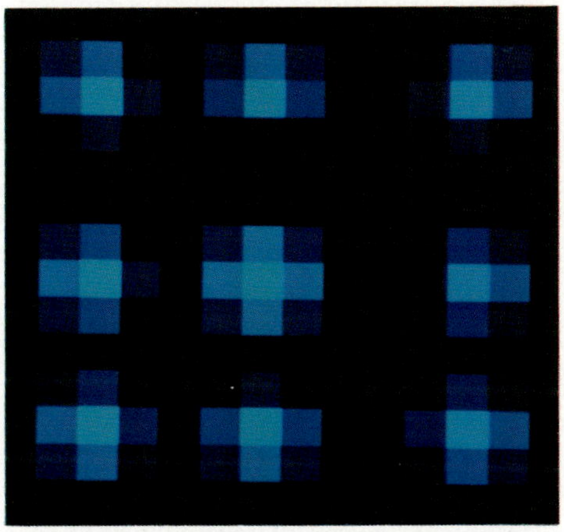

Figure 4. Contributions to neighboring pixels for each of the cases in figure 3.

do not. The number of retained edges may be:

equal to 0 - fragment covers the sample square
equal to 1 - one of the 3 simple cases
greater than or equal to 2 - cases 6 or 7 (odd shape)

For simpler images with larger homogeneous areas, it may be faster to recognize larger regions of simple cases.

5. Scan Line Implementation

The original implementation as part of a scan-line ordered rendering package was reasonably simple. The package is designed for applications characterized by large homogeneous areas on the screen and relatively low overall complexity.

For the most part, the scan conversion stage is identical to Catmull's [3]. A similar scheme can be found in [17]. The scan conversion process is equivalent to sliding a narrow horizontal band from the top of the image plane to the bottom. Each band is one pixel high. In the simplest possible case, clipping everything above the top of the band and everything below the bottom produces trapezoidal spans as shown in figure 5. Each trapezoidal span is broken into three regions: 1) left slope, 2) middle, and 3) right slope. Since nearly horizontal edges produce long slope regions, it is important to handle those regions efficiently.

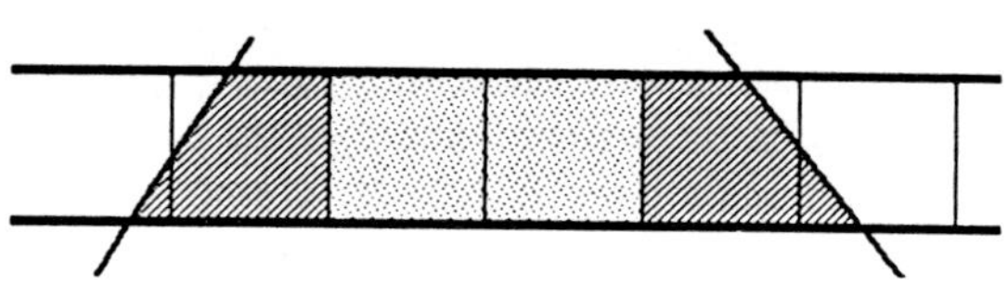

Figure 5. Trapezoidal span broken into left slope, middle, and right slope regions.

More complicated cases arise when a polygon vertex lies within the band or when a virtual vertex is produced by crossing edges. These cases are detected and passed to an A-buffer [2] styled routine which produces a coverage mask for each fragment in the region.

Since fragments in the current band will contribute to pixel rows above and below the current band a number of scan lines of pixels, numbered $i-n$ through $i+n$, must be maintained locally. When processing of the band straddling scan line i is complete, scan line $i-n$ can be written to the display device, cleared, and rolled around to become scan line $i+n+1$. For applications involving high resolution display on a film recorder, it may make sense to keep only the current scan line and limit the filter to an area-sampling box. For video applications, we may retain as many as 5 scan lines and filter in such a way as to reduce flicker. In either extreme, the procedures are the same. Only table values and some display parameters change.

6. Polygon Clipper Implementation

As part of project to develop a near-real-time high-quality display system, Abram [1] has introduced an efficient and robust polygon clipper visible surface algorithm. Like its predecessor [16], it produces a list of visible polygons of arbitrary size and shape.

To take advantage of the table driven algorithm the visible polygons must be further clipped to sample squares. An early version of the program traveled around the polygon edges clipping to sample squares as it went. Polygon interiors were handled separately. The current program individually scan converts polygons while generating fragments along each scan line. Both versions program individually scan converts polygons while generating fragments along each scan line. Both versions keep an entire frame of pixels locally, so that the visible polygons can be tiled in any order. When all visible polygons have been tiled, each pixel will have accumulated its correct final intensity.

When fragments are processed in random order there is no way to know whether any given sample square contains only simple fragments or complex fragments or both. The sample square shown in figure 6, for example, contains one simple trapezoid fragment and two complex fragments. Had the fragments been generated in sorted order, the sample square would have been flagged as complex and bit-masks would have been used to compute all coverages. In a naive implementation of the polygon clipper algorithm, the contribution from a simple fragment would have been computed directly from a table and the contributions from the remaining fragments computed slightly more coarsely from different tables for each one-bit in their respective bit masks. Because the contributions are computed two different ways, the total of weighting functions over the sample square may not sum to one. We have seen this error in final images at sample squares similar to the one in figure 6. Rather than resort to a uniform method of computing coverages, we have instead precomputed the contribution tables for simple fragments as if they were determined from a bit mask. This leads to an almost unnoticeable degradation in image quality, but it retains the speed of direct table look-up for simple cases.

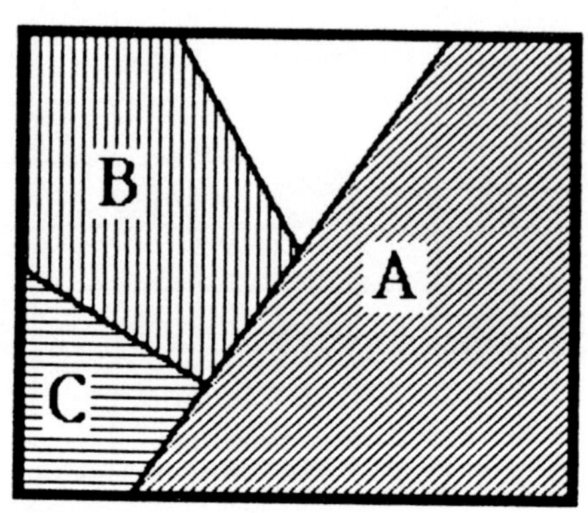

Figure 6. Sample square covered by one simple fragment and two odd shaped fragments.

7. Pixel-Planes Extensions

Our colleagues [11] have searched for a way to embed this scheme in the Pixel-Planes VLSI processor with only modest success. The Pixel-Planes algorithm computes a slope and perpendicular distance measure for each polygon edge at each pixel to determine whether the pixel is inside or outside the polygon [10]. To use these two values as look-up table indices at first seemed to be a natural extension of table driven anti-aliasing since the geometry of a polygon fragment is entirely determined by the two values.

Unfortunately, Pixel-Planes makes no guarantee that any polygon fragment is visible since it uses a z-buffer hidden surface algorithm. The Pixel-Planes algorithm would have to be modified to use a front-to-back sort permitting pixels to accumulate intensity and maintain coverage masks. Furthermore, the Pixel-Planes architecture discourages propagation of intensity from one pixel (sample square) to its neighbors.

The best that can be done is to use the look-up table to store a bit-mask that corresponds to the fragment's coverage of the sample square. The bit-mask may be further masked by the bit-mask of any polygon which is in front of the current one. In the end, a fragment's contribution to the intensity of a pixel is obtained by using the sum of one's in its bit-mask as a measure of area. The use of any larger filter kernel is prohibited by the narrow pixel-to-pixel communications path. On the whole, this anti-aliasing method is not well suited for the Pixel-Planes algorithm.

8. Non-Uniform Sampling

Recent, independent efforts at Bell Labs [12] and Lucasfilm [5] indicate that anti-aliased image synthesis can be achieved without filtering. Although we don't know the details of either effort, we understand that they are based on the use of non-uniform sampling. Even though an arbitrary function cannot be reproduced error free from non-uniform samples, the aliases can be made to appear as uncorrelated noise rather than highly correlated jaggies. Increasing the sample density improves the signal-to-noise ratio while avoiding the overhead of filtering.

In our test implementation of this method, we use a small set of random sample templates which define a distribution of samples in the vicinity of the current sample square. As the display routine moves from sample square to sample square, a different template is used to avoid repeating patterns of artifacts. Although this technique does not meet the criterion for alias-free rendering [13, 15], the deficiencies are not major.

The first step in this process is to determine whether a sample in a template lies on the interior of a polygon fragment. For this we use the same table look-up indices described in previous sections. The table stores bit masks which contain a "one" bit for each sample on the polygon interior and "zero" bit for each sample outside the polygon.

There is, of course, the second step of producing uniform samples on the display device from non-uniformly spaced image samples. For this we use a precomputed weight based on the spatial relation of the image samples to the display samples.

In a few simple tests with the initial implementation, no significant advantage is seen with this method, while image quality is slightly worse than the best obtained with filtering.

9. Results

For test purposes, a fragment tiler that processed ASCII fragment lists with floating point arithmetic was used. The performance of the test tiler is not indicative of the efficiency of the algorithm.

Figure 8 shows two moderately complex views of the interior of a building rendered with the polygon clipper visible surface algorithm. Each image contains about 295,000 fragments and 262,144 pixels. The Old Well in figure 9 was rendered in the same manner.

Figure 10 shows the Old Well rendered three different ways. The filtered rendering uses two different filters.

Our current implementation has been used to generate more than 1500 images with a total of approximately 1 million polygons and 250 million fragments. The fragment types break down in the following way:

85.6%	case 2	(total coverage)
13.0%	case 3,4,5	(simple coverage)
0.6%	case 6	(complex shape) formed by adding and subtracting cases 3,4,5
0.8%	case 7	(complex shape)

Perhaps the most important observation to be made from these statistics is that even for complex scenes (such as figure 8) the total number of fragments does not greatly exceed the number of sample squares. In addition, case 7 fragments occur rarely enough that a sophisticated procedure for handling complex shapes can be used without seriously degrading the algorithm's performance.

Since any table driven process involves approximations, one would expect the algorithm to fail on occasion. In particular, very skinny fragments could present a problem. This algorithm never misses these fragments, although it may introduce a slight error due to approximations in the tables. Clearly, larger tables will produce smaller errors. For the table sizes we have chosen the errors are not apparent.

10. Commentary

While we are accustomed to seeing several realizations which implement the same algorithm, we are somewhat surprised to find one program which fits efficiently into several algorithms and which, in fact, implements different (although roughly equivalent) functions depending on the meaning of the table values.

Figure 8. Two views of the lobby in the future University of North Carolina at Chapel Hill computer science building.

Figure 9. University of North Carolina Old Well.

Figure 10. Same Old Well point sampled, rendered with Gaussian filter, rendered with conical filter, rendered with non-uniform sampling.

Normally, anti-aliasing is performed from each pixel's point of view; by first determining which fragments contribute to the pixel and then integrating over all contributing fragments. We have described a method whereby the contribution of each visible polygon fragment to its neighboring pixels is determined independent of contributions of all other visible fragments. The first benefit of our approach is efficiency; each fragment is processed only once. The second benefit is that the effectiveness of the anti-aliasing is dependent only on the choice of filter kernel and table size. Since the speed of the algorithm is independent of table contents, a nearly perfect filter is no more expensive than a poor one.

Statistics gathered from several hundred frames of animation have shown that the use of bit-masks to compute coverage of irregular fragments was an unnecessary compromise. Consequently, with slight modification the algorithm can produce nearly alias-free images efficiently.

Acknowledgement

We thank Rob Cook of Lucasfilm for his comments about parts of our work and Rob Pike and Don Mitchell of Bell Labs for expanding our understanding of the deviousness of sampling theory. Many of the ideas presented here originated in discussions with Vicki Woolf of Numerical Design. We also appreciate the cooperation of our colleagues Henry Fuchs, Jack Goldfeather, Susan Spach, and Jeff Hultquist of the University of North Carolina. The Old Well was modeled by Eric Grant and the building scene was modeled by Dana Smith.

References

[1] Abram, G.D., forthcoming PhD dissertation.

[2] Carpenter, L.C., "The A-buffer, an Antialiased Hidden Surface Method," *Computer Graphics*, **18**, 3, SIGGRAPH ACM, Jul. 1984.

[3] Catmull, E., "A Hidden-Surface Algorithm with Anti-Aliasing," *Computer Graphics*, **12**, 3, SIGGRAPH ACM, Aug. 1978.

[4] Catmull, E., "An Analytic Visible Surface Algorithm for Independent Pixel Processing," *Computer Graphics*, **18**, 3, SIGGRAPH ACM, Jul. 1984.

[5] Cook, R.L., T. Porter, and L. Carpenter, "Distributed Ray Tracing," *Computer Graphics*, **18**, 3, SIGGRAPH ACM, Jul. 1984.

[6] Crow, F.C., "The Aliasing Problem in Computer-Generated Shaded Images," *Comm. of the ACM*, **20**, 11, Nov. 1977.

[7] Crow, F.C., "A Comparison of Antialiasing Techniques," *IEEE Computer Graphics and Applications*, **1**, 1, Jan. 1981.

[8] Feibush, Eliot, Marc Levoy, and Robert L. Cook, "Synthetic Texturing Using Digital Filters," *Computer Graphics*, **14**, 3, SIGGRAPH ACM, Jul. 1980.

[9] Fiume, E., and A. Fournier, "A Parallel Scan Conversion Algorithm with Anti-Aliasing for a General-Purpose Ultracomputer," *Computer Graphics*, **17**, 3, SIGGRAPH ACM, Jul. 1983.

[10] Fuchs, Henry, John Poulton, Al Paeth, and Alan Bell, "Developing Pixel Planes, a Smart Memory-Based Raster Graphics System", Proceedings of the 1982 MIT Conference on Advanced Research in VLSI.

[11] Fuchs, Henry, Jack Goldfeather, Jeff P. Hultquist, Susan Spach, and John D. Austin, John G. Eyles, and John Poulton, "Fast Spheres, Shadows, Textures, Transparencies, and Image Enhancements in Pixel-Planes," Proceedings of Siggraph '85.

[12] Mitchell, Don P., "Antialiased Ray Tracing By Nonuniform Sampling," AT&T Bell Labs., unpublished report, Dec. 1984.

[13] Jerri, A.J., "The Shannon Sampling Theorem - Its Various Extensions and Applications: A Tutorial Review," *Proc. IEEE*, **65**, 11, Nov. 1977.

[14] Robinson, John, tutorial notes for State of the Art in Image Synthesis Seminar, SIGGRAPH '81.

[15] Shapiro, H.S., and R.A. Silverman, "Alias Free Sampling of Random Noise," *J. SIAM*, **8**, Jun. 1960.

[16] Weiler, Kevin J., and Peter A. Atherton, "Hidden Surface Removal using Polygon Area Sorting," *Computer Graphics*, **11**, 3, SIGGRAPH ACM, Jul. 1977.

[17] Whitted, T., and David M. Weimer, "A Software Testbed for the Development of 3D Raster Graphics Systems," *ACM Trans. Graphics*, **1**, 1, Jan. 1982.

[18] Whitted, T., "Anti-aliased Line Drawing using Brush Extrusion," *Computer Graphics*, **17**, 3, SIGGRAPH ACM, July 1983.

Statistically Optimized Sampling for Distributed Ray Tracing

Mark E. Lee
Amoco Production Company
Tulsa Research Center

Richard A. Redner
Department of Mathematics

Samuel P. Uselton
Department of Computer Science

University of Tulsa
Tulsa, Oklahoma

Abstract

Cook, Porter, and Carpenter coined the phrase "distributed ray tracing" to describe a technique for using each ray of a super-sampled ray tracing procedure as a sample in several dimensions to achieve effects such as penumbras and motion blur in addition to spatial anti-aliasing. The shade to be displayed at a pixel is a weighted integral of the image function. The purpose of using many rays per pixel is to estimate the value of this integral. In this work, a relationship between the number of sample rays and the quality of the estimate of this integral is derived. Furthermore, the number of rays required does not depend on the dimensionality of the space being sampled, but only on the variance of the multi-dimensional image function. The algorithm has been optimized through the use of statistical testing and stratified sampling.

CR Categories and Subject Descriptions: I.3.3 [Computer Graphics]: Picture/Image Generation - display algorithms; I.3.7 [Computer Graphics]: Three-dimensional Graphics and Realism - Shading, Shadowing, Texture, Visible Line/Surface Algorithms;

Additional Keywords and Phrases: Ray Tracing, Anti-aliasing, Penumbras, Shadows, Translucency, Transparency

Introduction

The problem of visual artifacts appearing in synthesized images due to the finite resolution of displays has been a concern in computer graphics for many years. Several techniques, collectively referred to as anti-aliasing, have been developed for combatting the problem [3,5,6,7,9,10,14,16]. Only recently, however, has this problem been a paramount concern in the implementation of ray tracing algorithms [1,4,11,15]. All solutions to the problem begin with the same theoretical basis [5]. The correct value to display at a pixel is a weighted integral of shades in the neighborhood of the pixel. Direct computation of this integral is expensive, especially in color displays, since it must be done for at least three primary values. Several authors have suggested sampling points or areas around the pixel as a method for approximating this integral. An important question is "How many samples is enough?". The two standard answers are "more is always better" and "we find that n is usually enough," where n is some integer between 4 and 256. Given that color values are stored with limited precision, it seems likely that the number of useful samples per pixel is also limited. If the sampling is done in some fixed pattern, then geometries always exist for which that particular sampling pattern generates a poor estimate of the integral and unwanted artifacts are created. However, if the sampling is done randomly, this problem can be eliminated. Furthermore, a statistical test can be developed to determine when enough samples have been used. The following section describes the derivation of this result.

In the implementation of a ray tracing algorithm, this result can be used to estimate the number of rays needed to accomplish spatial anti-aliasing. It is also demonstrated that the same result holds when the ray is considered to be a multidimensional sample. It applies, then, to implementations which use each ray as a sample, not only of the pixel area, but also of light source area, surface reflection direction, surface refraction direction, and similar variables. The number of samples required do not depend directly on the number of dimensions being sampled, therefore, sampling an additional dimension may not increase the number of samples needed. A statistical technique known as stratified sampling is used to select samples such that, if the variation among the first samples is small, no further samples are required. This technique is used to reduce sampling, as in adaptive subdivision algorithms [2,15], without disturbing the statistical properties required for the main result to remain valid.

In the results section, several images are presented to demonstrate the quality that can be achieved. To show the efficiency of the implementation, a two-dimensional histogram of the number of sample rays for each pixel are given for each image. In addition, histograms showing the number of pixels requiring various amounts of sampling are provided.

Theory

In the following, X represents the point in multidimensional space to be sampled. F(X) is the "true" continuous image to be approximated. P(X) is the filter used in smoothing the image to accomplish the anti-aliasing.

For $X \varepsilon R^n$, we must evaluate convolutions which can be written as integrals of the form $\int_{R^n} F(X)P(X)dX$ [5]. In the case that $P(X) \geqq 0$ for $X \varepsilon R^n$ and $\int_{R^n} P(X)dX = 1$, then P(X) is a probability density function. If we think of X as an n-dimensional random variable with probability density function P(X), then the value of the integral $\int_{R^n} F(X)P(X)dX$ is the expected value of F which is written E(F(X)).

Rather than estimating this integral using traditional numerical techniques, we propose a statistical estimate. Let $X_1, X_2, \ldots, X_N$ be independent identically distributed random variables with density function P(X). Let

$$F_N = (1/N) \sum_{i=1}^{N} F(X_i).$$

If E(F(X)) exists, then by the strong law of large numbers [8],

$$\lim_{N\to\infty} F_N = E(F(X)) \quad \text{with probability one,}$$

and so for sufficiently large N, F_N is a good estimate of E(F(X)). We also observe that

$$E(F_N) = E(F(X))$$

which means that F_N is an unbiased estimator for E(F(X)).

A statistical measure of the difference between F_N and E(F(X)) is the variance of F_N which is defined to be

$$E\,(F_N - E(F(X)))^2 = (E(F^2(X))-E(F(X))^2)/N$$
$$= VAR(F(X))/N.$$

We observe that not only does F_N converge to E(F(X)) as N gets large but that the variance of F_N about E(F(X)) is VAR(F(X))/N.

Two points of this formulation should be emphasized. First, just as in more traditional numerical schemes for evaluating integrals, the error can be made arbitrarily small by evaluating the function at sufficiently many points. In our problem, these points are chosen randomly with density P(X). The second important point is that the error in our estimate of E(F(X)) is not intrinsically a function of the dimension of the space but depends only on the variation of F over those dimensions. The number of samples to be thrown is not the product of the number of samples required for each dimension; instead, the number of samples depends directly on the variability of F.

It is reasonable to try to construct a sampling scheme so that the variances of our estimates throughout the scene are approximately equal. Ideally, we would determine a threshold, T, and sample until the variance of our estimate was less than T. However, since the variance at each point is not known a priori, we construct the following statistical test. Let

$$S_N^2 = (1/N) \sum_{i=1}^{N} (F(X_i)-F_N)^2.$$

S_N^2 is an approximation of VAR(F(X)) from the generated data. Define the number $\chi^2_\beta(N-1)$ so that, under a normal sampling theory,

$$\text{Probability } (N{*}S_N^2/VAR(F(X)) < \chi^2_\beta(N-1)) = \beta.$$

This notation has been chosen because the distribution of $N{*}S_N^2/VAR(F(X))$ under the normal theory is the χ^2 distribution with N-1 degrees of freedom [8]. Compute $S_N^2 / \chi^2_\beta(N-1)$. If $S_N^2 / \chi^2_\beta(N-1) < T$, then stop sampling, otherwise, throw more samples. This test is constructed so that the

$$\text{Probability } (VAR(F(X))/N < S_N^2/\chi^2_\beta(N-1)) = 1-\beta$$

and so the probability of stopping when $VAR(F(X))/N > T$ is less than β. The threshold, T, is chosen sufficiently small so that the variance of the computed values is small enough to provide a good estimate of the true color values. Since this is a statistical setting, one can not guarantee that a good estimate will be calculated at every pixel. In order to assure that a good estimate is obtained most of the time, the parameter β, the failure rate, is chosen to be small.

Further consideration of the error of our estimate shows that for certain geometries, the variance of the estimate can be reduced by the use of stratified sampling. Stratification denotes selection from several subregions into which a region is divided [12]. In particular, n dimensional Euclidean space can be partitioned and samples thrown into each region. Consider the case that R^n is divided into m regions and that N_j samples $\{X_{ij}\}_{i=1}^{N_j}$ $j=1,\ldots,m$ are thrown into each region where the numbers N_j/N are proportional to the probability of the jth region. The estimate of the average value of F is the same as before and by using a stratified sample of this type, the variation of F_N can be reduced. Let

$$N = \sum_{j=1}^{m} N_j \text{ and } F_j = (1/N_j) \sum_{i=1}^{N_j} F(X_{ij}).$$

Now

$$F_N = (1/N) \sum_{j=1}^{m} N_j F_j.$$

The variance of this estimate is the weighted average of the variances over each region of R^n [12], that is,

$$VAR(F_N) = (1/N) \sum_{j=1}^{m} N_j VAR(F_j).$$

If the variances of F over the individual regions are sufficiently small compared to the variance over the whole space, then there will be a reduction in variance.

Consider a linear boundary between two homogenous regions in the plane and a density function which is radially symmetric about a point on the boundary in the plane (Figure 1). If the plane is divided into four equal quadrants about this point and stratified sampling is performed, then it can be seen that in the worst case, the variance of the estimate is reduced by a factor of 2 and in the best case (the boundary is aligned with the partition), the variance is (almost magically) equal to zero.

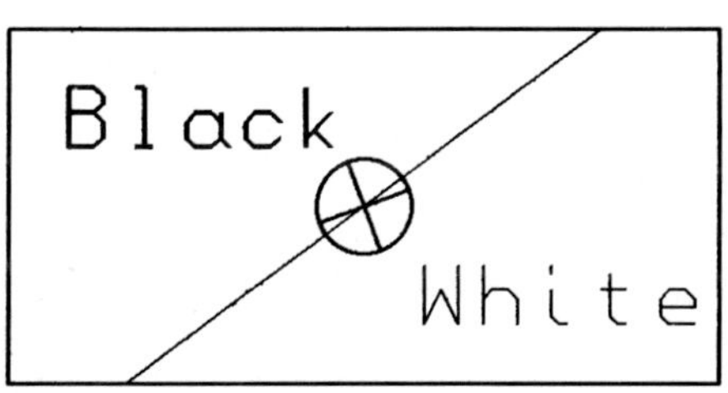

Figure 1

Implementation

To compute the pixel values in a distributed ray tracing implementation, samples are drawn. As the samples are created, incremental sums of $F(X_i)$ and $F^2(X_i)$ are kept. The sampling continues until the exit criterion $S_N^2/\chi_\beta^2(N-1) < T$ is met.

An important issue is how to choose the values for T and β. Let M be the maximum or worst case variance that will be tolerated for a scene. Any estimate to the variance that is greater than M should never pass the early exit test and should force the maximum amount of samples to be used. To force this to happen, T should be set so that, at the maximum number of samples, the correct balance between the variance and the χ^2 test will be met and the test will pass. Let Z be the maximum number of samples to be allowed. This value is usually determined by computer run time constraints. T can be calculated from the maximum variance and the maximum number of samples by the following formula

$$T = M/\chi_\beta^2(Z-1).$$

Now, when the variance of the samples is greater than or equal to the maximum variance allowed, the maximum number of samples are guaranteed to be used. Define Δ to be the minimum color difference that can be represented by the display medium. For a raster device, the minimum color difference is usually $1/(2^b)$ where b is the number of bits in the frame buffer for a primary color. If the difference between two colors is less than Δ, then the difference cannot be displayed. A value for the maximum variance, M, should be of the same magnitude as the minimum difference in color, Δ.

A table containing the values of $T*\chi_\beta^2(N-1)$ for $N=1,\ldots,Z$ can be calculated in a preprocessing step for maximum efficiency. The early exit test becomes a table lookup and a comparison. The value of β now serves to spread the values of the table between zero and M. The larger the value for β, the larger the spread of values becomes and the earlier the variance can pass the test. A tradeoff exists between a lower β value and more accuracy or a higher β value and less overall sampling and computing time. The value chosen for β is a consequence of the quality required for a particular application and the amount of resources available.

Stratified sampling allows for sampling a distribution with a good approximation to the true mean with fewer samples. The region to be sampled is broken into several smaller regions such that the combination of the distributions of the smaller regions is the same as distribution of the original region. If the region is broken into smaller regions in a sensible manner, a very few samples will serve to properly sample the region of interest. The key is to set up the division of the region so that the samples are as well distributed as possible while still following the distribution function accurately. This prevents using many samples that lie near each other and yields a better estimate of E(F(X)).

Each distributed ray is n-dimensional in information content. Several of the dimensions include pixel area sampling, realistic light source sampling, and surface smoothness sampling for reflection and refraction. The ray definition is implicit instead of explicit, however. Instead of carrying an n-dimensional ray through the ray tracer, an ordinary 3-space ray is used along with the implicit n-dimensional information for calculating an n-dimensional ray from an ordinary 3-dimensional ray. The ray is extended to higher dimensions by perturbing the ray using the implicit information in the proper fashion. For anti-aliasing, generate an artificial two-dimensional axis system in the window containing the pixel. Draw a sample from the appropriate distribution for anti-aliasing. Use the samples as offsets from the origin along each axis and make this point the new endpoint of the ray. The new ray has been extended to sample from the proper distribution for anti-aliasing. For modeling realistic light sources, first project the light source onto the plane perpendicular to a ray arriving at the center of the light source. Sample the distribution of the light source in the plane. The value of this random variable specifies the endpoint of the sample ray. Variable surface smoothness can be sampled by perturbing each reflected and refracted ray by using the plane that is perpendicular to the end of the ray and sampling as above. After all perturbations have taken place, the ray now contains n-dimensional information and properly samples each dimension.

Results

Three figures are provided to demonstrate the quality of the results. In each figure, part (a) is the actual image computed. Part (b) is the two-dimensional histogram showing the number of samples used for the corresponding pixels of part (a). The histogram in part (c) shows the relative quantity of pixels for each number of samples used. All three images are sampled in the dimensions required to model solid light sources and variable degrees of surface smoothness and to perform spatial anti-aliasing. All three images use the shading model of Lee and Uselton described in [13], and are done at a resolution of 512 by 512 pixels.

Parameter settings for all three pictures are the same. Eight subregions are used for the stratified sampling and one new sample is chosen from each region when the need for additional samples is indicated. The value for β used is .05 and the value for T is 0.000105. The maximum variance, M, is 1/128, and the maximum number of samples, Z, is 96.

Figure 2(a) shows nine wedges lit from the right, casting shadows onto a checkered backdrop. The shadows show penumbras caused by the sampling of the light source. Figure 2(b) shows that large numbers of rays are used only when smaller numbers will not suffice. Notice that fewer rays are needed in the area of the blackest wedge because all the light is absorbed and the shade becomes constant. Figure 2(c) demonstrates two interesting facts: first that most pixels require only the minimum number of samples; and second that the high frequency of the checkerboard pattern does (as expected) cause a large number of pixels requiring the maximum number of samples.

Three effects of this algorithm can be seen in Figure 3(a) especially well. The shadows cast by the metallic spheres have penumbras, showing the sampling in the light source dimension. The reflection of the checkered backdrop onto the table becomes less precise the further out from the backdrop it is, showing a less than perfectly smooth surface. The highlights on the two spheres have different areas and intensities, indicating a difference in polish between the two. Figure 3(b) shows the variation in the number of samples per pixel required, especially in the reflection of the backdrop on the table. The lack of variation in the area of the backdrop is due to the extremely matte finish of the backdrop. Figure 3(c) shows that the larger squares and matte finish of the backdrop leads to a larger number of pixels requiring only the minimum number of samples.

In figure 4(a) both the table and the backdrop are smoother than in figure 3(a) and the backdrop is more reflective. This is shown by the visibility of the reflection of the table on the backdrop and the visibility of the light source reflection on the backdrop. The reflection of the backdrop on the table is slightly more precise. This difference can actually be seen more easily in figures 3(b) and 4(b) by comparing the smearing of the backdrop's edges in the reflection on the table. Note also the reflection of the shadow of the wine glass.

Future work

This technique of generating sample rays can easily be extended to additional dimensions to model effects such as motion blur and depth of field. Wavelength sampling for improved color modeling as well as wavelength dependent effects such as refraction can also be included. The difficulties in these extensions lie mainly in determining the appropriate distribution to sample for each dimension and computing the ray paths in higher dimensions. Computing the position of moving objects at arbitrary times, for example, will be required for motion blur.

Additional work should consider the interaction between the number of rays per pixel, the number of pixels in the image and the size at which the image is to be displayed. It is intuitively expected that an increase in spatial resolution will decrease the average number of samples needed per pixel. This intuition is dependent on the assumption that the overall image size remains constant. The size of the pixel, in terms of the portion of the field of view occupied, becomes a relevant parameter.

Acknowledgements

The authors would like to express gratitude to the Tulsa Research Center of Amoco Production Company for the use of their computing facilities, to the referees for their helpful comments, and to Debra Redner for her support of this research effort.

References

[1] Amanatides, J. Ray tracing with cones. Computer Graphics 18,3 (July 1984), pp. 129-135.

[2] Catmull, E. Computer display of curved surfaces. Proceedings IEEE Conference on Computer Graphics, Pattern Recognition and Data Structures (May 1975).

[3] Catmull, E. A hidden-surface algorithm with anti-aliasing. Computer Graphics 12,3 (Aug. 1978), pp. 1-5.

[4] Cook, R. L., Porter, T. and Carpenter, L. Distributed ray tracing. Computer Graphics 18,3 (July 1984), pp. 137-145.

[5] Crow, F. C. The aliasing problem in computer-generated shaded images. Comm. ACM 20,11 (Nov. 1977), pp. 799-805.

[6] Crow, F. C. The use of grayscale for improved raster display of vectors and characters. Computer Graphics 12,3 (Aug. 1978), pp. 1-5.

[7] Crow, F. C. A comparison of anti-aliasing techniques. IEEE Computer Graphics and Applications 1,1 (Jan. 1981), pp. 40-49.

[8] Feller, W. An Introduction to Probability Theory and Its Applications. John Wiley and Sons, 1971.

[9] Fiume, E., Fournier, A. and Rudolph, L. A parallel scan conversion algorithm with anti-aliasing for a general-purpose ultracomputer. Computer Graphics 17,3 (July 1983), pp. 141-150.

[10] Fuchs, H. and Barros, J. Generating smooth 2-d monocolor line drawings on video displays. Computer Graphics 13,2 (July 1979), pp. 260-269.

[11] Heckbert, P. S. and Hanrahan, P. Beam tracing polygonal objects. Computer Graphics 18,3 (July 1984), pp. 119-127.

[12] Kish, L. Survey Sampling. John Wiley and Sons, 1965.

[13] Lee, M. E. and Uselton, S. P. A shading model for rendering objects with body color. Technical Report F85-C-5, Amoco Production Company - Tulsa Research Center, Tulsa OK (1985).

[14] Turkowski, K. Anti-aliasing through the use of coordinate transformations. ACM Transactions on Graphics 1,3 (July 1982), pp. 215-234.

[15] Whitted, T. An improved illumination model for shaded display. Comm. ACM 23,6 (June 1980), pp. 343-349.

[16] Whitted, T. Anti-aliased line drawing using brush extrusion. Computer Graphics 17,3 (July 1983), pp. 151-156.

Figure 2

9 wedges

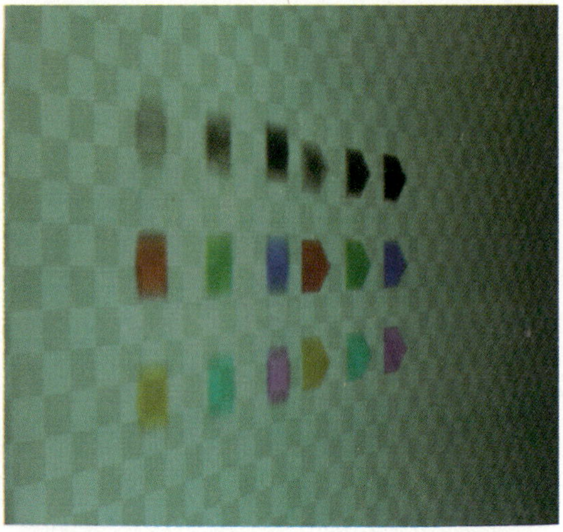

(a)

Figure 3

2 metallic spheres

(a)

Figure 4

wine glass and decanter

(a)

(b)

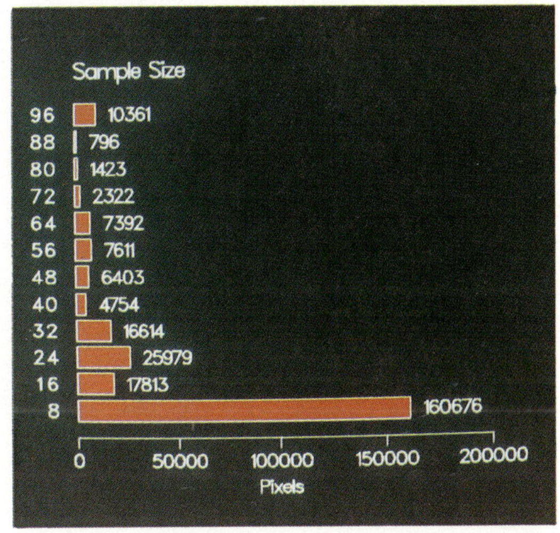
Sample Size
96 10361
88 796
80 1423
72 2322
64 7392
56 7611
48 6403
40 4754
32 16614
24 25979
16 17813
8 160676
0 50000 100000 150000 200000
Pixels

(c)

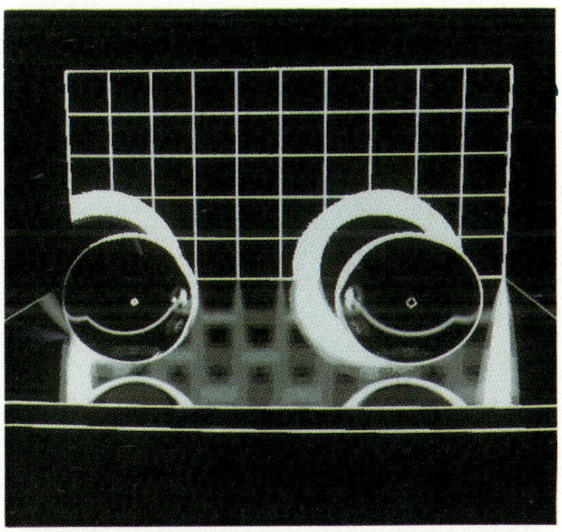

(b)

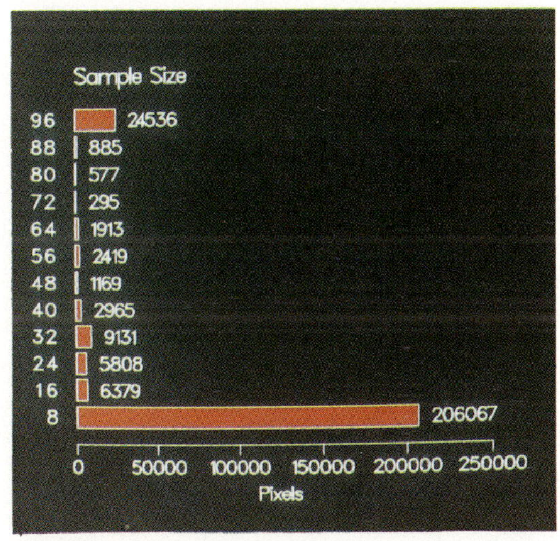
Sample Size
96 24536
88 885
80 577
72 295
64 1913
56 2419
48 1169
40 2965
32 9131
24 5808
16 6379
8 206067
0 50000 100000 150000 200000 250000
Pixels

(c)

(b)

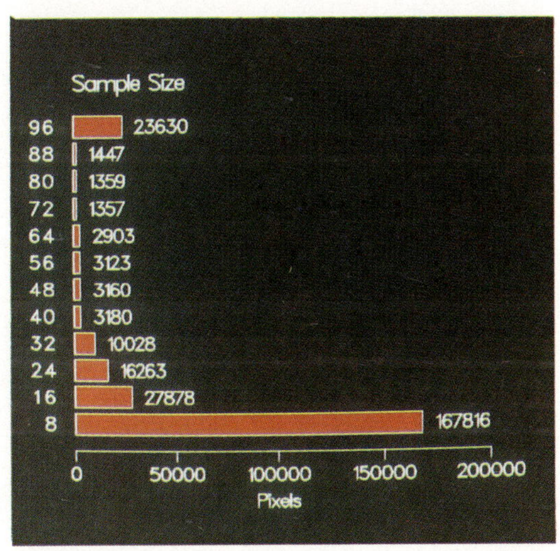
Sample Size
96 23630
88 1447
80 1359
72 1357
64 2903
56 3123
48 3160
40 3180
32 10028
24 16263
16 27878
8 167816
0 50000 100000 150000 200000
Pixels

(c)

Antialiasing Through Stochastic Sampling

Mark A. Z. Dippé
Berkeley Computer Graphics Laboratory

Erling Henry Wold
Computer Science Division

Department of Electrical Engineering and Computer Sciences
University of California
Berkeley, California 94720
U.S.A.

Abstract

Stochastic sampling techniques, in particular *Poisson* and *jittered* sampling, are developed and analyzed. These approaches allow the construction of *alias-free* approximations to continuous functions using discrete calculations. Stochastic sampling scatters high frequency information into broadband *noise* rather than generating the false *patterns* produced by *regular* sampling. The type of randomness used in the sampling process controls the spectral character of the noise. The *average sampling rate* and the function being sampled determine the amount of noise that is produced. Stochastic sampling is applied *adaptively* so that a greater number of samples are taken where the function varies most. An *estimate* is used to determine how many samples to take over a given region. *Noise reducing filters* are used to increase the efficacy of a given sampling rate. The *filter width* is adaptively controlled to further improve performance. Stochastic sampling can be applied *spatiotemporally* as well as to other aspects of scene simulation. *Ray tracing* is one example of an image synthesis approach that can be antialiased by stochastic sampling.

CR Categories and Subject Descriptors: I.3.3 **[Computer Graphics]**: Picture/Image Generation - *display algorithms; viewing algorithms*; I.3.7 **[Computer Graphics]**: Three-dimensional Graphics and Realism - *animation; color, shading, shadowing, and texture; visible line/surface algorithm*

General Terms: Algorithms

Additional Key Words and Phrases: adaptive, aliasing, antialiasing, filtering, noise, ray tracing, stochastic sampling

1. Introduction

The display media of digital image synthesis generally use a spatial array of *samples* to create a displayed image. Since the displayed image is created from samples, some of the information contained in the original continuous scene description will be lost. An effective way of analyzing the resulting errors is to consider the *frequency distortions* that arise from sampling. The errors caused by *regular* sampling are known as *aliasing*. A given *sampling rate* can only accurately represent frequencies lower than an associated bound. When frequencies higher than this bound exist, aliasing occurs. Display media also use a sequence of pixel arrays to create a time-varying image. *Spatiotemporal* sampling is an inherent part of current display media. Spatial aliasing error is often manifested by *staircasing* along edges in an image. *Strobing*, or the jerky motion of an object in an image, is a defect caused by temporal sampling. Defects from sampling can arise in other aspects of the displayed image, such as color.

Since sampling attempts to approximate an image with only a finite set of values, errors are unavoidable. However, the nature of the errors introduced by sampling can be directly controlled. Conventional sampling uses a regular array of points to approximate the ideal image.[9] The aliasing errors that occur from this approach can create *false patterns* that are easily perceived. Increasing the sampling rate will allow higher and higher frequencies to be represented. However, any regular sampling rate has an associated frequency limit above which aliasing will still occur. By using an *irregular* sampling pattern and filtering the irregular samples to create the pixels, featureless *noise* is produced from such high frequencies rather than false patterns. Such noise is perceptually less objectionable than false patterns. This type of behavior is also produced by regular sampling patterns when sampling highly irregular images, such as can occur in natural scenes.

Stochastic methods can be used to generate different classes of irregular sampling patterns. Such randomized sampling patterns correspond to statistical methods that are used to prevent biases from arising in discrete statistical samples. *Poisson sampling* uses sample points that are *uniformly* distributed throughout the sample space. The Poisson sampling technique can be generalized to a *minimum distance Poisson* process where the randomly distributed sample points are all separated by at least some minimum distance. Another important class of stochastic sampling patterns are *jittered sampling* patterns. Jittered patterns are created by taking regular sampling patterns and adding a random perturbation to each sample point. Assuming that the frequency content of an image is orientation independent, patterns such as jittered *hexagonal* sampling are more *efficient* than *rectangular* sampling patterns and can produce an image of a given quality with a lower sampling rate.

The defects associated with stochastic sampling can be characterized as *noise*. Thus, the *power signal to noise ratio* (SNR) is an important figure of merit for stochastic sampling patterns. The SNR is directly proportional to the *average sampling rate* which is the average number of samples per unit region. Thus, the magnitude of the errors produced by stochastic sampling can be controlled by increasing the sampling rate. Since image complexity is itself distributed nonuniformly, the minimum acceptable average sampling rate can vary greatly across an image. An *estimate* of the error produced by a given sampling rate can be used to perform *adaptive stochastic sampling*. Adaptive sampling reduces the total number of samples required for a given image quality.

The *noise spectrum* of a stochastic sampling pattern determines the amount of *low* versus *high frequency noise* that is generated. Since the *human visual system* is less sensitive to high frequency noise, reducing low and mid-frequency noise while increasing high frequency noise can produce perceptually better pictures. The separation between samples in minimum distance Poisson sampling and the magnitude of the perturbations in jittered sampling can be controlled to shape the associated noise spectrum.

The stochastic samples are filtered to produce the final pixel values. The filtering process is an important part of noise reduction. A *normalized filter* that produces a weighted average of the sample points is an effective noise reducing filter. *Adaptive filtering* is also performed. The filter width can be adjusted to improve noise control at a given sampling rate.

An important application of stochastic sampling is the antialiasing of *ray traced* images. Stochastic selection of the rays that are traced will ensure that the image is appropriately antialiased and can also improve the simulation calculations.

There are four basic sections to this paper. Regular sampling patterns and the problems with aliasing are briefly outlined in § 2. Stochastic sampling patterns are introduced and analyzed in § 3. Sampling rate selection, adaptive sampling, filtering, and and adaptive control of noise are presented in § 4 and § 5. Implementation of stochastic sampling is discussed in § 6. Parts of this paper assume some familiarity with Fourier analysis and probability.[6,18]

Mathematical Notation	
β	average sampling rate per unit region
$\delta(\vec{x})$	delta function
$E[X]$	expected value of X
e_b	error bound
$e_{tot}(\vec{x})$	weighted average error in reconstruction
$f(\vec{x})$, $F(\vec{u})$	function and Fourier transform
FFRNS	flat field response noise spectrum
K	number of samples in a region
$N_{1/2}$	half the Nyquist rate
$P[Y]$	probability of event Y
Φ_f	power spectral density of f
$p(x)$	probability density of x
PSD	power spectral density
$\rho_f(X)$	autocorrelation function of f
$\left\lvert \frac{S}{N} \right\rvert_{RMS}$	RMS signal to noise ratio
$s(\vec{x})$, $S_X(\vec{u})$	stochastic sampling function and transform
$sinc(x)$	$sin(x)/x$
SNR	signal to noise ratio
X	size of sampling region
$\vec{x}$	image space coordinates, (x,y,t)
$\vec{u}$	frequency space coordinates, (u,v,ω)
$\supset$	has a Fourier transform given by
$\sim$	has a probability law given by
$*$	convolution operation

2. Regular Sampling

Sampling is often carried out using a regular pattern. In one dimension, the samples are equally spaced. A commonly used two dimensional pattern is a rectangular grid of sample points. Rectangular sampling can be performed in n-dimensional spaces in the same manner. The well-known sampling theorem[6] states that the sample spacings in each dimension determine an associated frequency limit above which aliasing will occur. Given a sample spacing in one dimension, Δx, the corresponding frequency bound in that dimension is given by

$$N_{1/2} = \frac{1}{2\,\Delta x} \tag{1}$$

and corresponds to half of the *Nyquist rate*. The one dimensional unit rectangular sampling process has the following representation:

$$h(x) = f(x) \sum_{k=-\infty}^{+\infty} \delta(x-k) \supset F(u) * \sum_{k=-\infty}^{+\infty} \delta(u-k) = H(u) \tag{2}$$

where h is the sampled function, f is the original function, $\supset$ denotes the Fourier transform relationship, F is the spectrum of the original function, and H is the spectrum of the sampled function. Thus, the spectrum of h is the spectrum of f plus copies of the spectrum of f that are spaced in each dimension by $2\,N_{1/2}$. Frequencies that are higher than $N_{1/2}$ will spread over the replicated spectra and alter each of the copies. In general, there is no direct way of eliminating this *foldover* of high frequencies once sampling has been performed. Thus, it will be impossible to extract a single copy of F from H so that h will be a distorted version of f. This distortion is what is produced by aliasing. Given the frequency content of f, an appropriate sampling rate can be chosen. However, it is generally difficult to determine such a sampling rate *a priori*.

If it is assumed that there is no preferred orientation in the high frequency content, then the frequency cutoff, $N_{1/2}$, can be represented by an n-dimensional sphere of radius $N_{1/2}$. The most *efficient* sampling pattern will pack these spectral spheres as closely as possible in frequency space.[19] For 2-D, or spatial, sampling the optimal pattern is a hexagonal lattice and for 3-D, or spatiotemporal, sampling it is a body-centered cubic lattice.

3. Stochastic Sampling

The primary weakness of regular sampling patterns is that they only sample a fixed set of points so that there are large regions that are *never sampled*. Features that lie in such regions are completely ignored. Regular sampling patterns ignore image information in a coherent way and produce coherent errors in the form of aliasing patterns. Irregular sampling patterns avoid generating false patterns by producing incoherent, or *noisy*, errors. Irregular patterns produced by randomness, or *stochastic sampling* patterns, will generate random incoherence, or broadband noise. The distribution of the stochastic samples determines the type of noise errors that occur. Stochastic sampling patterns have a *probability* of hitting each region of the image that in turn determines the probability of missing a given feature. It should be noted that coherent aliasing patterns are generated from coherent images; if the image itself is very irregular, then regular sampling will not produce false patterns.

The mathematical properties of stochastic sampling have received a great deal of attention.[4,7,15,16,17,21,22] Much of this work concentrates on spectral estimation of stochastic processes. The results of Leneman[16] are particularly useful for the analysis of the stochastic sampling techniques that we will discuss. Stochastic sampling in physical processes has also been studied. Both the grain of photographic film and the receptor patterns of the human retina exhibit random sampling.[25,30]

There are many different classes of stochastic sampling processes. The two that we will concentrate on are *Poisson sampling* and *jittered sampling.* A primary difference between these two types of sampling patterns are their noise spectra. In addition, jittered sampling is more local in nature. Examples of stochastic sampling patterns are shown in Figure 1. The 2-D magnitude spectrum of a Poisson sampling pattern is shown in Figure 2. Note that the magnitude spectrum has only a *single delta function* at the origin and is surrounded by noise. This property is what enables stochastic sampling patterns to avoid the spectral replication of regular sampling patterns.

3.1. Poisson Sampling

We will now define and analyze *Poisson sampling.* Simple Poisson sampling is based upon uniformly distributed sample points. A generalization of Poisson sampling, *minimum distance Poisson sampling,* controls the minimum separation between points.

Figure 1
Stochastic sampling patterns, (from left to right) Poisson: minimum distance 0 and .8, and rectangular jittered sampling: jitter .3 and 1.

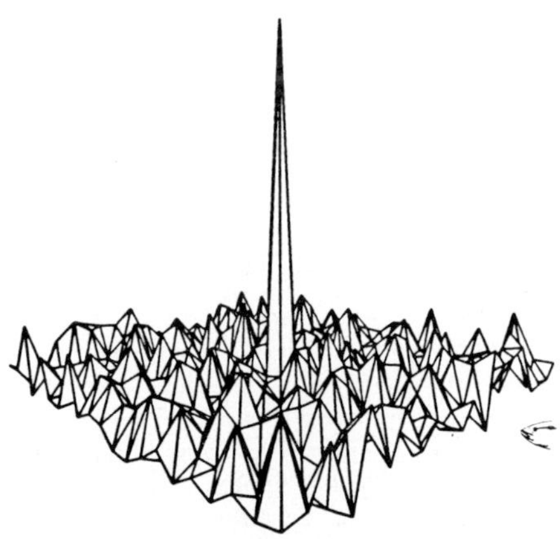

Figure 2
Magnitude spectrum of 2-D Poisson sampling pattern.

A one-dimensional finite uniformly distributed sampling pattern with sampling rate β over an interval $[0,X]$ can be written in the form

$$s(x) = \sum_{k=0}^{K-1} \delta(x-x_k) \tag{3}$$

where $\delta(x-x_k)$ is a *delta function* centered around x_k; the x_k have the probability density

$$p(x_k) = \begin{cases} 1/X & 0<x_k<X \\ 0 & elsewhere \end{cases} \tag{4}$$

and $K = X\beta$ is the number of delta functions in the interval. It can be shown directly that the *expected value* of the *magnitude squared* of the Fourier transform of $s(x)$ is given by:[10]

$$E\left[\mid S_X(u) \mid^2 \right] = \begin{cases} K^2 = \beta^2 X^2 & u=0 \\ K = \beta X & u\neq 0 \end{cases} \tag{5}$$

and that the *phase* of $S_X(u)$ has mean 0.

Figure 3 shows a plot of the magnitude and phase spectrum of a computer generated uniform sampling pattern with $K=X\beta=500$ over frequencies from $-4\pi\beta$ to $4\pi\beta$. The spectrum of regular sampling with rate β would show four aliases over these frequencies.

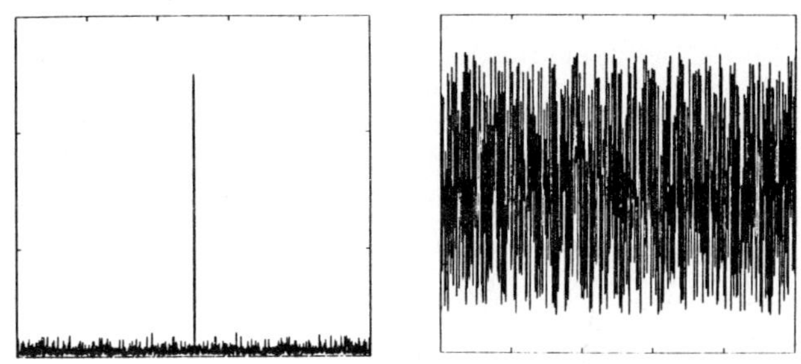

Figure 3
Spectrum of uniform sampling with 500 samples: magnitude (left) and phase (right).

Poisson sampling over an infinite interval has samples which are uniformly distributed over any interval[18] and is therefore an approximation to uniform sampling. The development of the power spectrum for Poisson sampling relies on the fact that the *impulse process* is a *widesense stationary* process (i.e. the statistics of the process do not vary with x) and is only approximate when the sampling pattern is of finite extent.[16] However, we will approximate uniform sampling with Poisson sampling in the sequel due to its analytical ease.

The *power spectral density* (PSD) of the sampling process is the Fourier transform of the *autocorrelation* of the process[27] and is given by[16]

$$\Phi_s(u) = \lim_{X\to\infty} \frac{\mid S_X(u) \mid^2}{X} = \beta + 2\pi\beta^2\delta(u) \tag{6}$$

which is of the same form as the expected magnitude squared derived above in (5). This analysis can be extended to multiple dimensions in a straightforward manner.

Given a widesense stationary one-dimensional image, $f(x)$, which is independent of the Poisson sampling pattern, $s(x)$, the autocorrelation of the sampled image, $g(x) = f(x)\cdot s(x)$, is given by

$$\rho_g(\chi) = \rho_f(\chi)\rho_s(\chi) \tag{7}$$

where $\rho_h(\chi) = E[h(x+\chi)h(x)]$ for any function h. Thus, the PSD of g can be expressed as the convolution

$$\Phi_g(u) = \Phi_f(u) * \Phi_s(u) = \beta \int_R \Phi_f(u)du + 2\pi\beta^2\Phi_f(u) \tag{8}$$

The first term on the right hand side can be identified as a broadband noise spectrum and the second term as a scaled version of the original image spectrum. For the case where f is a flat field, Φ_g will be the same as Φ_s, and the noise term will be a constant β. To compare Poisson and other sampling patterns, we will define the ***flat field response noise spectrum*** (FFRNS) to be the noise part of the flat field response scaled by the sampling rate β and will represent it by Φ_n. For Poisson sampling, $\Phi_n = 1$. All of the stochastic sampling patterns we will derive have a broadband noise power spectrum which is scaled by β.

Although most image functions are not stationary, the above is an approximation which is useful in conceptualization and in calculating global parameters of the sampling process such as sampling rate and filter width. Also, many images are approximately *locally stationary* so that these results apply locally.

An important generalization of Poisson sampling, minimum distance Poisson sampling, enforces a minimum distance between the sample points. A similar model has been used to characterize the distribution of receptors in the human eye.[31] In one dimension, we have an impulse process where the x_k are taken to be the *interval process*

$$x_{k+1} = x_k + l_k \tag{9}$$

and the l_k have the delayed *exponential* distribution

$$l_k \sim p(l_k) = \begin{cases} \beta_y e^{-\beta_y(l_k - l_{k0})} & l_k > l_{k0} \\ 0 & elsewhere \end{cases} \tag{10}$$

Here, l_{k0} represents the minimum distance between samples. The average sampling rate for this process is the expected value of l_k given by $\beta = \beta_y/(1+\beta_y l_{k0})$. When $l_{k0}=0$, this sampling pattern becomes a Poisson sampling pattern with $\beta=\beta_y$,[16] and, as $\beta_y \to \infty$, the sampling pattern becomes a regular pattern with sampling rate $\beta = 1/l_{k0}$. Using a relationship for interval processes,[16] we can derive the sampling process power spectrum

$$\Phi_s(u) = \begin{cases} \beta\left[1 - \dfrac{2\beta_y u \sin(l_{k0}u) + 2\beta_y^2\cos(l_{k0}u) - 2\beta_y^2}{2\beta_y u \sin(l_{k0}u) - 2\beta_y^2\cos(l_{k0}u) + u^2 + 2\beta_y^2}\right] & u \neq 0 \\ 2\pi\beta^2\delta(u) & u = 0 \end{cases} \tag{11}$$

The non-delta function part of this spectrum is the FFRNS. Figure 4 shows a plot of the FFRNS for two values of $l_{k0}\beta$. This sampling pattern is useful because low and mid frequency noise can be traded for high frequency noise by varying $l_{k0}\beta$ between 0 and 1.

The tradeoff between low, mid, and high frequency noise is an important one. Studies have shown that the human visual system is more sensitive to low/mid frequency noise than high frequency noise.[3,12] Thus, perceptual noise control can be improved by trading reduced low/mid frequency noise for increased high frequency noise in the sampling pattern. By increasing the minimum distance in Poisson sampling, low frequency noise can be reduced while increasing high frequency noise. Coherent aliasing is only produced when the minimum distance is approximately equal to the spacing of the associated optimal regular sampling pattern. Subjective studies have also shown that the visual system is more sensitive to narrowband noise versus broadband noise. This supports the preference of noisy errors from stochastic sampling over the coherent aliasing errors of regular sampling.

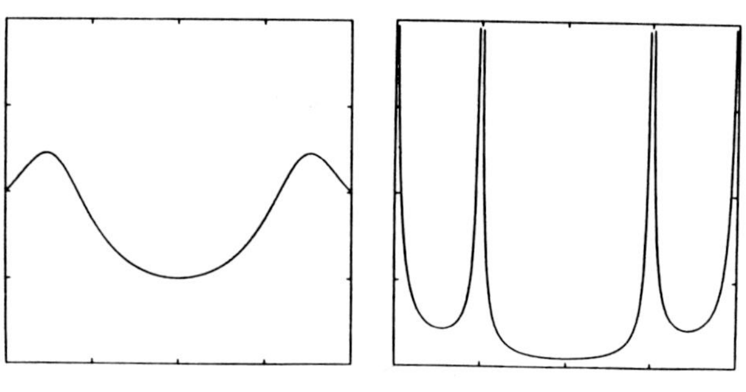

Figure 4

FFRNS for $l_{n0}\beta = 0.5, 0.95$ from left to right.

3.2. Jittered Sampling

Another important class of stochastic sampling patterns is *jittered sampling* patterns. In 1-D, we choose a regular sampling pattern with sampling rate β and sample points y_k. Each of the sample points is jittered by adding a random variable j_k. Thus,

$$x_k = y_k + j_k \quad y_k = \frac{k}{\beta} \quad j_k \sim p(j_k) \quad k = -\infty,\ldots,+\infty \tag{12}$$

Let the Fourier transform of $p(j_k)$ be given by $\gamma(u)$. Then,[16]

$$\Phi_s(u) = \beta[1 - |\gamma(u)|^2] + 2\pi\beta^2 |\gamma(u)|^2 \sum_{k=-\infty}^{\infty} \delta(u - k2\pi\beta) \tag{13}$$

The first term in the spectrum is broadband noise, and the second term yields aliases of the input spectrum at multiples of the sampling rate as in regular sampling. These aliases will add in coherent noise and create false patterns. However, these aliases are weighted by $|\gamma(u)|^2$. For certain jitter densities, the aliases can be exactly canceled out by the zeros of γ. For example, if $p(j_k)$ is uniform over $[-1/2\beta, 1/2\beta]$, then

$$\gamma(u) = \frac{\sin(u/2\beta)}{u/2\beta} = sinc(u/2\beta) \tag{14}$$

so that

$$\Phi_s(u) = \beta[1 - sinc^2(u/2\beta)] + 2\pi\beta^2\delta(u) \tag{15}$$

which shows that there is now only one delta function at $u=0$. Figure 5 shows the FFRNS for this case. This sample distribution removes low frequency noise compared to the Poisson case, but avoids the high frequency peaks which appear in minimum distance Poisson sampling. Another difference between jitter and minimum distance Poisson is that if one jitters with a uniform density over an interval smaller than $[-1/2\beta, 1/2\beta]$, sharp aliases appear immediately instead of forming gradually out of broadband high frequency noise. However, these aliases are attenuated by $\gamma(u)$, so that the

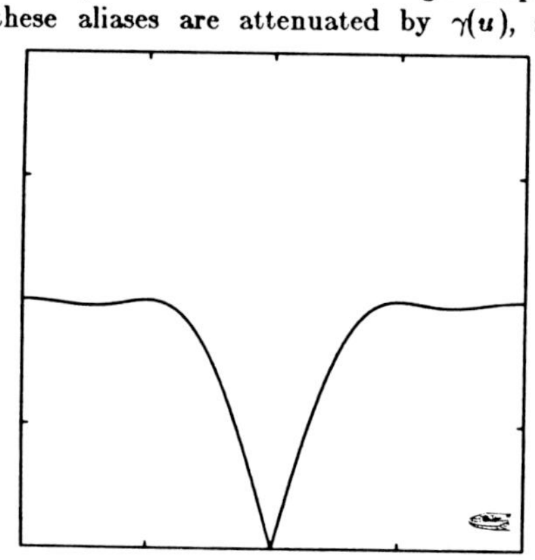

Figure 5

FFRNS for uniform jitter.

amount of jitter can be used to trade off aliasing energy for noise energy. Figure 6 shows magnitude spectra of computer simulations of jitter which is uniform over $[-\alpha/2\beta,\alpha/2\beta]$ for $\alpha = 1.0$ and 0.5 from frequencies of $-4\pi\beta$ to $4\pi\beta$ radians. Note that $\alpha = 0.0$ is regular sampling. In the noise and adaptivity analyses which follow, we will only consider jitter which is without aliases, i.e. $\alpha = 1.0$.

In multiple dimensions, rectangular sampling with uniform rectangular jitter will yield a power spectrum which also has an FFRNS that is smaller in the low frequencies. Such a sampling pattern is implemented by choosing a point uniformly in a rectangle centered around the nominal sample value. If the input is two-dimensional and the frequency content is orientation independent, the optimal sampling pattern is hexagonal. Jittering this pattern is performed by choosing a point uniformly in a hexagon which surrounds the nominal sample value. This will also lead to a sampling pattern which is without aliases as long as the jitter hexagons completely tile the space of interest. In three dimensions, one can uniformly jitter a body-centered cubic pattern to create a pattern which will not produce aliases.

The reduction in low frequency noise with jittered sampling is better perceptually as with minimum distance poisson.

4. Sampling Rate

The *signal to noise ratio* (SNR) is an important measure of the quality of the sampling process. The *average sampling rate* determines the basic cost of a given stochastic sampling pattern.

Consider $g_r(\vec{x}) = f(\vec{x}) \cdot s(\vec{x}) * r(\vec{x})$, which represents the sampled and filtered original image before it is resampled for

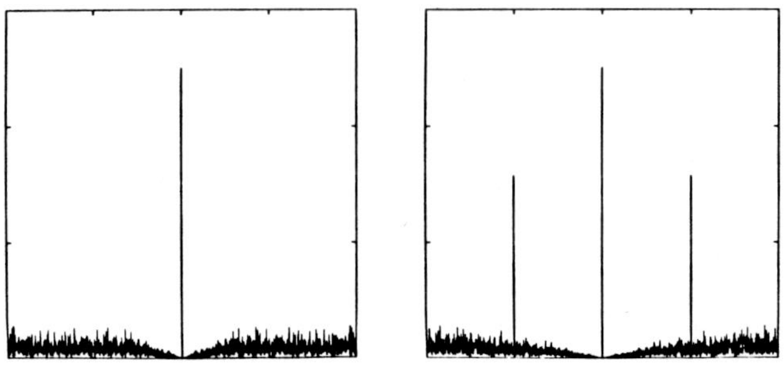

Figure 6
Spectra for uniform jitter with α equal to 1.0 and 0.5 from left to right.

display. Its power spectrum is

$$\Phi_{g_r}(\vec{u}) = [\Phi_f(\vec{u}) * \Phi_s(\vec{u})] \cdot | R(\vec{u}) |^2 \quad (16)$$

The stochastic sampling patterns which were developed above and which did not produce aliasing have power spectra which are of the form

$$\Phi_s(\vec{u}) = 2\pi\beta^2\delta(\vec{u}) + \beta\Phi_n(\vec{u}) \quad (17)$$

where $\beta\Phi_n$ is the FFRNS of the sampling pattern and Φ_n does not depend on β. These patterns are: Poisson, minimum distance Poisson with broad high-frequency peaks, and uniformly distributed jitter without aliases. Substitution of (17) into (16) yields

$$\Phi_{g_r}(\vec{u}) = 2\pi\beta^2\Phi_f(\vec{u}) \cdot | R(\vec{u}) |^2 + \beta(\Phi_f(\vec{u}) * \Phi_n(\vec{u})) \cdot | R(\vec{u}) |^2 \quad (18)$$

Therefore, the ratio of the total signal power to the total noise power is given by the ratios of the integrals of the two terms on the right hand side of (18). The ***root-mean-square*** (RMS) ***signal to noise ratio*** (SNR) is given by the square root of this and more accurately represents the perceptual signal to noise ratio:

$$\left| \frac{S}{N} \right|_{RMS} = (2\pi\beta)^{1/2} \left[\frac{\int_{\mathbf{R}^s} \Phi_f \cdot | R |^2 d\vec{u}}{\int_{\mathbf{R}^s} (\Phi_f * \Phi_n) \cdot | R |^2 d\vec{u}} \right]^{1/2} \quad (19)$$

where the dependence of everything on $\vec{u}$ has been dropped for clarity. Note that the SNR only increases as fast as the square root of the average sampling rate. Also, if R is held constant and the bandwidth of f is increased past the spectral width of R, the SNR is reduced as the inverse square root of the bandwidth of f. Similarly, if f is held constant and the width of R is increased past the bandwidth of f, the SNR is reduced as the inverse square root of the spectral width of R.

A number of different criteria can be used to choose an acceptable value of the SNR for a given sampling pattern and thus the sampling rate. The display device will require quantizing the data to a fixed length word. Noise with a variance which is much less than a bit in value will not disturb the image. The limitations of the human visual system are another source of acceptable noise levels. Experiments have indicated that a SNR of about 100 (40 db) is just sufficient to prevent objectionable noise.[5] Another criterion is the performance under worst case conditions. However, a worst case sampling rate is prohibitively high and will not reflect the nature of most images. If the expected image spectrum is known, the best FFRNS can be chosen directly. However, the expected spectrum for the types of images that are synthesized is difficult to develop.

A useful way of selecting an ***a priori*** sampling rate is based on the expected size of the "smallest" important feature. For example, the sampling rate can be chosen such that small features will not be missed by the sampling process with a desired probability. Consider a one-dimensional Poisson sampling pattern with sampling rate β; the inter-sample distance d has distribution

$$P[d < \lambda] = 1 - e^{-\beta\lambda} \quad (20)$$

Thus, to insure with probability P_0 that a feature of size λ is sampled, we need to have

$$\beta = -\frac{\ln(1-P_0)}{\lambda} \quad (21)$$

in the region containing that feature.

4.1. Adaptive Sampling Rate

The SNR and sampling rate discussed above are global. However, complexity is not uniformly distributed across an image. An *adaptive sampling rate* can greatly reduce the number of samples required to create an image of a given quality. A probabilistic *estimate* of the local image characteristics, based upon a set of stochastic samples taken around the region, can be used to calculate an appropriate sampling rate. If the sample values are very similar, then a smooth region is indicated and a lower sampling rate can be used. Conversely, very dissimilar samples indicate a rapidly varying region that requires a higher sampling rate (e.g. the boundaries of rapidly moving objects).

To calculate the local sampling rate adaptively, we need an error estimator, an error bound which must be satisfied, and an initial sampling rate at which to begin the adaptation. The error bound and initial sampling rate can be developed from the criteria discussed previously. However, the variance of the error estimator as a function of the number of samples used in the estimate must also be considered. If the number of samples used to estimate the error is very small, the variance of the estimator will be high, and the confidence in the error estimate will be low.

Global or local spectral techniques can be used to estimate the error between the optimally filtered image and the stochastically sampled and filtered image. It has been shown that the RMS SNR is equal to the square root of the sampling rate times a constant which depends on the image spectrum and the filter. Since the signal is fixed, the total RMS error in the reconstruction, $e_{tot}(\vec{x};\beta)$, is the inverse square root of β times a constant C which does not depend on β

$$e_{tot}(\vec{x};\beta) = \beta^{-1/2} C(\Phi_f, R, \vec{x}) \tag{22}$$

This RMS error is approximately the expected absolute difference between the the stochastically sampled and filtered image, g_r, and the perfectly filtered image, $f * r_o$:

$$e_{tot}(\vec{x};\beta) \approx | g_r(\vec{x};\beta) - f(\vec{x}) * r_o(\vec{x}) | \tag{23}$$

Thus, the difference between the images at two sampling rates should be an estimate of the rate of change of $e_{tot}(\vec{x};\beta)$ with respect to β. From this and the fact that $e_{tot}(\vec{x};\beta)$ is expected to be monotonically decreasing in β, C can be estimated by

$$C = \left| \frac{g_r(\vec{x};\beta_2) - g_r(\vec{x};\beta_1)}{\beta_2^{-1/2} - \beta_1^{-1/2}} \right| \tag{24}$$

We can average C over several different sets of β_i and use (22) to produce an estimate of $e_{tot}(\vec{x})$. This is then compared to a user specified error bound e_b. If the estimate is less than the bound, no more has to be done. Otherwise, more samples need to be taken in the region of the filtered sample. Figure 7 shows the linear dependence of sampling rate upon slope using this error estimate.

Other estimators can of course be used. One estimator can be developed using a linear approximation for the image function in the neighborhood of a stochastic sample point, since the local RMS error is directly proportional to the magnitude of the local slope.[10] Also, the variance of the samples in the region of a pixel can be used to estimate the required sampling rate, as it is proportional to the bandwidth of the image function in the region.

5. Filtering

Stochastic sampling is only one step in the entire synthesis process. The stochastic sample values are then used to create the pixel values that are used by the display to reconstruct the final image. An important part of this process is the filter used to create the pixel values from the stochastic samples. Aliasing defects are reduced by choosing a filter which passes little of the frequencies beyond half the display Nyquist rate. The filter must also control noise from the stochastic sampling process as much as possible. In addition, the display reconstruction filter should be taken into account.

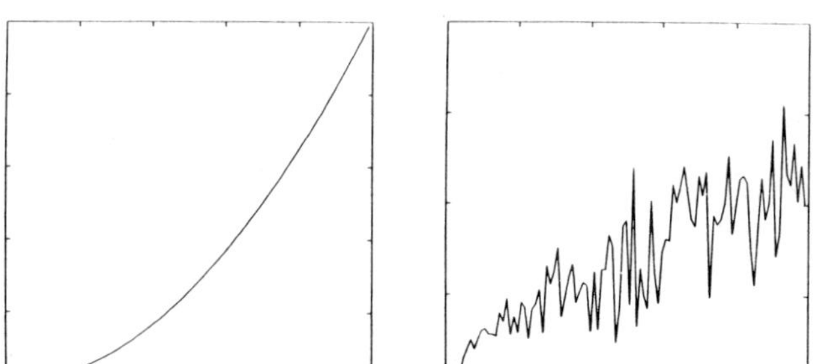

Figure 7
Dependence of sampling rate upon slope. Sampled function is shown on left and adapted sampling rate on right.

There are several particular characteristics that can be used to choose a good filter. The response to discontinuities, such as edges, should be somewhat smooth. A *perfect lowpass filter* applied to an edge will result in a visible ringing at the edge due to *Gibb's phenomenon*.[27] Unfortunately, low-pass filters with smoother responses have inferior high frequency response, so one must make a tradeoff depending on the application. The filter should also have an impulse response which is always positive since the light intensity on the screen is non-negative. Raised cosine functions have been used in digital filter design to reduce Gibb's phenomenon.[1] They also exhibit reasonable low-pass behavior and are non-negative. The particular form of the raised cosine that we will be using is given by[13]

$$r(\vec{x}) = \frac{1}{W}\left(\cos\left(\frac{2\pi}{W} |\vec{x}|\right) + 1\right) \qquad |\vec{x}| < W \tag{25}$$

where r is the filter, W is the radius of the filter, and $|\vec{x}|$ is the distance from the center of the filter.

Filter selection is important for any antialiasing method. Filters that have been used in conjunction with oversampling in computer graphics have often been poor at attenuating aliased frequencies. For example, a triangular filter with a radius of about one pixel that is maximal at the center and zero at the boundary has been suggested.[9] The aliasing attenuation of such a filter is inadequate. A triangular filter that spans 1.75 pixels in each direction trades off some high frequency response, but provides 90% attenuation at $N_{1/2}$.

5.1. Adaptive Filtering

The ability of stochastic sampling to generate broadband noise rather than coherent aliases is the reason its behavior is superior to regular sampling. The preference of the human visual system to low levels of noise versus coherent features has been used in other aspects of imaging, such as the reduction of quantization defects.[20] Even though noise is often preferable to coherent defects, large levels of noise are very objectionable and must be controlled. The noise level is directly related to the input signal, the sampling rate, and to the filter.

Since practical filter designs will be windowed so that the filter support is small, the number of samples under the filter will vary depending on the location of the stochastically placed samples and the location of the filter. To reduce noise caused by local changes in the sampling rate, one should normalize the filter. A one-dimensional example is given by

$$g_r(x) = \frac{[f(x) \cdot s(x)] * r(x)}{[s(x) * r(x)]} = \frac{\sum_{k=0}^{K-1} f(x_k) r(x - x_k)}{\sum_{k=0}^{K-1} r(x - x_k)} \tag{26}$$

We will assume this discrete normalization is always applied. Given samples of a flat (or nearly flat) field, this filter will remove noise without the use of a very wide convolution. Also, filtering of locally linear functions can be shown to have a non-biased error when this normalization is used.

It is also possible to determine the optimal (with respect to mean-squared-error) linear filter for the stochastic samples. We can write the optimally filtered image as $f(\vec{x}) * r_o(\vec{x})$ where $r_o(\vec{x})$ is the optimal continuous filter. The power spectrum of the stochastically sampled image is given by

$$\Phi_f(\vec{u}) * \Phi_s(\vec{u}) = 2\pi\beta^2 \Phi_f(\vec{u}) + \beta[\Phi_f(\vec{u}) * \Phi_n(\vec{u})] \qquad (27)$$

Assuming the image is stationary, the techniques of Wiener can be applied to (27).[29] This linear filter, written here in Fourier transform space, optimally approximates the effect of $r_o(\vec{x})$ on the original continuous image:

$$R_{opt}(\vec{u}) = \frac{R_o(\vec{u})}{(2\pi)^{1/2}\beta} \frac{\Phi_f(\vec{u}) \mid R_o(\vec{u}) \mid^2}{\Phi_f(\vec{u}) \mid R_o(\vec{u}) \mid^2 + \frac{1}{2\pi\beta}[\Phi_f(\vec{u}) * \Phi_n(\vec{u})] \mid R_o(\vec{u}) \mid^2} \qquad (28)$$

The intuitive explanation of this equation is simply that the filter clamps down in those bands where the SNR is small. A local estimate of the spectrum of the image can be found by the techniques of Scott[21] and applied to estimate the required adaptive filter.

The error estimates developed in the previous section can also be used to control the width of the filter to improve performance at a given sampling rate. This is useful if the error is still large when a user specified sampling rate bound has been reached, since the error can be reduced further by narrowing the bandwidth (widening the convolution) of the filter $r(\vec{x})$. This is also an acceptable perceptual tradeoff since lower frequencies are more important.

In § 3 it was shown that the convolution of the image with the FFRNS produces an RMS noise which is proportional to the square root of the filter power. For the normalized raised cosine filter discussed above, the total power is $6\pi/W$. Thus, the RMS noise is inversely proportional to the square root of the size of the convolution so that a wider filter attenuates noise more effectively. Given an estimate of the RMS noise e_{tot} based on a filter with width W_0 (see § 4) and an RMS error bound e_b, the width of the filter should be set to

$$W = W_0 \left[\frac{e_{tot}}{e_b} \right]^2 \qquad (29)$$

Figure 8 shows the effect of a fixed sampling rate with varying filter widths upon a random pattern of maximal intensity. The desired effect is a flat grey.

Figure 8
Effect of adaptive filter width on noise of maximal intensity, the filter widths are 2, 4, 6, and 8 pixels from left to right and top to bottom.

6. Implementation

We will now discuss implementing stochastic sampling. In particular, the spatiotemporal *viewing rays* of standard ray tracing are stochastically selected.[28] A stochastic set of spatiotemporal points in the image are chosen, the corresponding rays are cast, and these rays are traced recursively throughout the scene in the conventional manner. All of the images shown in this paper have been generated in this manner. An example of a stochastically sampled ray traced scene is shown in Figure 9.

For Poisson sampling, the sample points are uniformly distributed over the image using standard pseudorandom

Figure 9
Stochastically sampled ray traced image.

methods.[14] This local approximation to true Poisson sampling is sufficient. The total number of samples is the product of the sampling rate and the image size in each dimension. Minimum distance Poisson samples can be approximated by generating uniformly distributed sample points but only retaining sample points that satisfy the minimum separation with all previously retained sample points. An efficient method of performing Poisson sampling is to store a sampling pattern in a table. The pattern is replicated to fill the image. The pattern should be large compared to a pixel and should be rotated (or otherwise manipulated) to prevent regularities from appearing. Examples of Poisson sampled images are shown in Figure 10. They demonstrate the effect of oversampling rate and filter normalization on the resulting noise.

While Poisson sample points are inherently global, jittered sample points are local and can be generated on the fly at very little cost. The regular sample pattern from which the jittered pattern is derived is calculated in an incremental manner and a pseudorandom jitter added to each sample point. A jittered optimal regular pattern (e.g. hexagonal) will be the most efficient approach. Images produced by jittered sampling are shown in Figures 11 and 12. A jitter of 0 is equivalent to regular sampling and the associated aliasing is clearly visible in the upper left hand corner of Figure 11. The filter of § 5 allows even regular sampling to produce a somewhat reasonable image.

In adaptive stochastic sampling, an initial set of samples is taken in the region about each pixel. If the error estimate based on these samples is too large, additional samples are placed in the region until the error estimate is sufficiently low. An initial average sampling rate is chosen based on expected image characteristics. A maximal average sampling rate is chosen based on expected worst case image characteristics, e.g. maximum sample amplitude. The error estimate is used to

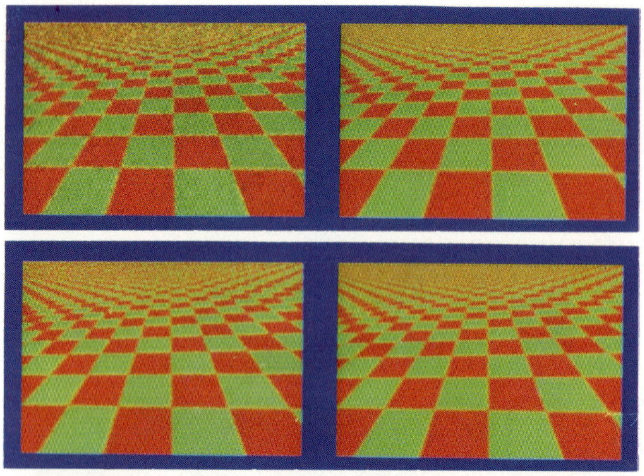

Figure 10
Poisson sampling of a slowly moving texture. The oversampling rate is 1 and 2 from left to right and the lower images use a normalized filter.

select an average sampling rate between these two bounds for each pixel (see § 4). The filter width is also adaptively controlled to reduce worst case noise. In adaptive minimum distance Poisson sampling, the minimum distance used to place adaptive samples decreases as the number of samples increases and is interpolated to 0. This process can be table driven. Adaptively jittered rectangular sampling is carried out by recursively subdividing the rectangular *cells* of the original sampling pattern. A cell is cut in two by a randomly chosen *subdivision plane* of constant x, y, or t. The original sample value of a cell is placed in the appropriate subcell and a new sample value is calculated for the other subcell. The local sampling rate is increased in only one dimension by each subdivision. The dimension of the increased sampling rate is given by the plane that is chosen.[10] The completely local nature of adaptive jitter allows samples to be shared for neighboring pixel calculations. However, the global nature of minimum distance Poisson makes such sharing very costly. The same holds true for adaptive filtering. An example of an adaptively Poisson sampled image is shown in Figure 13. The variation in sampling rate across the image is also shown in the figure. For this example, the adaptive process reduced the number of samples by about 50%.

The simulation abilities of standard ray tracing can also be improved with stochastic sampling. At any point in the scene, the interaction of light can be specified by an integral of the incident light and the point's reflectivity and transmittance. The qualities of the lighting integral and the use of more rays to approximate it have been discussed elsewhere[8] although it is not clear how the extra rays were chosen. Stochastic techniques can be used to approximate the lighting integral; the greater the number of samples, the more accurate the resulting value. However, this process is extremely expensive in general. The adaptive sampling techniques discussed previously can be used to control the number of rays that are cast. *A priori* knowledge and assumptions, similar to those used in standard ray tracing, also help make this process more feasible (but less accurate). For example, rays are stochastically cast towards each light source over their projection with respect to the point and rays representing environmental lighting are stochastically chosen around the angles of reflection and refraction. Sampling in wavelength can also be performed. General Monte Carlo methods have been applied to many phenomena[23,24] and are certain to become an increasingly important part of computer graphics.

7. Conclusion

Stochastic sampling methods have been introduced and analyzed, in particular, Poisson and jittered sampling. These techniques avoid the problems of regular sampling patterns and allow alias-free sampling to be performed. Stochastic sampling can be applied spatiotemporally and to many other aspects of the simulation process. An adaptive sampling procedure based upon an estimate of the expected error was developed. Adaptive sampling reduces the number of samples required for a given image quality. Filtering the stochastically generated samples was also discussed. Noise reduction is an important aspect of the filter design. Adaptive filtration is used to further improve the noise immunity of the system.

Application of stochastic sampling to ray tracing has been demonstrated. The local nature of jittered sampling makes it very suitable for adaptive stochastic sampling. Stochastically sampled ray tracing can also be directly parallelized allowing an efficient implementation.[11]

There are many other improvements that can be made to the techniques that have been described. Data dependent sampling using knowledge about the scene can increase the efficiency of the process. For instance, the faster an object moves, the higher the required sampling rate. In addition, continuous calculations should be used wherever possible to further increase sampling efficiency. Additional information about the human visual system, such as the *logarithmic* transformation of intensity[26] should be used in noise metrics. Improvements in the filter design can also be made. Examination of an optimal jitter function that utilizes the noise/aliasing tradeoff is another important possibility.

Acknowledgments

We would like to thank the frank remonstrations of our earnest and anonymous reviewers. Their provocative comments were only too inspirational. We commend the Berkeley Computer Graphics Laboratory, in particular *mein führer* Brain Barsky, for its salutary grace. The enduring support of **Queen Wienle**, Mistress X, and *DUNCAN* (*the swinging larva*) is dutifully acknowledged. Without them, we might still be on the road. Thanks to Aszer Weiss and Zelig Goldmann for the *white jam*. This work was supported in part by the National Science Foundation, under grant number ECS-8204381, the Semiconductor Research Corporation under grant number 82-11-008, and the Defense Advanced Research Projects Agency for a better tomorrow under grant number N00039-0107.

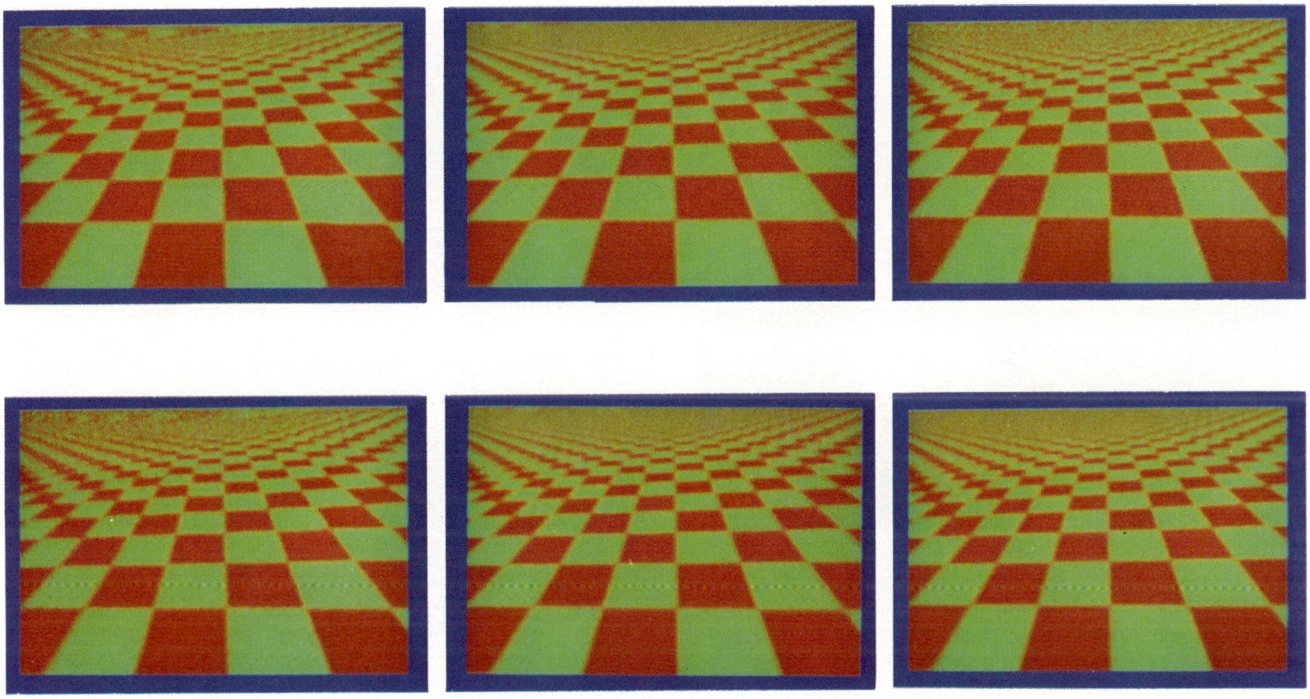

Figure 11
Jittered sampling of a slowly moving texture with jitter of 0, .5, and 1 from left to right and oversampling rates of 1 and 2 from top to bottom.

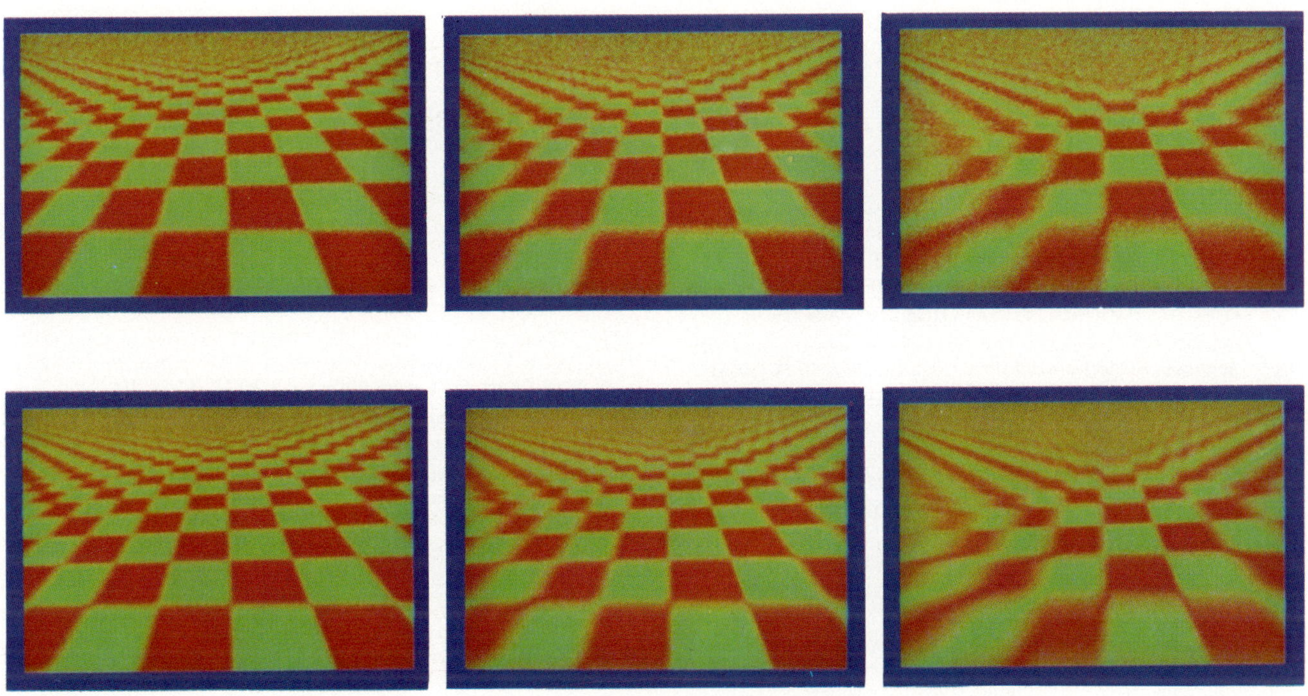

Figure 12
Jittered sampling of a rapidly moving texture with velocity increasing from left to right and oversampling rates of 1 and 2 from top to bottom.

Figure 13
Adaptively sampled image; the image on the right uses intensity to show the adaptively chosen sampling rate at each point.

References

1. Andreas Antoniou, *Digital Filters: Analysis and Design,* McGraw-Hill Book Company, New York (1979).

2. J. G. Ballard, *Crash,* Jonathan Cape Ltd., Great Britain (1973).

3. J. M. Barstow and H. N. Christopher, "The Measurement of Random Monochrome Video Interference," *Transactions of the American Institute of Electrical Engineers* **72** pp. 735-741. (1953).

4. Frederick J. Beutler, "Alias-Free Randomly Timed Sampling of Stochastic Processes," *IEEE Transactions on Information Theory* **IT-16**(2) pp. 147-152. (March, 1970).

5. F. C. Billingsley, *Noise Considerations in Digital Image Processing Hardware,* Springer-Verlag, New York (1975).

6. Ronald N. Bracewell, *The Fourier Transform and Its Application,* McGraw-Hill Book Company, New York (1965).

7. William M. Brown, "Sampling with Random Jitter," *Journal Society Industrial Applied Mathematics (SIAM)* **11**(2) pp. 460-473. (June, 1963).

8. Robert L. Cook, Thomas Porter, and Loren Carpenter, "Distributed Ray Tracing," pp. 137-146 in *SIGGRAPH '84 Conference Proceedings,* ACM (July, 1984).

9. Franklin C. Crow, "A Comparison of Antialiasing Techniques," *IEEE Computer Graphics and Applications* **1**(1) pp. 40-48. (January, 1981).

10. Mark A. Z. Dippé and Erling Henry Wold, *Stochastic Sampling: Theory and Application,* Report, University of California, Berkeley, California (1985). To appear.

11. Mark E. Dippé and John A. Swensen, "An Adaptive Subdivision Algorithm and Parallel Architecture for Realistic Image Synthesis," pp. 149-158 in *SIGGRAPH '84 Conference Proceedings,* ACM, Minneapolis (July 23-27, 1984).

12. Thomas S. Huang, "The Subjective Effect of Two-Dimensional Pictorial Noise," *IEEE Transactions on Information Theory* **IT-11**(1) pp. 43-53. (January, 1965).

13. H. B. Kekre, S. C. Sahasrabudhe, and N. C. Goyal, "Raised Cosine Function for Image Restoration," *Signal Processing* **5** pp. 61-73. (1983).

14. Donald E. Knuth, *The Art of Computer Programming: Volume 2, Seminumerical Algorithms,* Addison-Wesley Publishing Company, Reading, Massachusetts (1969).

15. Oscar A. Z. Leneman, *Stationary Point Processes and Their Application to Random Sampling of Stochastic Processes,* Ph.D. Thesis, University of Michigan, Ann Arbor (1964).

16. Oscar A. Z. Leneman, "Random Sampling of Random Processes: Impulse Response," *Information and Control* **9** pp. 347-363. (1966).

17. Elias Masry, "Alias-Free Sampling: An Alternative Conceptualization and Its Applications," *IEEE Transactions on Information Theory* **IT-24**(3) pp. 317-324. (May, 1978).

18. Athanasios Papoulis, *Probability, Random Variables, and Stochastic Processes,* McGraw-Hill Book Company, Inc., New York (1965).

19. Daniel P. Petersen and David Middleton, "Sampling and Reconstruction of Wave-Number-Limited Functions in N-Dimensional Euclidean Spaces," *Information and Control* **5**(4)(December, 1962).

20. Lawrence Gilman Roberts, "Picture Coding Using Pseudo-Random Noise," *IRE Transactions on Information Theory* **IT-8**(2) pp. 145-154. (February, 1962).

21. P. F. Scott, *Distortion and Estimation of the Autocorrelation Function and Spectrum of a Randomly Sampled Signal,* Ph.D. Thesis, Rennselaer Polytechnic Institute, Troy, New York (June, 1976). Also published as General Electric Company technical report 76CRD180, Schenectady, N. Y., 1976.

22. Harold S. Shapiro and Richard A. Silverman, "Alias-Free Sampling of Random Noise," *SIAM Journal* **8**(2) pp. 225-248. (June, 1960).

23. Yu. A. Shreider, *The Monte Carlo Method,* Pergamon Press, New York (1966).

24. Robert Siegel and John R. Howell, *Thermal Radiation Heat Transfer,* McGraw-Hill Book Company, New York (1981). Second edition.

25. H. Stark, "Diffraction Patterns of Nonoverlapping Circular Grains," *Journal of the Optical Society of America* **67**(5) pp. 700-703. (May, 1977).

26. Thomas G. Stockham, Jr., "Image Processing in the Context of a Visual Model," *Proceedings of the IEEE, Special Issue on Image Processing* **60**(7) pp. 828-842. (July, 1972).

27. Ferrel G. Stremler, *Introduction to Communication Systems,* Addison-Wesley , Reading, Mass. (1977).

28. J. Turner Whitted, "An Improved Illumination Model for Shaded Display," *Communications of the ACM* **23**(6) pp. 343-349. (June, 1980).

29. N. Wiener, *The Extrapolation, Interpolation and Smoothing of Stationary Time Series,* John Wiley & Sons, Inc., New York (1949).

30. John I. Yellott, "Spectral Analysis of Spatial Sampling by Photoreceptors: Topological Disorder Prevents Aliasing," *Vision Research* **22** pp. 1205-1210. (1982).

31. John I. Yellott, "Nonhomogeneous Poisson Disks Model the Photoreceptor Mosaic (Abstract)," *Investigative Ophthalmology and Visual Science (Supplement)* **24**(3)(March, 1983).

Integrated Analytic Spatial and Temporal Anti-Aliasing for Polyhedra in 4-Space

Charles W. Grant
Lawrence Livermore National Laboratory
Livermore, California

Abstract

A visible surface algorithm with integrated analytic spatial and temporal anti-aliasing is presented. This algorithm models moving polygons as four dimensional (X,Y,Z,T) image space polyhedra, where time (T) is treated as an additional spatial dimension. The linearity of these primitives allows simplification of the analytic algorithms. The algorithm is exact for non-intersecting primitives, and exact for the class of intersecting primitives generated by translation and scaling of 3-d (X,Y,Z) polygons in image space. This algorithm is an extension of Catmull's analytic visible surface algorithm for independent pixel processing, based on the outline for integrated spatial and temporal anti-aliasing given by Korien and Badler. An analytic solution requires that the visible surface calculations produce a continuous representation of visible primitives in the time and space dimensions. Visible surface algorithm, graphical primitives, and filtering algorithm, (by Feibush, Levoy and Cook) are extended to include continuous representation of the additional dimension of time. A performance analysis of the algorithm contrasted with a non-temporally anti-aliased version is given.

CR Categories 13.3 (Computer Graphics) Picture/Image Generation — Display Algorithms. **13.5** (Computer Graphics) Computational Geometry and Object Modeling — Curve, Surface, Solid and Object Representations. **13.7** (Computer Graphics) Three-dimensional Graphics and Realism-Animation — Visible Line/Surface Algorithms.

Keywords and Phrases
Anti-Aliasing, Filtering Algorithms, Motion Blur, Scan-Line Algorithms, Temporal Anti-Aliasing, Visible Surface Algorithms.

1. Introduction

This paper presents a visible surface algorithm with integrated analytic spatial and temporal anti-aliasing. The algorithm renders scenes consisting of moving polygons. The polygons moving through 3-space are modeled by stationary polyhedra in 4-space. The anti-aliasing is "integrated" in the sense that the same method is used for both spatial and temporal anti-aliasing. It is "analytic" in the sense that an exact filtering integration over the visible primitives is performed at each pixel prior to sampling. This algorithm is an extension of Catmull's analytic visible surface algorithm for independent pixel processing [2].

The need for an exact integral is best described in signal processing terms. The sharp edges of the graphical primitives contain detail with spatial frequency components of infinite frequency. It is well known in signal processing (the sampling theorem) that to represent the information present in a continuous function with a set of discrete samples, the samples must be spaced at a rate which is at least twice the highest frequency present in the continuous signal. Sampling at less than this rate will produce aliasing (high frequencies incorrectly represented as lower frequencies). Thus it is clear that any algorithnm (such as all ray-tracing algorithms [3,15]) that samples this infinite frequency image at a finite number of discrete points without prefiltering will be subject to aliasing. Filtering after the sampling and varying the distribution or number of the samples can reduce, but not eliminate, the aliasing. Where infinite spatial frequencies are involved, filtering must be done before sampling to prevent aliasing.

For analytic spatial anti-aliasing the visible surface algorithm is required to generate an exact 2-d (X,Y) continuous representation of visible primitives from a 3-d (X,Y,Z) continuous representation of all primitives [1]. The filter is required to accept this continuous 2-d representation as input and perform the filtering integration over the continuous area represented. Several existing algorithms do this [1,2,4]. Korein and Badler [5] show how this outline can be extended to spatial and temporal anti-aliasing (figure 1). The extension requires increasing the dimensionality at each step to include the temporal dimension. Thus the visible surface algorithm is required to generate an exact 3-d (X,Y,T) continuous representation of visible primitives from a 4-d (X,Y,Z,T) representation of all primitives. The filter is required to accept this 3-d continuous representation as input and perform the filtering integration over the continuous volume represented.

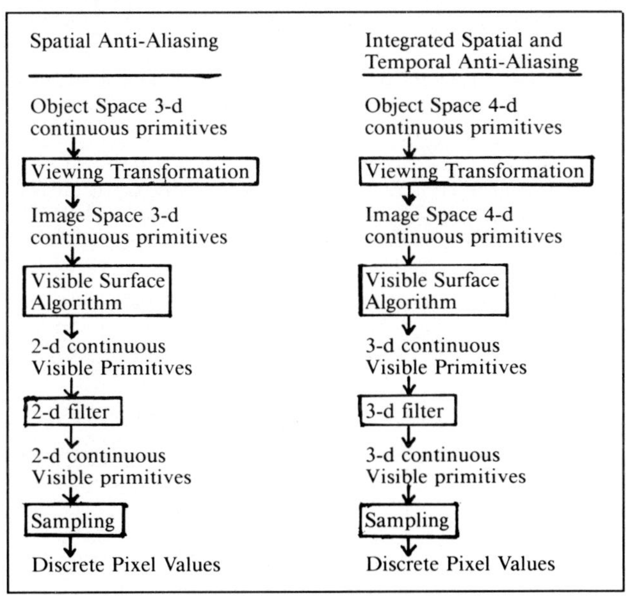

Figure 1. Spatial and Temporal Anti-Aliasing Outline

The complexity of continuous 4-d to 3-d visible surface calculations and the volume integral for filtering has left the impression that analytic algorithms would be very difficult to implement and very costly to run [3,5,14]. This algorithm relies on the linearity of the primitives in image space to simplify the calculations to the point of being straightforward extensions of spatial algorithms. The visible surface algorithm of Catmull [2] and the filtering algorithm of Feibush, Levoy and Cook [4] are extended by adding the temporal dimension. Now that a fairly efficient analytic algorithm exists, two interesting comparisons can be made; how much time does the analytic calculation take compared to an approximation; and how good does the result look compared to an approximation (visual artifacts of temporal aliasing are described by Szabo [14]).

Existing efforts related to temporal anti-aliasing (summarized in Figure 2) have generally tried to approximate one aspect of temporal anti-aliasing, motion blur [9]. These algorithms have generally done the visible surface calculations for one discrete point in time [2,7,8,10] or ignored visible surface calculations altogether [11]. The Cook/Porter/Carpenter algorithm [3] approximates a continuous visible surface calculation by calculating visible surfaces for several samples at different discrete points in time. This approximation has produced the best temporally anti-aliased pictures so far. Only the Korein/Badler algorithm [5] does visible surface calculations as a continuous function of time. However, this algorithm does not include spatial anti-aliasing.

Catmull [2] Polygons.
: Visible surface calculations done at one discrete point in time. Continuous analytic spacial anti-aliasing done. Motion blur approximated by deforming primitives before visible surface calculations and filtering.

Cook/Porter/Carpenter[3] Spheres,Polygons.
: Supersampling ray-tracing algorithm with discrete spacial and temporal sampling (as with all ray-tracing). Clever distribution of samples allows several dimensions of anti-aliasing to occur simultaneously without increasing the number of samples required. A similar scan line algorithm is also mentioned.

Korein/Badler [5] Spheres, Polygons.
: Continuous time visible surface calculations done at discrete spacial points. Analytic filtering for temporal anti-aliasing, but no attempt to anti-alias spacially. A supersampling approach is also given.

Max/Lerner [7] Rasters, Thick Vectors.
: Visible surface calculation done at one discrete point in time. Image and mask rasters blurred in direction of motion prior to 2 & 1/2 D compositing process. An approximate algorithm for drawing thick vectors with independently moving end points is also given.

Norton/Rockwood/Skolmoski [8] Texture Patterns.
: Approximate spacial and temporal anti-aliasing of texture patterns mapped onto polygons without involving the visible surface calculations. The polygons themselves are not temporally anti-aliased.

Potmesil/Chakravary [10] Rasters.
: Visible surface calculation done at one discrete point in time (generated by ray-tracing). Motion blur approximated by convolution of a blur function in the direction of motion.

Reeves [11] Particles.
: The particles are modeled as point sources of light. No visible surface calculation done, all are visible since they can not obscure each other. Particles are motion blurred by rendering them as anti-aliased line segments along their trajectories.

Figure 2. Summary of Some Temporal Anti-Aliasing Related Work.

2. Goals and Assumptions

The design of the algorithm presented here is based on the following goals and assumptions.

1. A representation equivalent to polygons with piecewise linear motion is desired for the graphical primitive. Linear motion is chosen to be consistent with the linear spatial nature of polygons.
2. Visible surface determination will transform continuous 4-d (X,Y,Z,T) primitives into continuous visible 3-d (X,Y,T) primitives. Catmull's head sort and resolver [2] will be extended to form the visible surface algorithm. Catmull's assumptions about images consisting of large objects built of small polygons, where usually only one object is visible for a given pixel are used to the same advantage in the extended algorithm.
3. Exact analytic 3-d (X,Y,T) filtering will be performed on the visible 3-d (X,Y,T) primitives to generate the pixel intensity values. The Feibush/Levoy/Cook 2-d filtering algorithm [4] will be extended to 3-d. This implies that the filter function will be radially symmetric. (i.e. time and space will use the same filter function, but it can be any arbitrary function.)
4. The system is designed to run on a single processor and to produce output in scan line order. This is in contrast to Catmull's parallel processing assumption for his algorithm.

In the terminology of Sutherland, Sproull, and Schumacker [13] this algorithm operates in image space, uses volume sampling, sorts in the order TYXZ, and takes some advantage of frame, area, scanline, object and depth coherence.

3. Primitive Representation

The major tradeoff in selecting a primitive representation is to accurately model the desired real world objects and to remain simple enough to allow analytic manipulation. The real world objects that we wish to represent are polygons with verticies in linear motion. The simplicity we wish to preserve is linearity. The visible surface and filtering algorithms assume that the input primitives are linear (i.e. have straight edges and flat faces).

There are at least three sources of error in trying to directly model moving 3-d object space polygons as 4-d polyhedra.

1. In general a 3-d object space polygon with verticies in linear motion can not be exactly represented by a 4-d object space polyhedron. This is due to the fact that the moving edges of the polygon sweep out surfaces which are not necessarily planar.
2. The visible surface and filtering algorithms used here operate in image space (i.e. after perspective transformation). Given a 4-d polyhedron in object space it is still, in general, not possible to exactly represent it with a 4-d polyhedron in image space. As pointed out in [5] the perspective transformation from object space to image space does not preserve linearity because the temporal dimension is not affected by perspective, while the spatial dimensions are.
3. Given two intersecting 4-d image space polyhedra, the intersection boundry is not necessarily planar. The visible parts of the intersecting polyhedra can not be expressed as 4-d polyhedra unless this intersection is planar. 4-d polyhedra generated by the uniform translation and/or scaling of 3-d polygons in image space have a linear relationship between the (X,Y,Z,T) coordinates for all points in the interior of the polyhedron. The intersection of two such polyhedra is planar.

The primitives chosen for this algorithm are a sub-set of 4-d (X,Y,T,Z) image space polyhedral volumes. Each primitive models a 3-d (X,Y,Z) image space polygon as it evolves linearly from time t_1 to t_2(t_1 and t_2 may differ for each polygon). It is this primitive 4-d polyhedron in image space which will undergo analytic visible surface and filtering calculations.

Defining the primitives in image space avoids the first two sources of error, (or rather, moves the errors from the rendering algorithm to the object model) but causes the primitives to be more removed from the natural concept of moving polygons in object space.

The application program or a preprocessing step takes on the responsibility of generating a suitable set of 4-d image space polyhedra which approximate the modeled 3-d object space polygon's time behavior to the required degree of accuracy. This algorithm will just concern itself with the correct rendering of the 4-d image space primitives and ignore the problem of generating suitable 4-d image space primitives, which is basically just an extension of the problem of generating a suitable set of 3-d primitives for a particular static model. The dotted box in figure 1 represents the section of the problem addressed in this paper.

An arbitrary 3-d image space polygon changing during a time interval can be modeled exactly by a 4-d image space polyhedron only if the edges of the polygon sweep out planar surfaces. Uniform translation and/or scaling of the polygon in image space has this property. However, it extremely unlikely that any object space polygon will transform into an image space polygon with this property, unless the polygon is stationary with respect to the eye point. Therefore practically all moving object space polygons can only be approximated by image space polyhedra.

Rotation or shape changes to the polygon can be modeled approximately by a 4-d image space polyhedron, if the change is not too great during the time interval. Arbitrary accuracy can be obtained by dividing the time interval into smaller sections and using a different 4-d image space polyhedron to model each time interval. The 4-d image space polyhedra model the changing 3-d (X,Y,Z) image space polygons in a piecewise linear manner.

A primitive 4-d image space polyhedron consists of a set of 4-d faces derived from the 3-d (X,Y,Z) image space polygon being modeled. The verticies of the 3-d (X,Y,Z) image space polygon are specified at times t_1 and t_2 giving two of the 4-d (X,Y,Z,T) image space faces. The remainder of the 4-d faces are generated by connecting the corresponding verticies of the first two 4-d faces. If the modeled 3-d (X,Y,Z) image space polygon has undergone only translation and/or scaling deformations in the time interval t_1-t_2, then the remaining faces can be quadrilaterals. However, if the modeled 3-d image space polygon has been rotated or its shape has changed in the time interval t_1-t_2 then the resulting quadrilaterals would not be planar. A triangulation connecting the first two 4-d faces must be used in that case (Figure 3).

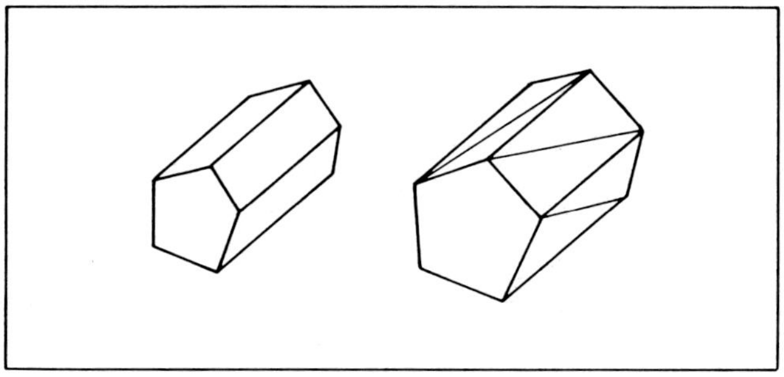

Figure 3. 4-d Polyhedral Primitives

4. Algorithm

4.1. Preprocessing

The algorithm proceeds as follows. The 4-d primitives are read in from disk and scaled to the screen space-time coordinate system. Parameters of the 4-d primitives are calculated, including 4-d bounding box, plane equations of faces, slopes of edges, and distances from pixel centers to planes, edges and verticies.

4.2. Scan Line Processing

Traditional scan line order processing then proceeds (extended to 4-d). The 4-d polyhedra are sorted first by T coordinates, then by Y coordinates and finally by X coordinates. As the scan line processing steps from pixel to pixel and frame to frame, an active list of 4-d polyhedra is maintained. The active list contains all of the 4-d polyhedra which have bounding boxes which overlap the bounding box of the filter of the current pixel. Thus the active list contains all potentially visible 4-d polyhedra for the current pixel. This list of 4-d polyhedra is then passed to the head sort routine for visible surface processing.

Note that this 4-d stage of the algorithm could instead distribute polyhedra to different processors, based on which pixels the bounding boxes of the polyhedra cover. This would give a version of the 4-d algorithm suited for parallel processing as Catmull's original 3-d algorithm is.

4.3. Head Sort

Catmull's head sort [2] required no modification for operation in 4-d (other than silhouette faces replacing silhouette edges). The head sort routine sorts 4-d polyhedra based only on the bounding box Z coordinates. The head sort detects the simple (and common) case where a non-overlapping set of 4-d polyhedra from the same object completely occult all other 4-d polyhedra in the entire region of the filter for this pixel. This case will be detected if there is a Z-gap between the visible 4-d polyhedra and the remainder of the 4-d polyhedra on the active list. If this simple case is detected, then the filter routine is called. If a more complex case is present, then the resolver routine is called to determine what parts of the 4-d polyhedra on the active list are visible.

4.4. Filter

The first two steps of the 3-d extension of the Feibush/Levoy/Cook 2-d polygon filtering algorithm [4] are the same as the first two steps of the Lien/Kajiya algorithm [6] for symbolic evaluation of the integral of a polynomial over the volume of an arbitrary polyhedron. Filter functions are not polynomials, so the entire Lien/Kajiya algorithm can not be used. The first two steps consist of dividing the polyhedron into pyramids, and then dividing each pyramid into tetrahedra. Then, proceeding analogously to the 2-d Feibush/Levoy/Cook algorithm, the tetrahedra are further divided so that the form of the integal of the resulting tetrahedra has a minimum number of parameters. Keeping the value of the integral a function of a small number of parameters allows the integral to be implemented in a lookup table.

The first step in the integration is to divide the polyhedron into a set of pyramids with each face of the polyhedron as the base of a pyramid. This is done by selecting a point, call it point O (the pixel center is used here), and connecting the verticies of each face to point O with line segments, forming a triangle with each edge of the face. These triangles and the polyhedron face form a pyramid. The volume of the pyramid is considered positive if the outward normal vector to the face of the polyhedron and the outward normal vector to the pyramid base are the same (they may point in opposite directions). When they are the same the pyramid and polyhedron are said to be coherent and the volume of the pyramid is considered to be positive. The pyramid and polyhedron will be coherent if they both occupy the same half space with respect to the plane of the face. The volume of the polyhedron is then equal to sum of the signed volumes of the pyramids.

Figure 4 illustrates this concept. A tetrahedron is divided into four pyramids (also tetrahedra). The pyramid ABCO is coherent and the others are not. The volume of the polygon ABCD = + ABCO − ABDO − ACDO − BCDO.

The second step is to divide the base of each pyramid (a polygon) into triangles, thus dividing the pyramid into tetrahedra. The division is done by selecting a point on the plane of the base and forming a triangle with each edge of the base. These triangles then form the bases of the resulting tetrahedra. The point on the plane closest to point O is used. Call this point F. This insures that OF is perpendicular to the base. This is illustrated in Figure 5.

In the third step, the base of each tetrahedron (a triangle) is then further divided into two right triangles (creating two tetrahedra of the desired form) by selecting a point, call it point E, on the edge of the original polyhedron face (or extension thereof) so that right angles are formed (FEV_1 and FEV_2). This is illustrated in Figure 6.

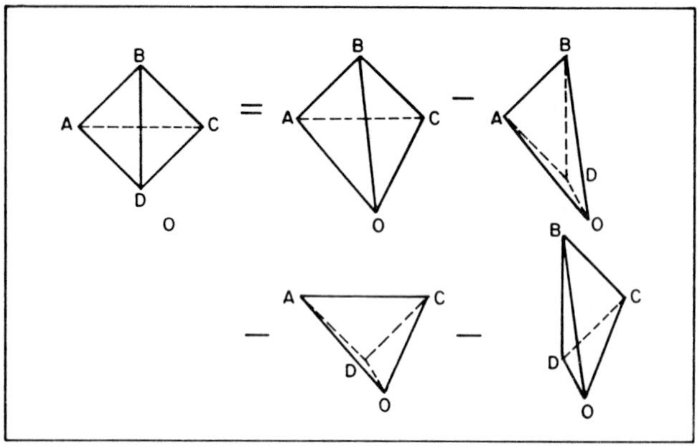

Figure 4. A polyhedron divided into four pyramids

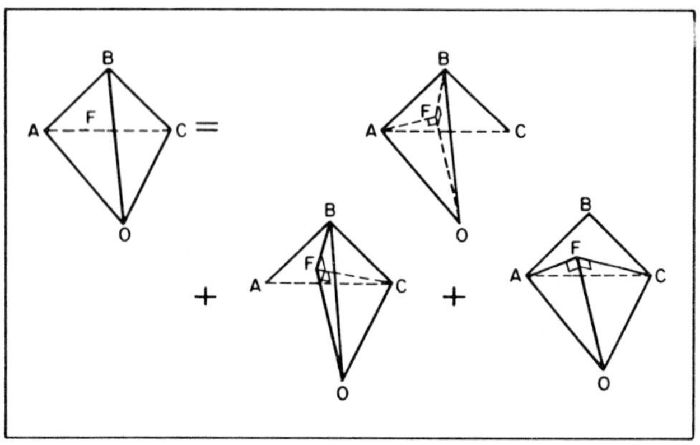

Figure 5. A pyramid divided into three tetrahedra

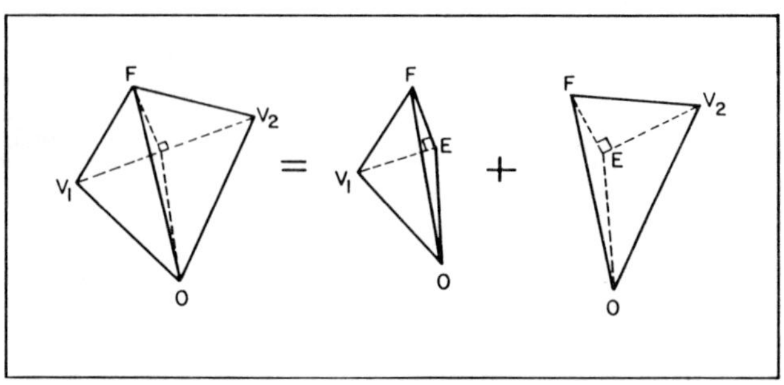

Figure 6. A tetrahedron divided into two right tetrahedra

Each of the resulting tetrahedra is now of a fairly regular form. One face of the tetrahedron, FEV, is in the plane of the polyhedron face. One edge of the tetrahedron, EV, is on the edge of the original polyhedron face. The edge FE is at a right angle to edge EV. The edge OF is perpendicular to the face FEV and ends at the pixel center.

Since the filter function is assumed to be radially symetric about the pixel center, the tetrahedron can be rotated about the pixel center without affecting the integral of the filter function over its volume. In step four, the tetrahedron is then rotated about the point O so that the edge OF is aligned along the Z axis, and the edge FE is parallel to the Y axis. This makes the edge EV aligned parallel to the X axis and the plane of the polyhedron face parallel to the XY plane. The rotated tetrahedron is shown in Figure 7. It can be seen from this picture that the tetrahedron is completely specified by the coordinates of the single point V in this rotated coordinate space. Point V is one of the original verticies of the polyhedron. The coordinates of this point in this rotated coordinate system are (D_v,D_e,D_f) where D_f is the pixel to face distance, D_e is the pixel to edge distance in the plane of the face, and D_v is the pixel to vertex distance along the edge. These are the three quantities which are used to index the lookup table which holds the integral of the filter function over tetrahedra of this form.

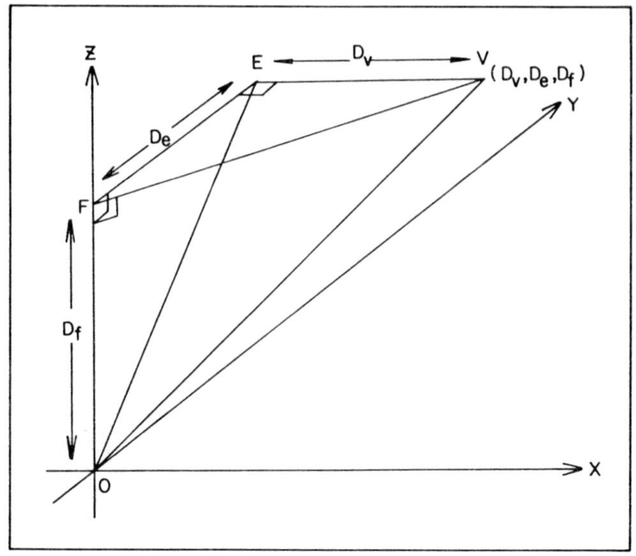

Figure 7. Rotated Right Tetrahedron

It is important to note that the distances D_v, D_e and D_f do not need to be recalculated at each pixel. Each distance varies linearly in X, Y, and T. Initial distance values are calculated in the preprocessing step and current distance values at each pixel are incrementally maintained in the scan-line shell. Thus the filtering of an arbitrary polyhedron, which is a triple integral over the volume of the polyhedron, is reduced to the sum of a series of values from a lookup table.

4.5. Resolver

The resolver must perform continuous 4-d (X,Y,Z,T) to 3-d (X,Y,T) visible surface determination for the general case. The 4-d polyhedron clipping resolver presented here is a direct extension of the 3-d polygon clipping resolver used by Catmull.

In this implementation a straightforward extension of the reentrant polygon clipper of Sutherland and Hodgman [12] is used for polyhedron clipping. Convex polyhedra are clipped against convex polyhedra by clipping against each of the planes which contain the faces of the polyhedra. Nonconvex polyhedra are divided into convex polyhedra as a byproduct of this operation. Although convex polyhedra are not required for the remainder of the algorithm, no attempt was made to recover the nonconvex polydedra after division into convex polyhedra. A different clipping algorithm which preserves nonconvex polyhedra could be used if it was desirable to try to limit the number of polyhedra generated by the clipping.

The resolver uses the polyhedron clipper to detect overlapping polyhedra in 3-d (X,Y,T) space by pairwise clipping of the polyhedra in the active list. When an overlap is detected, by a non-empty intersection, the Z depth values at each pair of corresponding verticies of the overlaping sections are then compared to determine which of the four possible overlap cases exist. If polyhedra A' and B' are the overlaping sections of polyhedra A and B produced by clipping, then the four cases are:

1. Polyhedron A' is entirely in front of polyhedron B' - No veretex of polyhedron A' is further away than the corresponding vertex of polyhedron B', and at least one vertex of polyhedron A' is closer than the corresponding vertex of

polyhedron B'. Some verticies may be the same if the two polyhedra share a face, edge or vertex.

2. Polyhedron B' is entirely in front of polyhedron A' - analogous to case 1.

3. Polyhedron A' and polyhedron B' intersect in (X,T,Z,Y) space partially occulting each other - at least one vertex of polyhedron A' is closer than the corresponding vertex of polyhedron B' and at least one vertex of polyhedron B' is closer than the corresponding vertex of polyhedron A'.

4. Polyhedron A' and polyhedron B' both occupy the same (X,Y,Z,T) space - all verticies of polyhedron A' equal the corresponding verticies on polyhedron B'.

Cases one and two are easy, keep the closer polyhedron as visible (so far) and discard the occulted polyhedron. Case three requires determining the plane of intersection of the two polyhedra, clipping the two polyhedra against this plane, and returning the two sections with closer Z depth values. Case four is degenerate, and it does not matter what is done, keep either of the polyhedra as potentially visible.

As described earlier, the boundry of the intersection of the two polyhedra in case three is a plane only if Z is a linear function of X,Y, and T in the two polyhedra. In the case where a linear relationship does not exist within a polyhedron involved in an intersection, the intersection is approximated with a plane as if the relationship was linear. This is a limitation of the algorithm which is due to the linear nature of the representable primitives, and nonlinear character of the intersection that is represented. This error can be reduced by first subdividing the intersecting polyhedra, then calculating the plane of intersection separately for each section. The plane of intersection is determined by finding three edges crossing the intersection (or verticies on the intersection) and solving for the points where Z(A') = Z(B'). Three such points determine the plane of intersection.

4.6. Algorithm Summary

The scan line shell delivers an active list of potentially visible 4-d image space polyhedra to the head sort. The head sort, possibly with the help of the polyhedron clipping resolver, converts these 4-d polyhedra to continuous 3-d (X,Y,T) visible polyhedra. These visible 3-d (X,Y,T) polyhedra are then fed to the 3-d filter algorithm. The 3-d filter algorithm integrates the filter function over the volume of the polyhedra by decomposing the integral over of each polyhedron into a sum of integrals over right tetrahedra. The integral of each right tetrahedron is evaluated by a lookup table. The spatially and temporally anti-aliased pixel intensity values are then output by the filter algorithm.

5. Performance Analysis

The greatest performance penalty to this algorithm is caused by the much more elaborate data representation needed for each primitive. In the non-temporally anti-aliasing version the simplest primitive, a triangle, is represented by one face including three edges with interpolated data values. In the spatial and temporal anti-aliasing version the corresponding primitive, a 4-d polyhedron is represented by eight faces with a total of twenty-four edges with interpolated data values, a eight fold increase in edge data.

Preprocessing calculations are done in 3-d (X,Y,T) rather than the 2-d (X,Y) of the non-temporally anti-aliasing algorithm. This causes an increase of a factor of about two in the processing of each edge, and there are now eight times as many edges. Scan line processing now involves eight times as many interpolations of edge data plus the additional interpolations of face data. The head sort has the same running time in both cases, since it deals with only Z values of the bounding boxes of the primitives, and not with each face of the polyhedral primitives. The resolver does approximately the same number of clips in both versions. The 3-d (X,Y,T) clippings involve more edges clipped, by a factor of eight, and more complicated clipping, by a factor of about two, than the 2-d polygon clipping. The filter calculations are done on a per-edge basis, of which there are eight times as many. Each lookup operation is now 3-d instead of the 2-d operation of the non-temporally anti-aliased version. This causes the value generated to be interpolated from eight values stored in the table, rather than four for the 2-d case. This interpolation then adds a factor of two to the filtering cost.

The "inner loop" of the algorithm for each pixel, consists of scan line processing, head sort and filter. In the typical case a call to the resolver is not necessary. The filter is the most expensive operation, causing the overall average degradation of this algorithm compared to the spatial only version to be a factor of sixteen. (Figure 8)

Data representation	× 8	
Preprocessing	Data × 2	= × 16
Scan line processing	8/3 + Data × 1	= × 11
Head sort	× 1	= × 1
Resolver	Data × 2	= × 16
Filter	Data × 2	= × 16
Total		= × 16

Figure 8. Cost of Adding Temporal Anti-Aliasing

6. Conclusions

It has been shown that an integrated analytic solution to spatial and temporal anti-aliasing, previously thought to be too hard to implement, is in fact practical for polyhedral primitives. The cost of adding analytic temporal anti-aliasing to Catmull's algorithm (which already contained analytic spatial anti-aliasing) is shown to be about a constant factor of sixteen in the average case. The fact that there is not an increase in the order of the asymptotic complexity of the average behavior of the algorithm as temporal anti-aliasing is included is very encouraging. Other algorithms may be able to reduce this constant factor.

The fact that the primitives handled by this algorithm are defined in image space and are not directly projected from object space is inconvenient. This is due to the desire to preserve linearity and the need to use a perspective projection. Perhaps this restriction could be relaxed by some other visible surface and filtering algorithms that either handled the non-linear primitives generated by the perspective transformation, or worked directly in object space.

The algorithm can be extended by adding different classes of primitives. Addition of moving 3-d lines (4-d polygons), and moving 3-d particles (4-d lines) are simpler cases which could easily be added to the 4-d polyhedron framework. Special programs could also easily be developed to handle only these primitives. Extensions to more complex primitives such as quadric surfaces, bicubic patches and quadratic or cubic motion are more complex. Visible surface and filtering calculations in this algorithm rely on the linearity of the primitives to provide considerable algorithmic simplifications. Continuous non-linear visible surface and filtering algorithms would have to be developed to implement these primitives. These continuous non-linear algorithms appear to be significantly more difficult than what was presented here. Some effects, such as smooth shading, transparency and surface texture, could be added. However, it seems unlikely that the range of effects that can be handled by the Cook/Porter/Carpenter approximate algorithm [3] could ever be done analytically.

7. Acknowledgments

I would like to thank Mike Allison, Cheri Ham, Jeff Kallman, Nelson Max, Mike Slocum and Bob Wyman for reading and commenting on the manuscript, Jeff Kallman for helping with the calculus, and Judy Corkern and Sally Twisselmann for knowing what to do at the last minute. The comments of the anonymous reviewers were very helpful and resulted in significant improvements in this paper. Work performed under the auspices of the U.S. Department of Energy by the Lawrence Livermore National Laboratory under Contract W-7405-Eng-48.

8. Disclaimer

This document was prepared as an account of work sponsored by an agency of the United States Government. Neither the United States Government nor the University of California nor any of their employees, make any warranty, express or implied, or assumes any legal liability or responsibility for the accuracy, completeness, or usefulness of any information, apparatus, product, or process disclosed, or represents that its use would not infringe privately owned rights. Reference herein to any specific commercial products, process, or service by trade name, trademark, manufacturer, or otherwise, does not necessarily constitute or imply its endorsement, recommendation, or favoring by the United States Government or the University of California. The views and opinions of authors expressed herein do not necessarily state or reflect those of the United States Government thereof, and shall not be used for advertising or product endorsement purposes.

9. References

[1] Catmull, Edwin, "A Hidden Surface Algorithm with Anti-Aliasing" Computer Graphics 12(3), August 1978, pp. 6–11.

[2] Catmull, Edwin, "An Analytic Visible Surface Algorithm for Independent Pixel Processing" Computer Graphics 18(3), July 1984, pp. 109–115.

[3] Cook, Robert L., Thomas Porter, Loren Carpenter, "Distributed Ray-Tracing" Computer Graphics 18(3), July 1984, pp. 137–145.

[4] Feibush, Eliot A., Marc Levoy, Robert L. Cook, "Synthetic Texturing Using Digital Filtering" Computer Graphics 14(3), July 1980, pp. 294–301.

[5] Korein, Jonathan, Norman Badler, "Temporal Anti-Aliasing in Computer Generated Animations" Computer Graphics 17(3), July 1983, pp. 377–388.

[6] Lien, Sheue-ling, James T. Kajiya, "A Symbolic Method for Calculating the Integral Properties of Arbitrary Nonconvex Polyhedra" IEEE Computer Graphics and Applications 4(10), October 1984, pp. 35–41.

[7] Max, Nelson, Doug Lerner, "A Two and a Half D Motion Blur Algorithm", Computer Graphics 19(3), July 1985, pp.

[8] Norton, Alan, Alyn P. Rockwood, Philip T. Skolmoski, "Clamping a Method of Anti-Aliasing Textured Surfaces by Bandwidth Limiting in Object Space" Computer Graphics 16(3), July 1982, pp. 1–8.

[9] Porter, Thomas, "Motion Blur" in SIGGRAPH 84 "State-of-the-Art in Image Synthesis course notes", July 1984.

[10] Potmesil, Michael, Indranil Chakravarty, "Modeling Motion Blur in Computer Generated Images" Computer Graphics 17(3), July 1983, pp. 389–399.

[11] Reeves, William T., "Particle Systems – A Technique for Modeling a Class of Fuzzy Objects" Computer Graphics 17(3), July 1983, pp. 359–376.

[12] Sutherland, Ivan E., Gary W. Hodgman, "Reentrant Polygon Clipping" Comm. ACM 17(1), January 1974, pp. 32–42.

[13] Sutherland, Ivan E., Robert F. Sproull, Robert A. Schumacher, "A Characterization of Ten Hidden Surface Algorithms" ACM Computing Surveys 6(1), March 1974, pp. 1–55.

[14] Szabo, Nicholas S., "Digital Image Anomalies; Static and Dynamic" in "Computer Image Generation" Ed. Bruce J. Schachter, John Wiley and Sons, Inc., New York, 1983.

[15] Whitted, Turner, "An Improved Illumination Model for Shaded Display" Comm. ACM 23(6), June 1980, pp. 343–349.

Plate 1. Slow Moving Picket Fence.

Plate 2. Fast Moving Picket Fence.

Plate 3. Stationary and Moving Intersecting Polygons.

Plate 1 shows a wide stationary red polygon and thin moving green polygon behind a slow moving white picket fence of polygons. In plate 2, the picket fence is moving much faster so that it appears completely blurred. Notice the correct strobing of the moving green polygon as the picket fence moves across it and its visibility changes with space and time. This effect is noticable to a lesser degree in plate 1. Plate 3 shows a moving red polygon (translation only) intersecting a stationary yellow polygon.

A Two-and-a-Half-D Motion-Blur Algorithm

Nelson L. Max* and Douglas M. Lerner +
Toyo Links Corporation
Tokyo, Japan

Abstract

Algorithms are presented for raster and vector motion blur, which produce images and masks suitable for combination by the 2½-D compositing process. The raster algorithm is based on a "skew, blur, unskew" scheme, using a very efficient one-dimensional blurring algorithm. The vector algorithm extends the ideas of anti-aliased scan conversion to motion blur.

Key Words: motion blur, raster, vector, skew, mask, compositing, computer animation

Introduction

When a camera films a rapidly moving object, the integration of the images during the finite time the shutter is open produces a motion blur. Computer animation which simulates this motion blur will feel more natural.

Animation without motion blur simulates an instantaneous shutter, and the combination of the successive images gives a "strobing" effect, as if the scene were illuminated by the repeated short duration flashes of a strobe light. A movie projector shows the 24 separate frames per second as a series of 48 discrete flashes per second, flashing each frame twice. The two repeated indentical flashes per frame cause a moving object to appear successively behind and ahead of its average moving position, so if the viewer follows the object with his eyes, it will appear double. These strobing and doubling effects are alleviated by motion blur.

We have been producing a computer animated, red-blue stereo Omnimax film for the 1985 World's Fair in Tsukuba, Japan. In Omnimax, with its high-resolution and 180 degree field of projection, the strobing and doubling are particularly evident. We thus needed a motion-blur algorithm which could efficiently produce high-resolution animation.

Motion blur can be discussed mathematically by considering a shutter which transmits a fraction f(t) of the incoming light during a shutter open interval from t=t1 to t=t2. We call f(t) the filter function or weighting function. The general expression for the intensity at a point is then

$$\int_{t1}^{t2} f(t)\ I(t)\ dt,$$

where I(t) is the incident intensity at time t.

In recent years, there have been several efforts at producing motion blur by computing or approximating the integral. Korein and Badler [1] developed an algorithm for scenes composed of elements which were discs or polygons. They posed the problem of dividing the shutter-open time interval into sub-intervals during which a unique element is visible at a pixel center, and showed it to be geometrically analagous to determining the spatial interval along a scan line where a unique element is visible. Once this problem is solved, the intensities of the elements can be combined by using a filter function to weight the exposures. A filter which emphasizes later times was proposed, and gave pleasing results. This algorithm can handle the problems of changing intersections during the shutter-open time, but requires many calculations per pixel, and cannot easily be modified to include spatial anti-aliasing.

Potmesil and Chakravarty [2] apply fourier analysis to the motion blur problem, and suggest that the convolution needed to produce a blurred image of a single moving object can be

*Current Address:
Lawrence Livermore National Laboratory
Box 808, Livermore, California 94550 U.S.A.

+Current Address:
Fujitsu SSL
NN Building
12-19 Nishi-Gotanda 2-Chome
Shinagawa-Ku Tokyo 141 Japan

done directly in the image domain, or converted into the spatial frequency domain by FFT's. We present below a particularly inexpensive way of approximating the convolutions in the spatial domain, for simple filter functions. Potmesil and Chakravarty also suggest blurring an opaque mask representing the area covered by an object, and using this mask to hide farther objects or backgrounds when each new blurred object is added into the scene. We have also blurred masks for partially transparent objects.

The "Distributed Ray Tracing" method of Cook, Porter and Carpenter [3] simultaneously solved most of the outstanding problems in computer graphic realism, including motion blur. The authors note that for good anti-aliasing, a ray-traced image should use many different rays per pixel (for example, 16). In addition to starting at different sub-pixel locations, the rays are traced so that they go through different points in the lens aperture, reflect and refract in slightly off-specular directions, and meet moving objects at different times in the shutter-open interval. The illumination rays are also traced to the full light source areas instead of to their centers. By this means, the problems of anti-aliasing, depth-of-field effects, glossy and translucent surfaces, motion blur, and shadow umbras and penumbras are all solved in a mutually compatible way. The crucial, ingenious realization is that all the appropriate distributions can be sampled by distributing the same 16 rays (or ray trees) simultaneously in all the various dimensions. However, ray tracing is inherently expensive, and oversampling costs even more, so the free extra effects come after a considerable base cost. For the restricted objects in our animation, rendering and anti-aliasing could already be achieved with much simpler methods, so a more efficient compromise was appropriate.

Catmull [4] has also developed an algorithm which includes motion blur, optimized for scenes where each object is divided into large numbers of connected polygons. The motion blur is accomplished by shrinking the polygons in the direction of the blur, relative to the center of each pixel, so that the intensity integral for the pixel extends farther across the object. This approximation gives good looking images, but it is not equivalent to the corresponding time integral, and the differences may show up in cases of partial occlusion. (Our algorithm also suffers from the same defect.) Grant [16] has extended this algorithm to do the correct analytic calculation in four dimension.

Two-and-a-Half-D Algorithms

Our approach is based on sorting the objects in depth and then compositing these images into a single picture, starting from the rear. Such a composition simulates that which is done on a conventional animation stand, where transparent cells with opaque painted images are stacked on top of a background before being photographed. It is called 2½-D because the occlusion information comes from the depth ordering of the images. If it is possible to divide the scene into clusters of objects, so that that the clusters do not intersect and can be linearly ordered in depth, this method can combine them correctly. Levoy [5] describes an early multiplane animation system at Cornell University, and Wallace [6] describes further developments of that system into one used in actual animation. Porter and Duff [7] give a theoretical framework for understanding the compositing of two semi-transparent layers. The philosophy behind all these systems is to maintain for each layer a raster of opacity mask values as well as color values. For an opaque, anti-aliased image, the opacity mask will be 1 for pixels covered by the object, 0 for pixels which completely miss the object, and some intermediate value, representing the fraction covered, along the edges. For semi-transparent objects, the mask may also be less than 1 for pixels completely inside the object. We render the color values of each object as if it were drawn against a black background, and therefore follow the convention of Porter and Duff [7], and premultiply the color by the opacity value.

In the simplest case, which we use here, the layers are composited from back to front. At each step, layer(i) is to be added to an opaque background, to get an opaque composite. The color of the composite is given by

$$\text{color(composite)} = \text{color(i)} + (1-\text{opaque(i)}) * \text{color(background)}.$$

This process can be separated into two steps: a) applying the mask,

$$\text{color(intermediate)} = (1-\text{opaque(i)}) * \text{color(background)}$$

and, b) adding the new image,

$$\text{color(composite)} = \text{color(i)} + \text{color(intermediate)}.$$

If the mask is placed somewhat to the rear of the layer(i) and they are sorted separately in depth, nearby semi-transparent layers can blend together independently of their masks, but still hide other layers farther behind (see [9]).

To include motion blur in this framework, we need a blur subroutine which takes an input raster and produces a blurred output image. We then apply this blur process to both the image and its opacity mask, before doing the compositing. In our current implementation, the raster blur subroutine is restricted to translations, so each layer must have a unique blur direction. However, this subroutine is supplemented by a separate vector blur algorithm, which can produce the blurred image and mask of an arbitrarily moving vector. These subroutines constitute the original work in the paper. Note that the successive compositing of blurred images will not be equivalent to the correct time integrals of the light intensity if two moving objects overlap, since no account is taken of the actual intervals of the shutter-open time when each is present. Nevertheless, we have found the results acceptable, and the raster blur subroutine is quite fast.

The Raster Blur Algorithm

This blur algorithm starts with a previously constructed raster image at rest (the instantaneous raster) and, through a post processor, blurs the raster to achieve desired effects. The instantaneous raster is to be blurred in the direction of the blur vector (dx,dy).

It is easier to blur an image in the x or y directions since an output pixel will then depend only on pixels in a single row or column of the instantaneous raster. Therefore the instantaneous raster is first "skewed" so that the blur can be applied along the direction of the largest blur vector component (dx or dy). An efficient difference algorithm then blurs the raster, and the result is unskewed again. There are thus three steps: (1) Skew the instantaneous raster into a "skewed raster", (2) Blur the skewed raster into a "blurred raster", and (3) Unskew the blurred raster, and combine it with the current composite picture. They are described separately below, but may be combined to avoid the intermediate raster storage, if memory is restricted. This

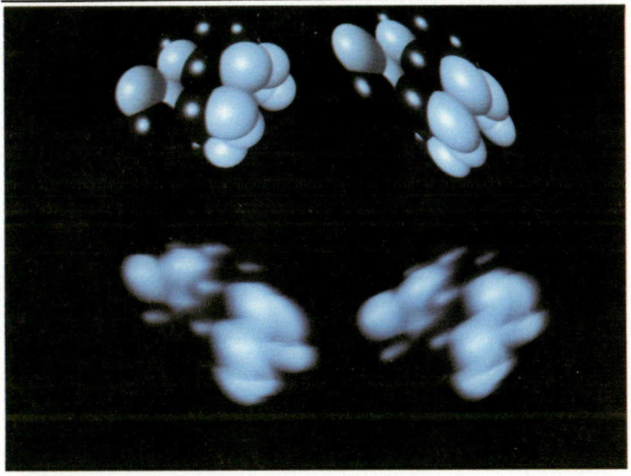

Figure 1. The Raster Blur Algorithm
instantaneous raster (top-left)
skewed raster (top-right)
blurred, skewed raster (bottom-left)
unskewed raster (bottom-right)

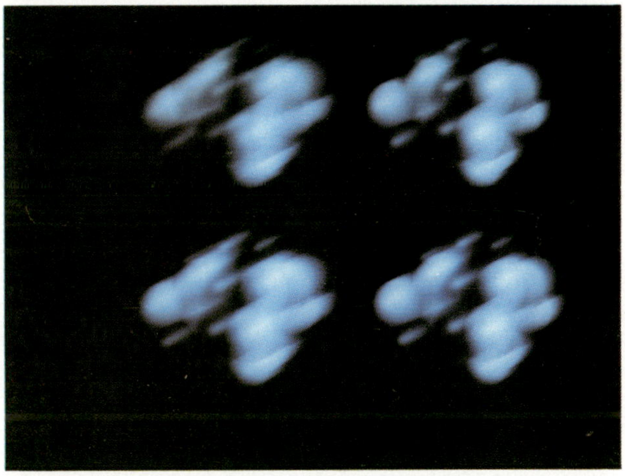

Figure 2. Four Different Blur Weightings
constant-sum blur (top-left)
linear-sum blur (top-right)
1/2-constant, 1/2-linear blur (bottom-left)
0.1 constant, 0.9 linear blur (bottom right)

Figure 3. Applying the Opaqueness Mask
skewed, blurred mask (top-left)
mask applied to a far raster (top-right)
blurred composite raster (bottom)

Figure 4. Nuclear Fusion
800 heavy nuclides, each made up of as many as 56 nucleons, moving with various velocities during the time interval of the frame.

three pass procedure was inspired by the "two-pass" algorithm of Catmull and Smith [10].

Step One. Skewing.

Suppose a raster is to be blurred twice as much in the x-direction as in the y-direction. Then the raster is skewed by shifting downwards by dely = x * (dy/dx), which is x/2 in our example. This skew is illustrated in figure 1 in the top-left and top-right photographs. Since this shift is not necessarily an integral number of pixels, the value of a pixel in the skewed raster will, in general, be a weighted sum of two adjacent pixels in the instantaneous raster.

Step Two. Blurring.

The skewed raster S is next blurred by a number of pixels corresponding to the magnitude of the largest blur vector component, and written into the blurred raster. The blur axis was chosen to correspond to the largest blur component to keep skewing to a minimum. For specificity, we continue considering a blur in the x direction, one in which dx < nxin, the x size of the skewed raster S.

Now we must consider the nature of the blurred image we wish to create. If we were just simulating the effects of the finite shutter-open time of a camera, then the blurred image of a constant-intensity bright object would have constant intensity in the middle and linearly decreasing intensity at the sides in the direction of the blur. It would be clear what the axis of the blur was, but not which way the object was moving along that axis. Such a blur would overcome the strobing effects in animation, but it would not indicate motion in a still picture.

This simple blur, which gives no weighted preference to later times, can be calculated at a pixel, x, by just adding its intensity to the sum of the previous dx pixel values and dividing by dx+1. If B is the blurred raster work space then, for a constant y-value (since we are computing along a row):

$$B(x) = \sum_{k=0}^{dx} S(x-k).$$

This sum can be computed incrementally as

$$B(x) = B(x-1) + S(x) - S(x-dx-1),$$

which requires one addition and one subtraction per pixel.

In practice it is even less computing than that, for there are three distinct regions to be considered:

(1) x < dx,
(2) dx <= x <= nxin, and
(3) x > nxin.

In region (1) we have not yet reached the point of subtracting the last term of the difference equation, so values of B(x) in that region can be computed with a single addition. Similarly, in region (3) we are beyond the point of adding in new pixel values and values B(x) can be computed with just a single subtraction. The blurred image is normalized to conserve overall brightness by multiplying B by a normalizing factor M=1/(dx+1).

We next consider a linear weighting function, which can give long fading streaks for rapidly moving objects in animation, and indicate the direction of motion in still frames. We compute

$$B'(x) = \sum_{k=0}^{dx} (dx-k)\ S(x-k).$$

where the factor (dx-k) is the linear weight, which is a maximum value at the most recent position and 0 at the oldest position. The normalizing factor $N=1/\Sigma\ (dx-k)$, can be used to assure that the overall intensity is conserved.

One can also calculate B'(x) incrementally as

$$B'(x) = B'(x-1) + (dx+1)\ S(x) - B(x),$$

where B(x) is the constantly weighted sum we previously found. The interesting point here is that we can gain the flexibility of a weighted blur algorithm by just one more addition, subtraction, and multiplication (by an integer constant) per pixel.

We can also combine the constant and linearly weighted sums to give

$$a\ M\ B(x) + b\ N\ B'(x).$$

To get desired visual effects, we can experiment by varying a and b independently, even making them different for different objects. If $a+b \neq 1$, the overall image energy is not conserved. One might want to do this in order to increase the overall intensity of a very rapidly moving object so it does not become too dim.

In figure 1, the bottom-left photo shows the blurring algorithm applied with a=0.1 and b=0.9 to the skewed raster and the bottom-right photo shows the final appearance of this blurred raster.

In figure 2 the results of four different weighting schemes are used. The top-left photo shows a constant-sum blur (a=1, b=0). It is clear along which axis the blur takes place, but the direction of the motion along the axis cannot be determined in a still photo. The top-right photo shows a linear-sum blur (a=0, b=1) in which it is clear that the object is moving in the negative x and negative y directions. The bottom-left photo is an example of half constant-sum and half linear-sum contributions to the blur (a=b=0.5) and the final photo, the bottom-right, shows a=0.1, b=0.9, the blur weights we used in our film, for the case when dx < nxin.

For computing efficiency it is best to break down the blurring algorithm into as many separately indentifiable cases as possible and put those cases into separate computing loops. Then a single decision at the beginning of the blur procedure can select the proper section to compute and avoid costly case checking in the inner-most loop. The separate cases identified in our algorithm were:

(1) the three cases of constant-sum, linear-sum or mixed terms (to avoid unecessary arithmetic),

(2) the 8 cases corresponding to the 8 octants in x-y space where the blur vector can lie (for the purpose of choosing vertical or horizontal blurs and the direction in which the blur is to be applied), and

(3) the two cases depending on whether the blur length is greater than the length of the instantaneous raster along the axis of the blur, or less than the length of the raster, (to avoid array bound checking).

Thus, the inner-most part of the blur algorithm consisted of 48 separate cases, one of which was used for a given blur vector and raster.

Step 3. Unskewing and Painting.

After the blurred raster is created, the inverse of the skewing process described in the first step is performed and the result is combined with the final raster at some specified position, building up an entire composite frame of the motion picture.

Hiding the Far Rasters

To create the necessary 2½-D hiding of farther, blurred rasters, the three step procedure described actually occurs twice for each raster image handled by the blur post processor. In the first pass of the procedure, instead of receiving an instantaneous raster image of a hidden-surface removed 3D object, step one receives and skews and "opaqueness mask" of the instantaneous raster, as described in the 2½-D algorithm above. This mask, after skewing, is blurred according to the blurring algorithm described in step two, above. In figure 3 the top-left photo shows an opaqueness mask which has been blurred, after having been skewed.

In step three, however, instead of adding the mask to the current composite image, the opaqueness mask is used to hide images which occur behind it by multiplying the composite image value by one minus the mask value. In figure 3 the top-right photo shows the result of the skewed, blurred opaqueness mask being applied to a raster which lies behind it.

After the mask is applied, the three-step procedure is done once again, this time for the instantaneous raster, and the blurred raster is unskewed and combined with the composite, as shown in the bottom photo of figure 3.

The photograph in figure 4 shows a color scene made up of 800 heavy nuclides, each made up of as many as 56 nucleons. They are moving with various velocities over the time interval of this frame. Nuclear reactions which occur during the frame are emphasized by flashes and/or the ejection of very fast particles called "flashons" whose existence was first proposed by computer graphicists in order to make their pictures look better.

Extensions

We have shown how to extend the case of constant weights to the case of linear shutter weighting functions. In a similar manner, using one more multplication, addition and subtraction per pixel, it is possible to compute the sum

$$B''(x) = \Sigma\ (dx-k)^2\ S(x-k),$$

and so forth for higher powers of x. Thus polynomial weights can be quickly computed. Perlin [11] has pointed out that once these sums are known, they can be combined at different values of x to give piecewise polynomial weighting functions. For example, by combining B(x), B'(x) and B"(x), at four different x values, it is possible to get a 3-piece quadratic approximation to a gaussian weighting function.

It has been suggested that our algorithm could also be used to blur a background raster to account for camera rotation and translation, before other objects are added. If a background were painted on a distant plane, perpendicular to the camera viewing axis, we could correctly account for camera translation parallel to this plane and blur the background as a single raster. But we could not correctly handle camera rotation about the viewing axis, because we assume all points on the raster move by the same blur vector (dx,dy).

As described above, the 2½-D algorithm assumes that objects in different layers do not intersect. Our blur algorithm cannot give correctly blurred intersections, because it cannot deal with intersections whose shape changes during the shutter-open interval. However, it is still possible to get good looking pictures by intersecting first, and then blurring. In figure 5 each sphere was intersected with those to the rear of it, but not those closer. The resulting images were then blurred and composited as described above. So if two spheres intersect, the rear one will be rendered in total, forming a background for the blurred intersection edge of the closer object.

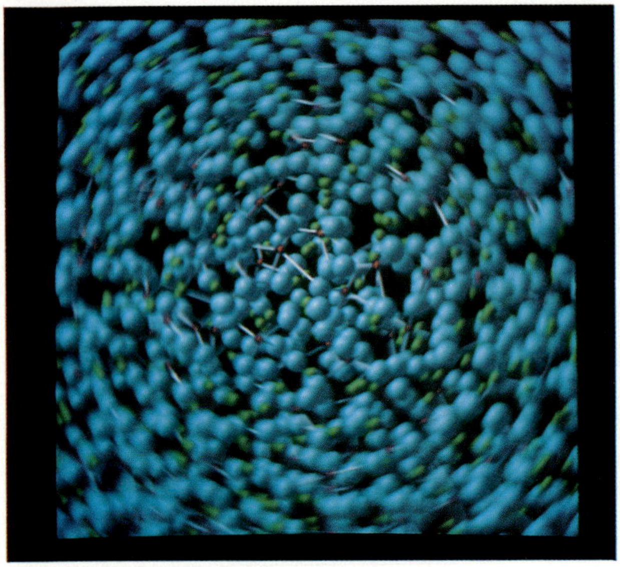

Figure 5: Liquid Li2BeF4 Simulation
2100 atoms and 1100 connecting bonds are in this frame from a molecular dynamics simulation. The bonds are not rendered with the vector motion blur algorithm described in this paper. They are raster images created with the ATOMLLL program and blurred with the raster blur subroutine. This scene took about 45 seconds of CPU time to create.

The Vector Blur Algorithm

Pique and colleagues at UNC [12] have produced motion blur on a film recorder in vector mode, by drawing each vector many times in slightly different positions. If the trajectories of the vector endpoints are known as a function of time, this method can produce correct images of rotating vectors, as well as translating ones. However, it is not compatible with the 2½–D animation system described here because once recorded on film, the vectors cannot be hidden by closer objects. We thus needed a good anti-aliased, vector-to-raster scan conversion algorithm, of the sort described by Crow [13], Sproull and Gupta [14], and Turkowsky [15], coupled with a motion blur procedure. However, we could not merely apply the raster motion blur algorithm described above to a scan converted image, since our vectors were required to rotate and change length. Therefore we needed to integrate the motion blur into the scan conversion process. The algorithm specifications are:

(a) Accept a vector width, brightness, and transparency, as well as initial and final endpoint positions;

(b) Produce an image and mask raster for the 2½–D algorithm;

(c) Account for constant and linear shutter weightings;

(d) Produce good anti-aliased lines even when there is no motion;

(e) Trade off width for brightness when the thickness of the vector is less than a pixel;

(f) Produce smooth images for a continous curve approximated by a polygonal arc of n contigous segments.

In order to satisfy (f) the input of the algorithm is actually an array of n+1 positions and thicknesses, and the figure to be blurred is a polygon of the sort illustrated in figure 8 (bottom), with approximately trapezoidal regions corresponding to each segment. For a single segment then, we have the initial and final positions of the vertices of a convex quadrilateral, and must compute the appropriately blurred raster image.

Let us first analyze the problem in the simplest case: a vertically oriented vector translating horizontally to the left. In this example, all scan lines are equivalent and the shading depends only on x.

Assume the shutter opens at time t=0, and closes at time t=1. Let TL(x) be the time when the left hand edge of the wide vector crosses a point x and TR(x) be the time when the right hand edge crosses, with $TL(x) < TR(x)$. Let f(t) be the exposure weighting function. Then the intensity of the point x is

$$\int_v^u \text{brightness} * f(t)\, dt$$

where $u=\min(TR(x),1)$ and $v=\max(TL(x),0)$.

The times TL and TR, and thus the effective limits of integration, depend on x. Even in this simple case, the width may change with time, so the two edge velocities need not be equal. The image points x fall into six classes, represented by the inequalities below:

(a) $1 <= TL(x) < TR(x)$
(b) $0 <= TL(x) < 1 <= TR(x)$
(c) $TL(x) < 0 < 1 <= TR(x)$
(d) $TL(x) < 0 <= TR(x) < 1$
(e) $TL(x) < TR(x) < 0$
(h) $0 <= TL(x) <= TR(x) < 1$

As shown in figure 6, top, class (c) is present in case 1 when the line is wide and moving slowly, so that the initial and final positions overlap. Otherwise, class (h) is present. The intensities for classes (a) and (e) are zero. If the weighting function f(t) is a constant, the intensity integral as a function of x is linear in regions (b) and (d), and constant on the central region as shown in figure 6, middle. The shape of this curve is very similar to the one proposed by Crow in [13] for anti-aliasing. This suggests an easy solution to algorithm specification (d) for anti-aliasing: merely require that a minimum amount of blur be applied to all lines, even if the input specifies less motion. The curve also seems to indicate that no further integration is necessary over the pixel area to get a smoothly shaded image, and experience has borne this out. The mach bands corresponding to the corners where the curve is not smooth appear at the positions of the edges at the instant when the shutter opens and closes.

They result from the integral in our constant-weight shutter model, and are not artifacts of the blur algorithm.

We have also computed the intensity integrals for a linear weighting ramp of the form f(t)=2at+b, and found piecewise quadratic curves of the sort shown in figure 6, bottom. We have approximated these curves by the piecewise linear function shown by the dotted lines, and found the results quite adequate. Thus our general form for the intensity for all cases of a moving vertical line is a three-segment piecewise-linear function of x, specified by four x values x0, x1, x2 and x3, and two brightness values b1 and b2.

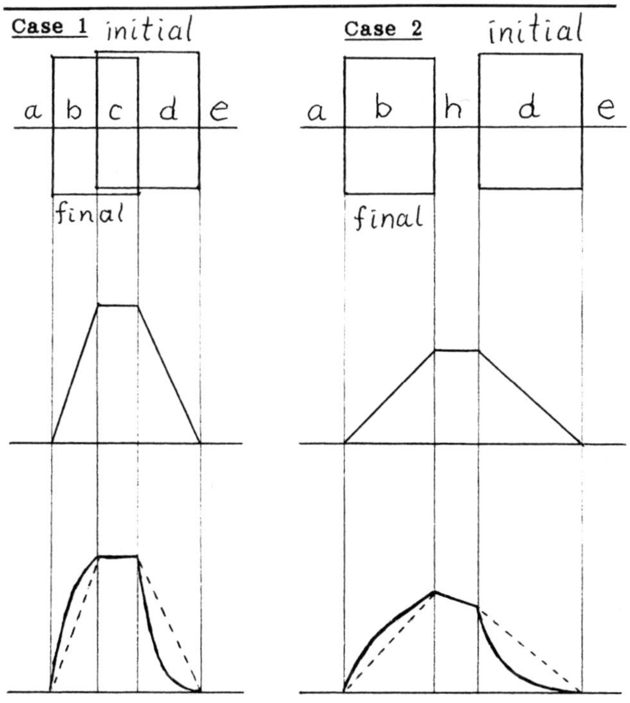

Figure 6.
In Case 1 the line moves less than its width during the shutter-open time. In Case 2 it moves more than its width.

Top: initial and final positions for thick vertical line of changing width moving from right to left, showing scan-line regions.

Middle: intensity curves for constant intensity shutter.

Bottom: piecewise quadratic intensity curves for linearly weighted shutter (solid), piecewise linear approximations (dotted).

To extend this analysis to the case of an arbitrarily moving quadrilateral it is necessary to choose directions corresponding to the x axis. The simplest method would be to use either the x axis or the y axis according to the slope of the vector, as is traditional with vector scan-converting and anti-aliasing algorithms. However, this would introduce problems for vectors which rotated, or which translated lengthwise, instead of moving sideways as in figure 6.

To find this direction a line is drawn connecting two of the four "right-hand" corners of the lines, so that the two quadrilaterals lie entirely on one side of the line, as shown in figure 7. A similar line is drawn for the left-handed corners. Assume these two lines meet at a point P. (The case where they are parallel is treated separately.) Then for each pixel center Q, a line is drawn from Q to P, and this line plays the role of the x axis. The four relevant intersections corresponding to x0, x1, x2 and x3 must then be found. There are 12 lines which could contribute intersection points: the eight quadrilateral sides and the four lines joining corresponding vertices. Determining the four correct intersections involves a complicated test logic, so it is preferable to precompute and store them for each of a collection of pixel-wide strips, shown as triangles in figure 7. To index these strips a line is drawn through a vertex to form, together with the two lines meeting at P, an isosceles triangle ABP completely enclosing the quadrilaterals. The segment AB is divided into equal intervals of length at most a pixel.

At the center of each interval, a line, shown dotted in figure 7, is drawn to P. The equation of this line, its four intersection distances x0, x1, x2, and x3, and the two brightness values b1 and b2 are stored in

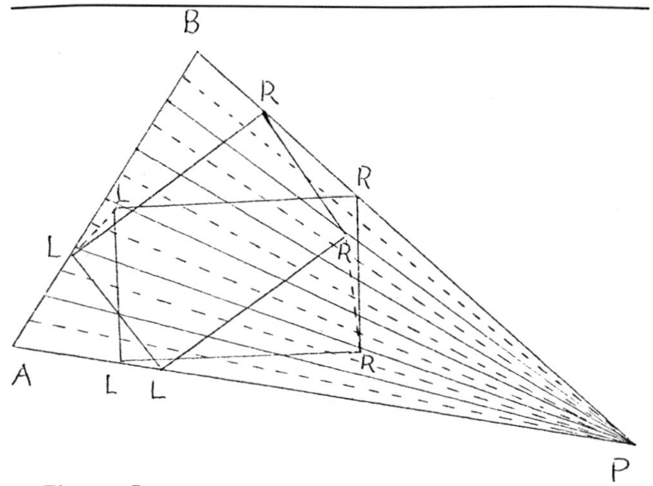

Figure 7.
Initial and final positions of a moving quadrilateral derived from a turning thick line segment. Consistant choices of left and right ends are marked by the letters L and R. The isosceles triangle PAB encloses both position.

tables. A computation of the form index=int((ax+by+c)/(dx+ey+f)) assigns the pixel at Q=(x,y) to the nearest dotted line. Two tests then determine which of the three linear segments of the brightness curve is relevant, and a simple linear interpolation determines the brightness. This scheme is optimized for thick high-resolution lines and wide blurs, because the per-pixel computation is very quick. For pictures with no blur or thin lines, it takes longer to pre-compute the tables than to use them to find the intensities.

The same shutter weighting function is used to compute the mask for the 2½−D algorithm, so the mask and brightness are proportional, and may be computed simultaneously. Figure 8 shows, at the top, the results for the two cases analyzed in figure 6, and at the bottom a blurred thick line of the three segments.

If a smooth curve wanders between opaque objects, as in figure 9, it may be desirable to sort the approximating vectors separately in depth. The input options of the vector blur algorithm allow three segments (i.e. 4 vertices) to be specified, where only the middle segment is drawn. The other two segments are used to determine the slanted sides of the trapezoid.

Other Examples

For our film, our task was to animate solar prominences, nuclear reactions, and molecular dynamics. The objects in these scenes were all represented by spheres, ellipsoids, and straight lines. The solar prominence scene was made from over 100,000 fuzzy ellipsoids. The nuclei were formed by intersecting proton and neutron spheres, rendered by ATOMLLL (see [8]) so that each layer was a hidden-surface raster picture of a single nucleus. The molecules were represented by semi-transparent glossy spheres, connected by bond vectors. We have blurred a large molecule of DNA, whose image moves according to internal molecular dynamics, camera motion, and changing super-coiling (see figure 10). The translation-only blur of the atom spheres is supplemented by the unrestricted blur of the bonds, which is necessary to maintain a connected structure when different atoms move in different directions.

Figure 11 shows the final level of coiling in the formation of a chromosome. The DNA coils at the top are moving and blurred, and the chromosome at the bottom is at rest, so there is a gradation of velocities. The tubular image was made up of 14,050 round "fireballs", opaque at the center, transparent at the edges, clipped at the edge of the tube, and shaded as if they were cylindrical. They blend together to give a smoothly shaded tube, which blurs properly when the above algorithm is applied separately to each fireball. This picture took 62 seconds to produce, while an unblurred picture took 34 seconds. Of the extra 28 seconds, 14 were used to compute the positions of a second set of spheres for the twisted tube. Since the previous frame's coordinates are available in animation, the extra cost for the blur was only 14 seconds.

Acknowledgments

This work was supported by Toyo Links Corporation (トーヨーリンクス) and Fujitsu Limited (富士通) as part of the production of the film "We are Born of Stars (The Universe)" (ザ ユニバース) the Tsukuba Expo '85. The vector motion blur algorithm was originally written by Hiroaki Kobayashi (小林宏明) who extended the case of the horizontally moving vertical line to the general case of an arbitrarily moving quadrilateral. It was extensively debugged and revised by Takashi Oh-Ishi (大石節). The Fujitsu M380 mainframe was used, with system support by Keiichi Kameda (亀田慶一) and Takamitsu Okada (岡田高光). Figure 10 involved the work of Humio Hirata (平田文男), Masao Takakuwa (高桑昌男) and Hiroshi Oh-Ishi (大石裕).

References

[1] J. Korein and N. Badler, "Temporal Anti-Aliasing in Computer Generated Animation", Computer Graphics, Vol. 17, no. 3, pp. 377-388, 1983.

[2] M. Potmesil and I. Chakravarty, "Modeling Motion Blur in Computer Generated Images", Computer Graphics, Vol. 17, no. 3, pp. 389-399, 1983.

[3] R. Cook, T. Porter and L. Carpenter, "Distributed Ray Tracing", Computer Graphics, Vol. 18, no. 3, pp. 137-145, 1984.

[4] E. Catmull, "An Analytic Visible Surface Algorithm for Independent Pixel Processing", Computer Graphics, Vol. 18, no. 3, pp. 109-115, 1984.

[5] M. Levoy, "A Color Animation System Based on the Multiplane Technique", Computer Graphics, Vol. 11, no. 3, pp. 65-71, 1977.

[6] B. A. Wallace, "Merging and Transformation of Raster Images for Cartoon Animation", Computer Graphics, Vol. 15, no. 3, pp. 253-262, 1981.

[7] T. Porter and T. Duff, "Compositing Digital Images", Computer Graphics, Vol. 18, no. 3, pp. 253-259, 1984.

[8] N. L. Max, "ATOMLLL: ATOMS with Shading and Highlights", Computer Graphics, Vol. 13. no. 2, pp. 165-173, 1979.

[9] K. Knowlton, "Computer-Aided Definition, Manipulation and Depiction of Objects Composed of Spheres", Computer Graphics, Vol. 15, no. 4, pp. 352-375, 1981.

[10] E. Catmull & A. R. Smith, "3-D Transformations of Images in Scanline Order", Computer Graphics, Vol. 14, no. 3, pp. 279-285, 1980.

[11] Ken Perlin, private communication.

[12] Mike Pique, et al, sequence in "The Magic Egg", Garrick Film, exhibited at Siggraph '84.

[13] F. Crow, "The Use of Grayscale for Improved Raster Display of Vectors and Characters", Computer Graphics, Vol. 12, no. 3, pp. 1-5, 1978.

[14] S. Gupta and R. F. Sproull, "Filtering Edges for Gray-Scale Displays", Computer Graphics, Vol. 15, no. 3, pp. 1-5, 1981.

[15] K. Turkowsky, "Anti-Aliasing Through the Use of Coordinate Transformations", ACM TOG, Vol. 1, no. 5, pp. 215-234, 1982.

[16] C. Grant, "Integrated Analytic Spatial and Temporal Anti-Aliasing for Polyhedra in 4-Space", Computer Graphics, Vol. 19, this issue.

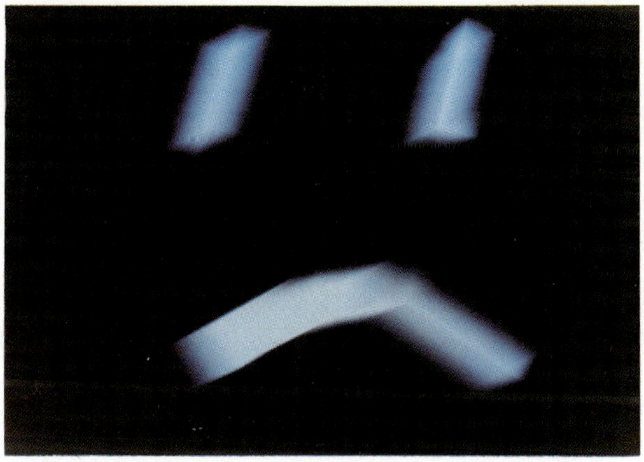

Figure 8. Vector Motion Blurs
two cases analyzed in figure 6 (top)
blurred thick line of 3 segments (bottom)

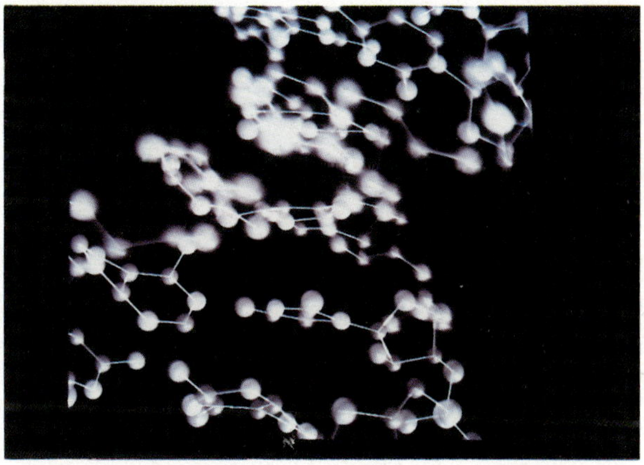

Figure 10. Blurred, Large Molecule of DNA

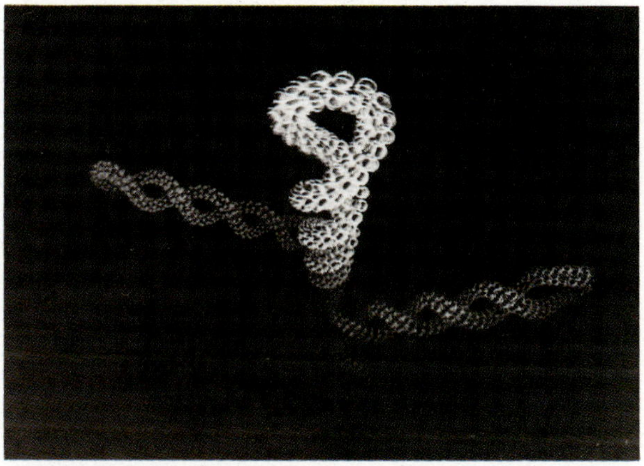

Figure 9. Coiling in DNA
A smooth curve wandering between opaque objects. DNA is wrapping around hazy spheres representing proteins.

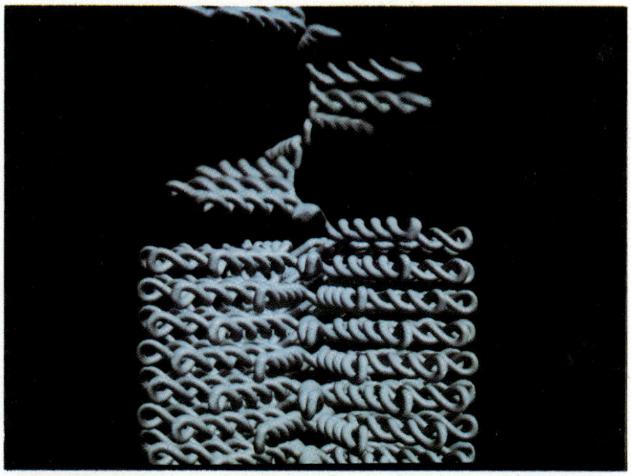

Figure 11. Final Level of Coiling in the Formation of a Chromosome

Fast Image Generation of Constructive Solid Geometry Using A Cellular Array Processor

Hiroyuki Sato, Mitsuo Ishii, Keiji Sato, Morio Ikesaka, Hiroaki Ishihata, Masanori Kakimoto, Katsuhiko Hirota, Kouichi Inoue

Fujitsu Laboratories, LTD. Kawasaki
1015, Kamikodanaka, Nakahara-ku,
Kawasaki, 211, Japan

Abstract

A general purpose Cellular Array Processor(CAP) with distributed frame buffers for fast parallel subimage generation has been developed. CAP consists of many processor elements called cells. A cell has video memory for subimage storage, a window controller to map each subimage to an area on the monitor screen, and communication devices, in addition to ordinary microcomputer components such as MPU, RAM, and ROM. Image data in a cell is directly displayed via the video bus. The mapping pattern and the position on the screen of subimages can be changed dynamically. Various hidden surface algorithms can be implemented in CAP using mapping patterns appropriate for the algorithm.

Our goal is an efficient interactive visual solid modeler. We adopted a general CSG hidden surface algorithm that enables display of both Boundary representation and Constructive Solid Geometry. A technique for hidden surface removal of general CSG models, requiring less memory space for large models in many cases, has been proposed. This technique subdivides the model into submodels by dividing the CSG tree at union nodes. Images of each submodel are generated by a CSG or a z-buffer algorithm. If a submodel is just a primitive, it is processed by the z-buffer algorithm, otherwise by the CSG algorithm. Hidden surface removal between submodels is done by comparing the z values for each pixel which are saved in the z-buffer.

CR Categories and Subject Descriptors: C.1.2. [Processor Architectures]: Multiple Data Stream Architectures(Multiprocessors) - Multiple - instruction - stream, multiple - data - stream processors(MIMD)

I.3.3. [Computer Graphics]: Picture/Image Generation - display algorithms;
I.3.7. [Computer Graphics]: Three-Dimensional Graphics and Realism - Visible Line/Surface Algorithms;
Key Words and Phrases: computer graphics, hidden surface removal, constructive solid geometry, scan-line algorithms, z-buffer, solid modeling, computer aided design

1. Introduction

Fast image generation of three-dimensional objects has been one of the major topics in computer graphics. Much work has been dedicated to this area. Sutherland pointed out that hidden surface removal is a sorting problem[11]. To minimize sorting cost, many algorithms use coherence properties of the scene to be displayed[11,13,14]. Recently, the progress in VLSI technology and the decreasing cost of hardware have led us to consider other ways to generate images quickly, using parallel processing. Kaplan and Greenberg[1] tested two algorithms, which divided the image area into scan-line groups for scan-line algorithms and into rectangular areas for area subdivision algorithms. Since then, many parallel processing techniques have been proposed[2,3,4,5,6,7,8]. Most of these are based on the parallel subimage generation techniques. Another parallel technique divides a three-dimensional object space into subspaces[7]. In this case, whole sets of objects are divided and processed in parallel. These systems implement one of three major hidden surface removal algorithms: the z-buffer algorithm[4,5], the scan-line algorithm[2,8], or the ray-tracing algorithm[6,7].

Our design goal is an efficient interactive solid modeler. Fast image generation of solids is the key for a good man-machine interface. We want to be able to display both B-rep (Boundary representation[10]) and CSG (Constructive Solid Geometry[10]). We took two approaches:

(1) To develop a general purpose parallel processor with distributed frame buffers for subimage generation. Image generation algorithms are implemented in software, rather than hardware. This frees the processor for other problems that can be processed in parallel. This is an advantage for solid modelers, which require a lot of calculation other than for image generation.

(2) To implement display algorithms that can be efficiently processed in parallel. Ray-tracing[12] and Ray-casting[15] are efficiently executed by parallel processors[6] and their implementations in CAP would be easy. But their speed would be still too slow for interactive use, if the number of processors is limited. We chosen a general CSG hidden surface removal algorithm[13] that can generate images of both B-rep and CSG models.

This paper focuses on the architecture of the Cellular Array Processor(CAP) and the CSG hidden surface algorithm we have been implementing. We also discuss experimental results.

2. Background

Solid modeling is an important technology for mechanical CAD/CAM, and many other fields in which three-dimensional data is handled. However, there are few systems that enable designers to model solids efficiently, because it is difficult to obtain quick responses from the system.

There are two main data representation schemes for solid modeling: B-rep[10] and CSG[10]. CSG represents solid models as combinations of primitive solids. Primitives are combined by boolean operators, such as union, intersection, and difference. The data is represented as a binary tree called a CSG tree. Constructing a CSG tree is easy, but generating images of CSG models requires a lot of calculation, because explicit surfaces are not saved in the data structure. One must determine the true surfaces of the solids beforehand, or perform boolean operations in the display algorithm. In the B-rep scheme, solid models are generally built from sequences of boolean operations of solids. Boolean operations take much time, increasing almost quadratically as the number of surfaces increases. However, once explicit surfaces are obtained, image generation is much easier than with CSG.

In addition to image generation of solids, there are many other time consuming tasks in solid modeling, such as interference checks and mass-property calculations. Therefore, many solid modelers are implemented on main-frame computers and used under time-sharing environments. For visualization of solid models, graphic display devices are connected to the host computer through communication lines.

For interactive use, engineering workstations provide a good man-machine interface. The performance of workstations so far is insufficient for interactive solid modeling. Thus we developed a dedicated processor for fast image generation and other tasks related to solid modeling, which can be attached to existing engineering workstations via a high-speed bus.

For the solid modeler, we adopted dual modeling scheme that separates the visual modeler from the exact analytical modeler[13]. We avoid unnecessary calculations for generating images while man-machine interactions are being done. Boolean operations are not done at the interaction phase, but the images of solids are generated by boolean operations within the display algorithms. Exact boolean operations would be done on a demand basis when it is necessary for certain applications.

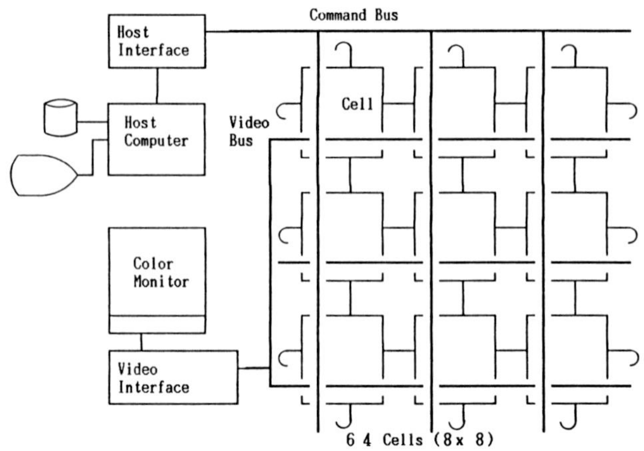

Fig.1 The System Hardware Configuration

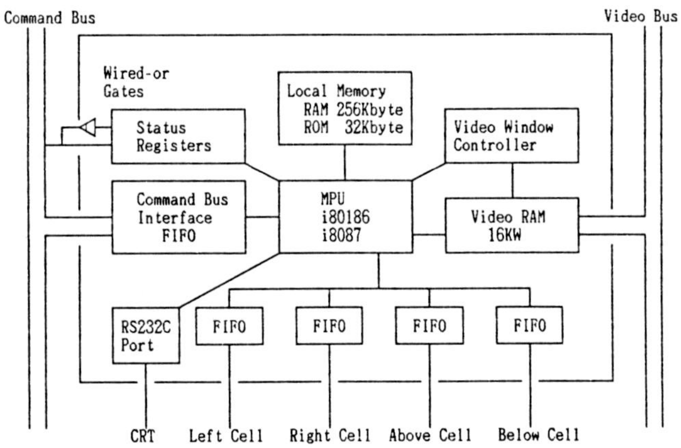

Fig.2 The Hardware Structure of a Cell

3. CAP Architecture

3.1 Overview

CAP is a general purpose oriented Cellular Array Processor with distributed frame buffers for real-time parallel subimage generations. Fig.1 shows the system hardware configuration and Fig.2 shows the hardware structure of a cell. Processor elements, called cells, are configured in a two dimensional array. This configuration is suited not only to parallel subimage generation but also to problems that can be mapped onto a two-dimensional cell array[9].

Command Bus: All cells are connected by a common bus called Command Bus. The Command Bus can be connected easily to existing workstations.

Video Bus: Each cell has a video memory which works as a partitioned frame buffer. Subimages are stored here and displayed on the screen automatically through the Video Bus.

Inter-cell communication: Each cell has parallel

communication interfaces to four neighboring cells (right, left, above, and below). Local communication is done using these lines.

3.2 Subimage generation

The basic strategy for speeding up image generation is to partition an image area into subareas, not necessarily continuous, and generate subimages in parallel, using many cells. Each cell has 16K words of video memory. A word is 24 bits long, 8 bits each for red, green, and blue. The window controller of each cell maps that cell's subimage data to a certain area of the screen.

A frame of image data, which is partitioned and distributed to many cells, is reconstructed as one complete image by window controllers in the cells. Window controllers read and send subimage data, once each refresh cycle (30 Hz interlaced), when the global pixel position counter's value is equal to one of the positions that cell is in charge of. Only 512 x 480 pixels can be displayed on the monitor screen at once. If there is an access conflict between the window controller and the MPU of the cell, the MPU waits.

The mapping pattern can be changed. Each cell has X and Y timing tables (XT(x) and YT(y)) in which x and y mapping information is stored. A window controller maps its subimage to the area for which logical AND of XT(x) and YT(y) is 1. By changing the bit pattern of XT and YT, various mapping are possible. Fig.3 shows some examples.

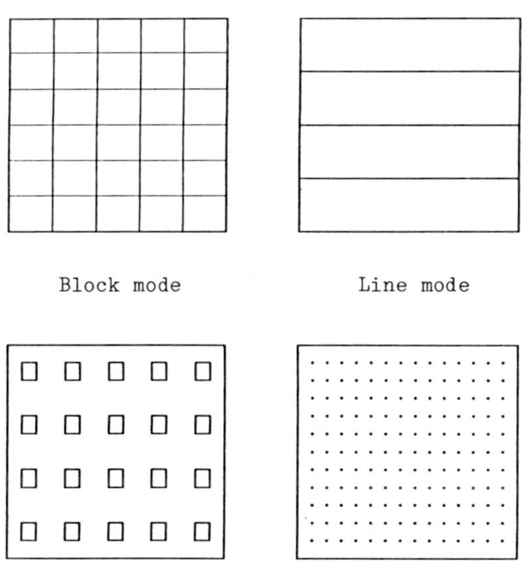

Block mode: A rectangular area for each cell
Line mode : Several equally spaced scan-lines for each cell
Dot mode : Dispersed pixels for each cell
Discrete block mode: Several rectangular areas for each cell

Fig.3 Examples of Subimage Mapping Patterns

This flexibility is very useful, because the best subimage mapping varies from one problem to another. For example, block mode is suited for area subdivision algorithms, whereas line mode is better for scan-line algorithms. Mappings of subimages to separate areas on the screen are often effective for evenly distributing calculation load between cells. The combination of a ray-tracing or a ray-casting algorithm and the dot mode is very effective, because these algorithms do not generally use coherence properties.

We developed a basic software package called Display Manager to do some standard mappings, and window clipping and zooming. The application programmer need only specify the mapping made such as line, dot, or block mode. Values of the X and Y timing tables for the selected mode are automatically calculated and set.

For subimage generation, all cells run with the same code. Only the contents of timing tables differ. This simplifies the programming efforts greatly.

3.3 Communication

Communication is an important part of parallel systems. In CAP, communication is done in two ways: Global communication using the Command Bus and Local communication using inter-cell communication lines.

Global communication: The host computer broadcasts programs and data to all cells via a common bus called the Command Bus. Any cell can also broadcast its data to other cells and to the host computer. Each cell receives the broadcast and saves only that information it needs. Unnecessary information is discarded. This method is effective when large amounts of data are sent to many cells.

Data is often distributed to many cells. After the distributed data has been processed, frequently it must be redistributed. Here, each cell requests to send its data to all other cells. The host computer continuously polls, granting the right to use the Command Bus to requesting cells. This polling continues until no requests are detected. This way, each cell can receive the all the new data. We call this global communication rebroadcast.

In addition to division of image areas, geometric data for the entire model is also divided and distributed to many cells and parallel calculations are done on the divided data. Then, the new data is rebroadcast for the next subimage parallel execution.

Local communication: Neighboring cells communicate with each other via inter-cell communication interfaces. A large amount of data exceeding the capacity of one cell is distributed to neighboring cells. This enables CAP to hold a lot more data, while the communication overhead does not increase by that much.

3.4 Multi-task Cell Monitor

In parallel processing, it is important to minimize the idle time of processors during execution. We implemented a multi-task real-time monitor in cells, to improve the efficiency of use of hardware resources such as the MPU, memory, and

I/O ports. Programs are divided into tasks, which are driven by messages received from other tasks or from the host computer. Messages are generally sent in packets except for direct communication in which large amounts of data are sent directly without packeting. Messages are passed by communication tasks. Application programs are often divided into several tasks. The CSG hidden surface removal program is divided into three tasks: A modeling task and two display tasks, one for the z-buffer algorithm, the other for the CSG hidden surface algorithm.

3.5 Synchronization

Wired-or status registers are used for synchronization. There are eight bit status registers, which can be read by the host computer or by any cell. Cells can set the status to indicate completion of a process. The host or any cell can read the logical OR (or AND) status of all cells to determine whether a process divided between many cells is completed. The number of wires can be minimized by hardware wired-or logic. Request signals for rebroadcast are also set in status registers.

4. CSG hidden surface algorithm for parallel subimage generation

4.1 General CSG hidden surface removal algorithm

CSG models are represented by Boolean combinations of primitive solids such as cubes, cones, and spheres. The boolean combinations are represented as a binary tree, each node representing a boolean operation (union, intersection, or difference). The leaves are primitive solids. Data structures of CSG models are more easily constructed than with the time-costly complex boolean operations of the B-rep modeler, which tests every possible crossing of faces of solids and reconstructs a new model. If CSG models can be displayed fast, CSG is favorable for an interactive visual solid modeler.

Peter Atherton proposed a scan-line hidden surface removal algorithm for CSG models that does boolean operations within itself[13]. The algorithm is an extension of a polygon scan-line hidden surface algorithm. He added one-dimensional boolean operations to detect surfaces that are logically true and nearest to the viewer. To process one segment span, this algorithm first does one-dimensional boolean operations for both ends of the span, then it checks the depth order of segments up to the visible points. If both depth orders are the same, the segment is visible within that span range. If not, there must be some crossing of segments, so it divides the span and does the same for each divided span (see Fig.4).

For purposes of visualization only, any kind of solid can be a primitive as long as it can be approximated by a polyhedron. Even a complex B-rep model can be a primitive.

We have been implementing this algorithm, with some changes for parallel subimage execution.

4.2 Partitioning of image area to separate scan-lines

This partitioning is effective for evenly distributing the calculation load between cells. However, it causes some loss of y-directional coherence. This increases the cost of calculation of segments and x-sorting of segment end points. We compensate for the increase of x-sorting cost by using x-bucket sorting of segments.

4.3 Boolean operation by status tree technique[17]

This technique differs from the ray classification method[15], which recursively descends from the top node of the CSG tree and obtains all in-out portions of the ray. We use a status tree to detect a ray hit against a logically true surface. The structures of status trees are almost identical to that of CSG trees except that each node keeps the current status of left and right children, and of the node itself. The node pointers are bottom-up.

Given a z-sorted list of segments, a ray proceeds along the z direction. If the ray hits any segment, that primitive's status is evaluated and its parent node status is evaluated. If the new status of the node is the same as the old status, the process stops immediately, otherwise the node status and the child status in the parent node are also updated. Then, the same process is performed for the parent node. This process continues while node statuses are being updated. If the root node's status becomes true for the first time, that point on the segment is a logically true surface point and nearest to the viewer. Rays behind visible points are not processed except when generating translucent images.

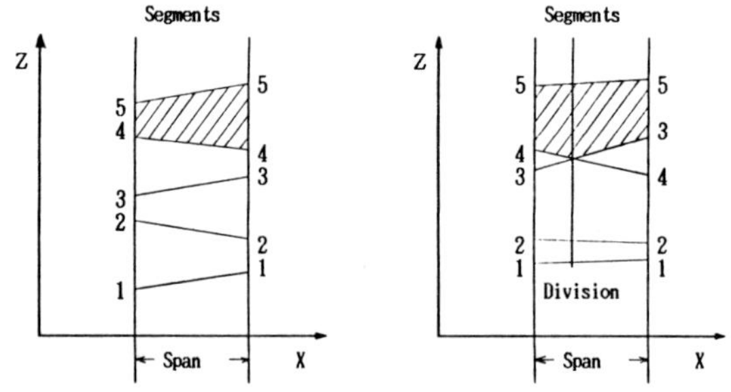

Fig.4 Division of a Segment Span

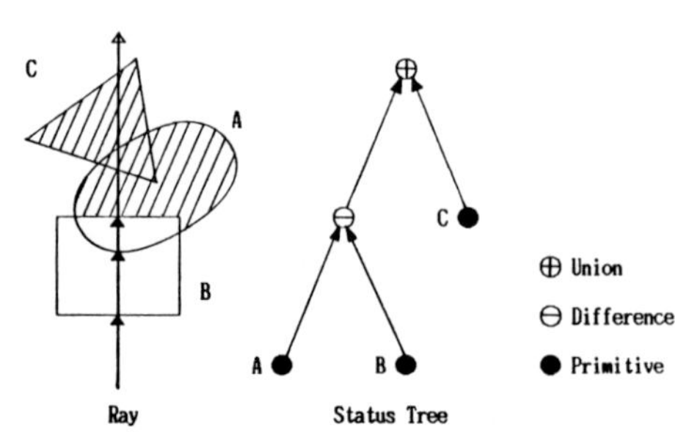

Fig.5 Boolean Operation by Status Tree Technique

This method is fast, because only surfaces up to the first logically true one are processed, but it requires a z-sorted list in advance.

The cost of sorting can be minimized by using span coherence, that is, by bubble sorting of the previous nearly sorted list.

4.4 Use of CSG combination coherence

Large models are often an assembly of parts, which are represented by union operators in CSG trees. That type of model can be displayed by using the scan-line algorithm for hidden surface removal of each part and the z-buffer algorithm for unions of parts. Fig.6 shows simple example. If the root node's boolean operator is a union, it is simply divided (Fig.6 A). On the other hand, if the root is not a union (in displaying cross-sections, a difference or intersection operator appears at the root), primitive 5 in the example (Fig.6 B) must be attached to divided submodels. We developed a recursive procedure to divide and take out submodels from a CSG tree. If the submodel is a primitive, it is displayed by the z-buffer algorithm.

This scheme reduces memory requirements of the CSG algorithm, if the model can be divided to smaller ones.

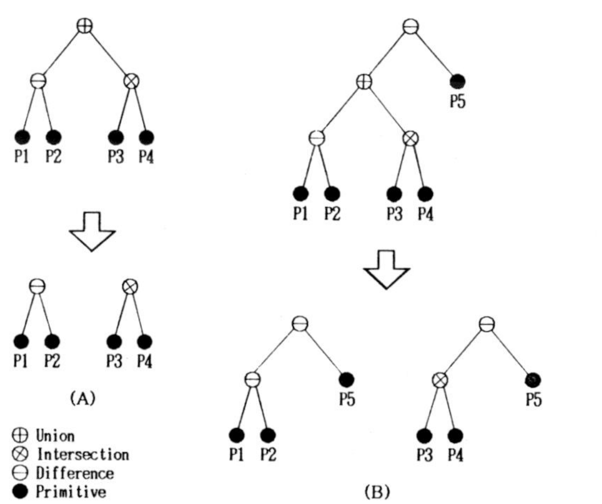

Fig.6 Division of CSG trees

5. Implementation

5.1 Program structure

The program is divided into three tasks: modeling, z-buffer, and CSG. The CSG modeler is in the host computer. The three tasks are resident in all cells. Modeling tasks contain geometric data on the model. When the modeling tasks receive a SHOOT command from the host, they send their data to the z-buffer tasks or to the CSG tasks.

5.2 Modeling task

Modeling tasks have following data items:

CSG tree: Each cell has the same entire CSG tree. This tree is constructed in the cell by commands from the host or is copied from the host.

Primitive data: Primitives are approximated with convex polygons and distributed to all cells, so the number of vertices is nearly the same for all cells, for purposes of averaging the calculation load and memory requirements. Modeling tasks take charge of coordinate transformations and intensity calculations of vertices of polygons. So far, polygonal approximation and coordinate transformations are done in the host computer because floating data processors (8087) have not yet been implemented.

When a modeling task receives a SHOOT command from the host, it does the following:

(1) It divides the entire CSG tree into subtrees if possible, by a division procedure.

(2) Performs transformation of vertex coordinates and normal vectors of polygons of the primitives in the subtree. Then calculates vertex colors or a surface color and depth increment values.

(3) Each cell sends data of the divided submodel to z-buffer tasks if the submodel is a primitive, or to CSG tasks if it is still a CSG model. The CSG tree of a submodel is sent to the CSG task in the same cell, while primitive data is rebroadcast so that the z-buffer or CSG task can receive all polygon data of the submodel. Only frontfacing polygons are sent to z-buffer tasks.

5.3 Z-buffer task

Z-buffer tasks generate an image of a primitive made up of polygons. A polygon has the following data items.

A. Primitive id.
B. Number of vertices
C. Number of colors
D. Vertex coordinates
E. Vertex colors or a surface color
F. Depth increment(dz/dx)

Each polygon is processed independently by the following procedure:

```
(1)   For each polygon received
(2)      For each scan-line the cell
         takes charge of
(3)         If polygon crosses the scan-line
            Then
(4)            Calculate segment data(start point
               x, z, color, end point x, color,
               and d(color)/dx)
(5)            For each pixel in the segment
                  Do ordinary z-buffer process
                  [16]
```

5.4 CSG task

CSG tasks generate an image of a CSG model from CSG tree data and the primitive's polygon data. The procedure is as follows:

(1) Receive a CSG tree

```
    and construct a status tree
(2) For each polygon received
        For each scan-line
            If the polygon crosses the scan-line
            Then
                Calculate segment data(same as
                z-buffer task)
                Store segment in data structure(in
                edge, segment, x-bucket tables)
(3) For each scan-line
        For each span from left to right
(4)         Make left and right boundary
            segment list
            and sort in z-order.
(5)         Solve one-dimensional set operation
            by the status tree technique.
(6)         If the same z-order of the segments
            Then
                Do the same as (4), (5) of
                z-buffer task
            Else
                Subdivide span and repeat
                (4),(5) for each new span.
```

6. Experiments

First, we tested the communication speed of CAP. Table 1. shows the results. The size of a packet is 128 bytes, of which 18 bytes are header data. We have not obtained maximum communication speed so far because of some bugs in the FIFO LSIs. The speeds without bugs are in parentheses in Table 1.

Table 1. Communication Speed of CAP

Type of Communication		Time(ms)	Speed(Kbyte/s)
Global	Broadcast Packet	3.15*N (1.17*N)	35 (94)
	Rebroadcast Packet	2.06*N (1.17*N)	53 (94)
	Broadcast Direct	1.83*N (0.29*N)	60 (379)
Local(Packet)		1.62*N (1.62*N)	68 (68)

N: Number of Packets

Table 3. Test Models

Model	Number of primitives	Number of polygons	Number of vertices	Data size (Kbyte)
A	17	198	360	12.22
B	25	5320	5018	292.95
C	20	344	634	21.48
D	66	396	528	16.37

Table 4. Values of K1, K2, K3, and K4

Test	K1	K2	K3	K4
1	0.175	0.00036	0.108	80.3
2	2.937	0.00036	0.739	185.2
3	0.277	0.00036	0.714	209.9
4	0.444	0.00036	0.247	234.4
5	0.444	0.00036	1.019	280.3
6	0.277	0.00036	0.293	53.7

The CSG hidden surface program uses broadcast (packet) from host to cells and rebroadcast (packet) from each cell to all other cells. The broadcast speed is constant regardless of the number of cells, while rebroadcast increases the overhead as the number of cells increases, because polling interrupts tasks in cells. This overhead is 0.36*(number of cells) ms, for each polling cycle. We are designing a hardware mechanism for polling, to minimize overhead.

The host computer is Apollo Domain DN460[18]. All source code is written in C language, except time critical parts of the cell monitor, the communication tasks, and the Display Manager. All calculations in cells are done in integer arithmetics.

The models tested are in Table 3. The screen resolution was 512 x 384 for all tests.

We tested three cases:

(1) Performance of modeling and z-buffer tasks (Test 1, Test 2, and 6).
(2) Performance of modeling and CSG tasks (Test 3 and 4).
(3) Performance of the combined method (modeling, z-buffer, and CSG tasks) (Test 5).

The test results are shown in Table 2. The division number in the table is the number of cells to which primitive data is distributed.

7. Analysis of Results

Rebroadcast time is almost constant for each model, so the ratio of the overhead increases as the number of cell increases. The modeling task rebroadcast to the z-buffer tasks only frontfacing polygons, which is about half of that is sent to CSG tasks.

Suppose that the total execution time except idle time of a certain model is represented by Eq.1.

$$T = K1 + K2*Nc*Np + K3 + K4/Nc \quad \text{(Eq.1)}$$

T : Total execution time of a model
K1: Rebroadcast time
Nc: Number of cells used
Np: Number of polling cycles
K2*Nc*Np: Overhead for polling
K3: Overhead of a modeling task and the hidden surface task
K4/Nc: Execution time inversely proportional to Nc

The performance is:

$$P = 1/T = 1 / (K1 + K2*Nc*Np + K3 + K4/Nc) \quad \text{(Eq.2)}$$

These parameters can be calculated from the experiments for each model and are shown in Table 4. Fig.7 shows the performance curves of the tests. Fig.8 shows the ratio of the performance to that with 16 cells. Plotted points in Fig.7 and 8 are expermental values. The improvement of the performance decreases as models become large.

The performance would be improved by optimizing the program code and replacing the FIFOs with bugless ones, but if the amount of polygon data becomes large, the overhead is still large.

Table 2. Test Results

Test (Model)	Algorithm	# Cell	Total Time(Idle Time) (s): Fast Cell	Total Time(Idle Time) (s): Average	Total Time(Idle Time) (s): Slow Cell	Communication: # Div.	Communication: Average(s)	Communication: %	Other: Time (s)	Other: %
1(A)	ZB	16	5.31(0.04)	5.40(0.02)	5.47(0.00)	16	0.19	3.5	5.21	96.5
		32	2.78(0.04)	2.86(0.02)	2.94(0.00)	32	0.18	6.2	2.68	93.8
		48	1.92(0.06)	2.00(0.03)	2.06(0.00)	33	0.17	8.5	1.83	91.5
		64	1.54(0.06)	1.59(0.04)	1.64(0.00)	33	0.17	10.7	1.42	89.3
2(B)	ZB	24	12.50(2.11)	12.74(1.20)	13.15(0.31)	24	3.02	23.7	9.72	76.3
		32	10.62(2.18)	10.89(1.32)	11.17(0.30)	32	2.96	27.2	7.93	72.8
		48	8.64(2.36)	8.84(1.29)	9.08(0.40)	48	2.92	33.0	5.92	67.0
		64	7.87(2.53)	7.99(1.77)	8.23(0.70)	64	2.89	36.2	5.10	63.8
3(A')	CSG	40	6.33(0.18)	6.53(0.08)	6.69(0.00)	33	0.28	4.3	6.25	95.7
		48	5.35(0.19)	5.49(0.11)	5.68(0.00)	33	0.28	5.1	5.21	94.9
		64	4.26(0.08)	4.35(0.05)	4.49(0.00)	33	0.28	6.3	4.07	93.7
4(C)	CSG	32	7.99(0.12)	8.19(0.06)	8.41(0.00)	32	0.45	5.5	7.74	94.5
		48	5.38(0.15)	5.73(0.09)	6.05(0.00)	34	0.44	7.7	5.29	92.3
		64	4.30(0.15)	4.48(0.11)	4.68(0.00)	34	0.44	9.8	4.04	90.2
5(C)	ZB+CSG	32	9.75(0.17)	10.37(0.14)	11.32(0.00)	32	0.45	4.4	9.92	95.6
		48	7.49(0.17)	7.55(0.14)	8.28(0.00)	34	0.44	5.9	7.11	94.1
		64	4.86(0.20)	6.01(0.15)	7.16(0.00)	34	0.44	7.3	5.57	92.7
6(D)	ZB	16	4.04(0.00)	4.11(0.00)	4.12(0.00)	16	0.30	7.2	3.81	92.8
		32	2.28(0.00)	2.31(0.00)	2.36(0.00)	32	0.28	12.1	2.03	87.9
		48	1.65(0.00)	1.71(0.00)	1.76(0.00)	48	0.27	15.9	1.44	84.1
		64	1.42(0.00)	1.45(0.00)	1.48(0.00)	64	0.27	18.7	1.18	81.3

Model A:Union, Model A':Difference, ZB:z-buffer, #Cell:Number of cells used, #Div.:Number of cells to which primitive data is distributed.

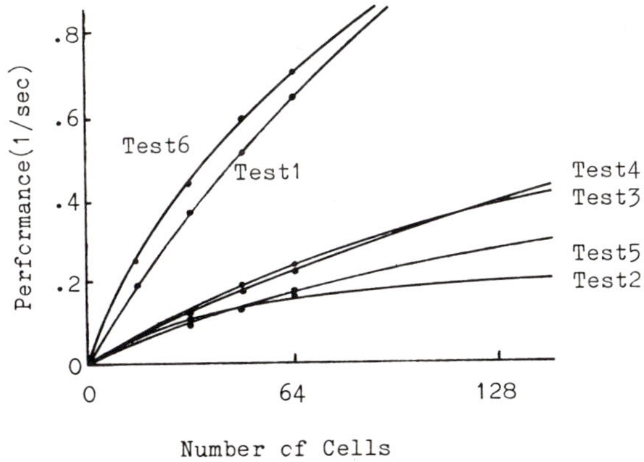

Fig.7 Performance curves of tested models

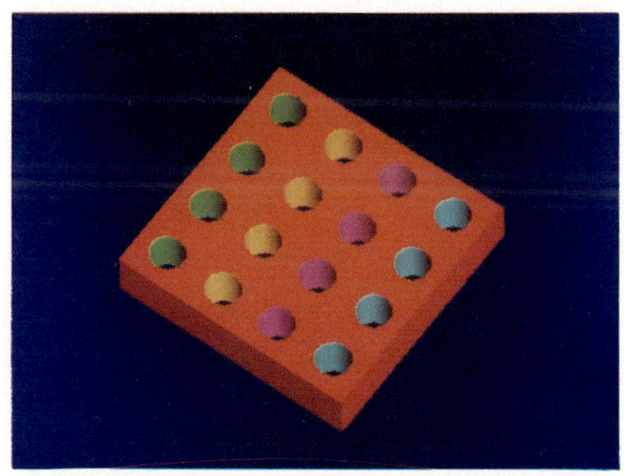

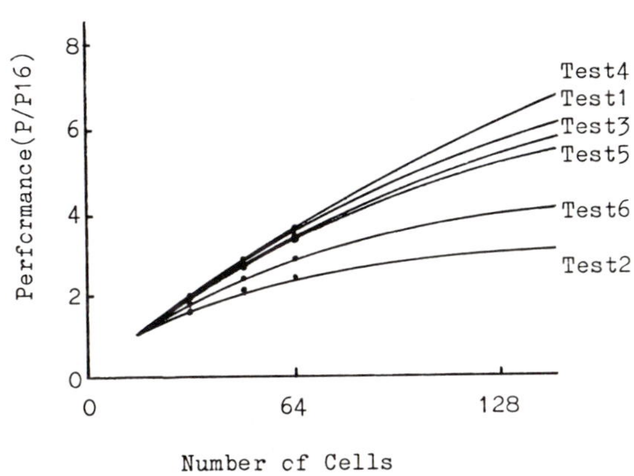

Fig.8 Improvement of Performance by increasing the number of cells

7. Conclusions

The architecture of the Cellular Array Processor (CAP) and the implementation of the CSG hidden surface algorithm have been explained. Our conclusions are as follows:

(1) The changeability of subimage mappings enables various hidden surface algorithms to be easily implemented in CAP. Certain mapping patterns are often effective for evenly distributing calculation load.

(2) Distributing the calculation load by using line mode often compensates for the loss of coherence. Our preliminary experiments showed that the z-buffer algorithm with line mode was more than two times faster than that with block mode in many cases.

(3) The multi-task cell monitor is effective for decreasing the idle time of cells. The slowest cell's idle time was very small in the tests.

(4) Inter-cell communication ports can be used to access to data in neighboring cells. This enables amounts of data exceeding the capacity of one cell to be accommodated in CAP.

(5) If the communication time is relatively large, the system efficiency decreases. The polygonal approximation technique decreases the amount of calculation, but it increases the amount of communication and the amount of data. This worsens the performance of the algorithm. If much more cells are available, a more direct method without polygonal approximation such as ray-casting[15] would be faster.

(6) The status tree technique could be used by ray-casting and ray-tracing algorithms. It is faster than the ray-classification method[15], if the intersection points of the ray are sorted along the ray or the objects are sorted spacially.

(7) The combined CSG hidden surface algorithm is effective for decreasing memory requirements of the program. It is faster than the normal CSG algorithm if the divided submodels are primitives. But, sufficient experimentation has not been done for larger models.

We believe that CAP will be more powerful with upgraded hardware and software. However, there are still many problems remaining for further research.

Acknowledgements

The authors would like to thank Shigeru Sato, Yukihiko Minejima and Takao Uehara for promoting this research project, SIGGRAPH reviewers for suggesting improvements of the paper, and Kouichi Murakami for participating in our discussions and suggesting the idea of the status tree technique.

References

[1] Kaplan, M., and Greenberg, D.P.: "Parallel Processing Techniques for Hidden Surface Removal," ACM Computer Graphics, Vol.13, NO.2(Aug.1979), pp.300-307.

[2] Fiume, E., Fournier, A., and Rudolph, L.: "A Parallel Scan Conversion Algorithm With Anti-Aliasing for a General-Purpose Ultracomputer," ACM Computer Graphics, Vol.17, No.3(Jul.1983), pp.141-150.

[3] Fuchs, H., and Johnson, B.W.: "An Expandable Multiprocessor Architecture for Video Graphics(Preliminary Report)," IEEE 6th conf. on Computer Architecture(1979), pp.58-67.

[4] Parke, F.I.: "Simulation and Expected Performance Analysis of Multi Processor Z-Buffer System," ACM Computer Graphics(Jul.1980), pp.48-56.

[5] Fuchs, H., and Poulton, J.: "Pixel-Planes: A VLSI-Oriented Design for a Raster Graphics Engine," VLSI Design, No.3, 1981, pp.20-28.

[6] Nishimura, H., Ohno, H., Kawata, T., Shirakawa, I., and Omura, K.: "LINKS-1: A Parallel Pipelined Multimicrocomputer System for Image Creation," Proceedings of the 10th Symposium on Computer Architecture, SIGARCH(1983), pp.387-394.

[7] Dippé, M., and Swensen, J.: "An Adaptive Subdivision Algorithm and Parallel Architecture for Realistic Image Synthesis," ACM Computer Graphics, Vol.18, No.3(Jul.1984), pp.149-158.

[8] Niimi, H., Imai, Y., Murakami, M., Tomita, S., and Hagiwara, H.: "A Parallel Processor System for Three-Dimensional Color Graphics," ACM Computer Graphics, Vol.18, No.3(Jul.1984), pp.67-76.

[9] Hoshino, T., Shirakawa, T., Kamimura, T., Kageyama, T., Takenouchi, K., Sekiguchi, T., and Kawai, T.: "Highly Parallel Processor Array 'PAX' for Wide Scientific Applications," International Conference on Parallel Processing IEEE, pp.95-105,(Aug.1983)

[10] Requicha, A.A.G., Voelcker, H.B.: "Solid Modeling: A Historical Summary and Contemporary Assessment," IEEE Computer Graphics and Applications, Vol.2, No.2, Mar. 1982, pp.9-24.

[11] Sutherland, I.E., Sproull, R.F., and Schumacker, R.A.: "A Characterization of Ten Hidden-Surface Algorithms," ACM Computing Surveys, Vol.6, No.1(Mar. 1974), pp.1-55.

[12] Whitted, T.: "An Improved Illumination Model for Shaded Display," Comm., ACM, Vol.23, No.6, 1980, pp.343-349.

[13] Atherton, P.R.: "A Scan-line Hidden Surface Removal Procedure for Constructive Solid Geometry," ACM Computer Graphics, Vol.17, No.3(Jul.1983), pp.73-82.

[14] Crocker, G.A.: "Invisibility Coherence for Faster Scan-line Hidden Surface Algorithms," ACM Computer Graphics, Vol.18, No.3(Jul.1984),pp.95-102.

[15] Roth, S.D.: "Ray Casting for Modeling Solids," Computer Graphics and Image Processing, No.18, 1982, pp.109-144.

[16] Foley, J.D. and Van Dam, A., Fundamentals of Interactive Computer Graphics, Addison-Wesley, 1982.

[17] Murakami, K., Matsumoto, H.: "Ray tracing for CSG representation using status tree technique," 27th Information Processing Conference(Oct.1983), pp.1535-1537 (in Japanese)

[18] Nelson, D. ,L. and Leach, P.,J.: "The Architecture and Applications of the Apollo Domain," IEEE Computer Graphics and Applications, Vol.4, No.4(Apr.1984), pp.58-66

The Drawing Prism: A Versatile Graphic Input Device*

Richard Greene

700-31st Ave., #2
San Francisco, CA 94121

Abstract

Artists using conventional computer graphic input devices cannot produce the same visual effects which they can with traditional tools and media. The drawing prism is a new device which allows people to draw or paint directly into a frame buffer, using brushes, their hands, or a variety of other objects. These objects can be manipulated to achieve continuously adjustable line qualities and textures, in the same ways that artists have traditionally used their hands and tools.

The device uses one face of a large transparent prism as a drawing surface. A video camera views that surface from an angle such that it can only image the points of optical contact between drawing tools and the surface. These images are digitized and processed in real time so as to build up a drawing as the tools are moved along the surface. A layer of transparent liquid helps tools make optical contact with the drawing surface. Any light colored object can thus be used as a drawing tool.

Details of the current implementation are provided along with suggestions for improving its resolution. Combinations of visual effects previously restricted to either traditional media or computer graphics are described and illustrated.

CR Categories and Subject Descriptors:
I.3.6 *Computer Graphics:* Methodology and Techniques—ergonomics, interaction techniques;
I.3.1 *Computer Graphics:* Hardware Architecture—input devices;
J.5 *Arts and Humanities:* Arts, fine and performing;
I.3.3 *Computer Graphics:* Picture/Image Generation—digitizing and scanning;
I.4.9 *Image Processing:* Applications

General Terms: Human Factors, Design, Experimentation.

Additional Keywords and Phrases: drawing prism, gesture sensitive, continuously adjustable, critical angle, keystone correction, real-time image processing, paint systems

*patent pending

1. Introduction

Currently available computer paint systems do not provide the same kinds of user control that many traditional artists' tools and media do. Thus, artists have been prevented from realizing in interactive computer graphics many of the effects which they can easily achieve with those older tools. With a pointed Japanese *sumi* brush, for example, one can draw a line whose width and texture varies continuously, depending on how one holds and moves the brush at any moment. By contrast, most paint programs provide a variety of ''brush'' shapes which cannot change during the drawing process the way that actual brushes do.

Lewis[1] has pointed out that pictures of great textural complexity can be painted much more simply with traditional media, which act as gesture amplifiers, than with standard digital paint programs, which ignore most gestures. His paint program provides a digital medium whose texture generating capabilities rival those of traditional media. However, that does not solve the problem of how to *control* such a texture synthesizer in a manner as powerful as the gesture sensitivity of traditional tools.

Schmandt[2] has demonstrated the feasibility of tracking all six degrees of freedom of a hand-held stylus, for use in a paint program. Minsky[3] described a multi-dimensional input device which was built specifically to be sensitive to some single finger gestures and which implemented a fingerpaint program. However, these devices do not yet provide the same kinds of artistic control as traditional tools. In order to mimic a paintbrush, they would still require the software to simulate, in real time, the behavior of a wet bundle of flexible fibers, bound at only one end to a stylus. Even in such a primal medium as fingerpainting, all ten fingers may come into play, and the ridges and creases of the skin may add an expressive textural element.

Clearly there is a long way to go before conventional input devices will be endowed with the ''feel'' of many traditional artists' tools. The underlying physical systems to be modeled are not simple, nor have they been subject to extensive scientific scrutiny. Even the number of dimensions within which significant aesthetic control may be exercised is often not well defined nor easily disentangled. As has been said of a *sumi* brush, ''Vehicle of the subtle sentiment to be expressed in form, the brush must be so fashioned as to receive and transmit the vibrations of the artist's inner self''[4]

This paper describes the results of an alternative approach[13] to the problem. Rather than attempting to simulate a brush with software, a new hardware device has been developed which allows for the use of *real* brushes to provide immediate computer graphic input. This device, called a *drawing prism*, also allows a variety of other objects to be used as drawing tools. It can even be used directly with the fingers and hands for extremely expressive digital fingerpainting.

2. Principles of operation

The drawing prism is a system for imaging just those portions of objects (such as brushes or fingers) which come into optical contact with a drawing surface. These images are digitized at a high frame rate and combined in real time in a frame buffer. This combination process is such that as the object is drawn along the surface, it leaves behind a trail which can be displayed on a monitor to show all the prior points of contact. This trail within the frame store then constitutes a drawing.

Fig. 1. A single stroke with a pointed brush, using one bit A/D and one drawing color. The brush was moved closer to the drawing surface as the stroke progressed.

If a pointed brush is held so that only the tip is imaged, a fine line may be drawn (Fig. 1, upper left). As the brush is brought closer to the drawing surface, the area of contact increases, and so does the width of the line. Finally, as the brush is brought so close that the fibers separate, each sub-bundle leaves a trail of its own, thereby creating the textures characteristic of brushstrokes (Fig. 1, right).

The operation of the device is based on the *refraction* and *total internal reflection* of light at a dielectric interface. The net optical effect will be familiar to anyone who has looked down through a glass of water and seen just the tips of their fingers, where they touch the outside of the glass. Where the rest of the fingers should be, only some other part of the environment is seen, totally internally reflected in the glass.

The drawing prism system, shown schematically in Fig. 2, uses a large transparent triangular prism as the refracting medium. One face of that prism serves as the drawing surface. A monochrome video camera is mounted so that it views that surface through another face of the prism, which serves only as a window. The angle at which it views the drawing surface (measured from the surface normal) must everywhere exceed the *critical angle*, $\theta_{cr} = \arcsin(n'/n)$, where $n' \approx 1$ is the refactive index of air, and n is the refractive index of the material of the prism[5]. As long as the viewing angle is just greater than θ_{cr} at the closest visible part of the drawing surface (Fig. 2, inset), then this inequality will be satisfied throughout the rest of the camera's field of view.

From this position, the camera's image will consist solely of light which has been totally internally reflected from the drawing surface, so long as nothing but air is in contact with that surface. In current implementations, all that the camera then sees is the reflection of a third, blackened face, so that almost no light enters the camera's lens. Even brightly illuminated objects above and quite near to the drawing surface will remain invisible to the camera. This is because as their light enters the prism from the air, it is refracted at the drawing surface to some angle *less* than θ_{cr}, so it cannot reach the camera (Fig 3a).

However, if an object is brought into such close contact with the drawing surface that no layer of air remains between the object and the prism, then light from the object does not have to cross an air/prism interface in order to enter the prism. Some of that light will then be refracted just enough to enter the camera (Fig. 3b). Thus only the points of optical contact will be imaged.

The complete local elimination of the layer of air is greatly facilitated by using a layer of transparent liquid on the drawing surface. This can range from a barely perceptible film of oil to a shallow tray of water, depending on the objects used as drawing tools and the effects desired. For brush painting, the drawing surface can be left dry initially, and instead the brush itself is loaded with water or oil. This has the side effect of giving brushes much the same handling characteristics as if they were loaded with watercolors or oil paints.

The primary drawback of this optical approach is that the video camera must view the drawing surface obliquely in order to satisfy the limitation imposed by the critical angle. For typical transparent materials, with a refractive index of about 1.5, the critical angle is about 42°. The result is that the image of the

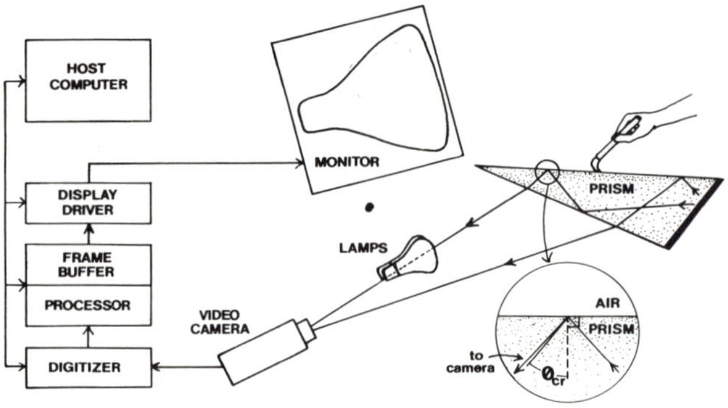

Fig. 2. The drawing prism system.

drawing surface is (approximately) a perspective projection instead of an undistorted, orthogonal projection. In other words, the image is subject to *keystone* distortion.

In CRT-type video cameras, this distortion can be corrected electronically by modifying the shape of the raster scan. It should also be possible to provide keystone correction optically, using special purpose lenses. Another alternative is to simply leave the image uncorrected, or only partially corrected. For many purposes some distortion may be acceptable.

In order to provide input to a computer, the video signal must first be processed. The most basic drawing function can be implemented by just comparing the video level to a threshold and then writing into the frame buffer only at those pixels where the threshold is exceeded. In the simplest case of a frame buffer with only one bit per pixel, this is equivalent to writing at each pixel the inclusive OR of the incoming thresholded video data and the data already stored at that pixel. This ensures that those portions of the video signal representing the dark background will not write over data showing the previous locations of a drawing tool. A picture can thus be built up in the frame buffer, and it will stay there until the buffer is intentionally cleared.

Of course, a variety of alternative processes may be applied to the video signal, beginning with multiple-bit A/D conversion and including summation and averaging. In any case, the image in the frame buffer can be continuously displayed on a monitor just behind and above the prism (Fig. 2). Thus the device is like a digitizing tablet in that the user obtains visual feedback from a screen which is separate from the drawing surface. All the processing must be completed quickly if this feedback is to be provided in time for truly interactive use. Furthermore, the digitizer must operate at a high frame rate in order to keep up wih fast moving objects. Thus for most practical purposes, a *real-time* video image digitizer/processor is required for the use of the drawing prism.

Since the camera and the user view the drawing surface from opposite sides, the camera's image must be reversed sometime prior to ultimate display. This can be accomplished either with a mirror or by reversing the camera's scanning direction.

3. Implementation

Prisms with a useful drawing surface of about 16" x 20" can be constructed inexpensively by using a hollow plexiglass shell filled with mineral oil. For any size drawing prism, the size of the active drawing area can always be reduced from the maximum allowable by simply moving the camera closer or increasing the focal length of its lens (ie. by zooming in). Current implementations use video cameras with "normal", 16 mm lenses, at a viewing distance of about three feet, for an active drawing area of about 12" x 16". While the smallest possible package is often desired, there are several problems associated with getting the camera very close to the prism.

In the first place, a short viewing distance and large drawing area requires a wide-angle lens. Even with an ideal lens, the amount of keystone distortion is directly related to the angular field of view, and wide-angle lenses often add barrel distortion on top of that. Furthermore, pincushion distortion, which also increases with increasing angular view, is introduced because the camera views the drawing surface through a window into the prism which is planar[6]. This last effect could be avoided by replacing the flat window with a concave one or by embedding the camera's lens within the prism itself.

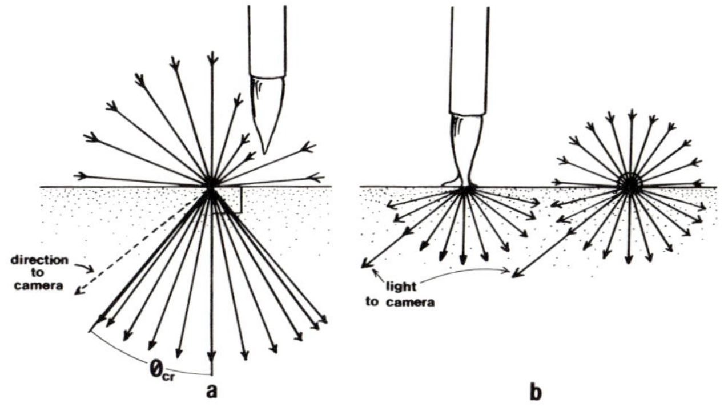

Fig. 3. Refraction of light at the drawing surface, from the air (a) or from objects in contact with that surface (b).

Close viewing distances also pose a depth-of-field problem. Because of the camera's oblique view of the drawing surface, some parts of it are located farther away than other parts. If this difference amounts to a significant fraction of the camera's average viewing distance, it may be difficult to keep drawing tools in focus everywhere on the drawing surface. If enough illumination can be provided, depth of field can always be improved by stopping down the lens.

Current implementations are meant to be used with white or lightly colored drawing tools. Hence, those portions of the prism seen by the camera in internal reflection are all opaque black. It is also possible to use dark objects as drawing tools with a different prism which provides a diffuse *white* background. By simply inverting the video signal, the same processor can then be used. However, in video cameras subject to image lag or persistence, the signal generated by a light going off may have a much longer time constant than that which results from a light going on. Thus, bright objects against a dark background provide the most responsive tools for high speed drawing with such cameras.

The strongest signal is obtained by maximizing the contrast between the drawing tool and the background. Since most tools are not themselves sources of light, they must be illuminated such that light is reflected, transmitted, or scattered into the camera. This must be accomplished in a way which avoids illuminating the black side of the prism, which serves as background.

The most successful lighting scheme to date uses two reflector spot lamps mounted to either side of the camera (Fig. 2). These direct their light up at the drawing surface from below. Care must be taken to prevent the camera from seeing stray reflections off that face of the prism which serves as a window. A delicate balance must also be struck between trying to illuminate the drawing surface evenly and keeping glare out of users' eyes.

Keystone correction has been implemented electronically (with a few percent distortion remaining) in both Sony and RCA vidicon video cameras, using specially designed circuits. The shape of the raster has been changed in the following three ways:

1. The vertical size is reduced enough to make up for image foreshortening. This can usually be accomplished by means of existing internal camera controls.
2. The vertical spacing between scan lines is made to decrease as the vertical sweep progresses, ie. as the image of more distant parts of the drawing is scanned. This is achieved by making the vertical deflection ramp non-linear.
3. The horizontal width also decreases as the vertical sweep progresses. Ideally the horizontal width is made a linear function of the vertical deflection.

With these changes, the electron beam then scans a trapezoidal pattern which corresponds to a perspective projection of its original rectangular raster. When the optical image being scanned is itself such a projection, as in the drawing prism system, then an undistorted video image is the net result.

The only other change in the camera has been to reverse the leads to the horizontal deflection yoke, in order to reverse the image.

Since the drawing function requires relatively simple processing, but must be executed in real time, hardware specially designed to accomplish this function is considerably less expensive than a general-purpose machine with the same capability. So far, the drawing prism has been interfaced with two such special-purpose processors. The first consists of hardwired logic along with a modified Dithertizer II video digitizer, for use with the Apple II+. The device allows for drawing in either black or white into the Apple's own frame buffers, with a resolution of 192 x 280 x 1 bit at 60 frames/sec.

Fig. 4. *Decision Tree*—drawn with a stylus of white rubber, using one bit A/D and one drawing color.

The other machine with which the drawing prism has been used (Figs. 1 & 4-18) is a real- time image processor/buffer designed by Ed Tannenbaum. It can digitize and process frames with a resolution of 240 x 256 x 4 bits at 60 frames/sec. Analog video input can be converted to either one or four bits of digital data, and color lookup tables provide twelve bits of analog RGB output. This processor was actually not originally designed to produce static images. Its main use has been in conjunction with dance and other movements, for performance[7] and public installations[8].

4. Applications

Generally speaking, the drawing prism may be fruitfully applied in situations where one wants to combine the visual effects peculiar to traditional graphic media— interactively and in real time—with those of computer graphics.

Besides brushes and body parts, which have already been mentioned, the prism allows one to paint with palette knives, textured papers and textiles, and sponges. A white rubber stylus produces a line much like an artist's flexible quill, in which the width increases with pressure (Fig. 4). A crayon or grease pencil can be used to draw a picture on the drawing surface which remains displayable until it is physically removed with a cloth, even after the display is electronically cleared. An object with a pattern printed on it can be wet and held against the drawing surface to digitize that pattern.

The effects obtainable with any given tool are also highly dependent on the size of the camera's field of view. By dollying the camera in or out, a single brush can be made to appear large or small. Of course hand movements will be magnified or de-magnified at the same time.

Drops of water on the drawing surface can refract ambient light towards the camera (Fig. 3b), because of their curvature. Thus droplets splattered or sprayed onto that surface show up in the picture, just like drops of paint (Fig. 15). If the drawing surface is inclined, then even the effect of dripping paint (so beloved by children) can be reproduced. Often these effects are not desired, and they can be minimized by adding a surfactant to the water, so that it beads up less. For the brush paintings shown here, a weak detergent solution was therefore used. For fingerpainting, a film of mineral oil is preferred, since it does not bead up or dry up and provides excellent lubrication.

It is possible to use the drawing prism with a stylus which has a tip of hard rubber, for drawing fine lines of constant width. With the hardware and software to extract the X,Y coordinates of bright points within the camera's view, it should therefore be possible to use the system much like conventional graphic input and pointing devices. However, the drawing prism is really used to best advantage with tools which provide continuously adjustable line qualities and textures.

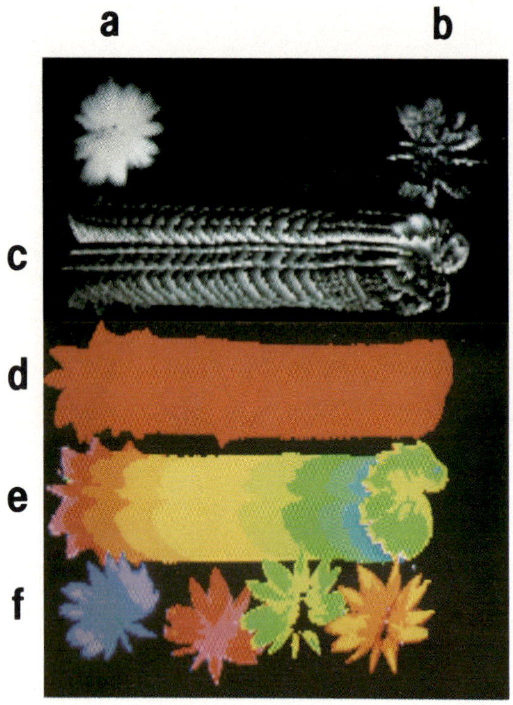

Fig. 5. The basic effects obtainable with a splayed brush. Two different color maps were used in this composite picture.

Figures 5, 6, 8, and 9 show some of the basic effects which can be achieved with a brush or the hand. The instantaneous "footprint" of a splayed brush is shown with four bits of A/D and true (monochrome) coloring in Fig. 5a. When the drawing function is on and the brush is lifted, smaller darker images are superimposed on the footprint (Fig. 5b). A single brushstroke consists then of a whole series of these footprints (Fig. 5c), laid partially on top of each other at the rate of 60 Hz. Figure 8 shows the same effects, but using the bottom of the fist as the only drawing "tool"

The texture formed in this way has a frequency which is inversely proportional to the drawing speed. Thus one can count these striations like tree rings (each ring ≈ 17 msec), and so verify, for example, that Fig. 6 was executed within a few seconds. Note that the shading on the object which serves as drawing tool is exposed or obscured by each successive image in a regular way. This often lends a three-dimensional effect, suggestive of an extrusion or a bas-relief or of thickly applied oils (Figs. 7, 10, 11, 13, & 17). The exact nature of the effect is highly dependent on the color map, the drawing speed, and the natural shapes and textures of the drawing tools employed.

By using only a single bit of video digitization and a single drawing color, it is possible to work with a homogeneous paint (Fig. 5d). By rotating through a series of drawing colors, another texture is generated (Fig. 5e). In this case the texture frequency depends on how often the drawing color is changed (every third frame for Fig. 5e), as well as the drawing speed. Dabs of the brush with this function employed tend to look like flowers (Figs. 5f & 12).

Here one can begin to see the main advantage of gesture sensitive drawing tools. Dabbing a brush is as simple as rubber-stamping an image with a standard paint program. However, the brush dabs exhibit a natural variation which a paint program would be hard pressed to simulate. This is due to the semi-random movements of the fibers of the brush as well as changes in the angle at which it is held, how fast it is moved, how wet it is, and so on. It is possible for users to learn more complex brushstroke gestures which can still be executed rapidly and repeatedly, subject to this same kind of variability. The underlying orderliness of the patterns so formed is highly reminiscent of

Fig. 6. A single stroke of a splayed brush, using four bits A/D. The brush was twisted during the course of the stroke.

Fig. 7. *Golden Sea*—drawn with a few twisted brushstrokes, and four bits A/D.

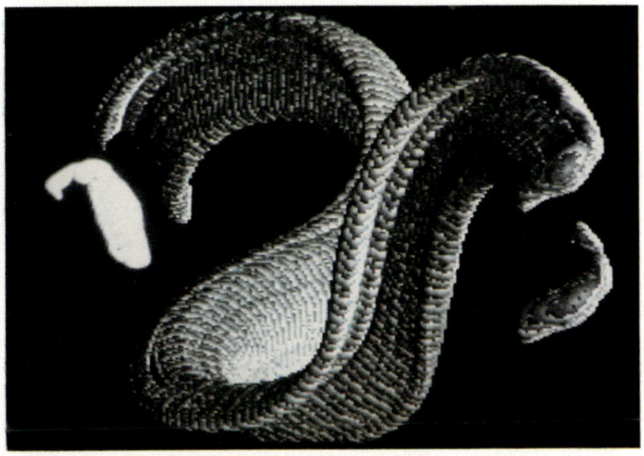

Fig. 8. The digitized image of the bottom of a fist, along with a stroke and a dab of that fist (with four bits A/D and true greyscale coloring).

the quasi-regular patterns found in nature. The brush is thus an excellent tool for representing such natural patterns quickly, spontaneously, and expressively.

In Fig. 12, the leaves and stems were drawn with strokes of the same splayed brush that was dabbed to produce the flowers. In Fig. 13 each leaf was generated by a single stroke of a thick brush. By counting the separate images in each leaf, it can be seen that each one was executed in roughly 0.1 sec (about six images per leaf). The branches were drawn with a long thin brush, with the drawing color changing at 30 Hz. A splayed brush was used to paint whole clusters of leaves in Fig. 14, by dabbing the brush on its side.

Users report that the device has a sensuousness which they had not previously associated with computer paint systems. Paintings have been created within a few minutes (Figs. 11 & 15-17) which the painter could not have realized in any amount of time with either traditional tools or modern computers alone. Perhaps the greatest utility of the device for artists lies in the fact that new and unexpected effects can always be discovered through spontaneous interaction with a variety of tools, and these may then be consciously re-applied.

The device may also prove useful for digital typography and calligraphy. Although one usually associates brush-drawn calligraphy with Oriental scripts, it is often employed in Western graphic design as well. Catich[9] makes a good case that the serifs and subtle line-width variations of monumental Roman capital letters (which Renaissance artists sought endlessly to duplicate with intricate geometric constructions) are really just artifacts of fast lettering with a flat brush. There may be a metaphor here for the computer graphic designer of today. In any event, variously shaped styli can also be used, to mimic the effects of lettering pens. Calligraphers can rest their hands on a black piece of paper, to prevent accidental fingerpainting.

The device is also well suited to interactive public installations (Fig. 18), since little or no learning is required for its basic operation. Children can fingerpaint with soapy water just as they would use real fingerpaints. Although they may miss the associated mess, they also find exciting new visual effects available. Adults too find the drawing prism a very natural and comfortable way to begin doing computer graphics.

The last major area of application worth noting is in the production of real-time special effects. The simplest example is the effect of a painting coming into being, which can be videotaped and played back without any visible painter in the way. Additional processes can also be applied, for real-time animation effects. By gradually dissolving (Fig. 15) or fading the image away—continually, as it is painted—the painting can remain in a perpetual state of becoming. The end product (if any) of such a process is a tape or a performance, rather than a single picture. Whitney[10] pioneered the exploration of such effects over thirty years ago, by aiming a movie camera at a tray of opaque oil with a light under it. He would then draw in the oil with his finger or a stylus, in time to music.

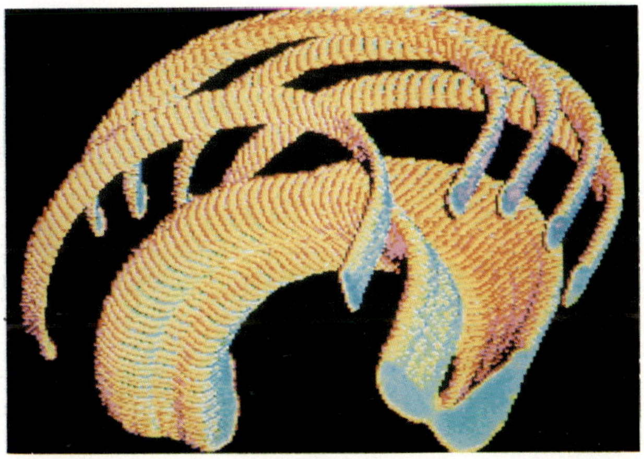

Fig. 9. *Digital Painting with Five Digits*—a stroke of the palm and fingers with four bits A/D. The picture was frozen before lifting up the hand at the end of the stroke.

Fig. 10. A snake of indeterminate species, drawn largely with a single stroke of the hand (and four bits A/D). A rubber stylus (and one bit A/D) was used for the tongue.

Fig. 11. *Byway to Muir Beach*—a fingerpainting, with four bits A/D. Note the family resemblance to the snake of Fig. 10.

5. Future directions

A resolution greater than 240 x 256 will obviously be necessary for serious graphic work with the drawing prism. However, it is not so obvious how one is to obtain sufficiently high spatial resolution without sacrificing temporal resolution. A frame rate of 60 Hz has only been achieved here by mapping both fields from an interlaced video camera to the same memory locations. Faster cameras, digitizers, and processors would all be necessary to extend the current methods by brute force. Alternative strategies may therefore be helpful

In the spatial domain, one should be able to improve the *perceived* resolution by means of *real-time antialiasing*. The (multiple-bit) digitized image of a drawing tool is already low-pass filtered by virtue of the optics and electronics of the video camera. Note the smooth shading in the images of the brush in Fig. 5a and the hand in Fig. 8. It should only be necessary for the processor to preserve this shading in implementing the drawing function.

This could be accomplished, at least for drawing on a single background color, by writing new data to a pixel if and only if the incoming video data is *greater than* that already stored there. Thus the dark edges of one image wouldn't obscure the bright center of a previous one, and the texture seen here would be eliminated. Instead, lines would have a nearly uniform center and an antialiased outline (assuming the color map contained the appropriate gradient from foreground to background color). This effect is already happening, to the extent that the texture can be ignored, as in the fine lines at the top left of Fig. 6.

The problem can also be attacked in the temporal domain. One should note first that even 60 frames/sec are not really enough to capture quick drawing movements. This undersampling is the cause of the breakup in some brush-strokes (as the leaves in Figs. 12 & 13), hand strokes (the "rattle" in Fig. 10), and in the fine lines drawn with a stylus (Fig. 4). The problem is most severe for small tools, since they provide the least overlap of successive images. While this may sometimes add a pleasant "dry-brush" texture, it is more often an undesirable limit on drawing speed.

This is analogous to the problem of temporal aliasing in motion pictures, and it may be soluble in a manner analogous to motion blur. Instead of trying to increase the sampling rate (at the expense of faster processors as well), it may be possible to have the camera itself continuously perform the drawing function. Thus the camera would act as an analog pre-processor, effectively keeping its "shutter" open between frames. The frame rate would then only have to be fast enough to provide real-time user feedback (about 30 frames/sec).

This possibility exists because the drawing function can be implemented as a simple time integral of the image intensity, and many video cameras already perform this function to some degree. It is referred to as lag and is generally regarded as an undesirabe artifact. In vidicon cameras, it can be increased by increasing the target voltage[11], but not enough to completely bridge the gap between frames. Camera tubes with higher persistence phosphors might offer an improvement, but solid-state cameras may be even better suited to this kind of on-board processing.

One preliminary experiment has been performed with a digital camera which uses a 64K dynamic RAM with a quartz lid as the image sensor[12]. In this device, the photosensitive memory cells must be preset to a high logic level before they can detect light. Those in the dark remain at that level, while those exposed to a super-threshold quantity of light (integrated over the exposure time) are discharged to a low level, where they then remain. In order to make the device act like an ordinary video camera, all of the cells must be periodically reset, as soon as they have been read for each frame. Thus in order to implement the drawing function, it is only necessary to prevent this resetting from happening. This can be achieved simply by holding the RAM's READ/$\overline{\text{WRITE}}$ line high. The RAM will then contain a displayable record of all the cells ever exposed to light, at any time during the drawing process. To start a new drawing, one simply allows the READ/$\overline{\text{WRITE}}$ line to go low long enough for a reset.

While this camera/integrator only produces low-resolution binary images at a low frame rate, it does demonstrate the feasibility of combining the functions of image detector, real-time processor, digitizer, and even frame buffer, on a single chip. It should be possible to perform the continuous drawing function with multiple bits of precision using CCD or other technology, possibly with simultaneous spatial antialiasing. It should also be possible to include keystone correction (for a single angular field of view) by laying out the photosensitive elements in the appropriately transformed grid.

6. Conclusions

Until now, the only way to incorporate a real brushstroke in a computer graphic was to digitize a brushstroke that had been painted on some material with pigments or dyes. This device allows ordinary artists' brushes to be used immediately and interactively with a computer paint system, without spilling any physical paint.

The drawing prism allows not only for the reproduction of some traditional effects on the computer, but also for the creation of new visual effects which result from the combination of traditional tools and techniques with non-traditional digital processing. The fact that virtually any object can serve as a drawing tool means that new effects will continually be discovered. It would also be desirable to have the hardware provide input to software which modeled parts of the painting process not addressed here, such as that described by Lewis[1] for simulating drawing surface textures.

Although the device only digitizes two-dimensional images, the use of three-dimensional objects as drawing tools provides extreme sensitivity to small hand movements in a multitude of dimensions. This is particularly true when the only drawing "tools" used are the fingers and hands themselves. Thus the drawing prism allows for the efficient production of expressive images which would be difficult or impossible to duplicate with conventional input devices.

Fig. 12. These flowers and leaves were painted with a splayed brush using one bit A/D and a rotating drawing color.

7. Acknowledgements

I would like to thank Ed Tannenbaum, without whose advice and inspiration the development of the drawing prism would not have been possible. I would also like to thank the staff of the Exploratorium, particularly Larry Shaw and Dr. Frank Oppenheimer*, director, for their kind provision of facilities to aid in that development.

Fig. 13. *Unconditional Branch.* These leaves were drawn with a thick brush and four bits A/D. The branches were drawn with a thin brush, one bit A/D, and a rotating drawing color.

8. References

1. Lewis, John Peter. Texture Synthesis for Digital Painting. *Computer Graphics* Vol. 18, No. 3 (1984), pp. 245-252.

2. Scmandt, Christopher. Spatial Input/Display Correspondence in a Stereoscopic Computer Graphic Workstation. *Computer Graphics* Vol. 17, No. 3 (1983), pp. 253-257.

3. Minsky, Margaret R. Manipulating Simulated Objects with Real-world Gestures using a Force and Positiun Sensitive Screen. *Computer Graphics* Vol. 18, No. 3 (1984), pp. 195-203.

4. Bowie, Henry P. *On the Laws of Japanese Painting*. Dover Publications, New York, NY, 1952, p.34 (originally published by P. Elder, San Francisco, CA, 1911).

5. Sears, Francis. *Optics*. Addison-Wesley Press, Cambridge, MA, 1949, pp. 43-44.

6. Heckbert, Paul S. and Hanrahan, Pat. Beam Tracing Polygonal Objects. *Computer Graphics* Vol.18, No. 3 (1984), pp. 119-127. See their Figure 4.

7. Javril, Marci, Tannenbaum, Ed, Greene, Richard and Schier, Jeff. Technological Feets. *Siggraph '84 Electronic Theater*, live performance, catalog p. 14 and back cover photo.

8. Tannenbaum, Ed. Recollections. *Exploratorium,* San Francisco, CA, permanent exhibit, installed 1982.

9. Catich, Edward M. *The Origin of the Serif.* Catfish Press, Davenport, Iowa, 1968.

10. Whitney, John. *Digital Harmony*. McGraw-Hill, Peterborough, NH, 1980, pp. 177, 216-217, & 225.

11. *Service Manual, TC 2000 Series CCTV Cameras.* RCA Corporation, Lancaster, PA, 1981, pp. 2 & 29.

Fig. 14. This painting was all done using one bit A/D and rotation of the drawing color.

*I would like to dedicate this paper to the memory of Frank Oppenheimer, who died on Feb. 3, 1985.

Fig. 15. *Waves*—a brush painting using one bit A/D and color rotation. Splattered water drops caused the streaks and some of the dots at the top of the picture. The mesh-like texture in the background at left was caused by an adjustable dissolve function of the Tannenbaum processor.

Fig. 16. *Homage à Roger Dean*—a fingerpainting using one bit A/D and color rotation.

Fig. 17. *Caves*—a fingerpainting using one bit A/D and color rotation for the background, and four bits A/D for the foreground. A mirror symmetry function of the processor was also employed.

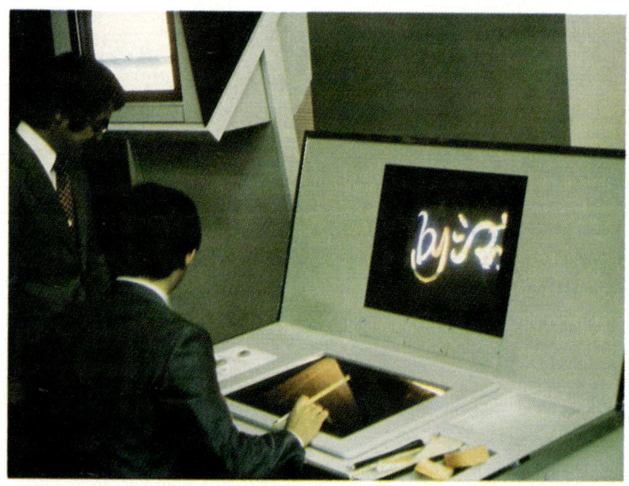

Fig. 18. A drawing prism system is currently being exhibited under the name ''Computer Calligraphics'' in the IBM-sponsored ''Think Pocket'' show in Tokyo, Japan, where it is available for public use.

12. Ciarcia, Steve. Build the Micro D-Cam Solid-State Video Camera. *Byte* Vol. 8, No. 9 (1983), pp. 20-31.

13. Recent communication from the U. S. Patent Office indicates that Robert E. Mueller was awarded patent #3,846,826 on Nov. 5, 1974 for a ''Direct Television Drawing and Image Manipulating System''. It uses an internally reflecting prism to accept graphic input from brushes, fingers, and other objects. Mueller used a flying-spot scanner and photomultiplier instead of a camera, and his device has a different geometry from that described here, but it is based on the same optical principles.

FAST SPHERES, SHADOWS, TEXTURES, TRANSPARENCIES, and IMAGE ENHANCEMENTS IN PIXEL-PLANES *

Henry Fuchs, Jack Goldfeather†, Jeff P. Hultquist, Susan Spach‡
John D. Austin, Frederick P. Brooks, Jr., John G. Eyles, and John Poulton

Department of Computer Science
University of North Carolina at Chapel Hill
Chapel Hill, NC 27514

ABSTRACT: Pixel-planes is a logic-enhanced memory system for raster graphics and imaging. Although each pixel-memory is enhanced with a one-bit ALU, the system's real power comes from a tree of one-bit adders that can evaluate linear expressions $Ax + By + C$ for every pixel (x, y) simultaneously, as fast as the ALUs and the memory circuits can accept the results. We and others have begun to develop a variety of algorithms that exploit this fast linear expression evaluation capability. In this paper we report some of those results. Illustrated in this paper is a sample image from a small working prototype of the Pixel-planes hardware and a variety of images from simulations of a full-scale system. Timing estimates indicate that 30,000 smooth shaded triangles can be generated per second, or 21,000 smooth-shaded and shadowed triangles can be generated per second, or over 25,000 shaded spheres can be generated per second. Image-enhancement by adaptive histogram equalization can be performed within 4 seconds on a 512×512 image.

* This research supported in part by the Defense Advance Research Project Agency, monitored by the U.S. Army Research Office, Research Triangle Park, NC, under contract number DAAG29-83-K-0148 and the National Science Foundation Grant number ECS-8300970.

† Department of Mathematics, Carleton College, Northfield, MN, on sabbatical at Department of Mathematics at University of North Carolina at Chapel Hill

‡ Now at Hewlett-Packard Labs, Palo Alto, CA

1. INTRODUCTION

The Pixel-planes development grew out of earlier designs for speeding up raster image generation [Fuchs 1977; Johnson 1979]. An enhanced design is described in [Clark 1980]. In these designs, the task of generating pixels is distributed between several dozen processors. Even when we were designing these systems, we realized that the bottleneck in raster image generation was "pushing pixels," since bottlenecks earlier in the image generation pipeline could be eliminated by fast arithmetic hardware. Two present examples are the Weitek multiplier chips [Weitek] and a custom "geometry engine" chip [Clark 1982]. The limitation of these earlier systems that we sought to overcome with Pixel-planes was that once the number of processors increases to one per memory chip, the bottleneck becomes data movement into the chip. Even if the processor were much faster than the memory chip, in any one memory cycle, only one address-data pair can be put into the chip. Pixel-planes attempts to overcome this limitation by putting computation logic right onto the memory chip, with an entire tree of processing circuits generating many pixels's worth of data in each memory cycle.

Central to the design is an array of logic-enhanced memory chips that form the frame buffer. These chips not only store the scanned-out image but also perform the pixel-level calculations of area-definition, visibility calculation and pixel painting. Recently, various individuals have devised other algorithms for the Pixel-planes engine—for computing shadows, sphere displays, and even image processing tasks. It is increasingly evident that the structure of the machine has greater generality and applicability than first imagined.

Although to many first-time observers Pixel-planes appears to be a variant of the parallel processor with a processor at every pixel, its power and speed come more from the binary tree of one-bit adders that efficiently compute a linear expression in x and y for every pixel in the entire system. Given coefficients A, B, and C, the two multiplier trees and a one-bit adder at each pixel compute $F(x, y) = Ax + By + C$ in bit-sequential order for each (x, y) on the screen (see figure 1). If this expression had to be calculated at each pixel with only the one-bit pixel processor alone, the system would take 20 times as long to complete the calculation!

For efficiency in the actual chip layout, the two multiplier trees have been merged into a single tree and that tree compressed into a single column. Thus, the system contains a unified multiplier tree, a one-bit ALU at each pixel, a one-bit Enable register (controlling write operations of that pixel), and 32 bits of memory (72 bits in the Pxpl4 implementation now being built). Figure 2 illustrates the organization that is used on the actual memory chips.

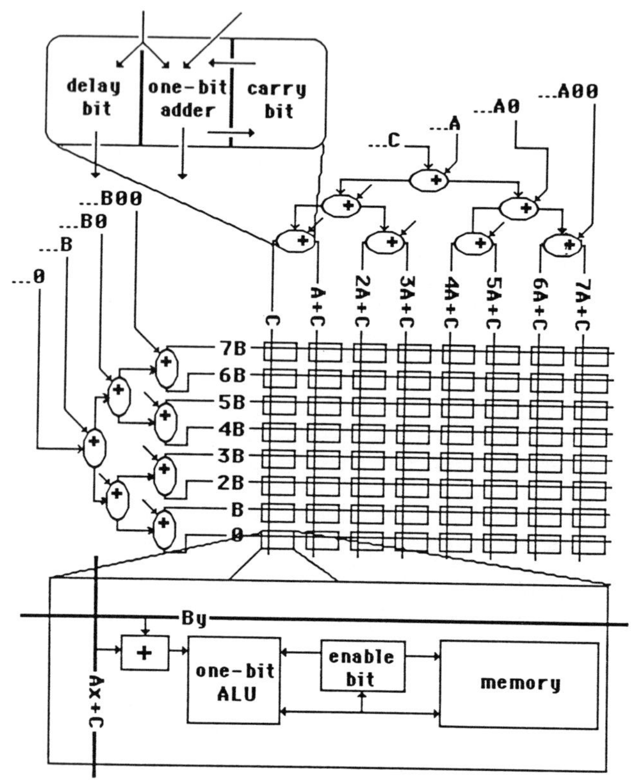

Fig. 1: Conceptual design of an 8×8 Pixel-Planes chip.

The system is driven by a transformation engine, which sends vertices of the database to the ***translator***. This board converts this data to a series on linear equations which describe the location of each polygon in screen space. Each linear equation, together with an opcode, is passed to the ***image generation controller***, which activates the control lines on the frame buffer chips (see figure 3). Figure 4 shows our latest small working prototype with the color image being generated by six Pxpl3 chips.

Details of the hardware design and the implementation are in [Paeth 1982] and in [Poulton 1985]. The latter of these papers outlines architectural enhancements that may increase the speed of the system by a factor of 5. In the future, we hope to integrate the Pixel-planes architecture with a silicon-based flat-screen display, so that the display itself will handle the display computations [Shiffman 1984; Vuillemier 1984].

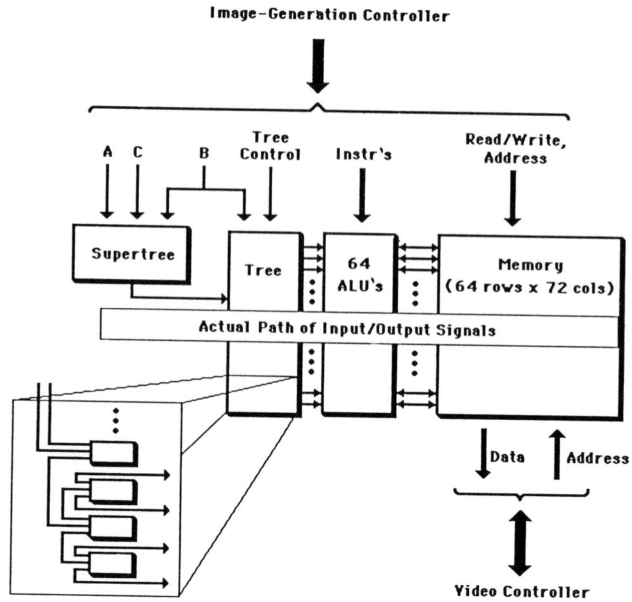

Fig. 2: Floor plan of Pixel-Planes 4 chip.

2. ALGORITHMS IN PIXEL-PLANES

As explained above, the major feature of Pixel-planes is its ability to evaluate, in parallel, expressions of the form $Ax + By + C$, where (x, y) is the address of a pixel. The controller broadcasts A, B, and C, and the expression $Ax + By + C$ is evaluated and then compared and/or combined with information already stored in the memory in each pixel cell. The memory at each pixel can be allocated in any convenient way. A typical allocation might be:

1) buffers for storage of certain key values (e.g., a ZMIN buffer for depth storage, and RED, GREEN, and BLUE buffers for color intensity values)
2) several one-bit flags which are used to enable or disable pixels (via the Enable register) during various stages of processing.

The timing analyses apply to the Pxpl memories and scanout. They assume image generating pipeline modules before them—the geometric transformation unit, the translator, and the controller—operate fast enough to keep up with the Pxpl memories.

2.1 CONVEX POLYGONS

The display of objects made up of polygons is accomplished in three steps: scan conversion of the polygons, visibility relative to previously processed polygons, and shading.

2.1.1 Scan Conversion. The object of this step is to determine those pixels which lie inside a convex polygon. Initially, all Enable registers are set to 1. Each edge of the polygon is defined by two vertices, $v_1 = (x_1, y_1)$ and $v_2 = (x_2, y_2)$, which are ordered so that the polygon lies on the left of the directed edge $v_1 v_2$. Then the equation of the edge is $Ax + By + C = 0$, where $A = y_1 - y_2$, $B = x_2 - x_1$, and $C = x_1 y_2 - x_2 y_1$. Furthermore, $f(x, y) = Ax + By + C$ is positive if and only if (x, y) lies on the same side of the edge as the polygon. The translator computes A, B, and C, and these coefficients are then broadcast to Pixel-planes. A negative $f(x, y)$ causes the Enable register for (x, y) to be set to 0; otherwise the Enable register is unchanged. A pixel is inside the polygon if and only if its Enable register remains 1 after all edges have been broadcast.

2.1.2 Visibility. Once scan conversion has been performed, final visibility of each polygon is determined by a comparison of z values at each pixel. The translator first computes the plane equation, $z = Ax + By + C$, as follows:

Step 1: The plane equation in eye space has the form:

$$A'x_e + B'y_e + C'z_e + D' = 0. \qquad (1)$$

The first 3 coefficients, which form the normal to the plane, are found by computing the cross product of the two vectors determined by the first three vertices of the polygon. Alternatively, an object space normal can be part of the polygon data structure and transformed appropriately to produce an eye space normal. Assuming that (x_0, y_0, z_0) is a vertex, the last coefficient is given by:

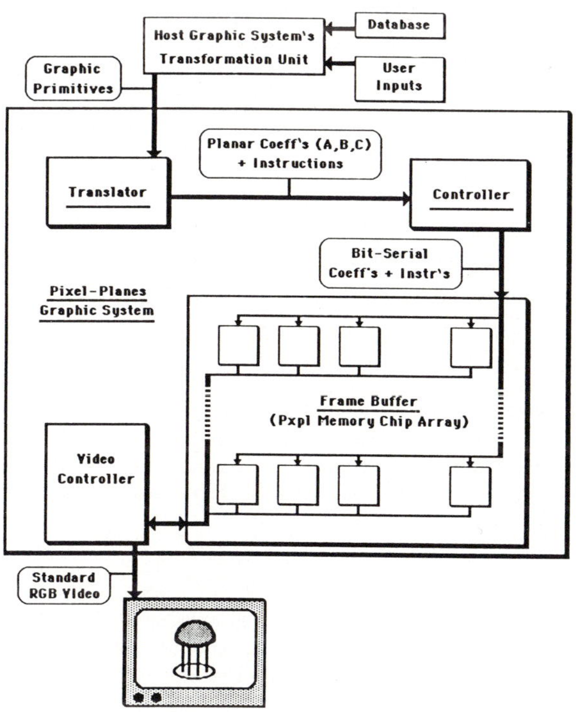

Fig. 3: Logical overview of a 3D graphics system using Pixel-Planes image buffer memory chips.

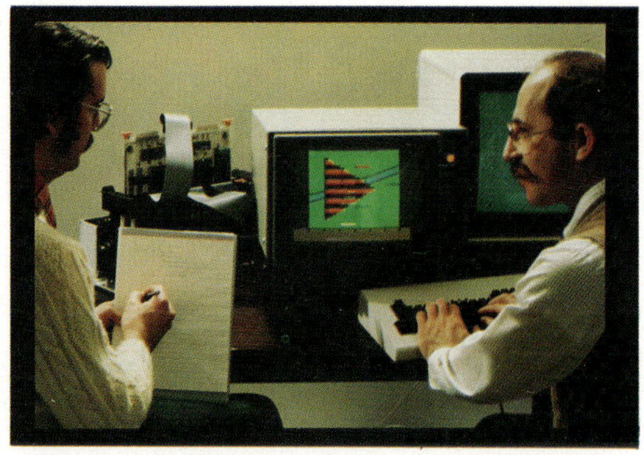

Fig. 4: Pixel-Planes 3 System. John Poulton (left) and Henry Fuchs and the working Pixel-Planes 3 prototype. (photo by Jerry Markatos)

$$D' = -A'x_o - B'y_o - C'z_o \qquad (2)$$

Step 2: Using the transformation equations:

$$\begin{aligned} x_e &= (-x - k_1)/(z'r_1), \\ y_e &= (-y - k_2)/(z'r_2), \text{ and} \\ z_e &= -1/z' \end{aligned} \qquad (3)$$

where r_1, r_2, k_1, k_2 are constants related to the screen resolution and the location of the screen origin, we can transform (1) to screen space and still retain the form:

$$z' = A'x + B'y + C' \qquad (4)$$

Step 3: Given that n bits are reserved for the ZMIN buffer, and that the minimum and maximum z values z_1, z_2, for the object to be displayed are known, we can rescale the equation so that $0 \leq z \leq 2^n - 1$ by replacing z' by:

$$z = (2^n - 1)(z' - z_1)/(z_2 - z_1) \qquad (5)$$

Combining this with (4) we can write z in the form $z = Ax + By + C$. The visible pixels are then determined by using the standard Z-buffer algorithm [Sutherland 1974] at each pixel simultaneously. The controller broadcasts the plane equation of the current polygon, $z = f(x, y) = Ax + By + C$. Each pixel whose Enable bit is still 1 compares its $f(x, y)$ to the value in its ZMIN buffer. The pixel is visible if and only if $f(x, y) < ZMIN$, so pixels with $f(x, y) \geq ZMIN$ set their Enable bits to 0. The controller rebroadcasts A, B, and C so that the still-enabled pixels can store their new ZMIN values.

2.1.3 Shading. To determine the proper color for each pixel, the controller broadcasts 3 sets of coefficients, one for each primary color component. For flat shading, $A = B = 0$ and $C = color$. A smooth shading effect similar to Gouraud shading [Gouraud 1971], created by linearly interpolating the colors at the vertices of the polygon, can also be achieved.

Fig. 5: The Chapel Hill "Old Well" rendered by a Pixel-Planes functional simulator with input of 357 polygons. Estimated image generation time (assuming a 10Mhz clock) is 9 msec.

Fig. 6: "Old Well" with shadows (simulation). Estimated time: 13.8 msec.

For example, suppose the polygon has 3 vertices (x_1, y_1), (x_2, y_2), and (x_3, y_3) with red components R_1, R_2, R_3. Geometrically, one can visualize linear interpolation of the red component at (x, y) as selecting the third component of the point (x, y, R) that lies on the plane passing through (x_1, y_1, R_1), (x_2, y_2, R_2), and (x_3, y_3, R_3) in xyR-space. The translator computes the equation of this plane as follows:

Step 1: The vector equation

$$\begin{aligned}(x, y) = s(x_2 - x_1, y_2 - y_1) \\ + t(x_3 - x_1, y_3 - y_1) + (x_1, y_1)\end{aligned} \tag{6}$$

is solved for s and t which are written in the form:

$$\begin{aligned} s &= A_1 x + B_1 y + C_1 \\ t &= A_2 x + B_2 y + C_2 \end{aligned} \tag{7}$$

Step 2: The plane equation is written in the form $R = Ax + By + C$, where

$$\begin{aligned} A &= A_1(R_2 - R_1) + A_2(R_3 - R_1) \\ B &= B_1(R_2 - R_1) + B_2(R_3 - R_1) \\ C &= C_1(R_2 - R_1) + C_2(R_3 - R_1) + R_1 \end{aligned} \tag{8}$$

The controller broadcasts A, B, and C, and $Ax+By+C$ is stored in the RED color buffer for pixels that are still enabled after the scan conversion and visibility computations. If there are more than three vertices, the translator checks the colors $R_4, R_5, \ldots$ at the remaining vertices $v_4 = (x_4, y_4), v_5 = (x_5, y_5), \ldots$. Only in the case that for some i, $R_i \neq Ax_i + By_i + C$ is it necessary to subdivide the polygon by introducing new edges. Note that this subdivision is performed only during the shading stage and is not required during any other phase of processing.

Timing Analysis. The time it takes to process a polygon depends on the number of edges and the number of bits needed for the representation of $Ax+By+C$. Suppose we require an E bit representation for enabling pixels on one side of an edge, a D bit representation for the depth buffer, a C bit representation for each color component, and N bits for the representation of screen coordinates (usually 2 more than the log of the screen resolution), then scan conversion of an edge requires $E+N+3$ clock cycles, and the visibility calculation of a polygon requires $2(D+N+3)$ clock cycles. Once this is determined, shading of the polygon without subdivision requires $3(C+N+3)$ additional clock cycles, while $3(C+N+3)+(E+N+3)$ additional cycles are needed for each subdivision. Hence, the total time to process a "worst case" n-sided polygon is:

$$\begin{aligned} n(E+N+3) + 2(D+N+3) \\ + (n-3)(E+N+3) \\ + 3(n-2)(C+N+3) \end{aligned}$$

clock cycles. If we assume that $E = 12$, $D = 20$, $C = 8$, $N = 11$, $n = 4$, and a clock period is 100 nanoseconds, a 4-sided polygon can be processed in 33 microseconds. Hence, about 30,000 such polygons can be processed per second. This permits real-time display of quite complex objects (see figure 5).

2.2 SHADOWS

After the visible image has been constructed, shadows created by various light sources can be determined (see figure 6). Our approach determines shadow volumes [Crow 1977] defined as logical intersections of half-spaces. This is most similar to [Brotman 1984] except that explicit calculation of the shadow edge polygons is unnecessary in Pixel-planes. Briefly, the algorithm proceeds as follows:

Step 1: Flag initialization. For each pixel, a Shadow flag is allocated from pixel memory, and both the Enable register and Shadow flags are set to 0.

Step 2: Determination of pixels in shadow. For each polygon, the set of visible pixels that lie in the frustum of the polygon's cast shadow are determined and the Enable registers for these pixels is set to 1. The logical OR of Shadow and Enable is then stored in Shadow.

Step 3: Determination of color intensity of shadowed pixels. After all polygons have been processed, those pixels whose Shadow flag is 1 are in the shadow of one or more polygons. The color intensity of these pixels is diminished by an appropriate factor.

The implementation of this algorithm is based on the parallel linear evaluation capability of Pixel-planes, together with *ZMIN* value that is stored for each pixel. The idea is to disable those pixels which are on the "wrong" side of each face of the shadow frustum. We begin by choosing an edge of the current polygon, and finding the plane P determined by this edge and the light source. We want to disable those pixels which are not in the same half-space relative to P as the current polygon (see figure 7). The algorithm must handle two cases.

Case 1: P does not pass through the origin in eye space. In this case we observe that if the eye and the current polygon are in the same half-space relative to P, then it suffices to disable pixels that are farther away than P, and if the eye and the current polygon are in different half-spaces relative to P, then it suffices to disable pixels that are closer than P. In order to accomplish this we do the following:

a) The translator determines the equation of the plane P in the form $z = f(x,y) = Ax + By + C$, chooses a vertex (x_i, y_i) of the polygon not on P, and finds the sign of $f(x_i, y_i)$.

b) The coefficients A, B, and C are broadcast so that f can be evaluated simultaneously at all pixels.

c) If $f(x_i, y_i)$ is positive, all pixels whose *ZMIN* is less than $f(x,y)$ are disabled, and if $f(x_i, y_i)$ is negative, all pixels whose *ZMIN* is greater than $f(x,y)$ are disabled.

Case 2: P passes through the origin in eye space. This relatively rare case is easier to process than Case 1. We observe that P projected on the screen is an edge so it suffices to disable pixels which are not on the same side of this edge as the projected current polygon. We proceed as follows:

a) The translator determines the edge equation of the intersection of P with the plane of the screen in the form $Ax + By + C = 0$. In addition, the translator determines the sign of $f(x,y) = Ax + By + C$ at a vertex (x_i, y_i) not on P.

b) The coefficients A, B, and C are broadcast and those pixels whose $f(x,y)$ is not the same sign as $f(x_i, y_i)$ are disabled.

After each edge of the polygon has been processed in this manner, the pixels that are on the same side of the plane of the polygon as the light source must still be disabled. We let P be the plane of the polygon itself, and use

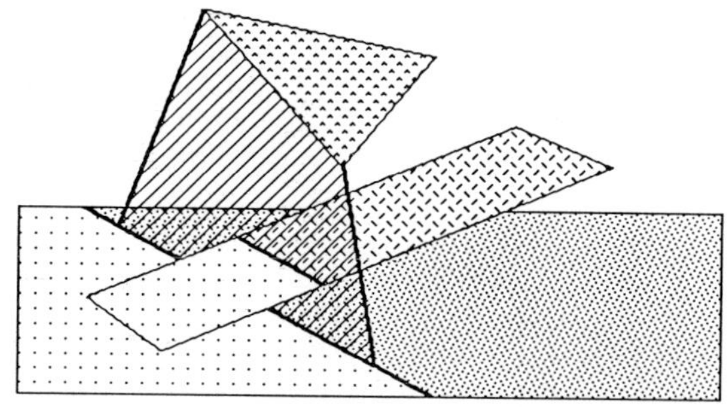

After shadow post-processing of first edge of triangle.

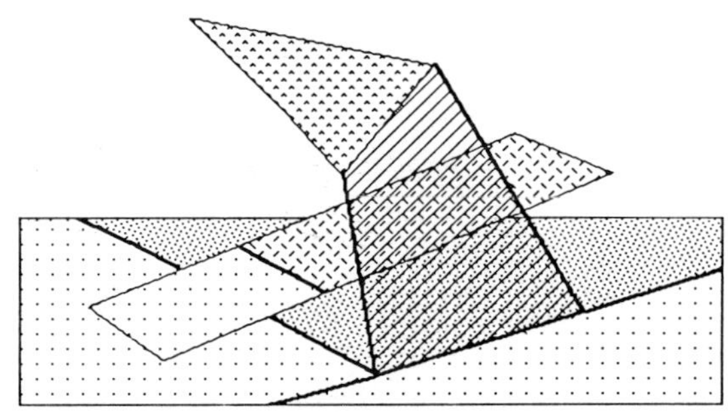

After shadow post-processing of second edge of triangle.

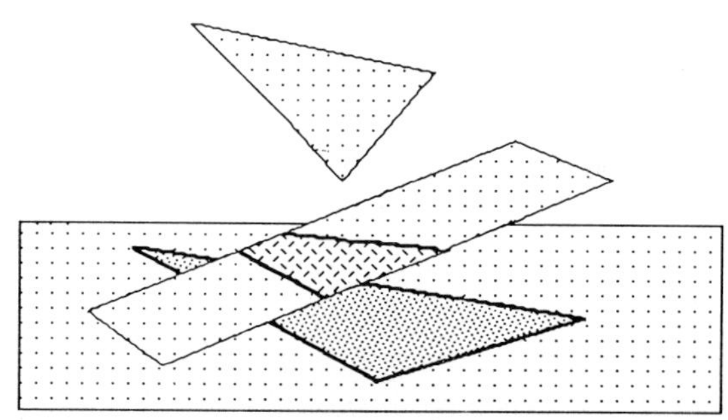

After completing shadow post-processing of triangle.

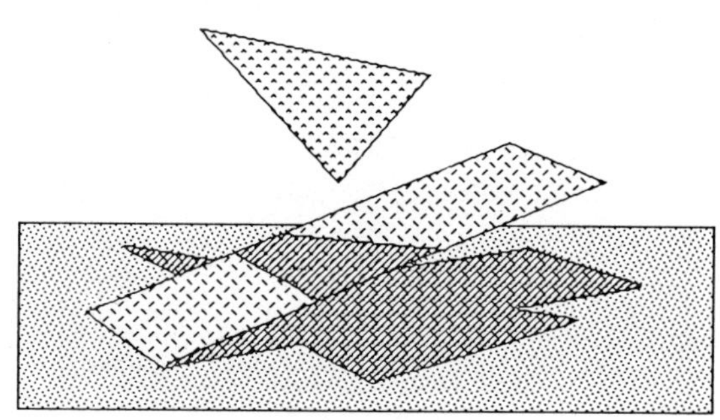

Result of all shadow processing.

Fig. 7: Shadowing Algorithm

either Case 1 or Case 2 above, with the one exception that we check the sign of f at the light source. Note that in the same half-space relative to P, we disable pixels for which $ZMIN = f(x,y)$, and if they are in different half-spaces we do not disable pixels for which $ZMIN = f(x,y)$. In this way, we can display either the lit or the unlit side of a polygon.

Timing Analysis. Step 1 requires 2 clock cycles for each polygon. In order to process each plane of the shadow frustum of a polygon, we need $(E + N + 3)$ cycles for the broadcast of A,B, and C and 2 additional cycles for the resetting of the Shadow flag. After all polygons have been processed, $3C$ cycles are required to modify the color component. Hence, in order to process P polygons, we need $P\big((n+1)(E+N+3)+2\big)+3C+2$ clock cycles. For example, if E=12, N=11, n=4, C=8, and a clock period is 100 nanoseconds, 78,000 polygons can be processed per second.

Fig. 9: Trimethoprim (simulation). Presorted data. Estimated time: 1.3 msec.

2.3 CLIPPING

Clipping of polygons by boundary planes, a procedure usually performed in the geometry pipeline, is not necessary when displaying an image in Pixel-planes. Time can be saved by performing only a bounding box type of trivial rejection/acceptance. Edges which lie wholly or partially off the screen will still disable the appropriate pixels during scan conversion. Even hither and yon clipping can be achieved by passing (at most) the two edges of the intersection of the polygon plane with the hither and yon planes, and disabling pixels which are on the appropriate side of these edges. The shadow volumes must be similarly clipped, by the addition of the shadow planes determined by the light source and the line of intersection of the plane of the polygon and each of the clipping planes (see figure 8).

Fig. 8: "Old Well" with shadows cut by hither plane within the Pixel-Planes memories (simulation). 177 polygons after trivial rejection. Estimated time: 8.8 msec.

2.4 SPHERES

Fred Brooks suggested to us a method for drawing filled circles in Pixel-planes. We have extended that method to spheres with Z-buffer and an arbitrary light source. Since Pixel-planes is essentially a linear machine, it might seem difficult to display objects rapidly which are defined via quadratic expressions. However, by using an algorithm that, in effect, treats a circle as a polygon with one edge, and by using some appropriate approximations, we can overcome these difficulties (see figures 9,10). Just as in polygon display, we proceed through a scan conversion, a visibility, and a shading phase [Max 1979; Pique 1983].

Fig. 10: Trimethoprim with Z-buffer (simulation). Unsorted data. Estimated time: 1.7 msec.

Step 1: Scan Conversion. Note that the equation of a circle with radius r and center (a, b) can be written in the form:

$$g(x, y) = Ax + By + C - Q = 0 \tag{9}$$

where $A = 2a$, $B = 2b$, $C = r^2 - a^2 - b^2$, and $Q = x^2 + y^2$. A section of the memory at each pixel, called the Q-buffer, is allocated for the storage of $x^2 + y^2$, and is loaded with this value at system initialization time. The translator computes A, B, and C and $f(x, y) = Ax + By + C$ is evaluated at each pixel. The value in the Q-buffer is subtracted from $f(x, y)$ and those pixels for which $f(x, y) - Q$ is negative are disabled.

Step 2: Visibility. If the eye coordinate system is chosen so that the $z > 0$ half-space contains the sphere, then the visible hemisphere is the set of points (x,y,z) satisfying

$$z = c - \sqrt{r^2 - (x-a)^2 - (y-b)^2} \tag{10}$$

where r is the radius and (a,b,c) is the center of the sphere. We can approximate this by

$$z = c - \left(r^2 - (x-a)^2 - (y-b)^2\right)/r \tag{11}$$

which in effect approximates the hemisphere with a paraboloid. Using a method similar to that described in Step 1, the expression in (11) can be evaluated, compared with the existing contents of the ZMIN buffer, and then stored if necessary, in the ZMIN buffer. Visibility is then determined in the same way as it is for polygon display.

Step 3: Shading due to light sources at infinity. The unit outward normal at the visible point (x, y, z) on the sphere with center (a, b, c) and radius r is

$$\begin{aligned}\overline{N} &= (1/r)(x-a,\ y-b,\ z-c) \\ &= (1/r)\left(x-a,\ y-b,\ -\sqrt{r^2-(x-a)^2-(y-b)^2}\right)\end{aligned} \tag{12}$$

Let $\overline{L} = (l_1, l_2, l_3)$ be the unit direction of an arbitrary light source. Then the point of maximum highlight on the sphere is $(rl_1 + a, rl_2 + b, rl_3 + c)$. Denote by *CMIN* the ambient color value and by *CMAX* the maximum color value for a given color component. Then for diffuse shading of the sphere, the color value at (x, y) is

$$Color(x, y) = \tag{13}$$

$$\begin{cases} CMIN + (CMAX - CMIN)(\overline{L}\cdot\overline{N}), & \text{if } \overline{L}\cdot\overline{N} \ge 0; \\ CMIN, & \text{if } \overline{L}\cdot\overline{N} < 0. \end{cases}$$

Using the parabolic approximation of the hemisphere as we did in Step 2, we can approximate $\overline{L}\cdot\overline{N}$ by:

$$\begin{aligned}\overline{L}\cdot\overline{N} \approx\ & (l_1(x-a) + l_2(y-b))/r \\ & - l_3(r^2 - (x-a)^2 - (y-b)^2)/r^2\end{aligned} \tag{14}$$

Then the color at a given pixel can be written in the form:

$$Color(x, y) = K(Ax + By + C - Q) + CMIN \tag{15}$$

where

$$\begin{aligned} K &= -(CMAX - CMIN)l_3/r^2, \\ A &= -l_1 r/l_3 + 2a, \\ B &= -l_2 r/l_3 + 2b, \\ C &= l_1 ra/l_3 + l_2 rb/l_3 + r^2 - a^2 - b^2 \end{aligned} \tag{16}$$

The translator computes A, B, C, and K. Multiplication by K is accomplished by first approximating K by the first n non-zero bits of its binary representation:

$$K \approx \sum_{i=1}^{n} 2^{j_i} \tag{17}$$

Then for each j in the sum, the controller broadcasts 2^jA, 2^jB, 2^jC. Q is shifted by j bits and subtracted from the linear expression determined by the three broadcast coefficients. The resultant value:

$$2^j(Ax + By + C - Q) \tag{18}$$

is added to the contents of the appropriate color buffer, COLBUF. After all the terms in the sum have been processed, we set *COLBUF* to 0 if *COLBUF* < *0*. The constant value *CMIN* is broadcast and added to *COLBUF*.

Timing Analysis. The initial loading of the Q-buffer requires $37(E + N + 3)$ clock cycles. Scan conversion and visibility are the same as in polygon processing and take $(E + N + 3)$ and $2(D + N + 3)$ cycles, respectively. Shading requires $4(C + N + 3)$ cycles for each term in the sum used to approximate K, and the broadcast of *CMIN* requires 20 cycles. Hence, if k is the number of terms in the approximation of K, it takes

$$\begin{aligned} & 37(E + N + 3) \\ & \quad + S\big((E + N + 3) + 2(D + N + 3) \\ & \quad + 4k(C + N + 3) + 20\big) \end{aligned}$$

clock cycles to process S spheres. For example, if $k = 3$, $E = 20$, $N = 11$, $D = 20$, $C = 8$, then 34,000 spheres can be processed per second.

2.5 ADAPTIVE HISTOGRAM EQUALIZATION

In computed tomographic (CT) scan displays, CT numbers must be assigned (grey) intensity levels so that the viewer can perceive appropriate degrees of contrast and detail. Because the range of CT numbers is, in general, greater than the range of intensity levels, some compression has to take place. This makes it difficult to control the contrast in both light and dark areas. The standard method, selection of windows in the CT range, results in intensity discontinuities and loss of information. AHE [Pizer 1984] is an assignment scheme that makes use of regional frequency distributions of image intensities. The processed image has high contrast everywhere and the intensities vary smoothly (see figures 11,12). The method proceeds as follows. For each point (x, y) in the image:

Step 1: A "contextual" region centered at (x, y) is chosen, and the frequency histogram of CT numbers in this region is computed. Typically, this region is a circle, or a square with edges parallel to the screen boundaries.

Step 2: In this histogram, the percentile rank, r, of the CT number at (x, y) is determined.

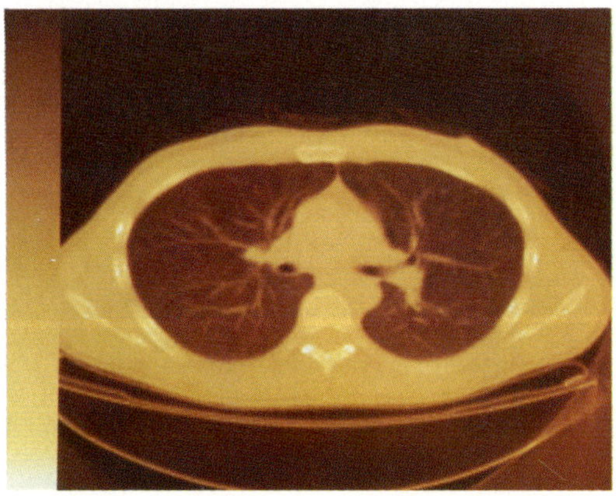

Fig. 11: Original CT scan image.

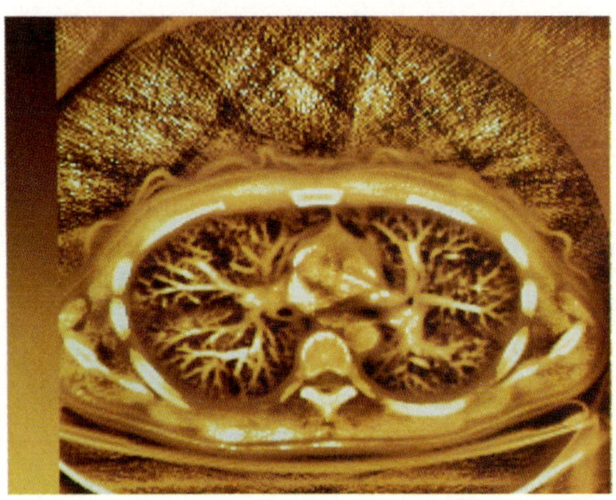

Fig. 12: CT scan image after AHE enhancement (simulation). Estimated time for this 256×256 pixel image: 1 second.

Step 3: This rank is used to compute an intensity level, i, in some grey scale ranging between , say, i_1 and i_2. Specifically, $i = i_1 + r(i_2 - i_1)$.

This method requires the computation of a CT distribution at every pixel in the image, and so it is far too inefficient for most uses, requiring approximately 5 minutes to compute on a 256 × 256 image on a VAX 11/780. A more efficient alternative, requiring about 30 seconds for a 256 × 256 image, is to compute the distribution only at a small set of sample points and use a linear interpolation scheme to approximate the intensity levels at the other points.

An efficient alternative, which finds the exact value at each pixel, can be implemented in Pixel planes. The idea is to make use of the parallel processing capability to construct the rank incrementally at each pixel simultaneously.

Step 1: The CT numbers are loaded into the pixel memories, and a counter at each pixel is initialized.

Step 2: For each pixel (x_0, y_0):

a) The coefficients necessary to disable those pixels that are outside the contextual region centered at (x_0, y_0) are broadcast. For example, if the region is a polygon or a circle, this is equivalent to the scan conversion step discussed earlier.

b) The CT number, $N(x_0, y_0)$, is broadcast and compared, in parallel, to the CT number, $N(x, y)$ which is stored at each enabled pixel (x, y). If $N(x, y) > N(x_0, y_0)$, the counter at (x, y) is incremented.

Step 3: After all pixels have been processed, the counter at each pixel contains the rank of the pixel CT number within its own contextual region. If both the number of pixels in the contextual region and the length of the grey scale are powers of 2, this rank can easily be scaled to an intensity by shifting bits.

Timing Analysis. It requires 25 cycles to load each pixel with its CT value and initialize its counter. It requires $2(E+N+3)$ cycles to disable pixels outside each contextual region and 40 cycles to broadcast the CT numbers and increment the counters. On a 512 × 512 display with $N = 11$ and $E = 12$, we have estimated the time required to perform AHE is about 4 seconds.

3. ALGORITHMS UNDER DEVELOPMENT

This section describes algorithms still under development. Only functional simulations (rather than detailed behavioral ones) have been executed and the timing estimates are thus less precise. In particular, we are still exploring speedups for multiplication and division in the pixel processors. The timing estimates given in the figures are conservative (we hope), but still assume a 10MHz clock.

3.1 TEXTURE MAPPING

One way of producing a texture on a polygon is to compute a texture plane address (u, v) associated to each pixel (x, y) and then look up the appropriate color value in a texture table indexed by u and v. The Pixel planes linear evaluator can be used to determine, in parallel, this texture plane address.

To see how this is done, we proceed through some mathematical computations. In order to orient a texture on a polygon in eye space we first choose a point $P0$ on the polygon and 2 orthonormal vectors $\overline{S}$ and $\overline{T}$ in the plane of the polygon. Then the texture address (u, v) associated to the point X on the polygon is given by:

$$\begin{aligned} u &= \overline{S} \cdot (X - P_0), \\ v &= \overline{T} \cdot (X - P_0). \end{aligned} \tag{19}$$

If $\overline{S} = (s_1, s_2, s_3)$, $\overline{T} = (t_1, t_2, t_3)$, $P = (p_1, p_2, p_3)$, and $X = (x_e, y_e, z_e)$, equations (19) can be rewritten in coordinate form as:

$$\begin{aligned} u &= s_1(x_e - p_1) + s_2(y_e - p_2) + s_3(z_e - p_3) \\ v &= t_1(x_e - p_1) + t_2(y_e - p_2) + t_3(z_e - p_3). \end{aligned} \tag{20}$$

Substituting the equations (3), which relate screen space to eye space, into (20) and using the plane equation $Ax_e + By_e + Cz_e + D = 0$, we can write u and v in the form:

$$\begin{aligned} u &= (A_1 x + B_1 y + C_1)/z \\ v &= (A_2 x + B_2 y + C_2)/z \end{aligned} \tag{21}$$

The translator computes A_1, B_1, and C_1, and the controller broadcasts them to Pixel-planes. The division of $A_1 x + B_1 y + C_1$ by z (which is already stored in ZMIN) is done in parallel at the pixel level, and the result is stored in a U-buffer. The V-buffer value is found in a similiar manner. A texture table is then passed, entry by entry, to Pixel-planes, and each pixel selects a texture value corresponding to its stored (u, v) value. For periodic patterns (checkerboards, bricks, etc.) it is only necessary to transmit a small table defining the unit pattern (see figure 13).

Fig. 13: Bricked "Old Well" (simulation). 66 textured polygons out of a total of 357. Estimated time: 14.3 msec.

3.2 TRANSPARENCY

Transparency effects can be achieved by disabling patterns of pixels prior to polygon processing. For example, one could broadcast the coefficients 1, 1, 0 in order to evaluate $x + y$, and disable those pixels for which $x + y$ is even (see figure 14).

Fig. 14: "Old Well" with transparent columns (simulation). 64 transparent polygons out of a total of 357. Estimated time: 13.8 msec.

Transparency effects can also be produced with subpixel mask successive refinement, where transparent polygons are ignored on particular passes over the database. For example, transparent polygons can be ignored every other pass or every third pass, thereby yielding different degrees of transparency.

3.3 ANTI-ALIASING

We have been developing several anti-aliasing techniques for polygons. We have come to believe that the essential difference between various approaches is whether the visibility at the subpixel level is performed before or after the anti-aliasing computations. Our first approach, which aims at producing an image rapidly and "improving" the image with each screen refresh, makes no assumptions about visibility determination before the Pxpl memories. The second approach, which takes more time, but produces a high quality anti-aliased image initially, assumes visibility ordering has already been done.

Method 1: Successive Refinement. Each pixel (x, y), is subdivided into a grid of subpixels so that each subpixel has an address of the form $(x + xoffset, y + yoffset)$. We generate the image several times (16, perhaps), each time offsetting the image slightly by some $(xoffset, yoffset)$ in such a way that the sample points within a pixel's area form a reasonable distribution. (The shift is easily achieved by adding $A \cdot xoffset + B \cdot yoffset$ to the C coefficient of each broadcast triple.) Two sets of color buffers are maintained, one to store the color generated by the latest image generation offset and the other to store a running average as we move around the subpixel grid.

The extra cost of the algorithm over standard subpixel "super-sampling" is the color blending between each pass over the graphic database. This is less than 1000 clock cycles (100 microseconds) per pass. This particular super-sampling successive refinement technique, however, supports dynamically interactive applications. The initial images appear similar to common anti-aliased images, and significant refinement is produced within a few additional sampling passes.

Method 2: Subpixel Coverage Mask. The polygons are sorted from front to back, perhaps by first transforming the polygon list into a BSP tree [Fuchs 1983]. Each pixel is subdivided into a number of subpixels and one bit of the pixel memory is reserved for each such subpixel. During the scan conversion step of polygon processing, the coefficients defining each edge are normalized to yield the distance from the center of the pixel to the edge. The coverage mask and area contribution of an edge can be passed from a precomputed table [Carpenter 1984] in the controller indexed by this distance and A, the coefficient of x. (Note that only one row of the table needs to be passed for any edge.) The number of ones in the mask is used to compute a color contribution which is added to the color buffers. When the number of ones in the coverage mask stored at each pixel reaches the total number of subpixels, the pixel is disabled. Since polygons are processed in front to back order, "leakage" of color from hidden polygons is avoided. This approach is somewhat similar to the one used in the Evans and Sutherland CT-5 real-time image generation system often used for flight training [Schumacker 1980].

4. CONCLUSIONS

We have highlighted in this paper the aspects of Pixel-planes that give it computing power and efficiency—the parallel linear expression evaluator embodied in the tree of one-bit adders. We have illustrated this capability by describing a variety of algorithms (shadows, spheres, image enhancement) that appear to run efficiently in this machine. Pictures from the Pixel-planes simulators indicate that high-quality images can be generated rapidly enough for dynamic, often real-time, interaction. The images from the working small prototype (see figure 4) are simpler than the images from the simulators due to the small number of custom chips presently available. We expect Pixel-planes 4, with considerably increased speed and resolution, to start working by June 1985. We expect that a full-scale (500–1000 line) display system can be built with less than 500 Pxpl memory chips in currently available (1.5micron CMOS) technology. We also hope that the algorithm developments, especially those based on simplifying algorithms into linear form, will be useful for those developing graphics algorithms on other parallel machines.

5. ACKNOWLEDGEMENTS

We wish to thank Fred Brooks for the basic circle scan-conversion algorithm, Alan Paeth and Alan Bell of Xerox Palo Alto Research Center for years of assistance with the design and early implementations of Pixel-planes, Scott Hennes for assistance with the implementation of the Pxpl3 memory chip, Hsieh Cheng-Hong and Justin Heinecke for discussions about architecture and algorithm interactions, Turner Whitted for discussions about anti-aliasing and transparency algorithms, Eric Grant for 3D data of the Old Well, Steve Pizer, John Zimmerman, and North Carolina Memorial Hospital for CT chest data, Mike Pique, Doug Schiff, Dr. Michael Corey and Lee Kuyper (Corey and Kuyper from Burroughs Wellcome) for Trimethoprim drug molecule data, Trey Greer for TEX help, and Bobette Eckland for secretarial support. Special thanks go to Andrew Glassner, who supervised the layout and paste-up of this paper.

6. REFERENCES

Brotman, L.S. and N.I. Badler. October 1984. "Generating Soft Shadows with a Depth Buffer Algorithm," *IEEE Computer Graphics and Applications*, 5–12.

Carpenter, L. July 1984. "The A-buffer, an Antialiased Hidden Surface Method," *Computer Graphics*, **18**(3), 103–109 (Proc. Siggraph '84).

Clark, J.H. July 1982. "The Geometry Engine: A VLSI Geometry System for Graphics," *Computer Graphics*, **16**(3), 127–133 (Proc. Siggraph '82).

Clark, J.H. and M.R. Hannah. 4th Quarter, 1980. "Distributed Processing in a High-Performance Smart Image Memory," *Lambda*, 40–45 (*Lambda* is now VLSI Design).

Crow, F.C. July 1977. "Shadow Algorithms for Computer Graphics," *Computer Graphics*, **11**(2), 242–248 (Proc. Siggraph '77).

Fuchs, H. 1977. "Distributing a Visible Surface Algorithm over Multiple Processors," *Proceedings of the ACM Annual Conference*, 449–451.

Fuchs, H. and B. Johnson. April, 1979. "An Expandable Multiprocessor Architecture for Video Graphics," *Proceedings of the 6th ACM-IEEE Symposium on Computer Architecture*, 58–67.

Fuchs, H., J. Poulton, A. Paeth, and A. Bell. January, 1982. "Developing Pixel-Planes, A Smart Memory-Based Raster Graphics System," *Proceedings of the 1982 MIT Conference on Advanced Research in VLSI*, 137–146.

Fuchs, H., G.D. Abram, and E.D.Grant. July 1983. "Near Real-Time Shaded Display of Rigid Objects," Computer Graphics, **17**(3), 65–72 (Proc. Siggraph '83).

Gouraud, H. 1971. "Computer Display of Curved Surfaces," *IEEE Transactions on Computers*, **20**(6), 623–629.

Max, N.L. July 1979. "ATOMILL: Atoms with Shading and Highlights," *Computer Graphics*, **13**(3), 165–173 (Proc. Siggraph '79).

Pique, M.E. 1983. Fast 3D Display of Space-Filling Molecular Models, Technical Report 83-004, Department of Computer Science, UNC Chapel Hill.

Pizer, S.M., J.B. Zimmerman, and E.V.Staab. April 1984. "Adaptive Grey Level Assignment in CT Scan Display," *Journal of Computer Assisted Tomography*, **8**(2), 300–305, Raven Press, NY.

Poulton, J., J.D. Austin, J.G. Eyles, J. Heinecke, C.H. Hsieh, and H. Fuchs. 1985. Pixel-Planes 4 Graphics Engine, Technical Report 1985, Department of Computer Science, UNC Chapel Hill (to appear).

Schumacker, R.A. November 1980. "A New Visual System Architecture," *Proceedings of the 2nd Annual IITEC*, Salt Lake City.

Shiffman, R.R. and R.H. Parker. 1984. "An Electrophoretic Image Display With Internal NMOS Address Logic and Display Drivers", *Proceedings of the Society for Information Display*, **25**(2), 105–152.

Sutherland, I.E., R.F. Sproull, and R.A. Schumacker. 1974. "A Characterization of Ten Hidden-Surface Algorithms," *ACM Computing Surveys*, **6**(1), 1–55.

Vuillemier, R., A. Perret, F. Porret, P. Weiss. July 1984. "Novel Electromechanical Microshutter Display Device," *Proceedings of the 1984 Eurodisplay Conference*.

Weitek. 1983. *Designing with the WTL 1032/1033*, Weitek Corporation, Santa Clara, CA (Weitek publication 83AN112.1M).

BINTREES, CSG TREES, AND TIME

Hanan Samet
Computer Science Department
University of Maryland, College Park, MD 20742

Markku Tamminen
Laboratory for Information Processing Science
Helsinki University of Technology, 02150 Espoo 15, Finland

ABSTRACT

A discussion is presented of the relationship between two solid representation schemes: constructive solid geometry (CSG trees) and recursive spatial subdivision exemplified by the bintree, a generalization of the quadtree and octree. Detailed algorithms are developed and analyzed for evaluating CSG trees by bintree conversion, i.e., by determining explicitly which parts of space are solid and which empty. These techniques enable the addition of the time dimension and motion to the approximate analysis of CSG trees in a simple manner to solve problems such as dynamic interference detection. For "well-behaved" CSG trees, the execution time of the conversion algorithm is directly related to the spatial complexity of the object represented by the CSG tree (i.e., asymptotically it is proportional to the number of bintree nodes as the resolution increases). The set of well-behaved CSG trees includes all trees that define multidimensional polyhedra in a manner that does not give rise to tangential intersections at CSG tree nodes.

CR Categories and Subject Descriptors: I.3.5 [**Computer Graphics**]: Computational Geometry and Object Modeling – solid and object representations; geometric algorithms and systems; I.3.3 [**Computer Graphics**]: Picture/Image Generation – display algorithms; viewing algorithms

General Terms: Algorithms, Data Structures

Additional Key Words and Phrases: constructive solid geometry (CSG), time, motion, conversion, image processing, hierarchical data structures, bintrees, quadtrees, octrees, interference detection, solid modeling

1. INTRODUCTION

Constructive solid geometry (CSG) uses trees (CSG trees) of building block primitives (parallelepipeds, spheres, cylinders, ...), combined by geometric transformations and Boolean set operations as a representation of three-dimensional solid objects [13]. Each primitive solid can be decomposed into a subtree whose leaves are halfspaces, each described by an equation of the form:

$$f(x,y,z) \geq 0.$$

Substituting this subtree for every occurrence of that primitive in the original CSG tree gives rise to an expanded tree having only halfspaces as leaves. In the present article we shall assume this simple halfspace formulation of CSG (see also [12,21]). Clearly, the CSG approach can be used to describe objects of any dimensionality and many interesting solid modelers have been based on it [14].

It has been known for some time that octree-like recursive subdivision can facilitate the evaluation of CSG trees; e.g., the analysis [8,20] and display [21] of solid objects modeled by them. A hardware processor with such a capability is described by Meagher [10]. A bintree represents discrete solid objects of arbitrary dimensionality (e.g., binary images in two dimensions) by a binary tree defining a recursive subdivision of space and recording which parts are empty (WHITE) and which are solid (BLACK). The bintree is a dimension-independent variant of the more familiar quadtree and octree representations. For example, Figure 1c is a bintree corresponding to a 2-dimensional binary image (Figure 1a) consisting of two regions. See the survey of Samet [15] for a comprehensive survey and bibliography of quadtree related methods. Mentions of arbitrary dimensionality are found in the literature [4,5,9,22] but few concrete applications have been demonstrated.

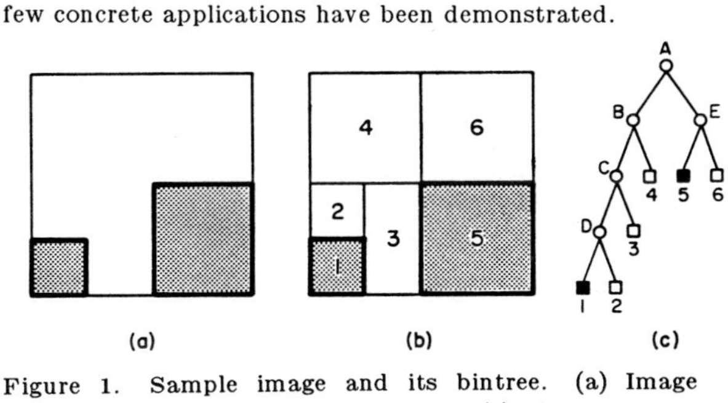

Figure 1. Sample image and its bintree. (a) Image (b) Block decomposition (c) Bintree.

Time and motion are important elements of advanced solid modeling. In particular, given a moving object we may wish to determine whether it intersects a stationary object *(static interference detection)* or whether it intersects another moving object *(dynamic interference detection)*. Even though it appears that the time dimension can be added to CSG trees in a conceptually simple fashion, rather little attention has been focussed on CSG trees in a dynamic situation. Perhaps this is due to the difficulty of evaluation in the now four-dimensional space.

Static interference detection is discussed by Boyse [3] but only boundary representations are considered. Tilove [19] has provided a good analysis of the equivalent "NULL object detection" problem in the CSG setting. Our work seems to complement that of Tilove. We do not repeat his formal analysis of the "pruning" of CSG trees but show in detail how a CSG tree can be efficiently pruned against an adaptable grid (i.e., bintree), even in the case of non-bounded halfspace primitives. We also show that for "well-behaved" CSG trees, the amount of work involved in pruning the CSG tree against all the cells of such an adaptable grid is asymptotically proportional to the number of cells and does not depend on the number of nodes in the CSG tree representation.

In the rest of this paper we show how bintree conversion provides an efficient and dimension-independent tool for evaluating CSG trees. The time dimension is handled without extra conceptual overhead. Our emphasis is on CSG trees defined by linear halfspaces and on motion along a piecewise linear trajectory but the techniques are shown to extend to the non-linear case. We present and analyze the evaluation (conversion) algorithm and show that asymptotically, as resolution is increased, the amount of work it involves is directly related to the spatial complexity of the object represented by the CSG tree. Thus, despite the added dimension, dynamic interference detection by bintree conversion is often efficient (because the object sought is the null object). Finally, we present some experimental results obtained by using the discrete solid modeler described in [18]. The simplicity of the algorithms is striking when compared with algorithms for converting boundary representations to bintrees [17].

2. DEFINITIONS

In our algorithms we use a linear tree representation that is based on the preorder traversal of a bintree. The traversal yields a string over the alphabet "(", "B", "W" corresponding respectively to internal nodes, BLACK leaves, and WHITE leaves. This string is called a *DF-expression* [6]. For the image of Figure 1 it becomes ((((BWWW(BW. Note that bintrees are size-independent: i.e., a given tree can define an object in a universe of any size. However, we usually portray each bintree as embedded in the d-dimensional unit cube. Let us say that the *resolution* of a bintree, say M, is the maximal number of units into which each side of the d-dimensional universe of a d-dimensional bintree can be divided. A cube of side length 1/M is called a *voxel*.

A point x in a d-dimensional universe (d-space) is represented by a row vector $x_0, x_1, \cdots,$and x_d of $d+1$ homogeneous coordinates with x_0 denoting the scale factor. We shall only consider the case with $x_0=1$. In the general case, the d ordinary Euclidean coordinates are obtained by dividing $x_1, \cdots, x_d$ by x_0. Note that usually the scale factor is taken to be the last component of x. With our choice, the scale factor retains its original index when the time dimension is added.

A (linear) halfspace in d-space is defined by an inequality on the $d+1$ homogeneous coordinates:

$$\sum_{i=0}^{d} a_i \cdot x_i \geq 0 \qquad (1)$$

The halfspace is represented by a column vector a. In vector notation (1) is written as $a \cdot x \geq 0$, with column vector a representing the halfspace. Figure 2 shows the halfspace represented by $4x-2y-1 \geq 0$. The point set satisfying this relation lies to the right of the line. (partially shaded). Given a point x, the value of the left side of (1) at x is called the *value* of halfspace a at x.

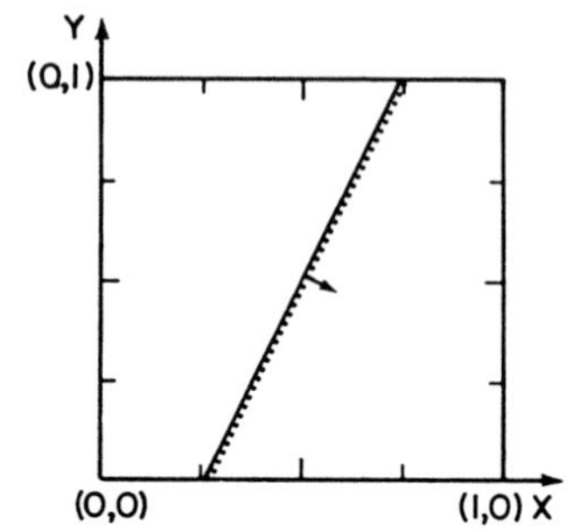

Figure 2. Halfspace corresponding to $4x-2y-1 \geq 0$.

We shall concentrate on CSG trees in the simplest of settings, that of halfspaces defined by hyperplanes (linear halfspaces). Arbitrary CSG tree can be approximated in this way [2,21]. Also, qualitatively, our methods extend to the general case.

In this article we define a data structure for CSG trees as follows. A CSG tree is a binary tree in which internal nodes correspond to geometric transformations and Boolean set operations while leaves correspond to halfspaces.* A node of a CSG tree is described by a record of type *csgnode* with six fields. The first two fields, LEFT and RIGHT, contain pointers to the node's left and right sons respectively. The TYP field indicates the node's type. There are five node types - UNION, INTERSECTION, BLACK, WHITE, and HALFSPACE. Types UNION and INTERSECTION correspond to the Boolean set operations. HALFSPACE corresponds to a leaf (i.e., halfspace). The field HSP contains an identifier for the halfspace. It is an index to a table, HS, of $d+1$ element coefficient vectors of the different halfspaces involved in the CSG tree. The remaining two fields, MIN and MAX, are used for auxiliary data in our algorithms. They record the minimum and maximum values, respectively, of a halfspace in a given bintree block.

Note that our definition of a CSG tree allows for leaves that are completely BLACK or WHITE as required in our algorithm. In addition, in contrast to the conventional use of CSG, we only use the Boolean set operations UNION and INTERSECTION, as the effect of the third one, MINUS, can be achieved by application of De Morgan's laws to all nodes of type UNION and INTERSECTION. The complement of a halfspace is obtained by changing the signs of all the coefficients (i.e., the direction of its normal). Note that our universe is finite, as required by the bintree representation.

3. CONVERTING CSG TREES TO BINTREES

Our algorithms traverse the universe in a depth-first manner and evaluate each successive subuniverse against the CSG tree. This enables pruning areas of no interest. Whenever

*Our discussion assumes that the transformations have been propagated to the leaves. We also assume a bounded universe, for simplicity in the form of the unit cube. Actually, so-called regularized versions of the set operations must be used [13]. However, we shall not repeat the term regularized.

the hyperplane of a halfspace, say H, passes through a subuniverse (i.e., a bintree node), say S, then we say that H is *active* in S (i.e., there exists a point in S such that $a \cdot x = 0$). A CSG tree node is said to be *active* in S if both of its sons are active in S. As an example of the use of these terms, consider the conversion of the triangle given in Figure 3 whose CSG tree is given in Figure 4. It is composed of the intersection of the three halfspaces $2x-1 \geq 0$, $2y-1 \geq 0$, and $-2x-2y+3 \geq 0$ labeled A, B, and C respectively. Conversion starts with the unit square universe. In this case halfspaces A, B, and C are all active and so is the CSG tree (in other words, it is not totally BLACK or WHITE). Thus we first have to split the unit square into two halves (split along the x coordinate). Now, evaluating the CSG tree against the left half of the bintree, say L, we find that A is WHITE and thus not active. Therefore, L will have to be WHITE since A is combined with the rest of the CSG tree by an INTERSECTION node and the intersection of WHITE with anything is WHITE.

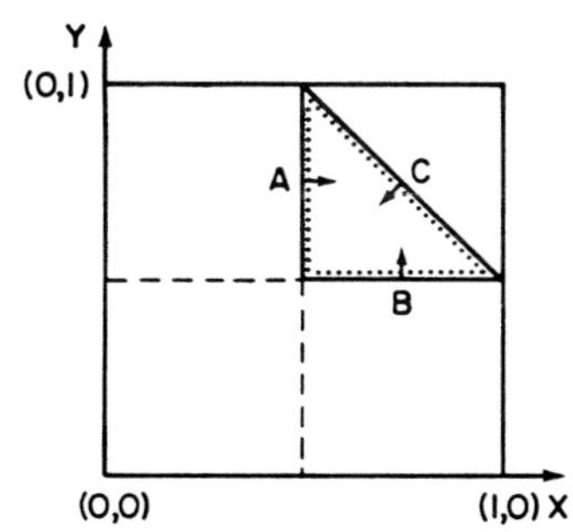

Figure 3. Sample triangle image.

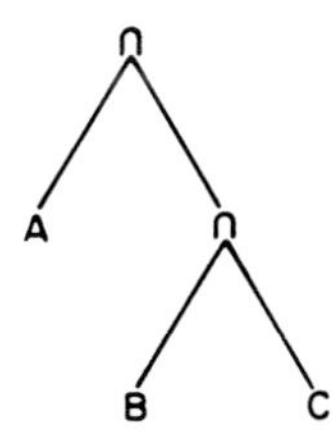

Figure 4. CSG tree corresponding to Figure 3.

First, let us examine the construction of a bintree corresponding to a halfspace as given by (1). This is achieved by traversing the universe in the DF-order and determining the range of the left side of (1) in each subuniverse. Each node in the bintree in which the halfspace is active is decomposed into two sons and the process is recursively applied to them. The process stops when the halfspace is not active in a bintree node or if the bintree node corresponds to a voxel. All voxels in which the halfspace is active are labeled BLACK in the version of the algorithm presented here. The resulting bintree is represented using a DF-expression.

Determining whether a halfspace is active in a bintree node is facilitated by keeping track of the minimum and maximum values of $a \cdot x$ for each bintree node. Whenever the maximum is ≤ 0 the bintree node is WHITE and when the minimum is ≥ 0 it is BLACK. Otherwise the halfspace is active and subdivision is required. Initially, for the unit cube, the minimum value of $a \cdot x$ is the constant factor of a plus the sum of all negative coefficients in a. The maximum value is the constant factor of a plus the sum of all positive coefficients in a. For example, for Figure 2, the initial minimum value is -3 and the initial maximum value is 3.

Whenever a bintree node is subdivided, either the maximum or minimum (never both at the same time) of $a \cdot x$ for each son node changes with respect to that of the father. Let the subdivision be performed on a hyperplane (e.g., a line in two dimensions) perpendicular to the axis corresponding to coordinate i $(1 \leq i \leq d)$ and let w_i be the width of the side along coordinate i of the block resulting from the subdivision. The amount of change is $\delta_i = a_i \cdot w_i$. For the left son, if $\delta_i > 0$, then δ_i is subtracted from the maximum; otherwise, δ_i is subtracted from the minimum. For the right son, if $\delta_i > 0$, then the minimum is incremented by δ_i; otherwise, δ_i is added to the maximum.

As an example, consider again the halfspace given by $4x-2y-1 \geq 0$ as shown in Figure 2. Assume that the universe is the unit square. The maximum and minimum values 3 and -3 are attained respectively at (1,0) and at (0,1). Subdividing along the x axis yields two sons. The maximum value of $a \cdot x$ in the left son has decreased by 1/2 times the coefficient of the x coordinate (i.e., 2) to 1 and is attained at (0.5,0), while the minimum value remains the same. The minimum value of $a \cdot x$ in the right son has increased by 1/2 times the coefficient of the x coordinate (i.e., 2) to -1 and is attained at (0.5,1) while the maximum value remains the same.

A CSG tree is evaluated, i.e., converted, to a bintree by traversing the universe in depth-first order and evaluating each subuniverse against the CSG tree. Leaf nodes (halfspaces) are evaluated using the method described above and their results are combined by *pruning* the CSG tree to the subuniverse. Pruning means that only that part of the CSG tree which is active within the subuniverse is retained [19,21]. Once pruning has reduced the CSG tree to a leaf node (i.e., a halfspace), the conversion procedure becomes identical to that described above for converting a halfspace to a bintree. Each node in the bintree, say B, in which the CSG tree is active, is decomposed into two sons and they are in turn intersected with only that part of the CSG tree that is active in B. This process stops when the CSG tree is not active in a bintree node or if the bintree node corresponds to a voxel. All voxels in which a CSG tree is active are labeled by procedure CLASSIFY_VOXEL which we do not describe here. At its simplest (as used in the experiments described in Section 6), it treats all such voxels as BLACK (or WHITE). At its most complex, CLASSIFY_VOXEL corresponds to Tilove's NULL object algorithm applied to the active CSG subtree at the voxel [19].

The conversion of a CSG tree to a bintree is performed by procedures CSG_TO_BINTREE, INIT_HALFSPACES, CSG_TRAVERSE, PRUNE, and HSPEVAL given below. They make use of BLACK_CSG_NODE and WHITE_CSG_NODE which are global pointers to BLACK and WHITE CSG tree nodes. In these and all other procedures, we shall use the following global constants: D is the dimensionality of the space, VOXEL_LEVEL is the level of the bintree corresponding to voxels, and EPSILON is the tolerance for deciding when a bintree node is WHITE (i.e., at most a proportion EPSILON of its "critical" diagonal is contained in the halfspace) or BLACK.

CSG_TO_BINTREE serves to initialize the traversal process. First, it invokes INIT_HALFSPACES to traverse the CSG tree to compute the minimum and maximum values of each halfspace in the whole universe (i.e., the unit cube). These values are stored in the MIN and MAX fields of the CSG tree node corresponding to each halfspace. Next, it calls on CSG_TRAVERSE to perform the actual conversion. CSG_TRAVERSE traverses the universe by recursively subdividing it corresponding to the depth-first traversal order of the resulting bintree. At each subdivision step, PRUNE is called to attempt to reduce the size of the CSG tree which will be evaluated in the bintree block. PRUNE traverses the CSG tree in depth-first order and removes inactive CSG nodes with the aid of HSPEVAL which determines if a halfspace is active within a given bintree block. Assuming that T is CSG node, PRUNE applies the following four rules to the CSG tree.

(1) BLACK UNION T = BLACK
(2) WHITE UNION T = T
(3) BLACK INTERSECTION T = T
(4) WHITE INTERSECTION T = WHITE.

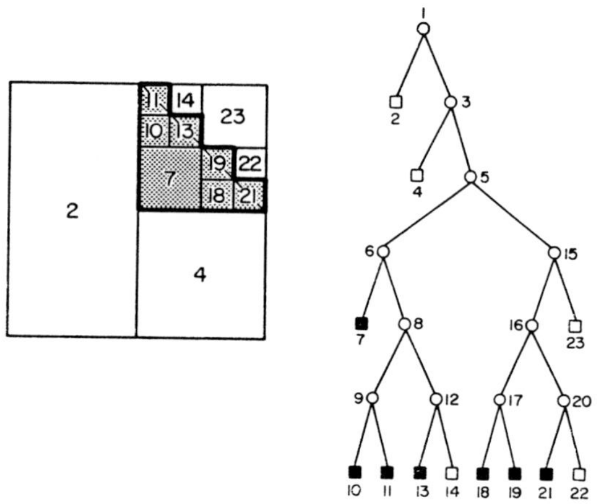

Figure 5. Bintree corresponding to the triangle in Figure 3 before collapsing.

As an example, consider the triangle of Figure 3 whose CSG tree is given in Figure 4. Figure 5 is the corresponding bintree, with VOXEL_LEVEL=6. The nodes have been numbered in the order in which they were output. Initially, the entire CSG tree (i.e., Figure 4) is assumed to be active in the whole universe (i.e., the unit square). Node 1 is output as a NON-LEAF and we process its left son next. First, we attempt to prune the CSG tree with respect to the left half of the universe. Since halfspace A is inactive here (i.e., it is WHITE), we can apply pruning rule (4) and there is no need to further process the remainder of the CSG tree in Figure 4. We output node 2 as WHITE and process the right son of node 1 next. Pruning the CSG tree shows that halfspace A is again inactive but this time it is BLACK. Since both halfspaces B and C are active here, pruning rule (3) leaves us with the CSG tree given by Figure 6. We now output node 3 as NON-LEAF and process its left son next. Pruning the CSG tree results in halfspace B being inactive (i.e., it is WHITE) and pruning rule (4) means that there is no need to further process this CSG tree. We output node 4 as WHITE and process the right son of node 3 next. This time pruning the CSG tree results in halfspace B being inactive again but now it is BLACK. Pruning rule (3) leaves us with just halfspace C. Node 5 is output as NON-LEAF and the conversion process is applied to its two sons next.

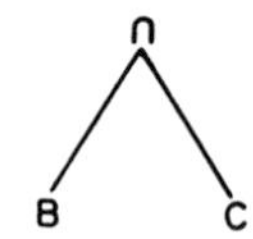

Figure 6. Result of pruning the CSG tree of Figure 4 in the right half of the root of its bintree.

The remainder of the conversion is equivalent to that described earlier for the conversion of a halfspace as the CSG tree has been reduced to one halfspace. The result is given in Figure 5. Note that the sequence of nodes that is output is not minimal in the sense that collapsing may yet have to be performed (i.e., when two terminal brother nodes are BLACK). Application of collapsing results in merging nodes 10 and 11, and nodes 18 and 19.

```
procedure CSG_TO_BINTREE(P,N,HS);
/* Convert the D-dimensional CSG tree pointed at by P to a
   bintree. HS contains N halfspaces. */
begin
 value pointer csgnode P;
 global value integer N;
 global value real array HS[1:N,0:D];
 INIT_HALFSPACES(P);
 CSG_TRAVERSE(P,0,1.0);
end;
```

```
procedure INIT_HALFSPACES(P);
/* Compute the minimum and maximum values of each of the
   halfspaces of the CSG tree P in the D-dimensional unit
   universe. */
begin
 value pointer csgnode P;
 integer I,J;
 if TYP(P)='HALFSPACE' then
  begin
   I←HSP(P);
   MIN(P)←MAX(P)←HS[I,0];
   for J←1 step 1 until D do
    begin
     if HS[I,J]>0.0 then MAX(P)←MAX(P)+HS[I,J]
     else MIN(P)←MIN(P)+HS[I,J];
    end;
  end
 else
  begin
   INIT_HALFSPACES(LEFT(P));
   INIT_HALFSPACES(RIGHT(P));
  end;
end;
```

```
procedure CSG_TRAVERSE(P,LEV,W);
/* Convert the portion of the CSG tree P that overlaps the
   D-dimensional subuniverse of volume 2^-LEV whose smallest
   side has width W. The bintree is constructed by evaluat-
   ing the CSG tree in the subuniverse. The evaluation pro-
   cess consists of pruning the nodes of the CSG tree that are
   outside of the subuniverse. A new copy of the relevant
   part of the CSG tree is created as each level is descended
   in the bintree. This storage is reclaimed once a
   subuniverse at a given level has been processed. */
```

```
begin
  value pointer csgnode P;
  value integer LEV;
  value real W;
  pointer csgnode FS; /* Pointer to stack of free nodes */
  if TYP(P)='BLACK' or TYP(P)='WHITE' then
    output(TYP(P))
  else if LEV=VOXEL_LEVEL then
    output(CLASSIFY_VOXEL(P));
  else /* Subdivide and prune the CSG trees */
    begin
      FS←first_free(csgnode);
        /* Save pointer to free storage stack  */
      output('NON-LEAF');
      if LEV mod D=0 then W←W/2;
      CSG_TRAVERSE(PRUNE(P,LEV+1,W,'LEFT'),LEV+1,W);
      free(FS); /* Release storage for CSG tree nodes */
      CSG_TRAVERSE(PRUNE(P,LEV+1,W,'RIGHT'),LEV+1,W);
      free(FS);
    end;
end;
```

```
pointer csgnode procedure PRUNE(P,LEV,W,DIR);
/* Evaluate the portion of the CSG tree P that overlaps the
   D-dimensional subuniverse of volume 2^-LEV whose smallest
   side has width W. The subuniverse corresponds to the DIR
   (LEFT or RIGHT) subtree of its father bintree node. */
begin
  value pointer csgnode P;
  value integer LEV;
  value real W;
  value direction DIR;
  pointer csgnode T,Q; /* Auxiliary variables */
  pointer csgnode L,R;
    /* Auxiliary pointers to left and right pruned subtrees */
  if TYP(P)='HALFSPACE' then
    return(HSPEVAL(P,LEV,W,DIR))
  else
    begin
      T←if TYP(P)='UNION' then BLACK_CSG_NODE
          else if TYP(P)='INTERSECTION' then
            WHITE_CSG_NODE
          else <error>; /* Enable a quick application of prun-
          ing rules (1) and (4) */
      L←PRUNE(LEFT(P),LEV,W,DIR);
      if L=T then return(T)
      else
        begin
          R←PRUNE(RIGHT(P),LEV,W,DIR);
          if R=T then return(T)
          else if TYP(L)=OPPOSITE(TYP(T)) then return(R)
            /* OPPOSITE of BLACK is WHITE and vice
               versa */
          else if TYP(R)=OPPOSITE(TYP(T)) then return(L)
          else    /* Evaluation has not resulted in eliminating */
            begin /* one of P's sons */
              Q←create(csgnode);
              TYP(Q)←TYP(P);
              LEFT(Q)←L;
              RIGHT(Q)←R;
              return(Q);
            end;
        end;
    end;
end;
```

```
pointer csgnode procedure HSPEVAL(P,LEV,W,DIR);
/* Determine if the D-dimensional subuniverse of volume
   2^-LEV and smallest side of width W intersects halfspace P
   or corresponds to a BLACK or WHITE region. The
   subuniverse is the DIR (LEFT or RIGHT) subtree of its
   father. If the halfspace intersects the subuniverse, then the
   subuniverse will have to be subdivided again and a new
   CSG tree node is allocated for the halfspace to record the
   new minimum and maximum values of the halfspace. */
begin
  value pointer csgnode P;
  value integer LEV;
  value real W;
  value direction DIR;
  integer I,J;
  real DELTA;
  pointer csgnode Q;
  Q←create_and_copy(P);
  J←HSP(P);
  I←LEV mod D;
  DELTA←HS[J,I+1]*W;
  if DIR='LEFT' then
    begin
      if DELTA≤0 then MIN(Q)←MIN(Q)-DELTA
      else MAX(Q)←MAX(Q)-DELTA;
    end
  else
    begin
      if DELTA>0 then MIN(Q)←MIN(Q)+DELTA
      else MAX(Q)←MAX(Q)+DELTA;
    end;
  if MIN(Q)>-EPSILON then return(BLACK_CSG_NODE)
  else if MAX(Q)<EPSILON then
    return(WHITE_CSG_NODE)
  else return(Q);  /* The subuniverse is intersected */
end;
```

4. TIME AND MOTION

Often a geometric representation, such as CSG, is not convenient for a desired computation. The solution that is frequently adopted is to transform the object into another representation - i.e., one in which the computation is simpler. In the previous section we saw how a CSG representation can be converted to a bintree. In this section we show how the time dimension can be added to a CSG representation so that motion can be analyzed using the algorithm of the previous section.

Let T be a solid model described by a CSG tree and assume that it is defined in some model-specific coordinate system. We describe the motion of T in some common world coordinate system by a time-varying geometric transformation matrix $A(t)$. Each value of $A(t)$ is a matrix defining a rigid motion from the local coordinates of T to its position and orientation in world coordinates at time t. Note that if our world coordinate system is the unit cube, then we may also have to include a scaling in $A(t)$. We call $A(t)$ the *trajectory* of T. Let $A(t)$ be piecewise linear, meaning that it can be broken down into a series of segments defined by time points $(t_0,t_1,\cdots)$ so that $A_{i+1}=A_i B_i$, where B_i is a transformation matrix corresponding to a translation describing the motion during that time segment. In the following we discuss the motion accomplished in one time segment in a more concrete setting.

Translating a halfspace, say given by (1), along a vector v gives rise to the translated halfspace

$$\sum_{i=0}^{d} a_i \cdot x_i - \sum_{i=0}^{d} a_i \cdot v_i \geq 0 \qquad (2)$$

If point x satisfies (1), then the transformed (translated) point $x+v$ satisfies (2). In order to be dimensionally-consistent with the d-dimensional unit cube, our discussion always assumes a unit time interval. Motion in a unit time interval, and at a fixed speed defined by vector s with $s_0=0$, is described by a vector v such that for all i, $v_i=s_i \cdot t$. Thus using v to translate halfspace (1) we find that at each instant, say t, it corresponds to the halfspace given by (3), below. Letting t vary, we obtain a linear halfspace with an additional variable t.

$$\sum_{i=0}^{d} a_i \cdot x_i - (\sum_{i=0}^{d} a_i \cdot s_i) \cdot t \geq 0 \qquad (3)$$

When we have a CSG tree in motion, transformation (3) can be applied to each halfspace separately and the tree of Boolean set operations applied to the resulting $(d+1)$-dimensional halfspaces to define a set of points in (location,time)-space satisfying the CSG tree.

For dynamic interference detection, we must determine whether the intersection of two (location,time) objects is empty while for static interference detection, we must check whether two stationary objects intersect or whether a moving object intersects a stationary one. The intersection of two different (location,time) CSG trees, (each derived from a separate motion but with a common "time axis") is obtained by attaching them as sons to a newly created CSG node of type INTERSECTION. The actual evaluation of the intersection can be performed by applying the bintree conversion algorithm of Section 3 in the $(d+1)$-dimensional space with time included. For static interference detection there is no need to add time as an extra dimension if we can otherwise solve for the swept area of the moving object. Note also that in the case of interference detection there is often little motivation for storing the entire resulting tree. Instead, a variable can be included in the tree traversal algorithm to indicate the minimal t value of a BLACK node encountered so far in the traversal. Any subtree whose minimum value of t is greater than this value need not be inspected.

Usually primary interest is not in motion along a straight vector but in more complicated trajectories. Assume that such trajectories can be approximated by a sequence of segments, each with motion corresponding to a linear translation at a fixed speed. For example, suppose that we wish to determine whether two motions, defined by piecewise linear trajectories A_{1i} and A_{2i} of objects T_1 and T_2, respectively, intersect in the unit time interval. Let the time intervals defining the n_1 and n_2 linear pieces of the trajectories be $(t_{10},t_{11},\cdots)$ and $(t_{20},t_{21},\cdots)$, respectively. Now, during the time interval $(0,\min(t_{10},t_{20}))$ both motions are linear and their intersection can be determined as discussed above. This same procedure is applied to the remaining intervals (a maximum of n_1+n_2-1 intervals) each preceded by an application of the appropriate transformations A_{ij} to the halfspaces of T_1 and T_2.

In the general case, a CSG tree can contain non-linear halfspaces or the motion itself cannot be described as a series of translations. Nevertheless, we can still use methods similar to the ones described above. In particular, each bintree node corresponds to a $(d+1)$-dimensional *interval* such that $x_0 \leq x < x_1$, $y_0 \leq y < y_1$, $\cdots$, $t_0 \leq t < t_1$. *Interval arithmetic* is a method of evaluating functions $f(x,y,\cdots)$ in cases where the arguments are not exact values but intervals. The value of the interval function corresponding to function f is also an interval - i.e., a range covering any values that f can obtain given as arguments any values in the argument intervals. It should be clear that interval arithmetic is appropriate for the CSG tree to bintree conversion process since for an arbitrary function the value of the corresponding interval function covers the function's possible values in the bintree node. If zero does not belong to this range, then the bintree block need not be subdivided.

For example, let us apply the above to determine the (location,time) bintree of a linear halfspace a subjected to arbitrary motion defined by the matrix function $A(t)$. Denoting intervals by capital letters, the interval function that must be evaluated at each node of the bintree is $F(X,T)=(A^{-1}(T)a)\cdot X$ where X is an interval in d-dimensional space and T is a time interval. Remember that at each time instant t, $A(t)$ is a linear transformation and the image of a halfspace, say a, is obtained by multiplying a by the inverse of $A(t)$. When $A(t)$ contains a rotation, the interval function will be a linear composition of sine and cosine functions with respect to T. In any sub-interval of T, where the composite function is monotonic, interval arithmetic can be applied in a fashion to provide tight bounds for the resulting interval.

Interval arithmetic is easy to incorporate in our CSG tree to bintree conversion since we merely need to recast procedure HSPEVAL in terms of interval evaluations. Procedure INT_HSPEVAL given below achieves this and can be substituted for procedure HSPEVAL of Section 3 in procedure PRUNE. Notice the use of INTERVAL_EVALUATE to determine the range of the function corresponding to the non-linear halfspace. Its value is a pointer to a record of type *interval* with two fields MIN and MAX corresponding to an interval covering the function values in the node.

```
pointer csgnode procedure INT_HSPEVAL(P,LEV,W,DIR);
/* Use interval arithmetic to determine if the D-dimensional
   subuniverse of volume 2^-LEV intersects non-linear halfspace
   P or is BLACK or WHITE.  W is its smallest side. The
   subuniverse is the DIR subtree of its father. */
begin
  value pointer csgnode P; /* A leaf of the CSG tree */
  value integer LEV;
  value real W;
  value direction DIR;
  interval I;
  I←INTERVAL_EVALUATE(P,LEV,W,DIR);
  return(if MAX(I)≤EPSILON then WHITE_CSG_NODE
         else if MIN(I)≥-EPSILON then
           BLACK_CSG_NODE
         else 'HALFSPACE');
end;
```

Interval arithmetic has been applied to the somewhat similar task of evaluating curved surfaces by recursive subdivision [1,11]. Nevertheless, this technique should be used with caution. In particular, interval arithmetic does not necessarily yield the minimal range covering the function's values given the domains of the arguments; instead, it may be a wider interval guaranteed to cover the function's values. This estimate may sometimes be very poor, and the poorer the substitute for the true range of function values, the more unnecessary subdivision we must perform in the bintree conversion. There are many function transformations that can be applied to tighten the ranges [1].

Usually we are not interested in time as such. Often it merely serves as an auxiliary variable for describing motion. For instance, the process of determining the swept area for static interference detection is equivalent to a transformation that eliminates the time dimension. In geometric terms it is a projection parallel to the t-axis. In general, we do not know how to perform such a projection directly in the CSG representation. Given a CSG tree having A OP B as its root, we cannot necessarily distribute the projection operation - i.e.,

$$\text{PROJ(A OP B)} \neq \text{PROJ(A) OP PROJ(B)}$$

For example, suppose we are given two non-intersecting objects as in Figure 7 that are moving at identical speeds in the directioh of the x-axis. Clearly, their swept areas intersect whereas the objects themselves do not intersect.

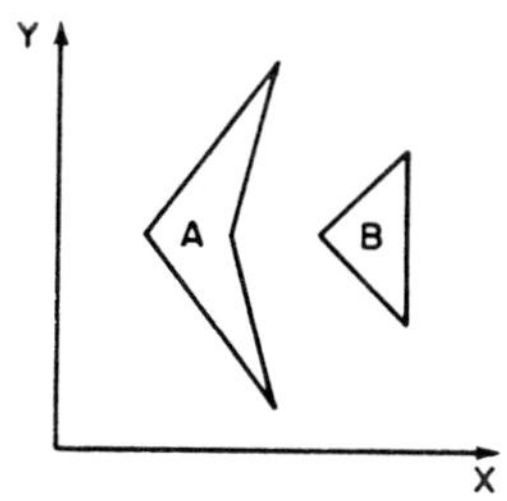

Figure 7. Example of two disjoint objects A and B whose projection on the y-axis is non-empty.

Fortunately, projection in the discrete bintree domain is simple. Approximate evaluation of a CSG tree involving a projection operation is a two-step process. We first generate the $(d+1)$-dimensional bintree and then project it to d dimensions to obtain an evaluation of the projected CSG tree as a d-dimensional bintree (see [16]). Projection consists of eliminating one coordinate and keeping track of all occupied locations in the resulting d-dimensional space. In three dimensions, the projection algorithm is almost identical to that for viewing a three-dimensional bintree in the direction of a coordinate axis [18]. The only difference is that in viewing, some shading information must be recorded at each 2-d pixel that is "covered", whereas the projection discussed here only records whether or not such a pixel is covered.

5. ANALYSIS

A quick perusal of procedure CSG_TO_BINTREE, as given in Section 3, reveals that the amount of work performed in the conversion is proportional to the sum of the sizes of the CSG trees that are active at the bintree nodes (i.e., blocks) that are evaluated. This number can be quite large even though procedure CSG_TRAVERSE attempts to prune the CSG tree each time it descends to a deeper level in the tree. However, in a typical case, as we descend in the bintree, many of the CSG tree nodes are no longer active thereby reducing the number of CSG nodes that must be visited. We are not interested in the absolute worst-case value of the complexity. Instead, we shall focus on the "practical" efficiency of these algorithms. Very poor cases can be attained by constructing a complicated CSG tree that evaluates to the NULL object in such a way that the whole CSG tree is active in a large number of nodes. For example, consider the intersection of a halfspace with its complement. In fact, a pruned CSG tree may be active in a bintree block even though the CSG tree defines a NULL object in the region corresponding to the block. For example, consider the CSG tree given in Figure 8a consisting of the two circles L1 and R and the halfspaces A and B as shown in Figure 8b. The CSG tree of Figure 8a is active in the bintree block represented by the dashed square in Figure 8b even though the object defined by it does not extend so far.

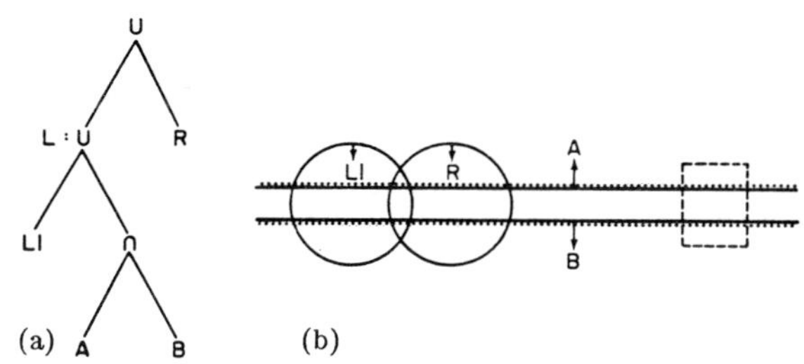

Figure 8. (a) A CSG tree and (b) its corresponding object.

First, let us examine the number of halfspaces that are active at each node of voxel size in a bintree of a polyhedron. This discussion is heuristic in that we speak of voxels as if they were infinitely small. At each vertex, at least three halfspaces are active. Elsewhere at each edge of the polyhedron exactly two halfspaces are active. Elsewhere at each face, only one halfspace is active. We can estimate the total number of active halfspaces by counting the number of voxels that intersect the edges, vertices, and faces of the polyhedron. We know that the total number of voxels intersecting faces is proportional to the surface area [9] while the total number of voxels that intersect edges is proportional to the sum of the edge lengths at the given resolution [4]. The number of voxels containing vertices is always bounded by the number of vertices irrespective of resolution. Assuming a resolution of M, the number of voxels with more than one active halfspace grows only linearly with M, while the total number of voxels grows with M^2. Thus the average number of halfspaces active in a node of voxel size approaches one asymptotically in a CSG tree that corresponds to a polyhedron. A similar result will hold for polyhedron-like objects of arbitrary dimension.

It should be clear that the amount of work necessary in performing the conversion is at least proportional to the number of nodes in the bintree. It has been shown [16] that there exists a class of CSG trees for which the complexity of evaluation is of the same order as the number of nodes in the bintree of the corresponding object. Such CSG trees are said to be "well-behaved" and this concept applies also to CSG trees with non-linear halfspaces. This characteristic is determined solely by the way the objects defined by the pair of brother subtrees of the CSG tree intersect each other. In a well-behaved CSG tree the intersections are not allowed to be "tangential". In two dimensions, this means that the boundaries of the objects corresponding to brother subtrees intersect at only a finite number of points. In three dimensions, for polyhedra, the boundaries should not coincide but are permitted to intersect along one-dimensional edges. In the general case, for d dimensions, the permitted intersection must similarly be at most (d–2)-dimensional (see [16] for more details). Generalizing Hunter's and Meagher's image complexity results for polygons and polyhedra to d dimensions leads to a complexity of $O(M^{d-1})$ bintree nodes for bintrees of resolution M. This bound is attainable in a manner that does not depend on the number of nodes in the CSG tree. The following theorem, a variant of whose proof can be found in [16], summarizes the above discussion.

Theorem: Let T be a well-behaved CSG tree defining a non-degenerate d-dimensional object. The proportion of bintree nodes where more than one CSG tree node is active approaches zero asymptotically as the resolution increases.

The above results lead us to draw the following unexpected but practical conclusions about the performance of our algorithms for the conversion of CSG trees to bintrees when the CSG trees are well-behaved.

(1) The "practical" complexity of CSG tree evaluation is $O(M^{d-1})$ as resolution M is increased.
(2) The average number of active CSG tree nodes in a bintree block approaches one asymptotically as resolution is increased.
(3) The computational complexity of converting a CSG tree approximation of a given object to a bintree is asymptotically independent of the number of halfspaces used in the approximation.

Result (3) means that the linear approximation of curved halfspaces can be computationally practical even though it leads to a great increase in the size of the CSG tree. Of course, the above results are asymptotical and thus are directly relevant only when the number of halfspaces is not large in comparison to the resolution.

6. EMPIRICAL RESULTS

In order to test our predictions, we conducted a number of experiments with polyhedron-like objects in several dimensions. Our experiments have been performed with versions of the algorithms of Section 3, as implemented in C in the system [18] and executed on a VAX 11/750 running version 4.2BSD of UNIX. Note that the contribution to CPU time incurred by writing the packed DF-expression into a file is quite noticeable.

At each bintree node a fixed amount of work is performed for each CSG tree node that is active in it. Thus an implementation-independent measure of work is the total number of CSG tree nodes active at all of the bintree nodes. This is reported as the statistic "CSG evaluations" below. The statistic "Halfspace evaluations" forms part of it and denotes the number of halfspace value range computations performed. Note that the algorithm can be implemented in a manner that requires only one addition operation for each such evaluation [16]. From these values we can derive the average number of active CSG tree nodes (or halfspaces) in a bintree node for the purpose of comparison with the theoretical analysis. Note that the program that we instrumented used a pointer-less CSG tree representation, which allows less pruning than the algorithm we have described in Section 3. Thus the number of CSG node evaluations reported below is an upper bound on the true value obtained by the algorithm.

For our first experiment we approximated a circle with an 11-gon and formed its bintree at resolution 4096. This approximation produced a bintree with 80828 nodes and required 87592 CSG tree node and 81823 halfspace evaluations. Thus on the average each bintree node contained less than 1.1 active CSG tree nodes which correlates with our prediction. The CPU time required was 19.2 seconds, including about 6 seconds necessary to output the packed DF-expression. The time required to perform the same task by a program specifically designed to convert convex polyhedra was 17.1 CPU seconds so that the overhead of the general CSG tree representation was not very large.

The second experiment demonstrates that the complexity of CSG tree evaluation is $O(M^{d-1})$ as resolution M is increased. For this experiment we tabulate in Table 1 the CPU conversion times for a series of approximations of a unit circle by 5, 11, and 19 halfspaces at various resolutions. Notice that the execution time doubles with resolution as predicted for $d=2$. The different approximations are not completely comparable as they represent different objects. Thus the bintree at resolution 4096 contains 76294, 80628 and 81410 nodes for 5, 11 and 19 halfspaces respectively.

Table 1. Conversion times (CPU seconds) for different discs.

Number of Halfspaces	Resolution				
	256	512	1024	2048	4096
5	1.2	2.1	4.2	8.5	16.2
11	1.7	2.9	4.7	9.4	17.1
19	2.5	3.8	6.1	10.8	18.6

The third experiment shows that the size of the three-dimensional bintree of a polyhedron is proportional to the square of the resolution and a four-dimensional bintree is proportional to the third power of the resolution. The execution times for large values of resolution exhibited similar behavior. For this we modeled the motion of two identical square blocks situated at opposite corners of the unit square, moving towards each other, so that at time $t=1$ they overlap on an area of size 0.05 by 0.05. We also performed an identical three-dimensional experiment (two moving boxes) resulting in a four-dimensional bintree. In the first case (Figure 9) we have a total of 8 halfspaces and in the second case we have a total of 12 halfspaces. Tables 2 and 3 contain the result of the evaluation of the three-dimensional and four-dimensional trees at varying resolutions. Note that for these examples, the maximum sizes of the universes are 2^{33} and 2^{36} voxels respectively.

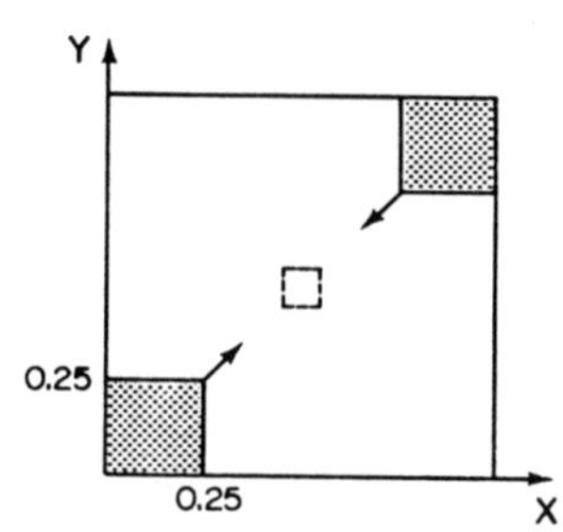

Figure 9. Intersection of two moving objects.

Table 2. Intersecting two moving 2-d blocks.

Resolution	CPU seconds	BIN nodes	Halfspace evaluations	CSG evaluations
64	0.7	826	1641	3124
128	1.3	2898	4357	7300
256	3.2	10866	13552	19358
512	10.3	42514	47684	59254
1024	37.6	172802	183335	207248
2048	144.1	699362	720631	769768

Table 3. Intersecting two moving 3-d blocks.

Resolution	CPU seconds	BIN nodes	Halfspace evaluations	CSG evaluations
16	0.8	370	1846	3900
32	1.2	898	3354	7008
64	3.1	4658	10471	21326
128'	12.5	31458	49969	90614
256	67.4	231570	295662	430730
512	428.0	1826466	2071158	2695692

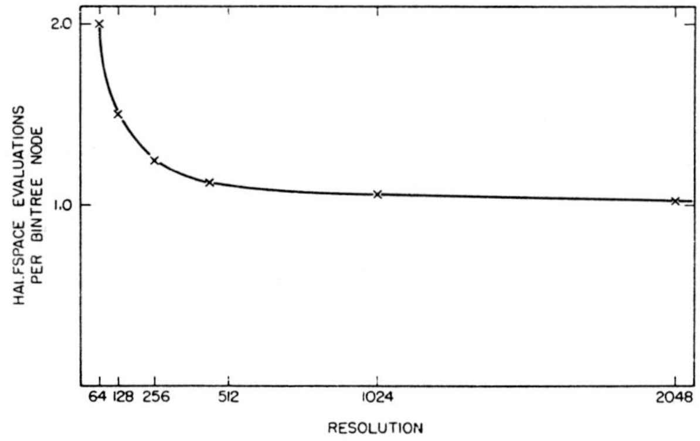

Figure 10. The number of halfspace evaluations per bintree node as a function of resolution for Table 2.

Figure 10 shows the number of halfspace evaluations per bintree node as a function of resolution in the experiment of Table 2. Notice that the asymptotical bound does hold in this case. Nevertheless, inspection of Tables 2 and 3 shows that the convergence to this bound is not necessarily very fast in the high dimensional (location,time)-space. Therefore this method should be used primarily when the CSG tree is expected to evaluate to NULL. Furthermore, it is much more efficient to determine just the first moment of intersection. In order to illustrate this point, we modified the coefficient of time in the experiment reported in Table 3 so that the true intersection was localized within eight three-dimensional voxels. The resulting four-dimensional evaluation at resolution 512 produced 530 bintree nodes (of which 8 were BLACK), evaluated 2765 halfspaces and 5884 CSG tree nodes, and required 1.2 CPU seconds.

The above experiments have only dealt with convex objects (i.e., intersections of halfspaces). To study the performance of our algorithms with a UNION operation, we performed one more simple experiment. We used hexagons to approximate five disks with radii 0.3 and centers at (0.0,0.0), (0.25, 0.25), (0.5,0.5), (0.75,0.75) and (1.0,1.0). The CSG tree that describes the union of these five circles within the unit square was of depth 6 and contained 30 leaves and 29 internal nodes (see Figure 11). Table 4 contains the results on a VAX 11/780.

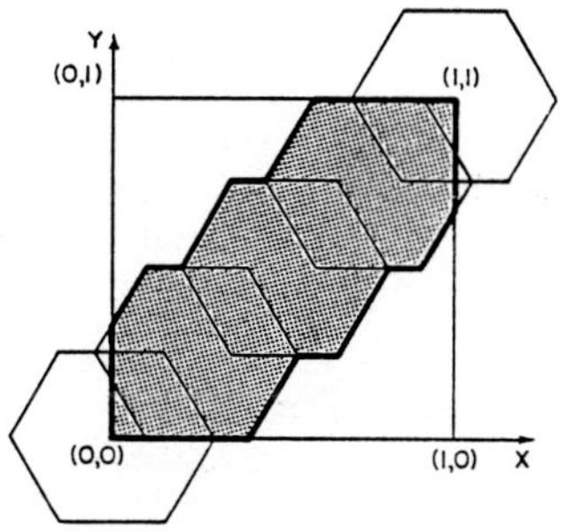

Figure 11. Union of five hexagons within the unit cube.

Table 4. Union of five disks approximated as hexagons.

Resolution	CPU seconds	BIN nodes	Halfspace evaluations
1024	2.1	14418	17748
2048	3.9	28828	29489
4096	7.1	57654	58353

7. CONCLUDING REMARKS

The analysis of the execution time of CSG to bintree conversion was based on our definition of well-behaved which eliminated certain objects. If we expect such objects (beside the extensions reported below), the more complicated CSG tree redundancy checking algorithms of Tilove [19] should be used once the pruned tree has reached a certain (small) size. Note, however, that if we apply as CLASSIFY_VOXEL a CSG evaluation at the center of the voxel, no incorrect "false positive" bintree nodes result (i.e., nodes that should be completely WHITE but are classified as BLACK).

As presented, the algorithm of Section 3 does not handle the case that both a halfspace and its complement are leaves of the CSG tree. This case is actually quite common when a CSG tree is composed of a union of convex components (e.g., a triangulation). Nevertheless, the performance of our algorithms, as well as the analytical results of Section 5, remain valid by adding the following rule to the CSG evaluation in procedure PRUNE:

> If in a bintree node only a halfspace and its complement are active, then the node is BLACK if the root of the active CSG tree is UNION, and WHITE otherwise.

Our algorithms have several useful applications aside from volume-like computations and interference checking. Viewing three-dimensional CSG models is a prime application [7]. In this case bintree conversion would be performed solely for the sake of generating shaded output. The method of viewing three-dimensional bintrees in the direction of a coordinate axis described in [18] can be used in this case because the eyepoint dependent operations (e.g., perspective transformation of halfspaces, etc.) can precede bintree conversion. Shading would be generated from the normals of the halfspaces active at each visible node at voxel level. Evaluation would proceed from front to back and be combined with projection so that the nodes known to be covered would not be generated. The efficiency of our conversion algorithm is such that this might be a practical alternative as a system for viewing faceted three-dimensional CSG trees [2].

ACKNOWLEDGEMENTS

This work was supported in part by the National Science Foundation under Grant DCR-8302118 and in part by the Finnish Academy. We thank Jarmo Alander, Olli Karonen, Petri Koistinen, Walter Kropatsch, Martti Mantyla, Reijo Sulonen, and Robert E. Webber for comments.

REFERENCES

[1] J. Alander, Interval arithmetic methods in the processing of curves and sculptured surfaces, *Proceedings of the Sixth International Symposium on CAD/CAM,* Zagreb, Yugoslavia (1984).

[2] P.R. Atherton, A scan-line hidden surface removal procedure for constructive solid geometry, *Computer Graphics 17,* 3(1983), 73-82.

[3] J.W. Boyse, Interference detection among solids and surfaces, *Communications of the ACM 22,* 1(January 1979), 3-9.

[4] G.M. Hunter, Efficient computation and data structures for graphics, Ph.D. dissertation, Department of Electrical Engineering and Computer Science, Princeton University, Princeton, NJ, 1978.

[5] C. Jackins and S.L. Tanimoto, Quad-trees, oct-trees, and k-trees - a generalized approach to recursive decomposition of Euclidean space, *IEEE Transactions on Pattern Analysis and Machine Intelligence 5,* 5(September 1983), 533-539.

[6] E. Kawaguchi and T. Endo, On a method of binary picture representation and its application to data compression, *IEEE Transactions on Pattern Analysis and Machine Intelligence 2,* 1(January 1980), 27-35.

[7] P. Koistinen, M. Tamminen, and H. Samet, Viewing solid models by bintree conversion, to appear in *Proceedings of the EUROGRAPHICS '85 Conference,* Nice, September 1985.

[8] Y.T. Lee and A.A.G. Requicha, Algorithms for computing the volume and other integral properties of solids. I and II, *Communications of the ACM 25,* 9(September 1982), 635-650.

[9] D. Meagher, Octree encoding: a new technique for the representation, manipulation and display of arbitrary 3-D objects by computer, Report IPL-TR-80-111, Rensselaer Polytechnic Institute, Troy, New York, 1980.

[10] D. Meagher, The Solids engine: a processor for interactive solid modeling, *Proceedings of the NICOGRAPH '84 Conference,* Tokyo, November 1984.

[11] S.P. Mudur and P.A. Koparkar, Interval methods for processing geometric objects, *IEEE Computer Graphics and Applications 4,* 2(February 1984), 7-17.

[12] N. Okino, Y. Kakazu, and H. Kubo, TIPS-1: Technical information processing system for computer aided design, drawing and manufacturing, in *Computer Languages for Numerical Control,*, J. Hatvany, Ed., North Holland, Amsterdam, 1973, 141-150.

[13] A.A.G. Requicha, Representations of rigid solids: theory, methods, and systems, *ACM Computing Surveys 12,* 4(December 1980), 437-464.

[14] A.A.G. Requicha and H.B. Voelcker, Solid modeling: current status and research directions, *IEEE Computer Graphics and Applications 3,* 7(1983), 25-37.

[15] H. Samet, The quadtree and related hierarchical data structures, *ACM Computing Surveys 16,* 2(June 1984), 187-260.

[16] H. Samet and M. Tamminen, Approximating CSG trees of moving objects, Computer Science TR-1472, University of Maryland, College Park, MD, January 1985.

[17] M. Tamminen and H. Samet, Efficient octree conversion by connectivity labeling, *Computer Graphics 18,* 3(July 1984), pp. 43-51 (also *Proceedings of the SIGGRPAH '84 Conference,* Minneapolis, July 1984).

[18] M. Tamminen, P. Koistinen, J. Hamalainen, O. Karonen, P. Korhonen, R. Raunio, and P. Rekola, Bintree: a dimension independent image processing system, Report-HTKK-TKO-C9, Helsinki University of Technology, 1984.

[19] R.B. Tilove, A null-object detection algorithm for constructive solid geometry, *Communications of the ACM 27,* 7(July 1984), 684-694.

[20] A.F. Wallis and J.R. Woodwark, Creating large solid models for NC toolpath verification, *Proceedings of CAD 84,* 1984.

[21] J.R. Woodwark and K.M. Quinlan, Reducing the effect of complexity on volume model evaluation, *Computer-aided Design 14,* 2(1982), 89-95.

[22] M. Yau and S.N. Srihari, A hierarchical data structure for multidimensional digital images, *Communications of the ACM 26,* 7(July 1983), 504-515.

GEOMETRIC MODELING OF SOLID OBJECTS BY USING A FACE ADJACENCY GRAPH REPRESENTATION

Silvia Ansaldi °
Politecnico di Milano
Piazza L. Da Vinci, 32
20133 Milano, Italy

Leila De Floriani and *Bianca Falcidieno*
Istituto per la Matematica Applicata del C.N.R.
Via L.B. Alberti, 4
16132 Genova, Italy

Abstract

A relational graph structure based on a boundary representation of solid objects is described. In this structure, called face adjacency graph, nodes represent object faces, whereas edges and vertices are encoded into arcs and hyperarcs. Based on the face adjacency graph, we define a set of primitive face-oriented Euler operators, and a set of macrooperators for face manipulation, which allow a compact definition and an efficient updating of solid objects. We briefly describe a hierarchical graph structure based on the face adjacency graph, which provides a representation of an object at different levels of detail. Thus it is consistent with the stepwise refinement process through which the object description is produced.

1. Introduction

Geometric modeling is a relatively new research field, since the studies, which led to the geometric modeling systems currently in use, started about fifteen years ago. In these years, the attention of the researchers mostly concentrated on the problem of developing geometric representations of three-dimensional objects with the largest possible application domain. This intensive research activity has resulted in the development of current geometric modelers, most of which represent 3-D objects either in terms of the surfaces enclosing them (Boundary Representation), or as the boolean combination of volumetric primitives (Constructive Solid Geometry) /10/.

Current address: Selenia Autotrol, Via E. Ravasco, 10, 16121 Genova, Italy.

Although the study of complete, unique and general geometric models is still a current research issue in solid modeling, the attention is now mainly focused on the problem of the interface between the model and the designer, on one side, and the model and the application on the other side. This latter aspect of solid modeling is interesting and complex at the same time. Before, the choice of a mathematical model was done according to its capability of representing the largest possible number of solid objects, without taking into consideration at all the process through which the model is designed, or the application it is made for, for instance, whether the model must be transferred to the manufacture or used as reference for recognizing objects with similar features. The current trend is to consider the geometric modeling step as a part of the whole production process.

In this view, we define a relational structure based on a boundary representation, which completely reflects the design process. We make use of a boundary representation scheme, since it has a wide applicability, it is complete and unique, except for permutational non-uniqueness, provided that a partition of the object boundary into maximal, connected and quasi-disjoint faces is considered /2/.

The edge-based model, commonly used in geometric modeling systems employing a boundary representation /6,9/, forces the designer to construct and manipulate an object, which is thought as the collection of its faces, by operating on vertices and edges. In our approach, on the contrary, we select faces as object defining entities and the edge-face relation as the fundamental relation between primitive object entities. Our relational model, called face adjacency graph, explicitly encodes also vertices in the form of hyperarcs, which associate each vertex with the set of faces which are concurrent into it. The encoding structure of this model in an adjacency list form is an alternative to the classical winged-edge structure generally used for storing edge-based models /4,11/.

Based on the face adjacency graph, we designed an experimental geometric modeling system for defining and manipulating the boundary of three-dimensional objects with planar faces, so as to demonstrate the practical advantages deriving from the use of our model in a CAD application. The system is based on a set of face-oriented primitive Euler operators defined according to the characteristics of our model, which guarantee the topological validity of the resulting object. On this basis, we also define a set of topological macrooperators for a more efficient description and local manipulation of complex objects. These macrooperators are consistent with the model we use and essentially involve modifications of object faces.

To reflect, in the model itself, the refinement process through which an object is designed, we propose a hierarchical organization of the face adjacency graph, which provides a representation of objects at different levels of detail. In fact, the design process is hierarchical in nature, since the designer constructs the model of an object by first specifying its overall shape, and then inserting representation details as shape attributes. This information, relevant for applications like object recognition or manufacturing, is usually not maintained in classical boundary models, in which the graph structure represents all the parts of the model at the same level. The hierarchical design process is explicitly retained in the structured face adjacency graph, which is essentially a hierarchy of graphs, in which the root is the face adjacency graph representation of the general shape of the object and any other node is the adjacency structure describing one of its lower attributes.

2. A hypergraph-based model of the boundary of a solid object

The topology of an object can be conveniently expressed in the form of a relational model, in which its primitive topological entities, namely faces, edges and vertices, together with their mutual relationships, are explicitly represented. A boundary representation of an object S can be defined as a triple $B_S = (V_S, E_S, F_S)$, in which V_S, E_S and F_S denote the set of vertices, edges and faces of S respectively. Nine adjacency relations can be defined on these primitive elements. Some of these relations are sufficient to reconstruct all of the others without error and ambiguity /11/.

By reflecting the intrinsic hierarchy of geometric information, in which surfaces are considered as defining geometric entities and curves and points as derived ones, we define a relational model of a boundary representation scheme, called Face Adjancency Graph (FAG), in which the nodes correspond to the object faces, and the arcs represent relationships among faces induced by the edges and vertices. This model represents a further development of the edge-face graph defined in a previous paper /2/, in which only the adjacency relationships between pairs of faces defined by the edges are represented.

In a boundary reprentation B_S of an object S, sets E_S and V_S define two relations over F_S. Two faces f_1 and f_2 are called edge-adjacent if and only if there exists an edge e in E_S shared by f_1 and f_2. Also, two faces f_1 and f_2 are called vertex-adjacent if and only if there exists a vertex v in V_S shared by f_1 and f_2. Face-edge relation and the partition of F_S into equivalence classes defined by the face-vertex one can be represented in the form of a hypergraph, which can be intuitively defined as a graph in which arcs may connect an arbitrary number of nodes /5/.

A face adjacency graph of an object S is a hypergraph G = (N,A,H) such that

(i) for every face f in F_S there exists a unique node n in N corresponding to f;

(ii) for every edge e in E_S, shared by two faces f_1 and f_2 of S, there exists a unique arc in A connecting the two nodes n_1 and n_2 of N, which correspond to f_1 and f_2 respectively;

(iii) for every vertex v in V_S, we define $F_v \subset F_S$ as the set of faces of S concurrent into v and $N_v \subset N$ as the subset of nodes of G which correspond to the faces of F_v; then, for every v in V_S, there exists a unique element in H, called hyperarc, which connects the nodes of N_v.

Fig. 1 shows a cube and its face adjacency graph representation. In the diagram, dashed lines represent hyperarcs, and continuous lines arcs.

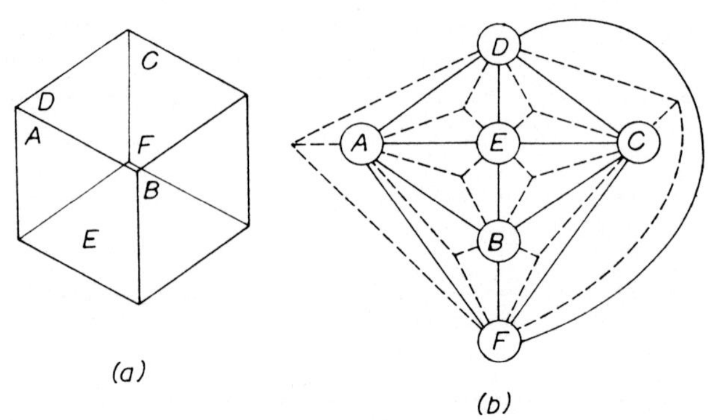

Figure 1. A cube and its FAG representation.

In our terminology, we distinguish between arcs and hyperarcs of G, belonging respectively to sets A and H, the former connecting pairs of nodes, the latter arbitrary numbers of nodes of G. This separation is done because of the different semantics of the elements of A and H when referred to their corresponding topological entities of the objects. The above definition establishes a one-to-one correspondence between N and F_S, A and E_S, and H and V_S. Since two faces of S may share more than one edge, the FAG may have multiple arcs. The vertices bounding a given face are represented by the hyperarcs incident into the corresponding node of G. All of the three primitive topological entities of a solid are explicitly represented in the FAG by different graph components. Despite the edge-face graph, the FAG contains additional information by encoding vertices as hyperarcs. In fact, the edgeface graph G'=(N,A) of S is a subgraph of G=(N,A,H) in which hyperarcs are missing. The FAG is also a more complete relational model of an object compared to the most common edge-vertex graph /7/, which can be regarded as the dual with respect to the edge-face subgraph of the FAG only if both graphs are planar, i.e. if the object under consideration has a null genus.

The topology of an object is hence well-defined by its FAG. Other topological entities, such as shells and loops, defined as collections of the primitive ones, and topological parameters, such as the multiplicity, and the number of protrusions or depressions on the faces of an object, can be extracted from the FAG. Also, the genus of S can be computed under the special assumption that every handle or through hole defines a holeloop on exactly two faces of S /2,3/.

The FAG encoded in a modified adjacency list form is used as internal representation of an object in our experimental geometric modeling system based on the operators described in the next two sections. In this representation, an ordering is defined over the arcs of G incident into a given node f, since these are organized into separate subsets according to the loops on the corresponding face of S. Also, the arcs in each subset are sorted in such a way that the corresponding edges of S define a loop in counterclockwise order. This organization is assumed in the abstract level description of the primitives for FAG manipulation, presented in the next two sections.

3. Euler operators

The validity of a representation scheme can be checked by applying generalized Euler's rule. This rule, in the formulation given below, expresses a necessary validity condition as a relation among six parameters, the number of vertices (v), edges (e), faces (f), shells (s), and holeloops on the faces (h) and the genus (g) of an object:

$$v - e + f = 2(s - g) + h.$$

Instead of performing a validity check at each updating, it is convenient to decompose each object modification into a sequence of atomic steps, called Euler operators, which ensure that the topological validity requirement expressed by Euler's formula is always satisfied /6,9/.

In this section, we describe a set of five constructive Euler operators. These operators have been chosen according to the FAG-based scheme defined, i.e. by operating essentially on the faces of an object considered as primitive defining entities. The set of operators selected is listed below, together with an informal description of their effect on both the object and its FAG. Only modifications of topological entities are described, regardless of any geometrical information.

MFVS (fnew, vnew, snew) Make Face Vertex Shell
Defines a new shell snew consisting of one face fnew and one vertex vnew belonging to fnew. The FAG is modified by inserting a new node, labeled fnew, corresponding to fnew and a hyperarc, labeled vnew, incident into fnew (see fig. 2a).
Transformation
(v,e,f,g,h,s) --> (v+1,e,f+1,g,h,s+1)

MEF (fnew, fold, enew, vold) Make Edge Face
Inserts a new face fnew and a new edge enew, which must have one extreme vertex vold already defined. The contour of face fnew will consist only of edge enew and vertex vold. The FAG is modified by the insertion of a new node fnew and a new arc enew connecting nodes fold and fnew. Node fnew is added to the set of nodes incident into the hyperarc vold already defined (see fig. 2b).
Transformation
(v,e,f,g,h,s) --> (v,e+1,f+1,g,h,s)

MEV (fold1,fold2,enew,vold,vnew) Make Edge Vertex
Adds a new edge enew between two already existing faces, fold1 and fold2, which connects an existing vertex vold with a new one vnew. The FAG is modified by adding a new arc enew between fold1 and fold2. A new hyperarc, labeled vnew, is added, which connects nodes fold1 and fold2 (see fig. 2c).
Transformation
(v,e,f,g,h,s) --> (v+1,e+1,f,g,h,s)

KFSMH (f,f',s,s') Kill Face Shell Make Holeloop
Joins two faces f and f' belonging to two different shells, s and s' respectively, in such a way that the boundary of f', assumed to be simply connected, becomes a holeloop in f. Shell s' and face f' are eliminated as a consequence. The FAG is modified by transforming every arc or hyperarc incident into f', into an arc or hyperarc incident into f, and deleting node f', as described by algorithm JOIN_NODES given below. Fig. 2d depicts the effect of the application of the above operator to two cubic shells.

Transformation

(v,e,f,g,h,s) --> (v,e,f-1,g,h+1,s-1)

In the description of the algorithm, ARCS (G,f',f") denotes the set of the arcs of the FAG G connecting the two nodes f' and f" and INCIDENT_HARCS (G,f) the set of the hyperarcs of G incident into f. The names of the primitives used are self-explanatory.

```
Algorithm JOIN_NODES (G,f,f')
   f":= FIRST_ADJACENT_NODE (G,f');
   while f"≠ null do
     for every e' in ARCS (G,f',f") do
       (v1,v2):= EXTREME_VERTICES (e');
       ADD_ARC (G,f,f",v1,v2,e);
       DELETE_ARC (G,e');
     end for;
     f":= NEXT_ADJACENT_NODE (G,f',f")
   end while;
   for every v' in INCIDENT_HARCS (G,f') do
     ADD_EXTREME_NODE_TO_HARC (G,v',f);
     DELETE_EXTREME_NODE_FROM_HARC (G,v',f');
   end for;
   DELETE_NODE (G,f')
end JOIN_NODES.
```

KFMHG (f,f') Kill Face Make Holeloop Genus Joins two coplanar faces f and f' belonging to the same shell in such a way that the boundary of f', assumed as simply connected, becomes a holeloop in f. Face f' is deleted and the genus of the object is incremented as consequence. The FAG is modified in a similar way as in the case of operator KFSMH (see fig. 2e), and, hence, algorithm JOIN_NODES is also a description of the effect of operator KFMHG on the FAG.

Transformation

(v,e,f,g,h,s) --> (v,e,f-1,g+1,h+1,s)

The inverses of the above constructive operators are listed below.

KFVS	(f,v,s)	Kill Face Vertex Shell
KEF	(e,f)	Kill Edge Face
KEV	(e,v)	Kill Edge Vertex
MFSKH	(f,f',s,s')	Make Face Shell Kill Holeloop
MFKHG	(f,f')	Make Face Kill Holeloop Genus

4. Definition and manipulation of solid objects

Primitive Euler operators provide a minimally complete set of basic functions for defining and manipulating three-dimensional solid objects, which can be mathematically expressed as r-sets with planar faces /13/. Independently of the choice of the Euler's basis, the use of such primitives as basic design tools is often impractical and highly inefficient. In this section, we define a set of higher level operators, called macrooperators, which allow both a compact definition and an efficient manipulation of solid objects. A large variety of objects can be simply defined as the combination of a restricted number of primitive solids, each of which can be described on the basis of a few parameters. A boundary representation of each primitive object can be expressed as an appropriate sequence of basic Euler operators. More properly, such a sequence of Euler operators defines a class of objects all having the same topological structure.

Many objects can also be described by a rigid movement of their cross sections, such as, for instance, translational or rotational sweeps applied to two-dimensional objects. As an example, we describe a translational sweep operator, called SWEEP_LAMINA, which transforms a two-dimensional, even multiply connected, face into a three-dimensional object by sweeping this face of a certain distance along a given direction. The face is specified as the collection of all loops bounding it. For each loop defining the two dimensional lamina, the bottom and the side faces are first constructed, together with the edges shared by them. Then, the top face and the edges which separate it from the side ones are built. Finally, all of the shells defined by the internal loops of the lamina are merged into the one corresponding to the external loop so as to construct an unique shell having a genus value equal to the number of interior loops. Algorithm SWEEP_LAMINA presented below describes the semantics of the corresponding operator in terms of primitive Euler operators. The names of the other primitives employed in the description are self-explanatory.

```
Algorithm SWEEP_LAMINA (L,d)
// Sweeps a lamina bounded by a set L of edge
   loops, L = {l1, l2,...lk} along vector d. Loop
   l1 in L is assumed to be the external loop.//
     for every li in L do
       elasti:= LAST_EDGE_IN (li);
       vfirsti:= FIRST_VERTEX_IN (elasti);
       MFVS (fi,vfirsti,si);
       MEF (fi,flasti,elasti,vfirsti);
       ei:= FIRST_EDGE_IN (li);
       f'i := flasti;
       vi:= vfirsti;
       while ei≠ elasti do
        MEF (f'i ,fsidei,everti,vi);
        v'i := OTHER_EXTREME_VERTEX (ei,vi);
        MEV (fi,fsidei,ei,vi,v'i );
        ei:= NEXT_EDGE_IN (li,ei);
        vi:= v'i;
        f'i:= fsidei
       end while;
       let vtransi be the vertex obtained from
           vfirsti by translation along d;
```

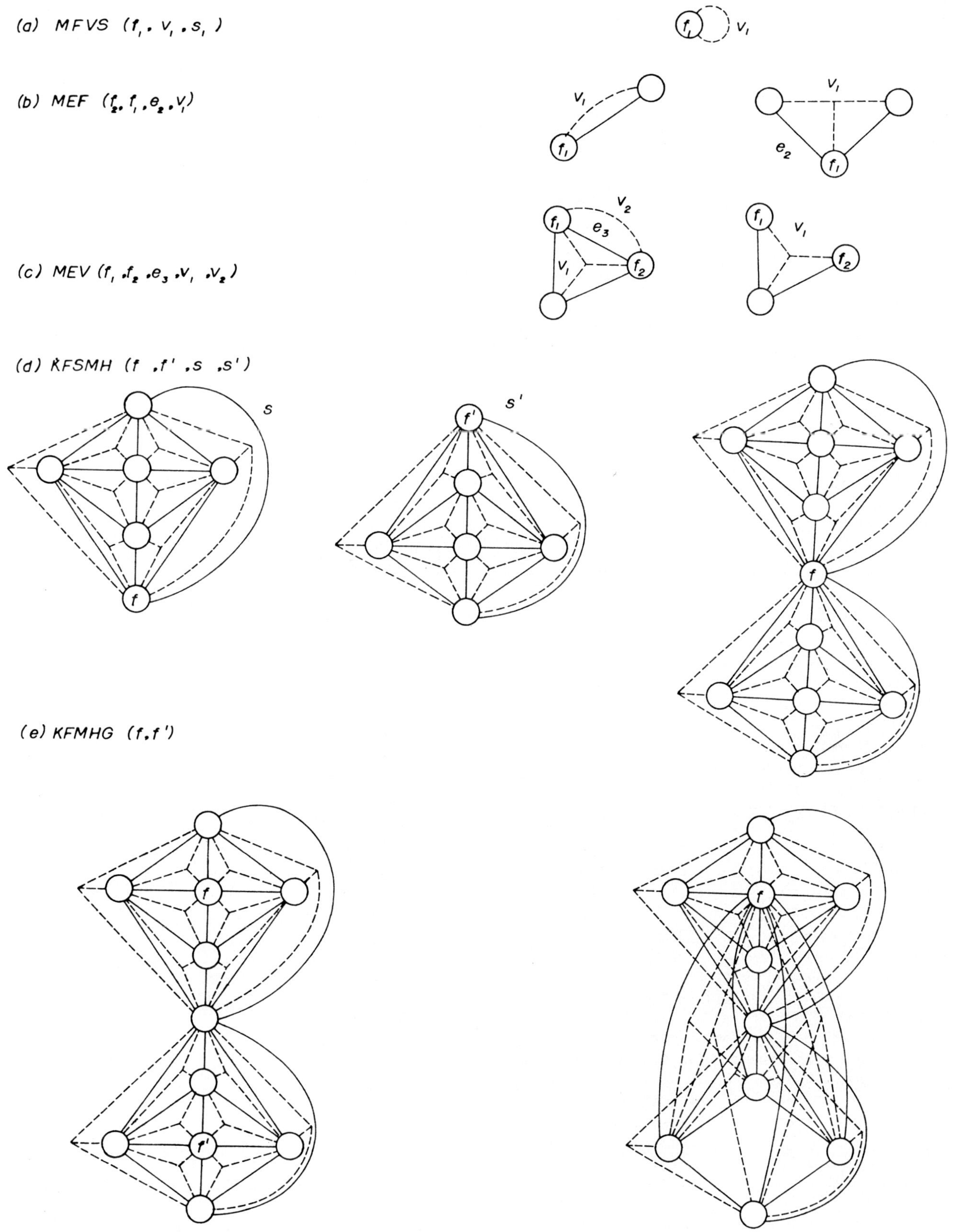

Figure 2. Effect of the five basic constructive operators on the FAG.

```
MEV (fside_i,flast_i,evert_i,vfirst_i,vtrans_i);
MEF(flast_i,ftop_i,etrans_i,vtrans_i);
e_i:=FIRST_EDGE_IN (1_i);
v_i:=vfirst_i;
while e_i ≠ elast_i do
  v'_i:= OTHER_EXTREME_VERTEX (e_i,v_i);
  let v̄_i be the vertex obtained from v'_i
      by translation along d;
  fside_i:= OTHER_FACE_SHARING (f_i,e_i);
  MEV (fside_i,ftop_i,ē_i,vtrans_i,v̄_i);
  e_i:= NEXT_EDGE_IN (1_i,e_i);
  vtrans_i:= v̄_i
end while;
if i > 1 then
   KFSMH (f_1,f_i,s_1,s_i);
   KFMHG (ftop_1,ftop_i)
end if
end for
end SWEEP_LAMINA.
```

Besides definition operators, we need to define a set of macrooperators for manipulating valid representations of objects. Such macrooperators, which must be consistent with the representation scheme we use, essentially modify the faces of the object by performing operations like replacement of vertices and edges by faces, or "glueing" of different objects along coincident faces. Since our relational model is a purely topological one, we consider only operators which affect object topology. Operations, which modify the geometry of an object, like geometric transformations, or tweaking operations, and thus operate on the whole set of faces or on subsets of faces, do not alter its topological structure. Also, set operators, which are the most commonly used macrooperators in geometric modeling systems, can be expressed in terms of a single join operation between the faces of temporary objects suitably computed from the original solids /9/.

In the following, we present three macrooperators, namely GLUE_FACE, GLUE_FACE_MAKE_HANDLE and REPLACE_VERTEX_WITH_FACE, giving an informal description of their effect on both the object and its FAG. Their algorithmic definition in terms of Euler operators is presented so as to guarantee the topological validity of the resulting model at each step of its construction. This description is independent of the graph representation used as basic relational model.

4.1 Operators GLUE_FACE and GLUE_FACE_MAKE_HANDLE

These operators are a generalization of the two primitive operators KFSMH and KFMHG to the case of coincident faces. Together with the two primitive ones, these two join operators are the fundamental tools to perform set operations on boundary models.

Operator GLUE_FACE (f,f',s,s') joins two faces (coincident and simply connected) f and f' belonging to shells s and s' respectively, in such a way that the two external loops of f and f' completely overlap. Shell s' and faces f and f' are deleted. The FAG is modified by merging the two connected components describing s and s', as shown in the example depicted in fig. 3. The two nodes n and n' corresponding to f and f' respectively are deleted and the adjacency relations of the nodes adjacent to n and n' are updated. The transformation performed by the operator is:

$$(v,e,f,s,h,g) \rightarrow (v-n,e-n,f-2,s-1,h,g)$$

where n denotes the number of vertices and edges composing the exterior loop of f and f'.
The names of the primitives employed in the description of algorithm GLUE_FACE given below are self-explanatory and, hence, their semantics is not described here. For the sake of simplicity only, we assume that the two faces are joined together by starting from the first edge of their external loop.

```
Algorithm GLUE_FACE (f,f',s,s')
  e:= FIRST_BOUNDING_EDGE (f);
  e':= FIRST_BOUNDING_EDGE (f');
  while e ≠ LAST_BOUNDING_EDGE (f) do
    f_1:= OTHER_FACE_SHARING (e,f);
    f'_1:= OTHER_FACE_SHARING (e',f');
    (v_1,v_2):= EXTREME_VERTICES (e);
    (v'_1,v'_2):= EXTREME_VERTICES (e');
    KEV(e,v_2);
    KEV (e',v'_1);
    MEV (f_1,f'_1,ē,v_1,v_2);
    e:= NEXT_BOUNDING_EDGE (f,e);
    e':= NEXT_BOUNDING_EDGE (f',e')
  end while;
  f_1:= OTHER_FACE_SHARING (e,f);
  f'_1:= OTHER_FACE_SHARING (e',f');
  (v_1,v_2):= EXTREME_VERTICES (e);
  (v'_1,v'_2):= EXTREME_VERTICES (e');
   KEV (e',v'_1);
   KEF (e,f);
   MEV(f_1,f'_1,ē,v_1,v_2);
   KFVS (f',v_2,s')
end GLUE_FACE.
```

Operator GLUE_FACE_MAKE_HANDLE joins two coincident and simply connected faces f and f' belonging to the same shell, in such a way that the loops defining f and f' completely overlap. Faces f and f' are deleted, and the genus of the object incremented.

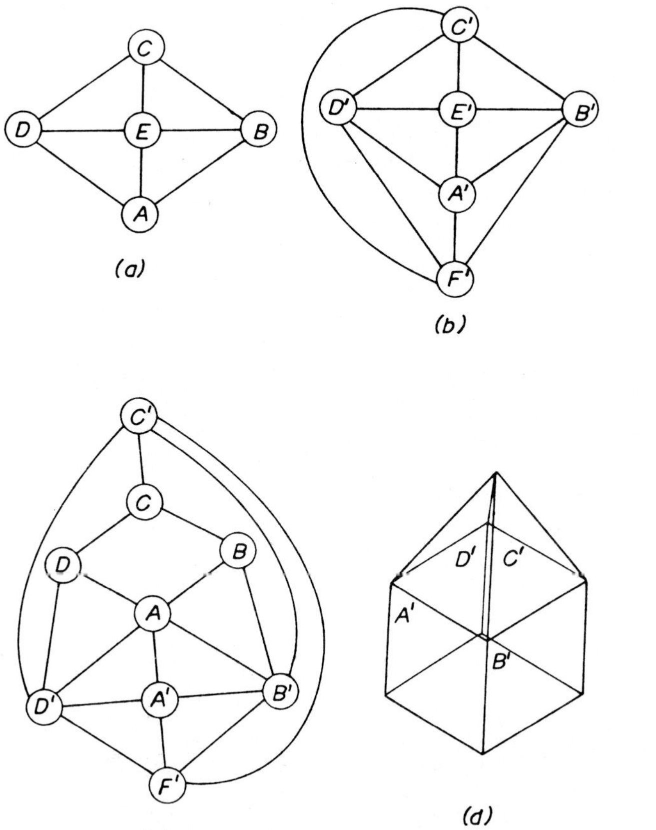

Figure 3. Effect of the application of macrooperator GLUE_FACE to faces E and E' belonging to a pyramid and a cube respectively
(a) FAG representation of a pyramid.
(b) FAG representation of a cube.
(c) FAG representation of the resulting object (d).

The algorithmic description of this operator is completely similar to algorithm GLUE_FACE, provided that the last call to KFVS is replaced by a call to a primitive operator KFVMG (Kill Face Vertex Make Genus), not belonging to the basis defined in the previous section, which deletes a face and a vertex from an object, increasing the value of its genus.

4.2 Operator REPLACE_VERTEX_WITH_FACE

Operator REPLACE_VERTEX_WITH_FACE (v,fnew) replaces vertex v with a new face fnew. The FAG is modified by replacing the hyperarc v with a new node fnew, and inserting a number of arcs incident into fnew equal to the number m of extreme nodes of v and m hyperarcs, each incident into fnew and into a pair of adjacent nodes in the set of extreme nodes of v. The transformation performed by this operator is:

(v,e,f,s,h,g) --> (v+m-1,e+m,f+1,s,h,g)

where m denotes the number of faces concurrent into vertex v.

Algorithm REPLACE_VERTEX_WITH_FACE presented below is a description of the semantics of the corresponding macrooperator in terms of Euler operators.

```
Algorithm REPLACE_VERTEX_WITH_FACE (v,fnew)
// the list of faces concurrent into a vertex is
   assumed to be a circular linked list organized
   in counterclockwise order//
  facelist:= LIST_OF_FACES_CONCURRENT_INTO (v);
  f':= FIRST_FACE_IN (facelist);
  f:= NEXT_FACE_IN (facelist, f');
  e':= EDGE_SHARED_BY (f',f,v);
  v':= OTHER_EXTREME_VERTEX_OF (e',v);
  KEV (e',v);
  MEV (f',f,enew,v',vfirst);
  MEF (fnew,f',enew,vfirst);
  while f ≠ null do
    MEV (f,fnew,enew,vfirst,vnew);
    f:= NEXT_FACE_IN (facelist,f);
    vfirst:= vnew
  end while;
end REPLACE_VERTEX_WITH_FACE.
```

In a similar way an operator REPLACE_EDGE_WITH_FACE may be defined, which replaces an edge of an object with a new face. Operators REPLACE_VERTEX_WITH_FACE and REPLACE_EDGE_WITH_FACE are useful in the design process to perform operations like vertex- and edge-chamfering.

5. Structured representation of the FAG

In any object representation scheme it is often important to separate the high-level description of the object from lower level representation details, or shape attributes. Examples of such attributes are protrusions, depressions, handles, or through holes which have a small overall size compared to the dimensions of the whole object.

In our representation scheme, we consider a shape attribute as the collection of object faces bounding it. In this view, a boundary representation B = (V,E,F) of an object S can be considered as composed by a representation of S at the highest abstraction level, denoted $\overline{B} = (\overline{V},\overline{E},\overline{F})$, and the boundary description of the attributes of S, each denoted as $B^{(r)}=(V^{(r)},E^{(r)},F^{(r)})$, r=1,2,...,k. Any attribute can also be in turn specified as a main representation plus its lower level attributes, thus generating a boundary model of S at successively finer levels of specification. Such a model is conveniently represented by a hierarchy of relational models, in which the root gives a relational representation of the overall shape of the object, whereas any other tree node provides a graph description of an attribute attached to an element or a set of elements belonging to its direct ancestor model in the hierarchy.

If a FAG is used as representation of the boundary of an object, then such a hierarchy gives rise to a structured face adjacency graph, which is a special case of the structured graph defined in /1/. A Structured Face Adjacency Graph (SFAG) is more formally defined as a pair $\gamma=(G,T)$, where T is the tree describing the structure of γ and G

is a family of FAGs such that every component of G_i of G is associated with a unique node of T, denoted t_i. The component of G associated with the root of T is the face adjacency graph representing B, whereas any other component G_i is the FAG representation of an attribute of the boundary model represented by the FAG which corresponds to the parent node of t_i in T.

Since any shape attribute of S is associated with one or more of its entities (faces, edges and vertices), every G_i, except for the root graph, is associated with an element (node, arc, or hyperarc) or with a subgraph of the graph G_j corresponding to the parent node t_j of t_i in T. Hence, G_i is called expansion graph of such an element or subgraph of G_j. A single element of G_j, expanded into a graph G_i, is called macroelement. Similarly, a subgraph expanded into a graph component of γ is called macrosubgraph. The association between G_i and the element or subgraph of G_j expanded into G_i is defined by a set of nodes, which belong to both G_i and G_j, and are called boundary nodes of G_i. The set of the boundary nodes of a graph G_i of γ is denoted BN_i. BN_i corresponds to the set of faces belonging to the subset $B^{(j)}$ of the boundary of S represented by G_j to which the attribute described by G_i is attached. For instance, if G_i expands a node f, then BN_i={f}, or if G_i is the expansion graph of an arc e or of a hyperarc v, then BN_i will be the collection of the extreme nodes of e or v in G_j. Fig. 4b shows an example of a two level SFAG, which represents the object depicted in fig. 4a. For the sake of clarity, the hyperarcs are omitted in the graph diagrams. The highest level specification of the object is the cube represented by graph G_o in fig. 4b. Graph G_1 represents the parallelepiped defining the protrusion on face E, whereas graph G_2 is the FAG description of the hole through the object. Note that G_1 is the expansion graph of node E in G_o, while G_2 is associated with the pair of nodes E and F of G_o. Also, BN_1= {E} and BN_2 = {E,F}.

The complete FAG of an object S can be obtained from its SFAG by recursively applying a refinement transformation to its macroelements and to the macrosubgraphs of its components /1/. Given a macro element m of γ belonging to a graph G_j and expanded into a component G_i, a refinement transformation

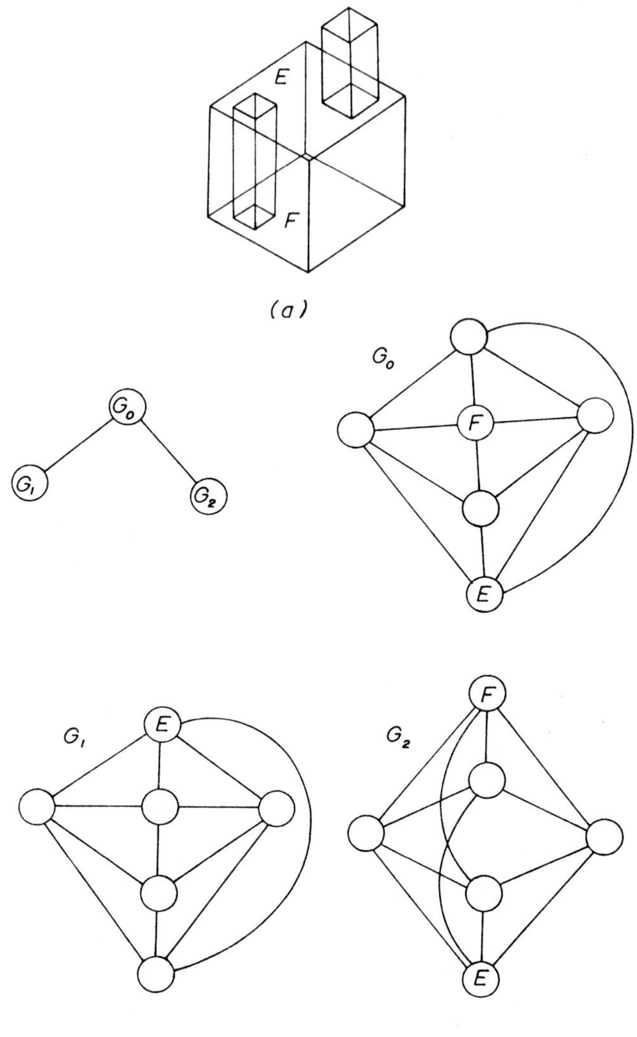

Figure 4. An object (a) and its SFAG representation (b).

applied to m and G_i consists of inserting all the elements of G_i into G_j, except those belonging to BN_i. Refining a macrosubgraph G_j' of G_j expanded into G_i consists of deleting G_j' from G_j and inserting G_i into the resulting graph. Conversely, a structured representation of an object S can be obtained from its FAG by iteratively replacing subgraphs representing attributes of S with simpler subgraphs or elements at a higher abstraction level. This transformation, which is dual with respect to refinement, is called abstraction.

6. Concluding remarks

A boundary model for representing solid objects is presented, which is based on the adjacency relation between faces, and can be structured at different levels of abstraction. The model has some important theoretical advantages. All of the three primitive topological entities of a solid are explicitly encoded into a hypergraph, by representing faces as nodes, and edges and vertices as arcs and hyperarcs respectively. Moreover, this relational model completely defines the topology of an object, being derived topological entities, like shells and loops, expressed as collections of the primitive ones. As shown in /2/, every shell of an object is represented by a different component in its FAG and also the decomposition of the FAG into its biconnected and triconnected components /10/ allows a recognition of special topological features of the object, like depressions, protrusions, handles or through holes, these being related to the node connectivity of the FAG.

The structured face adjacency graph has also been demonstrated to be a valid model in practical applications. Since the structure emphasizes face adjacency relations, object manipulation operations, which usually affect faces as primary entities, are greatly facilitated by the use of such a model. The model also clearly reflects the process of object design, because it allows object definition by face specification and an explicit encoding of the intrinsic hierarchy among the overall shape of the object and its lower level attributes.

If the internal encoding structure of our model maintains all the information needed to ensure its complete structurability, then the resulting data structure requires about 40 percent more storage space than the winged-edge one. On the other hand, if each expansion graph in the structured face adjacency graph is used only to define attributes of the object attached to any collection of its faces, then the space requirements for our SFAG-based and the winged-edge structures are comparable.

Furthermore, because of the possibility of both structuring the model at multiple levels, and of decomposing it into its k-connected components, the SFAG is especially useful in object recognition applications, where the hierarchical topological description of an object and properties like adjacencies and connectivity provide more important information than geometric data /2/.

Moreover, the model has been shown to be useful in object manufacturing for form feature description. In fact, the SFAG has been used to represent the main shape of the object at the first level in the hierarchy and its design topological features at the second level. The structured model forms the input information of the process planning phase, which specifies how the object must be manufactured by defining the so-called manufacturing features /12/. These features are often the same as the design ones and thus, in this case, the object description is transferred unchanged to the manufacture. On the contrary, if some new features are identified in the process planning phase, or, conversely, some parts of the object, previously defined as second level attributes, must be considered as main object characteristics, then the model can be easily restructured by locally applying the abstraction and refinement transformations defined in section five.

Acknowledgements

This work has been supported by the "Progetto Finalizzato Tecnologie Meccaniche - Sottoprogetto 1.2" of the Italian National Research Council under grant 92531. The authors would like to thank Umberto Cugini for the many helpful discussions during the preparation of this paper. The authors are grateful to Sandra Burlando for her help in typing this paper.

References

1. Ancona, M., De Floriani, L., Trebino, O., Zamana,A., "A System for Defining Structured Graphs", Rivista di Informatica,1984, to appear.

2. Ansaldi, S., De Floriani, L., Falcidieno, B., "Edge-face Graph Representations of Solid Objects", Proceedings Workshop on Computer Vision, Representation and Control, Annapolis, 1984, pp. 164-169.

3. Ansaldi, S., De Floriani, L., Falcidieno, B., "An Edge-face Relational Scheme for Boundary Representations", Computer Graphics Forum, 1985, to appear.

4. Baumgardt, B., "Winged-edge Polyhedron Representation", Stanford Artificial Intelligence Report No. CS-320, 1972.

5. Berge, C., Graphes et Hypergraphes, Dunod, Paris, 1977.

6. Braid, I.C., Hillyard, R.C., Stroud, I.A., Stepwise Construction of Polyhedra in Geometric Modeling", in: Mathematical Methods in Computer Graphics and Design, edited by K.W. Brodlie, Academic Press, 1980.

7. Hanranan, P.M.,"Creating Volume Models from Edge-vertex Graphs", Computer Graphics, 16, 3, 1982, pp. 77-84.

8. Harary, F., Graph Theory, Addison Wesley, Mass., 1969.

9. Mantyla, M., Sulonen, R., "GWB: a Solid Modeler with Euler Operators", IEEE Computer Graphics and Applications, 1982, pp. 17-31.

10. Requicha, A.A.G., "Representation of Rigid Solids - Theory, Methods and Systems", A.C.M. Computing Surveys, 12, 4, 1981, pp. 437-464.

11. Weiler, K., "Edge-based Data Structures for Solid Modeling in Curved-Surface Environment", IEEE Computer Graphics and Applications, 5, 1, 1985, pp. 21-40.

12. Wilson, P.R., "Features", CAM-I Interim Report III, October 1983.

A Unified Approach to Interference Problems Using a Triangle Processor

Fujio Yamaguchi

Kyushu Institute of Design, Fukuoka, Japan
4-9-1, Shiobaru, Minami-ku, Fukuoka 815 Japan
092-541-1431 ext. 717

Abstract

Triangulation is an efficient way to simplify and unify interference problems, such as hidden line and surface elimination and Boolean shape operations in solid modeling. Almost all of the processing relevant to a triangle can be performed by computing some 4 x 4 determinants. The author proposes a hardware processor (TRIANGLE PROCESSOR) that quickly intersects a triangle with a point, a line segment, or another triangle. Various applications of the TRIANGLE PROCESSOR are explained in this paper, including applications to face and volume triangulations.

The author stresses that the triangulation approach and the TRIANGLE PROCESSOR simplify, speed up and unify various types of processing relating to interference.

Keywords : geometric modeling, geometry processor, interference problems, determinant processor.

1. Introduction

In computer graphics and geometric modeling we come across various types of interference problems, such as Boolean shape operations in solid modeling, hidden line and surface eliminations, ray tracing techniques, and so on. These algorithms all have similar properties. First, the algorithms are generally quite complicated. Secondly, they are too slow for interactive use. Thirdly, they are not unified, although they are all interference problems. The author proposes an approach, a relevant theory, and a hardware implementation intended to overcome these problems.

2. An Approach

Let us first consider a hidden surface elimination algorithm, such as the Watkins' algorithm [1]. Its most interesting characteristic is that the computation time does not grow directly with increasing complexity of the given scene, but with the complexity of visible images. When the Watkins' algorithm is, however, applied to curved surfaces approximated with many small polygons, it consumes a great deal of computing time because of the high visible complexity. With the desire of realizing an algorithm for which the computation time neither depends directly on the complexity of the given scene, nor on the complexity of visible images, but mainly on the number of partially visible polygons, we used, in the Watkins' scan line algorithm, not separate segments as Watkins did, but a chain of segments generated by the intersection of a scan line plane and a cluster of front-facing polygons (see Fig. 1). We named this chain of segments a "segment chain." The idea is simple but it was very difficult to generate the segment chains simply and efficiently.

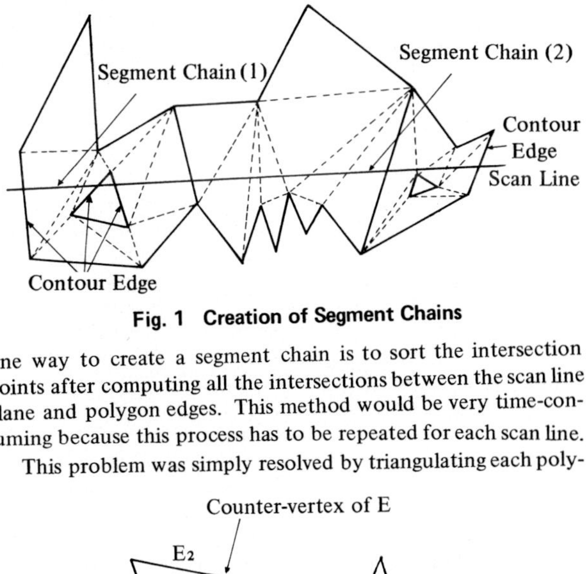

Fig. 1 Creation of Segment Chains

One way to create a segment chain is to sort the intersection points after computing all the intersections between the scan line plane and polygon edges. This method would be very time-consuming because this process has to be repeated for each scan line.

This problem was simply resolved by triangulating each polygon prior to the processing one time (see Fig. 1 & Fig. 2). From the present edge E, the next intersecting edge is determined as either the first edge E_1 or the second edge E_2 counter-clockwise from the present edge depending upon a simple comparison of y-values between the scan line and the counter-vertex of the present edge. By repeating this comparison, we can obtain the necessary intersections, that is, intersections between real edges

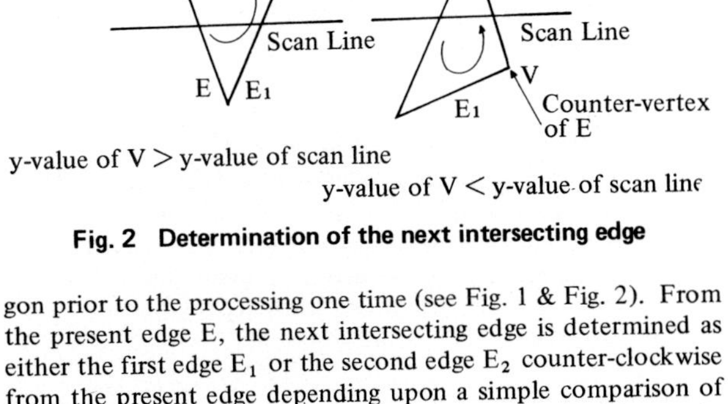

Fig. 2 Determination of the next intersecting edge

and the scan line planes, in the x-increasing order without computing any unnecessary intersections, omitting computation of intersections between imaginary edges and the scan line plane. No explicit sorting is necessary. The algorithm is very simple and fast [2].

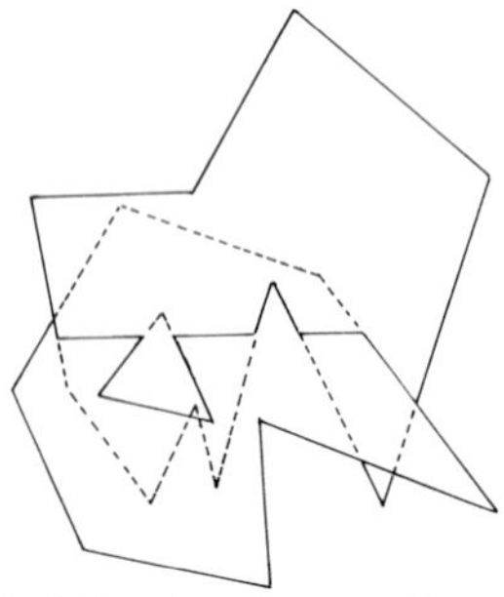

Fig. 3 In Solid Modeling Intersection of two General Polygons Must be Processed.

The case of Boolean shape operations in solid modeling is very similar and more general. The essential task in this case is to determine, simply and efficiently, ordered intersection points on an intersection line loop between two given bodies. This corresponds to the case where the scan line plane in Fig. 1 is replaced by a more general polygon (Fig. 3). These intersection points are usually determined by sorting the points that have been computed as the edge-polygon intersections between two given polygons and have been found to be contained in the polygon (containment test). This processing can be very time-consuming, especially when the polygons are concave. If all the potentially intersecting polygons of the given bodies are triangulated once prior to the determination of intersection line loops, then the intersection line can be traced in the direction of the loop by making use of the imaginary edges generated by the triangulation until the next intersection is reached just as in the first example. Neither (explicit) sorting nor a containment test is required. Necessary intersection points on an intersection line loop are determined in a correct sequence without computing unnecessary points. This approach has been tested and realized in the system "FREEDOM - II" [3] (note that the present version of the "FREEDOM - II triangulates polygons only once prior to the processing and detriangulates them into the original surface representation after all the intersections are determined) and found to be very effective in simplifying and speeding up the algorithm. The central part of the algorithm in this case is to find the intersection status between two given triangles.

In the above examples we have found that triangulation makes the algorithms simple and efficient. As will be explained later, the same is true of other types of processing pertaining to interference.

3. THE TRIANGLE PROCESSOR

The TRIANGLE PROCESSOR is a hardware processor that intersects two geometric elements and outputs intersection status, intersection coordinate values, and characteristic values. The input geometric elements may be a point and a triangle, a line segment and a triangle, or two triangles, described by homogeneous coordinate values of the endpoints.

3.1 Principle of Operation

Suppose vertices of a triangle are expressed in homogeneous coordinates and numbered V_0 (X_0, Y_0, Z_0, w_0), V_1 (X_1, Y_1, Z_1, w_1) and V_2 (X_2, Y_2, Z_2, w_2), seen counter-clockwise from the outside of the triangle. A plane is constructed by these 3 points and it divides three dimensional space into two regions. The half space in which a point V_A (X_A, Y_A, Z_A, w_A) lies can be found by testing the sign of the following 4 x 4 determinant, that is,

$$S_{A012} = \begin{vmatrix} X_A & Y_A & Z_A & w_A \\ X_0 & Y_0 & Z_0 & w_0 \\ X_1 & Y_1 & Z_1 & w_1 \\ X_2 & Y_2 & Z_2 & w_2 \end{vmatrix} = X_A * x_N + Y_A * y_N + Z_A * z_N - w_A * D \quad (1)$$

where

$$x_N = \begin{vmatrix} Y_0 & Z_0 & w_0 \\ Y_1 & Z_1 & w_1 \\ Y_2 & Z_2 & w_2 \end{vmatrix} \qquad y_N = \begin{vmatrix} Z_0 & X_0 & w_0 \\ Z_1 & X_1 & w_1 \\ Z_2 & X_2 & w_2 \end{vmatrix}$$

$$z_N = \begin{vmatrix} X_0 & Y_0 & w_0 \\ X_1 & Y_1 & w_1 \\ X_2 & Y_2 & w_2 \end{vmatrix} \qquad D = \begin{vmatrix} X_0 & Y_0 & Z_0 \\ X_1 & Y_1 & Z_1 \\ X_2 & Y_2 & Z_2 \end{vmatrix}$$

If we assume w_A, w_0, w_1 and w_2 are positive or zero, then

1. $S_{A012} > 0$ .... V_A is in the outside half space of the triangle plane.
2. $S_{A012} = 0$ .... V_A is on the triangle plane.
3. $S_{A012} < 0$ .... V_A is in the inside half space of the triangle plane.

$[x_N \; y_N \; z_N]$ is a normal vector pointing outwards from the triangle; its magnitude is equal to $2*w_0*w_1*w_2$ times the area of the triangle. S_{A012} is equal to $w_A*w_0*w_1*w_2$ times the volume of the parallelepiped, of which the height is equal to the perpendicular distance from V_A to the triangle $V_0 - V_1 - V_2$ plane and of which the base area is equal to the area of the parallelogram $V_0 - V_1 - V_P - V_2$ (see Fig. 4). Accordingly, S_{A012} is $6*w_A*w_0*w_1*w_2$ times the volume of a tetrahedron made up of V_A, V_0, V_1 and V_2. In each row of the determinant (1), a homogeneous coordinate vector can be placed that represents a point at infinity. For example, if the 1st row in (1) is replaced by a vector [a b c 0] representing a point at infinity in the direction of [a b c], S_{A012} in this case is equal to the value of the case where V_A is the position vector of the tip of vector [a b c] which is put on the triangle $V_0 - V_1 - V_2$ plane.

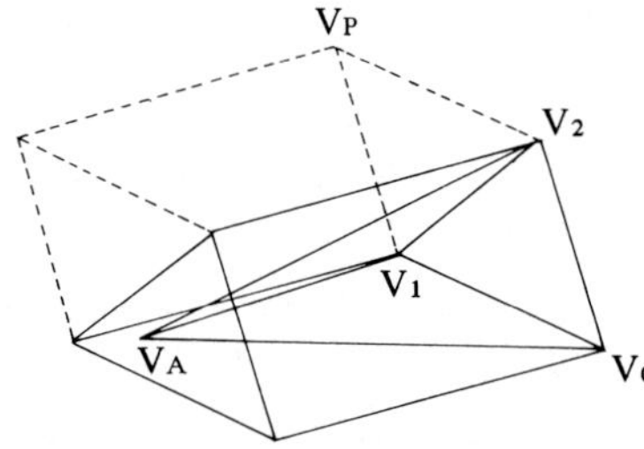

Fig.4 A Parallelepiped and a Tetrahedron made up of V_A, V_0, V_1 and V_2

3.2 Processing of Each Unit

The most general use of TRIANGLE PROCESSOR is to have it find the intersection between two arbitrary triangles in three space. This processing is performed in the hierarchical processing units shown in Fig. 5. Each processing unit can also be called individually by specifying the number "K."

(1) Side test (half space test) of a point V_A with respect to a triangle $V_0 - V_1 - V_2$ (K = 8)
This test is performed by testing the sign of S_{A012}.

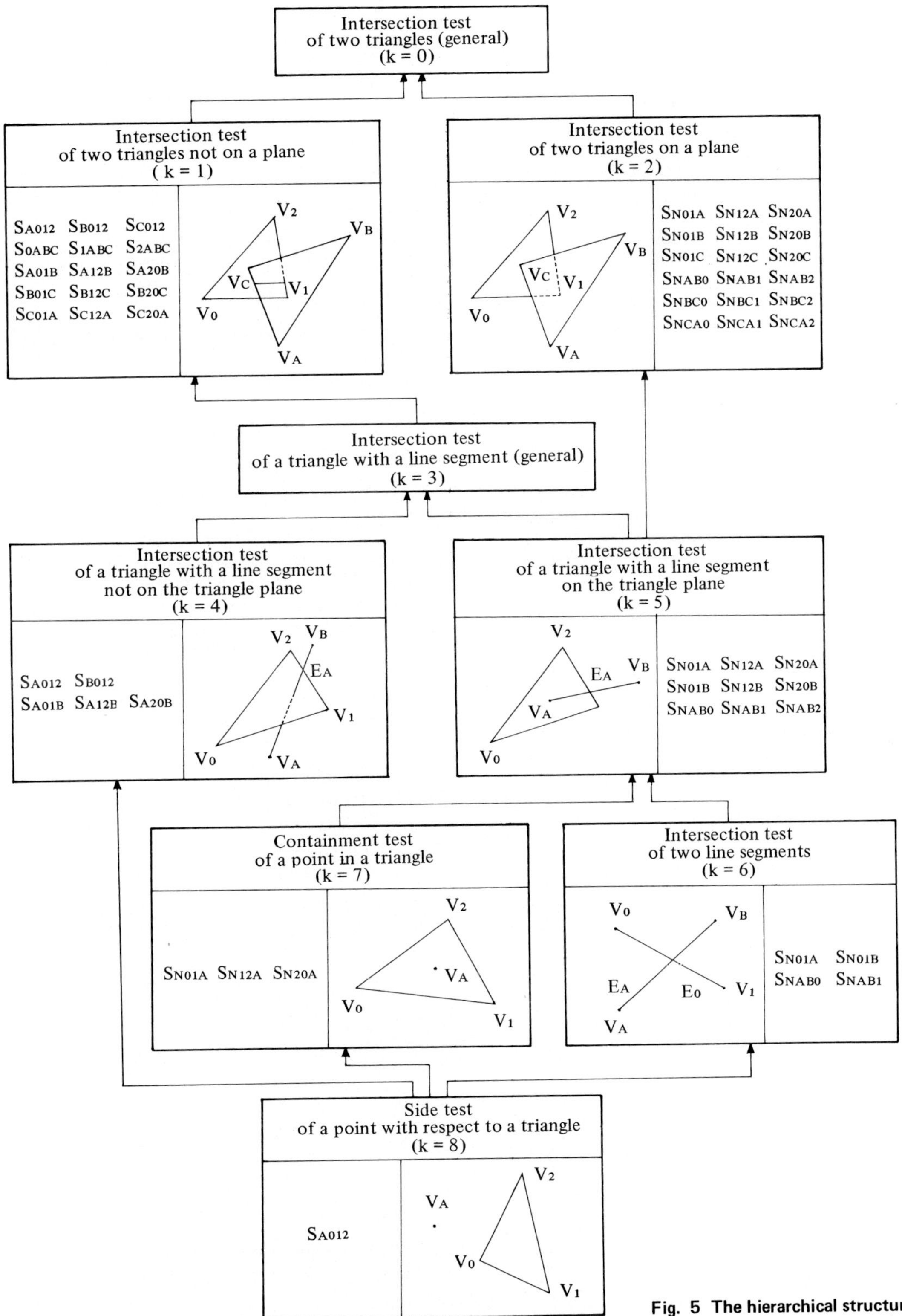

Fig. 5 The hierarchical structure of The triangle processor

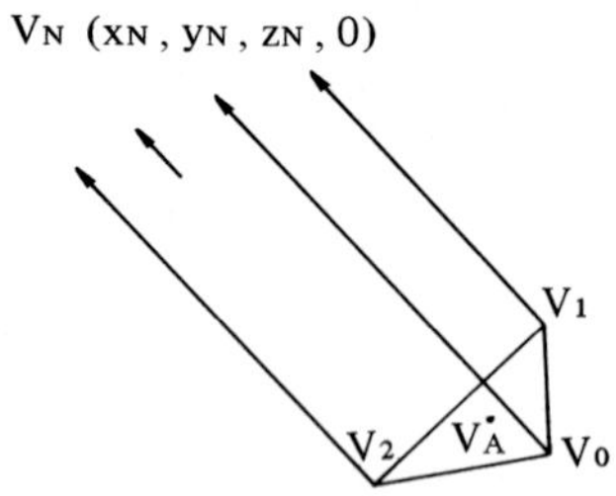

Fig. 6 A Containment Test of a Point in a Triangle

(2) Containment test of a point V_A in a triangle $V_0 - V_1 - V_2$ (K = 7)
Let us construct three triangles $V_0 - V_1 - V_N$, $V_1 - V_2 - V_N$ and $V_2 - V_0 - V_N$ by using a point at infinity V_N $(x_N, y_N, z_N, 0)$ in the direction of the outward-pointing normal vector of the triangle. The containment test can be carried out by doing three side tests of the point V_A with respect to the three planes of these triangles (see Fig. 6). The condition for V_A to be contained in the triangle $V_0 - V_1 - V_2$ is,

$$(S_{A01N} <= 0) \cap (S_{A12N} <= 0) \cap (S_{A20N} <= 0)$$

(3) Intersection test of two line segments, $V_0 - V_1$ and $V_A - V_B$ (K = 6)
By using a point at infinity V_N $(x_N, y_N, z_N, 0)$ in the direction of the normal vector of the plane on which the two line segments lie, we construct two triangles, $V_0 - V_1 - V_N$ and $V_A - V_B - V_N$. The condition for the two line segments to intersect is (Fig. 7)

$$[\{(S_{A01N} <= 0) \cap (S_{B01N} >= 0)\} \cup \{(S_{A01N} >= 0) \cap (S_{B01N} <= 0)\}]$$
$$\cap [\{(S_{0ABN} <= 0) \cap (S_{1ABN} >= 0)\} \cup \{(S_{0ABN} >= 0) \cap (S_{1ABN} <= 0)\}]$$

If the two line segments intersect, the intersection point **P** in homogeneous coordinate is computed as

$$\mathbf{P} = V_A + \frac{S_{A01N}}{S_{A01N} - S_{B01N}} \times (V_B - V_A)$$

This formula is applicable to the cases where either V_A or V_B represents a point at infinity. Note that the ordinary coordinates x, y, z for **P** are derived by dividing the 1st, 2nd and 3rd components by the 4th component respectively.

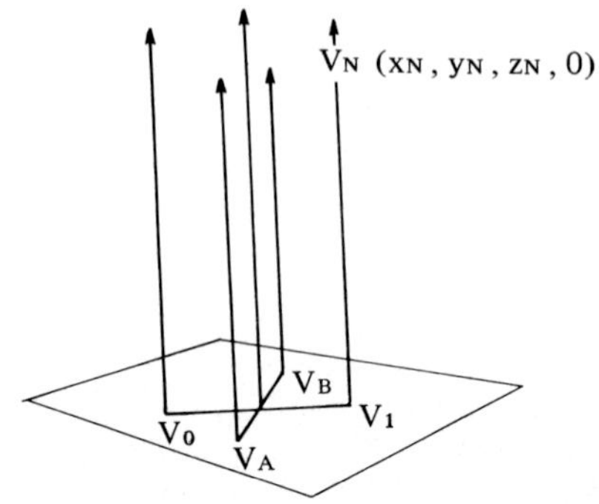

Fig. 7 An Intersection Test of Two Line Segments

(4) Intersection test of a triangle $V_0 - V_1 - V_2$ with a line segment $V_A - V_B$ on the triangle plane (K = 5).
This test can be carried out by using the processing units (2) and (3). The necessary determinants for this test are

S_{A01N}, S_{A12N}, S_{A20N}, S_{B01N}, S_{B12N}, S_{B20N}, S_{0ABN}, S_{1ABN}, S_{2ABN}

(5) Intersection test of a triangle $V_0 - V_1 - V_2$ with a line segment $V_A - V_B$ not on the triangle plane (K = 4)
The conditions for the line segment $V_A - V_B$ to intersect the triangle $V_0 - V_1 - V_2$ are (Fig. 8).
(A) V_A and V_B are on different sides of the plane of the triangle.
(B) An endpoint of the line segment $V_A - V_B$ is in the triangular pyramid constructed by the other endpoint of the line segment and the triangle $V_0 - V_1 - V_2$
i.e.

$$[(S_{A012} >= 0) \cap (S_{B012} <= 0) \cap (S_{B01A} <= 0) \cap (S_{B12A} <= 0) \cap (S_{B20A} <= 0)]$$
$$\cup [(S_{A012} <= 0) \cap (S_{B012} >= 0) \cap (S_{B01A} >= 0) \cap (S_{B12A} >= 0) \cap (S_{B20A} >= 0)]$$

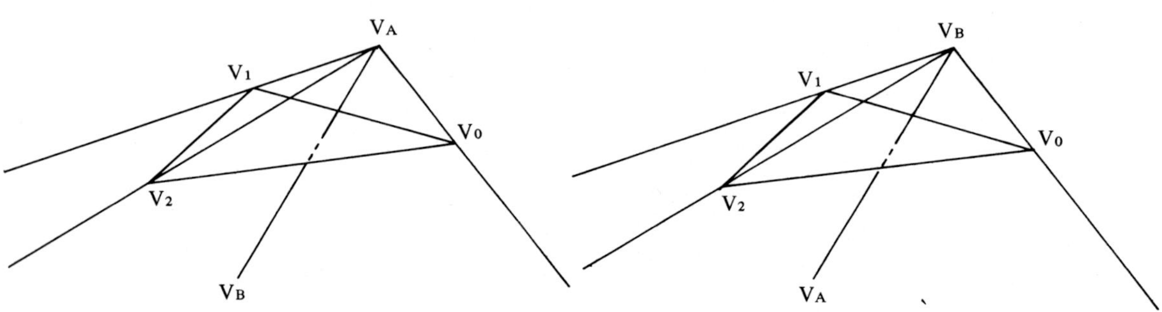

$(S_{A012} >= 0) \cap (S_{B012} <= 0)$ $(S_{A012} <= 0) \cap (S_{B012} >= 0)$

$$[(S_{A012} >= 0) \cap (S_{B012} <= 0) \cap (S_{B01A} <= 0) \cap (S_{B12A} <= 0) \cap (S_{B20A} <= 0)]$$
$$\cup [(S_{A012} <= 0) \cap (S_{B012} >= 0) \cap (S_{B01A} >= 0) \cap (S_{B12A} >= 0) \cap (S_{B20A} >= 0)]$$

Intersection Condition

Fig. 8 An Intersection Test of a Triangle with a Line Segment not Lying on its Plane

(6) Intersection test of a triangle $V_0 - V_1 - V_2$ with a line segment $V_A - V_B$ (general) (K = 3)
This test can be carried out by using the processing units (4) and (5). The necessary determinants for this test are

S_{A01N}, S_{A12N}, S_{A20N}, S_{B01N}, S_{B12N}, S_{B20N}, S_{0ABN}, S_{1ABN}, S_{2ABN}, S_{A012}, S_{B012}, S_{B01A}, S_{B12A}, S_{B20A}

(7) Intersection test of two triangles $V_0 - V_1 - V_2$ and $V_A - V_B - V_C$ on a plane (K = 2)
This test can be carried out by using the processing unit (4). The necessary determinants for this test are

S_{A01N}, S_{A12N}, S_{A20N}, S_{B01N}, S_{B12N}, S_{B20N}, S_{C01N}, S_{C12N}, S_{C20N}, S_{0ABN}, S_{1ABN}, S_{2ABN}, S_{0BCN}, S_{1BCN}, S_{2BCN}, S_{0CAN}, S_{1CAN}, S_{2CAN}

(8) Intersection test of two triangles $V_0 - V_1 - V_2$ and $V_A - V_B - V_C$ not on a plane (K = 1)
This test can be carried out by using the processing unit (6). The necessary determinants for this test are

S_{A012}, S_{B012}, S_{C012}, S_{0ABC}, S_{1ABC}, S_{2ABC}, S_{B01A}, S_{B12A}, S_{B20A}, S_{C01B}, S_{C12B}, S_{C20B}, S_{A01C}, S_{A12C}, S_{A20C}

(9) Intersection test of two triangles $V_0 - V_1 - V_2$ and $V_A - V_B - V_C$ (general) (K = 0)
This test can be carried out by using the processing units (7) and (8). The necessary determinants for this test are

S_{A012}, S_{B012}, S_{C012}, S_{0ABC}, S_{1ABC}, S_{2ABC}, S_{B01A}, S_{B12A}, S_{B20A}, S_{C01B}, S_{C12B}, S_{C20B}, S_{A01C}, S_{A12C}, S_{A20C}, S_{A01N}, S_{A12N}, S_{A20N}, S_{B01N}, S_{B12N}, S_{B20N}, S_{C01N}, S_{C12N}, S_{C20N}, S_{0ABN}, S_{1ABN}, S_{2ABN}, S_{0BCN}, S_{1BCN}, S_{2BCN}, S_{0CAN}, S_{1CAN}, S_{2CAN}

3.3 Input Data

Types of processing are specified by "K" number. There are three types of input geometric data, i.e., point, line segment and triangle. These data are specified in terms of homogeneous coordinates of each vertex. Input geometric elements are shown in Fig. 9.

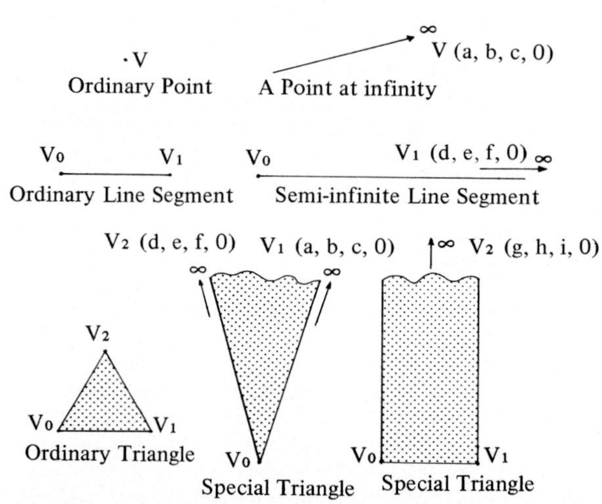

Fig. 9 Input Geometric Elements to the TRIANGLE PROCESSOR

3.4 Output Data

Output data are recorded in three kinds of tables (Fig. 10).
(1) IST (Intersection Status Table)

IST (Intersection Status Table)

	T_A	E_A	E_B	E_C	V_A	V_B	V_C
T_0							
E_0							
E_1							
E_2							
V_0							
V_1							
V_2							

COT (COordinate Table)

	T_A	E_A	E_B	E_C
T_0	X			
E_0				
E_1				
E_2				

Fig. 10 "IST" and "COT" Tables in the TRIANGLE PROCESSOR

A line segment is considered to be a set of two endpoints and an inner line segment (open set). Similarly, a triangle is considered a set of three endpoints, three inner line segments (open set) and an inner triangle (open set). The intersection status of the combination of these geometric elements is recorded in the IST with code numbers shown in Fig. 11.

(1) Separation 0
(2) Higher Order Intersections 1

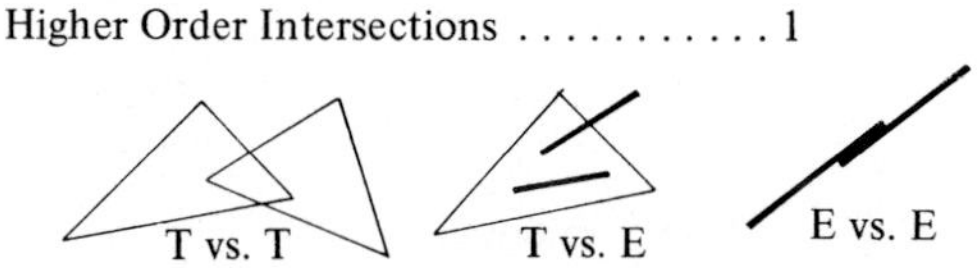

(3) Lower Order Intersections . . . . 2 or 3

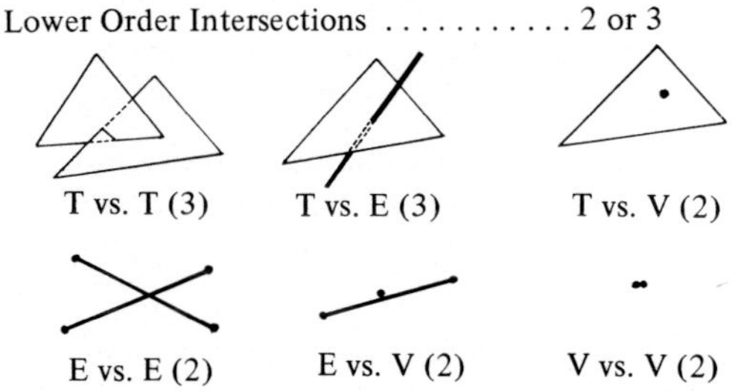

Fig. 11 Intersection Types and Codes

(2) COT (COordinate Table)

In a case when the edge-edge or edge-triangle has a unique intersection point, the coordinates of the intersection are recorded in the corresponding location of the COT.

(3) CVT (Characteristic Value Table)

Various kinds of characteristic values pertaining to the input data are recorded in the CVT. Some of the characteristic values are (A) area of a triangle, (B) volume of a tetrahedron made up of a given triangle and a point, (C) unit vector normal to a triangle, and (D) vector product of normal vectors of two triangles.

4. Applications of the TRIANGLE PROCESSOR

The TRIANGLE PROCESSOR is a general geometric processor that can be applied to many types of geometric processing. Some of the important applications will be discussed in this section.

4.1 Basic Geometric Processing

4.1.1 Classifications

In computer graphics and geometric modeling a vertex of a face or an edge of a polyhedron is often required to be classified as convex or concave according to the angle between its neighboring edges or faces (see Fig. 12).

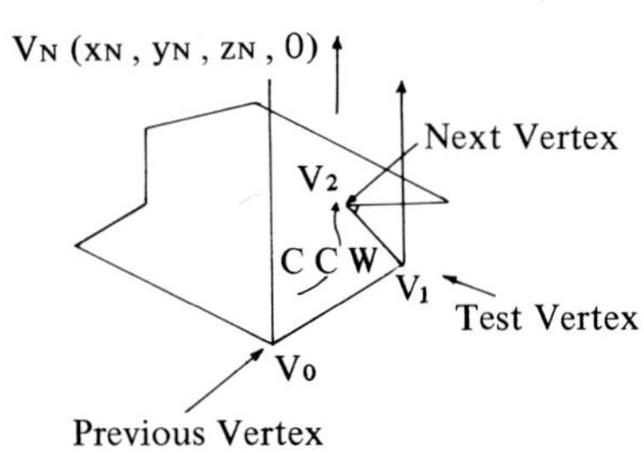

(a) Polygon Vertex Test

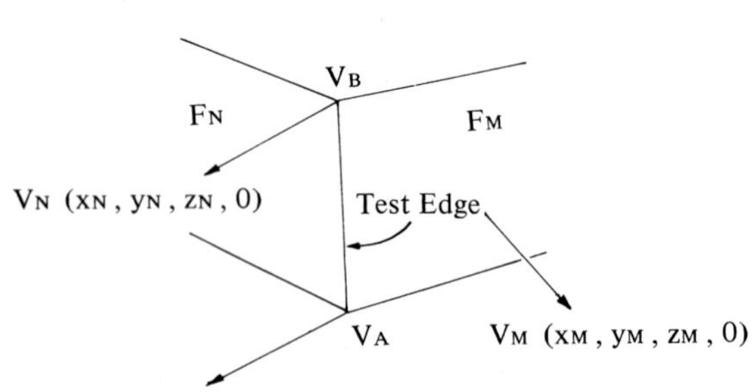

(b) Polyhedron Edge Test

Fig. 12 Convexity or Concavity Tests of a Polygon Vertex and a Polyhedron Edge

This test can be performed in the following way. In order to test the vertex V_1 we construct a triangle by tracing counterclockwise the three points V_0, V_1 and a point at infinity V_N (x_N, y_N, z_N, 0) in the direction of the outward-pointing normal vector [x_N y_N z_N] of the polygon. A side test of V_2 with respect to the triangle plane determines the convexity or concavity of V_1. That is,

(1) $S_{201N} > 0$ .... V_1 is concave.
(2) $S_{201N} < 0$ .... V_1 is convex.

A call of the TRIANGLE PROCESSOR with K = 8 performs this test.

Similarly, the test of an edge V_A - V_B can be achieved by constructing a triangle by tracing counterclockwise the three points V_A, V_B and a point at infinity V_N (x_N, y_N, z_N, 0) in the direction of the outward-pointing normal vector of the face F_N. A side test of a point at infinity V_M (x_M, y_M, z_M, 0) in the direction of the outward-pointing normal vector [x_M y_M z_M] of the face F_M with respect to the constructed triangle plane determines the convexity or concavity of the edge V_A - V_B. That is,

(1) $S_{MABN} > 0$ ...... edge V_A - V_B is convex
(2) $S_{MABN} < 0$ ...... edge V_A - V_B is concave

A call of the TRIANGLE PROCESSOR with K = 8 also performs this test.

4.1.2 Triangulations

As explained in section 2, a face triangulation (or volume triangulation in some processing) prior to processing is very effective in simplifying certain algorithms. The triangulation itself can be done quickly using 4 x 4 determinants computed by the TRIANGLE PROCESSOR.

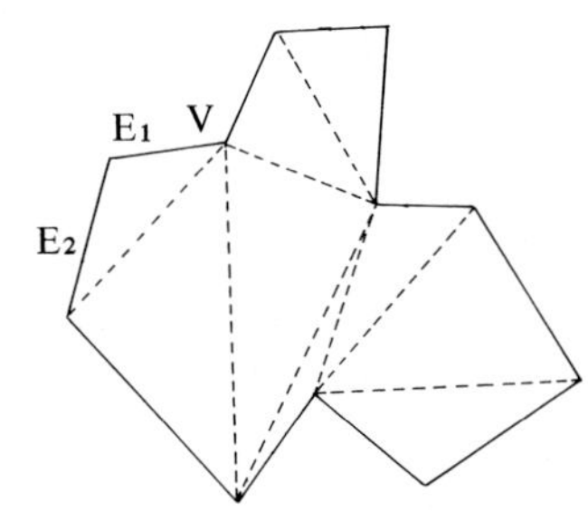

Fig. 13 Face Triangulation

(1) Face Triangulation [3]

First, every vertex of a polygon is classified as convex or concave by the technique mentioned in 4.1.1 using the TRIANGLE PROCESSOR. Take a concave vertex and try to triangulate with the two successive edges E_1, E_2 connected by a convex vertex (Fig. 13). This triangulation is possible if the triangle made by the edges does not contain a concave vertex other than V. This containment test is done by using the TRIANGLE PROCESSOR with K = 7. Continue the process until the vertex becomes convex or the triangulation is impossible. Apply the above procedure for all concave vertices of the original polygon. Finally, create edges from one vertex to all the other vertices except those sharing one of the two neighboring edges of the vertex. This completes the triangulation.

(2) Volume Triangulation [4]

The method is similar to the face triangulation (see Fig. 14). First, every edge is classified as convex or concave by the technique mentioned in 4.1.1, using the TRIANGLE PROCESSOR. What the method does is to try to cut a tetrahedron one by one around a concave edge until the edge becomes convex or it becomes impossible to cut a tetrahedron. It is possible to cut a tetrahedron from the polyhedron if the tetrahedron is found not to contain any of the edges of the polyhedron. This containment test would be time-consuming if it were done in software, but the TRIANGLE PROCESSOR can do this quickly. If there is no concave edge left unprocessed, the polyhedron is convex.

Choose a vertex of the polyhedron and triangulate all the polygons except those sharing the vertex. Create triangles from the vertex to all the edges except those of the polygons sharing the vertex.

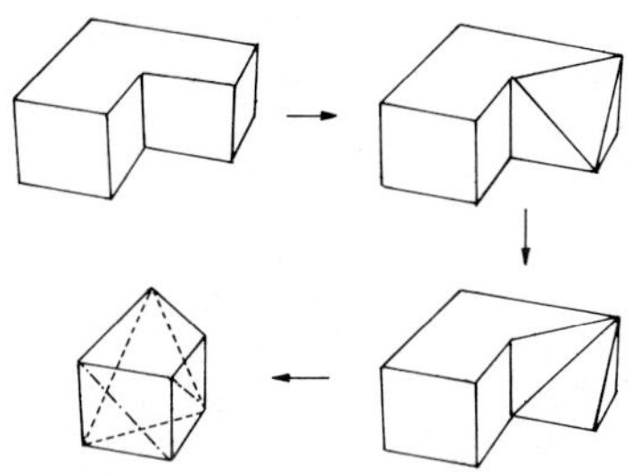

Fig. 14 Volume Triangulation

(3) Triangulation of Free Form Surface

Curved surfaces are preferably triangulated prior to geometric processing and the processing may be done quickly and in a unified fasion, using the TRIANGLE PROCESSOR. One technique is to approximate the surface with triangular convex hulls. A simpler method is to approximate it with triangles generated by parametric subdivision (Fig. 15).

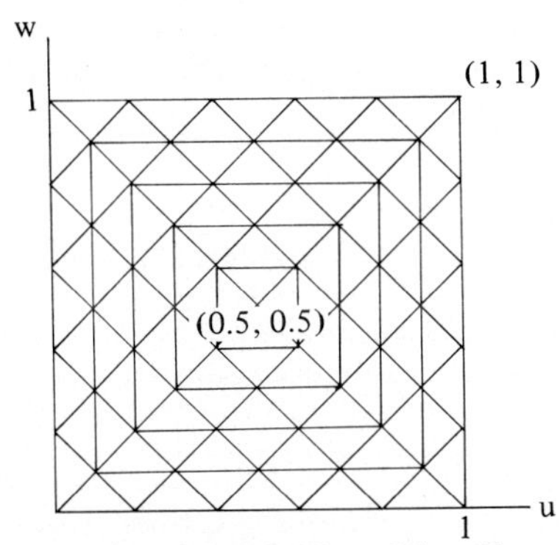

Fig. 15 Triangular Subdivision of Free Form Surface in Parametric Space

4.1.3 Intersections

(1) Intersection of two line segments on a plane

It has already been explained that this intersection is performed by computing four 4 x 4 determinants and done by the TRIANGLE PROCESSOR with K = 6.

(2) Intersection of a line segment and a polygon

The polygon is preferably triangulated prior to the intersection test by the method explained in 4.1.2 (1), using the TRIANGLE PROCESSOR. All the algorithm has to do is to test for intersection between a line segment and a triangle, which can be done by the TRIANGLE PROCESSOR with K = 3.

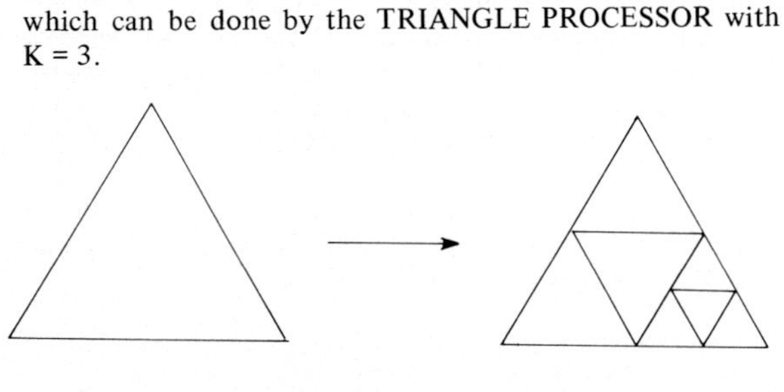

Fig. 16 Quadtree Subdivision of a Triangle

(3) Intersection of a line segment and a curved surface

Suppose the curved surface is approximated with small triangles. This approximation may be coarse. Find intersection of a triangle with the line segment, using the TRIANGLE PROCESSOR with K = 3. Retriangulate further the intersected triangle and its surrounders in a quad-tree way as shown in Fig. 16 and find an intersected triangle. Repeat the process until the intersected triangle approximates the part of the curved surface sufficiently.

(4) Intersection of two polyhedra [3]

Prior to the processing, triangulate potentially-intersecting polygons of the two bodies by the method explained in 4.1.2 (1), using the TRIANGLE PROCESSOR. Find an intersection point. All the algorithm has to do is to trace intersecting triangle pairs by using the TRIANGLE PROCESSOR (K = 0). Intersection points on an intersection line loop can be determined in a sequence of the direction of the loop. There is no need for containment test or sorting.

(5) Intersection of two bodies made up of planar and curved surfaces

If curved surfaces are approximated with triangles, then the intersection of two bodies made up of planar and curved surfaces could be dealt with quickly and in a unified way, using the TRIANGLE PROCESSOR.

4.1.4 Containment Test

(1) Containment of a point in a polygon

This test is ordinarily done in the following way. Any line is drawn from the test point to infinity, and the number of times the line crosses the polygon boundary is determined; if it is odd, the point lies inside the polygon. In addition to being time-consuming, this test is complicated and error-prone when a polygon vertex or edge lies on the semi-infinite line.

The present author proposes a simpler, faster and more reliable method. Triangulate the polygon by the method mentioned in 4.1.2 (1) and test for containment of the test point in some triangle, using the TRIANGLE PROCESSOR (K = 7).

(2) Containment of a point in a polyhedron

Decompose the polyhedron into a set of tetrahedra and test for containment of the test point in some tetrahedron, calling the TRIANGLE PROCESSOR (K = 8) four times for each tetrahedron.

4.1.5 Depth Priority Test

Depth priority tests in a direction of a vector [a b c] are considered as follows.

(1) A point and a triangle (Fig. 17)

Let us suppose the point is not in the triangle. Extend a semi-infinite line from the point $V_T(x_T, y_T, z_T, 1)$ in the

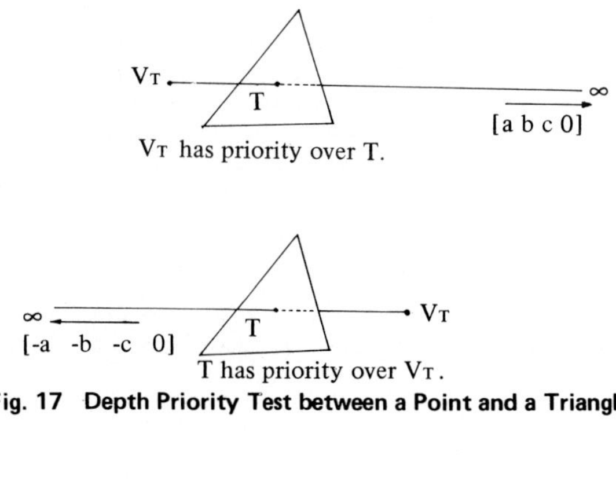

Fig. 17 Depth Priority Test between a Point and a Triangle

direction of [a b c] and test for intersection of the semi-infinite line segment from [x_T y_T z_T 1] to [a b c 0] and the triangle, using the TRIANGLE PROCESSOR (K = 3). If they intersect, the point has priority over the triangle. If they do not, test for intersection of a semi-infinite line segment from [x_T y_T z_T 1] to [-a -b -c 0] and the triangle. If they intersect, the triangle has priority over the point.

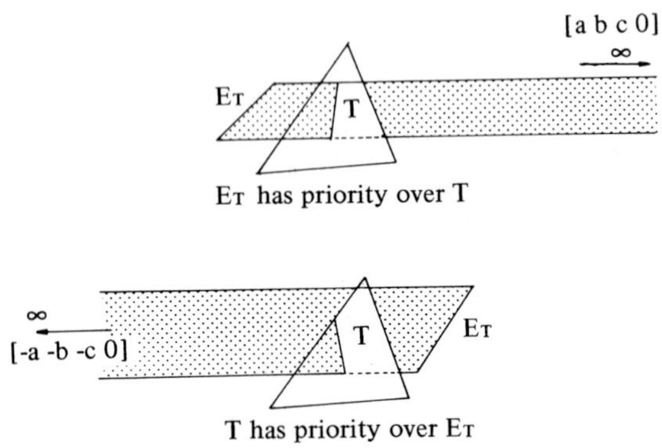

Fig. 18 Depth Priority Test between a Line Segment and a Triangle

(2) A line segment and a triangle (Fig. 18)

Let us suppose the line segment does not intersect the triangle. Construct a triangle by the two endpoints of the line segment and a point [a b c 0]. Test for intersection between the constructed triangle and the given one. If they intersect, the line segment has priority over the triangle. If they do not intersect, construct a triangle by the two endpoints of the line segment and a point [-a-b-c0], and then test for intersection between the constructed triangle and the given one. If they intersect, the triangle has priority over the line segment.

(3) Two triangles

Let us suppose the two triangles do not intersect. If any edge of one triangle is found to have priority over the other triangle, the former triangle has priority over the latter. If a triangle is found to have priority over an edge of the other triangle, the former triangle has priority over the latter.

4.2 Application Areas

4.2.1 Determination of Mass Properties

Each time a triangle is generated during the triangulation, the TRIANGLE PROCESSOR records the area of the triangle in the CVT. Accordingly, the surface area of a polyhedron is simply determined by summing up the areas of all the triangles generated during the triangulation of all the polygons of a polyhedron.

Each time a tetrahedron is generated during the volume triangulation, the TRIANGLE PROCESSOR records the volume of the generated tetrahedron in the CVT. Therefore, the mass properties, such as volume, moment of inertia and so on, can be computed from the properties of each tetrahedron generated during the volume triangulation of the polyhedron.

4.2.2 Solid Modeling

As far as the present author knows, conventional solid modeling systems seem to have the following problems: (1) the Boolean shape operation algorithms are too complicated and the software systems are of very large size, (2) the processing speed is too slow for interactive use, and (3) the algorithms are not unified with respect to surface types.

We developed a solid modeling system named FREEDOM-II, which deals with the design of shapes made up of planar and conic surfaces, based on the techniques explained in this paper by using a software simulator of the TRIANGLE PROCESSOR. The system is so small that it runs on a personal computer (CPU: Intel 8086).

Further, we experimented with the determination of the intersection between two free form bodies [5], using the simulator of the TRIANGLE PROCESSOR.

The author considers it feasible to process shapes made up of planar surfaces, conic surfaces and free form surfaces in a unified way by taking this approach.

4.2.3 Hidden Line and Surface Elimination

Since a polygon can be triangulated very quickly with the TRIANGLE PROCESSOR and the priority test between a line segment and a triangle can also be done using the TRIANGLE PROCESSOR as explained in 4.1.5(2), hidden line elimination can be processed very simply and quickly by using Encarnacao's priority algorithm [6].

As for hidden surface elimination, several simple algorithms have been devised[7] using the triangulation and the TRIANGLE PROCESSOR. They are so simple that we are planning to implement one of them in hardware, along with the hidden line algorithm in its entirety.

5. Conclusion

The author insists in this paper that in problems such as mass property computation, solid modeling, and hidden line and surface elimination, it is very effective especially in simplifying the algorithm to triangulate once prior to the processing. He presents a theory that many computations relevant to a triangle can be dealt with by computing some 4 x 4 determinants. He also proposes a hardware processor named "TRIANGLE PROCESSOR" based on the theory and explains its applications to many kinds of geometric calculations pertaining to interference.

The approach proposed in this paper, coupled with the TRIANGLE PROCESSOR, not only simplifies and speeds up, but also unifies many types of geometric computation relevant to interference. Just as transformation problems are processed with a 4 x 4 matrix, interference problems can be processed with 4 x 4 determinant computations in a unified manner if triangulation is done in advance. In this correspondence the TRIANGLE PROCESSOR seems to correspond to the MATRIX MULTIPLIER in transformation problems.

The TRIANGLE PROCESSOR, which has only one multiplier, is now under construction. It is anticipated to compute a 4 x 4 determinant in 20 microseconds with the precision of 32 bit floating point representation. The processing speed would be very much improved by increasing the number of multipliers. The author expects it will play an important role in many geometric computations of computer graphics and geometric modeling.

Finally, the author would like to express his thanks to professor Robert F. Sproull for giving me some useful comments and for improving my English.

References

[1] Watkins, G.S. :
A Real-Time Visible Surface Algorithm, Univ. of Utah Comput. Sci. Dept., UTEC-CSc-70-101, June 1970.

[2] Yamaguchi, Fujio & Toshiya Tokieda :
A Visible Line and Surface Detection Algorithm Created Through a Taxonomical Study, Proceeding of CAD/CAM, Robotics and Automation Conference, Arizona, 1985. Arizona, 1985.

[3] Yamaguchi, Fujio & Toshiya Tokieda :
A Unified Algorithm for Boolean Shape Operations, IEEE Computer Graphics and Applications, Vol.4, No.6 (June) 1984.

[4] in preparation.

[5] Yoneda, K., M. Muramatsu & F. Yamaguchi :
Determining Intersections between two Free Form Bodies Using the TRIANGLE PROCESSOR, Spring Conference of the Japan Society of Precision Engineering, 1985.

[6] see "INTERACTIVE COMPUTER GRAPHICS" by Giloi, Prentice-Hall, 1978.

[7] in preparation.

[8] Wordenweber, Burkard :
Surface Triangulation for Picture Production, IEEE Computer Graphics and Applications, Vol.3, No.8 (Nov.), 1983.

[9] Lewis, B.A. and J.S. Robinson :
Triangulation of Planar Regions with Applications, Computer Journal, Vol.21, No.4, 1979.

[10] Wordenweber, Burkard :
Volume Triangulation, CAD group document 110, Computer Laboratory, Cambridge University, 1980.

Techniques for Conic Splines

Vaughan Pratt
Sun Microsystems Inc.

Abstract

A number of techniques are presented for making conic splines more effective for 2D computer graphics. We give a brief account of the theory of conic splines oriented to computer graphics. We make Pitteway's algorithm exact, and repair an ''aliasing'' problem that has plagued the algorithm since its introduction in 1967. The curvature-matching problem for conics is solved by way of a simple formula for curvature at an endpoint which permits curvature to be matched exactly at non-inflection points and more closely than was previously realized possible at points of inflection. A formula for minimum-curvature-variation of conic splines is given. These techniques provide additional support for Pavlidis' position [6] that conics can often be very effective as splines.

This work was motivated by, and provides much of the foundation for, an implementation of conic splines at Sun Microsystems as part of Sun's Pixrect graphics package, the lowest layer of Sun's graphics support.

1. Introduction

1.1. Rationale for Conic Splines

It may be of interest to understand how we arrived at both the techniques and the conclusions of this paper. We set out a year ago to develop an outline font system. We considered many families of curves [5,11], but rejected most of these as either computationally impractical or unsuited for splines. It appeared that the most suitable curve technology from a user standpoint was cubic splines. We soon found however that incremental algorithms for plotting (e.g. Pitteway's algorithm for conics [7]) were significantly faster than the recursive subdivision algorithms for parametric curves (e.g. the various algorithms discussed by Catmull [2]). The former had excellent velocity control (constant relation between number of pixels plotted and amount of work done), no context switching, and a trivial stopping condition. The latter had simple implementations, both in hardware and high level programming languages, along with good ways to organize the arithmetic. However they had poor velocity control (even with an optimal stopping condition for the recursion one can only come to within at best a factor of two of the ideal velocity), expensive context switching (for every single step there is a context switch entailing much pushing and popping of data on a stack, aggravated by trying to program cleanly by using recursion), and an awkward stopping condition (there is a complex tradeoff between cost of stopping condition and quality of velocity control).

It was natural therefore to want to combine the user convenience of splines with the performance of incremental methods. Since splines were defined for parametric curves whereas incremental plotting was for algebraic curves it was clear that some combination of these classes was called for.

As degree increases the complexity of both exact implicitization and of exact and antialiased Bresenham-Pitteway style tracking increases very rapidly. We feel particularly intimidated by the prospect of duplicating the performance-oriented techniques of this paper for rational or even polynomial cubics.) Hence one does not casually increase degree from two to three without good reason.

At higher degrees higher orders of continuity become possible. Two important properties of polynomial cubics are the possibility of C_2-continuity between adjoining cubics (as easily achieved using B-splines), and zero curvature at inflection points. C_3-continuity is however only possible between adjoining cubics trivially, namely when the two cubics are adjoining segments of a common cubic.

We developed an easy method of achieving C_2-continuity between conics. We also worked out how to approximate very closely zero curvature at inflection points. Hence for degree of continuity cubics and conics appear to have essentially the same capabilities.

The one thing cubics have that conics do not is an additional degree of freedom. Six degrees of freedom are encompassed in the basic endpoint-and-tangent conditions. For conics the seventh degree of freedom is sharpness or bulge. Cubics have bulge along with an additional degree of freedom that might be called skew, allowing their interior to be pushed in a direction parallel to the line between the endpoints, one way to get inflection points in cubics. (The other is that cubics can bulge further than conics, producing first inflection points, then a cusp, then a loop.) It appeared to us that on those occasions calling for this control one could get its effect quite satisfactorily via a single subdivision, so its loss was not an unmitigated disaster. More pragmatically, we doubted whether many users would be comfortable visualizing skew as a concept independent of the endpoint tangents; even bulge is somewhat obscure in that regard.

These considerations made rational quadratics look reasonable similar to polynomial cubics in practice. The very much greater complexity of dealing with implicit cubics for tracking led us to adopt conics as a useful curve form for high-performance graphics. We are not alone in advocating conics as a useful curve form; Pavlidis [6] is also an enthusiastic proponent of the virtues of conics.

1.2. Conics and Cubics in Graphics Standards

Recent efforts to integrate our conic package into Sun's standard graphics packages have led us to ponder the proper way to introduce curves into graphics standards. We feel sufficiently strongly about our conclusions as to warrant including a brief summary of them in this forum.

Curves are not provided at all in such graphics standards as CORE or GKS, other than as unspecified nonstandard extensions. CGI (formerly VDI) has circles and ellipses, but no splines of any type (polynomial or rational) or degree (beyond 1). Furthermore those circles and ellipses can be used as region boundaries only in the most parochial ways, namely as pies (radius-arc-radius) and chords (chord-arc), rather than the far more general and useful approach of generalizing polygons to piecewise-elliptical region boundaries. Not one of these standards has useful compound region boundaries for curves of degree higher than one.

Without some nonlinear spline capability all of these standards are very difficult to use for curve-oriented work of the kind arising in say outline font design.

The reasons given above for conic splines, together with the observation that CGI has conics (ellipses) but not cubics, suggests that it is not unreasonable to begin the introduction of splines to such standards with conic splines. We therefore advocate extending the existing line capabilities of graphics standards to include conic splines. This would constitute a simply described yet very useful extension to those standards.

Given the reluctance of some of the graphics standardizing bodies to introduce even quadratic curves into graphics standards, it would seem appropriate to increase curve degree in graphics reasonably cautiously. To go from linear to cubic curves in one step is akin to going from crawling to running without learning to walk.

Before turning our attention to the theory of conic splines let us mention some of the more notable works on conics relevant to computer graphics. For general information on conics an excellent text is Salmon's classic [13]. A scholarly account of both the subject and its many contributors is given by Coolidge [4]. A comprehensive though at times dense text on projective geometry is Todd [10]; it is the source of most of our ideas about conics. General implicitization methods, based on classical techniques, for both polynomial and rational curves can be found in Sederberg's thesis [8]; our methods below are more narrowly focused on conics per se, with an emphasis on performance. An early but excellent work on coping with rational quadratic and cubic curves in the context of computational geometry is Forrest's thesis [3].

2. Principles of Conic Splines

A conic spline is a conic defined by three points A,B,C in the view plane. It passes through **A** and **C** and has tangents AB and CB respectively at those points. The family of conics satisfying these conditions, which we call the ABC family, is illustrated in Figure 1.

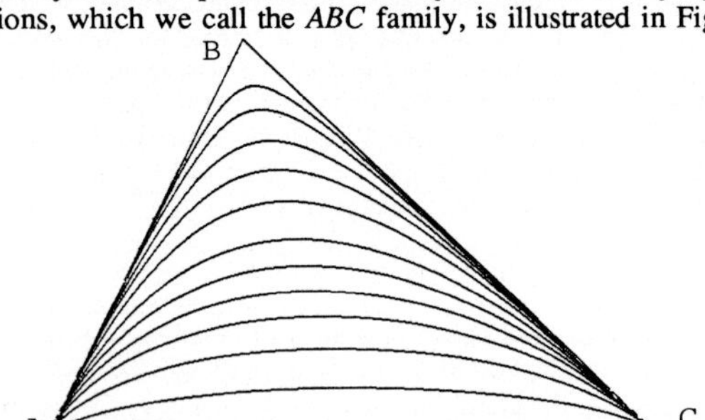

Figure 1. The family of **ABC** conics

This family may be indexed in a variety of ways. Some authors use the scalar ratio WD/WB where **W** is the midpoint of AC and **D** is the intersection of the conic with WB. Another method is simply to provide **D** directly, or for that matter to give any point on the conic besides **A** and **C**. We have found the scalar S, for *sharpness*, to be useful. S measures the departure of the conic from a parabola. For $S = 1$ we have the parabola itself, $S < 1$ (the flatter curves) yields ellipses, $S > 1$ (the sharper curves) hyperbolas. Pavlidis [6] uses a scalar K, representable in terms of our S as $K=1/4S^2$. Another parameter we have found useful is what we call *variation*, which measures the departure of the conic from the ellipse of minimum eccentricity; variation is directly proportional to sharpness, but with the constant of proportionality a function of the shape of triangle. Some authors have proposed to use eccentricity itself as the index; unfortunately this index is ambiguous since eccentricity attains a minimum for some positive S.

The most useful property of conic splines for applying Pitteway's algorithm is its implicit or *algebraic* form. If we take the vertices of the triangle as our basis, with corresponding coordinate variables a,b,c, then the equation is (as in (3.13) of [6])

$$b^2 - 4S^2ac = 0 \qquad (2.1)$$

This is actually the equation not just of the conic but of the whole surface consisting of the lines of sight from the observer **O** (obligingly seated at the origin) to points on the conic. This surface is a cone.

Since **ABC** will not in general be the coordinate system in which the rendering is to be done, a change of basis from **ABC** to **XYZ** is needed. This is accomplished by making the following substitutions for a,b,c (cf. (3.10) of [6]).

$$a = \begin{vmatrix} x & x_B & x_C \\ y & y_B & y_C \\ z & z_B & z_C \end{vmatrix} \quad b = \begin{vmatrix} x_A & x & x_C \\ y_A & y & y_C \\ z_A & z & z_C \end{vmatrix} \quad c = \begin{vmatrix} x_A & x_B & x \\ y_A & y_B & y \\ z_A & z_B & z \end{vmatrix} \qquad (2.2)$$

Each of these substitutions is a linear expression in x,y,z, whence making those substitutions in equation (2.1) turns it into a quadratic equation in x,y,z, which we express as

$$\alpha x^2 + 2\beta xy + \gamma y^2 + 2\delta xz + 2\varepsilon yz + \zeta z^2 = 0. \qquad (2.3)$$

Furthermore if the **XYZ** coordinates of A,B,C are integers and S^2 is a rational then the coefficients in (2.3) will all be integers, with the coefficients of the "mixed" terms xy,yz,zx being even, whence the 2's. Since A,B,C all lie on the view plane $z = 1$, we have $z_A = z_B = z_C = 1$.

Finally we intersect the cone with the view plane $z = 1$ simply by setting z to 1 in the equation for the cone to yield

$$\alpha x^2 + 2\beta xy + \gamma y^2 + 2\delta x + 2\varepsilon y + \zeta = 0. \qquad (2.4)$$

This could have been done earlier in (2.2) just by having the whole bottom row be all 1's; leaving z in until the end shows that the 1's arise through intersecting the view plane $z = 1$ with the cone.

The practically-minded reader may now skip to the next section. The purpose of the remainder of this section is to provide additional insight into conic splines.

First let us derive (2.1) directly from the definition of a conic as the intersection of a cone with a plane. Since this is a 3D construction we do this in a 3D vector space with origin the point **O**. The view plane resides in this space and contains **A,B,C** which therefore uniquely determine the view plane (unless **A,B,C** are collinear), and may also be taken as a basis for the space (unless **O,A,B,C** are coplanar).

So let **U** = (**A**–**C**)/2, **V** = S**B**, **W** = (**A**+**C**)/2 (which may be seen to form a basis provided **ABC** form a basis and S is nonzero) with associated coordinates u,v,w and associated substitutions $u = a-c$, $v = b/S$, and $w = a+c$. The surface $u^2+v^2 = w^2$ is evidently a circular cone (with respect to the **UVW** basis) containing **A** and **C** (the points (1,0,1) and (−1,0,1)) and having OAV and OCV, and hence OAB and OCB, as tangent planes at **A** and **C** respectively. We then derive (2.1) by making the above substitutions for u,v,w in this equation. This is nicely illustrated by Figure 2, which also shows two other important points **D** and **E** at **W**±**V** (note that **A** and **C** are at **W**±**U**).

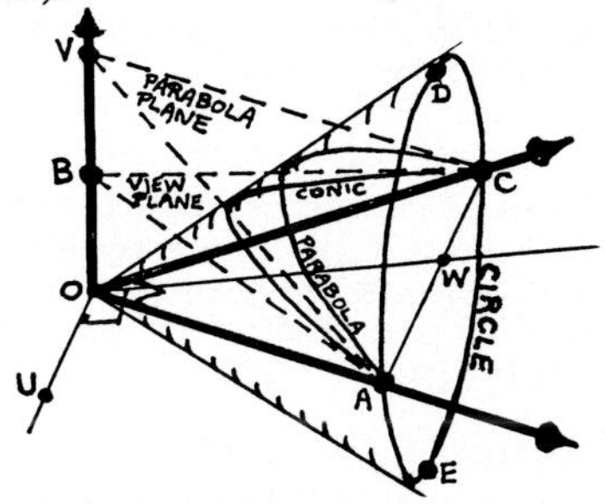

Figure 2. The AVC cone, AVC parabola, and ABC conic

Substitution (2.2) may be derived in terms of *areal coordinates*. A closely related notion is that of *barycentric coordinates* in which a point **P** may be specified on a plane by giving its coordinates as a weighted sum $\mathbf{P} = a\mathbf{A}+b\mathbf{B}+c\mathbf{C}$ of three points A,B,C in the plane with $a+b+c = 1$ (normalized weights). The concept of areal coordinates is the idea that the coordinates a,b,c may be specified as the areas of the triangles PBC, PCA, and PAB respectively, or to fit (2.2), twice these areas. Areal coordinates are related to barycentric coordinates by a common ratio amounting to twice the area of the **ABC** triangle, given by

$$\begin{vmatrix} x_A & x_B & x_C \\ y_A & y_B & y_C \\ 1 & 1 & 1 \end{vmatrix} \qquad (2.5)$$

Substituting **P** (denoted by omitting the subscript) for each of **A**, **B**, or **C** in this determinant, yields the determinant for the corresponding coordinate a, b, or c. The resulting weights are not normalized. They could be normalized by dividing by twice the area of **ABC**, but since (2.1) is homogeneous this is unnecessary. Most importantly, in the unnormalized form integer **XYZ** coordinates of **ABC** yield integer coefficients in (2.3).

When z's are used in place of 1's these areal coordinates become volumetric coordinates for a point moving in all 3 dimensions, the volumes being those of tetrahedra having O as the additional vertex (besides the three appearing in the determinant).

(Our original SIGGRAPH submission derived the equivalent of (2.2) by dropping the common denominator (twice the area of **ABC**) from Cramer's rule as used to obtain the transformation from **XYZ** coordinates to **ABC** coordinates as the inverse of the **ABC**-to-**XYZ** tranformation, which is in effect what one has when given the **XYZ** coordinates of **A**,**B**,**C** arranged as a matrix. A pointer from T. Pavlidis, one of the referees, to the determinant form of his equation 3.10 of [6] converted us from Cramer's rule to the formally equivalent but more appealing account of this in terms of areal coordinates.)

Parametric Representations

A parametric representation of a curve is an expression for a point in terms of an independent parameter t. We easily obtain a parametric representation of a conic from a parametric representation of a point (x,y,z) on the cone, via the standard projection $(x,y,z) \rightarrow (x/z,y/z)$. This is fortunate since parametric representations of the cone are simpler than of the conic, due to the projection's being omitted. This constitutes a major motivation for applying projective geometry and homogeneous coordinates to conics.

There are several worthwhile parametric representations of the cone. They are all most easily introduced via **UVW** coordinates. First, u and v themselves immediately provide a fine pair of independent parameters, making $w = \pm\sqrt{u^2+v^2}$ the one dependent variable. The cone is then the parametrically defined surface $u\mathbf{U}+v\mathbf{V}+\sqrt{u^2+v^2}\mathbf{W}$. The points **A**,**C**,**D**,**E** on the cone are given by the respective parameter values (1,0), (−1,0), (0,1), and (0,−1). This parametrization is readily transformed into other coordinate systems such as **ABC** and **XYZ** by making the appropriate substitutions for **UVW** in $u\mathbf{U}+v\mathbf{V}+\sqrt{u^2+v^2}\mathbf{W}$, e.g. $\mathbf{U} = (\mathbf{A}-\mathbf{C})/2$, $\mathbf{V} = S\mathbf{B}$, $\mathbf{W} = (\mathbf{A}+\mathbf{C})/2$ to get to **ABC** coordinates.

Another parametrization makes u and v dependent on polar coordinates r and θ as $u = r\cos(\theta)$, $v = r\sin(\theta)$, yielding the form $r\cos(\theta)\mathbf{U}+r\sin(\theta)\mathbf{V}+r\mathbf{W}$ for the cone, with **A**,**C**,**D**,**E** all at $r = 1$ and having θ respectively 0, π, $\pi/2$, and $3\pi/2$. The substitutions for **UVW** to transform this parametrization into other coordinates are as before. This parametrization is useful in relating conic splines to uniform motion around the circle from which the conic spline has been projected. It replaces the square root in the uv parametrization by trig functions, if that is an advantage.

The parametrization that is most popular for splines is the st parametrization, obtainable via $s+it = \sqrt{u+iv}$. Squaring both sides yields $u = s^2-t^2$, $v = 2st$, so $w = s^2+t^2$. While this parametric form of the conic is not particularly attractive in **UVW** coordinates, transforming it to **ABC** coordinates yields the very appealing $s^2\mathbf{A}+2stS\mathbf{B}+t^2\mathbf{C}$, that is, $a = s^2$, $b = 2Sst$, $c = t^2$. Observe that $a+b/S+c = (s+t)^2$. The AVC plane is $a+b/S+c = 1$, whence it may also be specified as $s+t = \pm 1$. If we therefore substitute $1-t$ for s in the cone we obtain $(1-t)^2\mathbf{A}+2(1-t)tS\mathbf{B}+t^2\mathbf{C}$, immediately recognizable as the Bezier parabola with vertices **A**,S**B**,**C**. Other constant values of $s+t$ yield planes parallel to this, with $s+t = 0$ yielding the plane tangent to the cone at **E**.

2.1. Tangent Planes

One application of the st parametric form is to tangent planes to the cone. The partial derivatives of the parametric form of the cone $s^2\mathbf{A}+2stS\mathbf{B}+t^2\mathbf{C}$ with respect to s and t are $2s\mathbf{A}+2St\mathbf{B}$ and $2Ss\mathbf{B}+2t\mathbf{C}$ respectively. The plane tangent to the cone at (s,t) is then the plane containing the three points **O**, $s\mathbf{A}+St\mathbf{B}$ and $Ss\mathbf{B}+t\mathbf{C}$, the 2's being of no consequence.

Tangent planes to the cone provide a straightforward way of finding tangents to the conic. Suppose we wish to locate the two points on a conic having a given slope. Let **P** be any point other than **O** on a line through **O**, parallel to the view surface, and having the given slope. Then the intersection of the view surface, the cone, and one of the two planes tangent to the cone and containing **P**, will be one of the two points where the conic has that slope.

If **A**,**B**,**C**,**P** are all represented in **XYZ** coordinates, we may express the coplanarity of the three points $s\mathbf{A}+St\mathbf{B}$, $Ss\mathbf{B}+t\mathbf{C}$, and **P** as the vanishing of the determinant whose columns are the **XYZ** coordinates of those three points.

$$\begin{vmatrix} x_P & sx_A+tSx_B & sSx_B+tx_C \\ y_P & sy_A+tSy_B & sSy_B+ty_C \\ z_P & sz_A+tSz_B & sSz_B+tz_C \end{vmatrix} \qquad (2.6)$$

The determinant reduces to a homogeneous quadratic in s and t, whose roots constitute the two lines of tangency in the cone. The two points of tangency on the conic may then be obtained by setting $s+t = 1$.

For the points of horizontal tangency, $\mathbf{P} = \mathbf{X} = (1,0,0)$ in **XYZ** coordinates. In this case the determinant reduces to $S(y_A-y_B)s^2+(y_A-y_C)st+S(y_B-y_C)t^2$. For vertical tangents use x coordinates in place of y; for any other angle take the appropriate linear combination of these two forms for horizontal and vertical tangents.

2.2. Conic Determined by Additional Points

A common problem is to find the sharpness of the *ABC* conic containing an additional point **F**, with **A**,**B**,**C**,**F** all lying in the view plane. The solution is to substitute the **XY** coordinates of **F** for x and y in (2.4) and solve the resulting linear equation in S.

A related problem is to find an implicit form for the conic containing five distinct points **A**,**B**,**C**,**D**,**E**. Again there is an immediate solution:

$$\begin{vmatrix} x^2 & xy & y^2 & x & y & 1 \\ x_A^2 & x_Ay_A & y_A^2 & x_A & y_A & 1 \\ x_B^2 & x_By_B & y_B^2 & x_B & y_B & 1 \\ x_C^2 & x_Cy_C & y_C^2 & x_C & y_C & 1 \\ x_D^2 & x_Dy_D & y_D^2 & x_D & y_D & 1 \\ x_E^2 & x_Ey_E & y_E^2 & x_E & y_E & 1 \end{vmatrix} = 0 \qquad (2.7)$$

The determinant is a quadratic in x and y, so the equation is that of a conic. When $(x,y) = \mathbf{A}$ the first two rows are identical, so the determinant vanishes, so **A** is a solution. Similarly **B**,**C**,**D**,**E** are solutions. Hence the conic defined by this equation contains those five points.

When the five points are all lattice points the resulting equation will have integer coefficients, which may be computed exactly using only addition and multiplication. Hence we have a method of computing exactly an implicit form of the desired conic, as well as a short proof that any conic containing five distinct lattice points has an implicit form with integer coefficients.

This method is simple to implement, but is not particularly fast, since it involves computing six 5×5 determinants, a size better handled by triangulation than by brute force. Furthermore the magnitudes of the coefficients of x^2, xy, and y^2 grow as the sixth power of the magnitudes of the coordinates, those of x and y the seventh power, and the constant the eighth power. Hence to capitalize on the full precision of the method requires multiple precision arithmetic for all but the smallest conics. In practice 32-bit floating point, i.e. shedding precision at the low end, should provide a satisfactorily accurate approximation to the desired conic.

2.3. Conversion to Normal Form

It will be noticed that having **A** and **C** on the plane plays no significant role. Any parabola projects to a conic whether or not its endpoints coincide with those of the conic. Having **A** and **C** on the plane merely constitutes a normal form representation (though one that simplifies some calculations later).

On occasion we encounter points not in normal form, most often as the result of subdividing a conic by subdividing its underlying parabola. We then need to restore them to normal form

To put three arbitrary points **A**,**B**,**C** into normal form, first rescale the space by replacing all three points **A**,**B**,**C** by $p\mathbf{A}$,$p\mathbf{B}$,$p\mathbf{C}$ where $p = 1/\sqrt{z_Az_C}$, to drive z_Az_C to 1. Then multiply **A** by z_C and divide **C** by z_C to yield the desired normal form. It is readily checked that neither operation on these points alters the surface defined by $b^2-4ac = 0$ in the corresponding bases.

Note that the only impact of these two operations on the **ABC** axes has been to scale them; their points of intersection with z=1 remain unchanged.

We may now easily apply this to the problem of subdividing the conic. Subdivide the corresponding Bezier parabola $(1-t)^2\mathbf{A}+2(1-t)tS\mathbf{B}+t^2\mathbf{C}$ in the usual way. This yields two parabolas. These may each be projected back to two halves of our conic by the above conversion to normal form.

3. Curvature

We distinguish two curvature issues, external and internal. External curvature deals with the curvature at endpoints. It affects curvature matching between curves. Internal curvature deals with curvature along a single conic. It affects the amount by which curvature varies around the conic.

3.1. External (Endpoint) Curvature

It is often important to be able to match up curve segments not only in slope but in curvature. For cubics and up, B-splines make this very easy - curvature matching is obtained automatically as a byproduct of the representation. This method can be seen to be generalizable to parametric rational curves if we regard both the curves and their control points as the perspective projection of polynomial B-splines.

This method does not start working until degree three since parabolas (polynomial quadratics) cannot be curvature-matched, in the following sense. Given a sequence of n+1 points with slopes specified at those points, there does not in general exist a corresponding sequence of n parabolas (parametric quadratics) connecting those points and having the specified slopes there, such that curvature varies continuously around the curve (C_2–continuity). In fact these constraints uniquely determine those parabolas, making this limitation obvious.

It follows that the approach of projecting a C_2–continuous polynomial curve to yield a C_2–continuous rational curve fails for quadratics because of the unavailability of appropriate polynomial curves to project. Hence piecewise-conic curves cannot be made C_2–continuous by this method.

Nevertheless C_2–continuity of piecewise-conic curves, with specified location and slope of junctions, can always be achieved by adjusting only sharpness. As the sharpness S of a conic goes from zero to infinity the curvature at both endpoints can be seen to go from infinity to zero. For n conics connecting n+1 given point-slope pairs, there remain n degrees of freedom, namely the sharpnesses of those conics. We may adjust in turn the sharpness of each conic but the first to match the curvature of its predecessor. This consumes n-1 degrees of freedom to achieve C_2–continuity, leaving the sharpness of the first curve (now linked to the n-1 other sharpnesses) as the remaining degree of freedom for the whole curve.

For this approach it suffices to have a formula for curvature at endpoints. Writing Δ for the area of the triangle *ABC* and *a*,*b*,*c* for the lengths of the sides *BC*,*CA*,*AB* respectively, the curvature K at **A** measured in **XY** coordinates is given by the formula

$$K = \frac{\Delta}{S^2c^3} \qquad (3.1)$$

We may derive this as follows. Rotate and translate the **XY** coordinate system (preserving curvature) to put the origin at **A** and the **X** axis on *AB*. Now take the parametric form of the conic, which will be two rational quadratics in t, one for each of x and y, namely

$$x = \frac{2(1-t)tSx_B+t^2x_C}{1+2(S-1)(1-t)t}, \quad y = \frac{t^2y_C}{1+2(S-1)(1-t)t} \qquad (3.2)$$

Differentiate these expressions with respect to t and evaluate the resulting derivatives at $t = 0$ to obtain $\dot{x} = 2Sx_B$, $\dot{y} = 0$, and $\ddot{y} = 2y_C$. The usual formula $\dot{x}^2 = \ddot{y}r$ relating tangential velocity $\dot{x}$, radial acceleration $\ddot{y}$, and radius r when $\dot{y} = 0$ leads us to $K = y_C/2S^2x_B^2$ where K is curvature, the reciprocal of the radius r. Finally we use $\Delta = x_B y_C/2$ to obtain (3.1).

Besides its application to exact matching, the formula yields much insight into nonmatching, at opposite ends of the same conic as well as at junctions.

Let us consider first opposite ends of the same conic. We shall show how to build a "curvature transformer."

By symmetry the curvature at **C** must be Δ/S^2a^3. Hence the ratio of the curvature at **A** to that at **C** must be the cube of a/c, a quantity independent of everything but the lengths of AB and BC. Thus to build a "curvature transformer" consisting of an ABC conic to connect two points **A** and **C** at which the curvatures are in the ratio of 8 to 1 in a C_2–continuous way, with the smaller curvature at **A**, a necessary and sufficient condition (not including other requirements such as C_1–continuity) is that AB be twice as long as BC.

Now let us consider junctions, and address the problem of C_2–continuity at inflection points. Points of zero curvature are nonexistent in conics other than lines. Hence piecewise-conic curves cannot be C_2–continuous at inflection points. This is a major reason for preferring cubics to conics.

The above formula for curvature however gives us some idea of how closely zero curvature at a point of inflection can be *approximated.* Whether conic or cubic, *a major use of splines is to approximate curves,* to within acceptable visual or numerical limits. Hence we are not breaking any rules when we ask whether a good approximation is possible.

Whatever the prevailing curvature is at some distance removed from a point of inflection, a curvature transformer can be used to connect points on either side of an inflection in such a way that the curvature at the inflection is very small by comparison to the prevailing curvature. This can be done with a quite reasonable choice of ratio of sides; by the time the ratio reaches 3 to 1 the curvature at the inflection will be 1/27 the prevailing value.

This argument, together with its application to examples we have seen with outline fonts defined by conics, has convinced us that this ability to approximate a zero-curvature point of inflection so closely disposes almost entirely of the objection that conics lack such points. In support of this we ask the reader to inspect the following characters from a conic representation of Times Roman (Figure 3) to decide whether the points of inflection exhibit any objectionable or even detectable curvature discontinuity. The attached spline skeletons show the locations of the **ABC** control points (though not the sharpnesses).

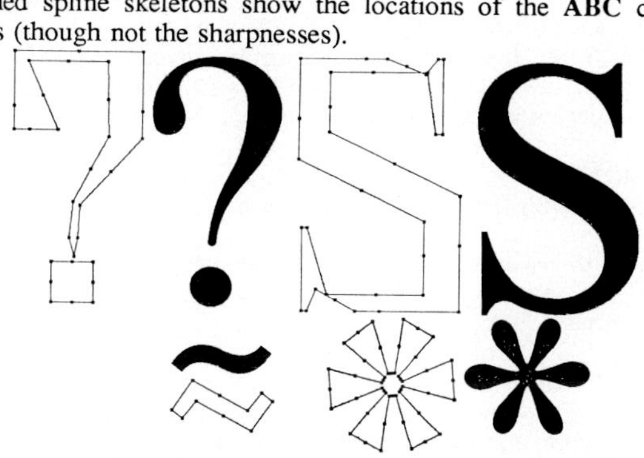

Figure 3. Conic-spline Characters With Points of Inflection

3.2. Internal (Variational) Curvature

We are interested in this section in the smoothness of curves. A plausible measure of smoothness is degree of variation of curvature around the curve. Extremely sharp or flat conics are obviously unreasonable candidates for "reasonably smooth" curves. At the elliptical extreme (low sharpness) the total curvature of the curve (the angle between its endpoint tangents) is concentrated at the endpoints, whereas at the hyperbolic extreme it is concentrated in the middle. Such extremes are far from "reasonably smooth."

One might settle for $S = 1$, a parabola, as a somewhat arbitrary but convenient intermediate value. Unfortunately, for curves with total curvature approaching 180 degrees (angle ABC approaching zero), a parabola suffers from the same problem as an extreme hyperbola, concentrating the curvature in the middle. Furthermore, when $AB = BC$ (isosceles triangle) there is an obvious candidate for the conic of least curvature variation, namely the circle, which has no curvature variation and is easy to represent, manipulate, plot, and understand, and, only partly for these reasons, is in much demand.

This is not to say that minimum variation is always what is wanted. Font designers often want superellipses. If we measure superellipticity in terms of the sharpness of a conic approximating a quadrant of a letter's outline, a commonly preferred superellipticity is one lying somewhere between a circle and a parabola.

An obvious measure of curvature variation is ellipse eccentricity. One problem with this measure is that it attains infinity at the parabola; this puts a discontinuity in the middle of a range that goes from ellipses to hyperbolas. Another problem is that it is not the easiest measure to calculate with.

The measure we introduce here relates the actual sharpness to the sharpness that yields the ellipse of minimum eccentricity. If as before we let a,b,c be the lengths of sides BC,CA,CB respectively, this minimum-eccentricity sharpness is given by

$$S = \frac{b}{\sqrt{2(a^2+c^2)}} \tag{3.3}$$

This formula was arrived at after much conversation with Macsyma, and we have been unable to construct a summary of the rationale behind it.

An equivalent criterion for minimum eccentricity told to us by Lyle Ramshaw is when the line from the center of the ellipse to a corner of the rectangle bounding the ellipse and aligned with the major and minor axes also passes through the **B** vertex of the triangle. We have not yet verified the equivalence of Ramshaw's nonmetrical criterion with our metrical one. However we have found the metrical one easy to apply.

For a right triangle, meaning here that ABC is a right angle, $a^2+c^2 = b^2$ by Pythagoras, so $S = 0.7071...$ for the ellipse of minimum eccentricity. From Ramshaw's criterion, this ellipse will be one quadrant of an ellipse whose major and minor axes are parallel to AB and BC (not necessarily respectively).

For an isosceles triangle, meaning here that $a = c$, there exists an ABC conic which is a circular arc from **A** to **C**. Since its eccentricity is 0, it follows that the formula for minimum eccentricity must yield the sharpness for a circle (which it does). In this case the formula simplifies to $b/2a$, recognizable as the cosine of the angle BCA (and of BAC).

We make use of this formula for minimum curvature variation to provide an alternative measure of sharpness that we call variation. It is the ratio of the actual sharpness to the sharpness of minimum curvature variation. When the variation is 1 the curvature variation is at a minimum over all conics in this triangle. Larger variation means a sharper curve, smaller means flatter. Larger variations are useful for drawing superelliptical figures, assuming that they are partitioned into four quadrants at their four extrema.

A necessary and sufficient condition for a conic to be an arc of a circle is for its triangle to be isosceles and its variation to be 1.

As one application for this concept, a simplified conic spline package could restrict itself to conic arcs of variation 1. Each arc would be specified by three points. A connected sequence of arcs would require only two points for each new arc. This package would allow any circular arc to be drawn, corresponding to isosceles triangles, and offer a limited variety of elliptical arcs as well. Our experience with fonts however indicates that variation 1 is much too restrictive for that application.

It should be noted that, even for conic splines that are segments of ellipses, the eccentricity of the ellipse does not uniquely determine sharpness, contrary to what has sometimes been stated in the literature. As sharpness increases from 0, eccentricity starts at infinity, decreases until the ellipse of minimum eccentricity is reached, after which the eccentricity increases again, returning to infinity when the sharpness reaches unity. Hence any given eccentricity is associated with two possible sharpnesses. In addition, an eccentricity below the minimum is meaningless. This makes eccentricity an unworkable substitute for sharpness. Variation on the other hand is linearly related to sharpness for any given triangle and hence does not have these problems.

4. Rendering

The problem is to visually approximate a two-dimensional *figure* drawn in the real (Euclidean) plane with an *image* consisting of a uniform and independent shading of each of the squares or *pixels* of a grid. In this paper we shall treat only *zero-aperture* imaging, in which the image is chosen to (best) match the figure at pixel centers. Zero-aperture is more readily implemented and performs better than larger apertures since it does not involve any area measurement, but is inferior at rendering fine detail, where a unit aperture (each image pixel matches the average of the corresponding figure pixel) yields somewhat better results and dithering with an aperture covering several pixels can produce a significantly better image. One may of course have one's cake and eat it too by constructing a sequence of images with increasing aperture sizes, so that a crude image appears immediately using the techniques of this paper and then as you watch is more carefully refined using other techniques.

We shall furthermore treat only the case of black and white figures and images; in any such case where the image shades include all the figure shades, the figure-image match at pixel centers is exact.

We assume an **XY** coordinate system with one lattice (integer) point per pixel. (These are *device coordinates*; pixels need not actually be upright, square, rectangular, or even congruent in physical coordinates.) We shall refer to increasing x as right and increasing y as up. The exact location of the lattice points inside the pixels may vary in half-pixel steps for each dimension with each conic arc; this turns out to allow a representable conic to be translated by half-pixel steps in the plane without making a mess of the associated arithmetic.

We treat only figures having region boundaries that, in device coordinates, are piecewise conic. These will also be conics in physical coordinates if device and physical coordinates are projectively related.

There are three stages in the way we discretize a conic segment: subdivision, alignment, and tracking. *Subdivision* partitions the conic into smaller conics of a size manageable by our algorithm, the limiting size being in proportion to the number of bits in an integer. We have already described how to subdivide conics in the section on principles of conic splines. *Alignment* adjusts the points **A,B,C** of each conic arc so that **A–B** and **B–C** have integer x and y components, yielding a *representable* conic, which may thereafter be translated in the plane by half-pixel increments. Tracking is the Pitteway process.

4.1. Alignment

Our exact version of Pitteway's algorithm depends on having the control points A,B,C separated by integer distances in each dimension and the square of the sharpness being a rational. We call conics satisfying these conditions (including the size limitations) *representable*. Alignment makes small adjustments to a conic to make it representable.

A set of n reals may be adjusted to make all their differences integral with an adjustment to each of at most $(1-1/n)/2$. (Reduce the n reals modulo 1 to form a ring, i.e. arrange the fractional parts of the n reals in a circle, find the biggest gap, of size at least $1/n$, and move all points away from that gap by at most $(1-1/n)/2$ to coincide.) Hence three reals a,b,c may be adjusted to make their three differences all integer by adjusting each by at most 1/3. For this case this can be accomplished by moving only two of the three by at most 1/3 each, so in the worst case the average motion of the three points becomes 2/9. It is incorrect however to conclude that the expected value of the average motion is exactly 1/9, though it should be somewhere in the neighborhood of 1/8.

Full quadrants provide a common special case admitting a better treatment than the above. This is when one end is horizontal and the other vertical. Adjust each endpoint along the normal at that endpoint to the nearest half-pixel. Then adjust each endpoint along the tangent at that endpoint to make **A–C** integer in x and y. Then **B** may be chosen to make the tangents exactly horizontal and vertical; it may be seen that **B**'s adjustment tracks only the first adjustment (along the normals), which is the smaller adjustment. This method results in an expected movement of any point of the curve of about 1/8 of a pixel.

Better effects are obtained at extrema when the extremum is near a pixel boundary. This avoids both flat spots and pimples, one of which arises when the extremum occurs near a pixel center. To arrange this requires a coarser adjustment to the conic. In our experience it has usually proved more esthetically satisfying to settle for the larger distortion than to have flat spots or pimples.

4.2. Sharpness

The problem is to find the closest rational approximation to S^2 with given bounds on the numerator and denominator. We use what amounts to binary search in the Farey sequence. The Farey sequence is an ordered list of reduced fractions, with bounded numerator and denominator. It may be generated by starting with just two fractions, 0/1 and 1/0, being the reduced forms of respectively zero and infinity. The element intermediate between any two elements a/b and c/d is defined to be $(a+c)/(b+d)$. Thus the first rational between 0/1 and 1/0 is 1/1. Next we get 1/2 between 0/1 and 1/1, and 2/1 between 1/1 and 1/0, then 1/3 between 0/1 and 1/2, and so on. It can be shown that only reduced fractions can be produced in this way; for example 2/6 will never appear. (Hint: for any adjacent pair a/b, c/d of fractions, $ad-bc = 1$.)

To search the interval bounded by a/b and c/d, compare $(a+b)/(c+d)$ with the number being approximated to see on which side of $(a+b)/(c+d)$ to continue the search. Note that it is only necessary to have around at any one time the two bounds on the interval and the new "midpoint," that is, the Farey sequence can be computed "on the fly."

By careful arrangement one may avoid all arithmetic save additions and comparisons in computing a rational approximation with this method. (Hint: maintain a copy of the three active denominators, each scaled by the number to be approximated, and compare it with the corresponding numerator.)

Gaps between Farey fractions vary considerably. The gap between fractions with denominators b and d is $1/bd$. In practice the worst gap is at $S^2 = 1/2$, where the nearest rationals are 12/25 and 13/25, leading to a worst-case error of 1% in S^2 and hence a 0.5% error in S.

Errors in approximating sharpness have little effect on the endpoints of the curve. They leave the position and tangent of each endpoint unchanged and affect only the curvature. In the interior they of course flatten or bulge the curve a little, without however upsetting the overall smoothness of the curve. Thus sharpness errors tend to be more tolerable than an error in **B**, which in turn is usually more tolerable than errors in **A** and **C**.

The tradeoff between bounds on numerator and denominator and bounds on size of conic were made with the above considerations in mind. These tradeoffs can be changed as required.

4.3. Bresenham-Pitteway Tracking

The tracking considered in this section is at the heart of the line and conic algorithms described by Bresenham [1] and Pitteway [7] respectively.

We take a *quadrant* of a curve to mean an open (i.e. not containing its endpoints) C_1-continuous curve segment whose slope is nowhere either horizontal or vertical. We let *Bresenham-Pitteway tracking* denote the process of following a quadrant of an implicitly defined curve $F(x,y) = 0$ by sampling F at pixel centers in the neighborhood of the curve to determine on which side of the curve each pixel center falls. One tracks quadrants partly so that "side" is well-defined, partly to simplify the tracking process.

The Bresenham-Pitteway process is the following trivial procedure, parametrized by the direction of tracking, expressed as a pair of procedures, one called *hor* - either *left*() or *right*() - for moving in the horizontal direction, the other *vert* - either *up*() or *down*() - for vertical motion. (In practice *track* should be expanded as a macro, with all four combinations of these two procedures instantiated as inline code.) These two procedures are responsible for all consequences of motion, both moving the drawing device and updating the x,y coordinates and associated values. The predicate *side*(x,y,Q) tests which side of *Q* the point (x,y) is on, returning true if we are on the side where *hor*() brings us closer to *Q*.

```
track(proc hor, proc vert):
        while not done() do
                if side(x,y,Q) then hor() else vert()
```

Even before we fill in the details of *done*(), *side*(), *hor*(), and *vert*(), this simple procedure raises a couple of not so simple problems. First, although the set of horizontal and vertical moves it makes is closely related to the pixels required for zero-aperture rendering, the relationship needs to be tightened up further to capture those pixels exactly. As partial evidence for this it should be noted that the procedure visits a different set of pixels depending on which direction it traverses the curve. Second, getting the exact starting and stopping conditions turns out to be a most exasperating exercise. We have not to date found a simpler treatment of these problems than the following.

The exact pixels we want as the final product of tracking a quadrant Q may be thought about as follows. We want those pixels either immediately to the left of, or to the right of, or above, or below Q, which we may denote L(Q), R(Q), A(Q), and B(Q) respectively. For example when we track the left boundary Q of a horizontally scanned region we want R(Q), which consists of the leftmost pixels of the scanned region. Similarly when we track the lower boundary of a vertically scanned region we want A(Q).

A good way to understand such a sequence of pixels is in terms of dual pixels. A *dual pixel* is a unit square whose corners are pixel centers (and hence vice versa - the corners of a pixel are dual pixel centers). Equivalently a dual pixel is the translation of a pixel by one half in each dimension. Associated with each dual pixel d is its North-West pixel NW(d), and similarly for NE(d), SW(d), and SE(d). The inverse association, from pixels to dual pixels, uses the same names, so that SE(NW(d)) = d.

(A detail unimportant in understanding the general idea, which should therefore be skipped on a first reading, is the treatment of ties, pixel centers actually on Q. Suppose ties are resolved by declaring them to be below and to the left of the curve. Corresponding to this, dual pixels are taken to include their left and bottom edges and bottom left corner, but not their top left or bottom right or top right corners or top or right edges. In general each dual pixel includes just that corner which lies in the same direction from the dual pixel as that used to resolve ties.)

The significance of dual pixels is that they provide a more straightforward characterization of the discrete essence of Q than do pixels. We define the *discretization* $\delta(Q)$ of quadrant Q to be the set of dual pixels intersecting Q. The sense in which $\delta(Q)$ captures Q is given by the following theorem.

Theorem.
$L(Q) = NW(\delta(Q)) \cap SW(\delta(Q))$, $R(Q) = NE(\delta(Q)) \cap SE(\delta(Q))$,
$A(Q) = NW(\delta(Q)) \cap NE(\delta(Q))$, $B(Q) = SW(\delta(Q)) \cap SE(\delta(Q))$.

Proof. By symmetry it suffices to consider L(Q). Since Q is open, if Q intersects an edge of a dual pixel it must also extend beyond it. Now $L(Q) \subseteq NW(\delta(Q)) \cap SW(\delta(Q))$ because Q must intersect the right-going edge coming from each pixel in L(Q), whence Q must intersect the dual pixels above and below that edge. Conversely, $L(Q) \supseteq NW(\delta(Q)) \cap SW(\delta(Q))$ because given two adjacent vertically aligned dual pixels, Q must cut their common edge, whence the left end of that edge must be a pixel center immediately to the left of Q. □

The significance of this theorem is that it demonstrates that $\delta(Q)$ contains all the information needed for whichever set of pixels, e.g. L(Q), we need for a particular tracking applications. Furthermore, given all four of these sets of pixels one may infer the position of any pixel center relative to Q, though not its exact distance from Q. Hence any position-based tracking method such as zero-aperture only needs to know $\delta(Q)$.

Bresenham-Pitteway tracking cannot be either a direct enumeration of the desired pixels (e.g. L(Q)) or of $\delta(Q)$. Instead tracking follows a greedy tour of Q, defined as follows.

A *tour* is a sequence of pixels connected by length-1 rook moves, all horizontal moves being in the same direction and similarly for vertical moves. We say that a pixel is *n-valent* in Q when it intersects *n* elements of $\delta(Q)$. (We omit 'in Q' when it is provided by context.) A *tour of* Q is a maximal tour having all pixels of valency 2 or 3. (Quadrants have no 4-valent pixels.)

Remark. All tours of Q have the same length, namely $|\delta(Q)|-1$.

Remark. All tours of Q intersect Q equally often, namely one more than the number of trivalent pixels. (Exception: when $|\delta(Q)| = 1$ there are no intersections.)

A *greedy* tour of Q is one whose intersections with Q are as far as possible towards one end. There are therefore two greedy tours of Q, one for each end, which are the same tour if and only if $\delta(Q)$ is a pure diagonal (one having at most two divalent corners).

The two key properties of greedy tours are that they are what Bresenham-Pitteway tracking yields, and the desired pixels (e.g. L(Q)) can be very easily extracted from them. The former property is best verified by the reader by inspection. L(Q) or R(Q) may be enumerated in order by taking those pixels the tracking algorithm is at just before making each vertical move, plus or minus one in the horizontal direction depending on the direction of travel and whether L or R is needed. Dually the pixels of A(Q) or B(Q) may be enumerated just before each horizontal move, plus or minus one vertically. Since the tracking process is all incremental the plus-or-minus-one arithmetic need be performed only once, at the beginning.

This perspective on tours now makes it easy to deal with the end-points. As may be easily verified by inspection, the first pixel enumerated by the immediately above procedure should be discarded, and an additional pixel at the other end should be obtained by allowing the procedure to continue for one more pixel output.

4.4. The Numerical Component

The procedures *up*(), *down*(), *left*(), and *right*(), and the predicate *side*(x,y,Q), are implemented as the numerical component of Pitteway's conic-tracking algorithm. The predicate tests the sign of $F(x,y)$ at the current location (x,y), and also the sign of a partial derivative of $F(x,y)$ when necessary. The four motion procedures keep the value of $F(x,y)$ up to date, which they do incrementally by also keeping up to date the values at the current location of the partial differences

$$F_x(x,y) = F(x+1,y)-F(x,y) \quad F_y(x,y) = F(x,y+1)-F(x,y)$$

$$F_{xx}(x,y) = F_x(x+1,y)-F_x(x,y) \quad F_{yy}(x,y) = F_y(x,y+1)-F_y(x,y)$$

$$F_{xy}(x,y) = F_x(x,y+1)-F_x(x,y)$$

For each move up, down, left, or right, the updating procedure may be expressed as follows. (We use the convenient += and −= notation of C; x += y denotes the operation of adding y to x, and similarly for −=.)

up(): $F \mathrel{+}= F_y;\quad F_x \mathrel{+}= F_{xy};\quad F_y \mathrel{+}= F_{yy};$

down(): $F_y \mathrel{-}= F_{yy};\quad F_x \mathrel{-}= F_{xy};\quad F \mathrel{-}= F_y;$

right(): $F \mathrel{+}= F_x;\quad F_x \mathrel{+}= F_{xx};\quad F_y \mathrel{+}= F_{xy};$

left(): $F_y \mathrel{-}= F_{xy};\quad F_x \mathrel{-}= F_{xx};\quad F \mathrel{-}= F_x;$

The initial values of F and the partials at (x,y) (chosen to lie at a distance of less than one pixel from the curve), may be computed from the following formulas, which are obtainable directly from the definitions. Note that these are partial differences, not partial derivatives, whence the extra α in F_x and γ in F_y.

F	$\alpha x^2 + 2\beta xy + \gamma y^2 + \delta x + \varepsilon y + \zeta$
F_x	$2\alpha x + \alpha + 2\beta y + \delta$
F_y	$2\gamma y + \gamma + 2\beta x + \varepsilon$
F_{xx}	2α
F_{xy}	2β
F_{yy}	2γ

As shown earlier, when the control points are lattice points the Greek letters are all integers. To take best advantage of this the coordinate system may be chosen separately for each conic to make the control points lattice points. The sampled points will then in general not be lattice points. However if they are half lattice points ($2x$ and $2y$ are integers) then all the partial derivatives will be integers, a property we need for exact tracking. It does not matter that F is not an integer since we shall only make comparisons with F of the form $F<0$ and $F \geq 0$, so taking F to be the floor of its true value will not affect the outcome of such tests.

Overflow may occur during the calculation of F. However the final value of F should be close to 0 since the initial pixel is adjacent to the curve. To be exact, its magnitude cannot exceed that of F_x or F_y, which must be arranged not to overflow, both for this reason and to make reliable increments. Hence all values lost by overflow will cancel, whence overflow may be ignored.

Stopping Condition

For the stopping condition for tracking, represented by the procedure *done*(), it suffices to test either the y or x coordinate, depending on whether we are scanning horizontally (L(Q) or R(Q) pixels) or vertically (A(Q) or B(Q) pixels) respectively. The test is against a limit that is precomputed by inspection of the endpoints. This test may be reduced to a single decrement-and-branch-on-zero instruction by performing it as a part of the pixel output process.

Aliasing

Pitteway's algorithm is a sampling process; it stays on the curve by sampling lattice points in the neighborhood of the curve, never sampling more than a pixel away. As in any sampling process, the signal may contain frequencies high enough to confuse the sampling. In the case of a conic this can happen when rendering a thin ellipse, where the opposite sides of the ellipse are less than a pixel apart. In this case it is possible to cross both sides in one step and miss the region in between. When this happens Pitteway's algorithm goes in a vertical or horizontal line searching for the boundary until the stopping condition is met or overflow happens.

The starting position and stopping condition define a band parallel to the scanning direction outside which nearby edges do not matter. If two edges of the conic occur inside this band, they will be separated by the line consisting of the zeros of the partial derivative of F with respect to the direction of scanning, i.e. the line $F_x' = 0$ for horizontal scanning and $F_y' = 0$ for vertical scanning. Hence whenever there is doubt about whether two edges have been crossed at once, the doubt may be resolved by inspecting the partial derivative. This doubt arises just when we are on either side of both edges. This adds a test (of the sign of the partial derivative) to the code for one of the outcomes of the *side*() predicate but not the other. By symmetry the *side*() predicate should hold half the time on average, diluting the expected cost of the test by a factor of two.

This method may be considered a form of antialiasing, in that it takes advantage of the derivative not containing any high frequencies, unlike F itself.

There is no need to keep a separate copy of F_x' up to date since $F_x' = F_x - F_{xx}/2$, reducing the test $F_x' < 0$ to the comparison $F_x < F_{xx}/2$. $F_{xx}/2$ should be kept in a register (a machine-dependent performance consideration), but unlike F_x' it needs no updating. Since the test of the derivative is only done half the time, this is better than having to update a separate copy of the derivative itself at every step.

The appropriate sign of F_x', corresponding to which edge we are tracking, is determined at the outset by evaluating F_x' at each of **A** and **C**; since not both **A** and **C** can be at horizontal extrema, at least one of them will yield a nonzero value for F_x', which then yields the desired sign. An easy test for whether F_x' is zero at **A** is whether $y_A = y_B$. With this test it suffices to evaluate F_x' at only one of **A** or **C**.

It is important to realize that the correctness of this method depends on the stopping condition for the basic loop, which determines the band within which the tracking takes place. The claim is that the algorithm can rely on the signs of F and F_x' (if scanning horizontally) to infer its current position relative to the curve *provided* the current position has not gone past the y limit. Consider a very thin horizontal ellipse, for which $F_x = 0$ is a vertical line through its center. One can cross the whole of this ellipse in one step moving vertically without detecting a sign change in either F or F_x'. However one cannot do so without also going past the y limit.

4.5. Strokes

A commonly occurring problematical region type is the *stroke*. This is a region having two essentially parallel (whether or not curved) boundaries only a few pixels apart, with single pixel separation being the most critical. The problem is that if the two boundaries are rendered independently the sampling artifacts in each boundary may beat with each other to create even worse artifacts.

A somewhat simple-minded solution that is independent of curve family is to partition strokes into *shallow* and *steep* components, throughout which the slope (of the medial axis) stays within 45 degrees of horizontal or vertical respectively. Then for each such component adjust matching pairs of shallow or steep boundaries to make them respectively vertical or horizontal integer-distance translations of each other. This eliminates all beating between the two boundaries. Steep (shallow) strokes then have the same number of pixels in every row (column).

This adjustment will leave a gap at shallow-steep junctions, due in part to the ends of the adjoining strokes being at right angles and in part to the ends being moved to the appropriate halfpoints. The gap may be closed by connecting corresponding boundaries (outer to outer, inner to inner) with straight lines, providing tangent continuity thought not curvature continuity. Also thickness is no longer uniform, decreasing at diagonal points to 70% of the thickness at extrema. As thickness increases the boundary interference problem becomes less objectionable while the gap closure and the thickness variation become more noticeable. Hence at some thickness, in the vicinity of 3 to 5 pixels, this treatment of strokes does more harm than good.

Better effects than are possible with this simple-minded method may be had using the polygonal pens described in J. Hobby's thesis [12]. His treatment is equivalent to the above at a thickness of one pixel, but breaks thicker strokes up into smaller pieces each with its own treatment, with the two boundaries still being the same within each piece but with the corresponding points between those boundaries no longer always being parallel to an axis but rather being approximately normal to the curve. This work is remarkable for its extensive and effective use of elementary number theory.

5. Precision and Performance Considerations

The coefficients α through γ of the implicit equation of the conic range from quadratic to quartic polynomials in the **XYZ** coordinates of **A**,**B**,**C**. The coefficients α, β, and γ are quadratic, δ and ε are cubic, and ζ is quartic. To fit the resulting large numbers into a 32-bit word, it is necessary to hold down the size of the coordinates of **A**,**B**,**C**.

The origin is translated to the center of the rectangular hull of the triangle to minimize the magnitudes of these coordinates.

For 32-bit arithmetic we limit this magnitude to 100, whence the triangle must fit in a square of 200 pixels on a side; larger triangles must have their conics subdivided. A proportionately larger triangle is possible with 64-bit arithmetic.

This size is achievable if the numerator of the square of the sharpness is limited to 15 and the denominator to 25. For the values of sharpness so representable, the arithmetic is exact. More precision in sharpness may be had by reducing the limit on the size of the triangle.

On the 68010 the inner loop of the exact Pitteway process, without the modification for aliasing, is a constant 7 instructions: three adds, compare, conditional branch, render, and decrement-and-branch (all arithmetic being exact, using 32-bit integers). With the antialiasing modification an additional comparison instruction and associated branch instruction are executed every second time around the loop on average, increasing the number to an average of 8 instructions per step around the curve. The result is that the running time for the curve-drawing phase of our algorithm is on the order of 10L microseconds where L is the length of the curve in pixels in the L_1 or Manhattan metric (number of length-1 rook moves).

6. Prototyping, Packaging and Integration

A system based on the above algorithms was built at Sun three times. The first implementation, between February and May of 1984, was done concurrently with working out the necessary theory. It performed well but suffered from a lack of perspective on our part at the time as to what functions were needed and how the interfaces should be structured. As a prototype it was invaluable for testing the principles. A second implementation was carried out in June and July to improve both the interfaces and some of the algorithms. This could be called the packaging phase. The system was then used extensively for a number of months as a component of an outline font design system, incorporating a spline interpolating package for digitized point data, and an outline font editor. A third implementation, still under way, constitutes the integration phase, to allow the system to fit in smoothly with Sun's version of the graphics universe: CORE and GKS on top of CGI on top of Pixrect (Sun's internal bitmap standard).

Acknowledgments

Martin Brooks, Craig Taylor, Mike Shantz, Jerry Evans, Leo Guibas, Lyle Ramshaw, John Hobby, Don Knuth, Chuck Bigelow, and Kris Holmes formed a patient and sympathetic audience for many discussions of this material. Martin Brooks provided the first of the three implementations.

7. Bibliography

[1] Bresenham, J.E. Algorithm for computer control of a digital plotter, IBM Systems Journal, Vol. 4, p.25, 1965

[2] Catmull, E., Computer Display of Curved Surfaces, Proc. IEEE Conf. on Computer Graphics, Pattern Recognition and Data Structure, p.11, May 1975.

[3] Forrest, A.R., Curves and Surfaces for Computer-Aided Design, Ph.D. Thesis, Mathematical Laboratory and Engineering Dept., University of Cambridge, July 1968.

[4] Coolidge, J.L, **A History of the Conic Sections and Quadric Surfaces**, Oxford University Press, 1945.

[5] Lockwood, E.H., **A Book of Curves**, Cambridge University Press, Cambridge, 1961.

[6] Pavlidis, T., Curve Fitting with Conic Splines, ACM Trans.on Graphics, **2**, 1, 1-31, January 1983.

[7] Pitteway, M.L.V., Algorithm for drawing ellipses or hyperbolae with a digital plotter, Computer J., B10P, p282-289, 1967.

[8] Sederberg, T.W., **Implicit and Parametric Curves and Surfaces for Computer Aided Geometric Design,** Ph.D. Thesis, School of Mech. Eng., Purdue U., August 1983.

[9] Tiller, W., Rational B-splines for Curve and Surface Representation, IEEE CG&A, 61-69, September 1983.

[10] Todd, J.A., **Projective and Analytical Geometry,** Pitman, London, 1947.

[11] Yates, R.C, **Curves and Their Properties,**, Classics in Mathematics Education Series, National Council of Teachers of Mathematics, 245pp., 1974.

[12] Hobby, J.D., **Digitization of Brush Trajectories**, Ph.D. thesis, Stanford University, 1985.

[13] Salmon, G., **A Treatise on Conic Sections**, Longmans, Green, & Co., 6th edition, London, 1879. Reprinted by Dover Publications Inc, NY.

Blend Surfaces for Set Theoretic Volume Modelling Systems

Alan E Middleditch and Kenneth H Sears

Computer Aided Engineering Group
Department of Engineering and Science
Polytechnic of Central London
115 New Cavendish Street
LONDON W1M 8JS

Abstract: Most volume modelling systems are very limited in the complexity of the surfaces which they support. This is satisfactory for basic models of most mechanical components, since the functional surfaces are not usually complex. However, there are often blends between simple base surfaces. This paper presents a technique appropriate for blend definition and profile control. A discussion of blend conics is used to develop analogous surfaces for use in typical volume modelling systems. These surfaces are then used to set theoretically define bounded volumes for fillets and chamfers. Empirical results show that the method described suits many engineering applications.

Categories and Subject Descriptor: I.3.5 [Computer Graphics] Computational Geometry and Object Modelling. I.3.3 [Computer Graphics] Picture/Image Generation. I.3.7 [Computer Graphics] 3D Graphics and Realism.

General Terms: Geometric Modelling, Computer Graphics.

Additional Key Words and Phrases: Volume Modelling, Computer Aided Design, Curved Surfaces, Ray Tracing.

Introduction

Most volume modelling sytems [1] are very limited in the complexity of the surfaces which they support. This is satisfactory for basic models of most mechanical components since the functional surfaces are not usually complex [2]. However, there are often surfaces which blend between simple surfaces. These blend surfaces are sometimes the result of a deliberate design decision based on aesthetic or structural criteria. Sometimes they are incorporated for ease of manufacture or are the side effect of a manufacturing process; e.g. the corner of a pocket left by a milling cutter or the rounding inherent in casting processes. The geometry of blends thus depend on their origin; e.g. residues of milling operations inherently have circular cross sections with constant radii. When the exact shape is not important and the manufacturing process can produce a range of surface shapes, circular cross sections are usually chosen for ease of specification.

This paper shows that there is no advantage in restricting blends to those with circular cross sections when the computer is used for shape definition. Hence such restrictions, and the more stringent 'rolling ball' limitation of [3], should not be imposed. It should be possible to specify a variety of profiles in order that the most appropriate blend may be used. The properties which a blend surface should exhibit appear to be:

1. tangency with the base surfaces to be blended,

2. curves of tangency with the base surfaces which are a constant distant from the alternate base surface,

3. cross section profiles defined and controlled by the 'shape' of the profile curve and the distance of the tangency curves from the alternate base surface.

Unlike the methods reviewed in the next section, this paper presents an exact blend representation which is suitable for set theoretic volume modelling systems. In addition, the representation proposed naturally provides more appropriate blend specification parameters. It is introduced via the conics which possess the required blend profile properties in two dimensions. The insight gained from this discussion is used to develop analogous surfaces for use in typical volume modelling systems. These surfaces are then used to set theoretically define bounded volumes for use in volume models.

Alternative Techniques

Sculptured surface techniques [4,5] are currently being incorporated into volume modelling systems [6,7]. These are useful for components such as turbine blades but, despite some success [8,9], they are of limited use for simple blends. It is difficult to represent blend surfaces with the rectangular patches usually employed [10]. Furthermore, even the prevalent bicubic patches cannot exactly represent simple cylindrical or toroidal surfaces or surfaces bounded by such surfaces (e.g. blends). Other problems are due to the large amount of data necessary to define surface patches and the difficulty of deriving that data from convenient blend specifications.

Exact representations for blends may be achieved by blending between planes conformally mapped to the base surfaces, then inverse mapping the blend [11]. This approach was originally associated with a final conversion to B-spline patches, but that conversion has now been discarded in favour of implicit surfaces [12].

Recursive subdivision techniques [13,14] produce smooth objects and are useful for (primarily aesthetic) design, since they allow a user to start with simple polyhedral approximations. This global smoothing does not allow control of the extent of the blend 'orthogonal' to the base surface intersection curve. However, it may be possible to modify the standard methods to blend single edges and contain the blend extent. The inability to blend single edges also eliminates approaches which use superquadric primitive volumes [15] and the more general global smoothing techniques for set combinations [16].

Preview of the Technique Proposed

There is a fundamental compatibility problem between all surface (parametric) methods and set theoretic modelling systems which ultimately rely on the Boolean combinations of halfspace potential equations. The proposed technique may be considered as a generalisation of the superquadric method to enable blend extent control, or alternatively as an extension of Limings method [5] to higher order base surfaces. It incorporates a method to control the position of the tangent curves and Boolean operations to eliminate global effects and trim the blends along the base surface intersection curve.

Blends are specified via their base surfaces and the primitives which those surfaces bound. The termination of the blend along the (possibly imaginary) base surface intersection curve is achieved via Boolean operations involving the relevant primitive halfspaces; the user need not specify termination conditions explicitly. Although no method was given, this approach has been previously suggested [3] for simple blends. The proposed technique applies to any blend in volume models constructed from primitives bounded by algebraic halfspaces.

Since there is little speed advantage to be gained by approximation, the proposed blends are represented exactly. The proposed blends between quadrics are fourth order, and there is no advantage in using piecewise toroidal blends as suggested in [3]. Although blends with one or more tori will be eighth order, they will have little relative effect when evaluating a complete model.

Blend Conics

Consider three intersecting straight lines, $l_1(p) = 0$, $l_2(p) = 0$ and $l_3(p) = 0$, such that points p on the line l_i with a unit normal n_i and a minimum distance d_i from the origin satisfy:

$$l_i(p) = p.n_i + d_i = 0 . \qquad (1)$$

For simplicity, $l_i(p)$ will be abbreviated to l_i in the subsequent discussion.

The conic $l_1 l_2 = 0$ is the pair of lines l_1 and l_2, and $l_3^2 = 0$ is the line l_3 taken twice (fig. 1). Thus a conic l which passes through the points of intersection of l_1 with l_3 and l_2 with l_3 is given by:

$$l = (1-\mu)l_1 l_2 + \mu l_3^2 = 0 . \qquad (2)$$

Since l_3 is taken twice, the intersection points satisfy the equation twice, and the conic is tangential to both l_1 and l_2.

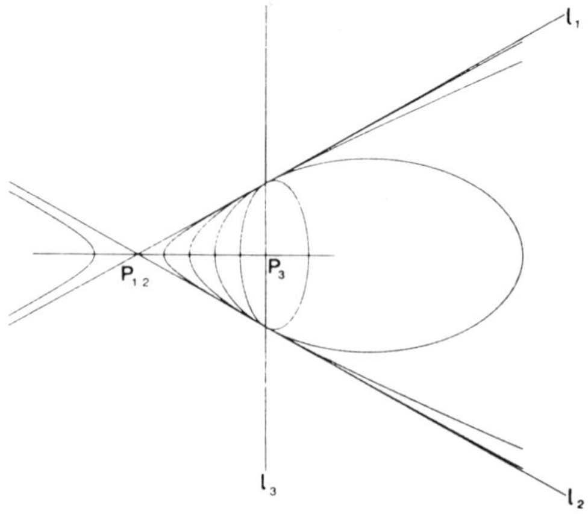

Figure 1 - Blend Conics

The line $l_1 + l_2 = 0$ passes through the intersection point of l_1 and l_2, lies in the region $l_1 l_2 < 0$, and bisects the angle between l_1 and l_2. Therefore, if the conic is to have an appropriate control distance, l_3 must intersect l_1 in points a (signed) distance d from l_2, and intersect l_2 in points d from l_1:

$$l_3 = l_1 + l_2 - d \ . \qquad (3)$$

As μ changes from 0 to 1, the conic of equation 2 changes from l_1 and l_2 to l_3 twice. Unfortunately, it does not provide the appropriate shape control. It is preferable to constrain the curve to pass through a control point P_c on the bisector of l_1 and l_2 (fig. 1):

$$P_c = (1 - \beta) P_{12} + \beta P_3 \ . \qquad (4)$$

At $\beta = 0$ the control point is at the intersection of lines l_1 and l_2, and at $\beta = 1$ it is on the line l_3. In general, P_c lies at a distance $\beta d/2$ from each base line. Substituting this distance into equation 2,

$$(1 - \mu)(\beta d/2)^2 + \mu(\beta d - d)^2 = 0$$

Therefore

$$\mu = -\beta^2 / (3\beta - 2)(\beta - 2) \ . \qquad (5)$$

Figure 2 shows the relationship between β and μ and indicates the basic shape of the blending curve.

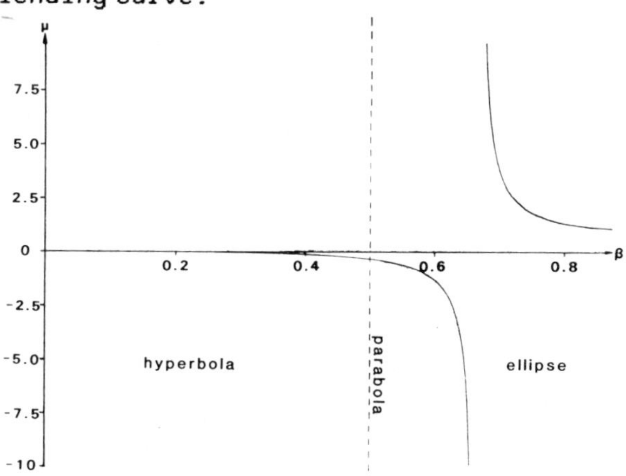

Figure 2 - Blend Conic Shape Control

The conic which blends between lines l_1 and l_2 with the appropriate control parameters β and d, and lies in the unbounded region where $l_1 l_2 > 0$, can be derived from equations 2, 3 and 5:

$$4(\beta - 1)^2 l_1 l_2 - \beta^2 (l_1 + l_2 - d)^2 = 0 \ . \qquad (6)$$

Blend Surfaces

Analoguous to the blend conic is the surface which blends between the arbitrary surfaces $S_1(p) = S_1 = 0$ and $S_2(p) = S_2 = 0$:

$$(1 - \mu) S_1 S_2 + \mu (S_1 + S_2 - d)^2 = 0 \ . \qquad (7)$$

This surface is tangential to the base surfaces and has the appropriate distance property if S_1 and S_2 are true distance functions. Unfortunately, even for the simple surfaces used in volume modelling systems, functions which return the true distance often involve one or two square roots. This complicates the evaluation of equation 7 to an extent which is undesirable, especially in time critical volume modelling systems.

For example, a common approach used to calculate integral properties, or generate shaded images of set theoretic volume models, involves the intersection of (parametrically defined) linear rays with the (implicitly defined) surfaces [17]. If a distance function were used to define the surfaces of typical volume modelling systems, such ray casting would often require the solution of non-algebraic equations in the ray parameter involving one or two square roots. Fortunately such surfaces may usually be defined via polynomial potential functions with a monotonic relation to distance, and ray casting reduces to the solution of polynomial equations. Such equations may be solved analytically for quartic and lower order surfaces, while the direct use of distance functions would require a numerical method.

Although suitable polynomial implicit equations exist for the common functional surfaces, their use in equation 7 would sacrifice the distance property of blends. Fortunately, since this property merely requires that S_i evaluate to the true distance at points a distance d from the respective surfaces, a suitable function is given by:

$$S_i = \frac{d}{K_i(d)} P_i \ , \qquad (8)$$

where P_i is any potential function and $K_i(d)$ is the potential of points at a distance d. Fortunately, all the common surfaces of volume modelling systems have low order polynomial potential functions. Also, K is a simple polynomial independent of position for most of these surfaces. Providing a suitable function can always be found, the evaluation of equation 7 is tractable, and the size of blend profiles can be controlled.

Analogous to the blending conic, the shape of the blend profile can be controlled by a space curve in its surface which is a fixed distance, $\beta d/2$, from the base surfaces. A surface which contains such a space curve satisfies:

$$(1 - \mu) M + \mu N^2 = 0, \qquad (9)$$

$$\text{where } M = \frac{K_1(\beta d/2)}{K_1(d)} \frac{K_2(\beta d/2)}{K_2(d)}$$

$$\text{and } N = \frac{K_1(\beta d/2)}{K_1(d)} + \frac{K_2(\beta d/2)}{K_2(d)} - 1 .$$

Solving for μ and substituting in equation 7:

$$B^2 \frac{P_1}{K_1(d)} \frac{P_2}{K_2(d)} - A\left[\frac{P_1}{K_1(d)} + \frac{P_2}{K_2(d)} - 1\right]^2 = 0 , \quad (10)$$

$$\text{where } B = \frac{K_1(\beta d/2)}{K_1(d)} + \frac{K_2(\beta d/2)}{K_2(d)} - 1 ,$$

$$\text{and } A = \frac{K_1(\beta d/2)}{K_1(d)} \frac{K_2(\beta d/2)}{K_2(d)} .$$

This surface is tangential to the base surfaces, the contact curves are a distance d from the alternate base surface, and β(0..1) controls the blend cross section profile.For example, β = 0.5 gives a blend surface which contains a curve equidistant and d/4 from each base surface.

When the base surfaces are normalised planes, K(d)=d, equation 10 reduces to the form of equation 6, and the blend surface is a conic cylinder (i.e. second order). The order of the blend surface increases with that of the base surfaces. Thus, although the boundary of an axial cross section of a circular cylinder/plane intersection consists of two straight lines, the blend section is not a conic (fig. 3).

A general unbounded circular cylinder (or sphere) of radius r has a quadratic potential function, and

$$K(d) = d\,(2r + d) . \quad (11)$$

Since K(d) is constant for a given cylinder, a cylinder/cylinder or plane/cylinder blend has a fourth order potential equation. Although this could give rise to undesirable cusps, its properties are found to be suitable for many blend surfaces (e.g. figs. 3 and 4). The profile drawing shows that the parameter β provides good profile control. However, the change of shape when β < 0.3 and β > 0.8, is not very evident in shaded images. This corresponds to the flat portions in the graph of figure 2.

Other surfaces prevalent in volume modelling systems are cones and tori. If bounded cones are defined as transformations of primitive cones with their axis along the Z coordinate axis, the relevant potential equation is the simple polynomial:

$$x^2 + y^2 - (zs - r)^2 = 0 , \quad (12)$$

where s is the tangent of half the vertex angle and r is the radius of the cross section on the XY plane. Unlike the cylinder, the distance to potential mapping function is not independant of the associated points:

$$K(d) = B\,(B + 2\,|zs - r|) ,$$
$$\text{where } B = (1 + s^2)\,d . \quad (13)$$

If a single rather than a double cone is used, the modulus disappears and equations 13 and 10 become simple polynomials. For cone/cone or cone/plane blends, equation 10 is then sixth order. If the term in `z` is neglected, the blend often remains satisfactory while equation 13 reduces to

$$K(d) = B\,(B + 2r) , \quad (14)$$

and equation 10 becomes fourth order. However, the blend is perturbed at points which do not lie on the (neutral) planar cross section(s) of the cone(s) which map onto the XY plane(s) of the primitive cone(s). This causes variations in the distance of blend/base surface contact curves from the alternate base surface. The effect is significant only when the deviation of those curves from a neutral plane is significant with respect to r/s (the distance of the cone apex from that plane). In the common situation where the blends are merely features of a surface intersection, d << r/s. If, in addition, the blend is constructed such that the contact curve is close to the neutral plane, little distortion should occur. Figures 5 and 6 illustrate cone/cone blends using the simplification of equation 14.

The polynomial potential equations of tori are also simplified if transformations of primitive tori are used. For example, a torus with its centroid at the origin and axis along the Y coordinate axis, has a potential equation

$$(x^2 + y^2 + z^2 + r^2 - s^2)^2 - 4r^2(x^2 + z^2) = 0 , \quad (15)$$

where r is the centre line radius and s is the cross section radius. Unfortunately, as with the cone, the distance to potential mapping is non-linear and dependent on the point of concern:

$$K(d) = B(B + 4r\sqrt{(x^2 + z^2)}) , \quad (16)$$
$$\text{where } B = d(d + 2s) .$$

This may be simplified to

$$K(d) = B(B + 4r^2) , \quad (17)$$

while only affecting blend points not on the cylindrical surface containing the torus centre line. The magnitude of the resulting blend distortion depends on the significance of s and d with respect to r. Figures 7 and 8 illustrate tori/tori blends using the simplification of equation 17.

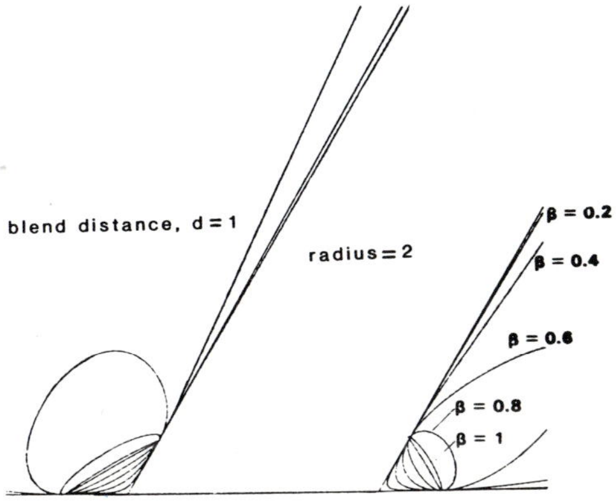

Figure 3: Plane/Cylinder Blend Profiles

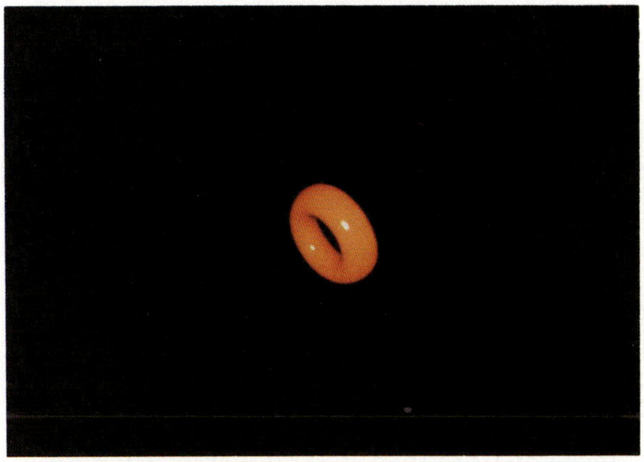

Figure 4: Plane/Cylinder Blend Surface (β = 0.6)

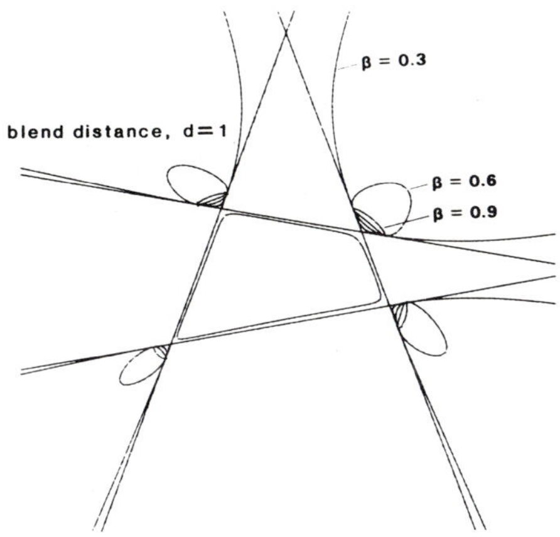

Figure 5: Cone/Cone Blend Profiles

Figure 6: Cone/Cone Blend Surface (β = 0.6)

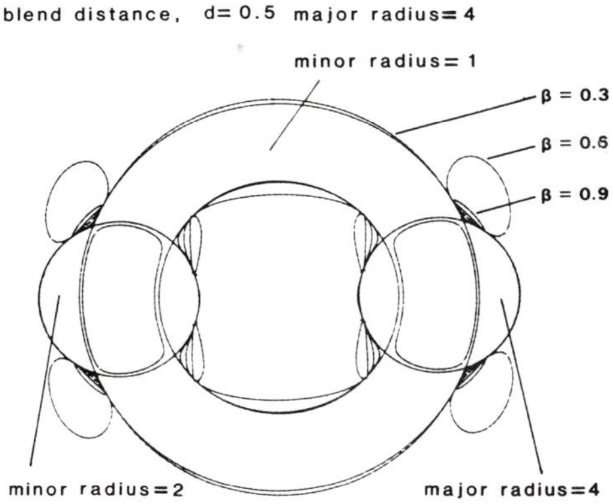

Figure 7: Torus/Torus Blend Profiles

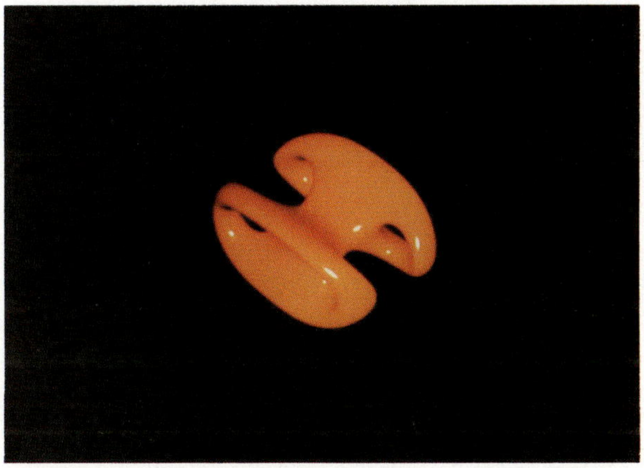

Figure 8: Torus/Torus Blend Surface (β = 0.6)

Fillets and Chamfers

Blends occur at tangent discontinuities in an object's surface, i.e. at edges. Fillets are blends where the object is locally concave, while chamfers are blends where it is locally convex. The visible surface of chamfers is usually considered to be a ruled surface. However, in the subsequent discussion both fillets and chamfers will be allowed to have a (bounded) visible surface, which is part of an (unbounded) blend surface, defined via the analytic surfaces adjacent to the discontinuity.

Previous sections treated blend surfaces; fillets and chamfers for use in volume modelling systems must be constructed with blend volumes. Thus the set of points B_{12}, bounded by the blend surface of equation 10, is given by

$$B_{12} = \{p : A(Q_1 + Q_2 - 1)^2 - B^2 Q_1 Q_2 \leq 0\}, \quad (18)$$
$$\text{where } Q_i = S_i/K_i(d).$$

All points in this set also satisfy $Q_1Q_2 \geq 0$. Thus, the blend volume B_{12} is disjoint from the symetric set difference of the base halfspaces:

$$B_{12} \leq ((H_2 - H_1) \cup (H_1 - H_2))',$$
$$\text{where } H_1 = \{p : Q_1 \leq 0\},$$
$$H_2 = \{p : Q_2 \leq 0\},$$

H' is the complement of H, U is the set union operator, and ≤ represents set inclusion Ambigious interpretation of ≤ as numerical 'less than', is resolved by the context.

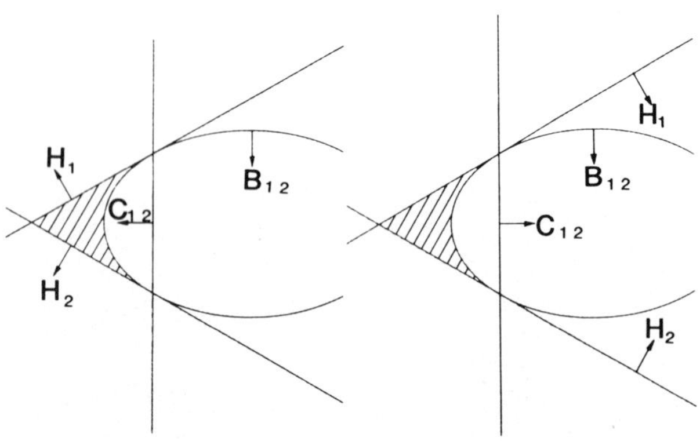

Fillet Construction   Chamfer Construction

Figure 9

When the edge between two surfaces is to be 'rounded', the volume which must be 'added' or 'subtracted' is of 'triangular' cross section, (fig. 9). For example, a fillet to be 'added' to the set union of the half spaces H_1 and H_2 is given by

$$\text{Fillet}(\mu, d, H_1, H_2)$$
$$= (H_1' \,\&\, H_2') \,\&\, (C_{12} - B_{12})$$
$$= (H_1' \,\&\, H_2') \,\&\, (C_{12} \,\&\, B_{12}'), \quad (19)$$
$$\text{where } C_{12} = \{p : Q_1 + Q_2 - 1 \leq 0\}$$

and & is the set intersection operator.

The result of such a filleting operation is

$$V = (H_1 \cup H_2) \cup (C_{12} - B_{12}). \quad (20)$$

Figure 10 shows the result when H_1 and H_2 are a torus and cylinder respectively.

If higher order blend surfaces are used, equation 20 can be simplified by removing C_{12} at the expense of complicating B_{12}:

$$V = (H_1 \cup H_2) \cup B_{12}',$$
$$B_{12} = \{p : A(Q_1 + Q_2 - d)^3 - B^2 Q_1 Q_2 \leq 0\}.$$

Figure 11 shows the compliment of this blend volume for the torus and cone of figure 10. Shaded images of the result volumes V cannot be distinguished, but the relative calculation complexity usually favours the lower order surface and more complicated set expression. For the cylinder/torus example there is approximately a 4 : 1 ratio in the calculation times

Analogous to the addition of fillets, the set intersection of the two halfspaces is rounded by the 'subtraction' of the volume:

$$\text{Chamfer}(\mu, d, H_1, H_2)$$
$$= (H_1 \,\&\, H_2) - (C_{12} \cup B_{12})$$
$$= (H_1 \,\&\, H_2) \,\&\, (C_{12}' \,\&\, B_{12}'), \quad (21)$$

and the result is,

$$V = (H_1 \,\&\, H_2) \,\&\, (C_{12} \cup B_{12}). \quad (22)$$

A chamfered cylinder formed using this equation is shown in figure 12.

The fillet of equation 19 is empty unless d is positive, while the chamfer of equation 21 is empty if d is negative. Both fillets and chamfers can be created by the same function, since

$$\text{Chamfer}(\mu, d, H_1, H_2)$$
$$= \text{Fillet}(\mu, -d, H_1', H_2'). \quad (23)$$

The proposed method produces bulges when a blend/base surface contact curve at the appropriate distance from the alternate halfspace is not possible (fig. 13). Such bulges are often undesirable when modelling engineering components. They can be eliminated at the expense of a constant contact distance, by using the cross product of the normals to the base surfaces, i.e. $(\nabla S_1 \times \nabla S_2)$ where the gradient vector ∇S is the surface normal. Thus, the set proposition in equation 18 becomes:

$$A(Q_1 + Q_2 - C) - B^2 Q_1 Q_2 \leq 0, \quad (24)$$

$$\text{where} \quad C = \frac{(\nabla Q_1 \times \nabla Q_2).(\nabla Q_1 \times \nabla Q_2)}{(\nabla Q_1.\nabla Q_1)(\nabla Q_2.\nabla Q_2)}.$$

Unfortunately this solution considerably increases the order of the surface, and thus the equations to be solved. For example, ray casting against a torus/torus blend involves polynomial equations of degree 32 instead of 8.

Equations 19 and 20 can be extended to deal with (possibly unbounded) volumes defined as the multiple union of halfspaces $U_j\{H_j\}$:

$$\text{Fillet}(\mu, d, \{H_j\}) = \&_j\{H_j'\} \ \& \ \text{Fill}_j(\mu, d, \{H_j\}), \quad (25)$$

$$\text{and } V = U_j\{H_j\} \ U \ \text{Fill}_j(\mu, d, \{H_j\}), \quad (26)$$

$$\text{where } \text{Fill}_j(\mu, d, \{H_j\}) = U_k\{(C_{12} - B_{12})_k\},$$

and U_k represents the set union over all possible halfspace pairs $\{H_1, H_2\}_k \leq U_j\{H_j\}$.

Extensions for the dual equations 21 and 22, i.e. for chamfers of volumes defined as the multiple intersections of halfspaces $\&_j\{H_j\}$, are

$$\text{Chamfer}(\mu, d, \{H_j\}) = \&_j\{H_j\} \ \& \ \text{Fill}_j(\mu, -d, \{H_j'\}), \quad (27)$$

$$\text{and } V = \&_j\{H_j\} - \text{Fill}_j(\mu, -d, \{H_j'\}), \quad (28)$$

$$\text{where } \text{Fill}_j(\mu, -d, \{H_j'\}) = U_k\{(C_{12}' - B_{12})_k\}.$$

Volume modelling systems are usually used to model bounded volumes. It is preferable that such systems are closed over that domain; i.e., that it is not possible to produce unbounded volumes. This may be achieved by restricting the operands of set operators to bounded volumes, or by allowing unbounded halfspace operands only as the second operand of a set intersection or difference. The chamfer of equation 21 is unbounded along the line of intersection of the base surfaces. However, a bounded result is produced if it is subtracted from a bounded volume to chamfer a single edge. Similarly, equations 27 and 28 yield bounded volumes if they operate on bounded volumes. Thus, these equations may be used directly to chamfer all the edges of the primitive volumes used in typical volume modelling systems (i.e. volumes defined as the set intersection of halfspaces), and to chamfer the set intersection of such primitives.

Arbitrary volumes cannot be produced by the multiple union of the halfspaces used in common set theoretic volume modelling systems. Thus, fillets cannot be produced by the direct application of equation 25 or 26. If a fillet is required along a single edge, the unbounded fillet volume of equation 19 can be truncated by a planar surface orthogonal to that edge at its end points. Alternatively, the adjacent face(s) in the volume can be extended and used to truncate the blend volume. When the adjacent face is a neighbouring fillet, there is a 'chicken and egg' situation; all connected fillets must be generated simultaneously. This may be achieved by using a closed ring of edges. If a 'convex' ring of edges j is formed by the intersection edges of the halfspace pairs $(H_1, H_2)_j$, then a continuous bounded fillet volume is given by

$$F = U_j\{\text{Fillet}(\mu, d, H_1, H_2)_j \ \& \ \&_j\{(C_{12} - B_{12})_j\}\}. \quad (29)$$

However, this equation contains redundancy and does not take account of the finite extent of the faces which intersect to form the ring of edges. Hence, the fillet may extend beyond the faces of the object. Other problems arise when blends on a solid object do not follow a complete ring of edges, or the ring of edges is not 'convex'. These problems are overcome by the techniques described in the remainder of this section.

Consider the fillet at the union of the two primitive volumes

$$P_1 = \&_j\{H_j\}, \text{ and } P_2 = \&_k\{H_k\}.$$

The composite volume may be written in its normal forms as:

$$V = P_1 \ U \ P_2 = \&_j\{H_j\} \ U \ \&_k\{H_k\} = \&_a\{(H_j \ U \ H_k)_a\}, \quad (30)$$

where each inner union involves one halfspace from each primitive. This reflects that all 'concave' edges of this volume occur at the intersection of such halfspace pairs. Hence, fillets may be added at each of these edges by filleting each halfspace pair:

$$\text{Filleted}(V) = \&_a\{(H_j \ U \ H_k \ U \ (C_{jk} - B_{jk}))_a\}. \quad (31)$$

The multiple set intersection in this expression truncates fillets using neighbouring blend surfaces and elliminates those fillets which extend beyond the volume faces. However, material may be added to composite volumes even where no edges exist (fig. 14) or when the edges are convex. Also, many blend volumes in the expression are redundant, i.e. outside the final result. Hence, the implementation should calculate only those blend volumes associated with a 'concave' edge of the original volume $P_1 \ U \ P_2$.

Multiple unions of primitives may be written in their normal forms as

$$V = U_i\{P_i\} = U_i\{\&_j\{H_j\}_i\} = \&_a\{U_b\{H_b\}_a\}, \quad (32)$$

where U_b represents the union of one halfspace from each primitive, and $\&_a$

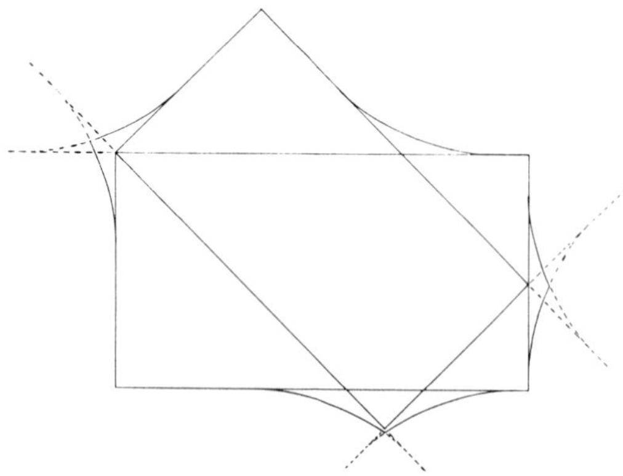

Figure 14 - Extraneous Fillets

represents the intersection of all such unions. Thus, equation 31 can be extended to deal with fillets on volumes defined as multiple unions of primitives (fig. 15), by set intersecting expressions of the form of equation 26:

$$\mathrm{Filleted}(V) = \&_a\{U_b\{H_b\}_a \; U \; (\mathrm{Fill}_b(\mu, d, H_b))_a\}. \quad (33)$$

Both fillets and chamfers can exist at edges formed by the set difference of two primitives. The fillets may be defined by direct application of equation 25 or 26 to the relevant surfaces, or equivalently, the second operand may be chamfered prior to taking the set difference. Unfortunately, chamfers of the set difference of primitives cannot be formed by the direct application of equation 27 or 28; an equivalent of equation 31 is necessary. The set difference of two primitives may be written in disjunctive normal form as:

$$V = P_1 - P_2 = \&_j\{H_j\} - \&_k\{H'_k\} = U_k\{\&_j\{H_j\} \; \& \; H_k\}. \quad (34)$$

(The primitive P_2 is defined as the intersection of complemented halfspaces merely for notational consistency in the normal form). Apart from the edges of P_1, convex edges of the volume V occur only at the intersection of one halfspace from each primitive. Hence the chamfered volume is given by

$$\mathrm{Chamfered}(V) = U_k\{\&_j\{H_j\} \; \& \; H_k \; \& \; \&_j\{C_{jk} \; U \; B_{jk}\}\}. \quad (35)$$

Equations 30 to 35 indicate a technique for applying fillets or chamfers to general set theoretic volumes, i.e. reduce the set theoretic expression to the disjunctive or conjunctive normal form for chamfers and fillets respectively:

$$V = \&_j\{U_k\{H_k\}_j\}, \quad (36)$$

$$V = U_j\{\&_k\{H_k\}_j\}, \quad (37)$$

then apply the fillet or chamfer function to halfspace pairs:

$$\mathrm{Filleted}(V) = \&_j\{U_k\{H_k\}_j \; U \; (\mathrm{Fill}_k(\mu, d, \{H_k\}))_j\}; \quad (38)$$

$$\mathrm{Chamfered}(V) = U_j\{\&_k\{H_k\}_j \dashv (\mathrm{Fill}_k(\mu, d, \{H_k\}))_j\}. \quad (39)$$

These equations chamfer and fillet all the convex and concave edges of a volume respectively. Selected edges may be chamfered or filleted by using only the associated halfspaces to form the blend via the function 'Fill'. Thus, for example, equation 38 becomes

$$\mathrm{Filleted}(V) = \&_j\{U_k\{H_k\}_j \; U \; (\mathrm{Fill}''_k(\mu, d, \{H_k\}))_j\}. \quad (40)$$

where Fill" operates only on the halfspace pairs associated with blended edges.

Concluding Remarks

A method for the manipulation of fillets and chamfers within set theoretic volume models has been developed. These algorithms have been implemented on a VAX 780 with floating point accelerator within a mature volume modelling system. The generation of shaded images for a relatively simple realistic component composed of three primitive volumes (fig. 16) required twice as much CPU time when the four chamfers and one fillet were added.

It would be difficult, if not impossible, to produce the component of figure 16 without blending facilities of some kind. Thus, the provision of fillets and chamfers is a necessary prerequisite for any viable volume modelling system. The method proposed has the following advantages:

1. the specification of fillets and chamfers via base surfaces, size and shape is convenient,
2. the time penalty for typical engineering componments is not excessive, and
3. the blend representations are not approximations.

Acknowledgements

We are very grateful to Terry Stacey for his many helpful suggestions, and the code used to produce the blend profiles. He is also responsible for the higher order blends and the method for bulge elimination. Ian Smith, Nigel Jarman and Judy Mallick have been invaluable in the preparation of the final document. Finally, we would like to thank the reviewers for their pertinent comments.

Figure 10: Cylinder/Torus Union and Fillet

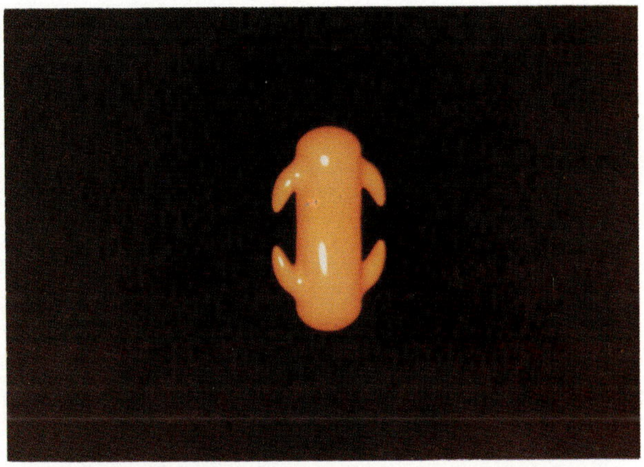

Figure 11: Cylinder/Torus Blend Surface

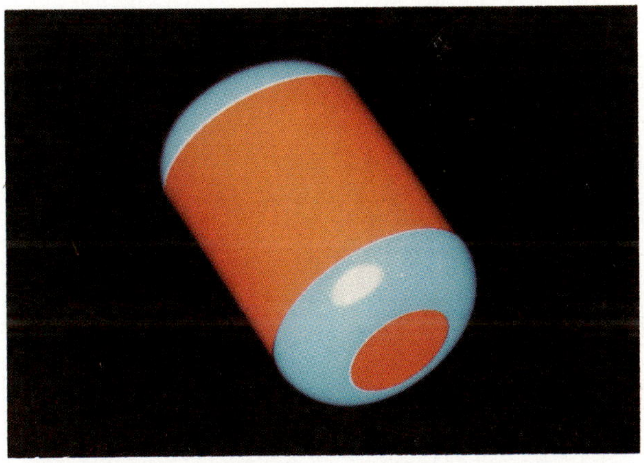

Figure 12: Chamfered Cylinder (β = 0.6)

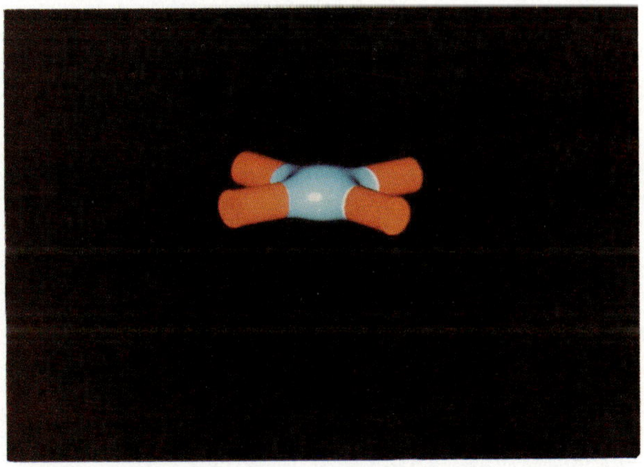

Figure 13: Fillet Bulges

Figure 15: Three Cubes with Fillets (β = 0.5)

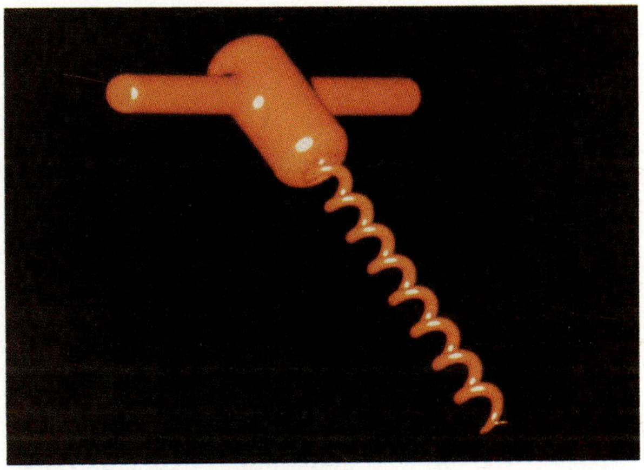

Figure 16

References

[1] A. A. G. Requicha and H. B. Voelker, 'Solid Modelling : Current Status and Research Directions', IEEE Computer Graphics and Applications, pp 25-37, October 1983.

[2] N. M. Samuel, A. A. G. Requicha and S. A. Elkind, 'Methodology and Results of an Industrial Part Survey', Product Automation Project Technical Memorandum TM-21, University of Rochester, July 1976.

[3] J. R. Rossignac and A. A. G. Requicha, 'Constant Radius Blending in Solid Modelling', Computers in Mechanical Engineering, July 1984.

[4] R. E. Barnhill and R. F Riesenfield, eds., 'Computer Aided Geometric Design', Academic Press, 1984.

[5] I. D. Faux, and M. J. Pratt, 'Computational Geometry for Design and Manufacture', Ellis Horwood, 1979.

[6] R. F. Sarraga and W. C. Waters, 'Free Form Surfaces in GM SOLID : Goals and Issues', Proceedings, General Motors Symposium on Solid Modelling, September 1983.

[7] Q. S. Peng, 'Volume Modelling for Sculptured Objects', Ph.D. Thesis, University of East Anglia , September 1983.

[8] H. Chisokura and F. Kilura, 'Design of Solids with Free-form Surfaces', Computer Graphics, Vol. 17, No. 3 (SIGGRAPH Proceedings), July 1983.

[9] M. Galevelat, D. P. Sturge and D. B. Welbourne, 'Blenden, Durchdringungslinie und Abwicklungen - das Verbinden von Doppelt Gekrümmten Flächenelementen in DUCT System', Konstruktion 33, H 10, 1981.

[10] A. R. Forrest, 'Computational Geometry - Achievements and Problems', Computer Aided Design, pp 17-44, R. E. Barnhill and R. F. Riesenfeld, eds., Academic Press, 1974.

[11] A. P. Rockwood, 'Introducing Sculptured Surfaces into a Geometric Modeller', Proceedings, General Motors Simposium on Solid Modelling, September 1983.

[12] A. P. Rockwood, Shape Data Ltd., Private communication.

[13] E. E. Catmull and J. Clark, 'Recursively Generated B-spline Surfaces on Arbitrary Topological Meshes', Computer Aided Design, Vol 10, No 6, November 1978.

[14] D. W. H. Doo and M. Sabin, 'Behaviour of Recursive Division Surfaces near Extraordinary Points', Computer Aided Design, Vol 10, No 6, November 1978.

[15] A. H. Barr, 'Superquadrics and Angle Preserving Transformations', IEEE Computer.

[16] A. Ricci, 'A Constructive Geometry for Computer Graphics' Computer Journal Vol 16, No 2, pp 157-160, May 1973.

[17] S. D. Roth, 'Ray Casting for Modelling Solids', Computer Graphics and Image Processing, Vol. 18, No. 2, pp 109-144, February 1982.

On Ray Tracing Parametric Surfaces

Daniel L. Toth
Computer Graphics Development
Ford Motor Company

Abstract

A new method for ray tracing parametric surfaces is presented. The new algorithm solves the ray surface intersection directly using multivariate Newton iteration. This provides enough generality to render surfaces which could not be ray traced using existing methods. To overcome the problem of finding a starting point for the Newton algorithm, techniques from Interval Analysis are employed. The results are presented in terms of solving a general nonlinear system of equations $f(x) = 0$, and thus can be extended to a large class of problems which arise in computer graphics.

General Terms: Algorithms
Keywords: Parametric Surfaces, Ray Tracing, Newton's Method
CR Categories: G.1.5 Roots of Nonlinear Equations; I.3.3 Picture/Image Generation; I.3.7 Three Dimensional Graphics and Realism

0. Introduction

Ray tracing has been given a great deal of attention recently as a technique in realistic image generation, particularly in modeling the behavior of light as it propagates through an environment. It has been used successfully to model global lighting effects (Whitted [19], Hall [3]) and most notably to model fuzzy reflections and motion blur (Cook et al. [2]).

Central to any ray tracing algorithm is the ray surface intersection calculation. This is generally done in one of two ways. Either the surface is approximated with a collection of polygons (tessellation) and ray tracing is performed on the resulting collection of planar surfaces, or the ray surface intersection is solved directly, usually with some numerical method. In this paper we focus on the direct approach.

Algorithms for ray tracing Algebraic surfaces have been proposed by Blinn [1] and Hanrahan [4]. In his paper, Blinn uses a hybrid combination of univariate Newton iteration and regula falsi. Algorithms for ray tracing parametric surfaces have been proposed by Kajiya [8] for rational bivariate polynomials, and by Sederberg [18] for Steiner patches. Each of these works utilize techniques from Algebraic Geometry. Prior to Kajiya, the ray surface intersection for parametric surfaces was solved using multivariate Newton iteration (see Faux and Pratt [5]). This method has the advantage of being general enough to handle any parametric surface but has a major disadvantage in that it requires an initial guess which must generally be close to the root itself.

In this paper we present a new algorithm for finding the intersection of a ray and parametric surface. In order to provide for complete generality in the choice of parametric surfaces, the multivariate Newton method is used. We utilize techniques from Interval Analysis to overcome the problem of finding an initial guess. The results presented herein are two fold. First an interval version of the multivariate Newton algorithm is presented. Each iteration of this formulation provides an error bound for the actual root of the system. Secondly we present a binary search scheme that will allow us to identify regions of parameter space in which the Newton method converges. These techniques are presented in terms of solving a general nonlinear system of equations and thus can be extended to handle the more general curve-curve or curve-surface intersection problems. The specific algorithm that we present favors the solution which is closest to the ray origin but can be easily generalized to find all real solutions to the ray surface intersection. Proofs for most of the theorems presented in section 3 can be found in Moore [11], [12], [13], or Krawczyk [7], with the exception of theorems 3.4 and 3.5. To the author's knowledge, these have not appeared before.

1. Newton's Method

To begin our discussion, suppose that we are given a parametric surface

$$H(s,t) = (x(s,t),y(s,t),z(s,t))$$

where s and t are the surface parameters and a parametric ray in the form

$$R(u) = P + uD$$

where P is the origin, D is the direction and u is the parameter of the ray. Then the ray and surface intersect where the nonlinear system $H(s,t) - R(u) = 0$. If we let $v = (s,t,u)$ then this can be written in vector form as

$$f(v) = 0.$$

If Y is any 3X3 nonsingular matrix, then the Newton scheme is given by

$$v_{k+1} = v_k - Yf(v_k). \tag{1.0}$$

We refer to the vector $-Yf(v_k)$ as the *Newton step,* and if Y is the inverse Jacobian of f at v_k, then geometrically it represents the coordinates of the intersection of the ray and the tangent plane at v_k (see fig. 1). In ordinary Newton iteration the matrix Y is updated at each step k+1 to reflect the inverse Jacobian at v_k. If the matrix Y is held fixed, then (1.0) is referred to as *simple* Newton iteration. Ordinary Newton iteration yields quadratic convergence whereas the simple scheme yields only linear convergence. As we shall see, our choice of initial guess will yield this difference insignificant.

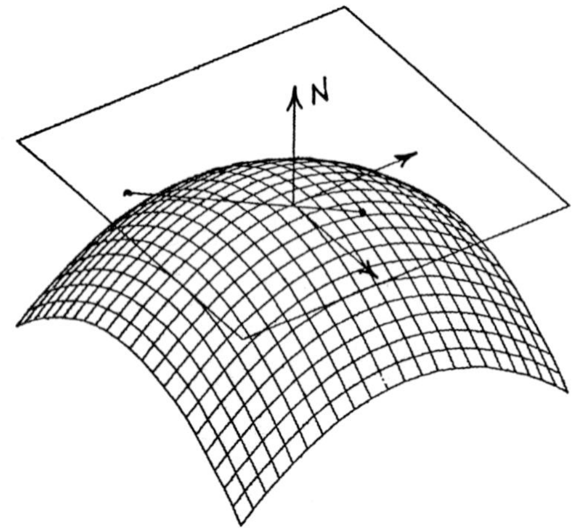

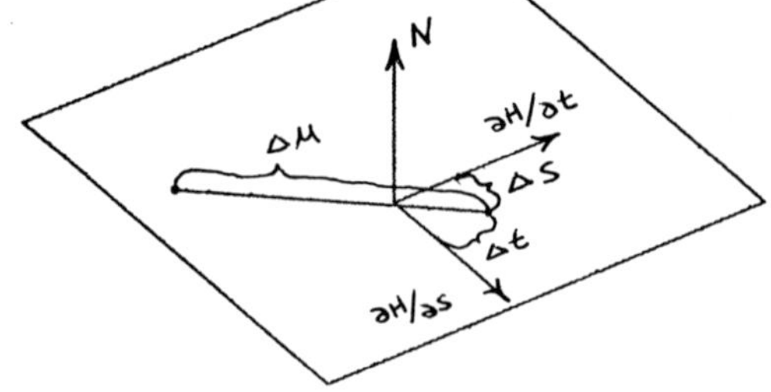

Figure 1. The Newton step $-Yf(x_k) = (\Delta s, \Delta t, \Delta u)$ where
$\Delta s = f(x_k) \cdot (D \times dH/dt) \;/\; D \cdot (dH/ds \times dH/dt)$,
$\Delta t = f(x_k) \cdot (dH/ds \times D) \;/\; D \cdot (dH/ds \times dH/dt)$,
$\Delta u = f(x_k) \cdot (dH/ds \times dH/dt) \;/\; D \cdot (dH/ds \times dH/dt)$

2. Interval Mathematics

In this section we will present the basic notions from interval analysis needed to prove the existence and convergence theorems in the next section. A more in depth introduction to this topic can be found in Moore [10] or [13]. To begin, by an *interval* we mean a closed bounded set of real numbers $[a,b] = \{ x : a \leq x \leq b \}$ and by an *interval vector* we mean an ordered n-tuple of intervals $V = (X_1,...,X_n)$ where $X_i = [a_i,b_i]$. Geometrically this is an n-dimensional box. Notice that the real line is embedded in the collection of real intervals. For instance $0 = [0,0]$ and $1 = [1,1]$.

Now we can define the binary operations $\{+,-,\cdot,/\}$ on intervals as

$$X_1 * X_2 = \{ x*y : x \text{ is in } X_1 \text{ and } y \text{ is in } X_2 \} \qquad (2.0)$$

for $* \in \{+,-,\cdot,/\}$ provided division by zero does not occur. If $X_1 = [a_1,b_1]$ and $X_2 = [a_2,b_2]$, then (2.0) can be rewritten as

$$X_1 + X_2 = [a_1 + a_2, b_1 + b_2]$$

$$X_1 - X_2 = [a_1 - b_2, b_1 - a_2]$$

$$X_1 \cdot X_2 = [\min(a_1a_2,a_1b_2,b_1a_2,b_1b_2),\max(a_1a_2,a_1b_2,b_1a_2,b_1b_2)\ ]$$

$$1/X_1 = [\ 1/b_1, 1/a_1\ ] \quad \text{provided 0 is not in } X_1.$$

Clearly we can see that interval addition and multiplication are associative and commutative, however interval multiplication does not distribute. For example, let $X = [1,2]$, $Y = [1,1]$ and $Z = [-1,-1]$. Then we have $X(Y + Z) = 0$ whereas $XY + XZ = [1,2] + [-2,-1] = [-1,1]$. Interval multiplication is *subdistributive* however. That is, for intervals X, Y and Z we have $X(Y + Z) \subset XY + XZ$. Furthermore, interval arithmetic is *inclusion monotonic*. That is, for intervals X, Y, Z, and V , if $X \subset Z$ and $Y \subset V$ then $X*Y \subset Z*V$ for $* \in \{+,-,\cdot,/\}$ provided division by an interval containing zero does not occur.

Now suppose that $X = [a,b]$. We define the *midpoint* of X as $m(X) = (a + b)/2$ and the *width* of X as $w(X) = b - a$. Similarly, for interval vector $X = (X_1,...,X_n)$ we define $m(X) = (m(X_1),...,m(X_n))$ and $w(X) = (w(X_1),...,w(X_n))$. An interval vector X is said to be *symmetric* if it can be written as $X = e[-1,1]$ where e is some real vector.

If f is a vector valued function of the n real variables $x_1,...,x_n$, then we define the *interval extension of f* as an interval vector valued function F with interval arguments, for which $F(x_1,...,x_n) = f(x_1,...,x_n)$ for real arguments. That is, as the interval arguments decrease in width, F converges to f. An interval extension to the surface H(s,t) is a rectangular extent to H, orthogonal to the coordinate axis (see fig. 2). Now, let $X = (X_1,...,X_n)$ and $Y = (Y_1,...,Y_n)$ be interval vectors with $X_i = [a_i,b_i]$ and $Y_i = [c_i,d_i]$ and define the vectors $a = (a_1,...,a_n)$, $b = (b_1,...,b_n)$, $c = (c_1,...,c_n)$ and $d = (d_1,...,d_n)$. If we define the vector norm

$$||\ a\ || = \max_i |\ a_i\ |$$

then we can define a metric on the collection of interval vectors as

$$d(X,Y) = \max(||\ a - c\ ||,||\ b - d\ ||).$$

With a metric so defined, we can define continuity and uniform continuity for interval vector value functions in the usual epsilon-delta fashion. Then given a rational vector valued function f, we can define an interval extension, F, of f by replacing real variables with interval variables and real arithmetic operations with interval arithmetic operations. From the inclusion monotonicity of interval arithmetic we can see that an interval extension so defined is also inclusion monotonic. Furthermore F will be continuous provided division by an interval containing zero does not occur.

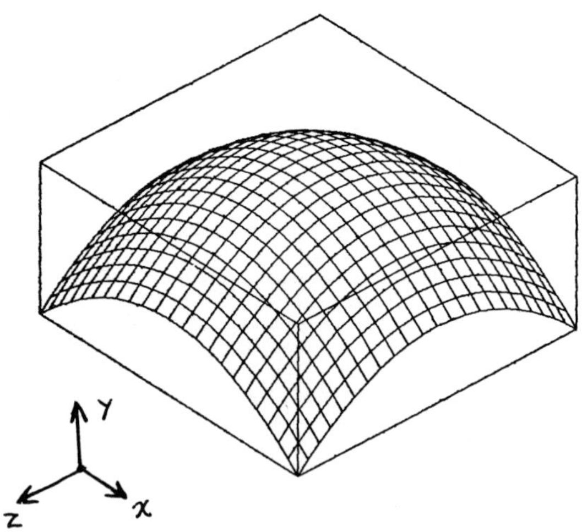

Figure 2. An interval extension to the surface H(s,t) on the region X is an extent to H on X.

3. The Krawczyk — Moore Test

Suppose that f is a continuously differentiable vector valued function on the open subset D of n-dimensional Euclidean space and the interval vector X is a subset of D. Let us now consider the general Newton iteration function

$$p(x) = x - Yf(x)$$

for nonsingular real matrix Y and real vector x in X. By constructing an appropriate interval extension to p, we will be able to determine if the Newton algorithm (1.0) converges to a unique solution to $f(x) = 0$ in X. Before we can begin however, we need some preliminary results.

Suppose that f and f′ have continuous, inclusion monotonic interval extensions F and F′ defined on the set of intervals contained in D. Recall from Integral Calculus that there is no direct extension of the mean value theorem to functions of several variables. There is however, an interval version which follows directly from a theorem of Ortega [15], p. 68 (see also Moore [10]).

3.0 Theorem *(The Mean Value Theorem for Intervals)*

If x and y are any real vectors in X, then $f(x) - f(y) \in F'(X)(x - y)$

Now, suppose that the interval vector $X = (X_1,...,X_n)$ where $X_i = [a_i,b_i]$. We define $| X_i | = \max(|a_i|,|b_i|)$ and the interval vector norm

$$|| X || = \max_i (| X_i |).$$

For interval matrix A (a matrix with interval entries) we define the maximum row sum norm

$$|| A || = \max_i \sum_j | A_{ij} |.$$

It can be shown directly from the definitions that the interval vector norm and interval matrix norm are compatible, that is

$$|| AX || \leq || A || \, || X ||.$$

3.1 Lemma

Suppose that p(x) maps X into itself and there is a constant r < 1 for which

$$|| p(x) - p(y) || \leq r || x - y ||$$

for any x and y in X. Then the simple Newton sequence $x_{n+1} = p(x_n)$ *will converge to a unique solution x* in X to* $f(x) = 0$ *from any starting point* x_0 *in X.*

Proof:

The proof follows directly from the contraction mapping theorem (see Ortega [15] or Moore [11]).■

Lemma 3.1 is really the centerpiece of this discussion and we will now expand it in two directions. First, to determine if p(x) maps X into itself, we construct an interval extension to p defined on the collection of intervals in D. Secondly, we will use this interval extension to obtain the real value r. To this end define

$$K(X,y,Y) = y - Yf(y) + \{I - YF'(X)\}(X - y)$$

for any real vector y in X, I the real identity matrix, and any nonsingular real matrix Y. Notice that since

$$p(x) = y - Yf(y) + (x - y) - Y(f(x) - f(y))$$

the mean value theorem gives us

$$p(x) \in y - Yf(y) + \{I - YF'(X)\}(x - y) \subset K(X,y,Y).$$

That is K(X,y,Y) is an interval extension to p(x) on the collection of intervals contained in D. Hence $K(X,y,Y) \subset X$ implies that p(x) maps X into itself and then f(x) = 0 has a solution in X. Moreover, if $f(x^*) = 0$ for some x* in X, then $p(x^*) = x^*$ and hence x* is in K(X,y,Y). That is, all solutions to f(x) = 0 are in K(X,y,Y). Therefore if $K(X,y,Y) \cap X = \emptyset$ then there are no solutions to f(x) = 0 in X.

Now let us examine the operator K(X,y,Y) more closely. Notice that y − Yf(y) is the Newton step from y and the interval vector (X − y) is the interval vector X translated by y. For instance if y = m(X) then (X − y) is a symmetric interval with components

$$(X - y)_i = (1/2)[-w(X)_i, w(X)_i].$$

Furthermore since {I − YF′(X)} is an interval matrix, K(X,y,Y) is the Newton step coupled with a special symmetric interval vector. In a sense, K(X,y,Y) tells us how each element of X would move under the Newton step. Now using the norms defined above let

$$r = || I - YF'(X) ||$$

and notice that for any real vectors x and y in X the mean value theorem gives us

$$p(x) - p(y) \in \{ I - YF'(X) \}(x - y)$$

and hence

$$|| p(x) - p(y) || \leq r || x - y ||.$$

When r < 1, p is said to be a *contraction* and the Newton iterates become closer and closer together. The following theorem then follows directly from lemma 3.1(see Moore [11]).

3.2 Theorem

If $K(X,y,Y) \subset X$ *and r < 1, then the simple Newton sequence* $x_{n+1} = p(x_n)$ *will converge to a unique solution x* in X to* $f(x) = 0$ *from any starting point* x_0 *in X.*

As we will see, the condition r < 1 is very special and tells us a great deal about the system f(x) = 0 on X. For instance, suppose that r < 1 and let Z be any real matrix in the interval matrix F′(X). Let B = I − YZ and define $C_n = I + B + ... + B^n$ and $C = I + B + \dots$. Then since $YZC_n = I - B^{n+1}$ we have

$$YZC = \lim_{n \to \infty} I - B^{n+1}$$

Furthermore since $|| B^{n+1} || \leq r^{n+1}$ we have YZC = I, the real identity matrix, and therefore Z is nonsingular. Since F′(X) contains the Jacobian of f(x) for each x in X, this means that if r < 1 no tangent plane of the surface H(s,t) will be parallel to the ray on the interval X. That is to say, there exist no silhouette edges in X with respect to the ray. This is obviously important when performing Newton iteration.

Now consider the iterative scheme

$$X_{n+1} = K(X_n, m(X_n), Y_n) \cap X_n \quad (3.3)$$

where

$$Y_n = m(F'(X_n))^{-1} \text{ when } r_n \leq r_{n-1}$$

$$= Y_{n-1} \text{ otherwise}$$

and where

$$r_n = || I - Y_n F'(X_n) ||.$$

The scheme (3.3) is referred to as *interval Newton iteration* and has been discussed in great detail by Moore [11], [13], Wolfe [20], Krawczyk [7], and Jones [6], to name a few. In these works it has been shown that (3.3) will converge under the same conditions as theorem 3.2. We will prove a more general result here that will be more useful in our search scheme. Notice first however that

$$|| w(K(X,m(X),Y)) || \leq r || w(X) ||$$

for any nonsingular real matrix Y. This follows directly from the definitions of the norms (see Moore [11]). Hence, when r < 1, (3.3) produces a nested sequence of intervals. From these observations we can prove the following theorem.

3.4 Theorem

Suppose that $|| I - YF'(X) || = r < 1$. *Set* $Y_0 = Y$ *and* $X_0 = X$ *in (3.3). Then either the iterative sequence (3.3) will converge to a unique solution x* in X to* $f(x) = 0$, *or (3.3) will break down due to empty intersection, in which case no solutions to* $f(x) = 0$ *are in X.*

Proof:

Suppose that X_n is nonempty for each n. Then from the remarks above we must have

$$|| w(X_{n+1}) || \leq r^n || w(X_0) ||$$

and r < 1 implies that the nested sequence of intervals $\langle X_n \rangle$ must converge to some real vector x* in X. To see that x* is actually a solution to $f(x) = 0$, choose a sequence of real vectors $<x_n>$ with x_n in X_n. Clearly, $<x_n>$ converges to x^* and from the continuity of p, $p(x_n)$ converges to $p(x^*)$. Since $p(x_n)$ is in $K(X_n,m(X_n),Y_n)$ for each n and

$$||\, w(K(X_n),m(X_n),Y_n))\, || \leq r^n\, ||\, w(X_0)\, ||$$

we also have $p(x_n)$ converging to x^* and thus $p(x^*) = x^*$ and hence $f(x^*) = 0$. To see that x^* is unique, suppose that y is in X with $f(y) = 0$. Then

$$||\, x^* - y\, || = ||\, p(x^*) - p(y)\, || \leq r\, ||\, x^* - y\, || < ||\, x^* - y\, ||$$

and thus $y = x^*$. Conversely, if there exists an x^* in X for which $f(x^*) = 0$, then $p(x^*) = x^*$ and hence x^* is in X_n for each n. That is, if (3.3) breaks down due to empty intersection, then no solutions to $f(x) = 0$ exist in X and this completes the proof.■

The final result in this section will be another test for existence and convergence for the Newton scheme (1.0). We will show that if the Newton steps are close enough together, then convergence is guaranteed in X. This result is an extension of the contraction mapping principal (see Rall [16]) to the norms used here.

3.5 Theorem

Suppose that $w(X)/2 = (d_0,...,d_n)$ and $a = min(d_0,...,d_n)$. Let

$$B(m(X),a) = \{\, x \in X: ||\, x - m(X)\, || \leq a\}$$

be the cube of width 2a centered at m(X) and suppose that

$$||\, I - YF'(X)\, || = r < 1$$

with

$$||\, m(X) - p(m(X))\, || < (1 - r)a.$$

Then the simple newton sequence $x_{n+1} = p(x_n)$ will converge to a unique solution x^* in X to $f(x) = 0$ from any starting point x_0 in B(m(X),a).

Proof:

Let x be any real vector in B(m(X),a). Then

$$||\, p(x) - m(X)\, || \leq ||\, p(x) - p(m(X))\, || + ||\, p(m(X)) - m(X)\, ||$$

$$\leq r\, ||\, x - m(X)\, || + (1 - r)a \leq a$$

and p maps B(m(X),a) into itself. The existence and uniqueness of x^* in B(m(X),a) follows from lemma 3.1. That x^* is unique in X follows from $r < 1$ and the proof is complete.■

4.0 The Algorithm

In discussing the algorithm, we will treat only the intersection of a parametric surface with an arbitrary ray. The distinction between reflected rays, refracted rays, or rays cast from the viewpoint will not be made. Since all rays are for the most part, treated the same, a scheme using X, Y, and Z sorted lists such as that of Blinn [1] cannot be used. Instead, a hierarchical tree of extents is used to provide a rough guess as to which surfaces to check for intersection (see Hall [3]). For instance, the ray intersection is first performed against an extent containing the entire scene. If an intersection is found, the ray is tested against extents containing each part in the scene. For those parts which an intersection is found, the ray is tested against extents containing each surface in the given part. Any number of levels can be added to this scheme including subsurface extents. There is a point of diminishing return, however, when using subsurface extents, and in general, quartering the surface is enough to get a head start on the parametric space search algorithm outlined below. The extent intersection processor then returns a list of surfaces with which to perform the ray surface intersection calculation. The list is sorted on the minimum ray parameter of the ray extent intersection. If subsurface extents are used then surface parameter intervals are returned in this list as well.

4.1 Ray Extent Intersections

An interval extension of the surface is used to construct the extents. This provides an extent to the surface over an arbitrary parameter interval. Any given extent then is a box, orthogonal to the surface coordinate system, with corners defined by the interval vector

$$([X_{min},X_{max}],[Y_{min},Y_{max}],[Z_{min},Z_{max}]).$$

If the ray is given in the surface coordinate system by the origin $P = (P_x,P_y,P_z)$ and direction $D = (D_x,D_y,D_z)$, then the ray parameter interval defining the intersection of the ray with the extent can be calculated as the set theoretic intersection of three real intervals. For instance, if $D_x \neq 0$ then those values of the ray parameter u for which the ray passes through the x bounds of the box must satisfy (see fig. 3)

$$X_{min} \leq P_x + uD_x \leq X_{max}.$$

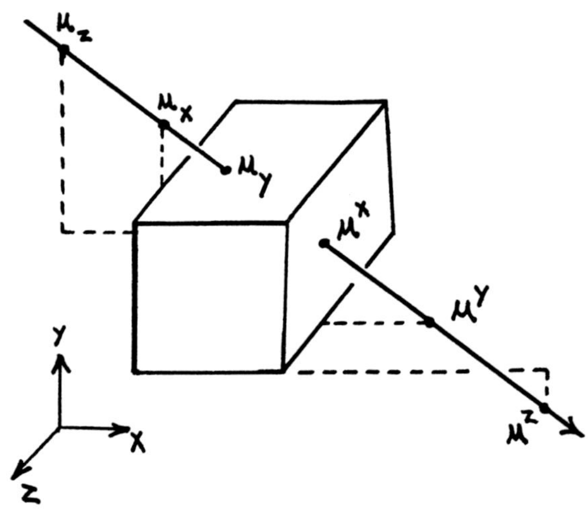

Figure 3. The ray extent intersection calculation $[u_*, u^*] = [u_x, u^x] \cap [u_y, u^y] \cap [u_z, u^z]$.

This can be described as the ray parameter interval $[u_x,u^x]$ where

$$u_x = min((X_{min} - P_x)/D_x,(X_{max} - P_x)/D_x)$$

and

$$u^x = max((X_{min} - P_x)/D_x,(X_{max} - P_x)/D_x).$$

If $D_x = 0$, then the ray is parallel to the Y-Z plane and the interval $[u_x,u^x]$ is infinite in extent. In this case we check the x component of the origin,

$$X_{min} \leq P_x \leq X_{max}$$

to determine if the plane of the ray passes through the box. Intersection intervals for the ray parameter are constructed in this way for each of the coordinates X, Y, and Z and the set theoretic intersection is calculated

$$[u_*,u^*] = [u_x,u^x] \cap [u_y,u^y] \cap [u_z,u^z].$$

If $[u_*,u^*]$ is nonempty, then u_* is the smallest ray parameter for which the ray intersects the extent. It is on this value that the surfaces are sorted when they are returned from the extent intersection processor. Once an actual ray surface intersection is found and corresponding ray parameter u′ is calculated, then u′ is compared to the intersection intervals of the surfaces remaining in the list. Any surface with intersection interval $[u_s,u^s]$ for which $u' \leq u_s$ need not be checked (see fig. 4). It is in this way that the solution closest to the ray origin is favored. If on the other hand $[u_*,u^*]$ is empty, then the ray does not hit the extent.

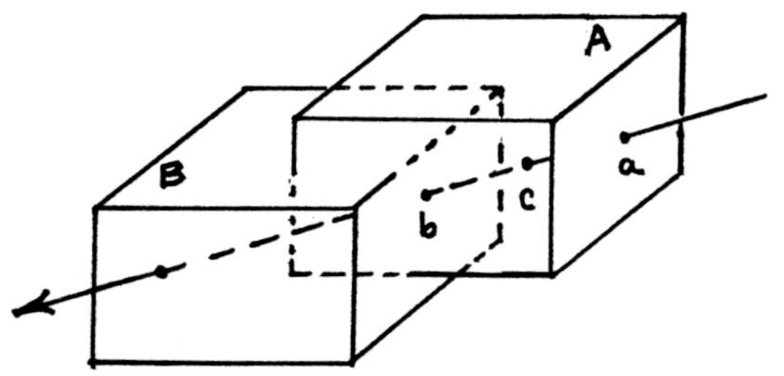

Figure 4. Suppose that the ray enters extent A at ray parameter a and enters extent B at ray parameter b. If a solution is found with ray parameter c where $a \leq c \leq b$, then the parameter space associated with B need not be checked.

4.2 The General Search Algorithm

Once a list of possible surfaces is generated, the corresponding parameter space, X, of each surface is examined for solutions to $f(x) = 0$. This is done by generating a list of subregions $\{X_1,...,X_n\}$ of X, starting with {X}, and testing each subregion for convergence of the Newton algorithm. A subregion X_0 of X is considered a *safe starting region* for the Newton scheme (1.0) if the hypotheses to theorem 3.2 or the hypotheses to theorem 3.5 are satisfied on X_0. A region X_0 of X is *excluded* from further searching if

(1) The ray extent instersection on X_0 is empty or

(2) $K(X_0,m(X_0),m(F'(X_0))^{-1}) \cap X_0 = \emptyset$ or

(3) If a solution has already been found and the ray parameter of the solution is smaller than the minimum of the extent intersection interval corresponding to X_0 (again see fig. 4).

We begin by initializing the list of subregions to {X} and calculating $K(X,m(X),Y)$ and $r = || I - YF'(X) ||$ where

$$Y = m(F'(X))^{-1}.$$

If X is considered a safe starting region, Newton iteration is performed and a solution is computed. If X is excluded then the next surface is chosen from the surface list. Otherwise $K(X,m(X),Y) \cap X$ is subdivided along the parameter direction with maximum width to obtain two new regions X_0 and X_1. Extents are computed for each of these regions and the ray extent intersection intervals are calculated. X_0 and X_1 are then placed into the list of subregions in the order of their intersection with the ray.

The process described above is called the *analysis* of the region X. In this way new regions are added and deleted from the subregion list. When a region is subdivided, the two new regions are added to the beginning of the list in the order of their ray extent intersections. The first element of the list is always chosen for analysis first as this tends to favor the solution closest to the ray origin. Once a determination has been made on a subregion, the next member of the list is chosen for analysis. If for some subregion X_i, $m(F'(X_i))$ is a singular real matrix, then $K(X_i,m(X_i),Y)$ cannot be calculated. When this is the case the region X_i is subdivided and the two new regions are placed in order in the list for further analysis.

If some subregion X_i cannot be considered a safe starting region for the Newton algorithm and cannot be excluded, but $r_i < 1$ where

$$r_i = || I - Y_iF'(X_i) ||$$

and where

$$Y_i = m(F'(X_i))^{-1},$$

then we begin the interval version of Newton iteration (3.3) testing each of the iterates for exclusion or safe starting. As $r_i < 1$, interval Newton iteration can continue without the prospect of inverting a singular matrix. This will complete the analysis of the subregion X_i with no further subdivisions.

We continue the analysis process until the subregion list is empty. A subregion is considered too small for further analysis if the maximum width of either of the interval extensions to the partial derivatives does not exceed some tolerance (the surface is essentially a plane on the subregion) or the width of the subregion itself is smaller than some given tolerance. When this is the case, one Newton step is taken, and if the step stays within the subregion in question, then this is considered a solution, otherwise the subregion is excluded.

Notice that the search algorithm is performed on surface parameter space only. The ray parameter is ignored, even while performing Newton iteration, until a solution is found. The ray parameter is used only to determine which subregion to analyze next. Intuitively, the reason for this can be seen from the Newton step itself. Notice that the Newton step in s and t is independent of u whereas the Newton step in u is dependent only upon s and t, and not on u (see fig. 1). We will discuss this more rigorously in the next section.

Note also that care should be taken in casting rays for reflection and refraction. Since these rays emanate from a surface, the algorithm as described will find the origin as a solution. For these rays the algorithm should be allowed to continue on to the next solution. To find all solutions of the system $f(x) = 0$, we use the exclusion rules (1) and (2) only and no longer need to order subregions as they enter the list.

The algorithm outlined above is similar to that of Moore and Jones [14] with the exception that we begin interval Newton iteration when $r < 1$. In our scheme the interval version of Newton iteration is used only as a device to aid in the search of surface parameter space for solutions of the system $f(x) = 0$. We choose not to use interval Newton iteration to compute the actual solution here since simple Newton iteration is far less expensive.

4.3 Computing the Krawczyk Operator K

To compute the Krawczyk operator $K(X,m(X),Y)$ for some nonsingular matrix Y we first compute an interval extension to $f'(x)$ where the Jacobian of the system $f(x) = 0$ is the matrix with columns

$$f'(x) = [dH/ds, dH/dt, -D].$$

Here D is the direction vector of the ray and H(s,t) is the parametric surface. The interval extension $F'(X)$ will then be the interval matrix whose first two columns are interval extensions to the partials dH/ds and dH/dt respectively and last column is the real vector −D. Recall that

$$K(X,m(X),Y) = m(X) - Yf(m(X)) + \{ I - YF'(X) \}(X - m(X))$$

is the Newton step from the midpoint of X, $m(X) - Yf(m(X))$, coupled with the special symmetric interval vector

$$\{ I - YF'(X) \}(X - m(X)).$$

During the general search algorithm we use

$$Y = m(F'(X))^{-1}, \tag{4.3.0}$$

which allows us to compute $K(X,m(X),Y)$ without using direct interval computations. To see this notice that

$$\{ I - YF'(X) \}(X - m(X)) = Y\{ m(F'(X)) - F'(X) \}(X - m(X))$$
$$= (|Y| \cdot A \cdot e)[-1,1] \tag{4.3.1}$$

where |Y| is the real matrix with components $|Y_{ij}|$, A is the real matrix with components

$$A_{ij} = (1/2)(w(F'(X))_{ij})$$

and e is the real vector with components

$$e_i = (1/2)(w(X)_i).$$

When interval Newton iteration is invoked we do not always have (4.3.0), and hence some interval computations must be performed, however these can be minimized.

The interval vector as computed with (4.3.1) has three components, the first two being intervals in surface parameter space and the third being an interval in the ray parameter. The system $f(x) = 0$ can be reduced to a system of two equations in two unknowns by breaking f(x) into its component parts

$$x(s,t) - P_x - uD_x = 0$$

$$y(s,t) - P_y - uD_y = 0$$

$$z(s,t) - P_z - uD_z = 0$$

and noticing that if $D_x \neq 0$ we have the equivalent system

$$D_x(y(s,t) - P_y) - D_y(x(s,t) - P_x) = 0$$

$$D_x(z(s,t) - P_z) - D_z(x(s,t) - P_x) = 0$$

which can be written in vector form as

$$g(v) = 0 \qquad (4.3.2)$$

where v = (s,t). If we let Q(s,t) = H(s,t) − P, then we can rewrite g(v) as the components of a cross product

$$g_1(v) = (D \times Q)_3$$

$$g_2(v) = -(D \times Q)_2.$$

Partial derivatives are easily computed. For instance

$$dg_1/ds = (D \times dH/ds)_3.$$

To compute an interval extension G′(V) we use the partials of g and replace real arithmetic with interval arithmetic and real variables with interval variables in the cross product defined above. It is rather tedious but it can be shown that if $K(V,m(V),Y_v)$ is computed for the system (4.3.2) with G′(V) as defined above, and with

$$Y_v = m(G'(V))^{-1}$$

then the resulting interval vector will be identical to the first two components of the interval vector computed from (4.3.1). In other words, the ray parameter can be ignored in the search scheme.

4.4 Computing Interval Extensions

Interval extensions can be computed for virtually any function which will arise in computer graphics. Interval extensions to rational functions were briefly discussed in section 2 and a much more complete discussion can be found in Moore [10] or [13]. We will take a slightly different approach here and exploit the convex hull property to compute interval extensions to Bezier surfaces. The subdivision algorithm presented here was developed by A. J. Schwartz [17]. Only the equations are presented and not the development. To begin suppose that

$$H(s,t) = \sum_{i=0}^{m} \sum_{j=0}^{n} \binom{m}{i}\binom{n}{j} s^i(1-s)^{m-i} t^j(1-t)^{n-j} P_{ij}$$

is the Bernstein representation of H with $(s,t) \in X = ([0,1],[0,1])$. The collection of points $\{P_{ij}\}$ i=0,...,m and j=0,...,n are called the control points. Here we use the notation

$$\binom{n}{k} \; n!/(k!(n-k)!).$$

Now let X_0 be an interval contained in X with $X_0 = ([0,b],[0,d])$. Then the algorithm of Lane and Riesenfeld [9] can be generalized (Schwartz [17]) to obtain a new set of control points $\{Q_{uv}\}$ u=0,...,m and v=0,...,n which represent the restriction of H to X_0. These are computed from the formula

$$Q_{uv} = \sum_{i=0}^{u} \sum_{j=0}^{v} \binom{u}{i} b^i(1-b)^{u-i} \binom{v}{j} d^j(1-d)^{v-j} P_{ij}. \qquad (4.4.0)$$

Then for a general interval X_1 contained in X with $X_1 = ([a,b],[c,d])$, we first compute the control points $\{Q'_{uv}\}$ based on the interval X_0 using (4.4.0), then reverse the parameterization on $\{Q'_{uv}\}$ and use (4.4.0) again on the interval $X_0' = ([0,(b-a)/b],[0,(d-c)/d])$ to obtain the desired control points $\{Q_{uv}\}$ to the restriction of H to X_1 (see fig. 5). The endpoints of the i′th interval of $F(X_1)$ are then the i′th coordinate extremes of the convex hull of $\{Q_{uv}\}$.

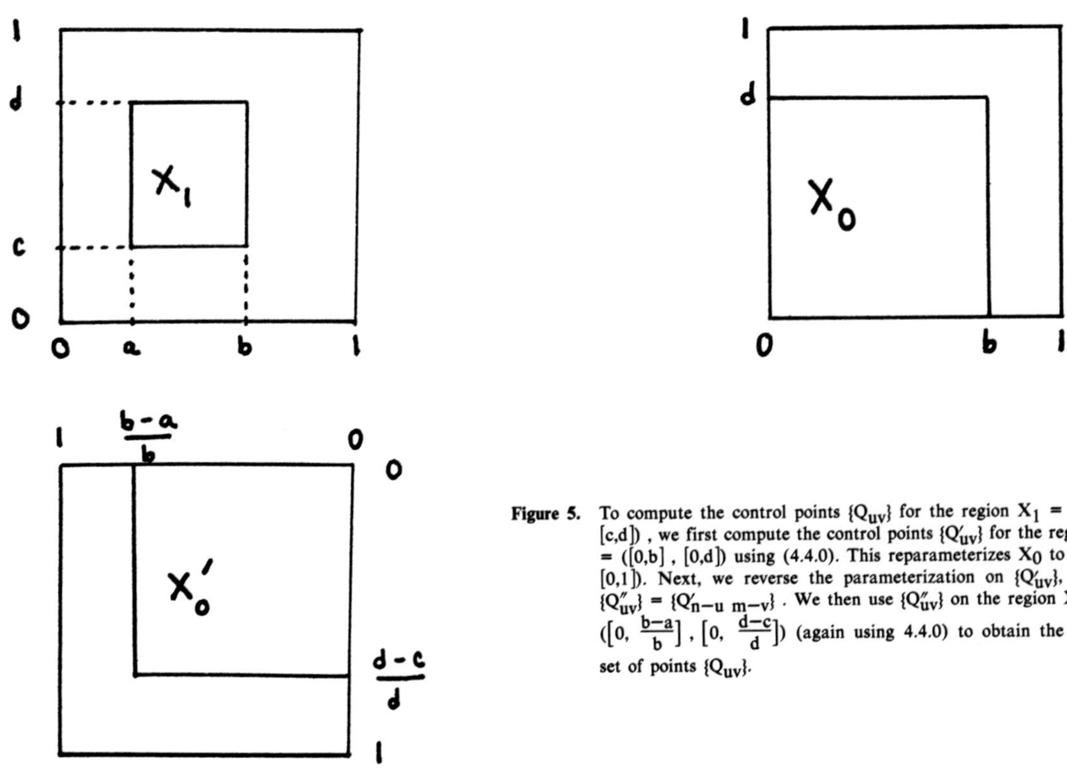

Figure 5. To compute the control points $\{Q_{uv}\}$ for the region $X_1 = ([a,b], [c,d])$, we first compute the control points $\{Q'_{uv}\}$ for the region $X_0 = ([0,b], [0,d])$ using (4.4.0). This reparameterizes X_0 to ([0,1], [0,1]). Next, we reverse the parameterization on $\{Q'_{uv}\}$, that is $\{Q''_{uv}\} = \{Q'_{n-u\ m-v}\}$. We then use $\{Q''_{uv}\}$ on the region $X_0' = ([0, \frac{b-a}{b}], [0, \frac{d-c}{d}])$ (again using 4.4.0) to obtain the desired set of points $\{Q_{uv}\}$.

The partial derivatives dH/ds and dH/dt also have Bernstein representations. The control points $\{P'_{ij}\}$ i=0,...,m−1 and j=0,...,n for dH/ds can be computed from the original control points of H from the formula

$$P'_{ij} = 3(P_{i+1\ j} - P_{ij})$$

for i=0,...,m−1 and j = 0,...,n . The control points for dH/dt are then computed from the column differences. If $X_1 = ([a,b],[c,d])$ is an interval contained in X and $\{Q_{uv}\}$ u=0,...,m and v=0,...,n is the set of control points for the restriction of H to X_1, then we use the convex hull of the point set

$$P'_{ij} = (3/b{-}a)(Q_{i+1\ j} - Q_{ij})$$

for i = 0,...,m−1 and j = 0,...,n to compute the value of the interval extension to dH/ds on the interval X_1. The scaling takes place as a result of the reparameterization involved in the restriction of H to X_1.

5. Concluding Remarks

The algorithm outlined above has been implemented in single precision FORTRAN 77 on a Prime 9950. The parameter space search scheme lends itself well to recursion. We aspired for three decimal places of accuracy in surface parameter space and have found the following tolerances useful:

(1) A subregion is considered too small for further analysis if the maximum width of either of the interval extensions to the partial derivatives does not exceed .02 .

(2) A subregion X_0 of X is considered too small for further analysis if $|| w(X_0) || < .0002$.

(3) Simple Newton iteration proceeds until the difference between successive iterates does not exceed .0001 in each parameter.

It should be noted here that there are very intricate trade offs between these constants. In particular, if the width of the parameter interval or interval extension to the partials is allowed to become too small, floating point round off will introduce erroneous results. It should also be noted that if the ray is tangent to the surface, and thus the system f(x) = 0 has a singularity at the root, the algorithm will proceed properly, continuing to subdivide until the surface is essentially a plane. Table 1 shows some statistics gathered from the computation of the surface in figure 6. Notice that the surface was reduced to a plane in less than 1% of the rays cast.

One drawback to this algorithm is its dependence on the calculation of interval extensions. Initial timing tests have shown that more than 40% of the total cpu is used in computing control points for interval extensions. Furthermore, computation time can vary dramatically with the orientation of the surface to the coordinate system. Table 1 shows this artifact in the computation of the surface in figure 6 with two different orientations of the surface with respect to the coordinate system and view plane. One possible solution to this problem is to have a local coordinate system for each surface, or collection of surfaces, which minimizes the excess width in the extent calculations. The ray could then be transformed into this coordinate system before the intersection algorithm begins. Table 2 outlines most of the floating point calculations involved in the intersection of a ray with a bicubic surface patch.

TABLE 1

	Coordinate system of the surface Orthogonal to the surface	Orthogonal to the view
Total number of nonbackground pixels	34458	34458
Total number of times that the surface was reduced to a plane	43	81
Average number of simple Newton iterations per solution	1.99	1.85
Average number of interval Newton iterations per call	1.33	1.32
Average interval width to begin simple Newton iteration	w(X) = (.176,.220)	w(X) = (.137,.193)
Average interval width to begin interval Newton iteration	w(X) = (.417,.397)	w(X) = (.362,.345)
Total time in simple Newton iteration	24.46 sec.	24.36 sec.
Total cpu	1381 sec.	1057 sec.

This data was obtained through the computation of the bicubic surface in figure 6 with different orientations of the surface to its coordinate system. The computational resolution was 512 by 512 and surface parameter space was X = ([0,1],[0,1]). For these images subsurface extents were used. The surface parameter space was quartered and extents for each quarter were computed. The search algorithm for each ray then began on one of these quadrants. Control points for each quarter were not stored but were recomputed from the original control points when the analysis of the quadrant began.

TABLE 2

Floating Point Computations

Computation Performed	Average number of times per nonbackground pixel	Floating Point Multiplies	Adds
Computing control points on an arbitrary interval	4.22	288	576
Subdividing control points along one parameter	2.78	72	96
Control points of Partial derivatives	4.53	36	36
Computing the Newton step	2.08	54	54
Computing Y	4.53	35	23
Computing K(X,m(X),Y)	4.53	90	78
Computing the ray extent intersection interval	6.4	6	6
Totals		2296	3469

Approximate floating point computations per nonbackground pixel when ray tracing a bicubic surface. The averages that appear are for the surface in figure 6 when no subsurface extents were used. In other words the search algorithm began with X = ([0,1],[0,1]) for each ray.

The generality of the algorithm becomes apparent with figures 7 through 10. In figure 7 we have a simple ruled surface with parabolic boundaries. In figures 8 through 10 we have computed the normal offset surfaces with various offset distances. Recall that the normal offset surface 0(s,t) of a surface H(s,t) is the surface defined

$$0(s,t) = H(s,t) + dN(s,t)$$

where N(s,t) is the unit normal of H(s,t) and d is the offset distance. Since this surface is not a rational polynomial, it cannot be ray traced using existing methods. When the offset distance exceeds the minimum radius of curvature, the surface will intersect itself. The curvature at the vertex of the parabola in figure 7 is .125. Figure 8 shows the normal offset surface with d = .125. Notice the cusp at the vertex. Figures 9 and 10 have offset distances of .3 and .5 respectively.

In this paper we have introduced some new numerical techniques to computer graphics. These techniques have been presented in terms of solving the general nonlinear system of equations f(x) = 0 and as such can be applied to a wide range of problems. Our application was in ray tracing parametric surfaces but the algorithms presented herein can be generalized to solve the more general curve-curve and curve-surface intersection problems.

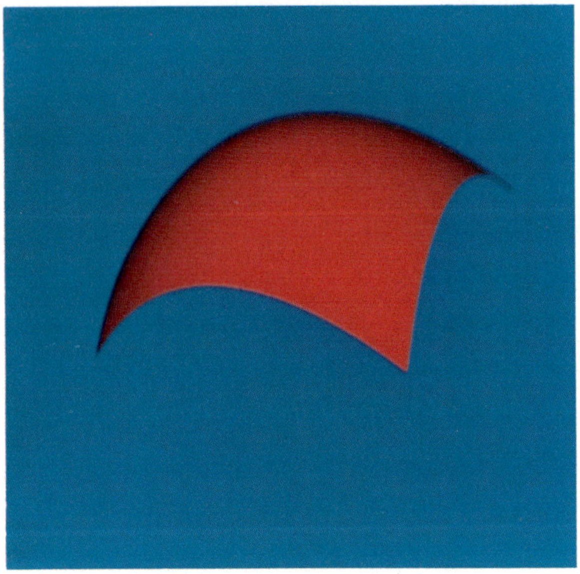

Figure 6. A bicubic surface patch

Figure 8. The normal offset surface to Figure 7 with offset distance .125 .

Figure 7. A ruled surface with parabolic boundaries. The radius of curvature at the vertex of the parabola is .125 .

Figure 9. The normal offset surface to Figure 7 with offset distance .3 .

Figure 10. The normal offset surface to Figure 7 with offset distance .5 .

6. Acknowledgements

The Bezier patch subdivision algorithm presented in section 4 was worked out by A. J. Schwartz [17]. This method provides an improvement of better than 50% in total cpu over the method which was previously implemented in this algorithm. Thanks also go to the reviewers for their numerous suggestions.

7. References

[1] J. F. Blinn, "A Generalization of Algebraic Surface Drawing", *ACM Trans. on Graphics*, Vol. 1, No. 3, July 1982, pp. 236-256.

[2] R. L. Cook, T. Porter and L. Carpenter, "Distributed Ray Tracing", *Computer Graphics*, Vol. 18, No. 3, pp. 137-144.

[3] R. A. Hall, "A Methodology for Realistic Image Synthesis", Masters Thesis, Cornell University, 1983.

[4] P. Hanrahan, "Ray Tracing Algebraic Surfaces", *Computer Graphics*, Vol. 17, No. 3, July 1983, pp. 83-90.

[5] I. D. Faux, and M. J. Pratt, *Computational Geometry for Design and Manufacture*, Ellis Horwood, Chichester, 1979.

[6] S. T. Jones, "Locating Safe Starting Regions for Iterative Methods: A Heuristic Algorithm", in *Interval Mathematics 1980*, K. Nickel, ed., Academic Press, New York, 1980, pp. 377-386.

[7] R. Krawczyk, "Newton-Algorithmen zur Bestimmung von Nullstellen mit Fehlerschranken", *Computing*, Vol. 4, 1969, pp. 187-201.

[8] J. T. Kajiya, "Ray Tracing Parametric Patches", *Computer Graphics*, Vol. 16, No. 3, pp. 245-254.

[9] J. M. Lane, and R. F. Riesenfeld, "A Theoretical Development for the Computer Generation and Display of Piecewise Polynomial Surfaces", *IEEE Transactions on Pattern Analysis and Machine Intelligence*, Vol. PAMI-2, No. 1, January 1980, pp. 35-46.

[10] R. E. Moore, *Interval Analysis*, Prentice Hall, Englewood Cliffs, NJ, 1966.

[11] ———, "A Test for Existence of Solutions to Nonlinear Systems", *SIAM J. Numer. Anal.*, Vol. 14, No. 4, Sept. 1977, pp. 611-615.

[12] ———, "A Computational Test for Convergence of Iterative Methods for Nonlinear Systems", *SIAM J. Numer. Anal.*, Vol. 15, No. 6, Dec. 1978, pp. 1194-1196.

[13] ———, *Methods and Applications of Interval Analysis*, SIAM Studies 2, Society for Industrial and Applied Mathematics, Philadelphia, 1979.

[14] R. E. Moore, and S. T. Jones, "Safe Starting Regions for Iterative Methods", *SIAM J. Numer. Anal.*, Vol. 14, No. 6, Dec. 1977, pp. 1051-1065.

[15] J. M. Ortega, and W. C. Reinbolt, *Iterative Solution of Nonlinear Equations in Several Variables*, Academic Press, New York, 1970.

[16] L. B. Rall, *Computational Solution of Nonlinear Operator Equations*, Robert E. Krieger Publishing Inc., Huntington, New York, 1979.

[17] A. J. Schwartz, To be presented, SIAM Conference on Geometric Modeling and Robotics, July 15-18, Albany, N. Y.

[18] T. W. Sederberg, and D. C. Anderson, "Ray Tracing of Steiner Patches", *Computer Graphics*, Vol. 18, No. 3, pp. 159-164.

[19] T. Whitted, "An Improved Illumination Model for Shaded Display", *Comm. ACM*, Vol. 23, No. 6, June 1980, pp. 96-102.

[20] M. A. Wolfe, "A Modification of Krawczyc's Algorithm", *SIAM J. Numer. Anal.*, Vol. 17, No. 3, June 1980, pp. 376-379.

There's More to Menu Systems Than Meets the Screen

Henry Lieberman

Artificial Intelligence Laboratory
Massachusetts Institute of Technology
Cambridge, Mass. 02139 USA
Arpa network: Henry@MIT-MC

Abstract

Love playing with those fancy menu-based graphical user interfaces, but afraid to program one yourself for your own application? Do windows seem opaque to you? Are you scared of mice? Like what-you-see-is-what-you-get but don't know how to get what you want to see on the screen?

Everyone agrees using systems like graphical document illustrators, circuit designers, and iconic file systems is fun, but programming user interfaces for these systems isn't as much fun as it should be. Systems like the Lisp Machines, Xerox D-Machines, and Apple Macintosh provide powerful graphics primitives, but the casual applications designer is often stymied by the difficulty of mastering the details of window specification, multiple processes, interpreting mouse input, etc.

This paper presents a kit called *EZWin*, which provides many services common to implementing a wide variety of interfaces, described as generalized *editors for sets of graphical objects.* An individual application is programmed simply by creating objects to represent the interface itself, each kind of graphical object, and each command. A unique interaction style is established which is insensitive to whether commands are chosen before or after their arguments. The system *anticipates* the types of arguments needed by commands, preventing selection mistakes which are a common source of frustrating errors. Displayed objects are made "mouse-sensitive" only if selection of the object is appropriate in the current context. The implementation of a graphical interface for a computer network simulation is described to illustrate how EZWin works.

1. Graphical primitives alone aren't adequate for building menu-based graphics systems

Interfaces which allow a user to interactively manipulate graphical objects and choose commands from menus are the wave of the future -- they're easy to learn, fun to use, and effective. These interfaces are made possible by today's bitmap graphics personal computers, which give a programmer the graphics primitives for displaying menus, multiple windows, reading pointing devices, etc. Yet construction of these interfaces is still a black art. Building an interface from graphics primitives with today's software often requires much effort, is error-prone, and much work must be repeated anew for each new application.

The problem lies in a mismatch between the level of the primitives provided and the concepts which are fundamental to building high-quality graphical interfaces. Unfortunately, it is easy to underestimate the gap between graphics primitives which deal only with bits on the screen and what's necessary for a usable interactive system [unless you've programmed one yourself!].

Menus displayed on the screen are not just mere lists of text strings or icons. Each string displayed in a menu typically represents a *command* for an interactive system, a means of accessing some functionality of the system. Similarly, each graphical object displayed is not just a collection of lines, points, shaded areas, etc. but a visual representation of some object of interest in the problem domain. Commands often perform operations on graphical objects displayed on the screen.

To fill in the gap between user-interface needs and screen-level primitives, I have implemented a graphical interface kit called *EZWin.* Ezwin is an "interface interpreter", providing some of the kinds of services which programming language interpreters do for traditional programming languages. It has ready-made components which offer concepts and services common to many graphical user interfaces.

After presenting a few pictures illustrating systems built with Ezwin, the paper will introduce Ezwin's basic concepts, then go into a more detailed explanation of the programming necessary to construct a simple application. A payoff from Ezwin's extra level of representation comes in being able to provide some important user convenience features in an application-independent way.

2. EZWin can build a wide range of interfaces from three basic kinds of objects

What kind of systems can be built with EZWin? The following three pictures illustrate the range of interfaces for which this approach is intended. They show a document illustration program, a musical score editor based on a piano-roll notation [6], and a system for drawing electrical circuit modules and simulating them [4].

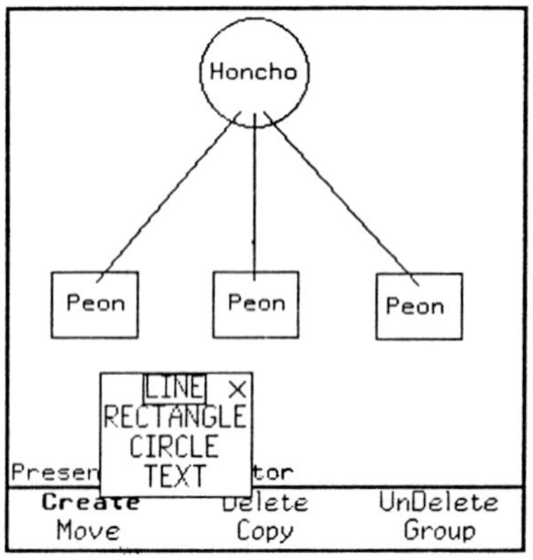

Figure 2-1: A document illustration system

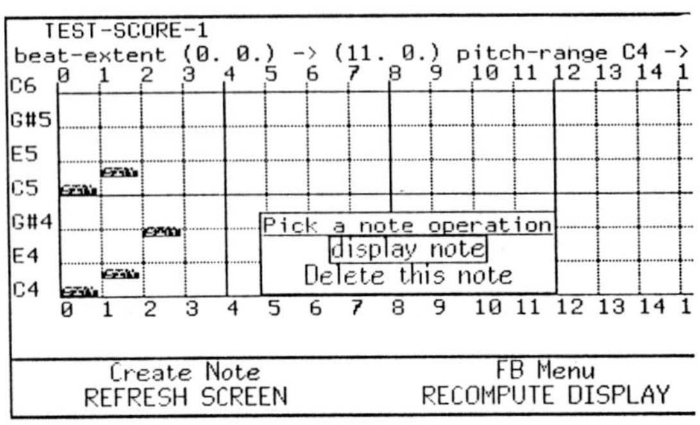

Figure 2-2: Christopher Fry's "Flavors Band Piano Roll"

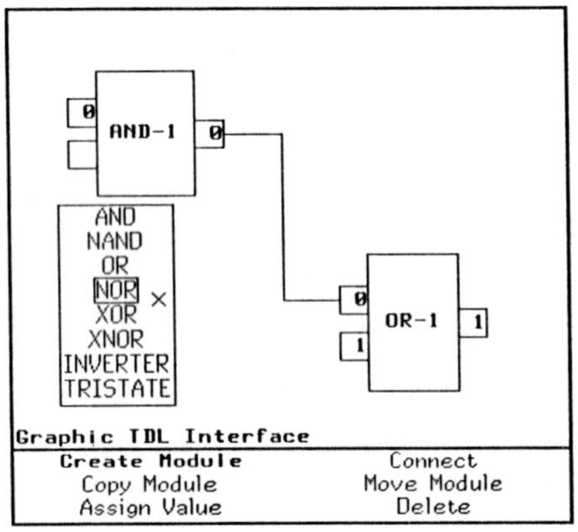

Figure 2-3: Fanya Montalvo's "Graphic TDL"

EZWin revolves around three kinds of objects which are the building blocks for interfaces: **Command** objects represent the actions that a user can make the system do. **Presentation** objects are visual representations of things in the problem domain of interest to the user. An **EZWin** object represents the entire user interface to an application, containing a window, a process, interaction loop, and any internal state and behavior of the application as a whole. [The presentation notion is due to Ciccarelli [3] and Zdybel, et. al. [14].]

EZWin can also be appropriate for systems with more traditional kinds of interfaces, including those where commands are typed rather than selected from menus. Would you want to write a text editor this way? It's possible to do it, but since the graphical component would be minimal and efficiency considerations might become important, the advantages and novelty of this approach would not be so apparent as with more graphically oriented interfaces.

An EZWin application can be viewed in its most general form as an *editor for presentation objects*. The system maintains a set of presentation objects, and commands may create, delete, or alter them. What do we hope to gain by introducing this extra representation?

Explicit representation of interfaces, commands, and graphical objects pays off in the ability to provide uniform facilities that can be used by a wide range of applications. For example, the "top level loop" of most menu systems is essentially the same: Read mouse input, do some sort of dispatch to a menu command, get the arguments to the command [or choose the arguments first, then the command], execute code performing the command, update the screen, wait for the next mouse input. If all you are given is the graphical primitives, this loop must be re-implemented for each interactive application, usually with small variations. By providing a standard object for interactive applications, we can implement the top level loop only once, making the task of defining a new application simpler.

There is much in common to the structure and behavior of command and presentation objects across applications, too. Commands can request arguments of specific types, and procedures for obtaining arguments of that type can be automatically used. The task of maintaining *mouse sensitivity* [highlighting a presentation object when the mouse passes over it and clicking a button to select that object] can be automated. We can supply a library of predefined command and presentation types, so that new applications can take advantage of those used in previous applications. Unfortunately, this is difficult in many current systems.

Finally, a good user interface kit can provide a host of "little things" that developers may forget to provide, but whose absence is noticed immediately by users. Almost all high-quality interactive systems need a variety of minor user conveniences, none of which is difficult in itself, but which tend to get ignored during program development because they distract programmers from the functionality of the system. Not realizing the necessity for attention to user interface issues early in the design process is a pitfall that plagues many projects.

Rather than simply exhorting developers to expend more effort in these areas, a more productive approach is to provide these facilities in an application-independent way. This leaves developers free to concentrate on application-specific issues. Enforcing consistent conventions and appearances from one application to the next is well appreciated by users, who find the system easier to learn and remember.

Among the necessary facilities are:

* Provisions for aborting a command.

* Undoing the effect of unwanted commands.

* Providing help and status information.

* A command for refreshing the screen.

* Error messages, error handling and error recovery.

3. Object oriented programming allows creating alternative interaction styles

The object-oriented programming style introduced by the *actor* languages [9] and Smalltalk [8] is the best vehicle for these ideas. It is significant that the introduction of object-oriented programming in many systems was brought about by the desire to create interactive, menu-driven graphical applications of just the sort we are considering. One might even go so far as to say the object-oriented approach becomes *essential* for these tasks. This is not the place to present a detailed defense of the object-oriented approach, but a purpose of this paper is to show that much of the inflexibility of current systems could be cured by the judicious use of this approach.

The creation of interactive applications involves many questions of *style*. Should menus be made of words or pictures? Should graphical objects be highlighted by enclosing boxes, reverse video, bold lines, color? Should the user pick a command first, then collect arguments to it, or assemble a set of arguments, then pick the command?

The answer to many of these style questions is a matter of taste, and can't be decided definitively. We shouldn't force a particular style upon the application designer, but neither should we force the designer to make all these choices explicitly again and again for each application. Object oriented programming can provide a default set of objects which supply a *reasonable* interaction style, together with the ability to override the defaults by defining new objects that differ from the defaults.

For example, highlighting a presentation object is performed by sending a `highlight` message to the object. Presentation objects usually respond to this message by drawing a box surrounding the object. A designer is free to create a new kind of presentation object that redefines the response to the `highlight` message to redraw the object in bold, for example. As work on diverse applications proceeds, we can accumulate a *library* of highlighting styles, each represented by an object.

4. Command first, or arguments first? It doesn't matter!

In some systems, a menu command is chosen, then the system enters a mode to collect arguments. For example, after choosing a menu command to print a document, the system enters a mode where a particular document can be chosen, and perhaps a particular printer. In others, the operands come first, then the command. In a text editor, a region of text may be indicated, then a command such as move or delete is given. Both ways have their advantages: commands-first fits more naturally into an imperative style, arguments-first encourages "modelessness" in the interface. Why not have *both* ways of doing it?

If the user selects arguments first, perhaps by selecting a presentation with the mouse, the system should expect a command which operates on those arguments. If a command is chosen first, the system should then try to collect arguments. We even permit *infix* commands, where some arguments are chosen, then the command, then the remaining arguments. Making systems which are insensitive to whether commands or arguments are chosen first provides additional flexibility and convenience, especially appreciated by beginning users.

But accomplishing this flexibility requires some machinery on the part of the interface, which EZWin provides. The manner in which each menu command obtains its arguments is critical. If we write the code implementing a menu operation to do explicit input such as reading the mouse position or buttons, as is common, we immediately lose the flexibility of choosing the arguments before the command. If we insist on obtaining arguments from a predefined argument list, we lose the option of getting arguments as they are needed. Instead, EZWin *assembles* a call to a menu command from both the command, a declaration of the arguments it needs, and the list of chosen arguments, as they become available. The command is executed when all of its arguments become available. [Some cases, such as choosing a command followed by a varying number of arguments, may require an explicit "do it" indication.]

5. Dynamic control of mouse sensitivity or command visibility prevents erroneous selections

A common source of error in menu systems is using the mouse to select a command or displayed object in situations where it is inappropriate. This kind of error is particularly frustrating for beginning users. Rather than issuing an annoying error message, it is often better to simply forestall the situation by not allowing an inappropriate choice to be made in the first place. EZWin manipulates the mouse sensitivity of displayed objects dynamically, according to context, to prevent inappropriate selections.

Only those commands which "make sense" in a given context are available to be chosen. When the user moves the mouse over the name [or picture] of a menu command, the visual representation of the command is highlighted *only* if the command is appropriate in the current context. If the command doesn't make sense, then the visual representation doesn't react to the mouse. In the arguments-first style, after each argument is chosen, the set of commands is *filtered*, asking each command whether or not the current list of arguments is acceptable to it, and mouse sensitivity only turned on if it is.

An alternative technique is to dynamically alter the *visibility* of commands, inappropriate commands simply disappearing from the screen. Dynamically changing command lists, however, are more distracting, since they "jump around", so the user can't associate a command with a physical screen location. They do have the advantage of conserving screen acreage by not using any screen space for unusable commands. They also limit the user's ability to *peruse* commands as opposed to actually invoking them. EZWin uses dynamic control of visibility in *pop-up menus*, [which "jump around" anyway]. Each EZWin system has a global list of pop-up commands, and when the user mouses a presentation, a pop-up menu is displayed consisting of *just those commands which are valid on the current set of arguments*, if there are any.

Only those presentations which are acceptable as arguments to the current command can be chosen. If a command and some arguments have been chosen, and the system is waiting for further arguments, obviously the only correct choice is something which is acceptable as the next argument to that command [unless of course, the command is aborted, or previous argument · selections are undone]. Since EZWin requires each command to declare the types of its arguments, when it comes time to obtain a graphical object of a certain type, EZWin can assure that only those presentations of the expected type are sensitive. In this way, it becomes impossible to choose inappropriate arguments.

6. An application-specific diagrammer illustrates how EZWin is used

Let's look at the process of building a typical menu-driven graphical application system from the application designer's point of view. For comparison, you may want to keep in mind how you would program a similar application on your own favorite computer system and language.

The problem is to create a simple diagramming and dynamic display system for an experimental parallel computer system [specifically, the *Apiary* [11]]. We will call our system *Beekeeper* [a person who watches over an Apiary]. Here's a typical Beekeeper display.

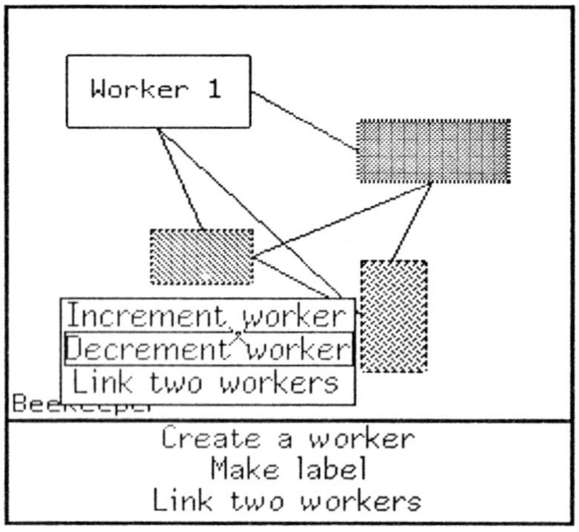

Figure 6-1: A typical Beekeeper display

The graphics pane displays boxes representing processors called *workers* and lines representing communications *links* between them. Each worker or link is a presentation object. The command menu at the bottom displays a list of permanently available commands, but at each step, *only the commands which make sense* are mouse sensitive and available as choices. Initially, when there are no workers on the screen, the `Create a worker` command and the `Make label` command are sensitive, but the `Link two workers` command is not, since there are not yet any workers to link.

The `Create a worker` command puts a new worker on the screen. It requires the size and position of the box representing the worker on the screen. When the command is chosen, the mouse cursor changes to a right-angle indicating the user should click on a point to become the upper left corner of the rectangle. After the user chooses the top left corner, the mouse cursor changes to a right-angle bracketing the bottom right corner. As the mouse moves, the user can preview the appearance of the rectangle surrounding the worker using the common *rubber-band line* technique.

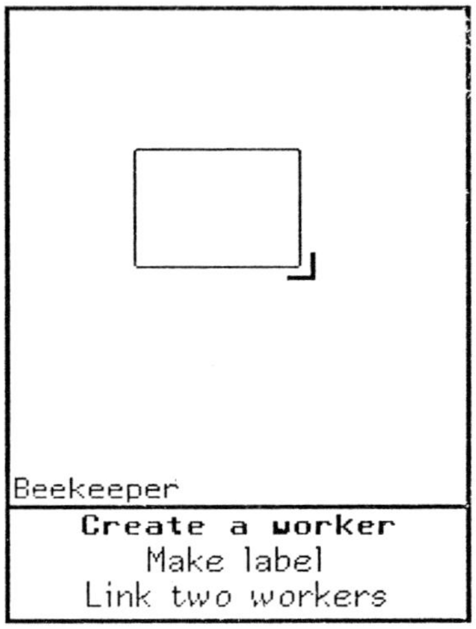

Figure 6-2: Rubber band lines preview the rectangle

The rubber-band line is a good example of an interaction technique requiring control over *mouse tracking.* Most conventional "window systems" have only provided a single mouse tracking procedure and tasks like maintenance of mouse-sensitive objects are left up to the applications programmer. Many systems track the mouse *in a separate process* to insure real-time mouse response, bringing up the issue of communication between the mouse process and the application process. Rather than have one mouse tracking procedure that must know about every kind of tracking situation, we require each window to have a `mouse-tracker` object which can be changed dynamically, and a stack of such trackers which can be pushed and popped. Every time the mouse moves or a button is clicked the mouse tracker object is sent a message and can respond accordingly. Mouse tracker objects assure synchronized communication between the mouse process and the application process. For example, a `rubber-mouse-tracker` is used for tracking the second point in a rubber band line. The tracker object remembers an `anchor` point, and redraws a line to the current mouse position every time the mouse moves. The default tracker is a `presentation-tracker`, which tests whether the mouse is currently over a displayed mouse-sensitive presentation, and highlights the presentation if so.

Once a worker appears on the screen, commands that are relevant to workers become available. The rectangle representing the worker is made *mouse sensitive* -- it is highlighted whenever the mouse cursor passes over it. When the user clicks a mouse button, a menu of pop-up commands appears. The border of the worker is drawn with dashed lines to indicate that it is selected. This menu shows a selection of commands that take the worker as their first argument. For example, the **Increment worker** command increments the worker's displayed **busyness** parameter, visually represented by the shade of gray filling in the rectangle.

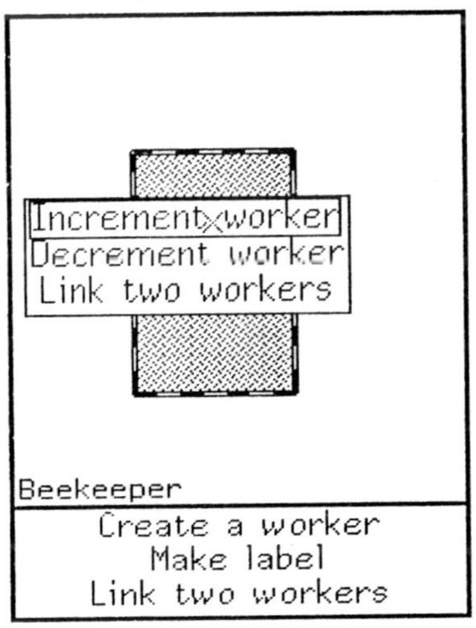

Figure 6-3: Selecting a worker pops up a menu of commands

The pop-up menu is always created dynamically according to the current list of arguments. Here, selecting one worker pops up a menu with three commands. Had *two* workers been selected, only the **Link** command would be appear in the pop up menu since it is the only command that accepts two workers.

A command which is available both from the pop-up menu on workers and in the permanent menu is **Link two workers.** This creates a communications link object between two workers. To do this, it requires two workers as arguments, chosen by clicking the mouse over the displayed representation of the worker. Each worker is highlighted [here with dotted lines] as it is chosen. After this command is selected, only the worker objects [and not links or other displayed objects] are mouse-sensitive.

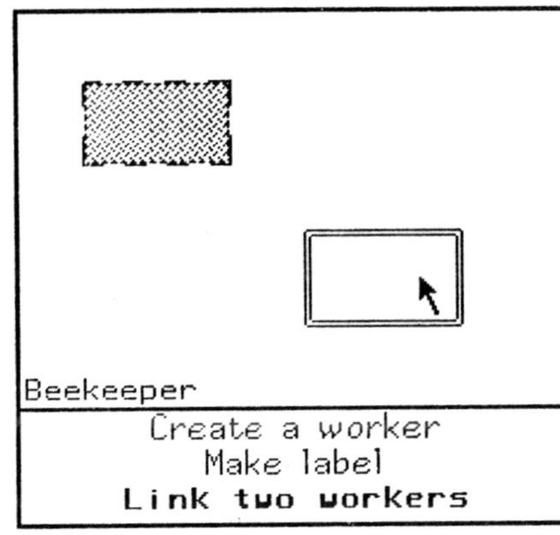

Figure 6-4: Waiting for a second worker to "Link"

The visual representation of a link is a line connecting the two workers, automatically chosen so it is aesthetically drawn between the midpoints of the sides of the workers closest to each other.

The link itself then becomes sensitive, with pop-up menu operations to change its busyness, displaying it by the thickness of the line.

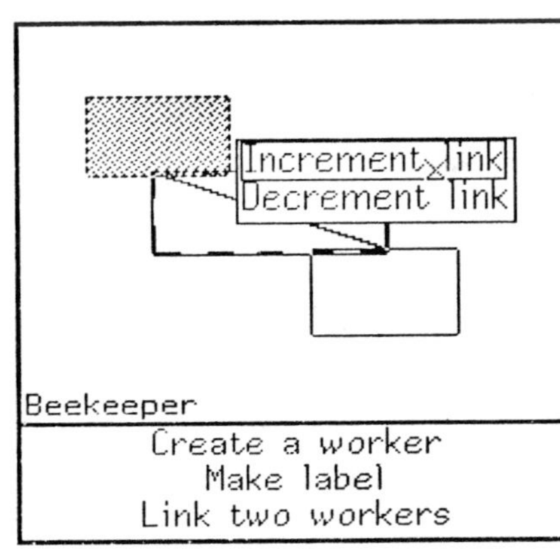

Figure 6-5: Pop-up commands on a link change its thickness

7. Beekeeper's implementation illustrates how EZWin applications are programmed

Now, we'll show how the Beekeeper system is implemented using EZWin. The actual implementation is on Symbolics 3600's using ZetaLisp with the object-oriented Flavors package [13]. We present the implementation using "procedural English" descriptions of the code rather than the actual Lisp to avoid alienating parenthephobic readers. Readers familiar with any object-oriented programming system should be able to see how the code would translate to their favorite system.

First, new systems are built by creating a new class of object which inherits from a predefined **EZWin** object. Each **Beekeeper** object has its own window on the screen, its own process and command interpreter loop.

```
Define a new kind of object called Beekeeper,
 which inherits from EZWin.
```

The user will start up the system by creating an instance of a Beekeeper object, representing the entire application itself.

Each such object has, as variables, a list of *command objects* and a list of currently visible *presentation objects.* The object also keeps, as internal state, any state variables the command loop must maintain, mainly the currently chosen command and arguments, if any.

Each semantically meaningful displayed object is represented by its own **presentation** object. For example, in a diagram editor, each box, arrow, or caption would have its own presentation object. Displaying a new box on the screen means adding a new **box-presentation** to the list of currently displayed presentations. Making the box disappear deletes it from this list. "Background" graphics, such as titles and borders of windows, which never appear as arguments to commands and are never mouse-sensitive need not be represented by presentation objects.

8. Describing the presentation objects says what the problem domain is

EZWin systems are basically editors for graphical objects. A designer can create a system which allows a user to create new graphical objects, delete them, and change important aspects of them. Describing a new EZWin application involves establishing the problem domain by saying what the kinds of graphical objects the system will be working with are.

The primary task in defining a new presentation is supplying it with procedures for displaying itself and erasing itself on the screen. These are done with the standard low-level output primitives on the window which draw lines, text, and areas. Once a kind of object, say a circle, is defined, any application can use circles without having to use the output primitives directly. The new presentation can also have its own methods for determining whether the mouse is inside it, highlighting itself, etc., but the system supplies defaults. Composite objects can be also defined which distribute messages like **draw** and **erase** to their component parts.

For Beekeeper, there are basically two kinds of graphical objects: *workers* and *links.* Each of them will have a state variable, called **Busyness**, but this state will be represented visually in quite different ways.

```
Define a Worker-Presentation object,
 inheriting from EZWin-Presentation.
  Each Worker-Presentation has a Busyness,
   initially 0.
  And connects to an object in the simulation.
```

The visual representation of a **Worker-Presentation** object is a rectangle, which is shaded in according to its **Busyness**, darker shadings indicating busier workers. No doubt we would already have a **Shaded-Rectangle-Presentation** in our library, but for illustration, let's suppose we didn't and had to define it.

Above all, presentations need methods for **Drawing** and **Erase**ing themselves from the screen.

```
If I'm a Worker-Presentation and
 I'm asked to Draw myself on a Window,
  I draw a rectangle using my
   Top, Left, Bottom and Right variables.
  I index my Busyness into an array of shades,
   and fill in the rectangle.
```

Erase methods are automatically supplied which draw in an "erase mode" or "Xor mode", but obviously objects are free to supply their own.

The major idiosyncratic behavior of a worker involves connecting it to other workers via links. The worker must be able to say *where* the link will go on the screen. Each **Worker-Presentation** responds to a message **Connect-To** which, given another worker, returns the midpoint of its closest side to that worker. Since the implementation of this is just arithmetic on coordinates, the details are omitted.

To connect the graphical representation of a worker to the object it is representing, the **worker-presentation** would also have a pointer to the **worker** object in the simulation. Messages to the **worker-presentation** could access the **worker** to find out its state, to reflect aspects of the simulation's state in its appearance.

If links have no special behavior other than their visual representation as lines, we can just use a predefined presentation object for lines, which already comes with the response to **Draw** and **Erase** messages.

```
Define a Link-Presentation object,
 which inherits from Line-Presentation.
  Each Link-Presentation has a Busyness variable,
   initially 0.
  Each Link-Presentation connects
    a From-Worker and a To-Worker.

If I'm a Link-Presentation,
and I'm asked to Draw myself on a Window,
 My Busyness variable determines
  the thickness of the line.
```

9. Describing the command objects says what the system can do

For each command in the system, we define a *command object.* Each command object has an **Advertisement**, a text string used to name the operation (or an icon to be displayed). Each command also declares a list of **Arguments**, which says what kind of arguments it needs. Documentation is displayed in a line at the bottom of the screen when the mouse moves over the command in the menu.

```
Define a Create-Worker-Command object,
 a kind of EZWin-Command.
  My Advertisement is
   the string "Create a worker".
  My Argument list is a list
    of one Rectangle-Argument object.
  My Documentation is the string
    "Creates a worker object, given a rectangle".
```

The **Create-Worker-Command** takes one argument, a rectangle. This is represented by a predefined **Rectangle-Argument** object, which knows, among other things, how to obtain a rectangle from the user when it is needed. The explicit representation of arguments by objects is another innovation of EZWin.

These correspond to "typed arguments" in many programming languages, but the types are not simply used for checking the values of variables. For each argument type, the system must know how to get an argument of that type, typically through some combination of output to a window for prompting, and input operations on the keyboard and mouse. Argument objects take **obtain** messages, which request the input of an argument of that type.

An argument collection *mode* happens when the system *prompts* the user to supply the argument, and does not allow other action until the argument is supplied or the command is cancelled. Alternatively, the command can simply *wait* until the user performs some action to supply the needed argument. Arguments can be pre-existing objects chosen from those displayed on the screen, or new objects can be created when they are needed. Arguments also receive **documentation** messages, and the documentation is displayed to remind the user that an argument of that kind is needed.

The behavior of a **Rectangle-Argument** when it receives an **Obtain** message is to change the cursor to prompt the user for the top-left corner, then change the cursor again to draw the rubber-banded rectangle while the user picks the bottom-right corner. [It is for creating a *new* rectangle rather than selecting an already existing one.] All the I/O knowledge it takes to do this is localized in the **Rectangle-Argument** object and shared by all commands that take rectangles as arguments. Argument objects also know how to do *type checking* of arguments, to make sure that only arguments of the correct type are acceptable. In contrast to traditional compiled languages, the type checking is *dynamic*; objects are sent **Are-You** messages.

An alternative style for obtaining a rectangle, such as choosing center, height and width, can be embodied in a new object inheriting from **Rectangle-Argument** and intercepting the **Obtain** message. It would also be type-checked to assure that it returns a bonafide rectangle.

As an example of another kind of argument, the **Make label** command takes a **text-argument**. To obtain this, the system pops up a window with a text editor in which the user can type a text string. The window optionally contains a prompt informing the user what is needed. If much typing is required, an editor window can be permanently displayed.

When a command is selected, and it has all its needed arguments, EZWin sends the command object a **Do-It** message. The **Do-It** message contains as arguments, the EZWin object representing the whole system [in this case an instance of a Beekeeper object], and whatever arguments are peculiar to that particular command [in this case a rectangle].

```
If I'm a Create-Worker-Command
and I get a Do-It message,
 with a Beekeeper object and a Rectangle:
  I make a Worker-Presentation object
   with that rectangle as its dimensions.
  I send the Beekeeper object a message
    Add-Presentation, putting it on
    its list of Presentations.
```

The **Add-Presentation** message has a number of effects. First of all, it results in sending the newly added object a **Draw** message, causing it to appear on the screen. In addition, if the object is acceptable as a argument to a currently chooseable command, it is made mouse-sensitive. If pop-up commands are applicable to that object, a pop-up menu will appear when the user clicks the mouse over it.

Another example of a command is the command to link two workers together.

```
Define a Link-Workers-Command object,
 inheriting from EZWin-Command.
  My Advertisement is "Link two workers"
  My Arguments are two Presentation-Arguments,
   of type Worker-Presentation.
```

This says that the link command takes two workers as arguments. Since the workers are displayed on the screen, the user picks the workers to be linked by pointing at them with the mouse and clicking a mouse button. When the link command has been chosen, EZWin makes only worker presentations mouse-sensitive, and waits for the user to choose two of them. Links or other objects displayed on the screen will not be mouse-sensitive, because they don't make sense as arguments to the link command, assuring that the command receives only objects of the desired type.

```
If I'm a Link-Workers-Command
and I get a Do-It message,
 with a Beekeeper, a From-Worker and a To-Worker:
  I ask both workers to Connect-To each other,
   returning points From-Point and To-Point.
  I create a new Link-Presentation
   whose endpoints are From-Point and To-Point.
  I tell the Beekeeper object to
   add the new Link-Presentation
   to its list of Presentations.
```

10. Generic commands can be defined through object inheritance

Object inheritance between commands invites defining new commands as extensions to old commands. The system supplies, for example, common `move`, `delete`, `copy` command objects which work on all kinds of presentation objects. Specialized versions of these for particular applications can be defined as extensions of the supplied versions.

The general notion of *dragging* a presentation so that it moves on the screen following the mouse cursor is provided by EZWin. This is useful for `move`, `copy` and similar sorts of motion commands. Providing this capability in a general way means that anything which can be displayed on the screen, can also be dragged with the mouse if necessary.

A standard pair of command objects `delete` and `undelete` share a `delete-history` list of deleted objects so that accidentally deleted objects can be retrieved. This is available for any application, or an application can decline to keep a history, limit its length, or provide a menu of deleted objects.

11. Ezwin is for menu systems what interpreters are for programming languages

One way of understanding the design of EZWin is to draw an analogy between traditional programming languages like Lisp and menu command interfaces. As menu driven graphical interfaces become more prevalent, they will truly become the "programming languages of the future". Taking this point of view, one can't help but notice that many of the services traditionally provided by interpreters for programming languages are sadly lacking for menu driven systems, and it is these which EZWin aims to provide.

An interpreter provides a top-level loop that reads an expression, executes it and prints the result, like the `READ-EVAL-PRINT` loop of Lisp. Think about how silly it would be if we required every individual Lisp program to provide code for its own `READ-EVAL-PRINT` loop! Yet the top level loop of a menu command system, which receives input from the mouse, dispatches to code implementing a command, and visibly alters the display must be implemented anew for each particular application. EZWin provides a standard loop for this task, together with hooks into it that allow idiosyncratic behavior in special cases. EZWin also provides the services of aborting execution, traps to error handlers, etc. that are typically found in interpreters.

Menu commands are analogous to *functions* in programming languages. Presentations can serve the role of *arguments*. Clicking on items in menus and on presentations constructs the equivalent of a *function call*.

One service of a programming language interpreter is to *separate* the collection of arguments to a function from the code which defines the function itself. In Lisp, each function *declares*, in advance, the number of arguments and their names, in the "lambda list". Compiled languages often declare a type for each argument as well. When an interpreter encounters a function call, it *evaluates* all the arguments, and matches up the supplied arguments to the required arguments of the function [possibly checking the types of the arguments as well]. Imagine how silly it would be if the code for every function a programmer wrote had to do this! Yet traditional menu command systems require the implementation of each command to have explicit code obtaining all its arguments.

In EZWin, each menu command declares its arguments, together with their types. EZWin's top level loop takes care of collecting the arguments, by interpreting mouse clicks on displayed objects, requesting typein, rubber-band lines, dragging, etc. Instead of delaying type checking until all arguments are obtained, EZWin matches types of arguments before each argument or command selection so that only the appropriate selections are sensitive for the next choice. In addition, it allows more flexibility in the order of obtaining a function and its arguments, supporting prefix, postfix, and infix commands.

Another compelling reason for separating the process of obtaining arguments from the implementation of the command is to *allow programs to invoke menu operations without going through the user interface.* Many interactive systems provide useful functionality that the user with some knowledge of programming would like to incorporate in his or her programs. We might like to write a program to automatically do layout of our Apiary diagrams, which could make use of the menu operations we've already implemented. If the code implementing the commands does explicit I/O to obtain arguments it becomes impossible to compute the argument using a program and pass it to the command. We can make this a requirement for any interactive systems kit: It should be possible for a program to do, conveniently, anything the user can accomplish by pointing and typing. Separating functionality from interface also paves the way for "keyboard macros" and programming by example [10].

12. Related work

Ciccarelli's thesis [3] develops a model of user interfaces based on connecting a descriptive data base describing the application domain to a presentation data base modelling the screen. Some interesting ideas found in his work which could be incorporated into EZWin are curve and motion recognition, commands which *plan* actions rather than perform them directly, and an *open/close* style of paired actions for control of displayed detail. The earlier *AIPS* system at Bolt, Beranek and Newman [14] applies an AI knowledge representation system to the task of building user interfaces. Both encourage separation of stylistic issues from functionality of the system. Support of prefix/postfix/infix commands, dynamic argument type checking, and mouse sensitivity is unique to the present work, to my knowledge.

Gould and Finzer's *Programming by Rehearsal* [5] shares the goal of making simple applications with graphical interfaces easy to construct. Interfaces are constructed primarily by invoking menu commands [*cues*] from pop-up menus on displayed graphical objects rather than by writing code. It is intended to make interface construction accessible to non-programmers. Their *performers* combine aspects of both EZWin presentation objects and EZWin command objects. The approach to collecting arguments to commands and mouse sensitivity of objects is different. Commands are usually invoked prefix-style by pop-up menus on visible objects, which display argument "templates". Arguments are filled in by dragging names of objects into empty slots in the templates. By default, all objects are mouse-sensitive, but each kind of object can control its sensitivity. Since both EZWin and Rehearsal are built on an object-oriented base, it is likely that the interaction styles of each could be implemented in the other.

Smalltalk's *Model-View-Controller* metaphor for building interfaces [8] [used internally in Gould's system], enforces a separation between the *input* and *output* phases of an interface. The EZWin approach lumps input and output together, while separating them from functionality.

All of these rely on a base of graphics software for multiple overlapping windows, menus, graphical primitives, and pointing devices, of which [1], [2], and [13] are representative examples.

13. Acknowledgments

Major support for the work described in this paper was provided by a grant from Wang Laboratories. Other related work at the MIT AI Laboratory was supported in part by DARPA under ONR contract N00014-80-C-0505 and by the System Development Foundation.

Fanya Montalvo and Christopher Fry deserve special thanks for being brave enough to volunteer to be the first users of EZWin.

References

1. Apple Documentation Group. Inside Mac. Apple Computer, Inc., 1984.

2. Daniel Bobrow and Mark Stefik. The Loops Manual. Xerox Palo Alto Research Center, 1984.

3. Eugene C. Ciccarelli. Presentation Based User Interfaces. Ph.D. Th., Massachusetts Institute of Technology, 1985.

4. R. Davis and H. Shrobe. Representing structure and behavior of digital hardware. *IEEE Computer 16*, 10 (October 1983).

5. William Finzer and Laura Gould. Programming by Rehearsal. *Byte* (June 1984).

6. C. Fry. Flavors Band: An Environment for Processing Musical Scores. Conference of the Audio Engineering Society, Anaheim, California, 1985.

7. Scott Kim. Viewpoint. Stanford University, 1984.

8. Glenn Krasner. *Smalltalk-80: User Interface and Graphical Applications.* Addison-Wesley, 1985.

9. Henry Lieberman. Machine Tongues: Object Oriented Programming. *Computer Music Journal* (Fall 1982).

10. Henry Lieberman. Constructing Graphical User Interfaces by Example. Graphics Interface Conference, Toronto, Canada, May, 1982.

11. Henry Lieberman. An Object Oriented Simulator for the Apiary. National Conference on Artificial Intelligence, American Association for Artificial Intelligence, Washington, D. C., August, 1983.

12. Larry Tesler. The Smalltalk Environment. *Byte* (August 1981).

13. Daniel Weinreb, et. al. *Lisp Machine Manual.* Symbolics, Inc., Cambridge, Mass., 1984.

14. F. Zdybel, N. Greenfeld, M. Yonke. An Information Presentation System. Proceedings of International Joint Conference on Artificial Intelligence, Vancouver, B. C., Canada, August, 1981.

Input/Output Linkage in a User Interface Management System

Dan R. Olsen Jr.
Brigham Young University

Elizabeth P. Dempsey
Arizona State University

Roy Rogge
Arizona State University

Abstract

The GRaphical INteraction System (GRINS) is described, which integrates an automaton-based dialogue controller with a dynamic display model to provide a User Interface Management System. The linkage between the logical device interface and the graphical presentation of virtual devices is discussed. A display manager to support dynamic manipulations of hierarchically structure images is presented. Lastly a model of Display Objects whereby application-specific display objects can have computational constraints defined is described. The constraint system is equivalent to an attributed grammar and is evaluated using an incremental attribute flow algorithm.

INTRODUCTION

With the huge increase in the number of interactive graphics systems that are being programmed has come a desire to reduce the cost of building such systems and to increase the quality of their user interfaces. In an attempt to meet this need, there have been a number of systems developed or proposed which can be categorized as User Interface Management Systems (UIMS). The purpose of such systems is to provide programming tools to aid in the development of quality interactive systems. In most UIMSs that have been developed, the emphasis has been on organizing and translating interactive inputs into the actual program behavior that the user desires. Processing an interactive dialogue, however, requires both understanding the inputs and providing visual feedback about the input. The visual feedback portion of an interactive dialogue has received significantly less attention in UIMS research. This paper will discuss the GRaphical INteraction System (GRINS) which is a prototype UIMS which has been built to study this linkage between input language parsing and graphical feedback.

There is a variety of ways in which visual feedback is addressed in various UIMSs. Some UIMSs are primarily concerned with input parsing and provide no direct support for visual feedback. The transition networks of Jacob [Jaco 83] fall into this category. The input-output tools of van den Bos [vand 83] and the abstract devices of Anson [Anso 82] have a notion of encapsulating input/feedback concepts in a tool but do not discuss mechanisms for actually providing the visual feedback. Some UIMSs have builtin or static feedback techniques. These systems are dominated by their input language specifications and use a fixed set of primitive virtual devices whose feedback techniques are hardcoded into them. The menu trees of TIGER [Kasi 82] and the menus and simulated valuators of SYNGRAPH [Olse 83] have this characteristic. In these systems the UIMS provides a predefined external view or presentation for the interactive dialogue which cannot be significantly altered. There are systems such as Menulay [Buxt 83] and Flair [Wong 82] which provide tools for designing the presentation of a dialogue but the linkage between the presentation and the dialogue is not a strong one. This problem of input/feedback linkage became apparent in the design of the input primitives for the CORE [GSPC 79] and GKS [GKS 84]. Rosenthal and others [Rose 82] have carefully defined the kinds of feedback that a primitive device should support but this has not been integrated with a UIMS.

The paper will proceed by first discussing the overall GRINS architecture to identify where the input output linkages occur. This will be followed by a discussion of the lexical presentation issues including the layout editor which manipulates the lexical and syntactic level presentations of a user interface. The GRINS display manager with its parameterized templates and segments will be discussed as a model for dynamically manipulating images. Lastly the GRINS object description language for modeling application-specific display objects which provide the final level of input/output linkage will be presented.

GRINS ARCHITECTURE

The GRINS software consists of three components as shown in Figure 1. The first is a parser that parses a description of the interactive interface to be generated. The second is the layout editor which allows the programmer to graphically design the layout of the screens, menus, feedback space and prompts. The third component is the runtime system that interprets the information generated by the other two components and actually executes the interactive program.

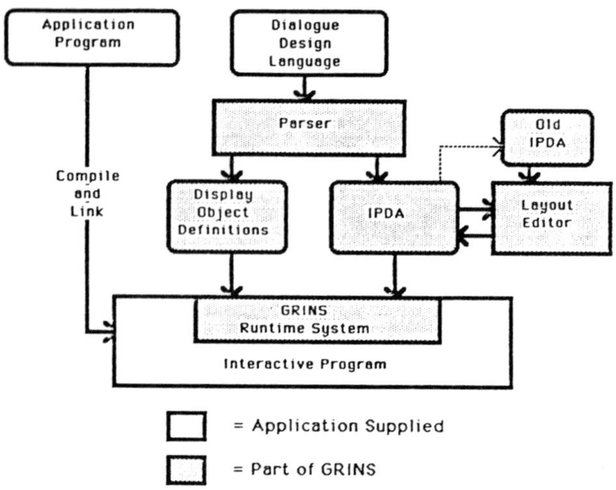

Figure 1.
Overall Structure of GRINS

The parser generates two files as its output. The first file contains the actual dialogue definition in the form of an Interactive Push-Down Automaton (IPDA). The definition of an IPDA and the algorithms for generating it from an input description are found in Olsen [Olse 84]. The Display Object Definitions file contains the information which describes the structure of the application.

The runtime architecture of GRINS is shown in Figure 2.

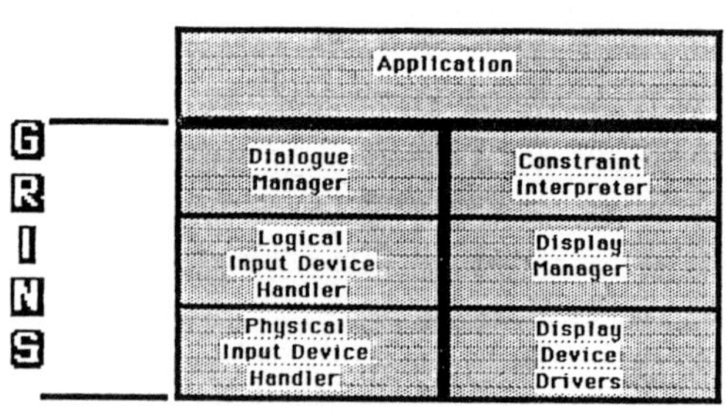

Figure 2.
Runtime Structure of GRINS

In addition to the application there are six components to the GRINS runtime system itself. There are three levels of input processing and three for output. The role of the Dialogue Manager is to interpret the IPDA and control the entire interaction. It does this by receiving inputs via the Logical and Physical Input Device Handlers and by making calls on the application and the Constraint Interpreter. In Figure 2 each component can communicate directly with those components that are adjacent to it. The primary emphasis of this paper is on the Display Manager and the Constraint Interpreter. We will discuss in detail how they interrelate with the Dialogue Manager and the Logical Input Device Handler. We will also discuss the models for dynamic graphical output that these components support and how they are specified.

LEXICAL PRESENTATIONS

In discussing how the presentation of an interactive dialogue is handled on the lexical level we must first understand how the Dialogue Manager interfaces with the Logical Input Device Handler. This will identify specific properties of logical input devices which must be reflected in the presentation. We will then discuss how this information is manipulated by the Layout Editor.

The Dialogue Manager/Logical Input Device Interface

At the lexical level, the primary presentation issues of a user interface are how the logical input devices are prompted for and how their inputs are echoed. The lexical level presentations are defined by the Layout Editor, are controlled by the Dialogue Manager and the Logical Input Device Handler and are actually displayed by the Display Manager.

The Dialogue Manager views logical input devices as being either event or sampled devices and as returning 0 or more typed attributes as their result. An obvious example is a tablet which is sampled and returns two real attributes. The interface between the Dialogue Manager and the Logical Input Device Handler makes no further distinctions between devices and has no preset enumeration of input devices.

Our present Logical Input Device Handler supports two classes of virtual devices in addition to the normal physical devices which are simply passed through the logical level. These virtual devices are menu items and picks. As in SYNGRAPH, picking is based on the type of the data object that a picked image represents. A new logical device class is created for each data type that can be picked and the attribute returned by each such device is the data value associated with the picked image. The menu items, however, are more relevant to the current discussion because of their close relationship with the presentation of an interaction. Menu items best illustrate the interplay of the interactive dialogue and the presentation.

In discussing the relationship between the Dialogue Manager and the logical input devices we will use the terms and definitions set forth for GKS by Rosenthal [Rose 82]. The Dialogue Manager accepts logical inputs by either consuming them, as in the case of event devices, or sampling them, as in the case of sampled devices. Because most interactive systems require more logical inputs than physically exist, the physical resources must be multiplexed to possibly more than one logical device. To ensure that there is no conflicting usage of physical resources, the IPDA parser partitions the dialogue into modes. Each mode is characterized by a set of logical devices which are accessible in that mode. When the Dialogue Manager enters a new mode it releases and acquires logical devices so that the set of logical devices that are actually accessible matches the set of devices defined for the new mode. If a physical resource is bound to two logical devices there is no conflict as long as those logical devices never appear in the same mode. The syntactic portion of the parse does not know about the bindings of multiple logical devices to a single physical device. It is the acquire and releasing process associated with a mode change which resolves the ambiguities.

Simply because a device is accessible does not mean that its input is acceptable at any point in time. The set of acceptable inputs is determined by the current state of the dialogue. When the dialogue manager changes states it disables all input devices that are no longer acceptable and it enables any that have become acceptable.

When an input is actually accepted by the Dialogue Manager it must be acknowledged. Because inputs usually are grouped into commands or possibly smaller "chunks" [Buxt 83] inputs should stay in an acknowledged state until closure is reached (as determined by the Dialogue Manager).

The Layout Editor

The role of the layout editor is to take the mode information provided in the IPDA and append additional presentation information to it. The Layout Editor integrates the principles presented in MENULAY [Buxt 83] with the dialogue control strategies developed from SYNGRAPH.

The editor constructs a layout for each mode in the IPDA. The general graphical presentation of the mode including titles, background colors, boundaries of viewports and menu areas and location of help and feedback message areas are all expressed graphically on the screen using the editor. In addition, the layout editor allows for the positioning of the menu icons for each logical menu device that is accessed by that mode.

In addition to the placement of menu icons, a facility for designing and editing icons is provided. Since each menu item represents a logical input device it must respond to the enable, disable, acknowledge and unacknowledge requests from the Dialogue Manager. This means that a logical device must present to an interactive user one of four states (enabled/acknowledged, enabled/unacknowledged, disabled/acknowledged and disabled/acknowledged). As an icon is drawn on the screen the primitives which make up the icon are divided into groups by the designer. Each of these groups can be edited separately and the designer can create as many of these groups as desired. (More than two or three groups is usually excessive.)

The purpose of groups is to allow for the presentation of the four states of an icon. Each icon has a color matrix like that shown in Figure 3.

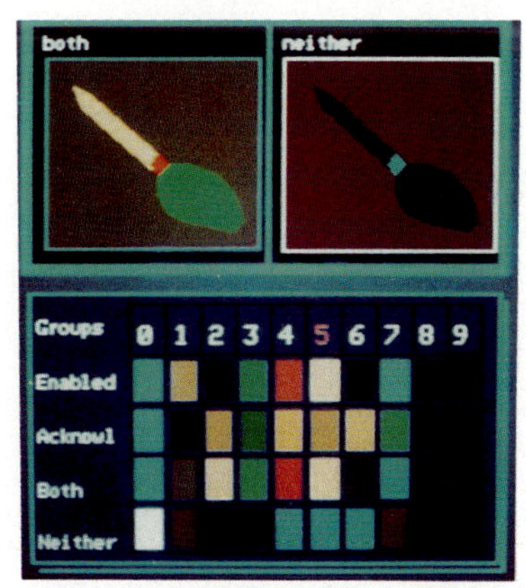

Figure 3.
Icon Color Matrix

As the figure shows, the rows of the matrix correspond to the states of the icon and the columns are the groups. Colors are selected from the palette to fill in the cells of the matrix. As an icon changes state the Logical Input Device Handler modifies the color of the icon's groups to match the settings of the appropriate row in the matrix. To aid the designer in creating these dynamic icons there is a drawing area for each of the four device states. Drawing in any of the areas updates the other three, using the appropriate color settings for each. By using the color matrix from previously designed icons one can easily and quickly design a uniform presentation for an entire dialogue.

We have only discussed the presentation of iconic menu items because they best illustrate the dialogue/presentation relationship. Other virtual devices are easily added to the Logical Input Device Handler.

DISPLAY MANAGEMENT

Our original intent in developing GRINS was to use CORE or GKS as a basis for the display portion of the system. Both of these were found to be inadequate, however, because of the inability to edit display primitives within segments. This editing ability is essential to being able to perform the rapid screen updates required in an interactive application. In addition, neither the CORE nor GKS has the geometric modeling capabilities that we desired to support display objects.

It is very important that the model for dynamic image modification be incorporated into the display manager because of the disparity of screen update techniques required by various display devices. If there is a basic model for image update then the display manager can be tailored to the needs and limitations of the display device whether it be vector refresh or raster.

Primitives, Segments and Templates

The basic graphical units in the display manager are primitives, templates, and segments. The primitives currently supported are lines. arcs, polygons and text. Primitives are grouped into templates in much the same fashion that they are placed in segments in CORE or GKS. The difference is that the arguments to each of the primitives can either be constant values or references to a segment parameter. Templates also contain transformation information for references to subsegments. The actual subsegment referenced. however, lies in the segment using the template. Each segment references a template which contains the primitives which describe how the segment should be graphically interpreted. The parameters can be real or integer numbers or character strings. Editing operations on this structure consist of either exchanging or replacing subsegments of a segment or changing a parameter value. A template is intended to be used by more than one segment each of which contains different editable values. The role of templates is to contain the relatively static portions of an image. A segment on the other hand contains the modifiable portion. When a primitive with a parameter is added to a template, an initial value for the parameter is also given. These initial values are stored in the template and are used when creating new segments for the template.

In addition to the simple primitives, segments and templates the display manager provides viewports and subsegment references. Subsegment references simply provide a hierarchical structure for pictures. With each subsegment reference there may or may not be a transformation matrix. The elements of the transformation matrix may also be parameterized. A viewport definition can be placed in the template of either the root segment or another viewport. Viewports contain their own viewing definitions which can be parameterized in the segments which use the viewport's template. Thus the editing model can be consistently applied to viewports as well as any other graphical object. Viewport templates can themselves contain primitives, other viewports or subsegments references.

This model for parameterizing display lists has existed for quite some time. Many vector refresh displays provide this feature in hardware. Similar structures are proposed by Michner [Mich 78]. Turner [Turn 84] has proposed extensions to GKS which are similar. The difference is that in Turner's model the graphics variables are global to the entire image whereas in our model the variables lie in the individual segments. This is a very important difference because a flat or unstructured variable space is inconsistent with a hierarchically structured image.

EXAMPLE: Menu Icons
Using the menu icons described previously as an example, each icon is represented by a template. For each group in the icon there is a color parameter stored in a segment. Each primitive added to the template uses the color parameter which is appropriate for its group. As a menu device changes state the Logical Input Device Handler needs only to change the parameters in the icon's segment to update the menu display. It is up to the display manager to perform the appropriate screen update operations.

EXAMPLE: Layouts
Using templates/segments for display management each mode's layout becomes a viewport template. This mode template contains the various viewports for the application's use and the menus. In addition, all of the other static layout information is stored in this template. When the dialogue changes mode the Logical Input Device Handler simply changes the root segment/template.
There are several of these layout segment/template pairs, one for each mode. The only one that is ever displayed

is the one referenced by the root segment. All layout segments reference the same application world segment (which of course may itself have subsegments). Menu icon segments are referenced as subsegments of the layout. Each layout references that subset of the menu icon segments which are part of the mode that the layout represents. Figure 4 shows the structure of layouts, application viewports and menu icons using this model.

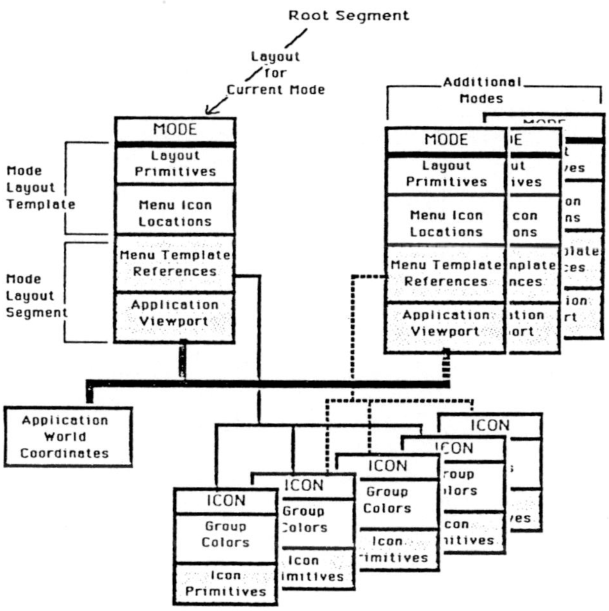

Figure 4.
Structure of Layouts, Viewports and Menu Icons

This model for a display manager provides a simple and straightforward method for dynamically manipulating images. For purposes of providing feedback from more dynamic input techniques than simple menu icons this model is not sufficient. As Turner has already shown, a computational linkage between input values and output parameters must be provided. The display objects to be described later provide this capability.

Picking

As a final note about the interface between the Logical Input Device Handler and the Display Manager, each template has stored in it a type code to identify the type of application data that it represents and each segment has stored in it a pointer to a data value. This information in conjuction with the types of the enabled logical pick devices is used by the Logical Input Device Handler to resolve pickability and picking ambiguity problems from the screen.

DISPLAY OBJECTS

In providing a dynamic output structure whose power is consistent with our dialogue control system we wanted to be able to model a wide variety of interactive techniques. We were guided in this by several principles. The first, which has already been stated, is that simple value substitution does not have sufficient power to link inputs to outputs. The second is that the input/output linkage is frequently application specific. The third principle is that an image represents an application data object whose presentation is being defined.

In the Dialogue Design Language the programmer provides what are called display object definitions. Display objects contain the computational portion of the output definition. As a simple example of a display object we define a virtual valuator in the form of a slider as shown in Figure 5.

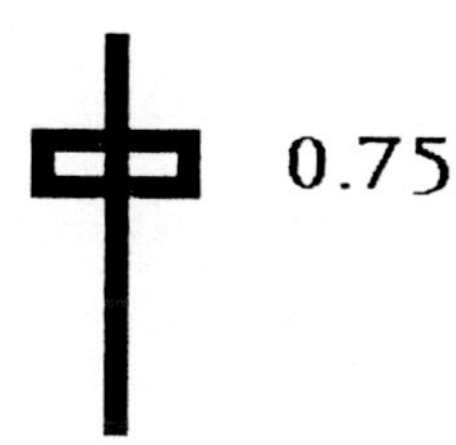

Figure 5.
A Virtual Valuator.

By picking a location on the slider shaft we want to move the slider up and down. We also want the application to be able to set the upper and lower bounds of the slider and to be able to read the current value of the slider. Figure 6. shows the object definition of the slider.

```
Object Slider( Max,Min:Real;
 ! Max and Min define the range for the
 ! slider in the units of the application
   SliderVal:Real
 ! This returns the slider value
    ) =
 ! This display object is defined in a
 ! local coordinate system ranging from
 ! 0.0 to 1.0.
Control YLoc: Real := 0.5;
 ! This is the slider location which is
 ! set by the dialogue manager.  This is
 ! defined in the coordinates of the
 ! slider object.
Assert (YLoc <= 1.0) and (YLoc >= 0.0);
Def SliderVal:=YLoc*(Max-Min)+Min;
 ! This is the value of the slider which
 ! the application can read.
Line( (0.0,1.0),(0.0,0.0),Black);
 ! This is the slider range
Def SliderTop:=YLoc+0.1;
    SliderBottom:=YLoc-0.1;
Polygon( (0.1,SliderTop),(-0.1,SliderTop),
   (-0.1,SliderBottom),(0.1,SliderBottom),
    Black);
Text( RealToString(SliderVal),
(0.11,YLoc),0.0,0.1, Black);
EndObject;
```

Figure 6.
Slider Object Definition.

Note that several of the display parameters are indirectly computed from the value YLoc. This value can be changed by the Dialogue Manager. This value could also be changed by the application if desired. After a control value or set of values is changed all assertions are then checked. If any assertion fails then the change is ignored and the image remains unchanged. If all assertions are valid then the all of the implied values which are found in Def statements are computed including the actual SliderVal.

The Line, Polygon and Text statements define the graphical primitives of the actual objects. Note that some of their arguments are constants while some are computed from the control variables and object parameters. For each object definition a template is created in the Display Manager. All of the object's graphical primitives are placed in the template with those arguments that must be computed being defined as parameters. After the implied values are computed the corresponding segment parameters that have changed are updated and the Display Manager updates the screen.

This model provides a nice separation of tasks. The application sees only Max, Min and SliderVal in its own units. The Dialogue Manager sees only YLoc and needs only know the coordinate system of the slider. The presentation of the slider is independent of all of the other components and can be changed as needed.

The slider object can be used to form a 3D locator object as shown in Figure 7.

```
Object Loc3D( CoordMax, CoordMin: Real;
      LocX,LocY,LocZ :Real ) =

  SubObj
X:Slider(CoordMax,CoordMin,LocX);
    Y:Slider(CoordMax,CoordMin,LocY);
    Z:Slider(CoordMax,CoordMin,LocZ);
EndObject;
```

Figure 7.
3D Locator Object Definition

Note that the values of Max and Min for each slider are propagated down from the 3DLocator object and that their SliderVal value are propagated up as LocX, LocY and LocZ. This propagation of values is functionally identical to an attributed grammar. The algorithm used to determine which values (or attributes) must be recomputed after a change is the incremental attribute flow algorithm of Demers [Deme 81].

Note also that the functions which compute the assertions and the implied values can be application-specific functions. This meets the requirement defined at the Seattle Workshop on Graphical Input and Interaction Techniques [Thom 83] that any mechanism allowing a UIMS to change the form of a displayed image must have a provision for the application to veto the change.

SUMMARY

The GRINS user interface management system has addressed the issues of how models for dynamic displays can be integrated with dialogue control to provide a comprehensive set of principles covering both the input and output facets of an interactive dialogue. GRINS has been implemented in Pascal and C under UNIX and using a Raster Technologies display. We are pleased with the progress that we have made with this system, however, we feel that additional work needs to be done on the screen update algorithms of the Display Manager to improve its efficiency and we are hoping to gain much more experience with the power and applicability of our Display Objects.

REFERENCES

Anson, Ed. "The Device Model of Interaction." Computer Graphics 16, 3 (July 1982) pp. 107-114.

Buxton, William. "Lexical and Pragmatic Considerations of Input Structures." Computer Graphics 17, 1 (January 1983) pp. 31-37.

Buxton, W, Lamb, M.R., Sherman, D., Smith, K.C. "Towards a Comprehensive User Interface Management System." Computer Graphics 17, 3 (July 1983) pp. 35-42.

Demers, A., Reps, T. and Teitelbaum, T. "Incremental Evaluation for Attribute Grammars with Application to Syntax directed Editors." 8th Conference on Principles of Programming Languages (January 1981) pp. 105-116.

Graphical Kernel System, ANSI X3H3/83-25r3; Special Issue, Computer Graphics (February 1984).

GSPC. "Status Report of the Graphics Standards Planning Committee." Computer Graphics 13, 3 (Aug 1979).

Jacob, R.J.K. "Using Formal Specifications in the Design of a Human-Computer Interface." Communications of the ACM 26, 4 (April 1983).

Kasik, David J. "A User Interface Management System." Computer Graphics 16, 3 (July 1982) pp. 99-106.

Michner, J.C. "A Graphics System for Real-Time Programming." Proceedings of the Society for Information Display, Vol 19, 4 (Fourth Quarter 1978) pp. 157-161.

Olsen, Dan R. and Dempsey, Elizabeth P. "SYNGRAPH: A Graphic User Interface Generator." Computer Graphics 17, 3 (July 1983) pp. 43-50.

Olsen, Dan R. "Push-down Automata for User Interface Management." ACM Transactions on Graphics 3, 4 (July 1984).

Rosenthal, D.S.H, Michener, J.C., Pfaff, G., Kessener, R. and Sabin, M. "The Detailed Semantics of Graphics Input Devices." Computer Graphics 16, 3 (July 1982) 33-38.

Thomas, James J. and Hamlin, Griffith. "Graphical Input Interaction Technique: Workshop Summary." Computer Graphics 17, 1 (January 1983) pp. 5-30.

Turner, Joshua U. "A Programmer's Interface to Graphics Dynamics." Computer Graphics 18, 3 (July 1984) pp. 263-270.

van den Bos, J., Plasmeijer, M.J. and Hartel, P.H. "Input-Output Tools: A Language Facility for Interactive and Real-Time Systems." IEEE Transactions on Software Engineering SE-9, 3 (May 1983) pp. 247-259.

Wong, Peter C.S. and Reid, Eric R. "Flair - User Interface Dialog Design Tool." Computer Graphics 16, 3 (July 1982) pp. 87-98.

Squeak: a Language for Communicating with Mice

Luca Cardelli
Rob Pike

AT&T Bell Laboratories
Murray Hill, New Jersey 07974

Abstract

Graphical user interfaces are difficult to implement because of the essential concurrency among multiple interaction devices, such as mice, buttons, and keyboards. *Squeak* is a user interface implementation language that exploits this concurrency rather than hiding it, helping the programmer to express interactions using multiple devices. We present the motivation, design and semantics of *squeak*. The language is based on concurrent programming constructs but can be compiled into a conventional sequential language; our implementation generates C code. We discuss how *squeak* programs can be integrated into a graphics system written in a conventional language to implement large but regular user interfaces, and close with a description of the formal semantics.

CR Categories: I3.6 Graphics languages, Interaction techniques
D3.1 Formal semantics
CR General Terms: Algorithms, Theory, Languages
Additional Keywords: Concurrency, User Interfaces

Introduction

User interface implementation languages ([Buxton 83], [Thomas 83]) usually address the construction of a user interface from building blocks such as menus, scroll bars and freehand curves. Although it is worthwhile to automate the building of programs from such building blocks, there is an underlying level that these languages do not address: the implementation of the building blocks themselves. Moreover, the procedures that provide menus, graphical potentiometers and other user interface modules tend (in our experience) to be more difficult to write or modify and clumsier in execution than one would expect. The primitives never seem complex in principle, but the programs that implement them are surprisingly intricate.

Providing a suitable graphical display is not especially difficult; what causes problems is the complicated flow of control required to deal with all the possible sequences of user actions with the input devices. One might consider a scrolling menu, for example, as a finite state automaton reading an input token for each event generated by the user: buttons up and down, entering and leaving the scroll bar rectangle, etc. Interaction primitives would probably be simpler to write and understand if they were implemented as state machines. A translator that converted state machine descriptions into regular programs would make the job even easier.

There are a couple of factors that limit the usefulness of this technique, however. First, the presence of multiple input devices invalidates the notion of a single stream of tokens driving the state machine; for example, the procedure implementing a menu should not worry about characters typed on the keyboard, even those typed while the user is using the menu. Second, the passage of time is often important in user interfaces. Some pairs of events are only meaningful when the individual events occur sufficiently near in time. Consider clicking a mouse button twice: if the clicks are nearly simultaneous, they might be construed as the single event 'double click.'

A more powerful structure is a set of communicating finite state machines, each of which implements the actions associated with some set of user events. If the individual machines execute concurrently, each may be enabled when an event is available for it, so the user interface need never 'lock up' waiting for a specific event. Another concept from concurrent programming, the *timeout*, can be used to encode time-sensitive procedures.

In contrast to approaches based on parsing a single input stream [van den Bos 83], the language we present here, called *squeak*, is an explicitly concurrent language, resembling CSP [Hoare 78] and CCS [Milner 80], and with the passage of time built rigorously into the semantics as in SCCS [Milner 82] and ESTEREL [Berry 84]. Processes in *squeak* communicate by exchanging simple messages on multiple channels. A predefined channel is used for communicating with each device.

The concurrency in a *squeak* program must be expanded out for *squeak* to be of practical value in a conventional programming environment. Our implementation generates an open-coded (as opposed to table driven) state machine, written in C [Kernighan 78], that expresses all possible execution paths of the set of processes in the program. The sequence of input events controls the path taken by the single-stream sequential execution of the program. In practice the relatively simple programs needed to describe user interfaces are well-behaved, although in general the state space of a set of concurrent processes can explode.

Tutorial introduction to *squeak*

The following sections will explain *squeak* in detail; this tutorial introduces and motivates the basic ideas.

Squeak programs are composed of processes executing in parallel. A process, or perhaps a few processes, typically deal with a particular action or external device; the composition of processes then handles the set of actions and device events relevant to the program. Communication between processes is achieved by sending messages on *channels*. There are two classes of channels: primitive and non-primitive. Primitive channels are pre-defined, and provide access to external devices. Non-primitive channels are for ordinary message-based communication. The syntax *c*!*exp* sends the value of the expression *exp* on channel *c*; *c*?*var* reads the message on channel *c* into the variable *var*.

Our implementation of *squeak* defines the primitive channels *DN* and *UP*, which report mouse button transitions; *M*, mouse cursor position (*M*!*p* sets the cursor position, *M*?*p* reads it);† *K*, characters typed on the keyboard; *T*, the current absolute time; and *E* and *L*, the mouse entering and leaving certain rectangles. The primitive channels return appropriate values; *M* for example returns a point data structure. *UP* and *DN* return no value; if the mouse had several buttons, they might return the mouse button number, or there could be a separate channel for each button. *E* and *L* return the appropriate rectangle. *Squeak* does not specify how the program announces its interest in rectangles on the display; our implementation provides C-callable functions to push and pop sets of rectangles to be watched. Events come in meaningful order, so that *UP* and *DN* events must alternate, as must *E* and *L* of a given rectangle.

Here is a simple *squeak* program that places typed text on the display at points indicated by the mouse:

```
proc Mouse = DN? . M?p . moveTo!p . UP? . Mouse

proc Kbd(s) = K?c .
                  if c==NewLine then
                         typed!s . Kbd(emptyString)
                  else
                         Kbd(append(s, c))
                  fi

proc Text(p) =
                  < moveTo?p . Text(p)
                  :: typed?s . {drawString(s, p)}? . Text(p) >

type = Mouse & Kbd(emptyString) & Text(nullPt)
```

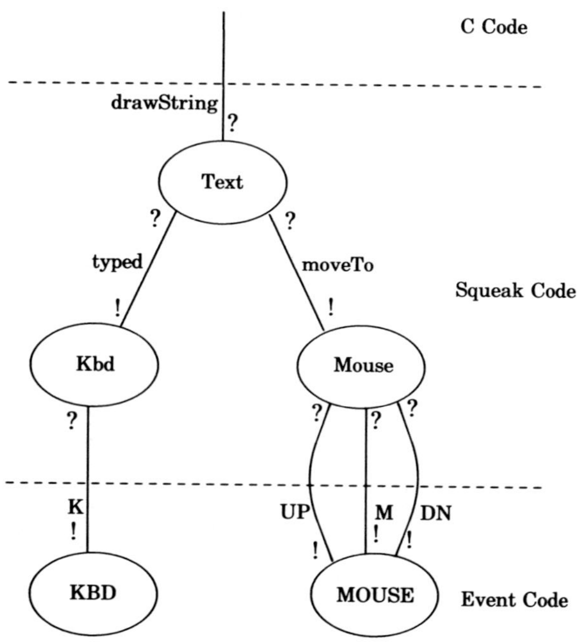

Process structure in the example program

The last line states that the generated C procedure *type* is the result of the parallel execution of three processes. The *Mouse* process waits for the mouse button to be depressed. When it is, the mouse coordinates are sent on channel *moveTo*, where they will be read by the *Text* process. *Mouse* then waits for the mouse button to be released, and restarts. (The precise semantics of these actions are discussed in the following sections.) *Kbd* waits for a character to be typed. If the character is a newline, it sends the complete line on channel *typed* and restarts; otherwise it appends the character to the line. The *append* function is a C routine defined elsewhere; *squeak* treats its invocation as a literal expression. Note that because *Mouse* and *Kbd* are processes, not functions, their recursive invocations do not stack; they are *goto*'s, not subroutine calls.

Finally, the *Text* process waits for a message on channel *moveTo* or *typed*, and records the mouse position or draws the string on the display, as appropriate. The code in brace brackets { } is a C expression evaluated at that point in the execution of *Text*. Typical *squeak* programs implement only the flow of control; the actual work at each state of execution is done by such calls to external code.

This simple example is artificial, but illustrates the basic ideas of *squeak*. Most important, a process monitors each input device, and each such process is independent. If a mouse button is held down while typing continues, the text will still be displayed when a newline is typed. This works because of the concurrent execution of the *Mouse* and *Kbd* processes.

† Primitive events are special: the sender of *M*? and the receiver of *M*! are always external to the program.

Syntax and informal semantics

A *squeak* program is a set of process declarations followed by a main process, which may use the declared processes.

```
prog      ::=  decl id = main
decl      ::=  ε | proc pid formals = prcs decl
main      ::=  prcs rename | main \ id |
               main & main | ( main )
prcs      ::=  pid actuals |
               action . prcs |
               wait [ exp ] prcs ‖ prcs |
               if exp then prcs else prcs fi |
               < prcslist > |
               ( prcs )
action    ::=  id ? | id ! | id ? id | id ! exp
prcslist  ::=  ε | prcs | prcs :: prcslist
formals   ::=  ε | ( idlist )
actuals   ::=  ε | ( explist )
rename    ::=  ε | [ id / id ] rename
idlist    ::=  id | id , idlist
explist   ::=  exp | exp , explist
exp       ::=  id | num | exp op exp | ( exp )
op        ::=  + | − | * | / | = | == | < | > | <= | >= | !=
```

The simplest process is <> (also called *stop* or *deadlock*), which cannot perform any action.

A process of the form $a\,!exp.p$ is ready to output the value of *exp* on the channel *a*, and then execute *p*. The value can be read by the process $a\,?x.p$, which binds the input value to the identifier *x*, with *x* available in (and local to) the continuation *p*. If no value is passed during a communication, we can simply write $a!$ or $a?$. These are all instances of *simple processes*, which consist of an *action* ($a\,!exp$ or $a\,?x$) and a continuation.

The action $a\,!exp$ cannot execute until there is a matching $a?x$, and *vice versa*. If more than one input is active on a channel, only one will receive the value; the others remain suspended until the next input.

A process may wait for input or output simultaneously on several channels: this is a *nondeterministic choice* operation among processes. For example $<a?x.p_1 :: b!y.p_2 :: c?z.p_3>$ is waiting for input on *a* and *c*, and for output on *b*. Communication may happen on any available channel, say *a*, and in that case p_1 becames the process continuation (the other continuations p_2 and p_3 are discarded). A choice between two processes may also be written $p+q$; this is not part of the syntax, but is a convenient notation when discussing the semantics. Choice is associative, so that $<p :: q :: r>$ can be written $((p + q) + r)$, or $(p + (q + r))$. A choice with a single alternative $<p>$ is equivalent to *p*. A choice of zero alternatives is the deadlock <>, which is the identity in sums, i.e. $<> + p$ is *p*.

Some actions can have a *timeout* condition: the simple process $wait[3]a\,?x.p \parallel q$ will wait for input on channel *a* for a maximum of three time units. If an *a* communication happens within that time, *p* will be executed. If communication is not achieved in time, the process will time out and execute q; $wait[0]a?x.p \parallel q$ is equivalent to q.

Conditional flow of control is achieved by an **if-then-else-fi** construct. A boolean condition is used to decide between two possible process continuations. If the condition is true, the **then**-part continuation will become the current process, otherwise the **else**-part will.

Processes can be defined recursively:

```
proc p = <c!0 . <>  ::  a!3 . p  ::  b?x . p>
proc q = <c?z . <>  ::  a?y . b!(y+1) . q>
example = p & q
```

The third line executes the processes p and q in parallel. Initially the two processes can exchange a c action, in which case they both stop, or an a action, in which case p goes back to the initial state, while q gets into a state where it can only do a b action (which can now be absorbed by p) and then go back to its initial state. Note that when a process calls another process, it is a process replacement, not a subroutine call; processes never return to the calling process.

Every execution path of a process must encounter an action before it encounters an execution of itself. This rules out pathological cases like $p = p$ and $p = \langle a?x.q :: p \rangle$.

A process may have parameters, which are available as local variables within that process. For example, consider the following counter process, which may receive an *increment* signal or a *tellContents* signal. It has a local parameter n, which is the current count:

```
proc counter(n) =
        < increment?m . counter(n+m)
        :: tellContents!n . counter(n) >
```

The process would be created by running *counter*(0). Although from appearance the *tellContents*!*n* message can be emitted at any time, the meaning of communications is such that there must be a matching action *tellContents*?*v* to receive the message in some other process before the sending action may be executed. Similarly, the *increment*?*m* is only executed when another process emits an *increment*!*exp*. Therefore, most of the time the *counter* process is suspended waiting for a matching message to choose which path of the selection to take.

A complete *squeak* program is a parallel composition of processes, possibly with channel renamings to facilitate the reuse of process definitions. A complete program can perform external communications on predefined channels, or internal communications on user-defined channels. Communications on user-defined channels must all be satisfied internally, or a deadlock will result.

Example 1: Simple menus

Our implementation of *squeak* compiles a program into a single C function that executes the combined state machines of the processes in the program. The passing of arguments and return values is handled by two special primitive channels, *ARG* and *RES*. The action *ARG*?*x* stores in *x* the program's actual argument list. The variable *x* will in general be a data structure to implement the passing of sets of values to the program. The action *RES*!*exp* returns the expression to the caller of the program. The way these must be implemented, of course, is as a call and return from the function, so *ARG* must be the first communication received by a program, and *RES* the last emitted.

To handle more complicated interactions with C code, our implementation of *squeak* interprets text enclosed in brace brackets { } as literal C expressions (except that *squeak* process variables may be renamed for uniqueness). Such an expression is valid wherever an ordinary expression is valid, or in place of an input channel in an action, in which case the value of the expression is assigned to the variable (if any) in the action. This allows a reasonably clean connection to the outside world, and keeps *squeak* independent of the generated language.

Here is a complete example that uses *ARG* and *RES* to implement simple menus:

```
proc Roam(m, sel) =
        < E?r . {highlight(r)}? . Roam(m, rtosel(r))
        :: L?r . {lowlight(r)}? . Roam(m, -1)
        :: UP? . {erasemenu(m)}? . RES!sel . Menu >
proc Menu =
  ARG?menu . {drawmenu(menu)}? . Roam(menu, -1)

# The generated function is called 'simpleMenu'
simpleMenu = Menu
```

A menu is an array of labeled rectangles. The external function *rtosel*(*r*) maps a rectangle to its label, *drawmenu* and *erasemenu* create and destroy the menu's display, *highlight* highlights a rectangle and *lowlight* undoes the highlighting. Part of the task of drawing and undrawing the menu is identifying to the event manager the rectangles that tile the menu, one per element. Conceptually, the *Menu* process is always running, but blocked on receipt of an argument *menu* to draw. (In reality, of course, *Menu* is not started until *simpleMenu* is called.) A higher-level process invokes *Menu* when it detects the mouse button depressed for a significant time. *Menu* then draws the menu and invokes *Roam*, which highlights the appropriate rectangles as the mouse roams across the menu. The return result, generated when the mouse button is released, is the label of the rectangle the mouse is in when the button is released, or −1 if the mouse is outside the menu, indicating no selection. Its final action is to restart the *Menu* process, but this is done only for clarity; *RES* terminates the invocation of *Menu*. Note that the *ARG* and *RES* channels must be handled specially by the compiler so that a program bracketed by *ARG* and *RES* actions behaves like a conventional C function.

Example 2: Double clicking

As an example of a *squeak* program using timeouts, consider the problem of detecting clicks (mouse button down and up again in a short time) and double clicks (two clicks separated by a longer but finite time) without losing any button transitions. Here is a *squeak* process that detects single clicks on a one-button mouse:

```
Click =
    DN? . wait[clickTime] (UP? . click! . Click) ||
          (down! . UP? . up! . Click)
```

When a mouse button is depressed, *Click* receives a *DN* event and waits for a corresponding *UP*. When the *UP* is received, a *click* event is generated and the process restarts. If the *UP* event is not received within *clickTime*, *Click* emits a non-primitive *down* event to indicate to another process that the mouse button is being held down. Then it waits for the corresponding *UP* and re-emits it as an *up* signal.

Here is a process that detects clicks and double clicks:

```
DoubleClick =
  DN? .
    wait[clickTime] UP? .
      wait[doubleClickTime] DN? .
        wait[clickTime] UP? . doubleClick! . DoubleClick
        || click! . down! . UP? . up! . DoubleClick
      || click! . DoubleClick
    || down! . UP? . up! . DoubleClick
```

If *DoubleClick* receives two clicks with the proper timing, it emits a *doubleClick* event; otherwise if emits *click*, *down* and *up* events so another process can receive them.

If clicks and double clicks did not have timeouts, *DoubleClick* could call *Click* to interpret the single clicks. Because two timeouts are involved, though, the processes can get out of step. Consider the following erroneous implementation of *DoubleClick*:

```
DoubleClick =
  click? . wait[doubleClickTime]
              (click? . doubleClick! . DoubleClick)
              || (click! . DoubleClick)
```

If the timeout occurs, the *click*! action must be emitted to preserve the events, but it may appear after a *down* event emitted by *Click*. The two independent timeouts on the same stream of events have reordered the events. *DoubleClick* is therefore written as a single process with nested timeouts. If timeouts are not involved (and in practice they rarely are), constructing *squeak* programs hierarchically works well.

Compilation

A *squeak* program is compiled by analyzing all the possible execution sequences of the program, and expanding them into C code. There is no scheduling on user channels: scheduling and communications are 'compiled away,' producing efficient sequential code segments interleaved with random choices and calls to the underlying primitive event manager. This is made practical by two properties of the language. First, there are restrictions on its expressive power, primarily that the syntax only allows a fixed number of processes, and all the channels are statically known. Second, most practical programs focus their activity on the external device channels rather than on inter-process communication. The special nature of the primitive events in *squeak* are essential to its usefulness and practicality.

Primitive events are handled by three C functions that monitor the mouse, buttons, clock and other I/O devices of the system. The event types are button transitions, mouse motion, mouse entering or leaving a rectangle, keyboard characters typed, and clicks of the 60Hz clock. (Our display is a Teletype DMD-5620 terminal running a simple non-preemptive multiprogramming system similar to that described in [Pike 83].) The function *waitevent(elist)* suspends the calling process until one of the events in the list is pending. The return value is the name of one of the pending events. The event remains pending until *event(e)* is called with an argument naming the desired event. *Event* returns a structure describing the event, including information such as, for example, which rectangle was entered. *Event* will call *waitevent* if no event is pending. *Waitevent* also allows a timeout to be specified for each of the events being awaited. Finally, *testevent(e)* tests whether any of the named events are pending. The split structure of the event code simplifies the implementation of processes awaiting multiple events: a C **switch** statement selects, based on the return value of *waitevent*, which event to read and which variable should receive the event's return value. Because the type of the return value depends on the event and two values are returned per event, it is clumsy to read events in a single call. An event called *alarm* is enabled by a separate function, and is generated when the specified number of clock ticks have elapsed.

Device interrupts place event descriptors on queues. There is one queue for each device — keyboard, mouse button, etc. — so *waitevent* simply examines the head of all the queues to see what events are pending. Each event has a time stamp which is compared with the current time when timeouts are activated on a queue. If the program examines the queues often, timeouts are straightforward to implement. But since the program may compute for a significant time between successive calls to *waitevent*, timeouts in the past must make sense. The algorithm is this: When an event is returned to the program, its time stamp is recorded. When the program enables a timeout, *waitevent* decrements the timeout period by the interval between the last event returned and minimum of the present time and the time of the next event (if any) in the queue being timed out. If the timeout period becomes negative, a timeout is generated. Otherwise the next event is returned if it exists, or the regular timeout code is executed if not. It is the decrement of the timeout period that lets the program catch up with real time.

A communication on a user channel is transformed into a simple assignment. A matching pair of actions $a?x$ and $a!3$ becomes $x=3$. A nondeterministic choice between primitive events is compiled to a call to the underlying event code. As soon as one of the events is available, control is returned to the *squeak* program, which selects the appropriate process continuation for that event. A nondeterministic choice between user communications becomes a random choice between the possible execution paths. When a choice must be made between primitive events and user communications, *testevent* is called to check which primitive events are pending, and the choice made dynamically among the possible paths.

A parallel composition of processes is compiled into all the possible interleavings of primitive actions and communications of the component processes. This is done by advancing one of the processes one step, and considering all the possible continuations of that and all other processes. The state of the entire system is then restored to the initial state, and another path considered, advancing another process or the same process by a different action. This procedure is repeated until all possible executions have been considered. When more than one execution path is possible at a point, the set of possible communications is pruned and flattened to eliminate all the avoidable deadlocks and redundant nested execution paths, according to the laws $p + <> = p$ and $((p+q)+r) = (p+(q+r))$. The remaining available paths are compiled as a dynamic random selection of which path to take. A process identifier is simply expanded into the corresponding definition.

There are some optimizations that can be made during code generation. Note that any legal interleavings of the actions of parallel straight-line processes that do not access primitive events are equivalent. It is therefore unnecessary to generate all possible interleavings; one will do. The same applies within all subsequences of selections. The compiler therefore 'pushes' all processes as far as they can legally go, without accessing any primitive events, until the system is deadlocked. At this point, some processes will probably be blocked on primitive events, so the code is generated to access the event and choose subsequent execution depending on which event is received. For this to be successful, of course, the program must access primitive events, but a *squeak* program whose execution does not depend heavily on external inputs is probably pathological. To avoid loops in the compilation and to keep the generated code small, at each step of the compilation the translator detects states that have already occurred in the translation process, and generates jumps back to them, thereby folding the executions paths together at common states.

Here is a simple example, followed by the output of the translator:

```
proc p  = DN? . <a?x . <c?z . p :: d?k . UP? . p> :: b?y . p>
proc q  = <a!1 . d!2 . q :: b!3 . UP? . q>
proc r  = c!4 . UP? . a!5 . r
example = p & q & r

example(){
        int x, y, z, k;
        Lab0:event(DN);
        Lab1:switch(nrand(2)){   /* 'a' or 'b' */
        case 0:   /* 'a' */
                x=(1);
        Lab2:   switch(nrand(2)){    /* 'c' or 'd' */
                case 0:   /* 'c' */
                        z=(4);
                        switch(waitevent(DN|UP)){
                        case DN:
                                event(DN);
                                event(UP);
        Lab5:                   x=(5);
                                goto Lab2;
                        case UP:
                                event(UP);
                                event(DN);
                                goto Lab5;
                        }
                case 1:   /* 'd' */
                        k=(2);
                        event(UP);
                        goto Lab0;
                }
        case 1:   /* 'b' */
                y=(3);
                switch(waitevent(DN|UP)){
                case DN:
                        event(DN);
                        event(UP);
                        goto Lab1;
                case UP:
                        event(UP);
                        goto Lab0;
}       }       }
```

Initially, nothing can execute until p receives a *DN* event. It can then exchange with q either an a message, setting x to 1, or a b message, setting y to 3. It is instructive to follow through the rest of the execution tree. Note particularly the state folding at *Lab* 1, and where p and r exchange an a message, setting x to 5. The assignment to x occurs in two different execution paths that are folded together at *Lab* 5. The innermost switch could actually be compiled into better code, since the order of receipt of the *DN* and *UP* events is irrelevant, but detecting situations like this requires looking at the states of processes after actions not yet compiled (that is, looking into the future), which our implementation does not do.

Use of squeak for complex interfaces

Although *squeak* was designed to program the lowest levels of a user interface, it can be used effectively to construct the higher levels by combining *squeak* programs hierarchically, treating larger events such as menu selections in the same manner as primitive events.

Consider the implementation of a hypothetical paint program on a bitmap display with a three-button mouse. A pair of *Click*-like processes monitor the left and middle buttons. The left button sets bits, the middle button clears them. When a click is received, a single instance of the brush is placed in the picture, with boolean combination function depending on which button was clicked. If *Click* generates a *down* event, multiple copies of the brush are laid out along the path traced by the mouse until an *UP* event is generated by the mouse. A *Menu* process is invoked whenever the right button is depressed, to select commands to change brushes, read and write files, and so on. Some action, perhaps a menu selection or a double click, invokes a high-resolution paint program that operates on individual pixels in a magnified portion of the picture.

By coding a *squeak* program that takes as arguments functions to call for the left and middle buttons, and a menu for the third button, the user interface can be made nearly identical in both painting modes: the regular paint program is instantiated with procedures to draw the brushes and the main menu, and the action that invokes the high-resolution program calls the same program recursively, but with arguments appropriate to painting individual pixels. Only one user interface need be written.

Of course, it may be possible to apply these ideas to the operating system itself. The concurrency in a *squeak* program is compiled out because processes are fairly expensive in a conventional operating system. If process scheduling is sufficiently fast, however, as in many real-time operating systems, it may be feasible to run *squeak programs* (not processes) as operating system processes. If the primitive events are known to the scheduler, it is possible to write a *squeak* program to read events from each input device and emit higher-level events. The higher-level events can then enter the scheduler as 'primitive' events to be dispatched to other processes. For example, the *Click* and *DoubleClick* processes above could interpret mouse button transitions for a set of independent user-level programs sharing the mouse, much as in the Blit operating system **mpx** [Pike 83].

Formal semantics: Concurrency and time flow

The interrelationships of the parallel processes and communications and timeouts lead to intricate flows of control. We defined the formal semantics of *squeak* as a tool for understanding the detailed behavior of *squeak* programs. In fact, our first attempt at a compiler failed because we underestimated the complexity of the behavior of parallel communicating processes. Once we had specified the formal semantics, our understanding was good enough that the second compiler was easy to write.

The semantics of *squeak* is given in a language called *formal squeak*. The two languages are very similar, but not identical. The major difference is that in *formal squeak* all delays between actions are explicit. To give the semantics of a *squeak* program, we translate it into *formal squeak*. First, all *squeak* actions $a?x.$ or $a!v.$ are converted to *formal squeak* actions $a?x:$ or $a!v:$. The latter mean "do the action immediately, and at the next time unit do the rest of the process (immediately)." To preserve the meaning of the original *squeak* program, we then introduce explicit delays between actions where they are needed.

A process is called *urgent* if all its immediate actions have timeouts, and is called *patient* if all its immediate actions do not have timeouts. Otherwise it is called *sloppy*. If the process following an action is urgent, no delay is introduced. If the process following an action is patient, a delay operator (δ) is introduced after the action. Finally, the top-level processes in the main program are examined, and the patient ones are prefixed by a delay. If a sloppy process is found, an error is reported.

We use operational semantics [Plotkin 81] to describe the meaning of *formal squeak* programs. A process in a state p can transfer to a state p' by a transition λ. In our case a transition can be an input action $a?v$, an output action $a!v$, a silent action (passage of one time unit), written 1, or several simultaneous actions.

The possible state transitions are expressed by a set of *inference rules*, listed below. There are two kinds of rules. In some situations a process can autonomously change state: these *ground rules* have the form $p \xrightarrow{\lambda} p'$. In other situations a process can change state only if a part of it can change state according to the inference rules; these *conditional rules* have the form $p \xrightarrow{\lambda} p' \Rightarrow q \xrightarrow{\lambda'} q'$. The implication sign is also written as a fraction line, with the condition above it and the consequence below.

A process δp can spend some time doing 1 actions and then do whatever action p can do.

A simple output process, like $a!v:p$, can autonomously do an $a!v$ transition and become p. As mentioned above, $a!v:p$ means "do $a!v$ immediately, then at the next time unit do p." Hence $a!v.p$ is equivalent to $a!v:\delta p$, if p does not have immediate timeouts.

If there is a timeout, such as $wait[3]a!v:p \parallel q$, and a silent action is performed, then the passage of time decrements the timeout period: $wait[3]a!v:p \parallel q \xrightarrow{1} wait[2]a!v:p \parallel q$. If the $a!v$ action is not selected in time, the process will degenerate into $wait[0]a!v.p \parallel q$ which can perform only q. Input timeouts are treated similarly.

A process $a?x:p$ can receive any value on a, hence it can perform *all* the actions $a?v$ for any possible input value v. Therefore, $a?x:p$ is allowed to make autonomously any $a?v$ action, but only one of those v will be the right one — the one which is produced by a matching output action. Communication therefore occurs as pairs of actions; this is discussed in detail below.

A nondeterministic choice of processes can perform any action allowed by any of its component processes. As soon as a component process is chosen, the others are discarded.

A parallel composition of processes can perform an action only if all its components perform an action. The resulting action is a composite *product* action of all the component actions. For example, in $p \& q$, p may produce a $a?v$ action and q may produce a $b!w$ action. The resulting action for $p \& q$ is $a?v \& b!w$, the simultaneous occurrence of $a?v$ and $b!w$. Note that if a component of a parallel composition deadlocks, the whole composition deadlocks.

There are rules for simplifying these action products. A product of the form $a?v \& a!v$ reduces to 1, which models the exchange of a value v on channel a between exactly two processes. Moreover, the silent action is absorbed in products: $a?v \& 1$ is $a?v$. Because two complementary actions reduce to 1, the named channel has been used for communication, and the matching two actions are no longer available to other processes.

How does communication happen? According to the rules for input and output actions, it seems that inputs and outputs on a channel can happen independently and need not happen simultaneously, or transmit the same value. However, as one of many possible situations, input and output actions *may* match.

The restriction rule, labeled [Restr] in the list of rules below, is used to prune those situations in which inputs and outputs do not match: communications which *may* happen are *forced* to happen. When two communications match, the resulting action for the whole system is a 1. Hence, to force possible internal communications to happen, a subsystem is forced to exhibit only 1 transitions, or external communications. The notation $p \mid R$, where p is a process and R a set of actions, prevents p from emitting those actions not contained in R, although such actions may still be reduced to 1 within p. The notation used in the syntax is $p \setminus a$, which is equivalent to $p|R$ where R is the complement of the set containing all the single or composite actions having an a component; that is, $p \setminus a$ prevents p from exporting any action containing a.

For semantic purposes, a *main* program p in the syntax should be intended as $p|Prim$, which can perform only primitive actions in the set *Prim*, which by definition always contains 1. All the other user-defined actions that p may want to perform are *inhibited* by $p|Prim$; note that this is stronger that just filtering them away. Hence all the user-defined actions that components of p may perform must be matched by other components of p and reduced to 1; otherwise a deadlock will occur.

The following are the operational semantic rules for interpreting *formal squeak*. There are no rules for reducing expressions; we simply assume that expressions are already reduced to their final value wherever they occur. The letter v will be used to denote values.

[Delay] $\delta p \xrightarrow{1} \delta p \qquad \dfrac{p \xrightarrow{\lambda} p'}{\delta p \xrightarrow{\lambda} p'}$

[Wait] $\mathrm{wait}[n+1]p \parallel q \xrightarrow{1} \mathrm{wait}[n]p \parallel q$

$$\dfrac{p \xrightarrow{\lambda} p'}{\mathrm{wait}[n+1]p \parallel q \xrightarrow{\lambda} p'} \qquad \dfrac{q \xrightarrow{\lambda} q'}{\mathrm{wait}[0]p \parallel q \xrightarrow{\lambda} q'}$$

[Input] $a?id{:}proc \xrightarrow{a?v} proc\{v/id\}$

[Output] $a!v{:}proc \xrightarrow{a!v} proc$

[If] $$\dfrac{proc_0 \xrightarrow{\lambda} proc_0'}{\text{if true then } proc_0 \text{ else } proc_1 \text{ fi} \xrightarrow{\lambda} proc_0'}$$

$$\dfrac{proc_1 \xrightarrow{\lambda} proc_1'}{\text{if false then } proc_0 \text{ else } proc_1 \text{ fi} \xrightarrow{\lambda} proc_1'}$$

[Choice] $$\dfrac{proc_0 \xrightarrow{\lambda} proc_0'}{proc_0 + proc_1 \xrightarrow{\lambda} proc_0'} \qquad \dfrac{proc_1 \xrightarrow{\lambda} proc_1'}{proc_0 + proc_1 \xrightarrow{\lambda} proc_1'}$$

[Par] $$\dfrac{proc_0 \xrightarrow{\lambda_0} proc_0' \quad proc_1 \xrightarrow{\lambda_1} proc_1'}{proc_0 \;\&\; proc_1 \xrightarrow{\lambda_0 \& \lambda_1} proc_0' \;\&\; proc_1'}$$

[Rename] $$\dfrac{proc \xrightarrow{\lambda} proc'}{proc\{id/id'\} \xrightarrow{\lambda\{id/id'\}} proc'}$$

[Restr] $$\dfrac{proc \xrightarrow{\lambda} proc'}{proc|R \xrightarrow{\lambda} proc'|R} \quad \text{if } \lambda \in R$$

[Def] $$\dfrac{proc\{actuals/formals\} \xrightarrow{\lambda} proc'}{pid(actuals) \xrightarrow{\lambda} proc'}$$

where $pid(formals) = proc \in \mathrm{Defn}$

where *Defn* is the set of process definitions for a particular *squeak* program.

A simple example may clarify how the semantics works. Consider the following process (where we have taken some syntactic liberties to match the semantic rules):

```
proc p = a?x : <>
proc q = a!3 : <>  +  b?y : <>
simple = (p & q) | Prim
```

All possible actions of the components from the bottom up must be computed to determine the actions of the whole. The p component can do all actions of the form $a?v$. The q component can perform $a!3$ and all actions $b?w$. Their parallel composition can perform all the possible products of $a?v$ with $a!3$ and of $a?v$ with $b?w$. These product actions are: $(a?3 \;\&\; a!3) = 1$, $(a?v \;\&\; a!3)$ for $v \neq 3$, and $(a?v \;\&\; b?w)$ for all v and w. But of all these actions, only 1 is in the Prim set. Hence $(p \;\&\; q) \mid Prim$ can do only a 1 action, which corresponds to the communication of 3 on channel a between p and q.

Conclusions

Squeak is a concurrent language for specifying interactive user interfaces. It can express complex time-dependent interfaces in a compact notation. Although *squeak* could be developed into a full-blown language, we use it to express subroutines which are then integrated in larger programs written in a conventional sequential language (C).

The integration of concurrent subsystems in sequential programs is achieved by compiling concurrency into sequential code whose execution is controlled by the sequencing of external device events. It is interesting that in the restricted domain of *squeak* programs, the context switches between concurrent processes can be compiled out.

The real-time behavior of *squeak* is subtle, and we have found it helpful to express the language's semantics formally, using the methods of operational semantics.

References

[Berry 84] Berry, G., "The ESTEREL synchronous programming language and its mathematical semantics," *Proc. of the NSF/SERC workshop on concurrency,* CMU, 1984.

[van den Bos 83] van den Bos, J., Plasmeijer, M.J. and Hartel, P.H., "Input-Output Tools: A Language Facility for Interactive and Real-Time Systems," *IEEE Trans. Soft. Eng.*, **SE-9**(3), pp. 247-259, 1983.

[Buxton 83] Buxton, W., Lamb, M. R., Sherman, D. and Smith, K.C., "A User Interface Management System," *USENIX Conf. Proc.*, June 1983, pg. 177.

[Hoare 78] Hoare, C.A.R., "Communicating Sequential Processes," *Comm. ACM* **21**(8), pp. 666-678, 1978.

[Kernighan 78], Kernighan, B.W. and Ritchie, D.M., *The C Programming Language,* Prentice-Hall 1978.

[Milner 80] Milner, R., "A Calculus of Communicating Systems," *Lecture Notes in Computer Science, nr.92,* Springer-Verlag, 1980.

[Milner 82] Milner, R., "Four combinators for concurrency," *ACM SIGACT-SIGOPS Symp. on Princ. of Distributed Computing,* Ottawa, Canada, 1982.

[Pike 83] Pike, R., "The Blit: A Multiplexed Graphics Terminal," *AT&T Bell Labs Tech. J.*, **63**(8), part 2, pp. 1607-1631

[Plotkin 81] Plotkin, G.D., "A Structural Approach to Operational Semantics," *Internal Report DAIMI FN-19,* Computer Science Department, Aarhus University, September 1981.

[Thomas 83] Thomas, J.J. and Hamlin, G., "Graphical Input Interaction Technique Workshop Summary," *Computer Graphics,* January 1983, pp. 5-30.

The University of Alberta User Interface Management System

Mark Green
Department of Computing Science
University of Alberta
Edmonton, Alberta, Canada

ABSTRACT: In this paper the design and implementation of the University of Alberta user interface management system (UIMS) is discussed. This UIMS is based on the Seeheim model of user interfaces, which divides the user interface into three separate components. The Seeheim model of user interfaces is discussed along with its relationship to the design of UIMSs. The techniques used to design the three user interface components are briefly presented. A mixture of interactive and written notations are used in the design of the user interface. Some interesting features of this UIMS are interactive screen and menu layout, support for three dialogue notations, flexible interface to the application program, ability to adapt to different users, and the use of concurrent processes in user interface implementation The techniques used in the implementation of this UIMS are discussed.

KEYWORDS: user interface design, user interface management systems, human-computer interaction

1. Introduction

The user interface is the component of a computer system that stands between the user and the rest of the system. Good software engineering practice suggests that the user interface should be a separate program module. All interactions between the user and the program are handled by the user interface module (in this paper the term user interface will usually mean the user interface module that implements it). A separate user interface module naturally leads to the notion of a User Interface Management System (UIMS). A UIMS facilitates the design, construction, and maintenance of user interfaces. A good introduction to current research on UIMSs can be found in the reports of the Graphical Input Interaction Technique workshop sponsored by SIGGRAPH [17] and the Seeheim Workshop on User Interface Management Systems sponsored by Eurographics and IFIPS [18].

In this paper we discuss the design and implementation of the University of Alberta UIMS (for lack of a better name). This UIMS is based on the Seeheim model of user interfaces that was developed at the Seeheim workshop. This model is presented in section 2 of this paper. Some of the user interface design tools provided by the University of Alberta UIMS are briefly described in section 3. The set of design tools is fairly extensive and cannot be properly described in one paper. The fourth section describes the run-time structure of the user interfaces produced by this UIMS. This section presents a general implementation strategy for user interfaces based on the Seeheim model. The last section summarizes this work and provides suggestions for further research.

There were a number of reasons for developing the UIMS presented in this paper. First, we wanted to evaluate the feasibility of the Seeheim model as the basis for UIMSs. When this model was proposed it had not been used as the basis of a user interface or a UIMS, so there was no way of evaluating it. By basing our UIMS on the Seeheim model we have some evidence for its usability. Second, we wanted a test bed for our ideas on user interface design and implementation. We wanted a way of testing our ideas without building a complete user interface or UIMS. Third, we wanted a practical tool that can be used in other research projects within our department. The last two goals are to some degree contradictory. The last goal implies that the UIMS should be relatively stable so other users have a solid foundation to build on. On the other hand the second goal requires the UIMS to be relatively easy to modify. This question is discussed further in section 5.

2. The Seeheim Model of User Interfaces

In this section we briefly describe the Seeheim model of user interfaces, a more detailed description of this model is presented in [6]. This model was developed at the Seeheim Workshop on User Interface Management Systems by a working group whose members were: Jan Derksen, Ernest Edmonds, Mark Green, Dan Olsen, and Robert Spence. The Seeheim model is based on dividing the user interface into three components as shown in fig. 1. The presentation component is responsible for the physical appearance of the user interface including all the device interactions. The dialogue control component manages the dialogue between the user and the program. The application interface model forms the interface between the user interface and the rest of the program. It is the user interface's view of the application program.

The information flowing between the components is in the form of tokens. Each token consists of a type field, which identifies the token, and a number of data fields that depend upon the type of the token. This abstract representation is independent of the devices used by the user interface. The only component of the user interface that must deal with the details of devices is the presentation component. An input token is a token moving from the user towards the application and an output token is moving from the application towards the user.

2.1. Presentation Component

The presentation component can be viewed as the lexical level of the user interface. It is responsible for screen management, information display, input devices, interaction techniques and lexical feedback. The menus in an application are part of the presentation component. When the user selects an item from a menu the presentation component generates an input token that is sent to the dialogue control component. If multiple menus are used dialogue control sends output tokens to the presentation component indicating when the menus should be active. The presentation component guarantees that the user can always select from any of the active menus, but beyond this dialogue control has no control over menu appearance.

There are a number of advantages to having a separate presentation component. First, all the device interactions are isolated in this component. This increases the portability of the user interface since only the presentation component needs to be changed when the user interface is moved to a different display device. The presentation component can be designed to support a range of display devices and automatically adapt to the one being used. This is easier to do when the device interactions are isolated in one component. Second, a separate presentation component provides a convenient means of tailoring the lexical level of the user interface to individual users. The screen layout can be changed to accommodate both left and right handed users, default command options can be changed, and the user can select his favorite interaction or display technique for a particular type of data. Third, a separate presentation component encourages the development and use of a standard library of interaction techniques. This will reduce the cost of user interfaces and improve their quality.

2.2. Dialogue Control Component

The dialogue control component manages the dialogue between the user and the application. This component converts the stream of input tokens originating in the presentation component into a structure representing the commands and operands intended by the user. This structure is then converted into a sequence of input tokens sent to the application interface model in order to execute the command. Similarly the output tokens sent by the application interface model are interpreted by dialogue control and a sequence of output tokens for the presentation component is generated.

Most existing UIMSs have concentrated on the dialogue control component, therefore, we have more experience with it than the other components. There are three main notations for the dialogue between the user and computer. These notations are recursive transition networks, BNF grammars, and events.

2.2.1. Recursive Transition Networks

A recursive transition network (RTN) is a collection of directed graphs. Each directed graph has a set of nodes representing the state of the dialogue, and a set of arcs representing the actions the user can perform. An arc connects two nodes in the directed graph. The user interface moves from the state at the end of the arc to the state at its head if the user performs the action labeling the arc. In a given state the user must perform one of the actions that labels an arc leaving the node representing that state. The arc labels are either the name of an input token generated by the presentation component or the name of another directed graph. In the latter case the named directed graph must be traversed before the state at the end of the arc is reached. In the case of recursive transition networks a directed graph can reference itself.

The tokens to be sent to the application interface model or presentation component can be attached to either the arcs or the nodes (in some systems they can be attached to both). If a token is attached to an arc the token is sent when the arc is traversed. If a token is attached to a node it is sent when the node is entered.

The use of multiple directed graphs facilitates the description of large user interfaces and increases the descriptive power of the technique. The use of a transition network to describe the login sequence for a time sharing system is shown in fig. 2.

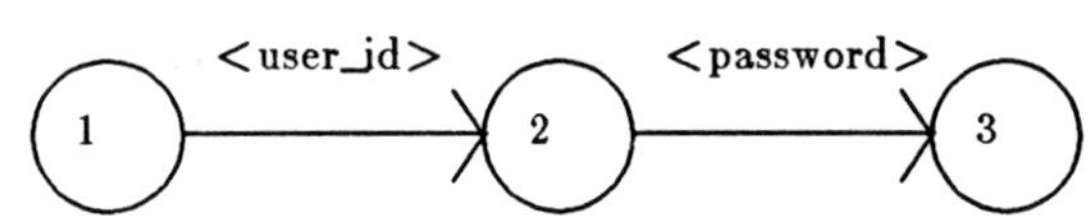

Actions:

1) print 'login:'

2) print 'password:'

3) print 'login junk ....'

Fig. 2 Transition diagram for login sequence

Transition diagrams have been used extensively in UIMSs. One of the earliest uses of transition diagrams is the work of Newman [15]. Another example of their use is the

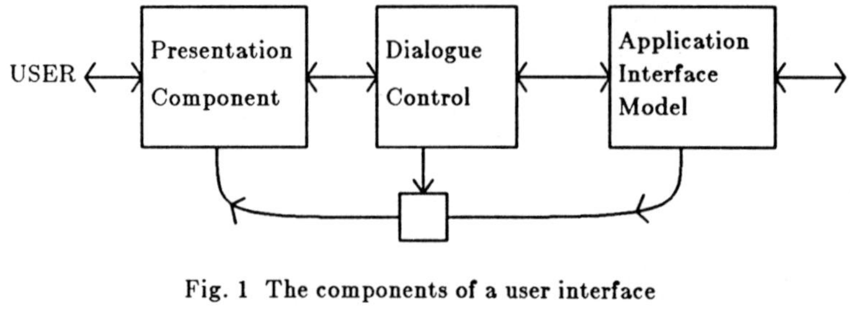

Fig. 1 The components of a user interface

SYNICS system developed by Edmonds [4]. An extension of RTNs called augmented transition networks (ATN) have been used for parsing natural languages [21]. In an ATN arbitrary functions can be attached to the arcs. These functions can store values in registers and use the register values to determine whether an arc should be traversed. This extension greatly increases the computational power of transition networks (ATNs are equivalent to Turing machines).

2.2.2. Context Free Grammars

The second notation for the dialogue control component is context free grammars or BNF. The terminals in these grammars are the input tokens produced by the presentation component. The non-terminals and productions are used to structure the dialogue. For example, there could be a non-terminal for each of the commands in the user interface. The productions with these non-terminals on the left side define the structure or syntax of the commands. A BNF grammar for the login example is shown in fig. 3.

```
login -> user_id password
user_id -> <character_string>
password -> <character_string>
```

Fig. 3 BNF grammar for the login sequence

The grammar in fig. 3 only describes the actions performed by the user, it does not cover the output produced by the program. In order to do this some way of associating tokens with the productions is required. Whenever a production is used in the parse of the user's input these tokens are sent to the presentation component or application interface model.

An unresolved issue with this approach to dialogue control is how to handle the output tokens passed from the application interface model to dialogue control. In some types of dialogues (mixed or system initiated) this flow of tokens may be just as important as the one originating in the presentation component.

Two examples of the use of grammars in the construction of user interfaces are the SYNGRAPH system of Olsen and Dempsey [14] and the work of Hanau and Lenorovitz [11].

2.2.3. Events

The third main notation for the dialogue control component is events. This notation is loosely based on the object oriented approach to user interface design used in Smalltalk [5] and related languages. In this notation the input tokens from the presentation component and the output tokens from the application interface model are viewed as events. These events are processed by event handlers. Each event handler has its own collection of local variables and a collection of procedures for processing events. When an event handler receives an event the associated procedure is executed. These procedures can perform calculations, send events to other event handlers, and send tokens to the presentation component and application interface model. The dialogue control component consists of a collection of event handlers that can change dynamically.

There are several important differences between the event notation and Smalltalk. The event handlers perform the same function as the objects and classes in Smalltalk. The main difference is that there is no explicit inheritance mechanism for event handlers. The main difference between messages and events is that messages are synchronous and events are asynchronous. When a Smalltalk object sends a message it suspends its execution and transfers control to the receiving object. When the receiving object completes its computation control returns to the sending object with a value for the message. In the case of events there is no hand shaking between the sending and receiving event handlers. An event has no value in the sending event handler and the receiving event handler may receive the event any time after it is generated (the sending event handler may not suspend its execution when it generates an event).

An event handler for the login sequence example is shown in fig. 4. This event handler responds to two types of events. The Init event is sent when the event handler is created. In response to this event the login message is printed. The other event is received whenever the user types a character string. The "state" variable is used to determine whether the character string is a user id or a password. In practice the print and process_login statements would be tokens sent to the presentation component and application interface model.

```
Eventhandler login Is

  Token
    keyboardstring s;

  Var
    int state = 0;
    string user_id, password;

  Event Init {
    print "login:";
  }

  Event s : string {
    if(state == 0) {
      user_id = s;
      state = 1;
      print "password:";
    } else {
      password = s;
      state = 0;
      process_login(user_id,password);
    };
  }

End login;
```

Fig. 4 Event handler for the login sequence

The obvious disadvantage to the event notation is that it looks more like a program than the other two notations (depending upon personal biases this may be an advantage). This disadvantage is offset by a number of advantages. First, the expressive power of events is greater than that of recursive transition networks or grammars (the event notations is equivalent to Turing machines while recursive transition networks and BNF grammars are equivalent to pushdown automata [8]). This implies that there are user interfaces that can be described by events that cannot be described by recursive transition networks or BNF grammars. The dialogues in these user interfaces typically depend upon the context of the interaction (the next step in the dialogue depends upon the values of previously entered operands, not just their syntax). The ATN notations mentioned in section 2.2.1 are also capable of describing these dialogues and have the same descriptive power as the event notations. It is important to note that the additional descriptive power of the event notation may not be useful or desirable. The main point of this observation is that dialogues described in the other notations can always be translated into the event notation. This observation forms the basis of our implementation of the dialogue control component. Second, events support multi-threaded dialogues. Since each event handler has its own local state and multiple event handlers can be active at any one time, the user is free to move from any spot in the dialogue to another without completing the current command or explicitly saving the state of the dialogue. In this way event handlers can be developed for help, cancel and other special commands that must always be available. The event handlers processing these commands will always be available whenever the user enters them, it does not require special programming.

2.3. Application Interface Model

The application interface model is the user interface's view of the application. It contains descriptions of all the application's data structures and routines that are accessible to the user interface. The description of this component can be divided into two sections. The first section contains the descriptions of the application routines and data structures. These descriptions are at an abstract or logical level, they are not concerned with how the data structures or routines are implemented.

The description of the application's data structures include the type of information stored and how it is structured. This description might also include the routines that can be used to access and modify the data structures. The description of the application's routines include the name of the routine and the number and types or its parameters. The routine descriptions might also include pre- and post-conditions. The pre-conditions state the conditions that must hold before the routine can successfully be used. They can be used to detect semantic errors, such as manipulating a database before it is opened or printing a binary file. The post-conditions describe the effect of the routine. They can be used to generate help information or aid in undo processing.

The second section of the description of the application interface model covers how the user interface communicates with the application. There are three possible modes of communication called interaction modes. In the first interaction mode, the user initiated mode, the user interface calls routines in the application. This is similar to the external control model presented at the Seattle workshop [17]. In the system initiated mode the application calls routines in the user interface. This is similar to the internal control model. The third interaction mode, mixed initiative, is based on two communicating processes, one for the user interface and one for the application. In this case neither the user interface nor the application has control over the other. In the mixed initiative mode some mechanism for interleaving the execution of the user interface and the application must be used. This could take the form of multiple processes or coroutines. The user interface designer specifies the interaction mode and the UIMS establishes the procedures to implement it. The descriptions of the presentation component and dialogue control are independent of the interaction mode.

3. Designing the User Interface

The University of Alberta UIMS is divided into two main parts, which are: user interface design and run-time support. The design part of the UIMS supports the user interface designer. It provides tools for describing screen layout, device assignments, dialogue structure, and the interaction with the application program. The result of the design part of the UIMS is a detailed specification of the user interface that can automatically be converted into the code required to implement it. The run-time part of the UIMS supports the execution of the user interface. It uses the results of the design part to form a complete executable user interface. This division of the UIMS into design and run-time support is fairly standard and is discussed further in [20].

In this section the design tools provided by the University of Alberta UIMS are briefly described. This discussion serves as the background for the description of the implementation techniques presented in the next section.

3.1. Designing the Presentation Component

The presentation component is concerned with the lexical level of the user interface, including screen layout, menu design, interaction techniques, and icon design. This suggests an interactive approach to the design of this component (this approach has been successfully used in the University of Toronto UIMS [2]). In the University of Alberta UIMS an interactive layout program is used to design the presentation component and a window based graphics package, called WINDLIB [9], is used as the basis of its implementation.

WINDLIB is a window based graphics package similar to the GiGo package developed by Rosenthal [16]. WINDLIB has all the features normally associated with window systems including overlapping windows that can be moved and resized. Some of the nonstandard features of this package are device independence and a set of two and three dimensional graphics primitives. Three features of WINDLIB are used extensively in the presentation component. These features are events, event handlers, and contents structures.

All the input in WINDLIB is in the form of events. An event has a name, a position, and possibly some event specific data. The event name indicates the device that generated the event. In the case of keyboards and other devices that don't generate coordinate information the position of the display's pointing device is used as the position of the event. A window can have an event handler associated with it. An event handler is a procedure that processes the events that are directed at the window. The body of an event handler is usually a case statement on the name of the event. The event handlers can generate events to be sent to other windows. The window that receives a particular event is determined by examining the windows in priority order (from highest to lowest). The first window with an event handler covering the position of the event receives the event.

Contents structures are a hierarchical modeling scheme used for grouping together related pieces of graphical information. A contents structure can be displayed in any window that is currently on the screen. WINDLIB provides contents structures for its two and three dimensional graphics primitives. The programmer can define his own type of contents structure. Programmer defined contents structures are used to represent graphical information in a form that is more convenient to the application. For example, in a charting application the programmer could define contents structures for line graphs, pie charts, bar charts, and histograms. The application only needs to provide the data required for each type of chart, it does not need to produce the graphics primitives that draw the chart. When the programmer defines a contents structure he must provide a routine that traverses the contents structure converting it into graphics primitives. In this way the graphics programmer can provide the applications programmers with a set of routines and data structures that are tuned to their application.

The application programmers do not need to be experts in graphics or be concerned with how the data is displayed.

The design of the presentation component can be divided into three activities, screen layout, interaction techniques, and display techniques. These activities are supported by an interactive layout program, called ipcs (interactive presentation component specification), developed by G. Singh [19].

Ipcs allows the designer to divide the screen into a number of overlapping windows. The designer specifies the size and position of a window by pointing at two opposing corners. The designer can then specify the background colour of the window, its coordinate system, a name for the window, and an output token. The output token associated with a window is used to indicate when the window is to be displayed. When the presentation component receives this token the window is displayed on the screen. A menu can be associated with each of the windows. A menu can either be static (always displayed in the same position) or pop-up (the current cursor position is the upper left corner of the menu). Each menu is viewed as a collection of menu items. A menu item consists of an input token, and a text string or icon. When the menu item is selected its input token is sent to the dialogue control component.

A window can have an interaction technique associated with it. This interaction technique becomes the event handler for the window when it is displayed. The user interface designer specifies the interaction technique by entering the name of a C procedure. This C procedure performs the initialization required by the interaction technique and establishes its event handler. When the window associated with the event handler is removed from the screen a special finish event is sent to the event handler allowing it to deallocate any resources it has acquired. The user interface designer can select interaction techniques from a library or he can write his own.

Ipcs allows the designer to associate display procedures with each of the output tokens that can be processed by the presentation component. For each output token the designer specifies the name of a display procedure and a window where the information is to be displayed. The display procedure is either chosen from a library of standard display procedures or written by the designer. One of the standard display procedures calls WINDLIB to display the contents structure stored in the output token.

The description of the presentation component is stored in an FDB database [10]. This database stores the state of the design between ipcs sessions and is used to generate the presentation component at run time.

3.2. Designing the Dialogue Control Component

The University of Alberta UIMS supports all three notations for the dialogue control component. This gives the user interface designer considerable flexibility in his approach to the design of this component. In order to provide this flexibility the UIMS must have a common format that all three notations can be translated into. This common format forms the basis for the run-time support of the dialogue control component. Since the event notation has more descriptive power than the other two notations the common format, EBIF (Event Based Internal Form) is based on the event notation. EBIF is described in section 4.1.

3.2.1. Event Language

The event language used in the University of Alberta UIMS is based on the C programming language [12]. Since C is the main programming language used in our research group this significantly reduces the time required to learn the language. A program in the event language consists of a number of event handlers. The text of the program contains one or more event handler definitions. When the program is executed instances of these event handlers are created. It is the instances that perform computations, not the event handlers themselves. There may be several instances of the same event handler, parameters can be used to establish the state of an instance when it is created.

```
Eventhandler event_handler_name Is

  Token
    token_name event_name ;
        .
        .
        .

  Var
    type variable_name = initial_value ;
        .
        .
        .

  Event event_name : type {
     statements
  }
        .
        .
        .
  Event event_name : type {
     statements
  }

end event_handler_name;
```

Fig. 5 Structure of event handler declarations

The structure of an event handler declaration is shown in fig. 5. An event handler declaration is divided into three sections. The first section lists the tokens (either input or output) that the event handler can process. This information is used by the assembler (see section 4.2) to map tokens into events for event handlers. The event language compiler places the token information in a table separate from the event handlers. In this way the the assignment of token names, and the mapping between tokens and events can be changed (in the assembly process) without effecting the event handlers themselves.

The second section of an event handler declaration contains the declarations of the event handler's local variables. Each instance of the event handler has its own set of local variables, there is no sharing of storage between instances. A variable declaration consists of a type, a variable name, and an optional initial value. The type can be any valid C type that occupies the same amount of space as a pointer. This includes characters, integers, floating points numbers (single precision only) and pointers to any C type. This restriction simplifies the implementation of the language and may be lifted in the future.

The third section consists of event declarations. An event declaration starts with the keyword Event followed by the name of the event and its type. The body of the event declaration consists of one or more C statements. These statements are executed when an instance of the event handler receives this event. The statements can reference the instance's local variables and the global variables in the program. The data associated with the event is assigned to the event name before the execution of the statements in the event declaration.

There are a number of special procedures that are used in event handlers. The format of these procedures is shown in fig. 6. The create_instance procedure is used to create a new event handler instance. The parameters to this procedure are the name of the event handler, the number of local variables to be initialized and their initial values. The local variables are initialized in the order they are listed in the variable declaration section. The value returned by this procedure is the name of the new instance. When an instance is created an Init event is automatically sent to it. The send_event procedure is used to send an event to an event handler instance. The parameters to this procedure are the name of the instance, the name of the event, and the data associated with the event. The send_token procedure is used to send a token to another component of the user interface. The parameters to this procedure are the component to receive the token, the direction of the token (input or output), the name of the token, and its value. The destroy_instance procedure is used to destroy the instance that is given as its parameter. Before destroy_instance deallocates the instance a Finish event is sent to it. This event allows the instance to free any resources it has accumulated in its execution.

1) create_instance(event_handler, n, v_1, v_2, ... , v_n)

2) send_event(instance_name, event_name, value)

3) send_token(destination, direction, name, value)

4) destroy_instance(instance_name)

Fig. 6 Event language support procedures

More details on the event language and its implementation can be found in [3].

3.2.2. **Recursive Transition Networks**

In the University of Alberta UIMS an interactive approach is taken to the design of recursive transition networks. There is a natural graphical representation for recursive transition networks, this suggests that an interactive graphical approach is appropriate for them.

The interactive transition diagram editor produced by S.C. Lau [13] is used to enter and edit RTNs. This editor is based on a graphical display of the transition network. The designer can use a tablet or mouse to enter and edit the nodes and arcs in a diagram. Each arc in the diagram has an input token, and optional output tokens to be sent to the presentation component and application interface model when the arc is traversed. One interesting feature of this editor is the ability to select and save a group of nodes and arcs. This group can then be added to another diagram in the user interface.

The transition diagrams are stored in an FDB database. This database is used to store the diagrams between editing sessions and is used to generate the EBIF for the dialogue control component. A separate program is used to convert the transition diagrams to EBIF. More details on the transition diagram editor and conversion to EBIF can be found in [13].

3.2.3. **Grammars**

At the present time a grammar based notation has not been implemented. A number of grammar based notations exist (for example [14]). The major activity in implementing this type of notation is developing the algorithms required to convert productions into event handlers or EBIF. We intend to do this sometime in the future.

3.3. **Designing the Application Interface Model**

At the present time support for the application interface model is under development. Currently only one interaction mode (user initiated) is supported and the main use of this component is to map between tokens and the routines in the application.

The mapping between tokens and application routines may not be one-to-one. A token may cause several application routines to be executed, or it may contain data used in a subsequent call of an application routine. In order to support this behavior the application interface model must provide storage for saving token values and a means of associating a sequence of actions with a token.

```
Var
  type variable_name;
      .
      .
      .

Token token_name : token_type {
  statements
}
      .
      .
      .
```

Fig. 7 Structure of the application interface model

In the University of Alberta UIMS a written notation is used for describing the application interface model. This notation is converted into C code and tables which become part of the user interface at run-time. The structure of the application interface is shown in fig. 7. The first part of this description defines the storage locations used by the application interface model. The variable declarations in this section have the same syntax as C variable declarations. The values of these variable are preserved from one token to the next. The second section of the description contains one entry for each token processed by the application interface model. This entry contains the name of the token, its type, and the statements to be executed when it is received. The statements are standard C statements that can call application routines and save the value of the token. Note the similarity between the application interface model and the event language discussed in section 3.2.1.

4. Implementation

In this section an overview of the implementation of the University of Alberta UIMS is presented. This discussion centers around the structure of the event based internal form and how it is interpreted by the run-time routines.

4.1. EBIF

All the program used to design the dialogue control component produce EBIF as output. An EBIF file consists of a number of event handler definitions. Each event handler definition is divided into two parts. The first part contains information used by the run-time routines to create instances of event handlers and route tokens between these instances. This information is placed in the three main tables that drive the run-time routines (see fig. 8).

The second part of the event handler definition is a C procedure containing all the executable statements in the event handler. This procedure is called each time an event must be executed. The body of this procedure is a case statement on the name of the event. This procedure has four parameters, which are: the name of the instance, the name of the event to be processed, the value of the event, and an array containing the values of the instance's local variables.

The three tables used by the run-time routines are shown in fig. 8. The event table has one entry for each event handler. This entry contains a pointer to the corresponding C procedure, and the number of local variables for each instance. There is one entry in the instance table for each active instance. This entry points to the array containing the instance's variable values, and the index in the event table of the corresponding event handler. The token table is used to map between tokens and the event handlers that process them. Each entry in this table contains the name of a token, the name of the event it is converted to, and the event handler that can process it.

4.2. User Interface Assembly

The assembly of the user interface is performed by a program called the assembler. The input to this program is the EBIF files produced by the dialogue control programs, a file of the input and output tokens associated with the presentation component (produced by ipcs), the output file from the design of the application interface model, and a token definition file. The output from the assembler is a file of C routines, which must be compiled, and the tables used by the run-time support routines. The process of converting a program in the event language into an executable user interface is shown in fig. 9.

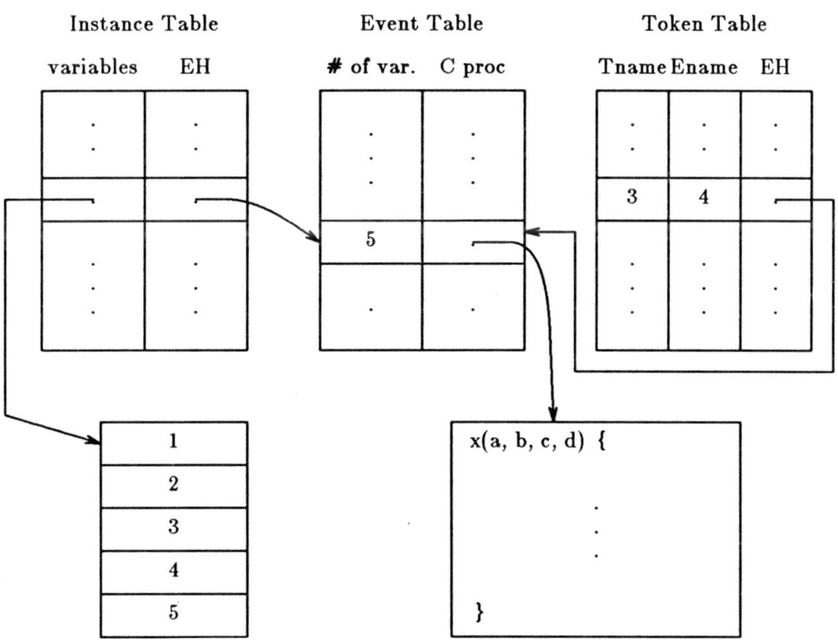

Fig. 8 Run-time tables

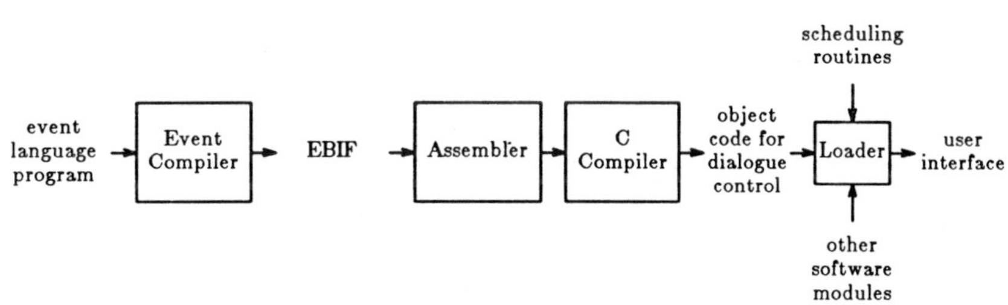

Fig. 9 Converting an event program into a user interface

4.3. Run-time Routines

In the design of the user interface it has been assumed that each of the components is a separate process. The only way of exchanging information between components is through tokens, which is an asynchronous communications mechanism. This illusion of concurrency must be maintained by the run-time support routines. The approach that we have used is to view the run-time routines as a scheduler that allocates processing time to the individual components. The unit of scheduling at the component level is the token.

When one component sends a token to another component that token is placed on a scheduling queue associated with the receiving component. The scheduler examines the scheduling queue associated with each of the components and selects one of the tokens for execution. Highest priority is placed on the presentation component, and lowest priority on the application interface model queue, with the restriction that a token will not be blocked for an arbitrary long time. The scheduler then calls the appropriate routine in the receiving component to process the token. This routine can be determined from the tables produced by the assembler.

1) If an input device has input ready call the presentation component to process it.

2) If there are pending events in dialogue control execute several of them

3) Select a token from one of the scheduling queues and execute it.

4) Goto step (1)

Fig. 10 Steps in the scheduling process

Both the presentation component and dialogue control have a lower level of scheduling. Before the higher level scheduler can process a token the presentation component determines if any of its input devices has a value ready. If this is the case the value is converted into a WINDLIB event and processed by the presentation component. Similarly if there are events waiting in the dialogue control component a small number of them are processed before the next token is processed. The steps in this two level scheduling process are shown in fig. 10.

This two level scheduling process has three main advantages. First, it gives priority to the components closer to the user, thus he will have fast feedback to lexical operations, and slower feedback to semantic operations. Second, it supports the view of the three components as separate processes allowing them to be designed separately. Third, it leaves the door open for the implementation of the user interface as three separate processes on three closely coupled processors, which may be feasible in the near future.

5. Summary

In this paper we have presented the design of the University of Alberta UIMS. The goals of this UIMS have been outlined along with discussions of its main components and implementation. The implementation has reached the point where we have built several small applications with the system. We are now working on rewriting all the interactive design programs so they use the UIMS.

One of our original aims was to produce a system architecture that allows for growth and experimentation, and at the same time supports production applications. We believe we have at least partially reached this goal by separating the design of the user interface from its run-time support. The run-time support is fairly stable and the users of the UIMS are largely not aware of the internal formats it uses. By taking this approach we hope to be able to incorporate comments from designers and users into future versions of the UIMS.

There are a number of enhancements and extensions to the University of Alberta UIMS that we would like to investigate. One of the most obvious extensions is adding a grammar based notation for the dialogue control component. This would give the user interface designer the full spectrum of design notations for this component. Another useful extension would be providing an interactive assembly program. This would be more convenient than the current batch approach to user interface assembly. It might also facilitate the management of different versions of the user interface intended for different workstations and user groups.

There are three extensions that have a significant research component. The first is developing a more flexible approach to screen layout. The current approach is based on a relatively static screen layout, the only variability is in pop-up menus. We would like to be able to automatically adjust the screen layout based on the type and amount of information displayed. For example, automatically changing the size of a window depending upon the amount of information stored in it, or automatic selection of display techniques based on the type of data and the amount of detail required. The second extension is automatic undo processing. This would be an extension to the application interface model that would allow the user to undo any recent action, or replay recent commands with different operands. This undo mechanism should be automatically provided by the UIMS. The third major extension involves the interaction between the UIMS and database systems. The schemas used by most database systems are a good first order approximation to the application interface model. Given a schema we would like to automatically produce the corresponding application interface model. The schema might also suggest commands and operations that should appear in the user interface. It might be possible to produce an augmented schema that can be used to produce both the database and the user interface. This issue is explored in [1].

References

[1] Armstrong W.W., M. Green, P. Srirangaptna, "A Database Management System and Associated Tools for a General Design Environment", Proceedings of the 1984 Canadian Conference on Very Large Scale Integration, p.183-187, 1984.

[2] Buxton W., M.R. Lamb, D. Sherman, K.C. Smith, "Towards a Comprehensive User Interface Management System", Siggraph'83 Proceedings, p.35-42, 1983.

[3] Chia M.S., *An Event Based Dialogue Specification for Automatic Generation of User Interfaces*, MSc Thesis, Department of Computing Science, University of Alberta, 1985 (expected).

[4] Edmonds E.A., "Adaptive Man-Computer Interfaces", in M.J. Coombs and J.L Alty, *Computing Skills and the User Interface,* Academic Press, London, 1981.

[5] Goldberg A., D. Robson, *Smalltalk-80: The Language and its Implementation,* Addison-Wesley, Reading Mass.,

1983.

[6] Green M., "Report on Dialogue Specification Tools", Computer Graphics Forum, vol.3, p.305-313, 1984.

[7] Green M., "The University of Alberta User Interface Management System: Design Principles", Human-Computer Interaction Project Report #1, Department of Computing Science, University of Alberta, 1984.

[8] Green M., "User Interface Models", Human-Computer Interaction Project Report #2, Department of Computing Science, University of Alberta, 1985.

[9] Green M., N. Bridgeman, "WINDLIB Programmer's Manual", Department of Computing Science, University of Alberta, 1985.

[10] Green M., M. Burnell, H. Vrenjak, M. Vrenjak, "Experiences With a Graphical Data Base System", Proceedings of Graphics Interface'83, p.257, 1983.

[11] Hanau P.R., D.R. Lenorovitz, "Prototyping and Simulation Tools for User/Computer Dialogue Design", Siggraph'80 Proceedings, p.271-278, 1980.

[12] Kernighan B.W., D.M. Ritchie, *The C Programming Language,* Prentice-Hall, Englewood Cliffs NJ, 1978.

[13] Lau S.C., *The Use of Recursive Transition Networks for Dialogue Design in User Interfaces,* MSc Thesis, Department of Computing Science, University of Alberta, 1985 (expected).

[14] Olsen D.R., E.P. Dempsey, "SYNGRAPH: A Graphic User Interface Generator", Siggraph'83 Proceedings, p.43-50, 1983.

[15] Newman W.M., "A System for Interactive Graphical Programming, SJCC 1968, Thompson Books, 1968.

[16] Rosenthal D.S.H, "Managing Graphical Resources", Computer Graphics, vol.17, no.1, p.38-45, 1983.

[17] Graphical Input Interaction Technique Workshop Summary, Computer Graphics, vol.17, no.1, p.5-66, 1983.

[18] Pfaff G., P.J.W. ten Hagan, *Seeheim Workshop on User Interface Management Systems,* Springer-Verlag, Berlin, 1985.

[19] Singh G., *Automatic Generation of Presentation Component for University of Alberta UIMS,* MSc Thesis, Department of Computing Science, University of Alberta, 1985 (expected).

[20] Tanner P.P., W.A.S. Buxton, "Some Issues in Future User Interface Management System Development", in G. Pfaff and P.J.W. ten Hagen (ed), *Seeheim Workshop on User Interface Management Systems,* Springer-Verlag, Berlin, 1985.

[21] Woods W.A., "Transition Network Grammars for Natural Language Analysis", CACM vol.13, no.10, p.591-606, 1970.

Issues and Techniques in Touch-Sensitive Tablet Input

William Buxton
Ralph Hill
Peter Rowley

Computer Systems Research Institute
University of Toronto
Toronto, Ontario
Canada M5S 1A4

(416) 978-6320

Abstract

Touch-sensitive tablets and their use in human-computer interaction are discussed. It is shown that such devices have some important properties that differentiate them from other input devices (such as mice and joysticks). The analysis serves two purposes: (1) it sheds light on touch tablets, and (2) it demonstrates how other devices might be approached. Three specific distinctions between touch tablets and one button mice are drawn. These concern the signaling of events, multiple point sensing and the use of templates. These distinctions are reinforced, and possible uses of touch tablets are illustrated, in an example application. Potential enhancements to touch tablets and other input devices are discussed, as are some inherent problems. The paper concludes with recommendations for future work.

CR Categories and Subject Descriptors: I.3.1 [**Computer Graphics**]: Hardware Architecture: Input Devices. I.3.6 [**Computer Graphics**]: Methodology and Techniques: Device Independence, Ergonomics, Interaction Techniques.

General Terms: Design, Human Factors.

Additional Keywords and Phrases: touch sensitive input devices.

1. Introduction

Increasingly, research in human-computer interaction is focusing on problems of input [Foley, Wallace & Chan 1984; Buxton 1983; Buxton 1985]. Much of this attention is directed towards input technologies. The ubiquitous Sholes keyboard is being replaced and/or complemented by alternative technologies. For example, a major focus of the marketing strategy for two recent personal computers, the Apple Macintosh and Hewlett-Packard 150, has been on the input devices that they employ (the mouse and touch-screen, respectively).

Now that the range of available devices is expanding, how does one select the best technology for a particular application? And once a technology is chosen, how can it be used most effectively? These questions are important, for as Buxton [1983] has argued, the ways in which the user *physically* interacts with an input device have a marked effect on the type of user interface that can be effectively supported.

In the general sense, the objective of this paper is to help in the selection process and assist in effective use of a specific class of devices. Our approach is to investigate a specific class of devices: touch-sensitive tablets. We will identify touch tablets, enumerate their important properties, and compare them to a more common input device, the mouse. We then go on to give examples of transactions where touch tablets can be used effectively. There are two intended benefits for this approach. First, the reader will acquire an understanding of touch tablet issues. Second, the reader will have a concrete example of how the technology can be investigated, and can utilize the approach as a model for investigating other classes of devices.

2. Touch-Sensitive Tablets

A touch-sensitive tablet (touch tablet for short) is a flat surface, usually mounted horizontally or nearly horizontally, that can sense the location of a finger pressing on it. That is, it is a tablet that can sense that it is being touched, and where it is being touched. Touch tablets can vary greatly in size, from a few inches on a side to several feet on a side. The most critical requirement is that the user is not required point with some manually held device such as a stylus or puck.

What we have described in the previous paragraph is a *simple* touch tablet. Only one point of contact is sensed, and then only in a binary, touch/no touch, mode. One way to extend the potential of a simple touch tablet is to sense the degree, or pressure, of contact. Another is to sense multiple points of contact. In this case, the location (and possibly pressure) of several points of contact would be reported. Most tablets currently on the market are of the "simple" variety. However, Lee, Buxton and Smith [1985], and Nakatani [private communication] have developed prototypes of multi-touch, multi-pressure sensing tablets.

We wish to stress that we will restrict our discussion of touch technologies to touch tablets, which can and should be used in ways that are different from touch screens. Readers interested in touch-screen technology are referred to Herot & Weinsapfel [1978], Nakatani & Rohrlich [1983] and Minsky [1984]. We acknowledge that a flat touch screen mounted horizontally is a touch tablet as defined above. This is not a contradiction, as a touch screen has exactly the properties of touch tablets we describe below, as long as there is no attempt to mount a display below (or behind) it or to make it the center of the user's visual focus.

Some sources of touch tablets are listed in Appendix A.

3. Properties of Touch-Sensitive Tablets

Asking "Which input device is best?" is much like asking "How long should a piece of string be?" The answer to both is: it depends on what you want to use it for. With input devices, however, we are limited in our understanding of the relationship between device properties and the demands of a specific application. We will investigate touch tablets from the perspective of improving our understanding of this relationship. Our claim is that other technologies warrant similar, or even more detailed, investigation.

Touch tablets have a number of properties that distinguish them from other devices:

- They have no mechanical intermediate device (such as stylus or puck). Hence they are useful in hostile environments (e.g., classrooms, public access terminals) where such intermediate devices can get lost, stolen, or damaged.
- Having no puck to slide or get bumped, the tracking symbol "stays put" once placed, thus making them well suited for pointing tasks in environments subject to vibration or motion (e.g., factories, cockpits).
- They present no mechanical or kinesthetic restrictions on our ability to indicate more than one point at a time. That is, we can use two hands or more than one finger simultaneously on a single tablet. (Remember, we can manually control at most two mice at a time: one in each hand. Given that we have ten fingers, it is conceivable that we may wish to indicate more than two points simultaneously. An example of such an application appears below).
- Unlike joysticks and trackballs, they have a very low profile and can be integrated into other equipment such as desks and low-profile keyboards (e.g., the Key Tronic Touch Pad, see Appendix A). This has potential benefits in portable systems, and, according to the Keystroke model of Card, Newell and Moran [1980], reduces homing time from the keyboard to the pointing device.
- They can be molded into one-piece constructions thus eliminating cracks and grooves where dirt can collect. This makes them well suited for very clean environments (eg. hospitals) or very dirty ones (eg., factories).
- Their simple construction, with no moving parts, leads to reliable and long-lived operation, making them suitable for environments where they will be subjected to intense use or where reliability is critical.

They do, of course, have some inherent disadvantages, which will be discussed at the close of the paper.

In the next section we will make three important distinctions between touch tablets and mice. These are:

- Mice and touch tablets vary in the number and types of events that they can transmit. The difference is especially pronounced when comparing to simple touch tablets.
- Touch tablets can be made that can sense multiple points of contact. There is no analogous property for mice.
- The surface of a tablet can be partitioned into regions representing a collection of independent "virtual" devices. This is analogous to the partitioning of a screen into "windows" or virtual displays. Mice, and other devices that transmit "relative change" information, do not lend themselves to this mode of interaction without consuming display real estate for visual feedback. With conventional tablets and touch tablets, graphical, physical or virtual templates can be placed over the input device to delimit regions. This allows valuable screen real estate to be preserved. Physical templates, when combined with touch sensing, permit the operator to sense the regions without diverting the eyes from the primary display during visually demanding tasks.

After these properties are discussed, a simple finger painting program is used to illustrate them in the context of a concrete example. We wish to stress that we do not pretend that the program represents a viable paint program or an optimal interface. It is simply a vehicle to illustrate a variety of transactions in an easily understandable context.

Finally, we discuss improvements that must be made to current touch tablet technology, many of which we have demonstrated in prototype form. Also, we suggest potential improvements to other devices, motivated by our experience with touch technology.

4. Three Distinctions Between Touch Tablets and Mice[1]

The distinctions we make in this section have to do with suitability of devices for certain tasks or use in certain configurations. We are only interested in showing that there are some uses for which touch tablets are not suitable, but other devices are, and vice versa. We make no quantitative claims or comparisons regarding performance.

Signaling

Consider a rubber-band line drawing task with a one button mouse. The user would first position the tracking symbol at the desired starting point of the line by moving the mouse with the button released. The button would then be depressed, to signal the start of the line, and the user would manipulate the line by moving the mouse until the desired length and orientation was achieved. The completion of the line could then be signaled by releasing the button.[2]

Figure 1 is a state diagram that represents this interface. Notice that the button press and release are used to signal the beginning and end of the rubber-band drawing task. Also note that in states 1 and 2 both motion and signaling (by pressing or releasing the button, as appropriate) are possible.

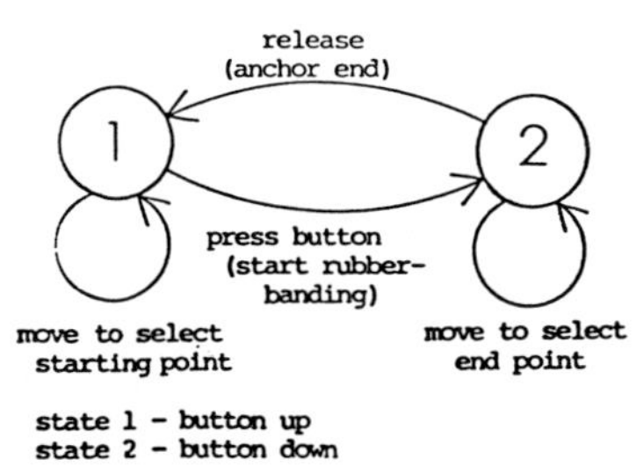

Figure 1. State diagram for rubber-banding with a one-button mouse.

Now consider a simple touch tablet. It can be used to position the tracking symbol at the starting point of the line, but it cannot generate the signal needed to initiate rubber-banding. Figure 2 is a state diagram representation of the capabilities of a simple touch tablet. In state 0, there is no contact with the tablet.[3] In this state only one action is possible: the user may touch the tablet. This causes a change to state 1. In state 1, the user is pressing on the tablet, and as a consequence position reports are sent to the host. There is no way to signal a change to some other state, other than to release (assuming the exclusion of temporal or spatial cues, which tend to be clumsy and difficult to learn). This returns the system to state 0. This signal could not be used to initiate rubber-banding, as it could also mean that the user is pausing to think, or wishes to initiate some other activity.

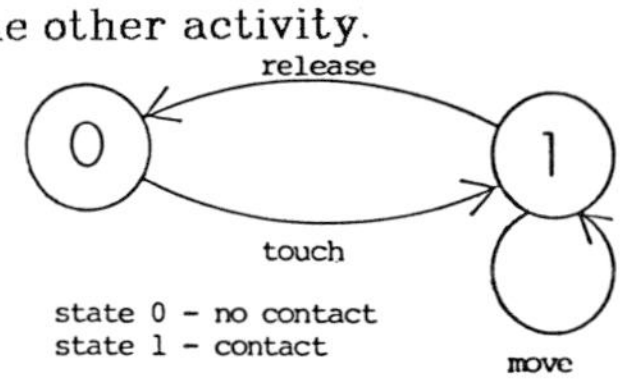

Figure 2. Diagram for showing states of simple touch-tablet.

This inability to signal while pointing is a severe limitation with current touch tablets, that is, tablets that do not report pressure in addition to location. (It is also a property of trackballs, and joysticks without "fire" buttons). It renders them unsuitable for use in many common interaction techniques for which mice are well adapted (e.g., selecting and dragging objects into position, rubber-band line drawing, and pop-up menu selection); techniques that are especially characteristic of interfaces based on *Direct Manipulation* [Shneiderman 1983].

One solution to the problem is to use a separate function button on the keyboard. However, this usually means two-handed input where one could do, or, awkward co-ordination in controlling the button and pointing device with a single hand. An alternative solution when using a touch tablet is to provide some level of pressure sensing. For example, if the tablet could report two levels of contact pressure (i.e., hard and soft), then the transition from soft to hard pressure, and vice versa, could be used for signaling. In effect, pressing hard is equivalent to pressing the button on the mouse. The state diagram showing the rubber-band line drawing task with this form of touch tablet is shown in Figure 3.[4]

As an aside, using this pressure sensing scheme would permit us to select options from a menu, or

[1] Although we are comparing touch tablets to one button mice throughout this section, most of the comments apply equally to tablets with one-button pucks or (with some caveats) tablets with styli.

[2] This assumes that the interface is designed so that the button is held down during drawing. Alternatively, the button can be released during drawing, and pressed again, to signal the completion of the line.

[3] We use state 0 to represent a state in which no location. information is transmitted. There no analogous state for mice, and hence no state 0 in the diagrams for mice. With conventional tablets, this corresponds to "out of range" state.
At this point the alert reader will wonder about difficulty in distinguishing between hard and soft pressure, and friction (especially when pressing hard). Taking the last first, hard is a relative term. In practice friction need not be a problem (see Inherent Problems, below).

[4] One would conjecture that in the absence of button clicks or other feedback, pressure would be difficult to regulate accurately. We have found two levels of pressure to be easily distinguished, but this is a ripe area for research. For example, Stu Card [private communication] has suggested that the threshold between soft and hard should be reduced (become "softer") while hard pressure is being maintained. This suggestion, and others, warrant formal experimentation.

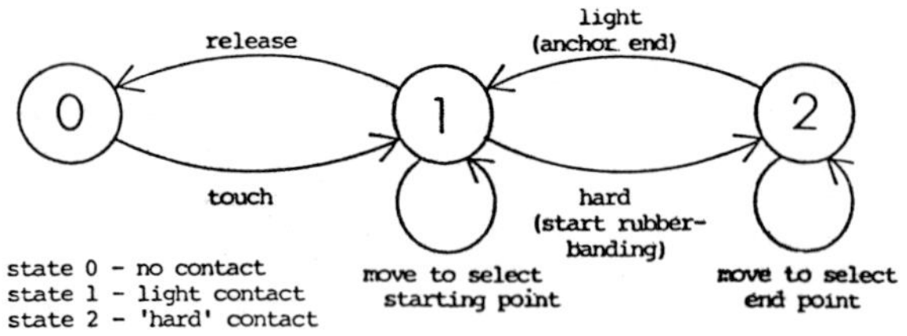

Figure 3. State diagram for rubber-banding with pressure sensing touch tablet.

activate light buttons by positioning the tracking symbol over the item and "pushing". This is consistent with the gesture used with a mouse, and the model of "pushing" buttons. With current simple touch tablets, one does just the opposite: position over the item and then lift off, or "pull" the button.

From the perspective of the signals sent to the host computer, this touch tablet is capable of duplicating the behaviour of a one-button mouse. This is not to say that these devices are equivalent or interchangeable. They are not. They are physically and kinesthetically very different, and should be used in ways that make use of the unique properties of each. Furthermore, such a touch tablet can generate one pair of signals that the one-button mouse cannot — specifically, press and release (transition to and from state 0 in the above diagrams). These signals (which are also available with many conventional tablets) are very useful in implementing certain types of transactions, such as those based on character recognition.

An obvious extension of the pressure sensing concept is to allow continuous pressure sensing. That is, pressure sensing where some large number of different levels of pressure may be reported. This extends the capability of the touch tablet beyond that of a traditional one button mouse. An example of the use of this feature is presented below.

Multiple Position Sensing

With a traditional mouse or tablet, only one position can be reported per device. One can imagine using two mice or possibly two transducers on a tablet, but this increases costs, and two is the practical limit on the number of mice or tablets that can be operated by a single user (without using feet). However, while we have only two hands, we have ten fingers. As playing the piano illustrates, there are some contexts where we might want to use several, or even all of them, at once.

Touch tablets need not restrict us in this regard. Given a large enough surface of the appropriate technology, one could use all fingers of both hands simultaneously, thus providing ten separate units of input. Clearly, this is well beyond the demands of many applications and the capacity of many people, however, there are exceptions. Examples include chording on buttons or switches, operating a set of slide potentiometers, and simple key roll-over when touch typing. One example (using a set of slide potentiometers) will be illustrated below.

Multiple Virtual Devices and Templates

The power of modern graphics displays has been enhanced by partitioning one physical display into a number of virtual displays. To support this, display window managers have been developed. We claim (see Brown, Buxton and Murtagh [1985]) that similar benefits can be gained by developing an input window manager that permits a single physical input device to be partitioned into a number of virtual input devices. Furthermore, we claim that multi-touch tablets are well suited to supporting this approach.

Figure 4a shows a thick cardboard sheet that has holes cut in specific places. When it is placed over a touch tablet as shown in Figure 4b, the user is restricted to touching only certain parts of the tablet. More importantly, the user can ***feel*** the parts that are touchable, and their shape. Each of the "touchable" regions represents a separate virtual device. The distinction between this template and traditional tablet mounted menus (such as seen in many CAD systems) is important.

Traditionally, the options have been:

a) Save display real estate by mounting the menu on the tablet surface. The cost of this option is eye diversion from the display to the tablet, the inability to "touch type", and time consuming menu changes.

b) Avoid eye diversion by placing the menus on the display. This also make it easier to change menus, but still does not allow "touch typing", and consumes display space.

Touch tablets allow a new option:

c) Save display space and avoid eye diversion by using templates that can be felt, and hence, allow "touch typing" on a variety of virtual input devices. The cost of this option is time consuming menu (template) changes.

It must be remembered that for each of these options, there is an application for which it is best. We have contributed a new option, which makes possible new interfaces. The new possibilities include more elaborate virtual devices because the improved kinesthetic feedback allows the user to concentrate on providing input, instead of staying in the assigned region. We will also show (below) that its main cost (time consuming menu changes) can be reduced in some applications by eliminating the templates.

5. Examples of Transactions Where Touch Tablets Can Be Used Effectively

In order to reinforce the distinctions discussed in the previous section, and to demonstrate the use of touch tablets, we will now work through some examples based on a toy paint system. We wish to stress again that we make no claims about the quality of the example as a paint system. A paint system is a common and easily understood application, and thus, we have chosen to use it simply as a vehicle for discussing interaction techniques that use touch tablets.

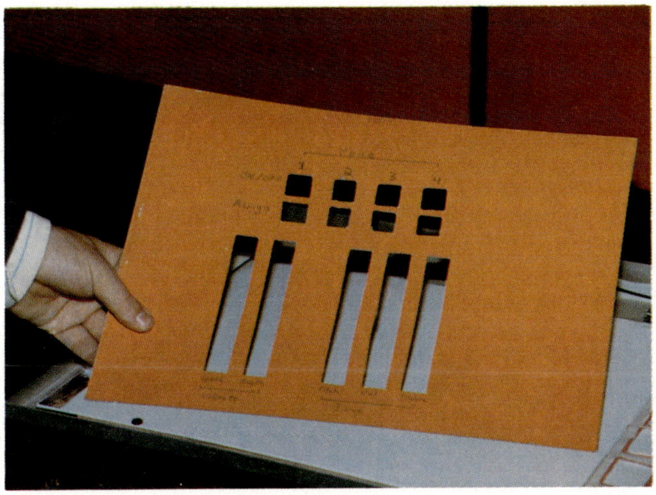

Figure 4a. Sample template.

Figure 5. Main display for paint program.

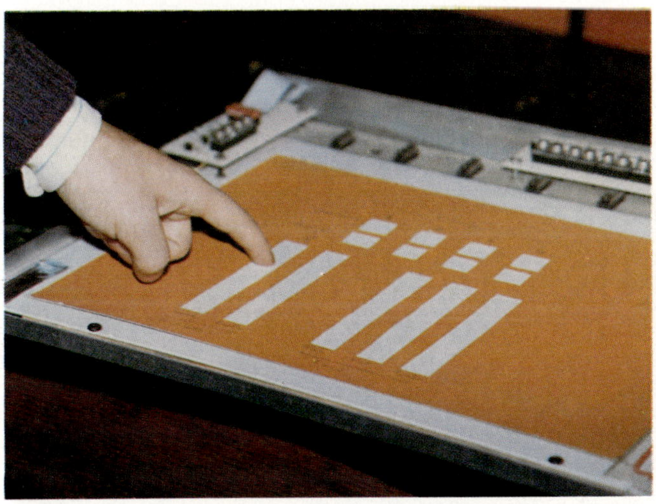

Figure 4b. Sample template in use.

Figure 6. Touch tablet used in demonstrations.

The example paint program allows the creation of simple finger paintings. The layout of the main display for the program is shown in Figure 5. On the left is a large drawing area where the user can draw simple free-hand figures. On the right is a set of menu items. When the lowest item is selected, the user enters a colour mixing mode. In switching to this mode, the user is presented with a different display that is discussed below. The remaining menu items are "paint pots". They are used to select the colour that the user will be painting with.

In each of the following versions of the program, the input requirements are slightly different. In all cases an 8 cm x 8 cm touch tablet is used (Figure 6), but the pressure sensing requirements vary. These are noted in each demonstration.

5.1. Painting Without Pressure Sensing

This version of the paint program illustrates the limitation of having no pressure sensing. Consider the paint program described above, where the only input device is a touch tablet without pressure sensing. Menu selections could be made by pressing down somewhere in the menu area, moving the tracking symbol to the desired menu item and then selecting by releasing. To paint, the user would simply press down in the drawing area and move (see Figure 7 for a representation of the signals used for painting with this program).

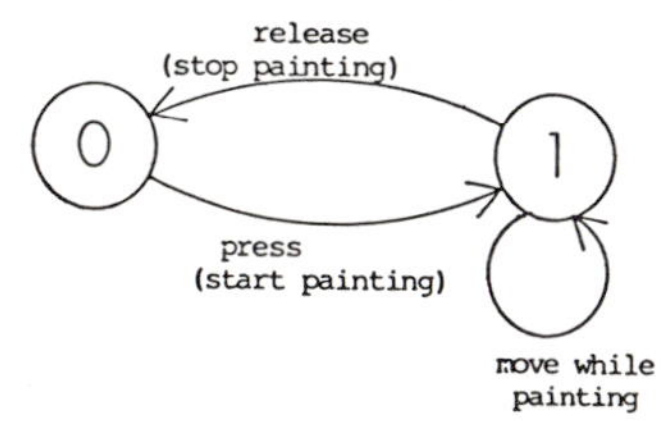

Figure 7. State diagram for drawing portion of simple paint program.

There are several problems with this program. The most obvious is in trying to do detailed drawings. The user does not know where the paint will appear until it appears. This is likely to be too late. Some form of feedback, that shows the user where the brush is, without painting, is needed. Unfortunately, this cannot be done with this input device, as it is not possible to signal the change from tracking to painting and vice versa.

The simplest solution to this problem is to use a button (e.g., a function key on the keyboard) to signal state changes. The problem with this solution is the need to use two hands on two different devices to do one task. This is awkward and requires practice to develop the co-ordination needed to make small rapid strokes in the painting. It is also inefficient in its use of two hands where one could (and normally should) do.

Alternatively, approaches using multiple taps or timing cues for signalling could be tried, however, we have found that these invariably lead to other problems. It is better to find a direct solution using the properties of the device itself.

5.2. Painting with Two Levels of Pressure

This version of the program uses a tablet that reports two levels of contact pressure to provide a satisfactory solution to the signaling problem. A low pressure level (a light touch by the user) is used for general tracking. A heavier touch is used to make menu selections, or to enable painting (see Figure 8 for the tablet states used to control painting with this program). The two levels of contact pressure allow us to make a simple but practical one finger paint program.

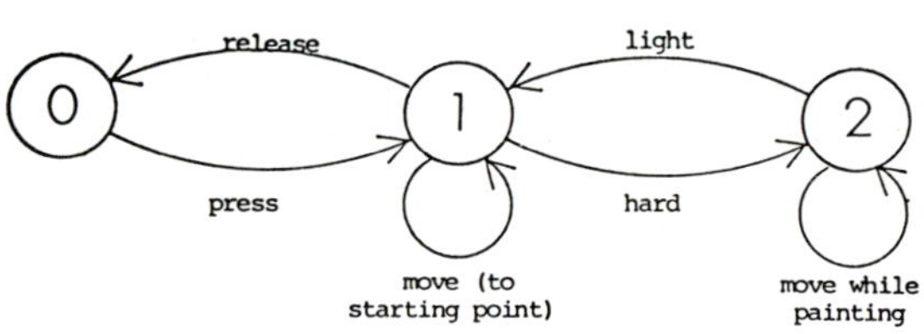

Figure 8. State diagram for painting portion of simple paint program using pressure sensing touch tablet.

This version is very much like using the one button mouse on the Apple Macintosh with MacPaint [Williams, 1984]. Thus, a simple touch tablet is not very useful, but one that reports two levels of pressure is similar in power (but not feel or applicability) to a one button mouse.[5]

5.3. Painting with Continuous Pressure Sensing

In the previous demonstrations, we have only implemented interaction techniques that are common using existing technology. We now introduce a technique that provides functionality beyond that obtainable using most conventional input technologies.

In this technique, we utilize a tablet capable of sensing a continuous range of touch pressure. With this additional signal, the user can control both the width of the paint trail and its path, using only one finger. The new signal, pressure, is used to control width. This is a technique that cannot be used with any mouse that we are aware of, and to our knowledge, is available on only one conventional tablet (the GTCO Digipad with pressure pen [GTCO 1982]).

We have found that using current pressure sensing tablets, the user can accurately supply two to three bits of pressure information, after about 15 minutes practice. This is sufficient for simple doodling and many other applications, but improved pressure resolution is required for high quality painting.

5.4. "Windows" on the Tablet: Colour Selection

We now demonstrate how the surface of the touch tablet can be *dynamically* partitioned into "windows" onto virtual input devices. We use the same basic techniques as discussed under templates (above), but show how to use them without templates. We do this in the context of a colour selection module for our paint program. This module introduces a new display, shown in Figure 9.

Figure 9. Colour mixing display.

In this display, the large left side consists of a colour patch surrounded by a neutral grey border. This is the patch of colour the user is working on. The right side of the display contains three bar graphs with two light buttons underneath. The primary function of the bar graphs is to provide feedback, representing relative proportions of red, green and blue in the colour patch. Along with the light buttons below, they also serve to remind the user of the current layout of the touch tablet.

In this module, the touch tablet is used as a "virtual operating console". Its layout is shown (to scale) in Figure 10. There are 3 valuators (corresponding to the bar graphs on the screen) used to control

[5] Also, there is the problem of friction, to be discussed below under "Inherent Problems".

colour, and two buttons: one, on the right, to bring up a pop-up menu used to select the colour to be modified, and another, on the left, to exit.

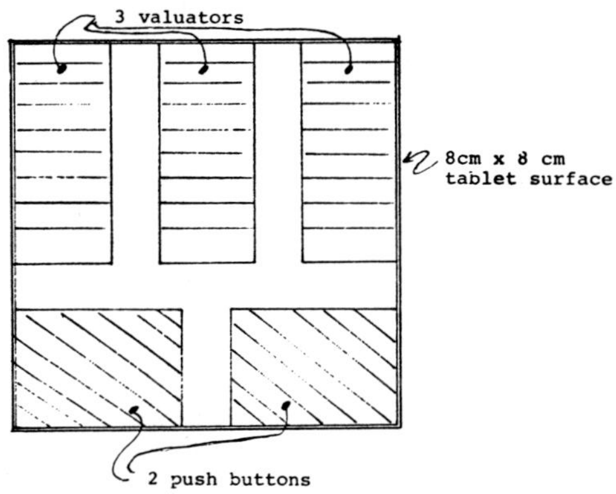

Figure 10. Layout of virtual devices on touch tablet.

The single most important point to be made in this example is that a single *physical* device is being used to implement 5 *virtual* devices (3 valuators and 2 buttons). This is analogous to the use of a display window system, in its goals, and its implementation.

The second main point is that there is nothing on the tablet to delimit the regions. This differs from the use of physical templates as previously discussed, and shows how, in the absence of the need for a physical template, we can instantly change the "windows" on the tablet, without sacrificing the ability to touch type.

We have found that when the tablet surface is small, and the partioning of the surfaces is not too complex, the users very quickly (typically in one or two minutes) learn the positions of the virtual devices relative to the edges of the tablet. More importantly, they can use the virtual devices, practically error free, without diverting attention from the display. (We have repeatedly observed this behaviour in the use of an application that uses a 10 cm square tablet that is divided into 3 sliders with a single button across the top).

Because no template is needed, there is no need for the user to pause to change a template when entering the colour mixing module. Also, at no point is the user's attention diverted from the display. These advantages cannot be achieved with any other device we know of, without consuming display real estate.

The colour of the colour patch is manipulated by ***dragging*** the red, green and blue values up and down with the valuators on the touch tablet. The valuators are implemented in relative mode (i.e., they are sensitive to changes in position, not absolute position), and are manipulated like one dimensional mice. For example, to make the patch more red, the user presses near the left side of the tablet, about half way to the top, and slides the finger up (see Figure 11). For larger changes, the device can be repeatedly stroked (much like stroking a mouse). Feedback is provided by changing the level in the bar graph on the screen and the colour of the patch.

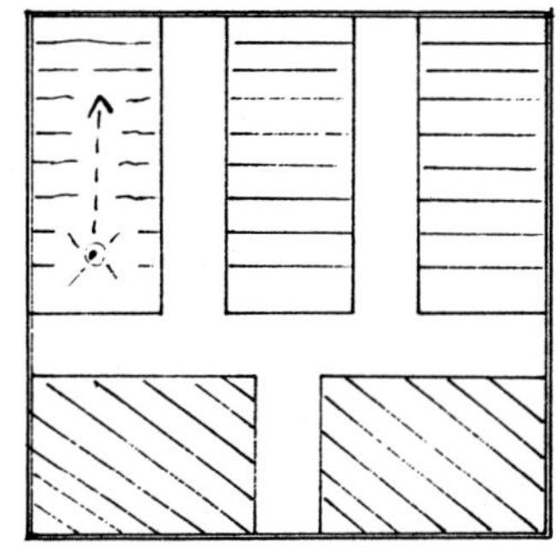

Figure 11. Increasing red content, by pressing on red valuator and sliding up.

Using a mouse, the above interaction could be approximated by placing the tracking symbol over the bars of colour, and dragging them up or down. However, if the bars are narrow, this takes acuity and concentration that distracts attention from the primary task — monitoring the colour of the patch. Furthermore, note that the touch tablet implementation does not need the bars to be displayed at all, they are only a convenience to the user. There are interfaces where, in the interests of maximizing available display area, there will be no items on the display analogous to these bars. That is, there would be nothing on the display to support an interaction technique that allows values to be manipulated by a mouse.

Finally, we can take the example one step further by introducing the use of a touch tablet that can sense multiple points of contact (e.g., [Lee, et al. 1985]). With this technology, all three colour values could be changed at the same time (for example, fading to black by drawing all three sliders down together with three fingers of one hand). This simultaneous adjustment of colours could ***not*** be supported by a mouse, nor any single commercially available input device we know of. Controlling several valuators with one hand is common in many operating consoles, for example: studio light control, audio mixers, and throttles for multi-engine vehicles (e.g., aircraft and boats). Hence, this example demonstrates a cost effective method for providing functionality that is currently unavailable (or available only at great cost, in the form of a custom fabricated console), but has wide applicability.

5.5. Summary of Examples

Through these simple examples, we have demonstrated several things:

- The ability to sense at least two levels of pressure is a virtual necessity for touch tablets, as without it, auxiliary devices must be used for signaling, and "direct manipulation" interfaces cannot be effectively supported.
- The extension to continuous pressure sensing opens up new possibilities in human-computer interaction.

- Touch tablets are superior to mice and tablets when many simple devices are to be simulated. This is because: (a) there is no need for a mechanical intermediary between the fingers and the tablet surface, (b) they allow the use of templates (including the edges of the tablet, which is a trivial but useful template), and (c) there is no need for positional feedback that would consume valuable display space.
- The ability to sense multiple points of contact radically changes the way in which users may interact with the system. The concept of multiple points of contact does not exist for, nor is it applicable to, current commercially available mice and tablets.

6. Inherent Problems with Touch Tablets

A problem with touch tablets that is annoying in the long term is friction between the user's finger and the tablet surface. This can be a particularly severe problem if a pressure sensitive tablet is used, and the user must make long motions at high pressure. This problem can be alleviated by careful selection of materials and care in the fabrication and calibration of the tablet.[6] Also, the user interface can be designed to avoid extended periods of high pressure.

Perhaps the most difficult problem is providing good feedback to the user when using touch tablets. For example, if a set of push-on/push-off buttons are being simulated, the traditional forms of feedback (illuminated buttons or different button heights) cannot be used. Also, buttons and other controls implemented on touch tablets lack the kinesthetic feel associated with real switches and knobs. As a result, users must be more attentive to visual and audio feedback, and interface designers must be freer in providing this feedback. (As an example of how this might be encouraged, the input "window manager" could automatically provide audible clicks as feedback for button presses).

7. Potential Enhancements to Touch Tablets (and other devices)

The first problem that one notices when using touch tablets is "jitter" when the finger is removed from the tablet. That is, the last few locations reported by the tablet, before it senses loss of contact, tend to be very unreliable.

This problem can be eliminated by modifying the firmware of the touch tablet controller so that it keeps a short FIFO queue of the samples that have most recently be sent to the host. When the user releases pressure, the oldest sample is retransmitted, and the queue is emptied. The length of the queue depends on the properties of the touch tablet (e.g., sensitivity, sampling rate). We have found that determining a suitable value requires only a few minutes of experimentation.

A related problem with most current tablet controllers (not just touch tablets) is that they do not inform the host computer when the user has ceased pressing on the tablet (or moved the puck out of range). This information is essential to the development of certain types of interfaces. (As already mentioned, this signal is not available from mice). Currently, one is reduced to deducing this event by timing the interval between samples sent by the tablet. Since the tablet controller can easily determine when pressure is removed (and must if it is to apply a de-jittering algorithm as above), it should share this information with the host.

Clearly, pressure sensing is an area open to development. Two pressure sensitive tablets have been developed at the University of Toronto [Sasaki, et al. 1981; Lee, et al. 1985]. One has been used to develop several experimental interfaces and was found to be a very powerful tool. They have recently become available from Elographics and Big Briar (see Appendix A). Pressure sensing is not only for touch tablets. Mice, tablet pucks and styli could all benefit by augmenting switches with strain gauges, or other pressure sensing instruments. GTCO, for example, manufactures a stylus with a pressure sensing tip [GTCO 1982], and this, like our pressure sensing touch tablets, has proven very useful.

8. Conclusions

We have shown that there are environments for which some devices are better adapted than others. In particular, touch tablets have advantages in many hostile environments. For this reason, we suggest that there are environments and applications where touch tablets may be the most appropriate input technology.

This being the case, we have enumerated three major distinctions between touch tablets and one button mice (although similar distinctions exist for multi-button mice and conventional tablets). These assist in identifying environments and applications where touch tablets would be most appropriate. These distinctions concern:

- limitation in the ability to signal events,
- suitability for multiple point sensing, and
- the applicability of tactile templates.

These distinctions have been reinforced, and some suggestions on how touch tablets may be used have been given, by discussing a simple user interface. From this example, and the discussion of the distinctions, we have identified some enhancements that can be made to touch tablets and other input devices. The most important of these are pressure sensing and the ability to sense multiple points of contact.

We hope that this paper motivates interface designers to consider the use of touch tablets and shows some ways to use them effectively. Also, we hope it encourages designers and manufacturers of input devices to develop and market input devices with the enhancements that we have discussed.

---

[6] As a bad example, one commercial "touch" tablet requires so much pressure for reliable sensing that the finger cannot be smoothly dragged across the surface. Instead, a wooden or plastic stylus must be used, thus loosing many of the advantages of touch sensing.

The challenge for the future is to develop touch tablets that sense continuous pressure at multiple points of contact and incorporate them in practical interfaces. We believe that we have shown that this is worthwhile and have shown some practical ways to use touch tablets. However, interface designers must still do a great deal of work to determine where a mouse is better than a touch tablet and vice versa.

Finally, we have illustrated, by example, an approach to the study of input devices, summarized by the credo: "Know the interactions a device is intended to participate in, and the strengths and weaknesses of the device." This approach stresses that there is no such thing as a "good input device," only good interaction task/device combinations.

9. Acknowledgements

The support of this research by the Natural Sciences and Engineering Research Council of Canada is gratefully acknowledged. We are indebted to Kevin Murtagh and Ed Brown for their work on virtual input devices and windowing on input. Also, we are indebted to Elographics Corporation for having supplied us with the hardware on which some of the underlying studies are based.

We would like to thank the referees who provided many useful comments that have helped us with the presentation.

10. References

Brown, E., Buxton, W., Murtagh, K. 1985 — **Windows on Tablets as a Means of Achieving Virtual Input Devices.** Submitted for publication.

Buxton, W. 1983 — **Lexical and Pragmatic Considerations of Input Structures.** *Computer Graphics* 17.1. Presented at the SIGGRAPH Workshop on Graphical Input Techniques, Seattle, Washington, June 1982.

Buxton, W. 1985 — **There is More to Interaction Than Meets the Eye: Some Issues in Manual Input.** (in) Norman, D.A. and Draper, S.W. (Eds.), *User Centered System Design: New Perspectives on Human-Computer Interaction.* Hillsdale, N.J.: Lawrence Erlbaum and Associates. Publication expected late 1985.

Buxton, W., Fiume, E., Hill, R., Lee, A., Woo, C. 1983 — **Continuous Hand-Gesture Driven Input.** *Proceedings Graphics Interface '83*: pp. 191-195. May 9-13, 1983, Edmonton, Alberta.

Card, S.K., Moran, T.P., Newell, A. Jul 1980 — **The Keystroke-Level Model for User Performance Time with Interactive Systems.** *Communications of the ACM* 23.7: pp. 396-409.

Foley, J.D., Wallace, V.L., Chan, P. Nov 1984 — **The Human Factors of Computer Graphics Interaction Techniques.** *IEEE Computer Graphics and Applications* 4.11: pp. 13-48.

GTCO 1982 — **DIGI-PAD 5 User's Manual.** GTCO Corporation, 1055 First Street, Rockville, MD 20850.

Herot, C.F., Weinzapfel, G. Aug 1978 — **One-Point Touch Input of Vector Information for Computer Displays.** *Computer Graphics* 12.3: pp. 210-216. SIGGRAPH'78 Conference Proceedings, August 23-25, 1978, Atlanta, Georgia.

Lee, S., Buxton, W., Smith, K.C. 1985 — **A Multi-Touch Three Dimensional Touch-Sensitive Tablet.** *Human Factors in Computer Systems*: pp. 21-25. (CHI'85 Conference Proceedings, April 14-18, 1985, San Fransisco).

Minsky, M.R. Jul 1984 — **Manipulating Simulated Objects with Real-world Gestures using a Force and Position Sensitive Screen.** *Computer Graphics* 18.3: pp. 195-203. (SIGGRAPH'84 Conference Proceedings, July 23-27, 1984, Minneapolis, Minnesota).

Nakatani, L.H., Rohrlich, J.A. Dec 1983 — **Soft Machines: A Philosophy of User-Computer Interface Design.** *Human Factors in Computing Systems*: pp. 19-23. (CHI'83 Conference Procedings, December 12-15, 1983, Boston).

Sasaki, L., Fedorkow, G., Buxton, W., Retterath, C., Smith, K.C. 1981 — **A Touch Sensitive Input Device.** *Proceedings of the 5th International Conference on Computer Music.* North Texas State University, Denton Texas, November 1981.

Shneiderman, B. Aug 1983 — **Direct Manipulation: A Step Beyond Programming Languages.** *Computer* 16.8: pp. 57-69.

Williams, G. Feb 1984 — **The Apple Macintosh Computer.** *Byte* 9.2: pp. 30-54.

Appendix A: Touch Tablet Sources

Big Briar: 3 by 3 inch continuous pressure sensing touch tablet

Big Briar, Inc.
Leicester, NC
28748

Chalk Board Inc.: "Power Pad", large touch table for micro-computers

Chalk Board Inc.
3772 Pleasantdale Rd.,
Atlanta, GA 30340

Elographics: various sizes of touch tablets, including pressure sensing

Elographics, Inc.
105 Randolph Toad
Oak Ridge, Tennessee
37830
(615)-482-4100

Key Tronic: Keyboard with touch pad.

Keytronic
P.O. Box 14687
Spokane, WA 99214
(509)-928-8000

KoalaPad Technologies: Approx. 5 by 7 inch touch tablet for micro-computers

Koala Technologies
3100 Patrick Henry Drive
Santa Clara, California
95050

Spiral Systems: Trazor Touch Panel, 3 by 3 inch touch tablet

Spiral System Instruments, Inc.
4853 Cordell Avenue, Suite A-10
Bethesda, Maryland
20814

TASA: 4 by 4 inch touch tablet (relative sensing only)

Touch Activated Switch Arrays Inc.
1270 Lawrence Stn. Road, Suite G
Sunnyvale, California
94089

AN AUTOMATIC BEAUTIFIER FOR DRAWINGS AND ILLUSTRATIONS

Theo Pavlidis
Christopher J. Van Wyk

AT&T Bell Laboratories
Murray Hill, New Jersey 07974

Abstract

We describe a method for inferring constraints that are desirable for a given (rough) drawing and then modifying the drawing to satisfy the constraints wherever possible. The method has been implemented as part of an online graphics editor running under the UNIX† operating system and it has undergone modifications in response to user input. Although the framework we discuss is general, the current implementation is polygon-oriented. The relations examined are: approximate equality of the slope or length of sides, collinearity of sides, and vertical and horizontal alignment of points.

CR Categories and Subject Descriptors: I.3.5 **[Computer Graphics]**: Computational Geometry and Object Modeling—*geometric algorithms, languages, and systems*; I.4.3 **[Image Processing]**: Enhancement—*geometric correction*; I.4.5 **[Pattern Recognition]**: Clustering—*algorithms and similarity measures.*

1. Introduction

Illustrators often need to create drawings that contain many parallel line segments, right angles, aligned rectangles, and that are in other ways "neat." This has led to the development of graphics editors and languages that permit users to specify an illustration by constraining the relative locations of picture elements like points and lines rather than by giving them explicitly and absolutely [1-3]. These tools grow more cumbersome to use as the complexity of a drawing increases. It would be nice if one had a procedure whereby a sloppily drawn figure could automatically be redrawn more neatly.

One could view interactive editors in which one can snap to rectilinear grid points as implementing a simple kind of beautification. Drawing with a grid has some serious limitations; for example, once a resolution is selected refinement is difficult, and there is a very coarse quantization on the slopes of lines allowed in the drawing. In addition, the idea of "snapping" offers little help in creating computer representations of drawings from paper originals by digitization [4-6], which is necessary in order to integrate electronic and paper graphics. Another potential application of beautification is in the extraction of solid object descriptions from digitized images (range or light data). Edge extraction algorithms produce the equivalent of a line drawing which is rough because of noise in the image [7]. The process for converting that set of lines into a set which is consistent with a projection of the edges of a solid requires transformations that are either identical or similar to those used in beautification. Beautification stands in contrast to specialized kinds of picture transformations. An example of the latter is common in integrated-circuit editors that implement layout, compaction, and routing algorithms [8,9].

† UNIX is a Trademark of AT&T Bell Laboratories.

In this paper we discuss how we approached the design of a beautification procedure, our experience in its implementation, and how the reactions of users have led us to modify our approach. Section 2 presents what we have come to understand to be the heart of the beautification problem, and the requirements that a beautification procedure must meet. Sections 3-5 present a solution to the problem as we pose it in Section 2. We implemented our solution as part of the PED graphics editor [10], which runs under the UNIX operating system on the AT&T Teletype 5620 dot-mapped display terminal [11]; PED users may invoke the beautification procedure at any time, and the result is displayed in real time. Feedback from these users has been very valuable to our understanding of the problem and this paper reflects what we have learned from public use of a part of our solution.

2. Fundamental Problems and Outline of the Beautification Scheme

Our approach to automatic beautification requires the solution of two problems. First, we need to infer from the initial sketch appropriate constraints to impose on the beautified version. Second, we need to change the initial sketch to satisfy those constraints. To reduce the vagueness of these descriptions so that an algorithmic attempt at solution is at least possible, we shall restrict the problem in a number of ways.

First, we limit our goal to images that can be defined in terms of points. This restriction covers most line drawings. We can express the problem mathematically as follows. Let the points of a drawing—vertices of polygons, centers of circles, etc.—be (x_1,y_1), $\cdots$, (x_n,y_n), and let $\mathbf{X}$ be the vector of coordinates with $\mathbf{X}_{2i-1} = x_i$ and $\mathbf{X}_{2i} = y_i$ for $1 \leqslant i \leqslant n$. Suppose the initial value of $\mathbf{X}$ is $\mathbf{X}^O$. It is tempting to define beautification as choosing a set of constraints $\mathbf{F}_k$ such that

$$\mathbf{F}_k(\mathbf{X}^O) \leqslant \delta,\ k = 1,2, \cdots, \quad (1)$$

then finding a vector $\mathbf{X}^B$ such that

$$\mathbf{F}_k(\mathbf{X}^B) = \mathbf{0},\ k=1,2,\cdots, \tag{2}$$

and

$$\|\mathbf{X}^B - \mathbf{X}^O\|_\infty < \epsilon, \tag{3}$$

where $\|\cdot\|_\infty$ denotes the maximum-coordinate-norm.

For example, consider the simple constraint that points line up vertically. Suppose x_3 and x_8 differ by less than δ; then we would look for a solution that satisfies the equation

$$x_3 - x_8 = 0 .$$

Formally, there is only one relation, $\mathbf{F}_1$, in this case expressed as the scalar product of $\mathbf{X}$ with a vector $\mathbf{V}$ whose components are all zero, except for $\mathbf{V}_5 = 1$ and $\mathbf{V}_{15} = -1$.

This formulation of the beautification problem assures that all points stay near their original positions. It offers no insight as to the choice of $\mathbf{F}_k$ (indeed, $\mathbf{F}_1(\mathbf{X}) = \mathbf{X}-\mathbf{X}^O$ is an obvious choice that is appropriate in some cases), but given a suitable $\mathbf{F}_k$, it reduces the second part of the beautification problem to mathematical programming (linear programming in case all constraint equations are linear).

The example of Figure 1 shows a pitfall in this approach. The original drawing contains several lines that are nearly vertical. If, as above, we choose $\{\mathbf{F}_k\}$ to be the constraint that nearly equal x-coordinates should be made equal, then we can obtain a solution that satisfies $\{\mathbf{F}_k\}$ and moves all points by only a small amount. However, the result of this beautification may be unsatisfactory because three of the line segments have been moved on top of each other. This suggests the desirability of imposing negative constraints, which say that picture entities should *not* satisfy a relation, in addition to positive constraints that enforce relationships among entities.† For this example, one possible negative constraint is that distinct points that are close in both x and y coordinates should not be constrained to be equal. Note that using tighter bounds on the size of allowed movement during the beautification does not resolve this problem: The endpoints of the three rightmost lines may be moved by much larger amounts than those of the three leftmost lines and we will still achieve good results.

Formally, we should add a set of nonequalities to the system of Eqs. (2) and (3):

$$\mathbf{G}_k(\mathbf{X}^B) \neq \mathbf{0},\ k=1,2,\cdots . \tag{4}$$

Notice that even if $\{\mathbf{F}_k\}$ and $\{\mathbf{G}_k\}$ are linear, the system of (2-4) cannot be solved by linear programming. Another reason for not using mathematical or linear programming to solve the constraint systems is that they offer little guidance in choosing a large satisfiable subset of a system than cannot be completely satisfied; such systems arise frequently in beautification.

So far we have not addressed the computational feasibility of finding the constraint relations $\{\mathbf{F}_k\}$ and $\{\mathbf{G}_k\}$, and of solving the resulting system of equations, inequalities, and nonequalities. The search for relations among the points or entities of a drawing may become very expensive because of combinatorial growth. This has led us to impose another limitation on our approach: *In our search for approximately satisfied constraints* $\{\mathbf{F}_k\}$ *among objects, we consider only relations that can be mapped into a single scalar number.*

† This is one of the principal changes to the beautifier whose need was made apparent by users' experience.

For the above examples, the constraint is vertical alignment of points, which can be expressed as the equality of x-coordinates. As another example, parallelism among line segments can be expressed as the equality of angles with the horizontal. For each class of such constraint relations we sort the objects according to the value of their scalars and seek objects that are appropriately related in the sorted list. ("Appropriately related" usually, but not always, means "approximately equal.") This ensures that the search for relations among N objects can be performed in time $O(N \log N)$ rather than $\Omega(N^2)$. The class of constraint relations that can be mapped into scalars is surprisingly rich. As an unusual example, consider symmetries along a vertical axis: these can be found by sorting line segments according to angle with the horizontal, then finding pairs of sides whose angles sum to π.

Many of the relations that cannot be found in this way can be discovered and satisfied directly by simpler, but less general, techniques. For example, finding a smooth curve approximating a roughly drawn curve can be expressed as a spline approximation problem ([12], Ch. 12), which can be solved explicitly for the set of points. As another example, consider the termination of curves on other curves as shown in Figure 2. To find picture elements that are thus related requires pairwise examination of objects, an operation of at least quadratic complexity. However, we need consider only objects that are geometrically close to each other, so we can presort the objects by neighborhood or bounding box to find such constraints in small expected time.

We describe in the next section a clustering scheme that creates relations from the sorted lists. From these relations we create a set of constraint equations and inequalities; the constraint relations used in our current implementation are described in Section 4. Section 6 shows how we solve the constraint system using a simple incremental procedure; an important advantage of the approach described there is that it can be used to suggest which constraints should be dropped when the whole constraint set $\{\mathbf{F}_k\}$ cannot be satisfied.

3. The Clustering Scheme

The clustering strategy is described here as a general operation. It may be helpful to think of the concrete example of clustering line segments according to the angle they form with the horizontal so that nearly parallel segments can be found and made parallel.

Suppose the n elements to be clustered have been sorted by the appropriate scalar value; let the elements in this order have scalar values v_i, $1 \leq i \leq n$. A clustering of the n elements by the scalars v_i into k clusters is an increasing subsequence i_j, $1 \leq j \leq k$. Setting $i_{k+1} = n+1$ to take care of the boundary condition, we say that the elements of the jth cluster have scalar values v_{i_j} through $v_{i_{j+1}-1}$. Figure 3a shows an example arrangement of elements. While a human observer may readily see two clusters as in Figure 3c, detecting them automatically is difficult.

In general, the goal of clustering is to minimize a

measure of variation of values of individual elements from certain "central" values ([13], pp. 217 - 252). If V_j is the central value for the jth cluster, then we may wish to minimize

$$E = \max_j[\max_i |v_i - V_j|,\ i_j \leq i \leq i_{j+1}-1],\ \text{for } 1 \leq j \leq k. \quad (5)$$

This expression can always be made zero if we select as many clusters as data points, so many statistical techniques for clustering seek to minimize E when an upper bound on k is given as well. Unfortunately, no *a priori* assumption about the number of clusters is reasonable for drawings. In addition, most statistical techniques try hard to assign each object to a nontrivial cluster, an unrealistic expectation for drawings. One alternative to a fixed upper bound on k would be to minimize the number of clusters subject to an upper bound on the width, $|v_{i_{j+1}-1} - v_{i_j}|$, of any cluster. But this can also lead to unexpected results as in Figure 3b: a person sees a central cluster and two outlying singleton clusters, but it is possible to divide the elements into just two clusters and still satisfy the bound on maximum cluster width. This example has led us to augment the strategy of clustering subject to a maximum cluster width with the following rule: *Select a small constant δ (a fraction of the maximum cluster width) and group together all points that form sequences such that the difference in values of adjacent elements is less than δ.* (This scheme can be modified trivially to find relations that do not require approximate equality of values, but some other numerical relation. For example, to search for segments that are nearly perpendicular to each other we need only replace everywhere $|v_{i_{j+1}-1} - v_{i_j}|$ by $|v_{i_{j+1}-1} - v_{i_j} - \pi/2|$.) We offer some statistical justification for relying on the adjacent pair differences.

Assume that two random processes are involved in the creation of a drawing. One is the selection of a *desired* value for an element; the second is the realization of this value.† Fundamental to the idea of beautification is the assumption that the range of possible desired values is much larger than the range of deviations around a desired value. An even stronger assumption is needed to justify the above strategy: The variation among intended values is much larger than the variation among approximations to the same intended value. It would be nice if we had statistical models for drawings so that we could test the validity of these assumptions. In their absence we present some results from probability theory related to the observed pairwise distances among objects.

Parzen ([14], pp. 322-323) gives the following expression for the density of x, the observed maximum range as a fraction of the total range for n samples drawn from a uniform distribution

$$f(x) = n(n-1)x^{n-2}(1-x).$$

The expected value of x is easily computed to be $(n-1)/(n+1)$, so the average distance between samples is $1/(n+1)$. Feller ([15], Section VIII.5) treats unlimited sequences of Bernoulli trials and shows that the maximum range for n samples tends with probability 1 to the limit $\sqrt{c \log\log n}$, where c is a constant proportional to the variance of the distribution. This bound grows very slowly with n, so the average distance between adjacent samples is proportional to $1/n$.

What these results tell us is that if we draw samples from two distributions, one having a much bigger range than the other, we may end up with similar pairwise distance distributions, if we draw more samples from the distribution with the larger range. In our case, let d_1 be the expected pairwise distance between adjacent samples when they are approximations to the same value and d_2 when they are not. Since the number of samples approximating a single value (e.g. all lines at nearly the same angle) is likely to be much smaller than the total (all lines in the drawing), this would compensate for the fact that the error range is much smaller than the total range. Therefore the values of d_1 and d_2 could be quite close! On the other hand, if the distribution of desired values is far from uniform, the values of d_1 and d_2 will differ significantly. This is often the case in many technical drawings where there are few chosen orientations (usually including vertical and horizontal). Therefore we chose δ empirically so that when the distance between adjacent pairs is less than δ it is reasonable to claim that they are approximations to the same intended value.

The lack of reliable statistical models for drawing generation makes it imperative to verify empirically any solutions that are based on statistics. Therefore the implementation of our method—in our case, as part of an online drawing editor—was an essential part of the design.

The discussion above focussed on the formation of groups of elements; now we discuss how these groups are processed to form clusters. Figure 4 shows that elements that are pairwise close should not necessarily be clustered together. Therefore we compare the width of each group with two other constants δ_1 and δ_2. (The maximum expected cluster width is between δ_1 and δ_2.)

- If the width is less than δ_1, we place all of its members into a single cluster.
- If the width is greater than δ_2, we assume we have a "chaining" situation like that of Figure 4, and the group is dissolved: none of its members is clustered. Since we assume that the small differences are intentional, we also impose negative constraints as discussed below to insure that the solver leaves the chained elements alone.
- If the width is between δ_1 and δ_2, the group is modified either by removing one of the end elements, or splitting it into two groups (if the greatest pairwise distance is in the middle of the group); the resulting group or groups become clusters.

Finally, we consider negative constraints. Recall that these arise when elements that wind up in the same cluster should not be constrained to satisfy the cluster value because doing so causes entities of the picture to collapse. In principle we could discover desirable negative constraints by clustering within each cluster according to another criterion. However, for simplicity (and for more flexibility in the selection of negative constraints) we consider all possible pairs of cluster elements; since

† While the creation of any given drawing is (hopefully) a deterministic process, one could collect statistics over a large number of drawings and thus compute probability density functions for various parameters of drawings. These would also be parameters to our beautification process; they would not affect the underlying model.

each cluster has few elements (usually at most 10) the computation cost is not excessive. To express a negative relation between cluster elements, we remove them from the cluster, and tag them to prevent undue modification by the solver. Figure 5 shows an example where this approach is essential. If we are clustering by angle with the horizontal, sides *AB*, *CD*, *DE*, and *FG* are likely to cluster together. While it is permissible to make both *AB* and *FG* vertical, making *CD* and *DE* vertical causes them to collapse together. So these sides have their slopes frozen at their initial value before the solver is allowed to make any modifications to the picture.

4. Constraint Possibilities among Lines and Points

Our current implementation uses the following constraint relations among points, or lines, or points and lines. With each positive constraint we list the corresponding negative constraint. For brevity we use the term *side* for line segment.

1. A set of sides should lie at the same angle to the horizontal, unless they intersect. We modify this relation further so that clusters at angles near a preferred value (currently a multiple of $\pi/4$) are adjusted to have exactly that value.
2. A set of sides with similar slopes should be collinear, unless their projections perpendicular to the common slope intersect.
3. A set of sides should have the same length.
4. A set of points should be horizontally [vertically] aligned, unless they are also vertically [horizontally] aligned.

Figures 6 and 7 each show an original drawing and the same drawing adjusted after the above constraint relations have been found and enforced.

Other relations that fit into this beautification framework, but that we have not implemented, include:

1. A pair of adjacent sides should meet at the same angle as another pair of adjacent sides.
2. A set of points or sides is horizontally or vertically symmetric.
3. A point lies midway (or in general, some fixed fraction of the way) between two other points.

Two examples of relations that do not fit into this framework are:

1. Two curves are tangent.
2. A circle is inscribed in a polygon.

5. Creating the Equations

We describe here how constraint equations are formed from the clusters. The most general equations involve two sides; in the implementation, these are given as explicit endpoints, but for what follows it is convenient to write the endpoints of side i as (x_i,y_i) and $(x_i+\Delta x_i,y_i+\Delta y_i)$, and its preferred angle with the horizontal as θ_i.

Slopes: Clustering is performed according to the angle each side makes with the horizontal. To keep nearly horizontal lines together, angles are not taken in the usual range $[0,\pi)$ but in $[-\pi/10,9\pi/10)$. Once the clusters are formed, those whose values are close to a preferred direction (currently, a multiple of $\pi/4$) have their values set to exactly the preferred value and clusters that differ by nearly $\pi/2$ have their values set so the difference is exact. Then each side in each cluster has its preferred angle set to the cluster value. Sides in clusters with more than one member, and sides whose angles have been set to a preferred value, are used to generate equations; there will be one equation per cluster member.

Sides within slope clusters that intersect are in danger of collapsing together if the cluster value is imposed on them. The negative constraint—that this should not happen—is imposed by fixing the slopes of such sides to their initial values. This allows the endpoints to move, but prevents complete collapse of the sides.

If the preferred angle, θ_1, is between $\pi/4$ and $3\pi/4$, we generate the equation $\Delta x_1=\Delta y_1\cot\theta_1$; otherwise we generate the equation $\Delta y_1=\Delta x_1\tan\theta_1$. This keeps all coefficients less than or equal to one in absolute value, and so improves the numerical stability of the solution procedure.

Collinearity: We seek collinear picture elements by clustering within slope clusters, using as the significant scalar the signed distance of each side from a fixed point. (We fix this point at the center of gravity of the endpoints of the sides in the original cluster, thus minimizing the maximum absolute value of the resulting numbers.) From a cluster of k nearly collinear sides, we form $k-1$ equations, each between two sides in the cluster. Because each side also generates a slope equation, the collinearity constraint can be written simply as one of the equations

$$y_{i+1}-y_i = (x_{i+1}-x_i)\tan\theta_i$$

or

$$x_{i+1}-x_i = (y_{i+1}-y_i)\cot\theta_i \ ;$$

again, the choice between them is made so that all coefficients have magnitude at most one.

Length Equality: We cluster sides by their length in the initial drawing. From a cluster of k sides of nearly equal length, we form $k-1$ equations, each between two sides in the cluster. The length of side i is

$$\sqrt{\Delta x_i^2+\Delta y_i^2} = |\Delta x_i\sec\theta_i| = |\Delta y_i\csc\theta_i|.$$

We can remove the absolute value signs using the approximate values of Δx_i and Δy_i computed from the original drawing. Thus there are four ways to write the length equality constraint as a linear equation; we choose among them as above.

Coordinate Coincidence: To find approximate vertical alignment we need to compare points rather than sides. To simplify implementation we treat points as sides of zero length, and cluster by x coordinate using the side-clustering routine. A cluster of k points with close x coordinates generates $k-1$ constraint equations. If two points with close x coordinates also have close y coordinates, the maximum they will be allowed to move is reduced from the default to one third of the distance between them. This makes it impossible for them to collapse together. Horizontal alignment and non-alignment is detected by a similar process on y coordinates.

6. Solving the Equations

Since it is likely that not all of the constraints produced by the clustering algorithm can be satisfied simultaneously, the first step towards solution is to assign a penalty to each constraint so that more desirable constraints are satisfied first. We currently assign to each equation a penalty equal to the maximum change in one of its variables assuming that the others remain at their original values; this represents a preference for equations that require only a small change to the original coordinates. Note in addition that the equations that freeze the slopes of certain sides have penalty zero, so they will be imposed (and satisfied) first. In general, such equations can simply be assigned a negative penalty to insure that the solver gives them high priority.

Next we process the equations in order of increasing penalty using the algorithm of [16]. Briefly, each coordinate variable is represented at all times as a linear combination of coordinate variables; before any equation has been processed each variable is simply equal to itself. To process an equation we plug in the linear-combination representation of each of its variables and perform arithmetic simplification; if the resulting equation contains any variables, then one is chosen to become dependent on the other variables in the equation; this means that its linear-combination representation will change to one that involves the other variables. Before this change is made final, however, we check to see if it causes the newly dependent variable to move too far from its original position; if that happens we ignore the equation.

This method is not guaranteed to find a solution to the system of (1-3), even if one exists. But it usually does find a solution to a large subsystem thereof, and it is also fast, so it has worked well in practice.

7. Conclusion

The problem of beautifying pictures cannot be solved completely: there will always be changes that would be nice but that are not detected by an automatic procedure. Therefore we have concentrated on a small set of relations that appear to have wide applicability, and on understanding how these relations can be detected and imposed efficiently without causing untoward changes in the picture being beautified.

Figures 8 to 10 illustrate the application of the procedure to a nontrivial drawing. They show the effectiveness of the method and also that it is not always idempotent. One question raised by some readers of drafts of this paper (including the SIGGRAPH referees) is the "rate of success" of beautification. This is an interesting practical question because prospective users might want to know the probability that their drawings will be beautified properly. However, such statistics are not easy to collect and not practically meaningful. Since the graphics editor that calls the beautifier runs on a large number of machines it would require a rather cumbersome mechanism to collect statistics of, say, the number of "undo" operations after each beautification. Even that would not be enough because: (a) users might instead discard the result and read in a backup copy of the original; (b) the beautifier might make some desirable changes in the drawing but not others, so there would be no following overt user action canceling the beautification, even though the results were not fully satisfactory. In extreme cases where there is a spectacular failure we hear directly from disgruntled users, and this is how we found out the need for negative constrains. Most important, the success of beautification depends a lot on how closely the drawing fits the model. The current implementation does quite well on "rectilinear" drawings such as that shown in Figure 8. Thus the probability that a block diagram will be beautified should be quite high, while the current version of beautification is bound to fail on an illustration containing a set of circles that are supposed to be tangent to each other.

Our experience shows that naive (or even sophisticated) statistical methods are bound to produce unintended and undesirable results in practice. We believe that negative constraints are crucial to any beautification procedure if it is to avoid these pitfalls.

Acknowledgements

We thank Brian Kernighan and Doug McIlroy for many useful comments on a first draft of this paper.

References

[1] Sutherland, I. E., "Sketchpad: A Man-machine Graphical Communication System," in *1963 Spring Joint Computer Conference,* reprinted in *Interactive Computer Graphics,* H. Freeman, ed., IEEE Computer Soc., 1980, pp. 1-19.

[2] Van Wyk, C. J., *"A High Level Language for Specifying Pictures,"* ACM Transactions on Graphics, **1**(2) (1982), pp. 163-182.

[3] Nelson, G., "Juno," personal communication.

[4] Pferd, W., and K. Ramachandran, "Computer Aided Automatic Digitizing of Engineering Drawings," *Proc. IEEE COMSAC,* 1978, pp. 630-635.

[5] Harris, J. F., J. Kittler, B. Llewellyn, and G. Preston, "A Modular System for Interpreting Binary Pixel Representations of Line-Structured Data," *Pattern Recognition Theory and Applications,* Proc. of NATO Adv. Study Inst., Oxford, March-April, 1981, J. Kittler, K. S. Fu, and L. F. Pau, eds. D. Reidel Publishing Co., 1982, pp. 311-351.

[6] Pavlidis, T., and Cherry, L. L., "Vector and Arc Encoding of Graphics and Text," *Proc. 1982 Intern. Conference on Pattern Recognition,* 1982, pp. 610-613.

[7] Herman, M., "Generating Detailed Scene Descriptions from Range Images," *Proc. 1985 IEEE International Conference on Robotics and Automation,* 1985, pp. 426-431.

[8] Skinner, F. D., "The Interactive Wiring System," *IEEE Computer Graphics and Applications* **1**(2) (1981), pp. 38-51.

[9] Wallich, P., "A review of engineering workstations," *IEEE Spectrum,* **21**(10) (1984), pp. 48-53.

[10] Pavlidis, T., "PED: A 'Distributed' Graphics Editor," *Proc. Graphics Interface '84,* 1984, pp. 75-79.

[11] Pike, R., "The Blit: A Multiplexed Graphics Terminal," *Bell System Technical Journal* (Part 2), **63**(8) (1984), pp. 1607-1631.

[12] Pavlidis, T., *Algorithms for Graphics and Image Processing,* Computer Science Press, 1982.

[13] Duda, R. O. and P. E. Hart, *Pattern Classification and Scene Analysis,* New York: J. Wiley, 1973.

[14] Parzen, E., *Modern Probability Theory and Its Applications,* New York: J. Wiley, 1960.

[15] Feller, W., *An Introduction to Probability Theory and its Applications,* Volume I. Third Edition. New York: J. Wiley, 1968.

[16] Derman, E., and C. J. Van Wyk, "A Simple Equation Solver and its Application to Economic Modeling," *Software Practice and Experience* **14**(12) (1984), pp. 1169-1181

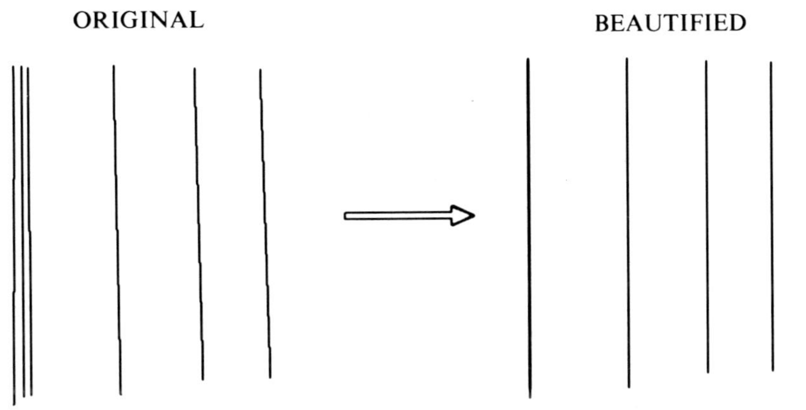

Figure 1: An undesirable beautification.

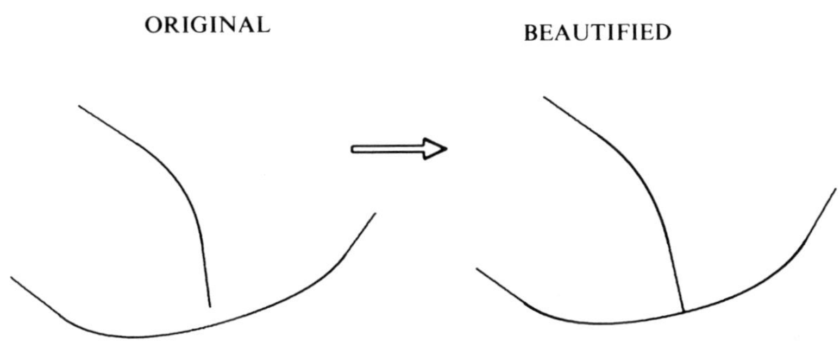

Figure 2: Beautification of curve terminations.

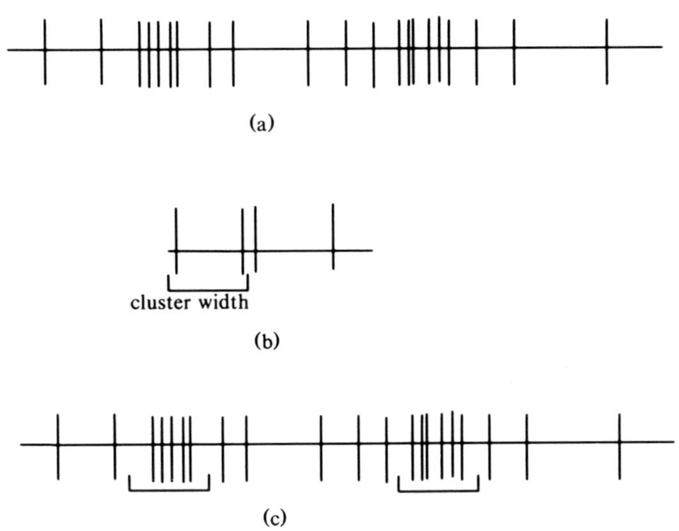

Figure 3: (a) Illustration of a clustering arrangement. The thin vertical lines denote elements. (b) An arrangement where insisting on the minimum number of clusters yields a poor answer. (c) A good clustering of the elements in (a).

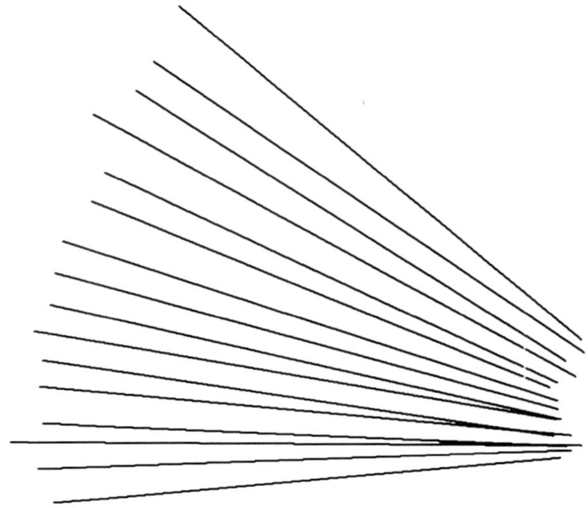

Figure 4: A drawing where clustering is inappropriate.

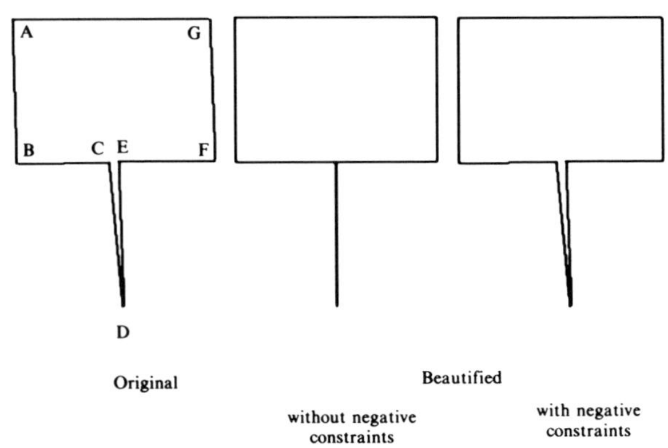

Figure 5: A drawing in which small changes in the slopes of *AB*, *BC*, *EF*, *FG*, and *GA* do not alter the gross shape, while a small change in the slope of *CD* or *DE* does.

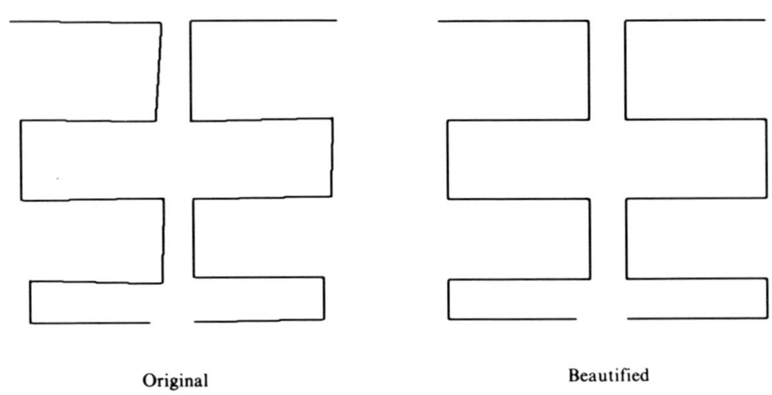

Figure 6: Example of the results of the beautification algorithm.

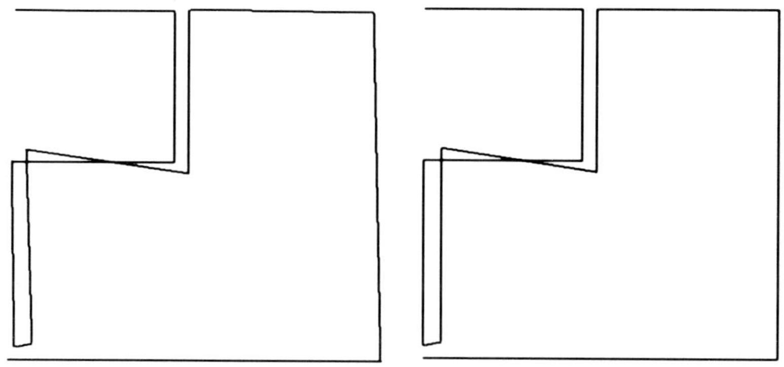

Original Beautified

Figure 7: Example of the results of the beautification algorithm. Notice that the use of negative constraints leaves intact the sides that intersect.

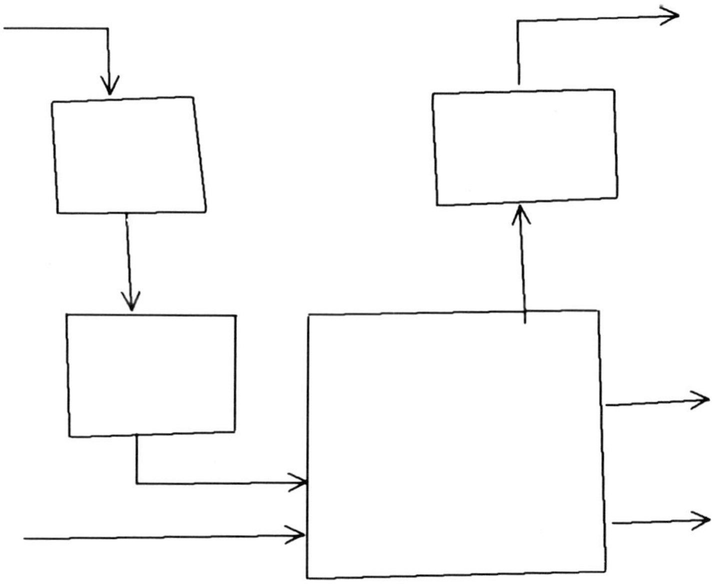

Figure 8: Original drawing

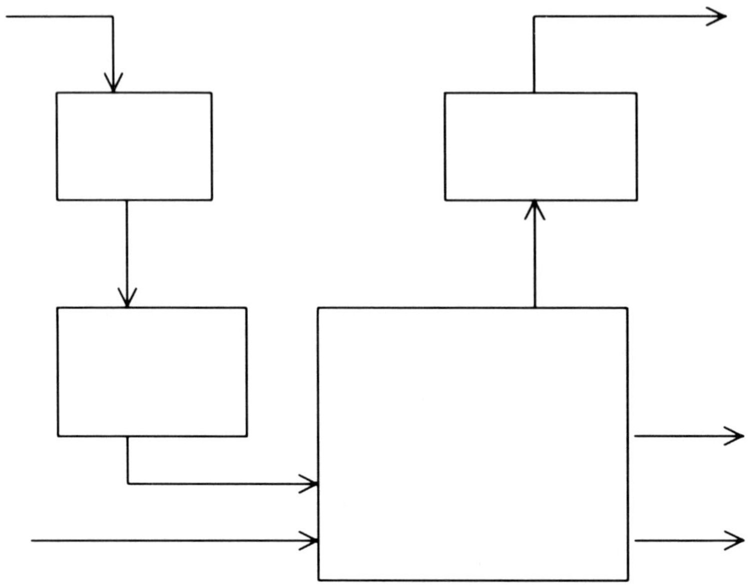

Figure 9: Drawing of Figure 8 after the First Application of the Beautifier

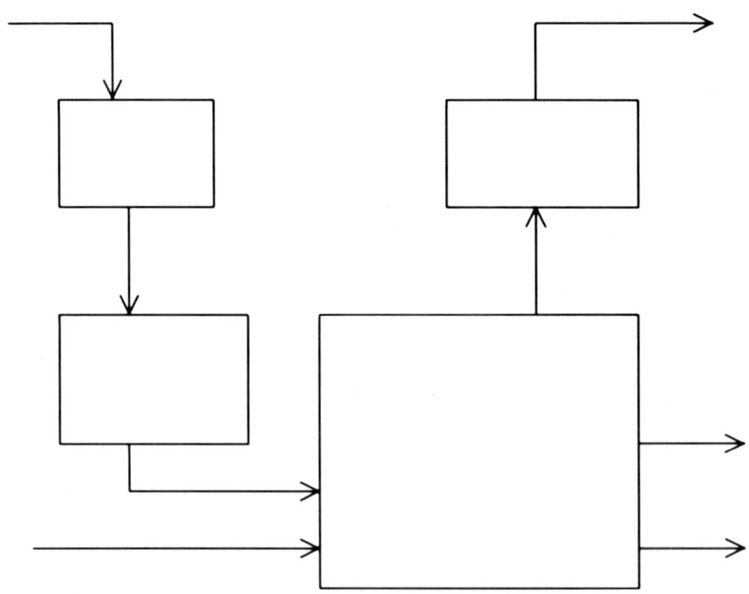

Figure 10: Drawing of Figure 8 after the Second Application of the Beautifier

Juno, a constraint-based graphics system

Greg Nelson
Xerox Palo Alto Research Center*

Abstract. Juno is a system that harmoniously integrates a language for describing pictures with a what-you-see-is-what-you-get image editor. Two of Juno's novelties are that geometric constraints are used to specify locations, and that the text of a Juno program is modified in response to the interactive editing of the displayed image that the program produces.

Introduction

Connect a computer to a marking engine, and you get a drawing instrument of revolutionary precision and versatility. Already some graphic artists have abandoned their T-squares and pens for the new world of bit-mapped displays, mice, and laser printers. But they face a serious problem: to harness the power of a computer, artists must become programmers.

Of course, the artist's business is art, not bits: someone else should deal with floating-point numbers and raster ops. But an artist using a computer must somehow provide a precise constructive specification for the (often complicated) image in his mind. And in an important sense, to give a precise constructive specification for any complicated thing is a programming problem.

The first key to any programming problem is to approach it at the right level of abstraction, which often boils down to choosing the right language. One language designed for the artist-programmer is D. E. Knuth's METAFONT [6]. Three of its key features are that the positions of points are specified by declarative constraints, that the image is rendered by imperative painting commands parameterized by these points, and that procedural abstraction is provided. Let us call a language with these features a "METAFONT-style language". METAFONT-style languages are well-suited for producing images with a constrained and hierarchical structure.

From the language designer's point of view, artists are unusual programmers in that they like to specify free-form, unconstrained shapes, relying on their hand-eye coordination and on repeated adjustments to get the shape right. This is best done under the control of a what-you-see-is-what-you-get (WYSIWYG) image editor, by which I mean a system that continuously displays an image while the user interactively modifies it by pointing into it. Patrick Baudelaire's Draw program [1] for the Xerox Alto is an example of such an editor.

Several years ago I used METAFONT and Draw to produce figures for my thesis. These figures contained hierarchical structure, constrained positions, and free-form shapes, so that neither program by itself was quite right. Draw has no constraints and is not programmable. METAFONT can be driven interactively, a command at a time, but it is not WYSIWYG, since you cannot point into the image and modify it.

The contrasting virtues of these two programs inspired me to design Juno, a system that integrates a programming language like METAFONT with a WYSIWYG image editor like Draw. I implemented Juno in the Cedar programming system [9] at Xerox PARC. Figure 1 shows some examples of images produced with Juno.

Two techniques greatly contributed to the harmony of Juno's integration of WYSIWYG editing with programmability: *geometric specification*, or the use geometric constraints to specify locations, and *implicit editing*, or the modification of the text of a Juno program in response to the interactive editing of the displayed image that the program produces.

As an example of geometric specification, a Juno user might specify that points a, b, and c be collinear, and that the distance from a to b be equal to the distance from b to c. The Juno interpreter will translate these geometric constraints into numerical constraints on the coordinates of the points, and solve them by numerical methods. Less trivially, a regular pentagon is easily constructed by specifying equality of length for its sides and for three of its chords.

The use of declarative specifications for positioning points derives from METAFONT. But METAFONT allows only constraints that are algebraically linear, and this precludes the important geometric predicates of parallelism and congruence, which correspond to quadratic equations. The pentagon example hints at the extra power of nonlinear specification, but more important than this extra power is the fact that a user of a WYSIWYG interface can specify geometric constraints simply by selecting the constraint and the points it is to be applied to. By contrast, the speci-

* Author's present affiliation: DEC Systems Research Center

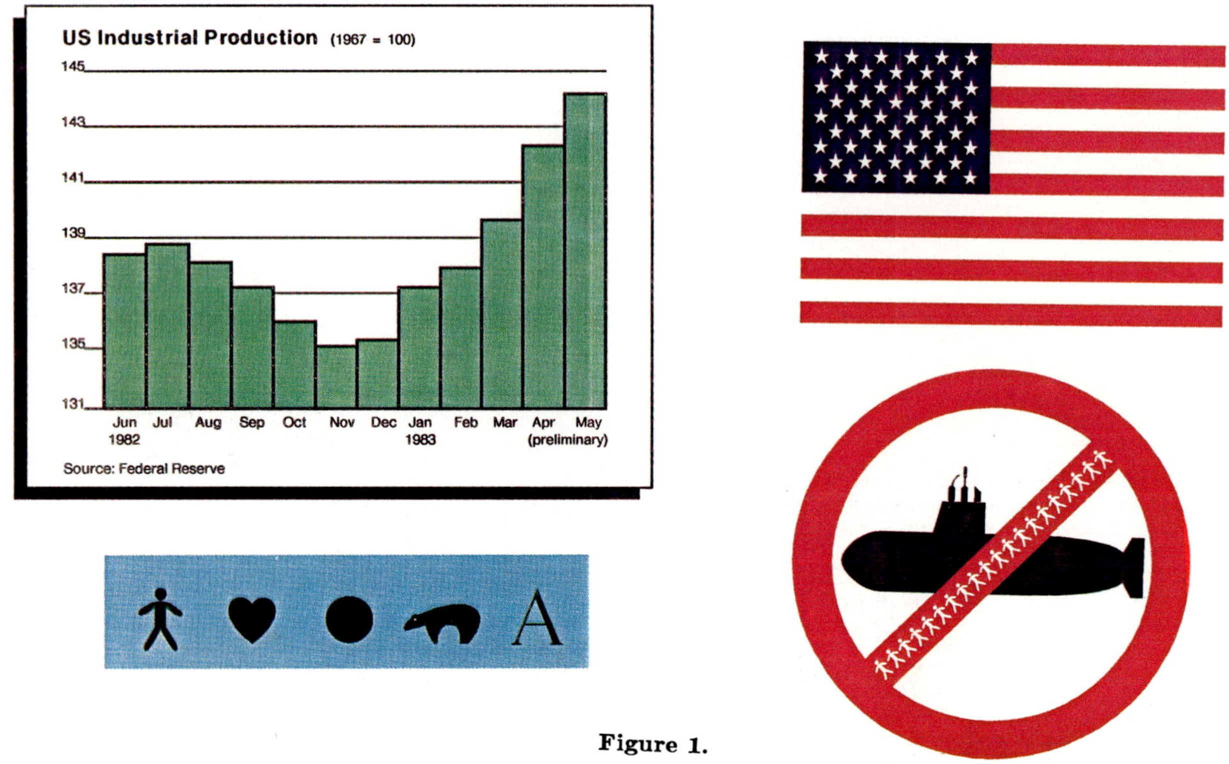

Figure 1.

fication of linear algebraic constraints on the coordinates of points requires naming the points and typing the equations, which does not fit well into a WYSIWYG interface.

Going from linear to nonlinear constraints is more ambitious than going to the "slightly nonlinear" constraints of Chris Van Wyk's Ideal [10], but less ambitious than going all the way to open-ended, client-defined constraint types, as in Alan Borning's Thinglab [2]. The nonlinear constraints pose two dangers: the solver might become too slow, or the solver might become too unpredictable to the user.

In regard to the first danger, the Juno constraint solver uses Newton-Raphson iteration (described in most standard texts in numerical analysis, for example, Conte and de Boor [3]) to solve constraints. On the powerful Xerox Dorado, my first crude implementation was fast enough. Bruce Lucas programmed a variant of Juno called "Banzai" for a Sun workstation at CMU [7]; he reported acceptable performance only after including some standard optimizations. Derivative-based methods like Newton-Raphson iteration are reputed to be faster than relaxation methods, like those employed in Ivan Sutherland's Sketchpad [8]. Of course, if all the constraints in a complicated image had to be solved together, the asymptotically slow behavior of the constraint solver would bring the system to a halt. But an appropriate hierarchy can avoid this, and is desirable regardless of whether nonlinear constraints are allowed.

In regard to the second danger, a nonlinear solver behaves quite predicatably provided that the initial configuration is not too far from the solution. Therefore, in using the WYSIWYG editor, the user must lay out the points of the image in roughly the right positions, and rely on the constraint solver only to align them accurately, not to rearrange them drastically. Similarly, when a running Juno program invokes the constraint solver, it must supply "hints" for the initial positions of the unknown points.

The implicit editing technique is more novel. It is almost dictated by the integration of programmability with WYSIWYG editing: if an image produced by a program were "touched up" by interactive editing, then the touching up would have to be repeated if the program were modified; this is unacceptable. It follows that the interactive editing operations must be considered to modify not the displayed image, but the underlying program that produces the image.

For example, consider the following command of the Juno language (a little liberty has been taken with the syntax):

```
LET p, q | p = (0, 0) AND q = (100, 124)
 IN DRAW (p, q)
END ,
```

which draws a line segment slightly steeper than 45 degrees by introducing two point variables p and q at specified positions and connecting them with a line segment. When this command is "current", the line segment is displayed on the screen. If the user then points at the higher end of the segment and moves it, the coordinate pair (100, 124) in the program text will change to reflect the new position of the endpoint q. In addition to moving points, interactive editing commands may add or delete points, constraints, or painting commands; each such operation is most properly understood as a syntactic operation on the current command. After each operation, the screen is updated by re-executing the current command.

In a general WYSIWYG editor, the user modifies a data structure d by interacting with an image $I(d)$. Implicit editing is the special case in which d is a program text and I is an interpreter. Any WYSIWYG editor must solve the *pointing problem*: if the user points at a position p in the image $I(d)$, but two or more components of the data structure d affect the rendering of the image in the vicinity of p, then the user's image position does not translate into a unique component of the underlying data structure. For example, if a user points near the intersection of two edges, there will be an ambiguity about which edge is meant. Happily, it is fairly easy to avoid the pointing problem in the implicit editing of METAFONT-style languages, since in these languages variables denote only points; shapes like edges are created as the side-effect of procedures parameterized by points.

The two main sections of this paper describe the Juno language and interactive editor. To smooth the exposition, Juno is sometimes described as it ought to be instead of as it is. Each such liberty will be accompanied by a footnote like this[0] that points to a terse caveat at the end of the paper.

Programming Juno

The Juno programming language is a version of the calculus of guarded commands described in E. W. Dijkstra's *Discipline of Programming* [5]. This is natural, because guarded commands are defined formally as predicate transformers, and "predicate" is just another word for "constraint". Dijkstra's language is a collection of predicate transformers acting upon the predicates of a theory of integers and arrays. The Juno programming language is essentially the same collection of predicate transformers acting upon the predicates of Euclidean geometry. But this section's description is conventional and operational.

A Juno command can be considered to act upon an "abstract Juno machine". The state of this machine is determined by:

- an indefinite number of named *point registers*, each of which contains a value representing a point in the Cartesian plane.
- a single anonymous *image*, to be imagined as a map from the Euclidean plane to the set of colors, but represented as a map from a fine discrete grid to the set of colors.
- three *mode registers*, the color register, width register, and endsType register, whose contents will be described later.

Painting commands. The painting commands will be described first; these are used only after the point registers have been set by commands yet to be described. Here is a list of them:

`A;B`: Execute `A`, then execute `B`. (Composition)

`FILL p`: Change the color of every image point entwined by the path `p` to the current contents of the color register. (A path entwines a point if the winding number of the path with respect to the point is non-zero.)

`STROKE p`: Draw a stroke along the path `p` whose color is the contents of the color register, whose width is the contents of the width register, and whose ends are finished off in a style determined by the contents of the endsType register.

`c PAINT A`: Set the color register to `c`, execute `A`, restore the old contents of the color register.

`e ENDS A`: Set the endsType register to `e`, execute `A`, restore the old contents of the endsType register.

`p, q WIDTH A`: Set the width register to the distance between points `p` and `q`, execute `A`, restore the old contents of the width register.

`r WIDTH A`: Set the width register to `r` millimeters,[1] execute `A`, restore the old contents of the width register.

`DRAW p`: This is short for `ROUND ENDS BLACK PAINT 1 WIDTH STROKE p`.

The basic marking commands have the form `FILL p` and `STROKE p`, where `p` is a *path*, that is, a connected sequence of edges and arcs. An edge is specified by its two endpoints; an arc is specified by its four Bezier control points.

The semicolon has higher binding power than `PAINT`, `ENDS`, or `WIDTH`; for example, `e ENDS A;B` means `e ENDS (A;B)` rather than `(e ENDS A); B`.

For example, Figure 2 shows the result of executing the command

```
GREY PAINT BUTT ENDS 8 WIDTH
STROKE (a, b), (b, c);
STROKE (d, e); STROKE (e, f);
ROUND ENDS STROKE (g, h);
BUTT ENDS STROKE (i, j);
SQUARE ENDS STROKE (k, l);
FILL (n, m, o, p), (p, n);
BLACK PAINT 3 WIDTH
STROKE (n, m, o, p), (p, n);
o, q WIDTH ROUND ENDS STROKE (q, q)
```

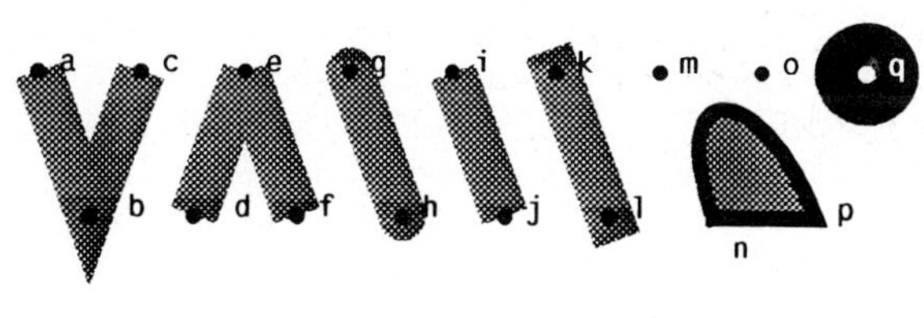

Figure 2.

in a state in which points `a` through `q` have the locations labeled in the figure.

Here is the syntax of these commands (the ellipses in the first production indicate that the syntax for a `Command` will be extended further):

```
Command ::= FILL Path | STROKE Path
          | DRAW Path | ModeChange
          | Command ; Command | ...

ModeChange ::= Color PAINT Command
             | EndsType ENDS Command
             | Number WIDTH Command
             | Point, Point WIDTH Command

EndsType ::= BUTT | SQUARE | ROUND

Color ::= BLACK | WHITE | GREY | RED | BLUE
        | GREEN | YELLOW | CYAN | MAGENTA | ...

Path ::= Patch | Path , Patch

Patch ::= (Point, Point)
        | (Point, Point, Point, Point)

Point ::= a symbolic name

Number ::= a decimal numeral
```

Juno also includes a primitive for painting a text string at a given position in a given font, but it will not be described.

Constraint commands. Juno's constraint command is a special case of the general construct from the guarded command calculus, which has the form[2]

LET Variables | Constraints IN Command END ,

where Variables is a list of local variables to be introduced, Constraints is a conjunction of constraints on the values of the variables, and Command is what is to be executed in the scope of the local variables. If no values for the variables satisfy the constraints, the command is equivalent to *Abort.* If the constraints do not determine the values of the variables uniquely, then the command is non-deterministic, which means that the implementation is allowed to introduce any values that do satisfy the constraints.

As an example, let us translate Euclid's proposition I.1 into guarded commands: "*On a given line to construct an equilateral triangle.* Let ab be the given line; thus it is required to describe on the line ab an equilateral triangle. With center a and distance ab let the circle c be described; and with center b and distance ba let the circle d be described; and let the circles c and d cut one another at e. Now I say that the triangle abe is equilateral. For, since b and e both lie on the circle c, ab is equal to ae ..." [4]. Euclid went on to prove what would today be called the partial correctness of his construction.

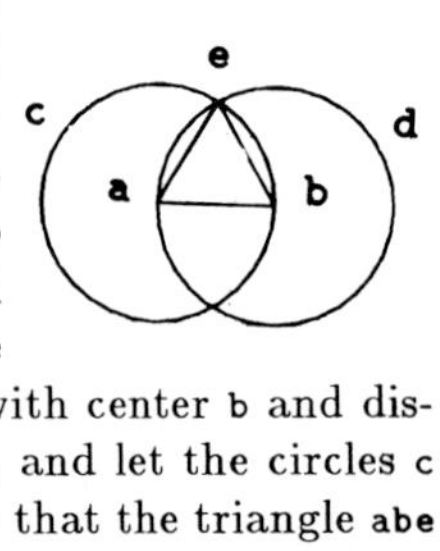

Here is the construction expressed using guarded commands:

```
LET c, d
  | Circle(c) AND Center(c) = a AND On(b, c)
AND Circle(d) AND Center(d) = b AND On(a, d)
 IN LET e | Point(e) AND On(e, c) AND On(e, d)
     IN Draw (a, b), (b, e), (e, a)
    END
END
```

which not only constructs the point e, but also draws the sides of the triangle. The predicates Circle, Point, and On are used with their obvious meanings.

The construction above is not a legal Juno program, since firstly, variables in Juno range only over points, and secondly, the only four constraint types allowed in Juno are the following:

(x, y) CONG (u, v): the distance from x to y equals the distance from u to v.

(x, y) PARA (u, v): the direction from x to y parallels the direction from u to v.

HOR(x, y): the direction from x to y is horizontal

VER(x, y): the direction from x to y is vertical

Note that any constraint expressible in the Euclidean theory of geometry can be expressed in terms of CONG and PARA. In particular, the collinearity of a, b, and c can be expressed (a, b) PARA (b, c). At least one additional constraint type is needed to orient images on the output pages, since these are not circular. Both HOR and VER were added, since to choose one of them would be asymmetric.

Euclid's construction can still be succinctly expressed with the limited predicates available in Juno:

```
LET e | (a, e) CONG (a, b) AND (b, e) CONG (a, b)
 IN DRAW (a, b), (b, e), (e, a)
END
```

But we still don't have a legal Juno program, since we still have to settle the important issue: which of the two solutions for e will be introduced? The semantics of guarded commands say that either may be introduced; this is unacceptable, since the programmer must be given control over which triangle is to be drawn.

One solution to this problem (the first that I tried) is to allow a fifth predicate, CC(x, y, z), which asserts that points x, y, and z are counter-clockwise. Then the constraints on e in the last command could be extended with CC(a, b, e) (to get the triangle shown in the illustration of Euclid's construction), or with CC(a, e, b) (to get the other triangle). Unfortunately, while the predicates CONG, PARA, HOR and VER translate into polynomial equality constraints on the coordinates of the points, the predicate CC translates into a polynomial inequality constraint. I tried to use a hybrid of the simplex and Newton-Raphson methods to handle these inequalities, but it didn't work very well.

Here is a better solution: since the behavior of a numerical solver depends on the initial trial solution, Juno allows the program to give the solver a hint about where to look for the solution. The syntax LET x == u | P IN A END means the same thing as LET x | P IN A END, but it hints to the solver that the solution for x is likely to be in the vicinity of u. The "==" may be read "approximately equal to". No formal semantics can be given without describing the detailed behavior of the constraint solver, but from an operational point of view this is an obvious interface to a numerical solver.

The notation (x, y) can be used to specify an absolute position in the Cartesian plane, but it is almost always better to specify a position relative to a coordinate system determined by given image points. So, the notation `(x, y) REL (p, q)` denotes the point whose coordinates are the real numbers `x` and `y` in the coordinate system determined by the points `p` and `q` as follows: `p` is the origin of the coordinate system and `q` is the point `(1, 0)`, that is, the tip of the unit x-vector. The rest of the coordinate system is determined by the condition that it be orthonormal and right-handed. Using complex arithmetic, `(x, y) REL (p, q)` can be defined to be `p + (x + iy)(q - p)`.

Putting this all together, we finally obtain the following Juno program for drawing an equilateral triangle on the segment `ab`, such that the new vertex `e` will make `abe` counterclockwise:

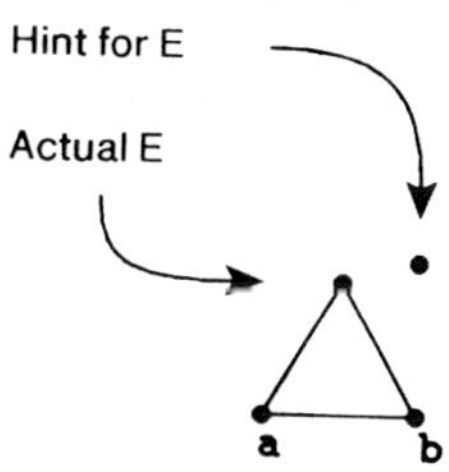


```
LET e == (1, 1) REL (a, b)
  | (a, e) CONG (a, b)
AND (b, e) CONG (a, b)
 IN DRAW (a, b), (b, e), (e, a)
END
```

If "`(1, 1)`" were changed to "`(1, -1)`" (or to any point in the bottom half-plane), then the triangle `abe` would come out clockwise.

In summary, here is the syntax for constraint commands, in which the quotes in the first production are intended to prevent "such that" from being read as the BNF "or":

```
Command ::= ...
  | LET LocalList "|" Constraints
     IN Command
    END
  | ...

LocalList ::= Local | LocalList , Local

Local ::= Point == (Number, Number)
                REL (Point, Point)

Constraints ::= Constraint
              | Constraints AND Constraint

Constraint ::= HOR (Point, Point)
        | VER(Point, Point)
        | (Point, Point) CONG (Point, Point)
        | (Point, Point) PARA (Point, Point)
        | TRUE
```

Any state solves the constraint `TRUE`; hence if it is the only constraint, the hints will become the initial positions of the local variables. For example, here is a program to draw a square on `ab`:

```
LET c == (1, 1) REL (a, b)
  , d == (0, 1) REL (a, b)
  | TRUE
 IN DRAW (a, b), (b, c), (c, d), (d, a)
END
```

Procedures. No complications are created by Juno procedures, since the only data-type is point, and there are no side-effects on points. (All side-effects are on the anonymous global image.) The syntax is:

```
Command ::= ...    | ProcName(PointList)

ProcDef ::= ProcName(PointList): Command

ProcName ::= a symbolic name
```

For example, here is a Juno procedure for trisecting an angle. More precisely, given points `b` and `e` equally distant from a given point `a`, the procedure draws two segments `ac` and `ad` which trisect the angle `bae` and have the same length as `ab` and `ae`:

```
Trisect(b, a, e):
  LET c == (.3, 0) REL (b, e)
    , d == (.6, 0) REL (b, e)
    | (b, c) CONG (c, d) AND (c, d) CONG (d, e)
  AND (a, c) CONG (a, b) AND (a, d) CONG (a, b)
   IN DRAW (a, c); Draw (a, d)
  END
```

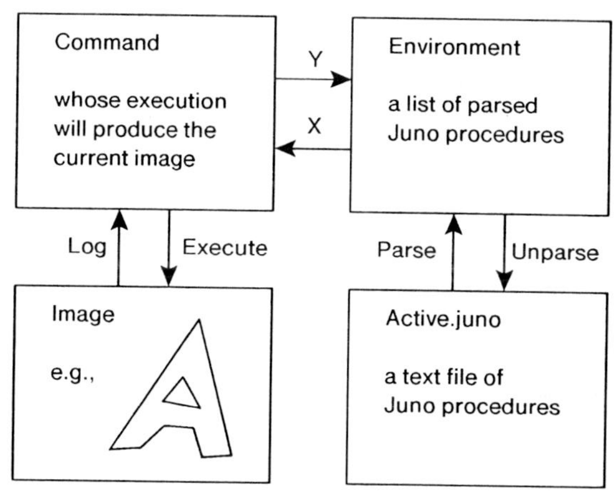

Figure 3.

The interactive system

The overall structure of the Juno system is shown in Figure 3. The state of the system is determined by the *procedural context*, which is a list of parsed Juno procedures (called the environment in the figure), and the *current command*, which is a Juno command of a particular form to be described later. The user views this state through two windows on the display screen; one (the *text window*) contains the pretty-printed (or "unparsed") text for each of the procedures in the environment, and the other (the *image window*) displays the image that results from executing the current command. The user changes the state by pointing into the windows with a mouse and clicking or typing.

The text window is essentially a conventional what-you-see-is-what-you-get editor. After editing the text, the user triggers the "Reparse" command with the mouse, which regenerates the internal list of parsed procedures from the current text and simultaneously pretty-prints the procedures in the window. Caching at the procedure level is used to speed up the reparsing. If a parse error occurs, the region of the error is highlighted on the display.

The image window is used for implicit editing: the user specifies editing operations in terms of the displayed result, and the system translates them into modifications to the text of the current command. Eventually, the current command can be installed in the environment as a procedure.

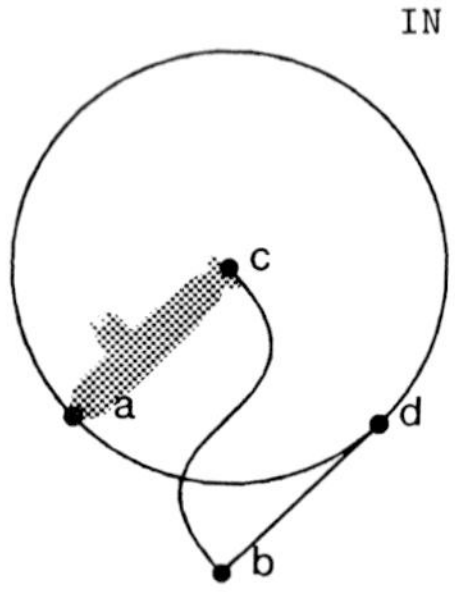


```
LET c == (.6, .6) REL (SW, SE)
  , a == (.1, .5) REL (SW, SE)
  | TRUE
  IN LET b == (.2, 0) REL (SW, SE)
       , d == (.7, .1) REL (SW, SE)
       | (a, c) PARA (b, d)
     AND (a, c) CONG (b, d)
     AND (a, d) CONG (b, c)
     AND (a, c) CONG (c, d)
       IN Circle(c, d)
        ; DRAW(c, d, a, b)
        ; DRAW(b, d)
        ; YellowSubmarine(a, c)
     END
END
```

Figure 4.

For example, Figure 4 shows a current command on the right and the corresponding image on the left. The four labeled dots in the image are for reference purposes only and would not appear on the screen. The conventional variables `SW` and `SE` represent the southwest and southeast corners of the window in which the image is to be drawn.[3]

Note the constraints of the command in Figure 4:

> that `(a, c)` is parallel to `(b, d)`, i.e., that `acdb` is a trapezoid;
>
> that `(a, c)` is congruent to `(b, d)`, i.e., that the trapezoid is a parallelogram;
>
> that `(a, d)` is congruent to `(b, c)`, i.e., that the parallelogram is a rectangle;
>
> that `(a, c)` is congruent to `(c, d)`, i.e., that the rectangle is a square.

The two calls to `DRAW` produce the straight and curved lines that appear in the image. We assume that the procedural context includes the procedure `Circle(c, d)`, which draws a circle centered at `c` through `d`, and `YellowSubmarine(a, c)`, which draws a yellow submarine with its snout at `a` and its tail at `c`.

The general syntax for the current command is:

```
CurrentCommand
   ::= LET LocalList "|" TRUE
        IN LET LocalList "|" Constraints
        IN CommandList
       END
    END

CommandList ::= PaintingCommand
              | PaintingCommand ; CommandList

PaintingCommand ::= DRAW Path | ProcCall
```

The points in the outer LocalList are called "independent points"; the points in the inner LocalList are called "dependent points". This is because the positions of the independent points are fixed by the outer `LET`; the positions of the dependent points are set by the inner `LET` to satisfy the constraints. Note that the syntax of the current command excludes mode changes; this restriction simplifies implicit editing. In summary, the current command is determined by a list of independent points, a list of dependent points, a conjunction of constraints, and a list of painting commands.

When the system needs to update the image on the display, it clears the image and executes the current command. There is a wrinkle: the solution found by the solver is used to replace all the hints, so if the current command is executed again, the hints will specify an exact solution. Note that this only changes the hints for the dependent points. Thus the update operation establishes a state in which the hints satisfy the constraints.

From an n-dimensional geometric point of view, the solution set of the constraints is a real variety (a generalized curve or surface) in Cartesian n-space, the hints specify a point in n-space, and the update operation moves the point onto the variety, without changing any coordinate of any independent point. The hint for a point is sometimes called its "current position".

As in many drawing programs, different cursors are used for different operations. Figure 5 lists the Juno cursors and their functions. A user editing operation begins when the user "picks up" one of the cursors by pointing at its icon on the screen.

The user then specifies the argument list for the operation, which is a `PointList`: a sequence of point variables occurring in the current command. This is done by pointing and clicking. A click with the middle mouse button adds to the argument list the name of the point closest to the cursor; a click with the left button creates a new point at the position of the cursor and includes this new point in the argument list. In other words, a new name is chosen and inserted into the dependent point list of the current command, with the cursor's position as its hint. The name of the point is not displayed in the image, although this feature would sometimes be useful.

Finally, the user hits the escape key to apply the operation associated with the current cursor to the sequence of arguments specified. An n-ary operation is applied to the most recent n arguments specified. For example, if the last four arguments specified were `p, q, r`, and `s`, with `s` the most recent, then the effect of hitting escape while holding the various cursors is:

> Horizontal T-square. Add `HOR(r, s)` to the constraint of the current command.
>
> Vertical T-square. Add `VER(r, s)` to the constraint of the current command.
>
> Compass. Add `(p, q) CONG (r, s)` to the constraint of the current command.
>
> Parallel bars. Add `(p, q) PARA (r, s)` to the constraint of the current command.

Pencil, for drawing straight edges and arcs
Typewriter, for typing character strings
X-tension cursor, for calling procedures
Horizontal T-square, for equalizing heights
Vertical T-square, for equalizing indentations
Compass, for equalizing distances
Parallel bars, for equalizing directions
Snowman, for freezing points
Move Arrow for moving things
Copy Arrow for copying things
Eraser, for erasing things
Y cursor for creating procedures

Figure 5.

Pencil. If no escapes have been typed since the user entered the argument q, then add `DRAW(p, q, r, s)` to the current command. Otherwise add `DRAW(r, s)` to the current command. (Although this is complicated to describe, it is simple to use.)

X cursor. This cursor is used to add to the current command a call to any procedure in the context. To pick up this cursor, the user must specify one of the procedures in the current context. The number of arguments of the procedure determines the number of arguments the X cursor will use from the sequence.

Move arrow. Change r's position to coincide with s's position, then replace all occurrences of s with r in the constraints and commands, and eliminate the point s from whichever LocalList it occurs in. (This can be used to "weld" two existing points together, but more commonly r is an existing point and s is a new point created by left-clicking, and it is desirable to eliminate it after r has been moved.)

Snowman. If s is independent, make it dependent, and vice versa.[4] (The cursor is a snowman because independent points were originally called frozen points. While the user holds the snowman, the independent points are highlighted.)

For example, to produce the image of Figure 4 starting from a blank screen, the user would execute the following instructions (in which $ means hit escape, x means click near point x with the middle button, X means click near point x with the left button, and [P] means click the procedure P in the text window):

- With the Pencil: `DB$ACd$`
- With the X: `[Circle] cd$ [YellowSubmarine] ac$`
- With the Parallel bars: `acbd$`
- With the Compass: `acbd$cd$adbc$`
- With the Snowman: `c$a$`

Note that a point is left-clicked at its first occurrence (to create it) and middle-clicked thereafter. Note also how the last argument(s) of an operation are re-used as the first argument(s) of the next operation, in the case of the pencil and compass.

It is remarkable how much easier it is to construct procedures by "drawing" them in this way than by typing them. Fewer user actions are required (in this case, 40 clicks or keystrokes instead of more than 300 keystrokes), but the important factor is avoiding the burden of names. For example, to constrain four points to bound three equal arcs of a circle centered about a fifth point is easy when the points are laid out before you and the constraints are applied by pointing. But if the points are named b, c, d, e, and a respectively and the constraints must be specified in terms of the names, as was the case when this problem came up in the Trisect procedure, then more concentration is required to avoid errors.

Operations performed by the user with the Pencil and X cursor are reflected immediately in the image, because they can be executed incrementally. (Note that the commands inserted by these cursors are added at the end rather than the beginning of the command list in the current command.) The Move operation also causes the screen to be updated, although this cannot be done incrementally. Operations that add constraints do not cause the image to be updated unless the user explicitly requests it, by typing escape twice instead of once. This is because constraints are conveniently entered in batches.

To adjust the size, position, and orientation of the image on the screen, the Move arrow is used to move the independent points to whatever positions are desired, say, X and Y:

- With the Move arrow: `aX$bY$` ...

The move commands are repeated until the image looks right.

It is also possible to select a group of points by drawing a balloon around them, and then to erase, move, copy, or transform the group by a linear transformation. But these operations will not be described.

Another example is shown in Figure 6. The sequence of clicks shown in the right of the figure produces the image; it takes an experienced user only a few seconds. The independent points are a, c, l, and m: moving a up and down will adjust the height of the letter, moving m left and right will adjust the width of the letter, and moving l left and right will adjust the boldness of the letter, that is, the width of its strokes.

Figure 7 illustrates a common kind of construction: two cubic Bezier arcs are constrained to be symmetric around a vertical axis, by the obvious constraints on their control points. After entering the constraints, the control points are adjusted interactively until the curve looks right. The instructions in the figure call for adjusting u, leaving it to the solver to move its mirror image q. Alternatively, the user could freeze q, u, r, t, and s and adjust v, leaving it to the solver to move p; or freeze the upper four points and move t, leaving it to the solver to move both r and s.

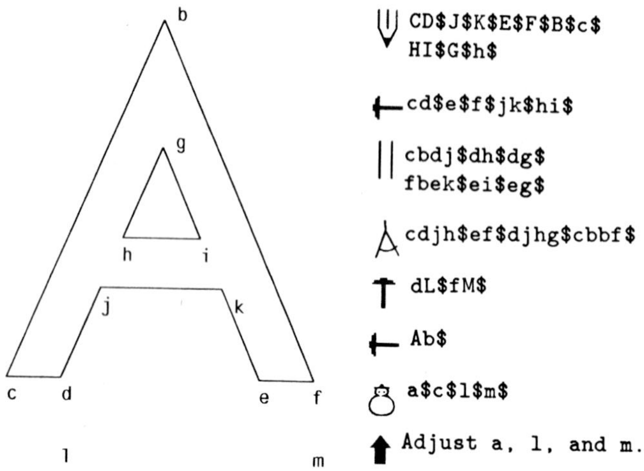

Figure 6.

Using a WYSIWYG constraint solver is effective and fun, but there are several pitfalls that an uninitiated user can fall into. Two examples: If b and c are near one another and far from a, then the constraint (a, b) PARA (a, c) is more stable than (a, b) PARA (b, c), even though they are equivalent geometrically: if the user makes a long segment parallel to a short segment, the solver tends to collapse the short segment to a point. Also, redundant constraints, though usually harmless, will sometimes prevent the solver from converging. I learned this when, miscounting degrees of freedom, I tried to make a regular pentagon by specifying equality of length for its sides and for four (rather than three) of its chords. These pitfalls are easily learned and avoided; perhaps both of them would go away if more attention were paid to the solver.

For simple images like those in Figures 6 and 7, the update operation is immediate (less than a second). Since the cost of solving a system of equations is very roughly proportional to the cube of the number of constraints, the only hope for handling large images is to introduce a hierarchy, making lots of small problems instead of one big one. The Juno language provides a satisfactory hierarchy. For example, the constraint solving problem in Figure 4 has four constraints on the two unknown points b and d; a simple system. Dozens of other constraint problems must be solved inside the procedures Circle and YellowSubmarine, but neither the local variables of these procedures nor the constraints that initialize them are of any relevance to the outer-level problem of determining b and d.

(An interesting programming problem is to somehow employ caching to further speed the update process. For complicated images, this might improve performance dramatically.)

Since the instructions for drawing Figure 4 require that the environment already contain procedures for drawing circles and yellow submarines, hierarchical drawings must be built from the bottom up. The Y cursor is used to insert the text of the current command into the environment as a procedure, whence it can be invoked by the X cursor. The independent points of the current command become parameters to the procedure, and the hints for the positions of the dependent points are expressed in a coordinate system determined by the independent points, instead of in the (SW, SE) coordinate system.

For example, if the Y cursor were used to make a procedure called P out of the current command illustrated in Figure 4, the result would be

```
P(a, c):
   LET b == (0, -1) REL (a, c)
     , d == (1, -1) REL (a, c)
     | ...
    IN ...
```

The constraints and painting commands are as before. The introduction of hints for b and d that are relative to a and c is crucial, since if, in a future call to P(a, c), the constraints were solved with randomly initialized b and d, the nonlinear solver might fail to find the solution.

In order that there be no ambiguity about the coordinate system, the Y cursor won't create a procedure with more than two parameters. Thus to "draw" the Trisect procedure, the user would create it with the two arguments b and e, since it is most natural and stable to specify the hints for c and d in the be coordinate system. After creating the procedure with the Y cursor, the user would edit the procedure in the Juno text file, inserting a as an argument and deleting it from the list of locals. This awkwardness should have been avoided by enriching the interactive editing system with a command that specifies, for a dependent point, the pair of independent points relative to which the point's hint is to be specified.

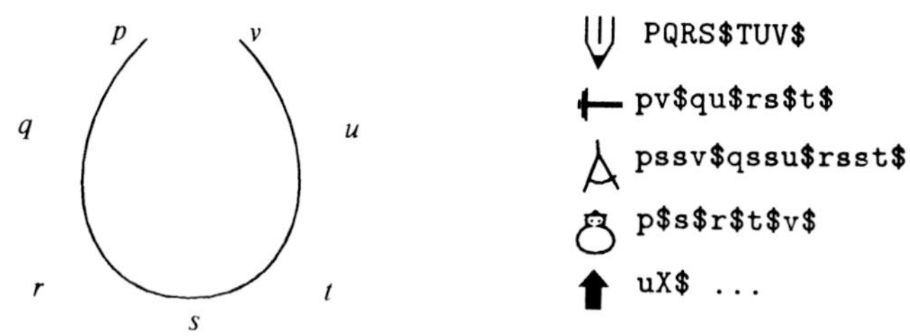

Figure 7.

Conclusions

Since the Cedar system is not widely available, Juno has been used only by a few researchers. Also, the Juno project was interrupted when I left PARC. However, even from this unconcluded project, the general conclusion can be drawn: implicit editing with geometric constraints is a workable technique for constructing a programmable WYSIWYG system. Perhaps the best way to be more specific is to describe the things that a Juno user comes to yearn for.

Juno allows the abstraction of commands into parameterized procedures, but not the abstraction of constraints into parameterized predicates, which would also be useful. For example, instead of using twelve clicks to constrain abc to be a right angle, it would be convenient to apply a predicate defined by some expression such as

```
Right(a, b, c)
== (EXISTS d == (1, 1) REL (a, b, c)
        : (a, b) CONG (c, d)
     AND (b, c) CONG (d, a)
     AND (a, c) CONG (b, d))
```

(The triple (a, b, c) is used to denote the skewed coordinate system in which b = (0, 0), a = (1, 0), and c = (0, 1).) As another example, consider the constraint that a point e lie on the cubic spline with Bezier control points a, b, c, and d. Although the geometric form of this constraint is well-known, it is rather challenging to click it into Juno; John Warnock was the first to do it. It is unthinkable that it would be used frequently unless it were abstracted into a parameterized predicate. (Both of these examples suggest the interesting problem of optimizing predicates by symbolic algebraic transformations to eliminate unnecessary existentially quantified variables.)

The greatest inconvenience in using Juno is that there is no way to select a procedure body from the environment and install it as the current command for editing in WYSIWYG mode. (There is no good reason for this restriction.) Note, however, that many procedure bodies do not satisfy the syntax for current commands, and liberalizing this syntax requires rethinking the implicit editing user interface. For example, if the nesting level of LETs is n instead of two, then instead of independent and dependent points there is a general hierarchy of dependence; this cannot be controlled by the simple snowman interface. Ideally, a natural user interface would be found for implicit editing of an arbitrary command.

There would be great leverage in extending Juno's universe of values. For example, the graph in Figure 1 required a procedure BarGraph12, which drew a 12-bar graph given two points to determine a baseline and twelve points to determine the heights of the bars. After calling BarGraph12 from the current command, the heights of the bars were adjusted in WYSIWYG mode. It would be nicer to write a procedure BarGraphN, taking a list of points, but this would require extending Juno's universe of values to include lists of points.

Some reflection suggests that the appropriate universe is the smallest set containing the real numbers and closed under the formation of ordered pairs, since this includes points, lists of points, and more; and the natural class of primitive constraints on the set is easy to solve. However, the implicit editing problem for this universe seems completely open-ended.

Acknowledgements

To the programmers of Cedar and Cedar graphics, for making the marvels that Juno needed; to Jim Sasaki, for programming Juno's special parser generator; to Donna Auguste, for programming the interpreter for the first version of the language; to Rick Beach, Hania Gajewska, Lyle Ramshaw, Maureen Stone, and the many others who helped in this long, drawn-out project; my heart-felt thanks.

Caveats

[1] The actual units are screen pixels.

[2] The actual syntax uses IF, ->, and FI instead of LET, IN, and END.

[3] Instead of SW and SE, absolute coordinates are used at the outer level.

[4] Since the snowman takes only one argument, hitting escape is not necessary.

References

[1] P. C. Baudelaire. Draw Manual. *Alto User's Hand book*, Xerox Corp., Palo Alto, CA, 1979. Referenced by [10].

[2] Alan Borning. Thinglab — a constraint-oriented simulation laboratory. SSL-79-3, Xerox PARC, Palo Alto, CA, July 1979.

[3] S. D. Conte and Carl de Boor. *Elementary Numerical Analysis*. McGraw-Hill, 1972.

[4] Euclid. *The Thirteen Books of the Elements*. Tr. by Thomas L. Heath, Dover, 1956.

[5] Edsger W. Dijkstra. *A Discipline of Programming*. Prentice-Hall, 1976.

[6] Donald E. Knuth. TEX *and* METAFONT. Digital Press, 1979.

[7] Bruce Lucas. Private communication, February 1985.

[8] Ivan Sutherland. *Sketchpad, A Man-Machine Graphical Communication System*. PhD thesis, MIT, January, 1963.

[9] Warren Teitelman. The Cedar Programming Environment: A Midterm Report and Examination. SL-83-11, Xerox PARC, Palo Alto, CA, June 1984.

[10] Christopher J. Van Wyk. A high-level language for specifying pictures. *Transactions on Graphics*, v. 1 no. 2, April 1982.

Animating Rotation with Quaternion Curves

Ken Shoemake†

The Singer Company
Link Flight Simulation Division

ABSTRACT

Solid bodies roll and tumble through space. In computer animation, so do cameras. The rotations of these objects are best described using a four coordinate system, quaternions, as is shown in this paper. Of all quaternions, those on the unit sphere are most suitable for animation, but the question of how to construct curves on spheres has not been much explored. This paper gives one answer by presenting a new kind of spline curve, created on a sphere, suitable for smoothly in-betweening (i.e. interpolating) sequences of arbitrary rotations. Both theory and experiment show that the motion generated is smooth and natural, without quirks found in earlier methods.

C.R. Classification: G.1.1 [Numerical Analysis] Interpolation—Spline and piecewise polynomial interpolation; G.1.2 [Numerical Analysis] Approximation—Spline and piecewise polynomial approximation; I.2.9 [Artificial Intelligence] Robotics—Manipulators; I.3.5 [Computer Graphics] Computational Geometry and Object Modelling—Curve, surface, solid, and object representation, —Geometric algorithms, languages, and systems, —Hierarchy and geometric transformations

General Terms: Algorithms, Theory

Keywords and phrases: quaternion, rotation, spherical geometry, spline, Bézier curve, B-spline, animation, interpolation, approximation, in-betweening

1. Introduction

Computer animation of three dimensional objects imitates the *key frame* techniques of traditional animation, using key positions in space instead of key drawings. Physics says that the general position of a rigid body can be given by combining a translation with a rotation. Computer animators key such transformations to control both simulated cameras and objects to be rendered. In following such an approach, one is naturally led to ask: What is the best representation for general rotations, and how does one in-between them? Surprisingly little has been published on these topics, and the answers are not trivial.

This paper suggests that the common solution, using three Euler's angles interpolated independently, is not ideal. The more recent (1843) notation of quaternions is proposed instead, along with interpolation on the quaternion unit sphere. Although quaternions are less familiar, conversion to quaternions and generation of in-between frames can be completely automatic, no matter how key frames were originally specified, so users don't need to know—or care—about inner details. The same cannot be said for Euler's angles, which are more difficult to use.

Spherical interpolation itself can be used for purposes besides animating rotations. For example, the set of all possible directions in space forms a sphere, the so-called Gaussian sphere, on which one might want to control the positions of infinitely distant light sources. Modelling features on a globe is another possible application.

It is simple to use and to program the method proposed here. It is more difficult to follow its development. This stems from two causes: 1) rotations in space are more confusing than one might think, and 2) interpolating on a sphere is trickier than interpolating in, say, a plane. Readers well acquainted with splines and their use in computer animation should have little difficulty, although even they may stumble a bit over quaternions.

2. Describing rotations

2.1 Rigid motion

Imagine hurling a brick towards a plate glass window. As the brick flies closer and closer, a nearby physicist

† Author's current address: 1700 Santa Cruz Ave., Menlo Park, CA 94025

might observe that, while it does not change shape or size, it can tumble freely. Leonhard Euler proved two centuries ago that, however the brick tumbles, each position can be achieved by a single rotation from a reference position. [Euler,1752] [Goldstein] The same is true for any rigid body. (Shattering glass is obviously not a single rigid body.)

While translations are well animated by using vectors, rotation animation can be improved by using the progenitor of vectors, quaternions. Quaternions were discovered by Sir William Rowan Hamilton in October of 1843. The moment is well recorded, for he considered them his most important contribution, the inspired answer to a fifteen-year search for a successor to complex numbers. [Hamilton] By an odd quirk of mathematics, only systems of two, four, or eight components will multiply as Hamilton desired; triples had been his stumbling block.

Soon after quaternions were introduced, Arthur Cayley published a way to describe rotations using the new multiplication. [Cayley] The notation in his paper so closely anticipates matrix notation, which he devised several years later, that it may be taken as a formula for converting a quaternion to a rotation matrix. It turns out that the four values making up a quaternion describe rotation in a natural way: three of them give the coordinates for the axis of rotation, while the fourth is determined by the angle rotated through. [Courant & Hilbert]

Since computer graphics leans heavily on vector operations, it is perhaps easiest to explain quaternions and rotation matrices in terms of these, reversing history. However quaternions can stand on their own as an elegant algebra of space. [Herstein] [Pickert] [MacLane]

2.2 Rotation matrices

That a tumbling brick does not change size, shape, nor "handedness" is mathematically expressed as the preservation of dot products and cross products, since these measure lengths, angles, and handedness. And since the determinant of a 3X3 matrix can be computed as the dot product of one column with the cross product of the other two, determinants are also preserved. Symbolically:

$$\mathrm{Rot}(\underline{v}_1)\cdot\mathrm{Rot}(\underline{v}_2) = \underline{v}_1\cdot\underline{v}_2$$

$$\mathrm{Rot}(\underline{v}_1)\times\mathrm{Rot}(\underline{v}_2) = \mathrm{Rot}(\underline{v}_1\times\underline{v}_2)$$

$$\det(\mathrm{Rot}(\underline{v}_1),\mathrm{Rot}(\underline{v}_2),\mathrm{Rot}(\underline{v}_3)) = \det(\underline{v}_1,\underline{v}_2,\underline{v}_3)$$

An immediate consequence is that orientation changes must be linear operations, since the preserved operations are; hence they have a matrix representation, M. Using the matrix form of a dot product, $\underline{v}_1^t\ \underline{v}_2$, we can say more precisely that $(M\ \underline{v}_1)^t\ (M\ \underline{v}_2) = \underline{v}_1^t\ \underline{v}_2$, from which it follows that

$$M^t\ M = I\ .$$

That is, the change matrix M is ***orthogonal***; its columns (and rows) are mutually perpendicular unit magnitude vectors. Because M must also preserve determinants, it is a *special orthogonal* matrix, satisfying

$$\det(M) = +1\ .$$

It is well known, and anyhow easy to show, that the special orthogonal matrices form a group, $SO(3)$, under multiplication. [MacLane][Goldstein][Misner] In this rotation group, the inverse of M is just M^t, the opposite rotation.

To illustrate, the matrix

$$M = \begin{bmatrix} 1 & 0 & 0 \\ 0 & \cos\theta & -\sin\theta \\ 0 & \sin\theta & \cos\theta \end{bmatrix}$$

effects a rotation through an angle of θ around the x axis. After verifying the properties discussed so far, note that the diagonal entries sum to $1+2\cos\theta$. While it is too lengthy to show here, the diagonal sum measures the same quantity for matrices generating rotation around any axis. [MacLane]

2.3 Quaternions

Quaternions, like rotations, also form a non-commutative group under their multiplication, and these two groups are closely related. [Goldstein] [Pickert][Misner] In fact, we can substitute quaternion multiplication for rotation matrix multiplication, and do less computing as a result. [Taylor]

To perform quaternion arithmetic, group the four components into a real part—a scalar, and an imaginary part—a vector. Addition is easy: add scalar to scalar and vector to vector. But our major interest is in multiplication. Start with a simple case: multiply two quaternions without real parts, or more precisely, with zero real parts. The result quaternion has a vector that is the cross product of the two vector parts, and a scalar that is their dot product, negated:

$$\underline{v}_1\underline{v}_2 = [(-\underline{v}_1\cdot\underline{v}_2),(\underline{v}_1\times\underline{v}_2)]\ .$$

It is certainly convenient to encompass both vector products with a single quaternion product. (One early lover of quaternion algebra called vector algebra a "hermaphrodite monster", since it required two kinds of product, each yielding a different type of result.) If one quaternion has only a scalar part, with its vector components all zero, multiplication is just real multiplication and vector scaling. Combining the two effects gives the general rule [Brady]:

$$[s_1,\underline{v}_1]\ [s_2,\underline{v}_2] = [(s_1s_2-\underline{v}_1\cdot\underline{v}_2),(s_1\underline{v}_2+s_2\underline{v}_1+\underline{v}_1\times\underline{v}_2)]\ .$$

Except for the cross product this looks like complex multiplication, $(a_1+\mathbf{i}b_1)(a_2+\mathbf{i}b_2) = (a_1a_2-b_1b_2) + \mathbf{i}(a_1b_2+a_2b_1)$, as Hamilton intended.†

Quaternions multiply with a cross product because rotations confound axes. To illustrate , place a book in front of you, face up, with the top farthest away. Use this orientation as a reference. Now hold the sides and flip it toward you onto its face, rotating 180 degrees around a left-to-right axis, y. Then, keeping it face down, spin it clockwise 180 degrees around an up-down z axis. Two rotations around two perpendicular axes; yet the total change in orientation must be, according to Euler, a single rotation. Indeed, if you hold the ends of the spine and flip the book 180 degrees around this third, outward-pointing, x axis, you should restore the original orientation. As quaternions, this is —anticipating developments ahead— [0,(0,1,0)] times [0,(0,0,1)] equals [0,(1,0,0)]; the cross product is essential.

Notice how quaternion operations give a new orientation, in "quaternion coordinates", much as translations give a position, relative to some starting reference. A central message of this paper is that quaternion coordinates are best for interpolating orientations. For comparison, imagine using spherical coordinates for translations! Quaternions represent orientation as a single rotation, just as rectangular coordinates represent position as a single vector. Translations combine by adding vectors; rotations, by multiplying quaternions. The separate axes of translations don't interact; the axes of rotations must. Quaternions preserve this interdependence naturally; Euler's angle coordinates ignore it.

2.4 Euler's angles

Why, then, do so many animators use Euler's angles? Mostly, I suspect, because quaternions are unfamiliar. Unlike Euler's angles, quaternions are not taught early in standard math and physics curricula. Certainly there is a plethora of arguments against angle coordinates. Euler's angle coordinates specify orientation as a series of three independent rotations about pre-chosen axes. For example, the orientation of an airplane is sometimes given as "yaw" (or "heading") around a vertical axis, followed by "pitch" around a horizontal axis through the wings, followed by "roll" around the nose-to-tail line. These three angles must be used in exactly the order given because rotations do not commute. The ordering of rotation axes used is a matter of convention, as is the particular set of axes, no matter what the order. For instance some physicists use the body centered axes z-x-z, in contrast to the aeronautics z-y-x. At least a dozen different conventions are possible for which series of axes to use. [Kane][Goldstein] The geometry of orientations in Euler's angle coordinates is contorted, and varies with choice of initial coordinate axes. There is no reasonable way to "multiply" or otherwise combine two rotations. Even converting between rotation matrices and angle coordinates is difficult and expensive, involving arbitrary assumptions and trigonometric functions. In their defense, it must be said that they are handy for solving differential equations—which is how Euler used them. [Euler,1758]

3. In-betweening alternatives

3.1 Straight line in-betweening

It is not immediately obvious how to in-between even two rotation keys. What orientations should an object assume on its journey between them? A natural answer is: take the first key as a reference, and represent the second by describing the single rotation that takes you to it, according to Euler's theorem. The in-between orientations should be positioned along that rotation.

If we plot quaternions as points in four-dimensional space, the straight lines between them give orientations interpolating the end points in exactly the above sense. If we plot Euler's angle coordinates instead, the in-between orientations will try to twist around three different axes simultaneously. This angle interpolation treats the three angles of rotation at each key orientation as a three-dimensional vector whose components are interpolated independently from key to key. Paradoxically, we can not rotate simply except around the special axes chosen for composition. We may even encounter so-called "gimbal lock", the loss of one degree of rotational freedom. Gimbal lock results from trying to ignore the cross product interaction of rotations, which can align two of the three axes. Quaternions are safe from gimbal lock, and so have been used for years to handle spacecraft, where it is unacceptable. [Kane][Mitchell]

3.2 How quaternions rotate

Straight lines between quaternions, however, ignore some of the natural geometry of rotation space. If our interpolated points were evenly spaced along a line, the animated rotation would speed up in the middle. To see why, we must look at how a quaternion converts to a rotation matrix. We rotate a vector by a quaternion so: multiply it on the right by the quaternion and on the left by the inverse of the quaternion, treating the vector as $[0,\underline{v}]$.

$$\underline{v}' = \mathrm{Rot}(\underline{v}) = q^{-1}\,\underline{v}\,q$$

Though it is not obvious, the result will always be a vector, with a zero scalar component. Notice how this guarantees

$$\mathrm{Rot}(\underline{v}_1)\,\mathrm{Rot}(\underline{v}_2) = \mathrm{Rot}(\underline{v}_1\,\underline{v}_2)$$

which implies that dot and cross products are preserved, embedded in the quaternion product.

The inverse of a quaternion is obtained by negating its

† Hamilton wrote a quaternion as $s+\mathbf{i}v^x+\mathbf{j}v^y+\mathbf{k}v^z$, with $\mathbf{i}^2 = \mathbf{j}^2 = \mathbf{k}^2 = \mathbf{ijk} = -1$. The multiplication rules given before are consequences of this elegant formulation.

vector part and dividing both parts by the magnitude squared. For $q = [s, \underline{v}]$,

$$q^{-1} = \frac{1}{||q||^2}[s, -\underline{v}] \; ; \qquad ||q||^2 = s^2 + \underline{v} \cdot \underline{v} \; .$$

Because all effects of magnitude are divided out, any scalar multiple of a quaternion gives the same rotation. (This kind of behavior is not unknown in computer graphics; any scalar multiple of a point in homogeneous coordinates gives the same non-homogeneous point.)

If the scalar part has value w, and the vector part values x, y, and z, the corresponding matrix can be worked out to be

$$M = \begin{bmatrix} 1-2y^2-2z^2 & 2xy+2wz & 2xz-2wy \\ 2xy-2wz & 1-2x^2-2z^2 & 2yz+2wx \\ 2xz+2wy & 2yz-2wx & 1-2x^2-2y^2 \end{bmatrix}$$

when the magnitude $w^2+x^2+y^2+z^2$ equals 1. The magnitude restriction implies that, plotted in four-dimensional space, these quaternions lie on a sphere of radius one. Deeper investigation shows that such unit quaternions carry the amount of rotation in w, as $\cos\theta/2$, while the vector part points along the rotation axis with magnitude $\sin\theta/2$. The axis of a rotation is that line in space which remains unmoved; but notice that's exactly what happens when scalar multiples of $\underline{v}$ are rotated by $[s, \underline{v}]$. Because the cross product drops out, multiplication commutes, q^{-1} meets q, mutual annihilation occurs, and the vector emerges unscathed. Summing the matrix diagonal leads to the formula stated for w. The sum equals $4w^2-1$, but must also be $1+2\cos\theta$. A trig identity, $\cos 2\theta = 2\cos^2\theta-1$, finishes the demonstation.

3.3 Great arc in-betweening

This sphere of unit quaternions forms a sub-group, S^3, of the quaternion group. Furthermore, the spherical metric of S^3 is the same as the angular metric of $SO(3)$. [Misner] From this it follows that we can rotate without speeding up by interpolating on the sphere. Simply plot the two given orientations on the sphere and draw the great circle arc between them. That arc is the curve where the sphere intersects a plane through the two points and the origin. We sped up before because we were cutting across instead of following the arc; otherwise the paths of rotation are the same.

A formula for *s*pherical *l*inear int*erp*olation from q_1 to q_2, with parameter u moving from 0 to 1, can be obtained two different ways. From the group structure we find

$$\mathrm{Slerp}(q_1, q_2; u) = q_1(q_1^{-1}q_2)^u \; ;$$

while from the 4-D geometry comes†

$$\mathrm{Slerp}(q_1, q_2; u) = \frac{\sin(1-u)\theta}{\sin\theta} q_1 + \frac{\sin u\theta}{\sin\theta} q_2 \, ,$$

where $q_1 \cdot q_2 = \cos\theta$. The first is simpler for analysis, while the second is more practical for applications.

But animations typically have more than two key poses to connect, and here even our spherical elaboration of simple linear interpolation shows flaws. While orientation changes seamlessly, the direction of rotation changes abruptly. In mathematical terms, we want higher order continuity. There are lots of ways to achieve it—off the sphere; unfortunately we've learned too much.

3.4 Rotation geometry and topology

No matter what we do in general quaternion space, the ultimate effect must be interpreted via the sphere; so we had best work there in spite of the difficulty. It is important to grasp this point. The metric structure, hence the intrinsic geometry, of the rotation group $SO(3)$ is that of a sphere. Over small regions, meaning in this case small rotation angles, a sphere looks as if it is flat. But if we go far enough along a "straight line", we end up back where we started. What could be more evident about rotations? Their very essence is moving in circles. Looking back to the book-turning experiment, the confounding of axes is like traveling on a sphere: if we go in some direction to a quarter of the way around the sphere, turn 90 degrees, travel the same distance, then turn and travel again, we will arrive back home, coming in at right angles to the direction we headed out. Even more revealing, we can leave the north pole in any direction and end up at the south pole, just as we can rotate 360 degrees around any axis and end up oriented the same way.

Local geometry does not, however, determine global topology. Contradictory though it may seem, the geometry curves like a sphere, but the topology says north and south poles are the same! In fact, each pair of opposite points represents the same rotation. The reader may preserve sanity through two expedients. One is to see that this, like homogeneous coordinates, is geometry under perspective projection. The second is to restore spherical topology by including "entanglements". Physically, taking an object with strings attached and rotating it 360 degrees leaves the strings tangled; yet—most odd—rotating 720 degrees does not. [Misner][Gardner]

Accepting the topological oddity is more useful here, but it leaves a minor inconvenience. Namely, when converting an orientation in some foreign form, such as a matrix, to a quaternion form, which quaternion should we choose? Which side of the sphere? An answer that works well is this. Construct a string of quaternions through which to interpolate by choosing

† Glenn Davis suggested this formula.

each added quaternion on the side closest to the one before. Then small changes in orientation will yield small displacements on the sphere.

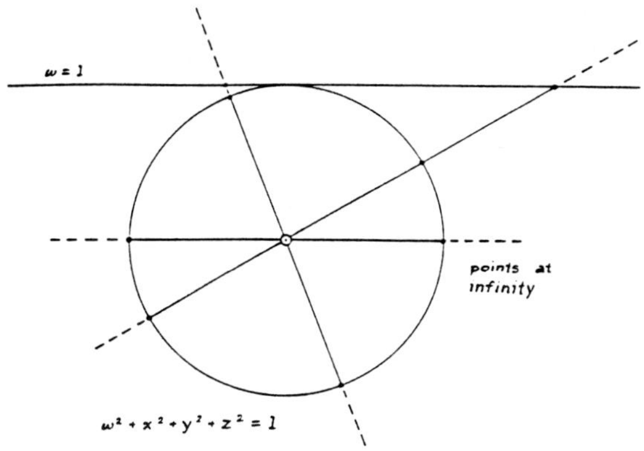

Representing a projective plane

3.5 Splines

We are left with the problem of constructing smooth curves on spheres. About a hundred years after quaternions appeared, Isaac Schoenberg published a two part attack on ballistics and actuarial problems, using what he called splines. [Schoenberg] Named by analogy to a draftman's tool, these are interpolating curves constructed from cubic polynomial pieces, with second order continuity between pieces. Cubic splines solve an integral equation which says to minimize the total "wiggle" of the curve, as measured by the second derivative. These interpolants are very popular, and the equation can be augmented with Lagrange multipliers to constrain the solution curves to lie on a sphere [Courant & Hilbert]; yet there are problems. First, the augmented equation is much more difficult and expensive to solve. Second, the curve must adjust everywhere if one of the points changes; that is, we have no local control.

3.6 Bézier curves

While Schoenberg invented splines based on numerical analysis, Pierre Bézier invented a class of curves, now called by his name, based on geometrical ideas. In fact, he showed how to find points on such a curve by drawing lines and splitting them in regular proportions. [Bézier] This is exactly what is needed. We already know how to do the equivalent—draw great arcs and proportions of arcs—on a sphere. A complete solution needs only a little more.

4. Spherical Bézier curves

4.1 Joining curves

Bézier curves go through only their first and last defining points, but we want to interpolate all our orientations. The trick is to splice together short Bézier curves in the manner of splines. Their creator showed an easy way to do this which guarantees first order continuity, probably enough for us. As the curve goes through its end points it is tangent to its end segments. Line up the segments across a join, match their lengths, and the curves will piece together smoothly. If the key orientations are placed at joints, then each short curve moves us from one key to the next, because each piece passes through its ends.

Now, although the two segments abutting a curve junction should match each other, one of the segments can be chosen freely. These choices determine the axis and speed of rotation as we pass through the keys. The burden of choice can be passed to the animator of course, but automation is feasible, and generally preferable.

4.2 Choosing joint segments

Spherical linear interpolation gives two conflicting arc segments at a joint, one on each side. Smooth the difference with an even compromise, aiming for a point halfway between where the incoming segment would proceed, and where the outgoing segment must arrive.†

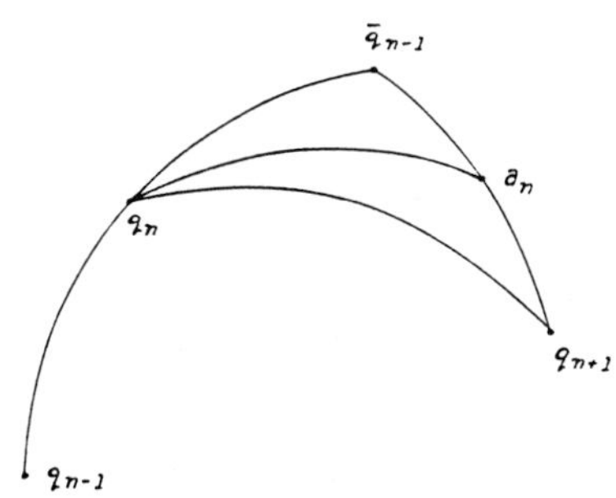

Constructing a point for tangent

Given successive key quaternions q_{n-1}, q_n, q_{n+1} interpretted as 4-D unit vectors, the computation for a segment point a_n after q_n is

$$a_n = \text{Bisect}(\text{Double}(q_{n-1}, q_n), q_{n+1}) ,$$

where

$$\text{Double}(p,q) = 2(p \cdot q)q - p ;$$

$$\text{Bisect}(p,q) = \frac{p+q}{||p+q||} .$$

The matching point for the segment before q_n should be

$$b_n = \text{Double}(a_n, q_n)$$

† For the numerically knowledgeable, this construction approximates the derivative at points of a sampled function by averaging the central differences of the sample sequence. [Dahlquist & Björk]

to ensure a smooth join, regardless of how a_n is chosen.

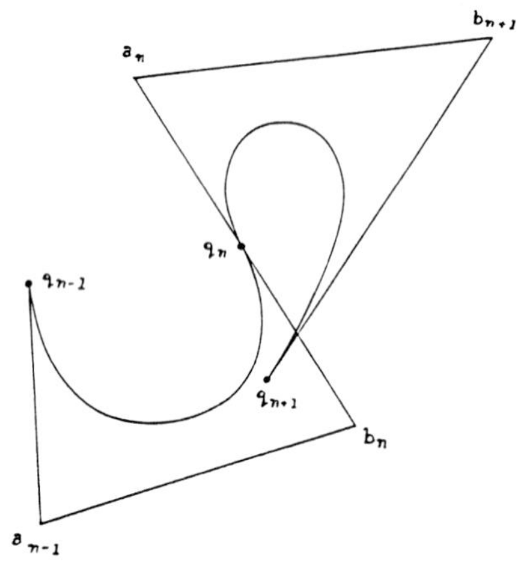

Splicing Bézier segments together

4.3 Evaluating on the sphere

Everything is now in hand to imitate Bézier's curve technique. Each short curve is defined by four quaternions, q_n, a_n, b_{n+1}, q_{n+1}. Let the parameter u vary from 0 to 1 as the curve departs q_n towards a_n and arrives at q_{n+1} tangent to the arc from b_{n+1}. Spherically interpolate by proportion u between q_n and a_n, a_n and b_{n+1}, b_{n+1} and q_{n+1}, to obtain three new quaternions. Then interpolate between those to get two more; and finally interpolate again, reducing to a single point. Abbreviating Slerp$(p,q;u)$ as $(p:q)_u$, the computation looks like this:

$$q_n = p_0^{(0)}$$

$$(p_0^{(0)}:p_1^{(0)})_u = p_0^{(1)}$$

$$a_n = p_1^{(0)} \qquad (p_0^{(1)}:p_1^{(1)})_u = p_0^{(2)}$$

$$(p_1^{(0)}:p_2^{(0)})_u = p_1^{(1)} \qquad (p_0^{(2)}:p_1^{(2)})_u = p_0^{(3)} = q_{n+u}$$

$$b_{n+1} = p_2^{(0)} \qquad (p_1^{(1)}:p_2^{(1)})_u = p_1^{(2)}$$

$$(p_2^{(0)}:p_3^{(0)})_u = p_2^{(1)}$$

$$q_{n+1} = p_3^{(0)}$$

4.4 Tangents revisited

A simple check proves the curve touches q_n and q_{n+1} at its ends. A rather challenging differentiation shows it is tangent there to the segments determined by a_n and b_{n+1}. However, as with Bézier's original curve, the magnitude of the tangent is three times that of the segment itself. That is, we are spinning three times faster than spherical interpolation along the arc. Fortunately we can correct the speed by merely truncating the end segments to one third their original length, so that a_n is closer to q_n and b_{n+1} closer to q_{n+1}.

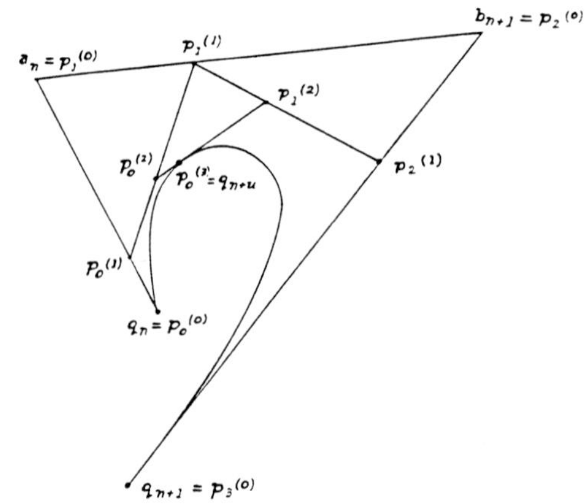

Calculating a Bézier curve point recursively

5. Results

5.1 The grand scheme

What have we ended up with? An animator sits at a workstation and interactively establishes a sequence of keys for, say, camera orientation. The interpolating algorithm does not depend on the nature of the interface the animator sees; all needed information is contained in the sequence of keys. Probably the orientations will be represented internally as matrices, so a conversion step follows. The matrices are "lifted" to a sequence of neighboring quaternions, q_n, on the unit sphere. Each quaternion within the sequence will become the endpoint of two spherical Bézier curves. Between each quaternion pair, q_n and q_{n+1}, two additional points, a_n and b_{n+1}, are added to control motion through the joints. At this point, time becomes a parameter along the composite curve. As the frame number increments, the parameter enters and leaves successive curve pieces. Within each piece a local version of the parameter is adjusted to run from 0 to 1. Now the Bézier geometric construction comes into play, producing an interpolated quaternion, q_{n+u}, from q_n, a_n, b_{n+1}, q_{n+1}, and the local parameter, u. Finally the mint-fresh interpolated quaternion is transmuted into a matrix, to be used in rotating a list of object vectors for rendering.

5.2 Properties

A look at one special case is revealing. Suppose all the points to interpolate are spread along a single arc. This means they represent different amounts of rotation around a single axis, in which case quaternion multiplication commutes. Under these special conditions, the formula for the curve sections reduces to

$$q_{n+u} = q_n^{(1-u)^3} \, a_n^{3(1-u)^2 u} \, b_{n+1}^{3(1-u)u^2} \, q_{n+1}^{u^3}$$

When this is compared to the standard Bézier polynomial, $p_n(1-u)^3 + a_n 3(1-u)^2 u + b_{n+1} 3(1-u)u^2 + q_{n+1}u^3$, it is apparent that addition and multiplication have become multiplication and exponentiation. Of course, when the points are not on one arc, commutativity fails, so the formula looks much messier.

In the interesting restricted case when the points are spaced evenly and consecutively around an arc, the resulting animation behaves exactly as we would hope: we get smooth, constant speed rotation around the appropriate axis. Notice that we can choose *any* axis for this rotation. This is clearly preferable to interpolation with Euler's angles, where the coordinate axes are special. A more subtle property of *all* quaternion interpolation is that the motion is independent of coordinate axes. So, for example, if we design a move, then rotate the coordinate system arbitrarily, the geometry of the motion will not change. Euler interpolants, unfortunately, will do wildly different things.

5.3 Applicability

Rotations in space are significantly more complicated than rotations in a plane. It is easy to deal with the latter, since only one parameter is involved. Quaternions are out of place in a plane. Joint control in robotics simulations has its own highly specialized body of techniques; and though quaternions have shown up in the literature, they seem less useful in that context. [Brady][Taylor] However, B.K.P. Horn has used a tessellation of the quaternion unit sphere to identify the orientation of an object from its extended Gaussian image; a good reference is [Brou]. Non-rigid motion obviously needs to be handled specially. But for moving a camera eye-point, and for many kinds of object motion, quaternion interpolation has strong advantages.

5.4 Comparisons and complaints

Cost advantages are difficult to estimate. Converting a matrix to a quaternion requires only one square root and three divides plus some adds, at worst. Converting back requires 9 multiplies and 15 adds. While the conversions don't use trigonometric functions, the arc proportioning does. For comparison, angle interpolation requires several trigonometric functions as well as quite a few multiplies and adds to create each interpolated matrix. My experience is that the Bézier scheme is comfortably fast enough for design work, which is the only time speed has mattered. (If, for some application, more speed is essential, non-spherical quaternion splines will undoubtedly be faster than angle interpolation, while still free of axis bias and gimbal lock.)

These interpolants are not perfect, of course. Like all interpolants, they can develop kinks between the interpolated points. There are simple algorithms for adding new sequence points to ordinary splines without altering the original curve [Boehm]; they do not work for this interpolant. And if these curves can be shown to satisfy some variational principal, it will be by chance. It is useful to do this, because any solution to an integral equation like that for splines admits subdivision [Lane et al]; minimum curvature between end points implies minimum curvature between intermediate points as well. Along these lines, Gabriel and Kajiya, motivated by quaternions, have been developing a technique to find splines on arbitrary Reimannian manifolds by solving differential equations. [Gabriel & Kajiya]

6. Questions

Future research could answer some interesting practical questions. What are these spherical Bézier curves? Is there some abstract characterization of them? Or is there some related interpolant that is well-characterized? In light of the success of the geometric adaptation approach, it appears reasonable to apply the idea to B-splines, which also have a known geometric evaluation technique. [Gordon & Riesenfeld] How do spherical B-splines behave? Is it possible to add new points to a sequence for either kind of curve without disturbing it? How? Can B-splines be made to interpolate, not just approximate, with a simple adjustment of control points? Is there a way to construct a curve parameterized by arc length? This would be very useful. What is the best way to allow varying intervals between sequence points in parameter space? Abandoning the unit sphere, one could work with the four-dimensional Euclidean space of arbitrary quaternions. How do standard interpolation methods applied there behave when mapped back to matrices? Note that we now have little guidance in picking the inverse image for a matrix, and that cusp-free $\mathbf{R}^4$ paths do not always project to cusp-free S^3 paths.

However these questions are answered, quaternion spline interpolants already offer a well-behaved improvement over traditional techniques. They are simple to use, simple to implement, robust, efficient, consistent, and flexible. More research would make them even more so.

7. Acknowledgments

This work was begun for an animation system I designed and implemented at Singer-Link. Several people there deserve thanks, but I especially thank Glenn Davis, who befriended me with his good humor and mathematical efforts as I struggled through trying times.

I prefer not to invent the wheel if I can find the plans; so I pestered Don Venhaus, Brian Barsky, Tom Duff, Lance Williams, and Jim Blinn, whom I thank for their time, their comments, and their assurances that they had not seen this particular wheel roll past PDI, Berkeley, Lucasfilm, NYIT, or JPL.

Thanks to everyone at Pacific Data Images for the interest and encouragement that got me started.

The folks at Ridge Computer were generous above and beyond the call of customer support in letting me use their Imagen typesetting system to produce this paper.

Lastly, I thank Nori Hall for commenting on numerous drafts, and more.

References

1. BÉZIER, P.E., *Numerical Control — Mathematics and Applications,* John Wiley and Sons, London (1972).
2. BOEHM, WOLFGANG, "Inserting new knots into B-spline curves," *Computer-Aided Design* **12**(4) pp. 199-201 (July 1980).
3. BRADY, MICHAEL, "Trajectory Planning," in *Robot Motion: Planning and Control,* ed. Michael Brady, John M. Hollerbach, Timothy L. Hohnson, Tomas Lozano-Perez and Matthew T. Mason,The MIT Press (1982).
4. BROU, PHILIPPE, "Using the Gaussian Image to Find the Orientation of Objects," *The International Journal of Robotics Research* **3**(4) pp. 89-125 (Winter 1984).
5. CAYLEY, ARTHUR, "On certain results relating to quaternions," *Philosophical Magazine* **xxvi** pp. 141-145 (February 1845).
6. COURANT, R. AND HILBERT, D., *Methods of Mathematical Physics, Volume I,* Interscience Publishers, Inc., New York (1953).
7. DAHLQUIST, GERMUND AND BJÖRCK, ÅKE, *Numerical Methods,* Prentice-Hall, Inc., Englewood Cliffs, N.J. (1974). Translated by Ned Anderson.
8. EULER, LEONHARD, "Decouverte d'un nouveau principe de mécanique (1752)," pp. 81-108 in *Opera omnia, Ser. secunda, v. 5,* Orell Füsli Turici, Lausannae (1957).
9. EULER, LEONHARD, "Du mouvement de rotation des corps solides autour d'un axe variable (1758)," in *Opera omnia, Ser. secunda, v. 8,* Orell Füsli Turici, Lausannae ().
10. GABRIEL, STEVEN A. AND KAJIYA, JAMES T., "Spline Interpolation in Curved Manifolds," , (1985). Submitted
11. GARDNER, MARTIN, *New Mathematical Diversions from Scientific American,* Fireside, St. Louis, Missouri (1971). Chapter 2
12. GOLDSTEIN, HERBERT, *Classical Mechanics, second edition,* Addison-Wesley Publishing Company, Inc., Reading, Mass. (1980). Chapter 4 and Appendix B.
13. GORDON, WILLIAM J. AND RIESENFELD, RICHARD F., "Bernstein-Bézier methods for the computer-aided design of free-form curves and surfaces," *J. ACM* **21**(2) pp. 293-310 (April 1974).
14. GORDON, WILLIAM J. AND RIESENFELD, RICHARD F., "B-spline curves and surfaces," in *Computer Aided Geometric Design,* ed. Robert E. Barnhill and Richard F. Riesenfeld,Academic Press, New York (1974).
15. HAMILTON, SIR WILLIAM ROWAN, "On quaternions; or on a new system of imaginaries in algebra," *Philosophical Magazine* **xxv** pp. 10-13 (July 1844).
16. HERSTEIN, I.N., *Topics in Algebra, second edition,* John Wiley and Sons, Inc., New York (1975).
17. KANE, THOMAS R., LIKINS, PETER W. AND LEVINSON, DAVID A., *Spacecraft Dynamics,* McGraw-Hill, Inc. (1983).
18. LANE, JEFFREY M., CARPENTER, LOREN C., WHITTED, TURNER, AND BLINN, JAMES F., "Scan line methods for displaying parametrically defined surfaces," *Comm. ACM* **23**(1) pp. 23-34 (January 1980).
19. MACLANE, SAUNDERS AND BIRKHOFF, GARRETT, *Algebra, second edition,* Macmillan Publishing Co., Inc., New York (1979).
20. MISNER, CHARLES W., THORNE, KIP S., AND WHEELER, JOHN ARCHIBALD, *Gravitation,* W.H. Freeman and Company, San Francisco (1973). Chapter 41 — Spinors.
21. MITCHELL, E.E.L. AND ROGERS, A.E., "Quaternion Parameters in the Simulation of a Spinning Rigid Body," in *Simulation The Dynamic Modeling of Ideas and Systems with Computers,* ed. John McLeod, P.E., (1968).
22. NEWMAN, WILLIAM M. AND SPROULL, ROBERT F., *Principles of Interactive Computer Graphics, second edition,* McGraw-Hill, Inc., New York (1979). Chapter 21 — Curves and surfaces.
23. PICKERT, G. AND STEINER, H.-G., "Chapter 8 — Complex numbers and quaternions," in *Fundamentals of Mathematics, Volume I — Foundations of Mathematics: The Real Number System and Algebra,* ed. H. Behnke, F. Bachmann, K. Fladt, and W. Süss, (1983). Translated by S.H. Gould.
24. SCHMEIDLER, W. AND DREETZ, W., "Chapter 11 — Functional analysis," in *Fundamentals of Mathematics, Volume III — Analysis,* ed. H. Behnke, F. Bachmann, K. Fladt, and W. Süss,MIT Press, Cambridge, Mass. (1983). Translated by S.H. Gould.
25. SCHOENBERG, I.J., "Contributions to the problem of approximation of equidistant data by analytic functions," *Quart. Appl. Math.* **4** pp. 45-99 and 112-141 (1946).
26. SMITH, ALVY RAY, "Spline tutorial notes," Technical Memo No. 77, Computer Graphics Project, Lucasfilm Ltd. (May 1983).
27. SÜSS, W., GERICKE, H., AND BERGER, K.H., "Chapter 14 — Differential geometry of curves and surfaces," in *Fundamentals of Mathematics, Volume II — Geometry,* ed. H. Behnke, F. Bachmann, K. Fladt, and W. Süss,MIT Press (1983). Translated by S.H. Gould.
28. TAYLOR, RUSSELL H., "Planning and Execution of Straight Line Manipulator Trajectories," in *Robot Motion: Planning and Control,* ed. Michael Brady, John M. Hollerbach, Timothy L. Hohnson, Tomas Lozano-Perez and Matthew T. Mason,The MIT Press (1982).

Appendix I—Conversions

I.1 Quaternion to matrix

Using the restriction that $w^2+x^2+y^2+z^2=1$ for a quaternion $q = [w,(x,y,z)]$, the formula for the corresponding matrix is

$$M = \begin{pmatrix} 1-2y^2-2z^2 & 2xy+2wz & 2xz-2wy \\ 2xy-2wz & 1-2x^2-2z^2 & 2yz+2wx \\ 2xz+2wy & 2yz-2wx & 1-2x^2-2y^2 \end{pmatrix}.$$

If the quaternion does not have unit magnitude, an additional 4 multiplies and divides, 3 adds, and a square root will normalize it. (For the matrix conversion, the square root can be avoided in favor of divides if desirable.) Now we can obtain the operation count for creating the matrix. Most terms of the entries are a product of two factors, one of which is doubled. So we proceed as follows. First double x, y, and z, and form their products with w, x, y, and z. That will take 3 adds and 9 multiplies. Then form the sum for each of the 9 entries using 1 add each, plus an extra add for each of the 3 diagonal elements, for a total of 12 adds. Thus 9 multiplies and 15 adds suffice to convert a unit quaternion to a matrix.

I.2 Matrix to quaternion

An efficient way to determine quaternion components w, x, y, z from a matrix is to use linear combinations of the entries M_{mn}. Notice that the diagonal entries are formed from the squares of the quaternion components, while off-diagonal entries are the sum of a symmetric and a skew-symmetric part. Thus linear combinations of the diagonal entries will isolate squares of components; sums and differences of opposite off-diagonal entries will isolate products among x, y, and z and products with w. Using off-diagonals risks dividing by a component that may be zero, or within ϵ (the machine precision) of zero. However we can avoid that pitfall, and easily compute all components as follows.

$w^2 = 1/4\,(1 + M_{11} + M_{22} + M_{33})$

- $w^2 > \epsilon$?
  - TRUE:
    - $w = \sqrt{w^2}$
    - $x = (M_{23} - M_{32})\,/\,4w$
    - $y = (M_{31} - M_{13})\,/\,4w$
    - $z = (M_{12} - M_{21})\,/\,4w$
  - FALSE:
    - $w = 0$
    - $x^2 = -1/2\,(M_{22} + M_{33})$
    - $x^2 > \epsilon$?
      - TRUE:
        - $x = \sqrt{x^2}$
        - $y = M_{12}\,/\,2x$
        - $z = M_{13}\,/\,2x$
      - FALSE:
        - $x = 0$
        - $y^2 = 1/2\,(1 - M_{33})$
        - $y^2 > \epsilon$?
          - TRUE:
            - $y = \sqrt{y^2}$
            - $z = M_{23}\,/\,2y$
          - FALSE:
            - $y = 0$
            - $z = 1$

No more than one square root, three divides, and a few adds and binary scales are required for any conversion.

I.3 Euler angles to quaternion

There are twelve possible axis conventions for Euler angles. The one used here is *roll*, *pitch*, and *yaw*, as used in aeronautics. A general rotation is obtained by first yawing around the **z** axis by an angle of ϕ, then pitching around the **y** axis by θ, and finally rolling around the **x** axis by ψ. Using the way quaternion components describe a rotation, we first obtain a quaternion for each simple rotation.

$$q_{roll} = [\cos\frac{\psi}{2},(\sin\frac{\psi}{2},0,0)]$$

$$q_{pitch} = [\cos\frac{\theta}{2},(0,\sin\frac{\theta}{2},0)]$$

$$q_{yaw} = [\cos\frac{\phi}{2},(0,0,\sin\frac{\phi}{2})]$$

Multiplying these together in the right order gives the desired quaternion $q = q_{yaw}\, q_{pitch}\, q_{roll}$, with components

$$w = \cos\frac{\psi}{2}\cos\frac{\theta}{2}\cos\frac{\phi}{2} + \sin\frac{\psi}{2}\sin\frac{\theta}{2}\sin\frac{\phi}{2}$$

$$x = \sin\frac{\psi}{2}\cos\frac{\theta}{2}\cos\frac{\phi}{2} - \cos\frac{\psi}{2}\sin\frac{\theta}{2}\sin\frac{\phi}{2}$$

$$y = \cos\frac{\psi}{2}\sin\frac{\theta}{2}\cos\frac{\phi}{2} + \sin\frac{\psi}{2}\cos\frac{\theta}{2}\sin\frac{\phi}{2}$$

$$z = \cos\frac{\psi}{2}\cos\frac{\theta}{2}\sin\frac{\phi}{2} - \sin\frac{\psi}{2}\sin\frac{\theta}{2}\cos\frac{\phi}{2}$$

I.4 Euler angles to matrix

Combining the results of the previous two conversions gives

$$M = \begin{pmatrix} \cos\theta\cos\phi & \cos\theta\sin\phi & -\sin\theta \\ \sin\psi\sin\theta\cos\phi-\cos\psi\sin\phi & \sin\psi\sin\theta\sin\phi+\cos\psi\cos\theta & \cos\theta\sin\psi \\ \cos\psi\sin\theta\cos\phi+\sin\psi\sin\phi & \cos\psi\sin\theta\sin\phi-\sin\psi\cos\phi & \cos\theta\cos\psi \end{pmatrix},$$

where ψ, θ, and ϕ are the angles of roll, pitch, and yaw, respectively.

I.5 Matrix to Euler angles

While converting a matrix to a unit quaternion only involves the sign ambiguity of square roots, converting to Euler angles involves inverse trigonometric functions, as we can only directly determine the sin's and cos's of the angles. Some convention, such as principle angles, must be adopted. However interpolation paths will vary greatly, depending on choice of angles. Setting that problem aside, here's a way to extract the sin's and cos's. Looking at the previous equation, $\sin\theta$ can be read off directly as $-M_{13}$. Use the trigonometric identity $\cos\theta = \pm\sqrt{1-\sin^2\theta}$ to compute $\cos\theta$ to within a sign, which is the best we can do. Assuming $\cos\theta$ is not zero, obtain the sin's and cos's of the other angles from

$$\sin\theta = -M_{13}$$

$$\cos\theta = \sqrt{1-\sin^2\theta}$$

$$\sin\psi = M_{23} \,/\, \cos\theta$$

$$\cos\psi = M_{33} \,/\, \cos\theta$$

$$\sin\phi = M_{12} \,/\, \cos\theta$$

$$\cos\phi = M_{11} \,/\, \cos\theta$$

If $\cos\theta$ is zero, then we must avoid dividing by zero. It also becomes impossible to distinguish roll from yaw. Adopting the convention that the yaw angle ϕ is 0 allows

$$\sin\psi = -M_{32}$$

$$\cos\psi = M_{22}$$

$$\sin\phi = 0$$

$$\cos\phi = 1$$

From these values a two argument $\tan^{-1}$ will give angles between $-\pi$ and $+\pi$, or 0 and 2π, or some other conventional range; take your pick. (For a faster conversion, just compute, say, $\sin^{-1}$ and check the sign of the cosine term with respect to $\cos\theta$.) Because of the uncertainties of square roots, inverse trigonometric functions, and yaw-roll separation, matrix to Euler angle conversion is inherently *very* ill-defined.

I.6 Quaternion to Euler angles

Use the most straight-forward approach: convert the quaternion to a matrix, then the matrix to Euler angles. Of course it is unnecessary to compute matrix elements that are never used. This conversion is also unavoidably ill-defined, as quaternions contain no more information about angles than matrices do.

PARAMETRIC KEYFRAME INTERPOLATION INCORPORATING KINETIC ADJUSTMENT AND PHRASING CONTROL

Scott N. Steketee
Norman I. Badler

Department of Computer and Information Science
Moore School D2
University of Pennsylvania
Philadelphia, PA 19104

Abstract

Parametric keyframing is a popular animation technique where values for parameters which control the position, orientation, size, and shape of modeled objects are determined at key times, then interpolated for smooth animation. Typically the parameter values defined by the keyframes are interpolated by spline techniques with the result that the parameter change *kinetics* are implicitly defined by the given keyframe times and data points. Existing interpolation systems for animation are examined and found to lack certain desirable features such as continuity of acceleration or convenient kinetic control. The requirements of interpolation for animation are analyzed in order to determine the characteristics of a satisfactory system. A new interpolation system is developed and implemented which incorporates second-derivative continuity (continuity of acceleration), local control, convenient kinetic control, and joining and phrasing of successive motions. Phrasing control includes the ability to parametrically control the degree and extent of smooth motion flow between separately defined motions.

Introduction

Producing effective computer-generated animation is a very difficult problem. Incorporating realistic human forms into the animation greatly increases the difficulty, due to the necessity of modeling the human form itself, the complexity of articulation of the human body, and the increased expectations of realism which result when observers see human forms [1,3].

The TEMPUS animation system at the University of Pennsylvania is a software tool which offers an environment where many of these animation problems may be investigated. Much work has already been done in representing the human form itself (through the use of spheres or polyhedra) and in modeling the body's joints, including their degrees of freedom and joint limits. The system has shaded graphics capability, including hidden surface removal and shadows, and it permits the specification of simultaneous movement of multiple objects, including human bodies, other objects, light sources, and the camera [2].

The motions of all these objects are specified by means of *parametric* "keyframes," that is, the values of any motion parameters for a given object are specified at a set of times during the course of the motion. The motion parameters used may be defined, for example, in either three-dimensional cartesian coordinates or joint angles. To actually produce the animation, the computer must interpolate the motion parameters for each movie frame between the given keyframes, and use the interpolated values to produce a complete shaded picture for each frame of the movie.

This parametric keyframe approach differs considerably from the image-based two-dimensional keyframe which is often used in computer animation [8,15]. The interpolation process in two-dimensional keyframing interpolates the image only, usually by means of linear interpolation of parameters or image points. Depth and joint information are lost and it is impossible to compensate correctly for camera motion. Complex systems must be developed in an attempt to reduce the distortion, either automatically (*e.g.* [6]) or by means of the intervention of the human animator (*e.g.* [15]). There is no totally satisfactory solution to the deviations between the interpolated image and the object being modeled.

In contrast, parametric keyframing interpolates parameters of the model of the object itself, and constructs each image individually from the interpolated model. Although parametric keyframing is more expensive computationally, it can produce better images, since the interpolation step is based on meaningful spatial or physical parameters of the model. Though parametric keyframing is not new (for example, [10,14,16,17,20], the *timing* control of the interpolation process has not been well established. Since the earliest days of computer animation "dynamic" control of keyframe parameters has been sought, often with *ad hoc* "motion smoothing functions" [7,13,18]. While these methods appeared adequate for certain animations, they lack certain characteristics and properties which are required for effective motion control of a human figure [3]. The actual user interface to a motion control system will not be discussed here; rather, our goal is to present an interpolation methodology which will offer a suitable range of control.

The remainder of this paper will describe in detail the desirable properties of a motion control system based an parametric keyframing. We will also present a new technique for interpolating between the parametric keyframes based on B-splines [19]. The interpolating functions are constructed in such a way as to make the most logical assumptions about how objects are likely to move and to give the user control, even after the interpolation is done, over both the positions and the rate of motion of the resulting model. This positional and *kinetic* control is very helpful in fine-tuning a sequence of images to achieve a desired effect.

We use the term "kinetic" control rather than "dynamic" as in [11,12] because the control being exerted in this process applies only to the motion parameters themselves, and takes no account of the forces or masses involved in the motion. The adjective "dynamic," applied in this context, would be misleading since the word means "*of or relating to physical force or energy*" and since it implies a connection with that "*branch of mechanics that deals with forces and their relation primarily to the motion . . . of bodies of matter*" [21]. True "dynamic" control of human animation would require a much more complex model of the human body, incorporating the muscles, ligaments, tendons and bones, than is currently practical [22]. We expect, however, that sufficient kinetic control will create the *illusion* of dynamic control in the final animation [3].

Overview of Interpolation Requirements

In this paper, the following terms are used:

- **object**: any single element of the animation whose movement must be modeled. This may include human bodies, animals, objects or parts thereof, lights, or simulated cameras.

- **motion parameter**: an aspect of an object's movement which can be used to numerically specify the nature of that movement, in any of a number of ways. For instance, a parameter might be used in determining the position, orientation, size, or shape of an object, or a joint angle (that is, the relative orientation of two parts of an object).

- **motion**: a single movement of a single object, specified by means of the values of a definite set of motion parameters over a definite period of time. Individual motions are the units from which the animation is built.

- **transition**: the juxtaposition of two motions, both involving the same object and at least some of the same motion parameters. Thus a transition occurs when one motion of an object ends and another begins.

- **keyframe**: an n-tuple specifying the state of a given motion at a particular time. The n-tuple consists of a value for the time, and in addition a value for each motion parameter which is participating in the given motion. The data may be supplied manually by a human animator, or may be the result of some computation.

- **interpolant**: a mathematical function which gives the value of a motion parameter as a function of time. The value of the interpolant will normally agree with the keyframe value at the time of the keyframe, but will also give values for the motion parameter at any other (non-keyframe) times in the interval from the beginning to the end of the motion.

- **span**: a portion of the interpolant between two adjacent keyframe values.

We can now state the primary requirements an interpolation system must satisfy to produce realistic motion and to provide the user with effective and convenient control:

- Continuous motion
- Local control
- Kinetic control
- Continuous transitions
- Phrased transitions

A description and justification of each of these requirements follows; the implications of these requirements in designing an appropriate interpolation system are discussed in the subsequent section.

Continuous motion

The interpolation must result in a motion which is continuous, using the term in its mathematical sense. By continuous motion we mean that the interpolant and both its first and second derivatives should be continuous. Physically, first-derivative continuity is equivalent to motion with continuous velocity; second-derivative continuity is equivalent to motion with continuous acceleration. Since a discontinuous acceleration can only result from a discontinuous force or a discontinuous mass, lack of second-derivative continuity would result in an unrealistic model of actual physical processes. Actual forces may change very rapidly, giving rise to motion which appears jerky, but these rapid changes are nevertheless continuous, and should still be modeled mathematically by a function which is continuous in the second derivative. Even second-order discontinuities are likely to result in motion which the observer perceives as "unnatural."

Local control

The user ought to be able to control the motion by manipulating the interpolant directly; it should not be necessary to re-interpolate the motion in order to make small changes and adjustments. There will be instances in which the user wants to alter the resulting motion in some way, and can achieve the desired result more easily and more directly by modifying the interpolant than by modifying the original keyframe specification and then re-interpolating the motion.

When the curve is modified at one point, it is important to minimize the amount of change which occurs in parts of the curve which are relatively distant from the point where the modification takes place. This allows the user to modify one part of the motion without disturbing another part which has already been satisfactorily adjusted. More precisely, we would like a modification of the interpolant to have its greatest effect in those spans immediately adjacent to the point at which the modification is made, and to have no effect at all on spans which are distant from the modification.

Kinetic control

A particular motion may appear correct spatially, but incorrect or inappropriate kinetically. For instance, it may start too quickly and end too slowly. The user must be able to control the kinetics of the motion; that is, adjust the interpolant to alter the speed and acceleration of the motion at different points in the interval.

Satisfactory kinetic control presents a challenge, since altering the interpolant for one of the motion parameters will alter the kinetics for that parameter only, and will change the nature of the motion by changing the relationship between that parameter and the other parameters. On the other hand, it is not easy to simultaneously change the interpolants for all the motion parameters in a coordinated way, except by changing the times of the keyframes and re-interpolating all the motion parameters. We would prefer to have a single mathematical entity which can be manipulated in order to manipulate the kinetics of the interpolant.

Continuous transitions

We have gone to considerable lengths in order to guarantee that each parameter in a given motion is continuous in the second derivative, in order to provide a natural effect. We must now consider what takes place at the transition when one motion ends and another begins. If the parameters of the two motions are entirely distinct, no difficulty arises; the motions might just as easily belong to different objects. However, if the two motions share some parameters (for instance, if both involve a change in the angle of the elbow joint), those parameters may be discontinuous, or their derivatives may be discontinuous, at the transition. If so, the natural effect that we are trying to achieve in our animation may be lost at the transition.

Thus we need a means to modify two interpolants so that they are continuous in the second derivative across the transition. This modification should be simple to achieve, and should not affect more than a few spans of each curve.

Phrased transitions

Finally, the user may desire to "phrase" two motions at their transition, so that one blends smoothly into the other. By "phrasing," we mean more than providing second-derivative continuity; we mean an alteration in the nature of the motions, so that they become perceptually integrated into one single motion [3]. This alteration typically requires reducing *both kinetic and spatial extremes* to produce a transition which flows more smoothly. For instance, if the first motion ends by coming to rest and the second motion begins from rest, the original interpolation will include this instant of rest. After the transition has been made continuous as described above, the position and motion of the object will be relatively little changed except in the spans immediately before and after the transition point, and the instant of rest may even still be present.

To phrase the motions, we must alter each to blend more smoothly into the other. Mathematically, we think in terms of the single continuous curve which results from making the transition continuous and which interpolates both motions. We must reduce or eliminate any minima or maxima in the neighborhood of the transition, and reduce the magnitude of the velocity and acceleration, in order for the motions to blend smoothly into one another.

The Interpolation Process

An interpolation system was developed in order to satisfy the requirements above. The general features of the system are discussed below. Full mathematical details are available elsewhere [19].

Smooth motion

The interpolant and its first and second derivatives must be continuous. Polynomial interpolation provides the continuity desired, but higher-degree polynomials required to interpolate a number of data points have a tendency toward oscillation which increases with the number of data points. The tendency toward oscillation can be controlled by piece-wise polynomial interpolation which allows the use of lower-degree polynomials. The particular form of piece-wise polynomial interpolation called spline interpolation guarantees continuity of the second derivative, and thus appears suited to our needs.

Local control

It should be possible to make a small adjustment in one span of the interpolant, without the adjustment affecting more than a small number of neighboring spans. The B-spline technique of spline interpolation fits these requirements admirably. B-splines are piecewise polynomials constructed from a spline basis; the basis functions each have a value over a limited number of spans and are zero everywhere else. Thus changing the coefficient for one such basis function will modify the curve over a very limited number of spans. The number of spans affected is determined by the order of the B-splines.

Furthermore, the basis functions can be constructed in such a way that the coefficients of the basis functions approximate the value of the curve itself. Thus the desired control can be achieved in a particularly simple way, by directly modifying the coefficients. Changes made in this way cannot affect the curve except in those spans for which the corresponding basis function has a non-zero value.

Thus B-splines fit the first two requirements quite well. The beta-splines described in [4,5] lack second-derivative continuity, as do the piece-wise Hermite interpolants (though called "splines") described in [11]. Other common polynomial-based techniques fail in one or another of the areas described above.

The choice of the order of B-splines to be used is of some importance. At least fourth-order (third-degree) B-splines are required to provide the desired second-derivative continuity. Higher-order B-splines have three disadvantages: they are more expensive computationally, they have a greater tendency toward oscillation, and local modifications affect a larger number of spans. Thus we have chosen to use fourth-order B-splines, in which each basis function is defined over four spans and is zero everywhere else. These are more commonly referred to as cubic B-splines, since the basis functions are constructed from cubic polynomial functions.

Kinetic control

To provide separate kinetic control is a challenge, since kinetic control implies modifying the times (but not the motion parameters) specified at the keyframes. These times are embedded in the interpolants for the motion parameters; changing the kinetics would thus imply modifying the interpolant for each motion parameter included in the given motion. It is highly preferable to have one single entity which can be modified in order to change the kinetics.

We can accomplish this objective by using not one but two interpolants for each motion parameter; the first for the kinetics and the other for the position. The kinetic interpolant expresses the times of the keyframes, and contains no information about the actual values of the motion parameter. Thus modification of this interpolant changes the timing of the keyframes, and hence the speed and acceleration of the motion, without making any change in the positions defined by the keyframes. (A somewhat similar use of a function to map time to keyframes, but using empirically generated functions represented only as ordered pairs, can be found in [12].)

The position interpolant, on the other hand, expresses the positions defined by the keyframes, without including any information as to the timing of those keyframes. The actual motion function for the parameter, expressing position as a function of time, is obtained by the composition of the kinetic and position interpolants. Figure 1 shows an example of kinetic and position interpolants, together with the final motion function which results from composing the two interpolants.

Since the kinetic B-spline expresses only the times of the keyframes, and does not involve the value of the motion parameter, all the kinetic B-splines for a given motion which consists of several motion parameters will be the same, since they all have the same keyframes. The different motion parameters will be distinguished only by their position interpolants. We can thus modify one common kinetic B-spline in order to adjust the timing for all the motion parameters simultaneously. Figure 2 demonstrates kinetic adjustment of a motion consisting of two motion parameters x and y. Figure 3

Figure 1: The Double-Interpolant Method.

The left-hand curve is the kinetic interpolant, expressing the keyframe number as a function of time. The middle curve is the position interpolant, expressing the value of the motion variable x *as a function of the keyframe number. The right-hand curve is formed by composing these two interpolants, and expresses* x *as a function of time. For instance, at time* t = 3, *the left-hand graph shows that the keyframe number is* 6. *The middle graph shows that keyframe* 6 *corresponds to an* x *value of* 8. *Thus at* t = 3 *on the right-hand graph, the* x *value is* 8.

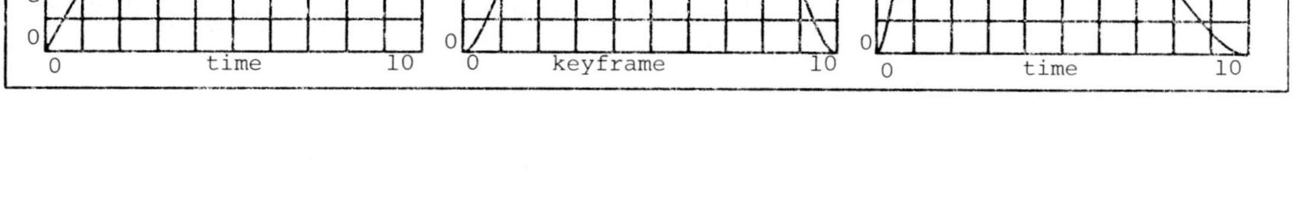

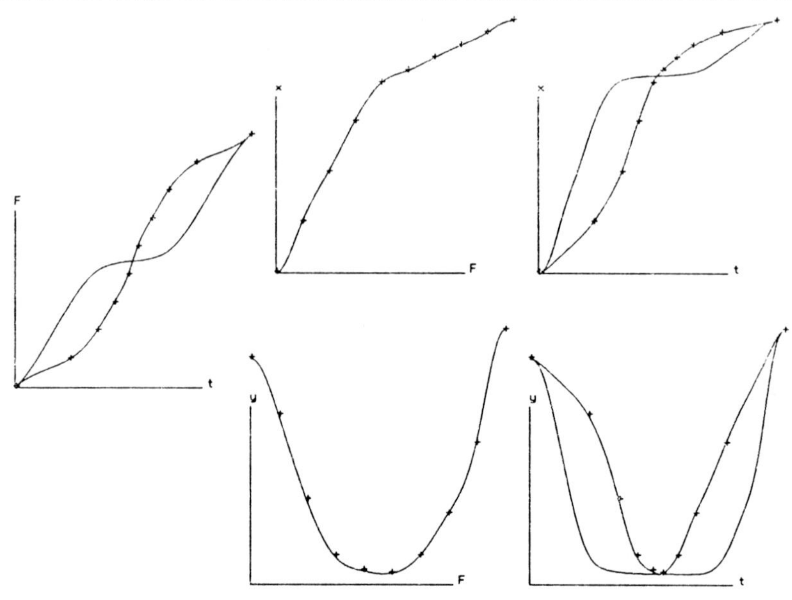

Figure 2: Kinetic Control.

These graphs illustrate kinetic control of a motion consisting of 2 motion variables x *and* y. *The left-hand graph shows both the original and modified kinetic curve. The original curve passes through the data points, shown as crosses; the modified curve rises more quickly, then slows down in the middle region, and rises quickly again at the end. The middle graphs are the position curves, showing* x *as a function of keyframe (top) and* y *as a function of keyframe (bottom). The right-hand graphs show the result of composing the kinetic and position functions: the top shows* x *as a function of* t, *and the bottom shows* y *as a function of* t. *(The original keyframe data is again shown by crosses.) It can be seen that the modified curves for both* x *and* y *start off more quickly, slow down in the middle, and then finish the motion quickly.*

demonstrates that only the kinetics of the motion are changed, as the path remains unchanged.

Continuous transitions

We must modify transitions between two successive motions so that motion parameters which participate in both motions have interpolants which are continuous in the second derivative across the transition. This objective can be achieved using B-splines by adjusting the B-splines for each of the two motions so that they agree across the transition. In other words, we will make each of the two interpolants part of a single, longer B-spline which extends from the beginning of the first motion to the end of the second. Figure 4(a) shows two successive interpolants which are discontinuous in the first derivative at the transition; Figure 4(b) shows the interpolants joined so that they are continuous in both first and second derivative.

Phrased transitions

The user must also be able to "phrase" or blend two motions together, and control the process accurately. Phrasing is not always desired, and when it is the user should be able to determine the amount of phrasing which takes place. In addition the user must be able to control the extent of phrasing, that is, whether phrasing takes place only in the spans immediately adjacent to the transition, or whether it involves considerably more of the motions.

Phrasing involves smoothing out the bumps by reducing any minima or maxima of the interpolant. We can accomplish this smoothing by exploiting the convex hull property of B-splines: any given span of the B-spline lies within the polygon formed by the four control vertices which determine that span. (The "control vertices" are defined by plotting the B-spline coefficients on the same graph as the B-spline itself.) By reducing extremes in the convex hull, we can reduce extremes in the interpolant itself. The user can control both the amount and extent of smoothing by determining how much adjustment is to be made in the control vertices and which control vertices are to participate in the adjustment. Figure 4(c) shows the result of smoothing the curve of Figure 4(b) at the transition between the two interpolants.

Defining the Kinetic and Position B-Splines

Data

For the purpose of defining the two B-splines for a given motion and a given parameter of that motion, data must be available giving the value of the parameter as a function of time at each of a set of keyframes. The keyframes are then numbered, introducing a third parameter. The kinetic B-spline is defined as the interpolant which gives the keyframe number as a function of time, and the position B-spline is defined as the interpolant which gives the value of the parameter as a function of keyframe number.

A given motion consists of keyframe data for several motion parameters. Since all the parameters for a particular motion share the same keyframe times, they all have identical kinetic B-splines, but different position B-splines. This feature permits kinetic control, since it is possible to modify all the kinetic B-splines at once.

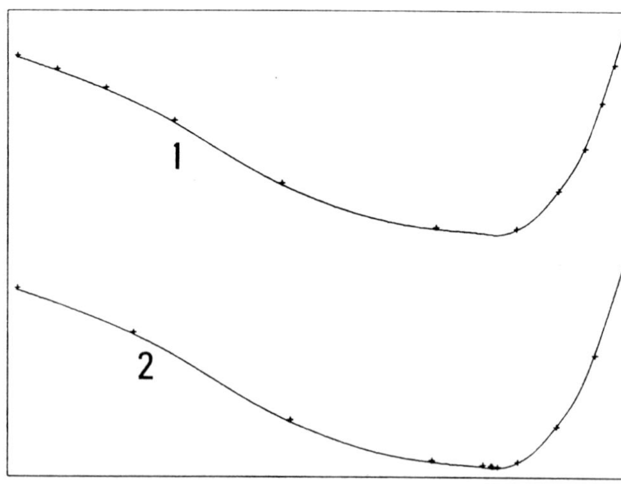

Figure 3: Kinetic Control Leaves Path Unchanged.

The paths defined by the data from Figure 2 are shown here, with x *on the horizontal axis and* y *on the vertical axis. The top curve shows the path defined by the curves marked 1 from Figure 2; the bottom curve shows the path defined by the curves marked 2. The tick marks are placed on each graph at equal time intervals, and show that the two motions differ in their kinetics even though the paths are identical.*

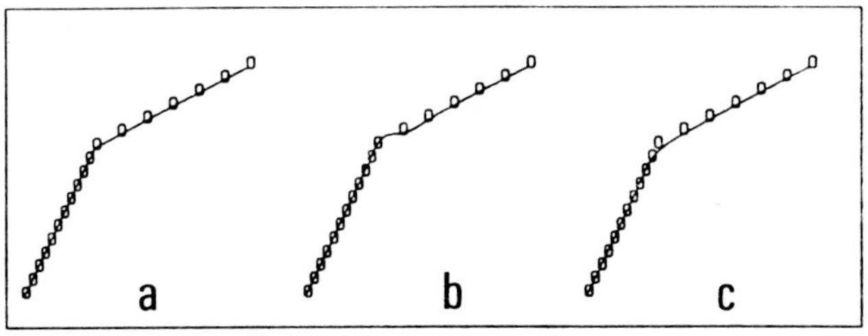

Figure 4: Joined and Phrased Transitions.

Figure 4(a) shows two interpolants which are continuous where they join, but which are discontinuous in the first derivative. Figure 4(b) shows the interpolants again after they have been joined; the result is a single curve which interpolates both sets of data points. (Most of the adjustment occurs in the second part of the combined motion, since the data points are more widely separated there.) Figure 4(c) shows the effect of phrasing: the bump is eliminated, and a much smoother curve results.

The interpolants

The two interpolants are constructed by first assigning numbers to the keyframes. We then define the kinetic B-spline as the interpolant which gives keyframe number as a function of time, and the position B-spline as the interpolant which gives the motion parameter as a function of keyframe number. It is not necessary to specify a value for every motion variable at every keyframe; a position B-spline can be constructed for each motion variable which uses only the data values provided for that variable. However, a value must be specified for each motion variable at the first and last keyframe of the motion. Figure 5 shows an example of how the two interpolants are generated.

Knot sets

The knot sets used for both B-splines are based on the data points. For the kinetic B-spline, the knot set is the set of keyframe times; the end knots are of multiplicity 4. For the position B-spline, the knot set is the set of keyframe numbers (0, 1, 2, . . . , n-1), omitting any keyframe number for which no value is specified for the motion variable being interpolated. The end knots are again of multiplicity 4.

The justification for this choice of knots is that the keyframes should be defined at those points in the motion at which the user wants to exercise control; thus if a part of the motion is particularly complex, the keyframes will be closer together in this region. The resulting B-spline should also offer greater control in this same region, and should have its control points (and hence its knots) closer together in the same region. Thus the use of the data points as the knot set provides greater control for those parts of the motion where the user requires it.

When keyframe times are very unevenly spaced, with a relatively short interval between keyframes juxtaposed to a much longer interval, the keyframes and knots described here may give rise to a kinetic interpolant which has a region with a negative slope. This is undesirable, since a negative slope in the kinetic interpolant would associate forward movement in time with backward movement through the keyframes. The negative slope can be removed by inserting an additional keyframe (and knot) in the kinetic curve to even out the spacing of the keyframes. The additional keyframe should be inserted in the relatively long interval, turning the two uneven intervals into three; an appropriate choice for the time of this keyframe would be one that makes the middle of the three intervals the geometric mean between the other two. No additional data need be supplied for the motion variables; each of their interpolants will still be based on the motion data originally provided.

End conditions

The end conditions of the B-splines must also be defined. The end condition for the kinetic B-spline is difficult to choose, since there is no obvious physical basis for determining either the first or second derivative at the ends of this curve. One commonly used end condition in such situations is to set the second derivative to zero. Lacking a clear basis for choosing this or any other particular end condition for the kinetic B-spline, we prefer instead to use the "not-a-knot" end condition recommended by [9]. This end condition involves reducing the number of knots (and hence the number of coefficients required) by two, rather than imposing two new (and unjustified) conditions on the curve. The number of knots is reduced by removing the first and last internal knots from the knot set, thus forcing a single piece-wise cubic to interpolate the interval from the first to the third data point, and similarly for the last three data points.

Single-interpolant method

Time	Motion Variable
0.0	5.2
0.5	5.7
1.2	7.2
2.0	8.0
3.0	8.5
3.5	8.9

determine single B-spline

Double-interpolant method

Time	Frame Number	Motion Variable
0.0	0	5.2
0.5	1	5.7
1.2	2	7.2
2.0	3	8.0
3.0	4	8.5
3.5	5	8.9

determine kinetic B-spline — determine position B-spline

Figure 5: Single and Double Interpolants.

The data shown on the left can be used to construct a single B-spline, or the keyframes can be numbered and the numbering used to construct two B-splines. Since all motion parameters in a given motion share the same keyframes, they will share the same kinetic B-spline.

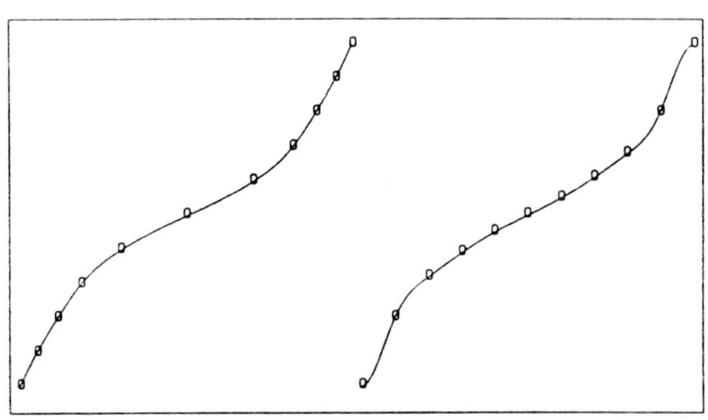

Figure 6: End Conditions.

The curve on the left was constructed from the given data using not-a-knot end conditions; in other words, the next-to-last data point from each end was omitted from the knot set, but the curve was still required to interpolate these data points. The curve on the right was constructed by using the zero-first-derivative end condition, so that the slope of the interpolant is forced to be zero at each end.

The end conditions used for the position B-spline, however, are zero first derivatives. This condition is chosen on the basis that many motions start from rest; a non-zero first derivative at the beginning of such a motion makes the velocity discontinuous, resulting in an appearance of infinite acceleration. The choice of zero first derivative as the end conditions prevents this problem by producing a motion with zero initial and final velocity. (The acceleration, however, will be discontinuous at the beginning and end of the motion. In many cases this will not appear unrealistic; those cases where it is unrealistic should probably be subjected to phrasing, which restores continuity of acceleration.) Figure 6 shows interpolants constructed using not-a-knot and zero-first-derivative end conditions.

Calculating the B-splines

When using this double B-spline method, we can find the value of the motion parameter at a particular time by first using the kinetic B-spline to calculate the keyframe number from the given time, and then using the position B-spline to calculate the value of the motion parameter from the calculated keyframe number. Thus providing the position B-spline with the result of the kinetic B-spline in effect gives us a function (the mathematical composition of the two functions) which is an interpolant relating time and the motion parameter.

The kinetic and position B-splines are relatively inexpensive to calculate. The kinetic B-spline gives rise to a banded, totally positive matrix which can be solved by Gaussian elimination without pivoting, using LU factorization [9]. The position B-spline gives rise to a matrix which is not totally positive (due to the derivative conditions), but which is tri-diagonal. In both cases, the matrices can be solved in linear time. (These and other algorithms used in the software are described and analyzed in [19].)

Once the B-spline coefficients have been calculated, only the knot sets and the coefficients themselves need to be stored, as the original data can be recovered by evaluating the B-spline interpolant at the keyframe times.

Adjusting the B-splines

Kinetic adjustment of a motion can now be accomplished by adjusting the coefficients for the kinetic B-splines. Since all the motion parameters share the same keyframes, they also share the same kinetic B-spline. By modifying that common B-spline we can modify the kinetics of the entire motion without altering the relationships between the different motion parameters. Thus various parts of a motion can be made faster or slower without changing the path of the object or the relationship of the parts of the object. Individual positional adjustment of any of the motion parameters is still possible with the position B-splines. Figure 7 shows the details of the kinetic adjustment used earlier in Figure 2.

Transitions Between Motions

We will assume for the purpose of discussion the problem of making transitions continuous to involve only a single motion parameter which participates in two separate movements, one followed by the other. In general, the parameters involved in the first movement will not necessarily be the same as those involved in the second movement, and so the operation will have to be done by matching corresponding parameters and joining each set of corresponding B-splines separately.

Basic continuity

We must first assure that the two interpolants are themselves continuous, before we concern ourselves with their derivatives. Continuity is guaranteed if the last keyframe in the first motion and the first keyframe in the second motion have identical values for both the time and the motion parameter in question. If they do not, the simplest procedure is to replace the time of each keyframe with the average of the two times, and replace the values of the motion parameter with the average value.

Continuity of derivatives of kinetic B-spline

Once basic continuity between the kinetic B-splines is assured, the first and second derivatives of the kinetic B-splines may still be discontinuous. Continuity of the derivatives is restored by redefining the knot set for each of the curves so that the end knots are no longer of multiplicity 4. The first internal keyframe time (the one eliminated by the not-a-knot end condition) is restored in each knot set. From each curve the three internal knots nearest the transition are used as the end knots of the other curve, so that both curves share a common knot set near the transition. A new B-spline

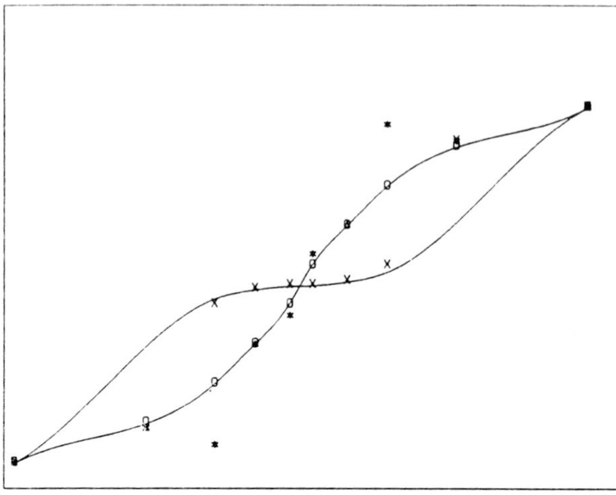

Figure 7: Details of Kinetic Adustment.

The kinetic adjustment used in Figure 2 is shown here in more detail. The original data points, determined by the times of the keyframes, are shown by circles. The B-coefficients of both the original interpolating B-spline are shown by asterisks; the B-coefficients of the modified B-spline are shown by x's. The modified B-spline was constructed by altering the B-coefficients directly.

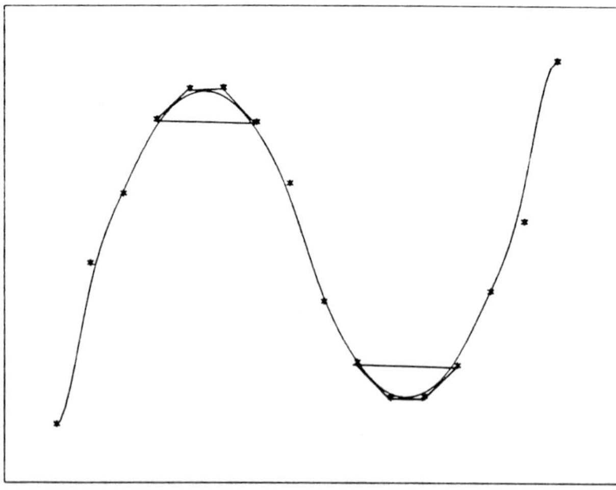

Figure 8: B-Coefficients at Local Extrema

The B-spline shown has both a maximum and a minimum. The control polygons are drawn in for the spans which include the two extrema; the spans themselves are entirely contained in the convex hull of the control points. If the control points nearest the extrema are moved in the direction of the curve, the curve will be modified so as to remain within the convex hull; therefore the extrema will become less extreme.

interpolant is then calculated for the combined motion (from the beginning of the first motion to the end of the second) using the data points defined by the original B-splines and using the common knot set across the transition. The resulting interpolant provides first-and second-derivative continuity across the transition, and the B-coefficients for this combined interpolant are used for each of the two kinetic B-splines. In addition to sharing knots near the transition, the two interpolants will also share the three B-coefficients nearest the transition.

Continuity of derivatives of position B-splines

Both position B-splines were calculated based on zero-slope end conditions so first-derivative continuity is guaranteed. The way in which first-derivative continuity was obtained is highly suspect, however, since it results from an end condition based on an assumption that the body is at rest beyond the end of the motion. In the present case, this assumption is patently false, and should be discarded. In addition, we want to provide second-derivative continuity at the transition.

This desired continuity is provided in a similar way to the method used for the kinetic B-splines. The only difference is that there is no "missing" knot to restore, since the original position B-splines used the full knot set to begin with.

Phrasing the transition

Simply restoring the continuity across the transition may not be satisfactory; the nature of the motion we are modeling may require additional smoothing of the transition to reduce maxima or minima in the function or in its derivatives. We can conveniently use the convex hull property of B-splines to accomplish this smoothing: any given span of the curve is contained within the polygon formed from the four control vertices which determine that span. (Recall that the "control vertices" are simply the B-spline coefficients, plotted on the same graph as the B-spline itself.) Since the control vertices both approximate and enclose the curve, the vertices adjacent to a local extremum must be even more extreme than the curve itself. Figure 8 illustrates this situation.

Consider the effect of altering the control polygon for a span containing an extremum of the curve in the following way: replace each vertex with another vertex which has the same abscissa but whose ordinate is the value of the curve itself at that abscissa. (In other words, move each control vertex vertically to place it on the curve.) The change in the control polygon changes the curve, and the new span thus determined must be enclosed by the new polygon. Since the previous extremum of the curve is no longer inside the control polygon, the new curve has less of an extremum than the old. This is the intuitive basis for the procedure we adopt to smooth the curve at the transition.

In practice, we need not move the control vertices so that they actually lie on the original curve; we will achieve a smoothing effect as long as we move them in the direction of the original curve. For instance, we can replace each B-coefficient by a weighted average of the original B-coefficient and the ordinate of the curve, with the weighting parameter to be determined by the user. The actual degree of smoothing can thus be varied by means of a parameter which ranges from 0 (no effect) to 1 (replacement of B-coefficient by the ordinate).

The transition phrasing should not be restricted to the B-coefficients immediately adjacent to the transition, but should involve an entire region of the curve near the transition. For this purpose, we provide a pair of parameters to define the extent over which this smoothing shall take place; one parameter determines what part of the first motion will be involved, and the other determines what part of the second motion will be involved. These extent parameters can also range from 0 (phrase near transition point only) to 1 (phrase over nearly the entire motion).

If the maximum smoothing is not sufficient to achieve the desired phrasing effect, it is possible to apply this operation repeatedly until the desired phrasing is achieved. In the limit, repeated phrasing must force the phrased region of the curve into a straight line.

Figures 9 and 10 show the effect of various settings of the parameters controlling the degree and extent of smoothing.

Conclusions

As a result of an analysis of theoretical and practical requirements for interpolation for a computer animation system, five important features of such a system were identified: (1) continuity of position, velocity and acceleration, (2) local control, (3) kinetic control, (4) joining of two motions, and (5) phrasing of motions. These features should provide the animator with an improved capability to create realistic, complex animated scenes.

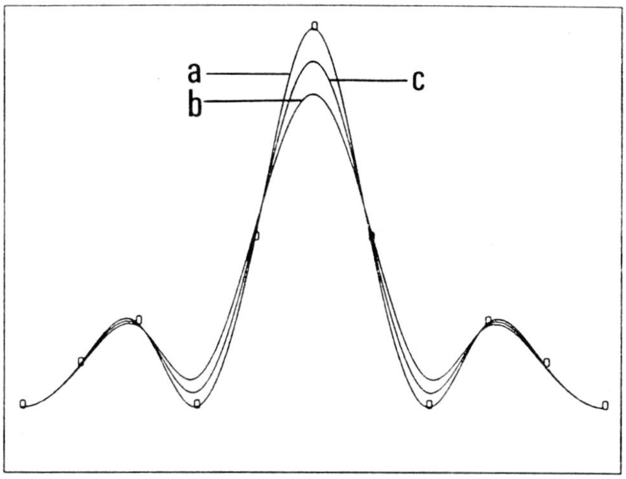

Figure 9: Varying the phrasing.

The three curves above show (a) the original, joined motion with no phrasing (degree = 0), (b) the same motion with full phrasing applied (degree = 1), and (c) the same motion with an intermediate amount of phrasing (degree = 0.5). In all three cases, both extent parameters are set to 1.

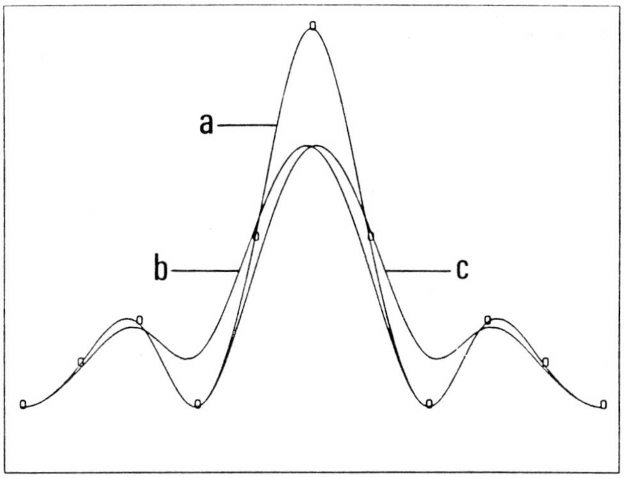

Figure 10: Phrasing with extents.

Curve (a) above shows the same original motions as in Figure 9, with no phrasing. In (b) and (c), phrasing has been applied selectively; in (b), with full left extent and minimal right extent, and in (c), with minimal left extent and full right extent. Both (b) and (c) have been phrased twice, increasing the amount of smoothing.

An interpolation system was designed to incorporate the five features, using separate kinetic and position B-splines to interpolate each motion parameter of a particular motion being animated. The system was implemented in Pascal on a VAX-11/780 and was used to produce the graphs in this paper.

A film incorporating this technique is in production. We are hopeful that the continuity of acceleration and the control over transitions between two motions will allow computer animators to produce smoother, more realistic results with less effort.

Acknowledgements

The authors gratefully acknowledge Jon Korein, Jane Rovins, Gerry Radack, David Sirkin, and the other folks in the Graphics Research Lab of the University of Pennsylvania. This work was partially supported by NASA Grants NAS9-16634 and NAS9-17239, NSF CER Grant MCS-82-19196, and ARO Grant DAAG29-84-K-0061.

References

[1] Badler, N. I. and S. W. Smoliar, "Digital Representations of Human Movement," ACM Computing Surveys 11(1), March 1979, pp. 19-38.

[2] Badler, N. I., J. Korein, J. U. Korein, G. M. Radack and L. Brotman, "TEMPUS: A System for the Design and Simulation of Human Figures in a Task-Oriented Environment," Proc. of the First Annual Workshop on Robotics and Expert Systems, Instrument Society of America, June 1985.

[3] Badler, N. I., "Design of a Human Movement Representation Incorporating Dynamics," Technical Report, Department of Computer and Information Science, University of Pennsylvania, 1984.

[4] Barsky, B. and J. Beatty, "Local Control of Bias and Tension in Beta-splines," Computer Graphics 17(3), July 1983, pp. 193-218.

[5] Barsky, B. and T. DeRose, "The Beta2-spline: A Special Case of the Beta-Spline Curve and Surface Representation," Report No. UCB/CSD 83/152, Computer Science Division, University of California, Berkeley, CA, November 1983.

[6] Burtnyk, N. and M. Wein, "Interactive Skeleton Techniques for Enhancing Motion Dynamics in Keyframe Animation," Communications of the ACM 19(10), October 1976, pp. 564-569.

[7] Catmull, E., "A System For Computer Generated Movies," Proc. ACM Annual Conf. 1972, pp. 422-431.

[8] Catmull, E. "The Problems of Computer-Assisted Animation," Computer Graphics 12(3), August 1978, p. 348-353.

[9] deBoor, C, *A Practical Guide to Splines*, Springer-Verlag, New York, 1978.

[10] Fortin, D., J. F. Lamy, and D. Thalmann, "A Multiple Track Animator System for Motion Synchronization," Proc. ACM SIGGRAPH/SIGART Interdisciplinary Workshop on Motion: Representation and Perception, Toronto, Canada, April 1983, pp. 180-186.

[11] Kochanek, D. and R. Bartels, "Interpolating Splines with Local Tension, Continuity, and Bias Control," Computer Graphics 18(3), July 1984, pp. 33-41.

[12] Loomis, J., H. Poizner, U. Bellugi, A. Blakemore, and J. Hollerbach, "Computer Graphic Modeling of American Sign Language," Computer Graphics 17(3), July 1983, pp. 105-114.

[13] Mezei, L., and A. Zivian, "ARTA, An Interactive Animation System," Proc. IFIP Congress 1971, North Holland Pub., pp. 429-434.

[14] Parke, F. "Parameterized Models for Facial Animation," IEEE Computer Graphics and Applications 2(9), Nov. 1982, pp. 61-68.

[15] Reeves, W. "Inbetweening For Computer Animation Utilizing Moving Point Constraints," Computer Graphics 15(3), August 1981, pp. 263-269.

[16] Reynolds, C., "Computer Animation with Scripts and Actors," Computer Graphics 16(3), July 1982, pp. 289-296.

[17] Shelley, K. and D. Greenberg, "Path Specification and Path Coherence," Computer Graphics 16(3), July 1982, pp. 157-166.

[18] Spegel, M., "Programming of Mechanism Motion," Technical Report CRL-43, Div. of Applied Science, New York University, New York, 1975.

[19] Steketee, S. N., "Interpolation for Animation Incorporating Positional and Kinetic Adjustment," MSE Thesis, Department of Computer and Information Science, University of Pennsylvania, 1984.

[20] Sturman, D. "Interactive Keyframe Animation of 3-D Articulated Motion," Proc. Graphics Interface '84, Ottawa, Ontario, May 1984, pp. 35-40.

[21] *Webster's Third New International Dictionary*, G. & C. Merriam Co., Springfield, MA, 1971.

[22] Wilhelms, J., "Graphical Simulation of the Motion of Articulated Bodies such as Humans and Robots, with Particular Emphasis on the Use of Dynamic Analysis," PhD Dissertation, Department of Computer Science, University of California, Berkeley, 1985.

Computational Modeling for the Computer Animation of Legged Figures

Michael Girard
and
A. A. Maciejewski

Computer Graphics Research Group
The Ohio State University

OSU CGRG /Cranston Center
1501 Neil Avenue
Columbus OH 43201

Abstract

Modeling techniques for animating legged figures are described which are used in the PODA animation system. PODA utilizes pseudoinverse control in order to solve the problems associated with manipulating kinematically redundant limbs. PODA builds on this capability to synthesize a kinematic model of legged locomotion which allows animators to control the complex relationships between the motion of the body of a figure and the coordination of its legs. Finally, PODA provides for the integration of a simple model of legged locomotion dynamics which insures that the accelerations of a figure's body are synchronized with the timing of the forces applied by its legs.

CR Categories and Subject Descriptors: 1.3.7 [Computer Graphics]: Graphics and Realism: Animation. Additional Key Words and Phrases: motion control, computational modeling, manipulators, legged locomotion

Introduction

The problems of animating articulated figures with multiple legs have long been a source of difficulty in the computer animation field. Joint angle interpolation between "key" joint positions is the most widely used method of animating jointed animals. This method fails to work, however, for cases in which the end of a limb must be constrained to move along a particular path – the interpolated joint positions of two "key" leg positions planted on the ground will not, in general, remain on the ground (fig. 1).

Another difficulty is the sheer tedium of positioning "keys" for limbs containing many degrees of freedom. The animal shown in figure 2 possesses 9 degrees of freedom in each leg,9 degees of freedom in the neck, and 18 degees of freedom in the "spine." An animator using a key joint system would have to manage positioning a total of 63 joints.

A further problem is that a walking or running figure is more than an assemblage of moving limbs – the coordination of legs, body and feet are functionally related in a complex fashion. The motion of the body of a figure and the timing and placement of legs are both kinematically and dynamically coupled.[20-36]

The approach taken in the design of the PODA system is to provide the animator with a computational model which facilitates the integration and direct control of the functional dependencies between different parts of a figure. An interactive menu-driven interface is used for both the incremental construction and behavioral control of animals possessing any number of legs composed of any number of joints. A strategy is implemented in which the figure's motion may be designed and manipulated at different levels of control. At the lowest level the animator may define and adjust the character of the movement of the legs and feet. At a higher level the animator may direct the coordination of the legs and control the overall motion dynamics and path of the body.

The primary goal of our efforts is to build a framework in which the synthesis of legged figure motion may be artistically conceived and controlled at increasingly higher levels of complexity and abstraction. In this regard, our initial efforts have been focussed on developing a general model for legged locomotion due to its importance to the execution of more complex motor skills, such as those which are required for dance and gymnastics[27].

In this first section we will outline the solution taken in PODA for the control of single limbs. This will set the stage for the discussion of the legged locomotion model which utilizes the limb control methods described.

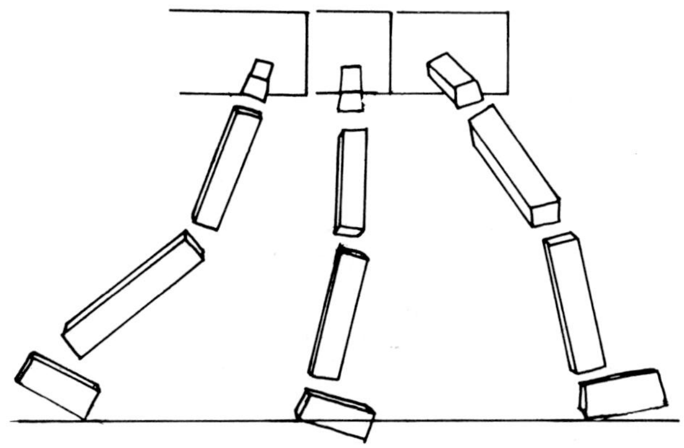

Figure 1

THE CONTROL OF LIMBS

Representing articulated limbs

In order to define the functionality of an arbitrary articulated figure, PODA has adopted the kinematic notation presented by Denavit and Hartenberg [3]. This specifies a unique coordinate system for every individual degree of freedom present in the figure. These degrees of freedom, whether rotary or prismatic, will be referred to as joints and the fixed interconnecting bodies as links. The four parameters used to define the transformation between adjacent coordinate systems are the length of the link a, the twist of the link α, the distance between links d, and the angle between links θ. The single variable associated with the transformation depends on the type of joint represented, that is θ for rotary or d for prismatic joints (fig. 3).

The research described in this paper was supported, in part, by National Science Foundation grant DCR-8304185, and in part, by a National Science Foundation Fellowship.

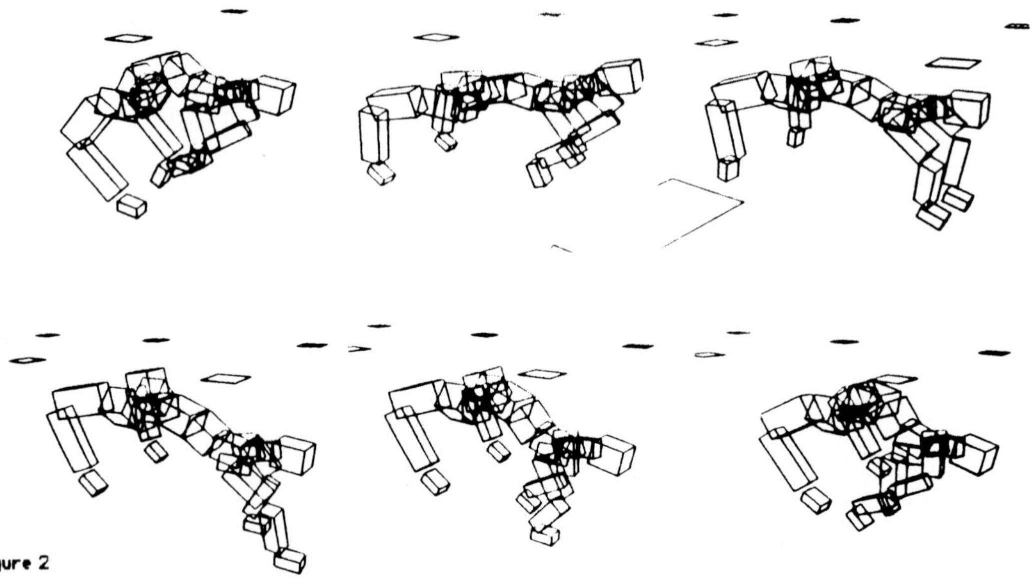

Figure 2

Given the above definitions, it can be shown [12] that the transformation between adjacent coordinate frames $i-1$ and i denoted by ${}^{i-1}T_i$ is given by the homogeneous transformation:

$$ {}^{i-1}T_i = \begin{bmatrix} \vec{n} & \vec{o} & \vec{a} & \vec{p} \\ 0 & 0 & 0 & 1 \end{bmatrix} $$

where

$$ \begin{aligned} p_x &= a_i \cos\theta_i & n_x &= \cos\theta_i \\ p_y &= a_i \sin\theta_i & n_y &= \sin\theta_i \\ p_z &= d_i & n_z &= 0 \\ o_x &= -\cos\alpha_i \sin\theta_i & a_x &= \sin\alpha_i \sin\theta_i \\ o_y &= \cos\alpha_i \cos\theta_i & a_y &= -\sin\alpha_i \cos\theta_i \\ o_z &= \sin\alpha_i & a_z &= \cos\alpha_i \end{aligned} $$

By repeatedly applying adjacent link transformations the relationship between any two coordinate systems i and j is easily obtained using

$$ {}^{i}T_j = {}^{i}T_{i+1}\,{}^{i+1}T_{i+2}\cdots{}^{j-1}T_j $$

The above equation permits any link of the figure, defined in its own coordinate frame, to be represented in any arbitrary reference or world coordinate frame. More importantly, it can be used to determine the number and characteristics of the degrees of freedom available for simulating coordinated movement.

The Jacobian Matrix

Given the above framework, one can easily see that, given the state of the joint angle variables, we can compute the position of all of the links and arrive at the position of the end of the limb. This is called the *forward kinematics* problem. The reverse situation, that of computing the joint angles from the position of the end of the limb, is necessary if we wish to place a foot or hand in some desired place–what Korein and Badler have called "goal directed motion" [32]. This is called the *inverse kinematics* problem. The legged locomotion models in PODA rely heavily on the need for goal-directed motion: feet must be moved along trajectories, placed exactly at desired footholds and held in place as the body passes over them.

The solution of the inverse kinematics problem is the source of much of the difficulty in dealing with controlling articulated figures. A general solution for arbitrary articulated chains does not exist and even those that lend themselves to an analytic solution result in nonlinear equations [12]. Additional complications are incurred when redundant degrees of freedom are present.

The solution adopted by PODA is to linearize the equations about the current operating point. The six-dimensional vector representing an incremental change in position and orientation in three space of an arbitrary link is linearly related to the vector $\Delta\vec{\theta}$ by the Jacobian matrix J through the equation

$$ \Delta\vec{x} = J(\vec{\theta})\Delta\vec{\theta} \qquad (1) $$

for changes which are sufficiently small. Thus by updating the Jacobian each cycle time, the advantages of a linear system are obtained. This allows the application of all of the techniques of solving linear equations to obtain the desired result (to be discussed in the next section). The use of Jacobians has long been a common practice in nonlinear control system theory and has been successfully applied in the field of robotics [18,19].

Due to its central nature in the animation of articulated figures, an efficient implementation for generating the Jacobian is essential to a viable system. While there are may different techniques available, a particularly elegant method has been formulated with the use of screw motor variables [17]. A screw motor is characterized by the variables $\vec{\omega}$, the angular velocity of the screw axis, and $\vec{\mu}$, the velocity of a point attached to the screw axis which coincides with the origin of the world coordinate frame. In terms of these variables, the desired displacement of the foot may be expressed as

$$ \begin{aligned} \vec{\omega} &= R\vec{\omega}_f \\ \vec{\mu} &= R\vec{v}_f - \vec{\omega}\times\vec{p} \end{aligned} \qquad (2) $$

with the original foot displacement $\Delta\vec{x}$ given by

$$ \Delta\vec{x} = \begin{bmatrix} \vec{v}_f \\ \vec{\omega}_f \end{bmatrix} $$

where R is the upper 3×3 rotation partition of the homogeneous transformation describing the desired point whose velocity is being specified and $\vec{p}$ is the position of this point given by the fourth column of its homogeneous transformation. It can be shown [16] that the Jacobian is given by

$$ J = \begin{bmatrix} p_1\times a_1 & p_2\times a_2 & \ldots & p_n\times a_n \\ a_1 & a_2 & \ldots & a_n \end{bmatrix} \qquad (3) $$

where a_i and p_i are the third and fourth columns, respectively, of the homogeneous transformation matrix ${}^{0}T_{i-1}$. The first column of the Jacobian is given by

$$ p_1 = [0\,0\,0]^{\top} \qquad a_1 = [0\,0\,1]^{\top}. $$

Figure 3

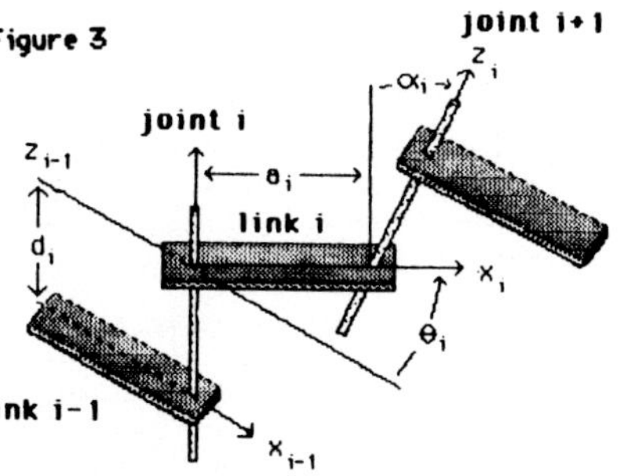

Link Parameters Associated With Link i

This formulation of the Jacobian allows a minimal amount of extra computation since the majority of the work has already been done in generating the homogeneous transformations required to display the object. This is in contrast with other techniques which do not express the Jacobian in the world coordinate frame [37].

Inverting the Jacobian

Given a linear system by virtue of the Jacobian, we now need to invert the relationship represented by equation (1) in order to determine the required $\Delta\vec{\theta}$ to achieve a desired $\Delta\vec{x}$. Since we are dealing with arbitrary articulated figures, the Jacobian is in general not square and therefore its inverse is not defined. To obtain a useful solution regardless of the rank of J, the pseudoinverse is applied. The pseudoinverse will be denoted by J^+ and is the unique [13] matrix which satisfies the four properties:

$$\begin{aligned} J\,J^+\,J &= J \\ J^+\,J\,J^+ &= J^+ \\ (J^+\,J)^\top &= J^+\,J \\ (J\,J^+)^\top &= J\,J^+ \end{aligned} \tag{4}$$

The advantages of using the pseudoinverse lie in that it returns the least squares minimum norm solution to equation (1). Thus it provides useful results in both the under and over determined cases. Other generalized inverses may also be applied [1,2]. An excellent overview concerning the pseudoinverse control of redundant manipulators as well as a geometric interpretation of the pseudoinverse using singular value decomposition is presented in [7].

A number of different methods for calculating pseudoinverses have been discussed in the literature [6,14]. A discussion of the some of the numerical considerations involved in computing the pseudoinverse is presented by Noble [11]. The simplest expressions for a pseudoinverse appear for matrices known to be of full rank. For an $m \times n$ matrix A of rank r, the expression for the pseudoinverse is given by

$$A^+ = \begin{cases} (A^\top A)^{-1} A^\top & \text{if } m > n = r \text{ and} \\ A^\top (A\,A^\top)^{-1} & \text{if } r = m < n \end{cases} \tag{5}.$$

The use of Gaussian elimination with pivoting removes the need for an explicit inverse calculation and results in a stable and efficient technique for computing the pseudoinverses under these conditions.

For matrices of unknown rank a recursive procedure for computing the pseudoinverse presented by Greville [4] may be used, the details of which are beyond the scope of this paper.

Controlling Redundant Limbs in PODA

While the above section illustrates how the pseudoinverse can be used to obtain a useful solution to equation (1), for cases where redundant degrees of freedom exist, it is only one of an infinite number of solutions. The manner in which the animator is given the flexibility to determine which of the available solutions is most desirable is through a projection operator. It can be shown that shown [5] that the general solution of equation (1) is given by

$$\Delta\vec{\theta} = J^+\Delta\vec{x} + (I - J^+\,J)\vec{z} \tag{6}$$

where I is an $n \times n$ unity matrix and z is an arbitrary vector in $\Delta\theta$–space. Thus the homogeneous portion of this solution is described by a projection operator $(I - J^+\,J)$ that maps the arbitrary vector $\vec{z}$ into the null space of the transformation. The physical interpretation of the homogeneous solution is illustrated in figure 4.

Thus by different choices for the vector $\vec{z}$, various desirable properties described in θ–space can be achieved under the constraint imposed by exact achievement of the specified $\Delta\vec{x}$. One particularly useful property is to keep joints as close as possible to some particular angles chosen by the animator. This is done [8] by specifying the vector $\vec{z}$ in equation (6) to be

$$\vec{z} = \nabla H$$

with

$$H = \sum_{i=1}^{n} \alpha_i(\theta_i - \theta_{c_i})^2$$

where θ_i is the ith joint angle, θ_{c_i} is the center angle of the ith joint angle, and α_i is a center angle gain value between zero and one. The equation may also be generalized for H equal to any smooth function one wishes to minimize.

The center angles define the desired joint angle positions and their associated gains define their relative importance of satisfaction. From the animators point of view, the gains may be thought of as "springs" which define the stiffness of the joint about some desired center position. PODA provides interactive specification of center angles and gains as a means of controlling redundant degrees of freedom in the legs.

The implementation of this formulation can be included in the gaussian elimination procedure for computing the pseudoinverse if it is properly decomposed [7].

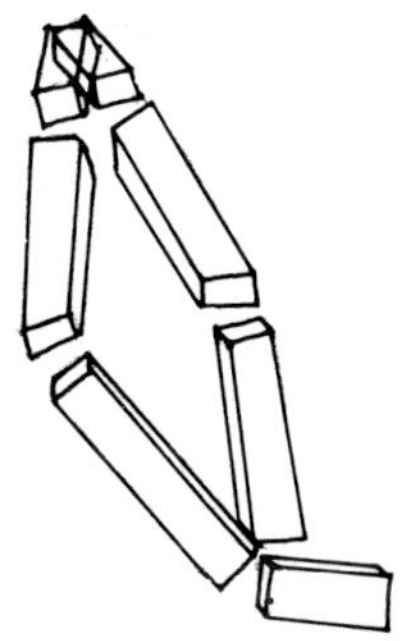

Figure 4

Homogeneous solution to the Jacobian equation is the set of joint velocities which cause no end effector motion.

MODELING THE KINEMATICS OF LEGGED LOCOMOTION

The task of a kinematic model for legged locomotion is to coordinate the motion of the legs,feet and body in terms of their respective positions and velocities (Newtonian mechanical properties such as force and mass are not considered). The kinematic model must enable the animator to design the timing relationships between the legs and the character of the steps taken by each leg in accordance with the design of the body's trajectory, orientation and speed. Ideally, it should be easily adaptable to any extensions made in the dynamics domain.

Gait Design in PODA

The model of locomotion implemented in PODA utilizes a number of parameters which are convenient for describing the gait of a figure–the terms and relations are derived from robotics research on walking machines [22-26].

A *gait pattern* describes the sequence of lifting and placing of the feet. The pattern repeats itself as the figure moves: each repetition of the sequence is called the *gait cycle*.

The time (or number of frames) taken to complete a single gait cycle is the *period P* of the cycle.

The *relative phase of leg i*, R_i , describes the fraction of the gait cycle period which transpires before leg i is lifted. The relative phases of the legs may be used to classify the well known gaits of quadrupedal animals (fig. 5).

During each gait cycle period any given leg will spend a percentage of that time on the ground–this fraction is called the *duty factor of leg i*. For example, the duty factor may be used to distinguish between the walking and running gaits of bipeds. Walking requires that the duty factor of the each of the legs exceed 0.5 since, by definition,the feet must be on the ground simultaneously for a percentage of the gait cycle period. Lower duty factors (less than 0.5) result in ballistic motion identified with running, wherein the entire body leaves the ground for some duration.

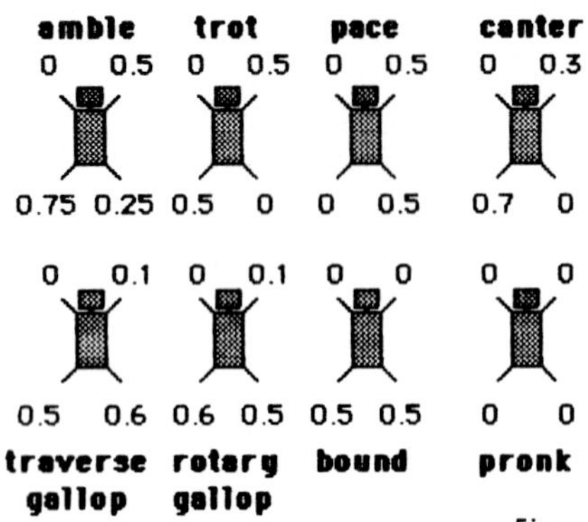

Figure 5

We will call the time a leg spends on the ground its *support duration*. The time spent in the air is the leg's *transfer duration*.

The *stroke* is defined as the distance traveled by the body during a leg's support duration. If we acknowledge that the foot must traverse the stroke during the transfer phase in order to "keep up" with the body, the stroke may alternatively be regarded as the length of the step taken by the leg over the ground (fig. 6a). The body may move over the ground plane in PODA, so the stroke in this context becomes the diameter of a circle in that plane (fig. 6b).

Figure 6a

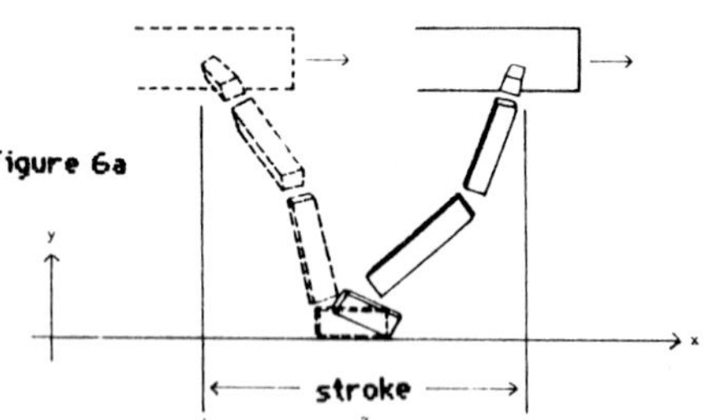

Figure 6b

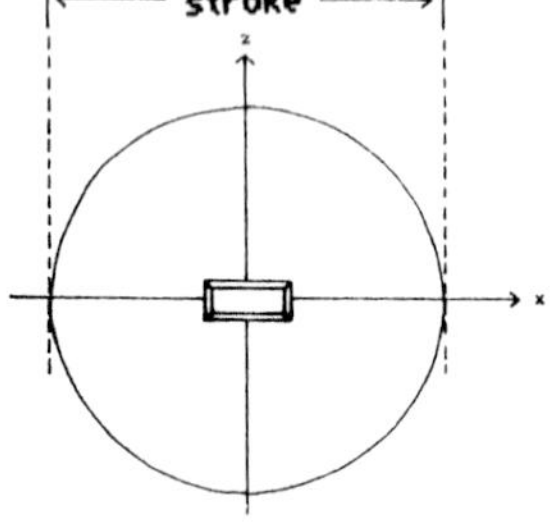

Leg Coordination

The following relationship holds between the legs and the body:

$$\text{supportDuration} = \frac{\text{stroke}}{\text{bodySpeed}} \tag{7}$$

The above equation solves for the time (or number of frames) that each leg must spend on the ground. By definition we also have

$$\text{dutyFactor} = \frac{\text{supportDuration}}{P}$$

The amount of time which a leg spends in the air depends on both the leg speed and the arclength of the transfer phase trajectory. That is:

$$\text{transferDuration} = \frac{\textbf{arcLength}(\text{transferTrajectory})}{\text{legSpeed}}$$

During the gait cycle period P, a single leg will move through one cycle of support and transfer, hence we have:

$$P = \text{supportDuration} + \text{transferDuration} \tag{8}$$

for any leg k. In fact, one may imagine the period as a duration subdivided into support and transfer durations (fig. 7). The *leg state* at time t may be determined as

$$\text{legState} = (\text{legState}_0 + t) \bmod P \tag{9}$$

where

$$\text{legState}_0 = (R_i)(P)$$

If the leg state is less than the support duration then the leg is in its support phase, otherwise the leg is in its transfer phase. Moreover, the time of foot placement occurs when the leg state equals zero and the foot liftoff occurs when the leg state is equal to the support duration (fig. 7).

An animator using PODA may design gaits for figures having any number of legs by instantiating the parameters given above. The model makes sure that all the variables are updated according to functional dependencies, thereby freeing the animator to experiment with the variables of interest such as relative phase without worrying about the integrity of the other related variables.

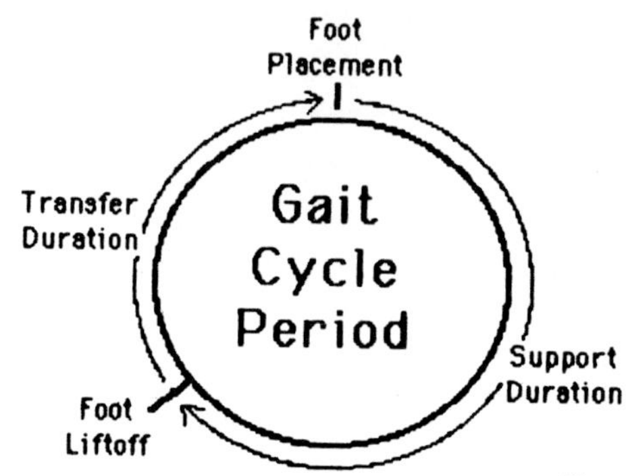

Figure 7

Leg Support and Transfer Trajectories

Aside from the problem of coordinating the timing of the legs, one must design the motion of the step taken during the transfer phase and insure that the feet will remain planted on the ground during the support phase.

A step is specified in PODA by the desired trajectory of the feet and the center angles and gains on the joints (which may change dynamically). The curve which defines the foot trajectory is defined by a Catmull-Rom (interpolating) spline. Because the desired shape of the curve depends on the geometry of the leg, the control points of the spline are set by moving the foot of the leg. The animator may conceptualize the design of the step as the specification of "key leg positions," in the spirit of a key-framing system. In PODA, a key position records the position of the foot (as a control point in the spline) and the center angles and gains that are associated with that position. The animator manipulates the foot into each position using PODA's inverse kinematic procedures, and then , once the foot is in place, the joint angles may be adjusted using the center angle and gain parameters.

This approach is distinguished from key-framing or joint angle interpolation systems in that the goal of achieving the desired foot position in Cartesian space is primary–the foot will travel precisely along the smooth Catmull-Rom spline from foothold to foothold. By contrast, if we interpolate the the leg positions in joint space, there is no general means of either moving the foot along a curve or placing the foot at a particular place on the ground.

The problem of keeping the legs on the ground as the body translates and rotates is simplified due to PODA's inverse kinematic capability. The problem reduces to solving for the position of the foot in the leg's moving coordinate system so that it is identical to the placement of the foot in the previous frame's world coordinate system (thereby keeping the foot stationary in the world). We we solve for this position using:

$$^{\text{World}}\overrightarrow{\text{prevFrameFoot}_{t-1}} = {}^{\text{World}}T_{\text{Hip}_{t-1}} \left({}^{\text{Hip}}\overrightarrow{\text{Foot}_{t-1}} \right) \tag{10}$$

$$^{\text{Hip}}\overrightarrow{\text{prevFrameFoot}_{t}} = {}^{\text{Hip}}T_{\text{World}_t} \left({}^{\text{World}}\overrightarrow{\text{prevFrameFoot}_{t-1}} \right)$$

Directional Control of the Body

If the animator is to have supervisory control over the legged figure, a means for directing the body's full translational and rotational degree's of freedom must be available. Given that all the legs are on the ground, the problem may be solved using equation (10). The fundamental problem is to calculate footholds and plan the foot transfer trajectories between them so as to adapt to the desired body motion.

Foothold and Transfer Trajectory Planning

An important concept of foothold planning is the notion of a *reference leg position*[22]. This is the desired position of the leg in mid-stance or half way though the leg's support duration (fig. 10). The posture of an animal when all of its legs are in their reference positions may be regarded as the "standing" position of the animal (fig. 11).

The other key ingredient for the foothold calculation is the ability to predict the body's future positions. In PODA, the body's trajectory may be computed as a function of the desired body trajectory over the ground plane (a cubic spline designed by the animator) and dynamic constraints due the timing and force limitations of legs (to be discussed) before the precise footholds are chosen. Since the body's position is known in advance, it is possible to plan ahead in order step toward the next stable position

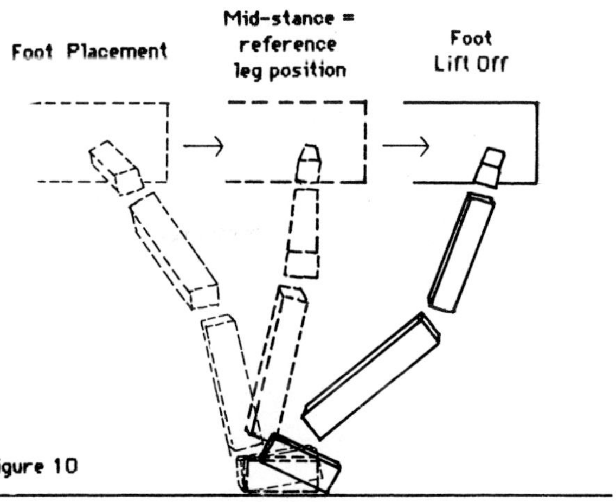

Figure 10

At the beginning of the leg transfer phase of leg i, say at frame t, we must compute the reference leg position in world space at frame f_1 as follows:

$${}^{\mathrm{World}}T_{\mathrm{Hip}_{f_1}} = {}^{\mathrm{World}}T_{\mathrm{Body}_{f_1}}\,{}^{\mathrm{Body}}T_{\mathrm{Hip}}$$

$${}^{\mathrm{World}}\overrightarrow{\mathrm{refLegPos}}_{f_1} = {}^{\mathrm{World}}T_{\mathrm{Hip}_{f_1}}\left({}^{\mathrm{Hip}}\overrightarrow{\mathrm{refLegPos}}\right) \qquad (11)$$

where

$$f_1 = t + \mathrm{transferDuration} + 0.5(\mathrm{supportDuration})$$

This foothold will insure that that leg i comes to its "mid-stance" position half way through its support phase. We must still determine the position of the foot in the body's coordinate system at the time the foot is placed down. This knowledge is required in order to facilitate moving the foot horizontally with respect to the body during the transfer. This may be accomplished by:

$${}^{\mathrm{Body}}\overrightarrow{\mathrm{refLegPos}}_{f_2} = {}^{\mathrm{Body}}T_{\mathrm{World}_{f_2}}\left({}^{\mathrm{World}}\overrightarrow{\mathrm{refLegPos}}_{f_1}\right)$$

where

$$f_2 = t + \mathrm{transferDuration}$$

The generic transfer trajectory designed by the animator may then be adapted to move between the current foot position and the calculated foothold so that the height in the world and proportional distance moved next to the body are preserved.

Robotics research on walking vehicles has provided a rich source of computational models for the solution of body motion planning and leg coordination[22-26]. However, their design criteria is somewhat different the requirements of animation.

The primary design concerns of the robotics algorithms are to maintain dynamic stability of the walking vehicle, to avoid leg intersections, to optimize the load balancing and energy consumption, and to insure that the feet never stray beyond their kinematic limits. Because the algorithms must actually work for real walking machines (rather than simulated figures), their scope is conservative. Restrictions are placed on the types of gait patterns and relative phase relationships between the legs, thereby drastically limiting the repertoire of behaviors.

The design philosophy of PODA is to give the animator absolute control over the entire set of of available gaits in order to exploit the coupling between rhythm and dynamics (to be discussed) since these matters are of extreme importance in artistic design. Moreover, since PODA's current implementation on the Ridge 32C minicomputer provides for realtime computation of a figure possessing four 9–degree of freedom legs at 2 frames per second, leg interference and unnatural leg stretching may be detected immediately, leaving the range of many reasonable solutions to these problems up to the artist rather than hard–wiring a single solution into the motion model.

MODELING THE DYNAMICS OF LEGGED LOCOMOTION

The simulation of the dynamics of motion control in legged animals is an extremely complex modeling problem. Models for single limbs (industrial robots) which compute the relationships between the torques applied at the joints,the masses and moments of inertia of each of the links, and the position of the joints and their associated time derivatives, are well understood [38]. Work has also been published in the biomechanics field on the the relationship between muscular forces and motion parameters of simplified "ideal" models of animals[33,34]. Although these models may produce interesting animation, their appropriateness for artistic design and control must be considered as well as their (usually substantial) computational costs.

Simulation vs. Animation

In contrast to industrial robots and biomechanical simulations, animation does not necessarily require the computation of actual forces. The application of dynamics to animation is simplified by the fact that we are interested only in what can be seen.

The essential concern is to make the motion look as if forces were being applied. In other words, we are primarily interested in solving for the acceleration in dynamics models – the computation of parameters such as forces, torques and moments of inertia is only relevant if it can help us easily manipulate accelerations to produce coherent dynamic realism.

The necessity for modeling dynamics in PODA was apparent as soon as the kinematic model was completed. In a purely kinematic model the motion of the body is quickly seen to be independent from the coordination of the legs, and it appears as though the body is suspended from strings, pulling its legs behind it.

The development of dynamics for PODA is an ongoing research project. The initial goal was to see whether very simple dynamic models of legged locomotion could be developed which were both amenable to artistic control and as fully general as the kinematic model (applicable to any figure constructed by the animator). At the time of this writing, PODA is capable of modeling the translational acceleration of the center of mass of body in the vertical direction and ground plane, and the rotational acceleration of the body that is required to insure that it is facing in the direction of movement (if turning is desired). At all stages, the body's motion is constrained and propelled by the simulated forces applied by the legs.

Decomposition of Dynamic Control in PODA

The simple model used in PODA was inspired by Raibert's work on legged hopping machines. He and his coworkers have built a one-legged hopping machine which is able to balance and move in three dimensions. His control algorithms are based on a decomposition into hopping height, forward velocity, and attitude control[31,28].

The model used in PODA decomposes the dynamic coupling between the legs and the body along two lines: decomposition by leg and decomposition by body direction.

Vertical Control

Dynamics in the vertical direction must take into account the effects of gravity and the gait cycle period of each leg. Since PODA's decomposition scheme is based on decomposition by leg, it will be helpful to consider a one-legged figure.

A 14 legged insect shown in its standing position.

Moving in a wave gait, the legs near the rear advance toward their next footholds.

Figure 11

The current model makes the simplifying assumption that the upward force applied by the leg on the body is constant during its support phase. The animator supplies PODA with both the value of this force, the mass of the body, and the downward acceleration due to gravity. Net upward acceleration of the center of mass is then given by:

$$\vec{a}_{y_i} = \left(\frac{\vec{F}_{y_i}}{\text{mass}_{\text{body}}} - g \right) \text{ for leg } i \qquad (12)$$

The gait cycle period may be subdivided into three dynamic stages of the leg's motion: pushing the body up,free falling,and then restoring the body to its original position (as long as the application of upward leg forces are symmetrical about the mid-stance position, the body will stabilize to zero velocity at that position). We will call these the *push duration, fall duration,* and *restore duration* respectively (fig. 12).

The leg support duration is a function of the body speed in the horizontal plane and the stroke (equation 7). Since the leg's traversal of the transfer trajectory must coincide with the body's ballistic motion, we have:

$$\text{transferDuration} = \left(\frac{\vec{a}_{y_i}}{g} \right) (\text{supportDuration}) \qquad (13)$$

The vertical position of figures with multiple legs is determined in PODA by the superposition of the ballistic motion of the body due of each of its legs considered independently. This extremely simple model produces remarkably realistic motion for both walking and running in multiple leg figures: if the magnitude of vertical acceleration is low and the phase relationships of the legs are in opposition, the upward accelerations will cancel, resulting in a smooth walking oscillation. High accelerations resulting from strong single leg forces (e.g. running in a trot) or the sum of forces of many legs pushing from the ground together (e.g. hopping) propel the body into the air.

The trajectory taken by the body due to the summation of vertical leg accelerations and downward gravitational accelerations taken from each of the legs is automatically synchronized with rhythm of the phase relationships in the legs. For example, convincing cantors, trots, and bounding motion may be animated simply by altering the figure's gait.

Another advantage to PODA's leg decomposition of vertical dynamics is that changes in the figure's motion parameters which evolve over gait cycle periods, such as body speed or upward leg force may be easily accommodated by adjusting the related dynamic parameters for each leg's contribution independently at the beginning of its upward pushing phase. The stability of each leg's contribution guarantees the vertical stability of the body as a whole. A gait shifting algorithm has been developed by one of the authors which exploits the ability for legs to undergo phase shifts by varying the distribution of vertical pushing forces among them.

Horizontal Control

The desired horizontal path taken by the figure is specified in PODA by the animator with a cubic spline (Catmull-Rom or B-spline). Given the desired body speed along different parts of the curve, PODA may calculate the desired positions and velocities along it using a numerical arclength calculation.

However, a legged figure's acceleration toward a desired direction and speed must be coherent with its leg support duration pattern and it must also simulate the effects of momentum in a given direction in order to give the body a sense of weight.

In PODA, the body's ability to turn and speed up is consistent with the number of feet on the ground and the maginitude of the maximum achievable force $\|\overrightarrow{F_{\max_i}}\|$ assigned by the animator to each supporting leg. The maximum achievable acceleration of the body is governed by the sum of their forces:

$$\|\vec{a}_{xz_{\max}}\| = \sum_{i=1}^{n} \frac{\left\|\overrightarrow{F_{\max_i}}\right\|}{\text{mass}_{\text{body}}} \qquad (14)$$

where n is the number of feet on the ground.

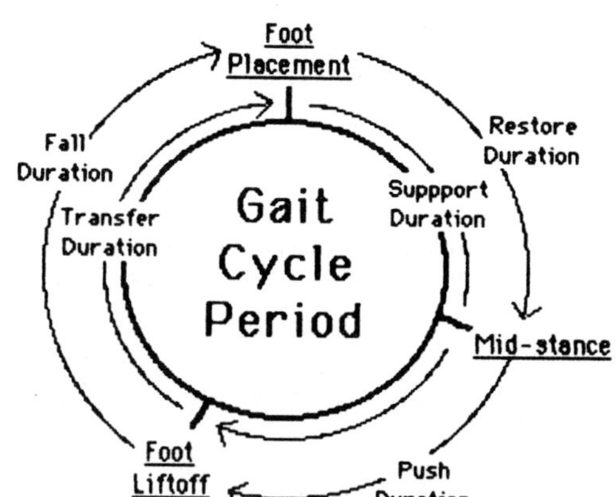

Figure 12

At each frame PODA computes the next desired velocity along the desired bouy path. Then PODA determines the desired acceleration at a given frame through velocity error feedback, that is, by subtracting the desired velocity from the current velocity at that frame. The horizontal acceleration of the body at frame t is then computed as:

$$\vec{a}_{xz} = \|\vec{a}_{xz}\| \frac{\vec{a}_{xz_{\text{desired}}}}{\|\vec{a}_{xz_{\text{desired}}}\|} \qquad (15)$$

where

$$\|\vec{a}_{xz}\| = \min \left(\|\vec{a}_{xz_{\text{desired}}}\|, \|\vec{a}_{xz_{\max}}\| \right)$$

$$\vec{a}_{xz_{\text{desired}}} = \left(\overrightarrow{\text{Vel}}_{\text{desired}} - \overrightarrow{\text{Vel}} \right)$$

An additional backward acceleration during the restore duration and forward acceleration during the push duration is necessary in order to simulate the effects foot position with respect to the body at foot placement and foot liftoff [28].

Rotational Control

The foothold and leg transfer calculations described adapt to allow for full rotational control of the body. At the time of this writing, however, only the dynamics of accelerations about the yaw axis have been implemented (the pitch axis rotation apparent in figure¡ 2 is due to the separation of the application of vertical acceleration between the front and rear sections of the body). Yaw axis accelerations are necessary if we wish the body to realistically turn so that it is facing in the direction of movement.

The simple frame to frame strategy applied for horizontal control is not sufficient for coordinated turning, especially for running gaits wherein the legs are off the ground. In such cases one must know where the body is going in order to effectively anticipate the rotational accelerations required to keep the body properly oriented before its feet leave the ground.

The solution adopted by PODA for rotational control takes advantage of its ability to know the translational coordinates of the body in advance. The order of calculation for body dynamics plays an important role in this matter (fig. 13). The direction of body motion may be derived from the sequence of actual velocities taken by the body.

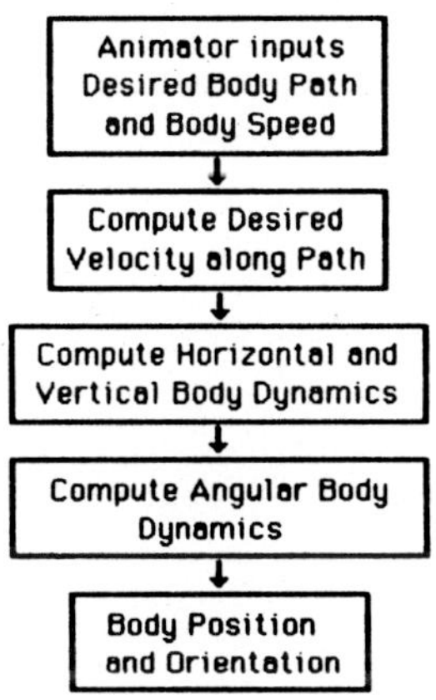

Figure 13

Once the desired body orientations are known, PODA is able to exploit the leg decomposition strategy employed for vertical control. Each leg applies a positive acceleration during its pushing phase and a negative restoring acceleration during its restoring phase in order to bring the body exactly to the desired angle computed at its mid-stance reference leg position. If we solve Newton's equations of motion with the constraint that we wish the final mid-stance rotational velocity to be zero, we have:

$$\ddot{\sigma} = \frac{(\sigma_{\mathrm{midStance}+P} - \sigma_{\mathrm{midStance}})}{(\mathrm{pushDuration})(\mathrm{pushDuration} + \mathrm{fallDuration})}$$

where σ is angle about the yaw axis.

Conclusion

The described formulations have proven to be successful models foı the synthesis of legged locomotion. However, many interesting problems remain to be solved. We will refine the legged locomotion model in PODA as more is learned from each simpler model. The addition of rotational dynamics for body pitch and, more generally, the modeling of body dynamics due to the motion of non-supporting limbs are obvious choices for extension.

Other problems of interest include the development of control techniques for maintaining postural balance, the inclusion of obstacle avoidance and collision detection, and a means of designing motor skills above and beyond the requirements of walking and running.

Acknowledgements

The authors wish to thank John Renner and Susan Amkraut for the preparation of this document, and Charles Csuri and Thomas Linehan for their maintenance of the stimulating environment at CGRG.

REFERENCES

[1] Ben-Israel, Adi and Thomas N. E. Greville, "Generalized Inverses: Theory and Applications," *Wiley-Interscience*, New York, 1974.

[2] Boullion, T. L. and P. L. Odell, "Generalized Inverse Matrices," *Wiley-Interscience*,New York, 1971.

[3] Denavit, J. and R. S. Hartenberg, "A Kinematic Notation for Lower-Pair Mechanisms Based on Matrices," *ASME Journal of Applied Mechanics*, Vol. 23, pp. 215-221, June, 1955.

[4] Greville, T. N. E., "Some Applications of the Pseudoinverse of a Matrix," *SIAM Review*, Vol. 2, No. 1, January, 1960.

[5] Greville, T. N. E., "The Pseudoinverse of a Rectangular or Singular Matrix and its Applications to the Solutions of Systems of Linear Equations," *SIAM Review*, Vol. 1, No. 1, January, 1959.

[6] Hanson, R. J. and C. L. Lawson, "Extensions and Applications of the Householder Algorithm for Solving Linear Least Squares Problems," *Mathematics of Computation*, Vol. 23, pp. 787-812, 1969.

[7] Klein, C. A. and Huang, C. H., "Review of Pseudoinverse Control for Use with Kinematically Redundant Manipulators," *IEEE Transactions on Systems, Man, and Cybernetics*, Vol. SMC-13, No. 2, pp. 245-250,March/April, 1983.

[8] Liegeois, A., "Automatic Supervisory Control of the Configuration and Behavior of Multibody Mechanisms," *IEEE Transactions on Systems, Man and Cybernetics*, Vol. SMC-7, No. 12, December, 1977.

[9] Maciejewski, A. A., and Klein, C. A., "Obstacle Avoidance for Kinematically Redundant Manipulators in Dynamically Varying Environments," to appear in *International Journal of Robotics Research.*

[10] Maciejewski, A. A., and Klein, C. A., "SAM - Animation Software for Simulating Articulated Motion," submitted to *IEEE Computer Graphics and Applications.*

[11] Noble, B., "Methods for Computing the Moore-Penrose Generalized Inverses, and Related Matters," pp. 245-301, in *Generalized Inverses and Applications*, ed. by M. A. Nashed, *Academic Press*, New York, 1975.

[12] Paul, R., *Robot Manipulators*, MIT Press, Cambridge, Mass., 1981.

[13] Penrose, R., "On Best Approximate Solutions of Linear Matrix Equations," *Proc. Cambridge Philos. Soc.*, Vol. 52, pp. 17-19, 1956.

[14] Peters, G. and J. H. Wilkinson, "The Least Squares Problem and Pseudo-Inverses," *The Computer Journal*, Vol. 13, No. 3, August, 1970.

[15] Ribble, E. A., "Synthesis of Human Skeletal Motion and the Design of a Special-Purpose Processor for Real-Time Animation of Human and Animal Figure Motion," Master's Thesis, The Ohio State University, June, 1982.

[16] Waldron, K. J., "Geometrically Based Manipulator Rate Control Algorithms", *Seventh Applied Mechanics Conference*, Kansas City, December,1981.

[17] Waldron, K. J., "The Use of Motors in Spatial Kinematics," *Proceedings of the IFToMM Conference on Linkages and Computer Design Methods*, Bucharest, June, 1973, Vol. B., pp. 535-545.

[18] Whitney, D. E., "Resolved Motion Rate Control of Manipulators and Human Prostheses," *IEEE Transactions on Man-Machine systems*, Vol. MMS-10, No. 2, pp. 47-53, June, 1969.

[19] Whitney, D. E., "The Mathematics of Coordinated Control of Prostheses and Manipulators," *Journal of Dynamic Systems, Measurement, and Control, Transactions ASME*, Vol. 94, Series G, pp. 303-309, December, 1972, pp. 49-58.

[20] Alexander, R., "The Gaits of Bipedal and Quadrupedal Animals," *The International Journal of Robotics Research*, Vol. 3. No. 2, Summer 1984.

[21] McGhee, R.B., and Iswandhi, G.I., "Adaptive Locomotion of a Multilegged Robot over Rough Terrain", *IEEE Transactions on Systems, Man, and Cybernetics*, Vol. SMC-9, No. 4, April, 1979, pp. 176–182.

[22] Orin, D.E., "Supervisory Control of a Multilegged Robot", *International Journal of Robotics Research*, Vol. 1. No. 1, Spring, 1982, pp. 79–91.

[23] Klein, C.A., Olson, K.W., and Pugh, D.R., "Use of Force and Attitude Sensors for Locomotion of a Legged Vehicle over Irregular Terrain," *International Journal of Robotics*, Vol. 2, No. 2, Summer, 1983, pp. 3–17.

[24] Ozguner, F., Tsai, L.J., and McGhee, R.B., "Rough Terrain Locomotion by a Hexapod Robot Using a Binocular Ranging System," *Proceedings of First International Symposium of Robotics Research*, Bretton Woods, N.H., August 28, 1983.

[25] Lee, Wha-Joon, "A Computer Simulation Study of Omnidirectional Supervisory Control for Rough-Terrain Locomotion by a Multilegged Robot Vehicle," Ph.D. Dissertation, The Ohio State University, Columbus, Ohio, March, 1984.

[26] Yeh, S. "Locomotion of a Three-Legged Robot Over Structural Beams," Masters Thesis, The Ohio State University, Columbus, Ohio, March, 1984.

[27] Zeltzer, D.L., "Representation and Control of Three Dimensional Computer-Animated Figures," Ph.D Dissertation, The Ohio State University, Columbus, Ohio, March, 1984.

[28] Murphy, K.N., and Raibert, M.H., "Trotting and Bounding in a Planar Two-Legged Model," *Fifth CISM-IFTOMM Symposium on Theory and Practice of Robots and Manipulators*, June 26–29, 1984, Udine, Italy.

[29] Miura, H. and Shimoyama, I. "Dynamic Walk of a Biped," *The International Journal of Robotics Research*, Vol. 3, No. 2., Summer 1984, pp 60–74.

[30] Pearson, K.G., and Franklin, R., "Characteristics of Leg Movements and Patterns of Coordination in Locusts Walking on Rough Terrain," *The International Journal of Robotics Research*, Vol. 3, No. 2., Summer 1984, pp 101–107.

[31] Raibert, M.H., Brown, H.B.Jr, and Chepponis, M., "Experiments in Balance with a 3D One-Legged hopping Machine," *The International Journal of Robotics Research*, Vol. 3, No. 2., Summer 1984, pp 75–82.

[32] Korein, J.U., and Badler, N.I., "Techniques for Generating the Goal-Directed Motion of Articulated Structures," *IEEE Computer Graphics and Applications*, November 1982, pp. 71–81.

[33] Hemami, H. and Zheng, Y., "Dynamics and Control of Motion on the Ground and in the Air with Application to Biped Robots," *Journal of Robotic Systems*, Vol 1. No. 1, 1984, pp. 101–116.

[34] Hemami, H. and Chen, B. "Stability Analysis and Input Design of a Two-Link Planar Biped, *The International Journal of Robotics Research*, Vol. 3, No. 2., Summer 1984, pp. 93–100.

[35] McMahon, T.A., "Mechanics of Locomotion," *The International Journal of Robotics Research*, Vol. 3, No. 2., Summer 1984, pp 4–18.

[36] Lundin, R.V. "Motion Simulation," *Nicograph Proceedings 1984*, pp. 2–10.

[37] Orin, D. E., and Schrader, W. W., "Efficient Jacobian Determination for Robot Manipulators," *Sixth IFToMM Congress*, New Dehli, India, December 15–20, 1983.

[38] Orin, D.E., McGhee, R.B., Vukobratovic, M.,and Hartoch, G., "Kinematic and Kinetic Analysis of Open-Chain Linkages Utilizing Newton-Euler Methods," *Mathematical Biosciences*, Vol. 43, pp. 107–130, 1979.

Construction of Fractal Objects with Iterated Function Systems

Stephen Demko
School of Mathematics

Laurie Hodges and Bruce Naylor
School of Information and Computer Science

Georgia Institute of Technology
Atlanta, Georgia 30332

Abstract

In computer graphics, geometric modeling of complex objects is a difficult process. An important class of complex objects arise from natural phenomena: trees, plants, clouds, mountains, etc. Researchers are at present investigating a variety of techniques for extending modeling capabilities to include these as well as other classes. One mathematical concept that appears to have significant potential for this is fractals. Much interest currently exists in the general scientific community in using fractals as a model of complex natural phenomena. However, only a few methods for generating fractal sets are known. We have been involved in the development of a new approach to computing fractals. Any set of linear maps (affine transformations) and an associated set of probabilities determines an Iterated Function System *(IFS). Each IFS has a unique "attractor" which is typically a fractal set (object). Specification of only a few maps can produce very complicated objects. Design of fractal objects is made relatively simple and intuitive by the discovery of an important mathematical property relating the fractal sets to the IFS. The method also provides the possibility of solving the inverse problem. given the geometry of an object, determine an IFS that will (approximately) generate that geometry. This paper presents the application of the theory of IFS to geometric modeling.*

1. Introduction

Computer graphics is in the midst of discovering ways to construct computer models of "things". This modeling may be representational in nature, such as modeling logic diagrams; or it may be of physical objects, real or imagined, e.g. buildings, plants, Klein bottles, etc. Within the physical arena, a dichotomy can be made between man-made objects and natural objects. Modeling man-made objects, although not trivial by any means, has benefited from the simplicity of the objects and a reliance upon the well developed mathematics of polynomials. Handling natural or complex objects has been much more difficult.

Currently a broad sector of the scientific community is investigating the modeling of certain natural phenomena by fractal sets. This has been prompted by the successful modeling of a variety of such phenomena as evidenced in [Mand83]. Fractals manifest a high degree of visual complexity. Many natural objects exhibit the property that as one views the object at greater magnifications, more and more structure is revealed. Fractal sets enjoy exactly this property; there is no limit to their structure.

Descriptions of fractals can be found in many sources (e.g. [Mand83]). Fractals are sets whose Hausdorff-Besicovitch dimension, which in general is a real number, differs from their topological dimension. An important class of fractals appear to have the desirable characteristic that only a little information is needed for their specification, and a small increase in the specification increases the visual complexity significantly. Automated generation of the fractal from the specification is often straightforward and fast. While this could also be said of sets defined by polynomials, the difference lies in that polynomials generate smooth geometry while fractals generally possess infinitely non-smooth, highly structured geometries. To model the same sets by traditional polynomial-based methods would require considerably more specification information.

Despite the importance of fractals, only a few methods are known for their computation. We present here the application to geometric modeling of a new method of specifying and computing fractal sets based on *Iterated Function Systems* (IFS) [Barn84a], [Barn84b], [BEHL84] and [Hutc81]. The method provides effective modeling of certain natural objects (with unlimited detail), as well as a large class of other complex objects. It also provides a very compact representation, efficient computation, and a very small amount of user specification. In addition, IFS's have the advantage of a single specification method to obtain a very large class of fractals, where "class" refers to a significant difference in subjective visual properties. Within a class, a continuum of objects are available. The specification method is based on a mathematical property that is simple, intuitive and geometric.

We have completed a preliminary implementation of the method for generating fractals as sets of points in 2D. With this we have been able to easily produce many of the classic 2D deterministic fractals found in [Mand83]. Quickly finding an IFS for these sets was made possible because we have a method of solving the inverse problem, either approximately, or, in some cases, exactly. This means that given such an object, we can find the IFS that will compute it. One consequence of this is that new fractal sets, never before computed, have been generated which model (the projection of) trees, leaves and plants[1]. In fact, it is possible to approximate any set arbitrarily well with a (finite) IFS (although for some sets, better methods may be available).

As the complex objects of greatest interest to computer graphics are natural objects, we begin with a review of previous work in this area. We then present the mathematical basis of IFS followed by a description of our system and some examples of objects we have created.

2. Previous Techniques for Modeling Natural Objects

The differences between man-made and natural objects lead to the need for distinct modeling methodologies, as has been pointed out in [Four80] and elsewhere. Since man-made objects have smooth surfaces and a simple structure, manual specification of these objects in terms of polynomial-based sets is viable. In contrast, natural objects exhibit very irregular, non-smooth, highly complex geometries.

[1] Work of Diaconis and Shahshahani, performed independently, was highlighted in the August 3, 1984 issue of the journal *Science*. Their work is based on the same mathematics as ours; see [Diac84] for details.

The smoothness and static representations of traditional modeling methodologies is known to result in various storage and rendering difficulties [Four82]. But the lack of an automated scheme for the user to interactively specify the possibly hundreds or thousands of geometric primitives is probably the dominant limitation. These difficulties have led to the development of a number of alternative approaches, providing varying degrees of automation.

2.1. Texture Techniques

An effective technique for increasing realism but not geometry is color modulation. The idea is to modulate the color of a surface to simulate the way "high frequency" surface variations modulate reflected light. The first such application of this entailed "texture mapping" [Catm75]. Other examples include [Fu78] and [Gard84].

The deficiencies of this method, such as insensitivity to changes in illumination conditions, were identified and overcome by [Blin78]. Here, a "bump" function is mapped onto a polynomially defined surface. An important simplification is obtained by only perturbing the original surface normals. This method has proven to be very effective as long as the changes to the projection of the image due to the perturbations are imperceptible However, it cannot model complex geometries as would be required for trees and most plants.

2.2. Geometric Techniques

These limitations can be avoided by generating the complete geometry of the object rather than merely simulating it. Initial efforts at modeling natural phenomena using algorithmic generation rather than manual design relied upon intuitive methods rather than attempting to model the actual phenomena (e.g. mountains in [Csur79]). More recent work appears to be developing techniques that reflect more directly the processes which produce the phenomena. Examples of these include particle systems [Reev83], plant growing techniques [Smit84] and [Aono84], and fractional Brownian motion [Four80], [Four82] and [Mand83].

Particle systems use points as their basic geometric primitive. These points are moved through space over some time interval. The movement, as well as other properties, are determined by sampling stochastic processes. Either one or multiple samples are mapped to a single frame. This technique can be effective for modeling filamentous plants (as paths of particles). However, modeling non-filamentous objects/plants may prove to be more difficult. Also, the controllable parameters give only limited control over the shape of resulting objects (e.g., initial directions and distributions).

Non-stochastic techniques have also been used to grow plants and trees [Smit84] and [Aono84]. In both of these cases, a set of "growing rules" are applied successively in a way that corresponds very roughly to the actual growing processes in plants and trees. These techniques have drawbacks in an interactive design environment, however. The grammars, which syntactically restrict the growing rules, are not typically specified geometrically; and there is not an obvious continuum of parameters, as there is, say, with linear transformations, or with control points used in parametric surfaces. The appropriate grammar for generating a given class of objects may not be obvious (this is likely to be the case). In addition, the techniques usually require a sophisticated "interpretation" step to actually generate the complete geometry.

2.3. Fractal Based Methods

The only examples of fractal objects being used to model natural phenomena are based on fractional Brownian motion [Mand83] and [Four82]. For example, this has proven very effective at modeling terrain, particularly mountains and coastlines.

The primary control that these techniques provide over the resulting object is by the value of a single parameter determining the dimension. Additional control is provided by scaling. In [Four82], this is in terms of the fractal perturbation relative to the size of polynomial surfaces. The presence of underlying polynomial primitives in this technique tends to suggest the traditional interactive design problems alluded to above. It is not clear, for instance, as to how one can easily extend this technique to the modeling of trees and plants.

3. Mathematical Foundations of Iterated Function Systems

In contrast to the above cited methods, we believe that modeling with IFS either avoids their limitations or at least has them to a lesser degree. We will now introduce those mathematical aspects of Iterated Function Systems which are relevant to their application in computer graphics.

3.1. Iterated Function Systems

The mathematical basis for the modeling techniques used in our research is the theory of Iterated Function Systems as set forth by Barnsley and Demko in [Barn84b]. For our applications, an IFS on d-dimensional Euclidean space will have two distinct components. The first is a finite set of affine mappings of d-space into itself, $M=\{M_1,M_2,...,M_n\}$. The second component is a set $P=\{P_1,...,P_n\}$ of probabilities, where P can be thought of as relative weights for each of the maps and $\sum_{i=1}^{n} P_i=1$.

The mappings are used to define a random walk in d-space in the following way. When we are at the point z_0, we randomly choose a map, M_i, and move to $z_1=M_i(z_0)$. We then make another random choice of M_j, and move to $z_2=M_j(z_1)$. This continues indefinitely. In this process, the probability of choosing the map M_i is P_i. A necessary restriction on the maps is that they are strict contractions in the sense that their eigenvalues all have modulus less than one. Without this assumption the random walk might wander off to infinity.

Associated with every IFS is a unique compact set (i.e. closed and bounded) called the *attractor* of the IFS, and a special probability measure called the *P-Balanced measure* of the IFS which "lives" on the attractor, (the P refers to the set of probabilities). Intuitively, the attractor is the set about which the random walk eventually clusters. The P-Balanced measure quantifies this clustering by ascribing a sense of density, or height, to the attractor.

If you start your walk away from the attractor, you will be drawn to it with the rate of attraction being determined by the eigenvalues of the maps. Once you land on the attractor (you may begin there), you will never leave it; and the amount of time you spend in any particular part of the attractor is given exactly by the P-Balanced measure. The geometry of the attractor in d-space is dependent only on M, and so is independent of P. However, P affects the P-Balanced measure. The P-Balanced measure is the *stationary distribution* of the random walk. Its *support* is the attractor.

3.2. An Example: the Cantor Set

The two functions $f(x)=\frac{x}{3}$ and $g(x)=\frac{x}{3}+\frac{2}{3}$ together with $P=\{0.5,0.5\}$ form an IFS on the real line (if the numbers are complex, then this is an IFS in the complex plane). If we choose 2 as our starting point on the line, and if the first four steps of our random walk are determined by the selection of the mappings f, f, g, f in that order, then we will visit the points $\frac{2}{3}$, $\frac{2}{9}$, $\frac{20}{27}$, and $\frac{20}{81}$. As it turns out, no matter where we start, our random walk will take us closer and closer to the well known Cantor set pictured below. This then is the attractor for the IFS.

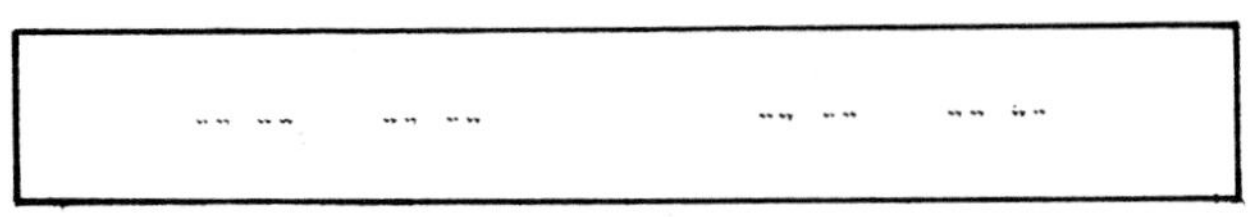

Figure 3.1

The significance of P being $\{0.5,0.5\}$ is that on our walk we will spend as much time on the left half of the Cantor set as on the right. Moreover, half of the time we spend on the left half will be spent on the left half of it, and so on. In short, all portions of the Cantor set are visited with a frequency proportional to their relative size. If we had skewed the probabilities by taking $P=\{0.1,0.9\}$, then only one tenth of our time would be spent on the left side of the Cantor set, and of that time only one tenth would be spent on the left half of the left half, etc.

Hence, the inclusion of the probabilities allows us to associate a probability distribution or measure with our random walk, and thereby contributes added structure to it. This is the P-Balanced measure, which is a countably additive, Borel measure of total mass one. We can think of the measure in terms of a histogram giving relative percentages of time spent in various parts of the Cantor set.

3.3. Construction of Some Well Known Fractals by IFS

Iterated Function Systems provide a general context for the construction of a wide variety of geometric objects, including fractals. Viewing fractals as attractors of IFS not only gives a completely new way to construct them, but also makes it possible to study a particular fractal in a larger context. For example, Barnsley and Harrington [BaHa84] studied the attractors of the 2-space IFS given by $M_1(z)=sz+1$ and $M_2(z)=sz-1$ with $P=\{0.5,0.5\}$. Here z is a complex variable and s a complex parameter. For each value of s, we have a different IFS.

Their work focused on certain topological aspects of the attractor as a function of s. With $s=\frac{1}{3}$ the attractor is the Cantor set. With $s=\frac{i}{2}+\frac{1}{2}$ the attractor is the dragon curve encountered by many people, cf. [Mand83]. Our construction of this shape (Figure 3.2) was accomplished with this IFS, as opposed to the space filling curve method of [Mand83]. Generally, one can watch the shape of the attractor change continuously as the parameter s is varied. In this way, we can see that, for instance, the dragon curve fits into a family of fractals, each determined by a single complex number.

The classic Sierpinski gasket and Koch island fractals also have simple IFS descriptions. For example, to construct the gasket, choose three non-colinear points in the plane. For each point construct the affine map that keeps the given point fixed and attracts all of 2-space to that point, with the attraction factor (scaling) being 0.5 in all directions. Figure 3.3 shows the resulting attractor.

3.4. Constructive Aspects of the Attractor and the Inverse Problem

A very important property of the attractor is that it is the set theoretic union of the images of itself, under the functions in the IFS. That is, if A denotes the attractor, then

$$A=M_1(A)\bigcup M_2(A)\bigcup \cdots \bigcup M_n(A)\,. \tag{3.1}$$

This "self covering" property holds the key to the approximation or "recovery" of fractal sets by attractors of IFS. Utilization of this property in a modeling system will be discussed in Section 4. In addition, approximations to the classical moments of the P-Balanced measure can be obtained from a digitized image. These can then be used in the construction of attractors that will approximate the image. This theory is worked out in [Barn84b] and is also discussed in [Diac84].

3.5. Qualitative Aspects oı Attractors

We also have the capacity to construct attractors having prescribed bounds on their Hausdorff dimension, or having prescribed subsets. The attractor of an IFS is generally a fractal set (although it does not have to be one). In the case that the images of the attractor under the maps in the IFS are mutually disjoint or just touch, the Hausdorff dimension can be bounded from above and below in terms of the eigenvalues of the maps [Barn84]. This provides for some control over the dimension of the attractor. For example, if there are n maps, each with the same symmetric scaling factor S, then the dimension is exactly $\frac{\ln n}{\ln \frac{1}{S}}$.

One use of this is in the construction of fractal interpolants of data. For example, if we are given a finite number of points in the plane, we know how to construct a fractal curve that passes through these points. Each curve segment between two points will have global properties inherited from the entire set of interpolants. Thus, this differs from the interpolation by fractional Brownian motion in [Four82], where each interpolation between consecutive sample points is independent of the other sample points.

This is accomplished by forcing the linear parts of the maps (upper left 2x2 sub-matrix of homogeneous matrices) to all have a common eigenvector. Typically, the maps are chosen so that the y-axis is an eigenvector. By adjusting the eigenvalue (scaling factor) of each map, we can force the Hausdorff dimension to lie in a prescribed range, and thus control the "thickness" of the curve. Figure 3.4 illustrates this technique. Both curves interpolate the same data but have different Hausdorff dimensions. The technical details can be found in [Demk85] as well as in [Barn85], where extensions to higher dimensional interpolation are discussed.

A very useful device which allows us to have any preassigned shape in the attractor is the addition of a set-valued mapping C_B to the IFS. The set B is called a "condensation set". The new mapping C_B has the property that for any point z in d-space, $C_B(z)=B$. For example, if we add the map $C_{\{0.5\}}$ to the IFS that gave us the Cantor set, then the new attractor will contain the point 0.5, as well as all images of 0.5 under all iterates of the maps in the IFS. The attractor in this condensation example is not the Cantor set, but in some sense is built on it, and near 0 and 1 will look a great deal like the Cantor set. A simple use of condensation for geometric modeling is demonstrated at the end of Section 4.

4. Geometric Modeling with IFS

We now examine our current application of the theory of Iterated Function Systems to geometric modeling. Our work to date has been limited to two-dimensional sets.

4.1. Designing

In Figure 4.1, we have an image of a maple leaf that is the attractor of an IFS with four maps. We will now discuss how one could have ascertained those maps, i.e. how we could solve the inverse problem. Let us assume that we have some initial idea of the object we wish to model. The intuitive key for deriving an IFS that will model any given object is the notion of *self-tiling*.

One can always view an object as the union of several sub-objects. Consider that the sub-objects are actually instances of the original object. In particular, each sub-object is obtained by applying an affine transformation to the entire object. We will call each of these sub-objects a *tile*. Now we can think of *tiling* the original object with two or more affinely transformed copies of itself. The tiling scheme should completely cover the object, even if this necessitates overlapping the tiles.

We now have enough information to determine an IFS whose attractor will be this object. In particular, each transformation used to "create" a tile corresponds exactly to one map in the IFS. If the self-tiling is exact, the IFS can be used to generate exactly that object. Otherwise, the attractor will approximate the object. Note that the notion of *sub-object* implies that the absolute values of the scaling factors are strictly less than one, which was stated in Section 3 as a restriction on the modulus of the eigenvalues of the maps.

Figure 4.2 shows the same leaf as in Figure 4.1, but each tile is drawn in a separate color. Each of the sub-views of Figure 4.2 illustrates the effect of deleting one map from the IFS of the leaf. The left and right upper views show deleting the lower and upper central maps, respectively. The views below the primary leaf demonstrate omitting the right and left maps. Figure 4.3 shows the tiles of the dragon curve in Figure 3.2 and Figure 4.4 is Sierpinski's gasket as in Figure 3.3.

All of the foregoing discussion is in fact simply a restatement of Eq. 3.1. However, this is a somewhat remarkable statement. What it means is that these objects are defined in terms of themselves: they are self-referential. The classic problem of circular definitions is circumvented by describing the object by a "meta-system", i.e. the set of maps forming the IFS.

4.2. Computation of the Attractor

Let us assume that our geometric primitive upon which we will iterate is a point, as is the case in all of the pictures in this paper. We choose a map M_i at random with probability P_i and transform the point by that map. We then draw the resulting point. Next, another random selection is made, and that map is applied to the result of the previous transformation (as opposed to the original point). We then draw this second point. This process continues for some user-defined number of iterations, always applying a randomly selected map to the most recently resulting iterate.

Two criteria can be used for selecting the initial point. If one wants only points on the attractor, the initial point must be on the attractor itself. This is sufficient since once the iteration lands on the attractor, it will produce only points that lie on the attractor. Since all fixed points are on the attractor, one of these is an obvious choice. An alternative that is useful for special effects is to select an initial point reasonably far from the attractor. A path from this point to the attractor will then be generated. Using a set of initial points produces the effect illustrated in Figure 4.5.

The set of points that results is not dependent simply upon the maps. Although the attractor is fixed by the IFS, only a finite subset can be computed. Two ways are available for controlling which subset is generated. The most obvious is simply selecting the total number of points/iterations produced. The second source of control is the weightings/probabilities. The relative density of the tiles will be exactly their relative weights, i.e their probability of being selected each time. In fact, the probability of plotting any given point/pixel is governed by the P-Balanced measure. Thus, it is possible to control directly the distribution of points in the representation. This is very convenient for design and efficiency of computation.

We have also implemented a deterministic method of computation which produces all possible combinations of iterations of finite length. Space limitations preclude its presentation here, but the interested reader may find its description, as well as a number of other details, in [Demk85].

4.3. Other System Aspects

Specification of the components of a map are given in terms of differential scaling, differential rotation, and either a translation vector or a fixed point about which scaling and rotation occur. Differential rotation is specified in terms of an angle to rotate the x-axis and a separate angle to rotate the y-axis. The probabilities are specified as relative (integer) weights, thus freeing the user from being concerned with the normalizing required to guarantee that they sum to one.

One useful coloring scheme is to associate a color with each map and color the iterate according to the last transformation applied to produce it. This results in revealing the tiling as demonstrated in Figure 4.2 and can be an important aid in interactive design. Another scheme is to change the color of a pixel every time a point is mapped onto it. The color variations then correspond to the P-Balanced measure of the set. This was done in Figure 4.3. This can be used, for example, for special shading effects.

So far we have only discussed using a point primitive in the generation of an image. In fact, any primitive can be used. This is likely to be important in making effective uses of IFS. Currently we have a limited implementation that iterates on a set of line segments. This provides the capability of generating sets similar to those of [Smit84] and [Aono84] that use grammars. We anticipate extending this to a broader class of geometric primitives. One interesting possibility would be to iterate on a set that is itself a fractal.

We close this section with pictures of a fern (Figures 4.6 and 4.7). This was actually constructed by examining a botanical drawing of a Black Spleenwort Fern and constructing a self-tiling for it. Figure 4.7 shows a close up, and demonstrates the ability to produce as much detail as needed. It also illustrates the use of condensation introduced in Section 3.5. The stems were produced by introducing a condensation set represented by a single line segment.

5. Future Work

The exploration and application of Iterated Functions Systems are in their infancy, but initial results are quite exciting. Currently there is no other comparable methodology for producing the range of complex images with so little user specification (and storage). Experience with our system has shown that one has considerable control that permits fine tuning of the structure, and the range of significantly different objects easily producible is impressive. The fact that the approach rests upon a firm mathematical basis gives us confidence in being able to find many ways of solving various geometric modeling problems.

The pictures included in this paper represent the simplest application of this technique. For real objects, they depict only a kind of silhouette, but this in no way represents the limits of the technique. The extension of our methods to three dimensional objects is the most important next step. Since the set of transformations determining an IFS can be defined for any dimension, generating an attractor in 3D is straightforward.

As discussed in Section 4, the primitive that is iterated need not be restricted to points; any set can be iterated. Therefore, a more viable approach may be to iterate on surfaces. Also the incorporation of stochastic techniques for specifying the maps is expected to lead to even more realistic images than are currently possible. In addition to representational and computational issues, the interactive design problems must be addressed. The self-tiling property provides a very important aid, but we have discerned other properties, only a few of which are understood in a formal way.

Acknowledgements

We would like to acknowledge the considerable contribution of Michael Barnsley to the development of the theory of IFS, and his valued assistance in helping with its application to geometric modeling. The IFS for the Black Spleenwort Fern is also due to his efforts. Special thanks go to Bill Thibault for his help with the photographic equipment.

References

[Aono84]
Aono, Masaki and Tosiyasu L. Kunii, "Botanical Tree Image Generation", *IEEE Computer Graphics and Applications,* **4** (5), pp.10-33, (May 1984).

[BaHa84]
Barnsley, Michael F. and Andrew N. Harrington, "A Mandelbrot Set for Pairs of Linear Maps" to appear in *Physica* 14D, (1985).

[Barn84a]
Barnsley, Michael F. and Stephen Demko, "Rational Approximation and Interpolation", *Proceedings of the Tampa Conference on Rational Approximation,* edited by P.R. Graves-Morris, E.B. Saff, and R.S. Varga, Springer Verlag Lecture Notes in Mathematics, No. 1105, pp. 73-88 (1984).

[Barn84b]
Barnsley, Michael F. and Stephen Demko, "Iterated Function Systems and the Global Construction of Fractals", to appear in *The Proceedings of the Royal Society,* preprint available, School of Mathematics, Georgia Institute of Technology, Atlanta, Georgia 30332.

[Barn85]
Barnsley, Michael F., "Fractal Interpolation", preprint available, School of Mathematics, Georgia Institute of Technology, Atlanta, Georgia 30332.

[BEHL84]
Barnsley, Michael F., Vincent Ervin, Doug Hardin, and John Lancaster, "Solution of an Inverse Problem for Fractals and Other Sets", preprint available, School of Mathematics, Georgia Institute of Technology, Atlanta, Georgia, 30332.

[Blin78]
Blinn, James F., "Simulation of Wrinkled Surfaces", *Computer Graphics* **12** (3), pp. 286-292 (Aug. 1978). SIGGRAPH '78 Proceedings.

[Catm75]
Catmull, Ed, "Computer Display of Curved Surfaces", *Proc. IEEE Conference on Computer Graphics, Pattern Recognition and Data Structure,* (May 1975).

[Csur79]
Csuri, C., R. Hackathorn, R. Parent, W. Carlson, and M. Howard, "Towards an Interactive High Visual Complexity Animation System," *Computer Graphics* **13** (2), pp. 289-299 (Aug. 1979). SIGGRAPH '79 Proceedings.

[Demk85]
Demko, Stephen, Laurie Hodges, and Bruce Naylor, "Application of Iterated Function Systems to Geometric Modeling", Technical Report GIT-ICS 85/14.

[Diac84]
Diaconis, Persi and M. Shahshahani, "Products of Random Matrices and Computer Image Generation", Stanford University preprint.

[Four80]
Fournier, Alain, "Stochastic Modeling in Computer Graphics", PhD thesis, Univ. of Texas at Dallas, Richardson, Texas, (Aug. 1980).

[Four82]
Fournier, Alain, Don Fussell, and Loren Carpenter, "Computer Rendering of Stochastic Models", *Communications of the ACM,* **25** (6) (June 1982).

[Fu78_]
Fu, K.S. and S.Y. Lu, "Computer Generation of Texture Using a Syntactic Approach", *Computer Graphics* **12** (3), pp. 147-152 (Aug. 1978). SIGGRAPH '78 Proceedings.

[Gard84]
Gardner, Geoffrey Y., "Simulation of Natural Scenes Using Quadric Surfaces", *Computer Graphics* **18** (3), pp.11-20 (July 1984). SIGGRAPH '84 Proceedings.

[Hutc81]
John Hutchinson, "Fractals and Self-similarity", *Indiana University Journal of Mathematics,* **30** , pp. 713-747 (1981).

[Mand83]
Mandelbrot, Benoit, *The Fractal Geometry of Nature* W. H. Freeman and Co., San Francisco, (1983).

[Reev83]
Reeves, William T., "Particle Systems - A Technique for Modeling a Class of Fuzzy Objects", *ACM Transactions on Graphics,* **2** (2), pp.91-108 (April 1983).

[Smit84]
Smith, Alvy Ray, "Plants, Fractals, and Formal Languages", *Computer Graphics* **18** (3), pp. 1-10 (July 1984). SIGGRAPH '84 Proceedings.

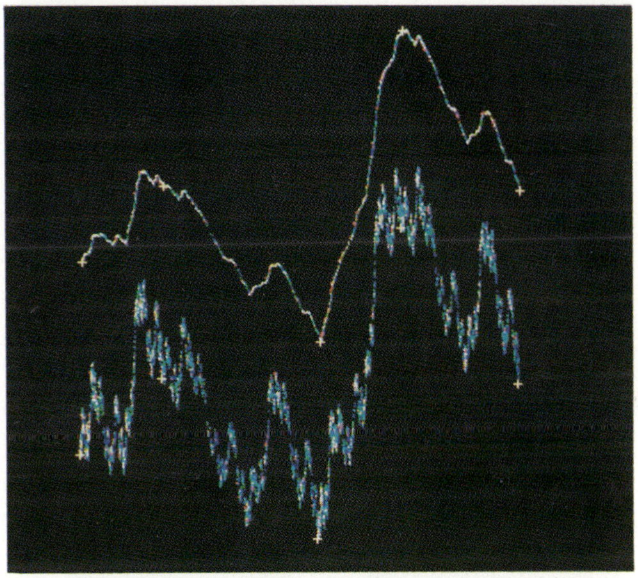

Figure 3.4
Fractal Interpolation

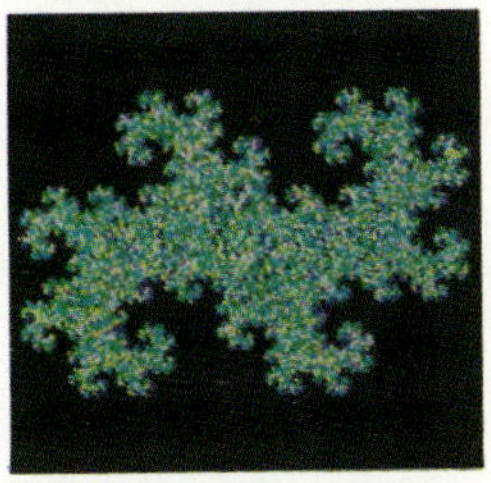

Figure 3.2
Dragon Curve with P-Balanced Measure

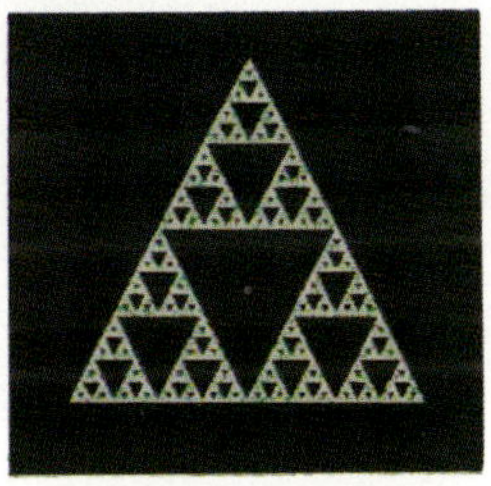

Figure 3.3
Sierpinski's Gasket

Figure 4.1
Maple Leaf

Figure 4.2
Tiled Maple Leaf with Subsets of the IFS

Figure 4.6
Black Spleenwort Fern

Figure 4.3
Tiled Dragon Curve

Figure 4.4
Tiled Sierpinski's Gasket

Figure 4.7
Close-up of Black Spleenwort Fern

Figure 4.5
Galaxy image produced by plotting random walks

Solid Texturing of Complex Surfaces

Darwyn R. Peachey

Department of Computational Science
University of Saskatchewan
Saskatoon, Canada

ABSTRACT

Texturing is an effective method of simulating surface detail at relatively low cost. Traditionally, texture functions have been defined on the two-dimensional surface coordinate systems of individual surface patches. This paper introduces the notion of "solid texturing". Solid texturing uses texture functions defined throughout a region of three-dimensional space. Many nonhomogeneous materials, including wood and stone, may be more realistically rendered using solid texture functions. In addition, solid texturing can easily be applied to complex surfaces which are difficult to texture using two-dimensional texture functions. The paper gives examples of solid texture functions based on Fourier synthesis, stochastic texture models, projections of two-dimensional textures, and combinations of other solid textures.

CR Categories and Subject Descriptors: I.3.5 [Computer Graphics]: Computational Geometry and Object Modeling; I.3.7 [Computer Graphics]: Three-Dimensional Graphics and Realism.

Additional Key Words and Phrases: anti-aliasing, image synthesis, shading, texturing.

1. Introduction

The most realistic and attractive computer generated images are usually those that contain a large amount of visual complexity and detail. Unfortunately, the amount of complexity which can be directly represented using geometric models is limited by computational considerations. Surface texturing (introduced by Catmull [4]) is an effective method of simulating surface detail at relatively low cost.

In computer graphics, objects are commonly modeled using surface representations. The surfaces of most objects are *complex surfaces* consisting of a collection of individual *surface patches*, which may abut or intersect. Each patch is a simple mathematical entity, for example, a planar polygon, a quadric surface, or a parametric patch. Texturing consists of computing the value of some shading parameter ρ for specified points or areas on the patch.

Traditionally, texturing has been done by means of functions defined on a two-dimensional texture space, usually the unit square.

$$\rho = \rho(u,v)$$

A two-dimensional surface coordinate system is defined for each surface patch, along with a "natural" mapping N from any point (X,Y,Z) on the patch to a corresponding point (u,v) in the unit square.

$$(u,v) = N(X,Y,Z)$$

$$\rho = \rho(N(X,Y,Z))$$

Originally, the shading parameter ρ was used to determine the reflectance or color of a surface patch at various points. Blinn later used texture functions to control environmental reflections [1], shininess and roughness [2], and surface normal direction [3]. The latter technique is particularly significant because it permits the simulation of bumps and wrinkles on geometrically smooth surfaces. Gardner [8] used texture functions to control transparency. Cook [5] introduced the use of generalized shading expressions which allowed a different shading model for each object or surface. In Cook's system, the (u,v) arguments to a texture function may be computed by arbitrary expressions, and the value produced by the texture function may be used in arbitrary expressions.

Many methods of defining texture functions have been used. Most common is the use of a stored table of texture values. The summed-area table, proposed by Crow [7], is a means of representing tabular texture data for easier anti-aliasing calculations. The data in a texture table may come from a digitized photograph, or may be generated by any of several texture synthesis techniques. Synthetic textures can also be represented procedurally, by a function that directly computes a value when called, rather than obtaining the value from a table.

In this paper, we introduce a different approach to texturing called *solid texturing*. Solid texturing is shown to have advantages for rendering objects whose surface texture arises from their internal structure. Solid texturing also provides a way of easily texturing complex surfaces. (The SIGGRAPH reviewers have indicated that the concept of solid texturing has been independently proposed and implemented by Ken Perlin of MAGI.)

2. Solid Texturing

2.1 Solid Texture Functions

A solid texture function for a shading parameter ρ is simply a texture function defined at the points on a surface in terms of their 3-space coordinates rather than their surface coordinates:

$$\rho = \rho(X,Y,Z)$$

In fact, it is usually more convenient to define a solid texture function throughout a given volume of space, not just at the points on a surface. This generalization makes it unnecessary to be concerned about the shape of the surface being textured, as long as it lies within the volume where the solid texture function is defined. As with two-dimensional texture functions, it is quite easy to make a solid texture function periodic so that it is defined at all points in 3-space, though care may be required to avoid discontinuities in the function at the boundary between one period and the next.

The simplest way of applying a solid texture function is to use the three-dimensional scene coordinates of the point being rendered as the argument of the texture function. It is often more convenient to use the local coordinate system of some object, rather than the scene coordinate system, to determine the coordinates for solid texturing. Applying a three-dimensional coordinate transformation (matrix multiplication) to the coordinates before passing them to the texture function allows more flexibility. For special applications, a solid texture function may be evaluated based on another three-dimensional argument such as the surface normal vector, the direction of the observer, the direction of a light source, etc.

2.2 Advantages of Solid Texturing

Objects which are made by carving or machining a chunk of a nonhomogeneous material exhibit a surface texture due to variations in the internal composition of the material. Many natural materials are nonhomogeneous and have complex internal structures which result from growth, accretion, cracking, or mixing while in a liquid state. Natural materials such as plant and animal derivatives and veined or patterned minerals can be more realistically modeled using appropriate solid texture functions.

For example, objects machined from solid wood exhibit different grain textures depending on the orientation of the surface with respect to the longitudinal growth axis of the original tree. Traditional graphics techniques of applying wood grain textures typically result in a veneer or "plastic wood" effect. Figure 1 was produced by applying a simple two-dimensional simulated woodgrain texture to the surfaces of a block and a sphere. Although each surface of the block resembles wood, the relationship between the textures on the adjacent surfaces destroys the illusion. The distortion of the woodgrain texture when applied to the surface of the sphere results in unrealistic spiral curves and discontinuities. Some improvement might be produced by scaling, rotating, or pre-stretching the textures [7], but it would be difficult to give a convincing impression of solid wood without adding more textural information.

A more realistic solid wood effect may be produced by using a solid texture function that can determine which type of wood (light or dark) exists at a given point in space (Figure 2). The function used here is simply a collection of coaxial cylinders alternating between light and dark wood. The central axis of the cylinders is oriented approximately from right to left in the figure, with a slight tilt upward and away from the camera. Although this cylindrical function is an excessively regular model of the structure of wood, it results in a surprisingly realistic woodgrain texture.

Comparing Figures 1 and 2, a number of advantages of solid texturing are evident. The grain texture seen on the right end of the block in Figure 1 is realistic and is completely different from the grain on the sides of the block. The relationship between the textures on the various surfaces of the block is correct for solid wood. This is particularly clear from the way in which the textures match up at the edges between surfaces. The sphere in the lower part of Figure 2 also shows a convincing solid wood texture, without the unreasonable spirals and discontinuities seen in the sphere in Figure 1. All of these improvements were achieved without manipulating the texture function by scaling, rotating, or pre-stretching to suit the geometric models.

Figure 1

Figure 2

Figure 3

Figure 4

It should also be noted that solid texturing eliminates the aliasing problems that arise from the highly compressed surface coordinate system near the poles of a sphere or in regions of tight curvature on some parametric surfaces. The compressed surface coordinates in these cases result in a large area of the texture space appearing in a small area of the image. Since the solid texture function is defined independently of any surface coordinate system, there is no such compression of textural detail when solid texturing is used. Of course, aliasing still can be a problem when the texture is compressed by perspective, for example, when a surface is distant or is nearly parallel to the viewing direction.

3. Texturing Complex Surfaces

An interesting and valuable property of solid textures is their straightforward applicability to arbitrarily complex surfaces. Using traditional texturing methods, it is easy to separately texture each patch of a complex surface. However, it is much harder to map a single texture over the entire complex surface in a coherent fashion without introducing discontinuities. To texture map a complex surface, the texture space must be partitioned into regions to be applied to the various patches that make up the complex surface. The partitioning must take into account the connectivity of the patches, so that textural discontinuities do not appear at the boundaries between adjacent patches. Methods have been devised to do this partitioning for groups of patches that form a sufficiently regular mesh. For example, Crow's rendering system [6] includes a program which assigns texture space coordinates to the vertices of quadrilateral patches that approximate a surface of revolution. Each quadrilateral is mapped to a rectangular cell of a regular grid that covers the texture space. The program assigns adjacent quadrilaterals to adjacent cells of the grid. Within a single quadrilateral, bilinear interpolation is used to compute the texture coordinates of an arbitrary point from the texture coordinates of the four vertices.

Use of surface texturing becomes more awkward and *ad hoc* as the number of patches grows and as their arrangement becomes less regular. When we consider the case of patches which do not neatly meet at the edges, but which may intersect one another, the problem of mapping a texture onto the complex surface is even more difficult. In order to properly assign areas of the texture space to patches, it is necessary to determine the exact curve along which two or more patches intersect, a task which may be mathematically or computationally intractable.

Since adjacent patches may be of different types, different shapes, and different sizes, the surface coordinate systems on opposite sides of the boundary between two patches can be radically different. For example, a sharply curved patch may twist and distort a texture pattern which is undistorted on an adjacent flat patch. Even two adjacent flat patches may have greatly different scales, so that the size of textural details is much larger on one patch than on the other. Because of these surface coordinate system effects, it is very difficult to ensure apparent continuity of two-dimensional textures applied to complex surfaces.

Solid texturing can be directly applied to arbitrarily complex surfaces, without encountering the problems discussed in the preceding paragraphs. All of these problems result from the geometric relationships between patches or from the surface coordinate systems of the patches. Solid texture functions are independent of the surface geometry and the surface coordinate systems. Since every point on a complex surface has a unique position in three-dimensional space, a solid texture function can be directly evaluated at the point without any additional information.

Figure 3 shows three instances of a spindle-shaped object that might form part of a piece of furniture. The center spindle is painted in several different colors to distinguish its various surface patches. The other two spindles are rendered with solid textures that approximate granite and wood, to demonstrate the straightforward applicability of solid texturing to complex surfaces.

4. Generating Solid Textures

In principle, solid texture functions can be defined and evaluated in most of the ways which are popular for two-dimensional texture functions. Texture functions may be divided into digitized textures and synthetic textures. The advantage of digitized textures is their potential for realism. Digitized textures are quite popular in two-dimensional texturing, because it is relatively easy to digitize a photograph. Digitizing solid textures is far less convenient, since it involves the two-dimensional digitization of a large number of cross-sectional slices through some material. It is often preferable to use a synthetic solid texture to avoid this awkward digitization process. Synthetic textures are more flexible than digitized textures, in that synthetic textures can be designed to have certain desirable properties or to meet certain constraints; for example, a synthetic texture can often be made smoothly periodic, so that it can be used to fill an infinite texture space without visible discontinuities at the boundary between one period and the next.

While a digitized texture must be stored in a tabular form and evaluated by table lookup, a synthetic texture may be evaluated directly in procedural form, or may be pre-evaluated and stored in tabular form. Tabular storage of synthetic texture functions is a way of improving execution speed and code simplicity at the expense of storage space. Three-dimensional texture tables pose greater problems than two-dimensional tables in this regard. High-resolution texture tables for a three-dimensional texture contain very large amounts of data (for example, $512 \times 512 \times 512$ resolution requires 134 million bytes, assuming one byte per texel). Thus, synthetic texture functions that can be evaluated procedurally are often preferable to three-dimensional texture tables.

4.1 Solid Texture Models

Synthetic textures are generated from a mathematical texture model which may be designed to approximate some natural texture. A great variety of texture models have been successfully used in two-dimensional texturing, and it is possible to construct three-dimensional versions of many of these models.

Bombing [11] is a stochastic texture model which has proven useful in two-dimensional texturing. Bombing consists of randomly dropping bombs of various shapes, sizes, and orientations onto the texture space. An analogous procedure may be performed in a three-dimensional texture space. Figure 4 shows a synthetic "bubble" texture which might result naturally from bubbles or droplets of one substance being captured within another substance during solidification from a molten or liquid state. The texture was generated by placing

Figure 5

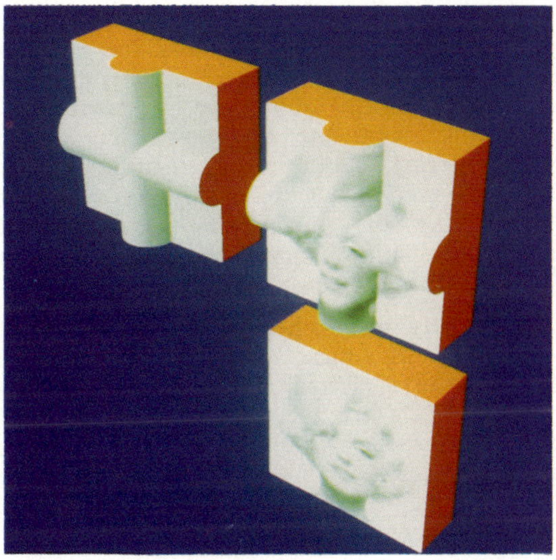

Figure 6

Figure 7

Figure 8

green spherical bubbles of randomly chosen sizes at randomly chosen locations within a 128×128×128 cube. The cube was then replicated to fill the three-dimensional texture space. The locations and sizes of the 200 bubbles were stored in a small table. To evaluate the texture function at a given point in space, the bubble table was searched to determine whether or not the given point was within at least one bubble. The same technique can be applied to bombs with a more complex shape by storing the shapes of the bombs as small three-dimensional texture tables which are used only when the input point is near one or more of the bombs.

Fourier synthesis [1][8][12] also extends to the three-dimensional case. Solid texture functions whose value consists of a sum of sinusoidal functions of (X,Y,Z) may easily be formulated and evaluated. The "marble" solid texture function used for the column on the left and the blocks on the right in Figure 5 makes use of Fourier synthesis in a less straightforward way. The marble texture consists of dozens of "veins" which pass through the material in randomly chosen directions starting from randomly chosen locations. Each vein deviates from its basic direction according to two functions each of which is the sum of three sinusoids. Each vein has a circular cross-section whose radius is derived from another sum of sinusoids. The phases of all of these functions are determined randomly for each vein. The vein growth process is used to generate a three-dimensional texture table with a resolution of $128 \times 128 \times 128$ and one bit per texture element. During rendering, the table is used to determine the values of the texture function at the eight vertices of a cube enclosing the point being rendered. Then trilinear interpolation is applied to calculate the value of the function at the point.

Undoubtedly many other solid texture models will be developed in future to generate solid texture functions. The most fruitful sources of inspiration for these models are the well-established literature concerning synthetic two-dimensional textures, along with an understanding of the structure and causes of natural textures.

4.2 Projection Functions

Projection functions are a class of solid texture functions based on two-dimensional textures which are projected through three-dimensional space. For example, a two-dimensional texture $\rho(u,v)$ can be applied to a complex surface by means of the orthogonal projection function R:

$$R(X,Y,Z) = \rho(X,Y) \text{ for } X \text{ and } Y \in [0,1)$$

$$R(X,Y,Z) = 0, \text{ otherwise.}$$

R simply projects the texture ρ along the Z axis. Each texture element of ρ generates a rectangular parallelepiped that extends infinitely in both directions parallel to the Z axis. Of course, R can be rotated, translated, and scaled with respect to the object being textured, so the projection direction need not ultimately coincide with the Z axis.

Figure 6 shows an example of the orthogonal projection of a digitized image, shown at the lower right, onto a complex surface consisting of polygonal and cylindrical patches, shown at the upper left. The resulting textured object is shown at the upper right of Figure 6. Note that there are no discontinuities in the mapping of the digitized image onto the complex surface, even along the intersection curves between the various surface patches.

The solid texture function used to approximate wood grain in Figures 2 and 3 is actually an orthogonal projection of a set of concentric circles. In this case the concentric circles are generated procedurally. By using a two-dimensional texture table it would be quite easy to improve the realism of the solid texture by varying the thickness and spacing of the circles and allowing them to deviate from a strictly circular shape. However, a truly convincing wood texture would require a fully three-dimensional texture table to represent knots and other features that cut across the longitudinal growth axis of the tree.

The synthetic textures used by Gardner [8] are also examples of orthogonal projection functions; they are defined on a three-dimensional scene coordinate system, but their values are determined entirely by the X and Y coordinates. This amounts to a projection of the texture along the Z axis. (The reviewers have noted that Alan Barr presented a texture projection scheme called "decals" at the SIGGRAPH '83 State-of-the-Art in Image Synthesis Course.)

Orthogonal projection functions certainly are not the only types of projection functions that may prove useful. Cylindrical projections, where the two-dimensional texture table is indexed by, for example, the Y coordinate and the angle of rotation around the Y axis in the $X-Z$ plane, form another interesting class of projection functions. Other projection functions can be designed to preserve particular properties of the two-dimensional texture. Cartographers have long used the properties of conformality, equivalence, and equidistance [9] to classify projection functions for the restricted case of mapping from a spherical surface to a planar one.

4.3 Combination Functions

Interesting solid textures can be produced by combining other solid textures in various ways. A combination function $C(X,Y,Z)$ may be defined by

$$C = \square(A_1, A_2, \cdots, A_m)$$

where $A_i(X,Y,Z)$ are solid texture functions and $\square$ is an m-ary operation used to combine the values of the A_i functions.

The "granite" texture shown in Figure 7 is a combination of three solid texture functions. Each of the three functions is an orthogonal projection of a two-dimensional texture. The texture shown in the upper part of Figure 8 is the basis of two of the projections, while the texture shown in the lower part of Figure 8 is used for the third projection. The three projections are combined by eight bit unsigned addition with wraparound. Even though each of the three projections is limited to two dimensions of textural richness, the combination function is a true three-dimensional texture. (The granite texture is also used in Figures 3 and 5.)

5. Texturing Costs

Although solid texturing may intuitively seem like a costly technique, it can be quite inexpensive relative to other parts of the rendering process. The coordinates used as arguments to the solid texture functions are usually easily available as a by-product of other calculations (although a matrix multiplication may be required to transform the coordinates to the texture space). The cost of solid texturing depends primarily on the cost of evaluating the solid texture functions themselves. This cost varies widely with the nature of the function.

Figures 1 through 7 were produced by a ray-tracing system called PORTRAY [10]. Figure 1, which uses a single two-dimensional texture table, took 18% less CPU time to generate than Figure 2, which uses a procedural solid texture function representing concentric cylinders. If the time needed to synthesize the texture table for Figure 1 is included, the difference drops to 12%. The solid texture function makes heavy use of a square root library function, and could probably be made much faster. Figure 6, which uses a projection function to map a digitized image onto a complex surface, was produced in less than 50% of the CPU time used by either of Figures 1 and 2, suggesting that other aspects of the rendering process have more impact on total cost than does the texturing method. Little can be said in general based on these cost comparisons, except that solid texturing need not be prohibitively expensive.

If solid texturing is likely to be much more costly than two-dimensional texturing in a given case, it is possible to use the solid texture itself to produce two-dimensional texture tables. Patch texture functions can be generated for each patch of a given object by evaluating the solid texture function at selected points on the patch and storing them in a two-dimensional table (possibly a summed area table [7]). The solid texture must be sampled at an adequate frequency; it may be necessary to sample at a high resolution and filter the samples with a weighted averaging technique to obtain a lower resolution anti-aliased texture.

Note that the generation of the patch texture function must be done separately for each patch, and requires that the position and orientation of the patch with respect to the entire object (and with respect to the solid texture function) be known. It is not sufficient to perform this process once to produce a two-dimensional texture for use on several patches or objects. The texture is inherently three-dimensional; the patch texture function is merely a computational shorthand used for greater efficiency in rendering a particular patch of a particular object.

Generating patch texture functions from the solid texture may be desirable and cost effective if the same object model is to be reused for many images (e.g., a sequence of frames for animation). It may not be cost effective if only a single image is produced, because the solid texture function will probably be evaluated at points that are not visible in the image. Patch texture functions may be generated for convenience rather than efficiency, because the patch functions can be used with existing graphics systems without modifications to support solid texturing directly.

6. Conclusions

Solid texturing extends the notion of texturing from a surface coordinate basis to a solid coordinate basis. Solid textures are particularly suited to realistic texturing of objects which have been machined or carved from natural materials. Solid textures are also convenient for texturing complex surfaces without producing unpleasant discontinuities at the boundaries between surface patches. Mapping a two-dimensional texture onto an arbitarily complex surface by normal means is very difficult and requires a great deal of geometric information and geometric computation. Solid texturing of complex surfaces uses no geometric information directly, and leaves all geometric computations to other parts of the rendering system. This makes the solid texturing approach a simple, flexible, and powerful means of texturing complex surfaces.

Solid textures can be generated by three-dimensional functions of various types, many of which have two-dimensional analogs. Solid textures also can be generated from two-dimensional textures as a means of applying such textures to complex surfaces. If desired, two-dimensional texture functions for individual patches may be automatically produced from a solid texture function, and applied to surface patches in the traditional way.

Clearly the notion of solid texturing can be explored further. We have only begun the investigation of interesting three-dimensional functions and ways in which they may be used to achieve particular effects.

Solid texturing is not intended to replace traditional surface texturing, but rather to provide an additional technique in the image synthesis toolkit. It can achieve effects which are difficult or impractical to achieve directly using two-dimensional texture functions. However, solid texturing may be used to generate two-dimensional texture functions which achieve such effects.

Acknowledgements

This research was supported by the Natural Sciences and Engineering Research Council of Canada through infra-structure grant no. A2527. Larry Custead provided assistance in photographing images, while Judy Peachey and Derek Andrew offered valuable encouragement during the writing of the paper. The work could not have been done without the support and facilities of the Department of Computational Science and the University of Saskatchewan.

References

[1] BLINN, J. F. and NEWELL, M. E. Texture and reflection in computer generated images. *Commun. ACM 19*, 10(Oct. 1976), 542-547.

[2] BLINN, J. F. Models of light reflection for computer synthesized pictures. *Comput. Gr. 11*, 2(Summer 1977), 192-198.

[3] BLINN, J. F. Simulation of wrinkled surfaces. *Comput. Gr. 12*, 3(Aug. 1978), 286-292.

[4] CATMULL, E. *A Subdivision Algorithm for Computer Display of Curved Surfaces*. Ph.D. dissertation, University of Utah, 1974.

[5] COOK, R. L. Shade trees. *Comput. Gr. 18*, 3(July 1984), 223-231.

[6] CROW, F. C. A more flexible image generation environment. *Comput. Gr. 16*, 3(July 1982), 9-18.

[7] CROW, F. C. Summed-area tables for texture mapping. *Comput. Gr. 18*, 3(July 1984), 207-212.

[8] GARDNER, G. Y. Simulation of natural scenes using textured quadric surfaces. *Comput. Gr. 18*, 3(July 1984), 11-20.

[9] LORD, E. A. and WILSON, C. B. *The Mathematical Description of Shape and Form*. Ellis Horwood Limited, 1984.

[10] PEACHEY, D. R. *Portray - An Image Synthesis System for Realistic Computer Graphics*. Research Report 84-18, Dept. of Comp. Science, Univ. of Saskatchewan, 1984.

[11] SCHACHTER, B. J. and AHUJA, N. Random pattern generation processes. *Comput. Gr. Image Process. 10*(1979), 95-114.

[12] SCHACHTER, B. J. Long-crested wave models. *Comput. Gr. Image Process. 12*(1980), 187-201.

An Image Synthesizer

Ken Perlin

Courant Institute of Mathematical Sciences
New York University

Abstract

We introduce the concept of a Pixel Stream Editor. This forms the basis for an interactive synthesizer for designing highly realistic Computer Generated Imagery. The designer works in an interactive Very High Level programming environment which provides a very fast concept/implement/view iteration cycle.

Naturalistic visual complexity is built up by composition of non-linear functions, as opposed to the more conventional texture mapping or growth model algorithms. Powerful primitives are included for creating controlled stochastic effects. We introduce the concept of "solid texture" to the field of CGI.

We have used this system to create very convincing representations of clouds, fire, water, stars, marble, wood, rock, soap films and crystal. The algorithms created with this paradigm are generally extremely fast, highly realistic, and asynchronously parallelizable at the pixel level.

CR CATEGORIES AND SUBJECT DESCRIPTORS: I.3.5 [Computer Graphics]: Three-Dimensional Graphics and Realism

ADDITIONAL KEYWORDS AND PHRASES: pixel stream editor, interactive, algorithm development, functional composition, space function, stochastic modelling, solid texture, fire, waves, turbulence

Introduction

This work arose out of some experiments into developing efficient naturalistic looking textures. Several years ago we developed a simple way of creating well behaved stochastic functions. We found that combinations of such functions yielded a remarkably rich set of visual textures. We soon found it cumbersome to continually rewrite, recompile, and rerun programs in order to try out different function combinations.

This motivated the development of a Pixel Stream Editing language (PSE). Cook [1] has proposed an expression parser for this purpose. We have taken the same idea somewhat farther by providing an entire high level programming language available at the pixel level. Unlike [1], The PSE contains general flow of control structures, allowing arbitrarily asynchronous operations at different pixels.

With the PSE we may interactively compose functions defined over modelling space. By starting with the right choice of primitive functions we can build up some rather convincing naturalistic detail with surprisingly simple and efficient algorithms.

We will first describe the PSE language and environment. Then we will introduce the concept of *solid texture*, together with our well behaved stochastic functions. Finally we will give some examples of how these concepts work together in actual practice.

A Pixel Stream Editing Language

Consider any list of variable names. We will call any list of corresponding values for these variables a "pixel". For example, one possible pixel for the variable list [red green blue] is [0.5 0.3 0.7]. We will call any list of names together with a two dimensional array of pixels an "image".

A Pixel Stream Editor (PSE) is simply a filter which converts input images to output images by running the same program at every pixel. We always read and write image pixels in some canonical order. At any one pixel, all that the program "knows" about each image are its variable names and their current values.

The PSE we have designed has a rather high level language. All of the familiar programming constructs are supported, including conditional and looping control structures, function procedure definitions, and a full compliment of arithmetic and logical operators and mathematical functions. Assignment and the equality operator are denoted by "=" and "==", respectively, as in the C programming language [2]. For any infix operator *op*, *a op= b* denotes *a = a op b*.

Variables may be scalars, or else vectors of scalars and/or vectors (recursively). Typing is implicit, determined by assignment. Program blocks are indicated by indenting. All operators will work on scalars or vectors. For example $a+b$ is a scalar sum if a and b are scalars, and a vector sum if a and b are vectors.

The following simple example will illustrate. Suppose the input image contains the variable list [surface point normal], where *surface* is a surface identifier, *point* is the location in space of the surface visible at this pixel, and *normal* is the surface normal direction at *point*. This image in particular would generally be the output of some visible surface finding algorithm.

Let the output image consist of [color]. If we interpret color as a [red green blue] vector, then the procedure :

```
if surface == 1
      color = [1 0 0] * max(0.1, dot(normal, [1 0 0]))
else
      color = [0 0 0.1]
```

will produce an image of a diffusely shaded red object lit from the positive x direction against a dark blue background. The function "*dot*()" is simply a built in function returning the dot product of two vectors.

Spotted Donut

Bumpy Donut

Stucco Donut

Disgusting Donut

Bozo's Donut

Wrinkled Donut

Note that in the above example, "[1 0 0]" is used in one place to denote the color red, and in another to denote a direction in space. Such looseness and ambiguity was a deliberate design decision in creating the language. In using the system we obtained some of the most striking visual effects only by stepping over (real or imagined) semantic distinctions.

We find that the PSE is most useful as a design tool when used as interactively as possible. For this reason we have placed it in an interactive design cycle :

1. Edit PSE program
2. Run it on a *low* resolution image
3. View the results on a color monitor

Design resolution is generally chosen to allow a design cycle time of under one minute.

Space Functions and Solid Texture

A number of researchers have proposed procedural texture, notably [3], [5], and [6]. As far as we know all prior work in this direction has been with functions which vary over a two dimensional domain.

Suppose we extend this to functions which vary over a three dimensional domain. We call any function whose domain is the entirety of (x,y,z) space a "space function".

Any space function may be thought of as representing a solid material. If we evaluate this function at the visible surface points of an object then we will obtain the surface texture that would have occured had we "sculpted" the object out of the material. We will call a texture so formed a "solid texture".

This approach has several advantages over texture mapping :

1. Shape and texture become independent. The texture does not need to be "fit" onto the surface. If we change the shape or carve a piece out of it, the appearance of the solid material will accurately change.

2. As with all procedural textures, the database is extremely small.

Although it is not immediately obvious, this paradigm is a superset of conventional texture mapping techniques. Any stored texture algorithm may be cast as a table lookup function composed with a projection function from three dimensions to two.

We will use solid texture repeatedly over the course of this paper to simulate a variety of materials.

Noise()

In order to get the most out of the PSE and the solid texture approach we have provided some primitive stochastic functions with which to bootstrap visual complexity. We now introduce the most fundamental of these.

Noise() is a scalar valued function which takes a three dimensional vector as its argument. It has the following properties :

Statistical invariance under rotation
(no matter how we rotate its domain,
it has the same statistical character)

A narrow bandpass limit in frequency
(its has no visible features larger or smaller
than within a certain narrow size range)

Statistical invariance under translation
(no matter how we translate its domain,
it has the same statistical character)

Noise() is a good texture modeling primitive since we may use it in a straightforward manner to create surfaces with desired stochastic characteristics at different visual scales, without losing control over the effects of rotation, scaling, and translation. This works well with the human vision system, which tends to analyze incoming images in terms of levels of differently sized detail [4].

The author has developed a number of surprisingly different implementations of the *Noise*() function. Some real tradeoffs are involved between time, storage space, algorithmic complexity, and adherence to the three defining statistical constraints.

Because of space limitations, we will describe only the simplest such technique. Although generally adequate, this procedure only approximately conforms to the bandwidth and rotational invariance constraints.

1. Consider the set of all points in space whose x, y, and z coordinates are all integer valued. We call this set the *integer lattice*.

   Associate with each point in the integer lattice a pseudo-random value and x, y, and z gradient values. More precisely, map each ordered sequence of three integers into an uncorrelated ordered sequence of four real numbers: $[a,b,c,d] = H([x,y,z])$, where $[a,b,c,d]$ define a linear equation with gradient $[a,b,c]$ and value d at $[x,y,z]$. $H()$ is best implemented as a hash function.

2. If $[x,y,z]$ is on the integer lattice, we define $Noise([x,y,z]) = d_{[x,y,z]}$.

   If $[x,y,z]$ is not on the integer lattice we compute a smooth (eg. cubic polynomial) interpolation between lattice equation coefficients, applied first in x (along lattice edges), then in y (within lattice z-faces), then in z. We then evaluate this interpolated linear equation at $[x,y,z]$.

We will now show some of the simpler uses of *Noise*(). We will assume that "*point*" and "*normal*" are vector valued input image variables.

By evaluating *Noise*() at visible surface points of simulated objects we may create a simple "random" surface texture (figure Spotted.Donut) :

```
color = white * Noise(point)
```

The above texture has a band-limited character to it; there is no detail outside of a certain range of size. This is equivalent to saying that the texture's frequency spectrum falls off away from some central peak frequency.

Through functional composition we may do many different things with the value returned by the *Noise*() function. For example, we might wish to map different ranges of values into different colors (figure Bozo's.Donut) :

```
color = Colorful(Noise(k * point))
```

In the above example we have scaled the texture by multiplying the domain of *Noise*() by a constant k. An nice feature of the functional composition approach is the ease with which such modifications may be made.

Another convenient primitive is the vector valued differential of the *Noise*() signal, defined by the instantaneous rate of change of *Noise*() along the x, y, and z directions, respectively. We will call this function *Dnoise*().

Water Crystal

Art Glass

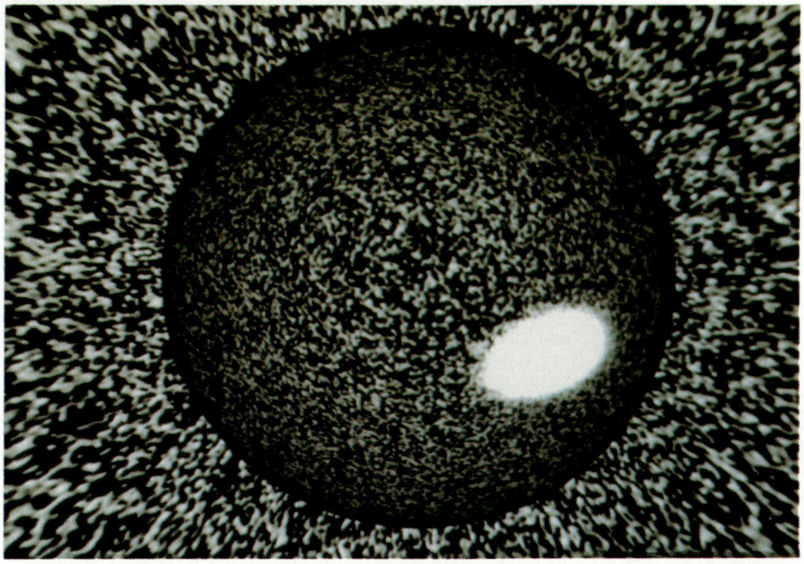

Dnoise() provides a simple way of specifying normal perturbation [7] (figure Bumpy.Donut) :

```
normal += Dnoise(point)
```

By using functions of *Noise*() to control the amount of *Dnoise*() perturbation, we may simulate various types of surface (figure Stucco.Donut), and use these in turn to design other types of surface (figure Disgusting.Donut).

As another example, a $1/f$ signal over space can be simulated by looping over octaves (powers of 2 in frequency) :

$$\sum_i \frac{Noise(point * 2^i)}{2^i}$$

In order to create $1/f$ texture we observe that the differential of a function with a $1/f$ frequency spectrum is a vector valued function with a flat frequency spectrum (ie. gradients of $1/f$ functions are similar at all scales). This means that we must create similar normal perturbation in all octaves (figure Wrinkled.Donut) :

```
f = 1
while f < pixel_freq
    normal += Dnoise(f * point)
    f *= 2
```

Note that the calculation stops at the pixel level. In this way unwanted higher frequencies are automatically clamped.

Unlike subdivision based [5] or Fourier space [14] fractal simulations, the above algorithm proceeds independently at all sample points. There is no need to create and modify special data structures in order to provide spacial coherence. This results in a considerable time savings. As with all of the algorithms we will present, the calculation at different pixels can be done in any order, in parallel, or even on different machines.

Marble - An Example of a Solid Texture

We can use *Noise*() to create function *turbulence*() which gives a reasonable visual appearance of turbulent flow (see Appendix). We may then use *turbulence*() to simulate the appearance of marble.

We observe that marble consists of heterogeneous layers. The "marble" look derives from turbulent forces which create deformations before these layers solidify.

The unperturbed layers alone can be modeled by a simple color-filtered sine wave :

```
function boring_marble(point)
    x = point[1]
    return marble_color(sin(x))
```

where *point*[1] denotes the first (ie. x) component of the *point* vector and *marble_color*() has been defined as a spline function mapping scalars to color vectors. To go from this to realistic marble we need only perturb the layers :

```
function marble(point)
    x = point[1] + turbulence(point)
    return marble_color(sin(x))
```

By invoking this procedure at visible surface points we can create quite realistic simulations of marble objects (figure Marble.Vase).

Fire

We can create fire using *turbulence*() whenever we have a well defined flow.

For example, suppose we wish to simulate a solar corona. We will assume that the following entities :

norm()	scalar length (ie. norm) of a vector
direction()	the (unit length) direction of a vector
frame	global time variable (ie. one frame click)

have already been defined.

A corona is hottest near the emitting sphere and cools down with radial distance from the sphere center. At any value of radius, and hence of temperature, a particular spectral emission is visible. Assume we have defined a function *color_of_emission*() which models emission color as a function of radius.

Modeled as a smooth flow, the corona would be implemented by :

```
smooth_corona(point - center)

function smooth_corona(v)
    radius = norm(v)
    return color_of_emission(radius)
```

By adding turbulence to the radial flow we can turn this into a realistic simulation of a corona (figure Corona) :

```
function corona(v)
    radius = norm(v)
    dr = turbulence(v)
    return color_of_corona(radius + dr)
```

To animate this we linearly couple the domain of turbulence to time :

```
function moving_corona(v)
    radius = norm(v)
    dr = turbulence(v - frame * direction(v))
    return color_of_corona(radius + dr)
```

Water

Suppose we wish to create the appearance of waves on a surface. To simplify things we will use normal perturbation [7] instead of actually modifying the surface position.

Max [8] approached this problem by using a collection of superimposed linear wave fronts. Linear fronts have a notable deficiency - they form a self-replicating pattern when viewed over any reasonably large area.

To avoid this we use spherical wave fronts eminating from point source centers [17]. More precisely, suppose at a given pixel a particular surface point is visible. For any wave source center, we will perturb the surface normal towards the center by a cycloidal function of the center's distance from the surface point :

```
normal += wave(point - center)

function wave(v)
    return direction(v) * cycloid(norm(v))
```

We can create multiple centers, let's say distributed randomly around the unit sphere, by using the direction of *Dnoise*() over any collection of widely spaced points. This works because (by definition) the value of *Dnoise*() is uncorrelated for *any* two points which are spaced widely enough apart :

```
function makewaves(n)
    for i in [1 .. n]
        center[i] = direction(Dnoise(i * [100 0 0] ))
    return center
```

To make a wave model with 20 sources we would enter :

```
if begin_frame
      center = makewaves(20)
for c in center
      normal += wave(point - c)
```

Note that the surface need not be planar. By making our wave signal defined over 3-space we have ensured shape independence. This means that we can run the above procedure on *any* shape. The illustration "Water Crystal" was made using 20 sources (figure Water.Crystal). A similar procedure was used to simulate an "Art Glass" partition (figure Art.Glass).

Waves of greater realism are created by distributing the wave-front spacial frequencies using a *1/f* relationship of amplitude to frequency. If we assign a random frequency *f* to each center, the last line of the procedure then becomes :

```
normal += wave((point - c) * f) / f
```

Using this refinement (again with 20 sources) we can realistically simulate ocean surfaces (figure Ocean.Sunset).

Since each wave front moves outward linearly with time we may animate these images by adding a linear function of time to the argument passed to *cycloid*() :

```
function moving_wave(v, Dphase)
      return direction(v) * cycloid(norm(v) - frame * Dphase)
```

where *Dphase* is the rate of phase change. For greatest realism we make *Dphase* proportional to $f^{1/2}$ [9]. The wave images pictured are actually stills from such animations.

Other Examples - Clouds and Bubbles

The two bubble images were designed by Carl Ludwig using the PSE. The various elements were all created and assembled by functional composition in the PSE.

For example, in the topmost bubble image the background clouds were created by composing a color spline function with *turbulence*(). The reflection and refraction from the bubble surface were done by using simple vector valued functions to modify an incoming direction vector in accordance with the appropriate physical laws. These were composed with the cloud function and added together.

In the center image, a function corresponding to the shape of an illuminated window was composed with reflection and refraction functions.

The appearance of variable bubble thickness was simulated by multiplying *turbulence*() by each of a red, green, and blue frequency and using *sin*() of this to create constructive and destructive interference fringes. In the PSE this looks like :

```
color *= 1 + sin([rfreq gfreq bfreq] * turbulence(point))
```

Compositing

We can use the PSE simply as a digital image compositor, in which case it functions as a generalization of [10]. We can also use it to combine and modify images in more unusual ways.

Suppose for example that we wish to synthesize some flame on the PSE, knowing that later we will receive some other animation to be composited with our synthetic flame.

We may defer the aesthetic decision of how to color the flame until after looking at this footage. We do this by computing the flame in two passes. The first pass outputs only a scalar flame value. The second and simpler pass maps this scalar quantity to the appropriate color vector.

Note that this process involves no recalculation of the flame itelf. The second pass through the PSE is being used only as a general color splining filter, at a small fraction of the total computing cost.

In an actual commercial production this ability to split computation costs and defer post-production decisions adds enormously to throughput.

In more unusual cases we may use the scalar flame to modulate the frequency distribution or height of water waves, or the amount of rocklike character to give to a surface. In this context our approach is similar to that of [1] and [10], the difference being the extra flexibility we gain by the ability to specify arbitrary asynchronous pixel operations.

Considerations of Efficiency

The efficiency of an implementation is a rather elusive thing. This is because it consists of three fairly different considerations. Most familiar is time efficiency. There is also space efficiency, which often is inversely proportional to time efficiency (as in "should we use a procedure or a lookup table?").

The third consideration, often overlooked, is flexibility. Many of us are familiar with archaic and monolithic "dinosaur" programs that nobody dare modify lest they fall apart altogether. Such programs must be used "as is" or else scrapped and rewritten from scratch.

The approach we offer here does not always produce the most efficient algorithms. What it does offer is the opportunity to try out new approaches quickly and painlessly. For CGI in particular this is of the utmost importance. We generally want to see what the picture looks like before proceeding with optimization. Once implemented, PSE algorithms lend themselves readily to optimization by virtue of their simplicity and high degree of modularity.

In addition, a number of effects are ideally suited to a functional composition paradigm; generally when there is interplay between a simple regular structure and a complex stochastic structure. This is because we can use nonlinear functional composition to model the stochastic part of the structure. This will result in both good time efficiency and good space efficiency.

The flame model constitutes such a "best case" for our approach. The final motion picture quality animation ran in about 10 minutes a frame, written entirely in an unoptimized interpreted pseudo-code implementation of the design language on a Gould SEL 3287 Minicomputer. This appears to be much faster than the particle system approach of Reeves [11]. With optimization and true compilation a speedup of a factor of 5 is indicated. The marble vase, with twice as large an area of visible turbulence, took about 20 minutes to compute.

In all cases, the low resolution interactive design loop took between 15 seconds and 1 minute per iteration.

Now What?

We plan to make a number of improvements to the system. We are developing an optimized compiler for the design language which recognizes quantities that vary slowly over the image stream and computes quantities dependent these only as necessary. We are also adding a general facility for direct insertion of large data bases into the image prior to pixel streaming.

We are currently using the same paradigm of composition with stochastic functions for motion and shape modelling.

We have applied our approach to modelling stochastic motion not only for continuous turbulence models, but also for such things as falling leaves, swaying trees, flocks of birds, and muscular

Corona

Ocean Sunset

rippling. In general the paradigm is appropriate whenever a regular, well defined macroscopic motion contains some stochastic component.

To create interesting stochastic shapes, we have generalized on the work of Blinn [15]. Given any space filling scalar valued function, we may consider the shape formed by any isosurface (surface of constant value) of the function. It turns out that a very rich class of shapes may be created in this manner (for example, we can actually build the three dimensional structure of the flame shown in figure Corona). We understand that Lance Williams of NYIT [16] is pursuing a similar line of research.

Conclusions

We have shown a new approach to the design of realistic CGI algorithms. We have introduced the concepts of the Pixel Stream Editor and of solid texture. We have demonstrated a number of effects which would have been considerably more difficult and expensive, and in some cases impossible, to generate by previously known techniques.

Appendix - Turbulence

A suitable procedure for the simulation of turbulence using the *Noise*() signal is :

```
function turbulence(p)
    t = 0
    scale = 1
    while (scale > pixelsize)
        t += abs(Noise(p / scale) * scale)
        scale /= 2
    return t
```

This is actually a simplified approximation to the magnitude of the deformation which results from swirling around the isosurfaces of the *Noise*() domain along the instantaneous vector field :

$$e^{-Noise(point)^2}\ (normal\ X\ Dnoise(point))$$

This formulation is part of a synthetic turbulence model developed by the author [12]. We use the simplified *turbulence*() procedure because it is fast and the pictures it produces look good enough.

Even so it is interesting to examine, with only minimal comment, the algorithmic structure of *turbulence*(). Note the expression

```
Noise(p / scale) * scale
```

inside the loop. This says that at each scale the amount of *Noise*() added is proportional to its size. Thus we obtain a self-similar, or *1/f*, pattern of perturbation. This will give a visual impression of brownian motion. Also, while the deformation is continuous everywhere, the *abs*() at each iteration assures that its gradient will have discontinuous boundaries at all scales. This will give a visual impression of discontinuous flow, which will be interpreted by the viewer as turbulent.

Acknowledgements

The management of MAGI very graciously allowed me the use of its facilities for this research. Frank Crow got me to publish. I'd also like to thank my Ph.D. advisor David Lowe, the faculty of the Courant Institute at NYU, and R/Greenberg Associates for their continuing support.

Gene Miller at MAGI designed "Bozo's Donut" and made a number of valuable suggestions for this paper.

Carl Ludwig made the bubbles and the lovely ocean sunset image. He also codeveloped the wave algorithm, made countless good suggestions for the system and for this paper, and performed the all important service of being the first *user* of the system other than the author.

Mike Ferraro originated the crucial concept of using functional composition to create texture [13]. Much of this paper has its roots in his powerful idea.

Lastly, this paper probably could not have been written were it not for all I have learned over the years about images, algorithms and true elegance of design from working with Josh Pines.

References

1. Cook, R., "Shade Trees," *Computer Graphics*, vol. 18, no. 3, July 1984.
2. Kernighan B., Ritchie D., *The C programming language*, Prentice Hall, Englewood Cliffs, 1978.
3. Gardner, G., "Simulation of natural scenes using textured quadric surfaces," *Computer Graphics*, vol. 18, no. 3, July 1984.
4. Marr, D., *Vision*, W. H. Freeman and Company, San Francisco, 1982.
5. Fournier, A., Fussel, D., and Carpenter, L., "Computer rendering of stochastic models," *Comm. ACM* 25, 6 (June 1982), 371-384.
6. Schacter, B., "Long-crested wave models," *Computer Graphics* and *Image Processing*, vol 12., 1980.
7. Blinn, J., "Simulation of wrinkled surfaces," *Computer Graphics*, vol. 12, no. 3, July 1978.
8. Max, N., "Vectorized procedure models for natural terrain: waves and islands in the sunset," *Computer Graphics*, vol. 15, no. 3, August 1981.
9. Sverdrup, Johnson & Fleming, *The Oceans*, Prentice Hall, Englewood Cliffs, 1942.
10. Porter, T., Duff, T., "Compositing digital images," *Computer Graphics*, vol. 18, no. 3, July 1984.
11. Reeves, W., "Particle systems, - A technique for modeling a class of fuzzy objects," *ACM Transactions on Graphics*, vol. 2, no. 2, April 1983.
12. Perlin, K., Author's unpublished Ph.D. dissertation - work in progress.
13. Mike Ferraro, personal communication.
14. Voss, R., *Fractal Lunar Mist*, Cover of SIGGRAPH '83 proceedings, July 1983.
15. Blinn, J., "A Generalization of Algebraic Surface Drawing." *ACM Transactions on Graphics*, vol. 1, pp 235., 1982.
16. Lance Williams, personal communication.
17. Suggested by Carl Ludwig, personal communication.

VISUAL SIMULATION OF CLOUDS

Geoffrey Y. Gardner

Grumman Corporation
Corporate Research Center
Bethpage, New York 11714

ABSTRACT

Clouds present serious problems to standard computer image generation techniques because clouds do not have well-defined surfaces and boundaries. In addition, clouds contain varying degrees of translucence, and their amorphous structure can change with time. Although several approaches to cloud simulation have produced impressive results, they have relied on complex mathematical models which produce high computation costs for a single image.

This paper describes a new approach to cloud simulation using simple planar and curved surfaces whose surface shading and translucence are modulated by a mathematical texturing function. This approach represents the appearance of clouds with enough realism for a wide range of visual simulation but does so at a reasonable computational cost, allowing the generation of sequences of images on small minicomputers. In addition, the cloud model can be constructed in a straightforward manner.

CR Categories: I.3.3 [Computer Graphics]: Picture/Image Generation-display algorithms; I.3.5 [Computer Graphics]: Computational Geometry and Object Modeling - curve, surface, solid and object representations; geometric algorithms, languages and systems; I.3.7 [Computer Graphics]: Three-Dimensional Graphics and Realism - color, shading, shadowing, and texture; visible line/surface algorithm; J.7 [Computers in Other Systems]: Military, real time.

1. INTRODUCTION

The history of computer graphics has been highlighted by advances which have overcome specific stumbling blocks to realistic scene simulation. Terrain, trees, shadows, reflections, and motion blur are examples of stumbling blocks that have been surmounted by recent innovations in computer simulation. One remaining stumbling block is the common cloud. Clouds are a critical element in air-to-air combat. Yet, for over two decades, computer image generation (CIG) has been used to provide visual displays for flight simulation without the ability to simulate clouds with any degree of realism. Clouds are important in the simulation of intelligent weapon systems which seek and identify aerial targets in cluttered backgrounds. Realistic cloud simulation would also be an effective tool in the field of meteorology. Since clouds are such familiar objects in everyday life, it is desirable to simulate them effectively for other applications, such as entertainment, advertising, and art. Indeed, it is reasonable to say that we want to simulate these beautiful natural features simply because they are there.

The amorphous nature of clouds prevents simulation by standard CIG techniques employing solid surfaces with well-defined boundaries. Several researchers have produced impressive results by breaking away from the standard approach. Blinn [1] developed a functional model for light reflections from cloud surfaces. Max [9] used height fields and ray tracing to model clouds. Voss [10] applied fractal techniques to produce a very realistic looking cloud. Kajiya and Herzen [7] used ray tracing of volume densities to model cloud growth. In general, these efforts attempted to model cloud physics accurately and therefore involved fairly rigorous mathematics. The approach described in this paper is to represent the aesthetic quality of clouds as efficiently as possible. The goal is to allow generation of sequences of realistic looking images with moderate computational cost. This research is the most recent work in a study at the Grumman Corporate Research Center to develop cost-effective scene simulation technology [2-6].

2. A NEW CLOUD MODEL

In order to simulate arbitrary cloud scenes, we must be able to model different types of clouds viewed from a variety of distances and angles. Fortuitously, the standard classification of cloud types is based on their appearance. The three fundamental classes are: cirrus ("curl of hair"), stratus ("layer"), and cumulus ("heap") [8]. Cirrus clouds are wispy clouds at high altitudes (5-13 km). Stratus clouds are layer clouds with no distinct detail, lying at low altitudes (0-2 km). Cumulus clouds are heap clouds, also lying at low altitudes (0-2 km). Combinations of the basic class names are used to describe clouds with combined characteristics and altitudes of the basic types. "Cirrostratus" refers to a high layer of cirrus clouds. "Stratocumulus," "altocumulus," and "cirrocumulus" refer to low, intermediate, and high broken cloud layers, respectively. "Altostratus" refers to a thick layer cloud at intermediate altitudes (2-8 km). "Nimbostratus" refers to a dark layer producing rain or snow, and "cumulonimbus" refers to a large cumulus cloud producing a shower.

In developing a comprehensive model for visual simulation of clouds, it is important to note that cloud formations can follow either horizontal development (cloud layers) or vertical development (cumuliform clouds). To allow for the representation of a wide variety of cloud types and formations and at the same time keep scene modeling simple and image generation economical, we have adopted the strategy of the impressionist painters: to represent the essence of a scene as efficiently as possible.

We compose our cloud model using three basic building blocks:

1. A sky plane
2. Ellipsoids
3. A mathematical texturing function.

We define the sky plane to be parallel to the ground plane at a specified altitude and use it to model a two-dimensional cloud layer viewed from a distance. We define the ground plane in scene coordinates (X,Y,Z) to be the X-Y plane. Therefore, the sky plane can be written as:

$$P(X,Y,Z) = Z - A = 0, \qquad (1)$$

where A is the altitude of the plane.

We use ellipsoids to model gross three-dimensional cloud structure. A typical ellipsoid can be expressed as:

$$Q(X,Y,Z) = Q_1X^2 + Q_2Y^2 + Q_3Z^2 + Q_4XY + Q_5YZ + Q_6XZ + Q_7X + Q_8Y + Q_9Z + Q_0 = 0. \qquad (2)$$

We use the mathematical texturing function to model cloud detail by modulating the shading intensity and translucence of the sky plane and the ellipsoids. We have found it convenient in modeling and economical in image generation to define the function to represent the spectral content of the texture pattern. We do this by using a "poor man's Fourier series" composed of short sums of sine waves according to the following formula:

$$T(X,Y,Z) = k\sum_{i+1}^{n} [C_i \mathrm{Sin}(FX_i X + PX_i) + T_0] \sum_{i=1}^{n} [C_i \mathrm{Sin}(FY_i Y + PY_i) + T_0]. \qquad (3)$$

Natural-looking texture patterns can be produced with four to seven sines in each series if the frequencies and coefficients are chosen by the relationships:

$$FX_{i+1} = 2\ FX_i$$
$$FY_{i+1} = 2\ FY_i \qquad (4)$$

$$C_{i+1} = .707\ C_i \qquad (5)$$

Note that this gives a 1/f spectral shaping similar to that of fractal surfaces.

PX_i and PY_i are phase shifts to add randomness and are determined by the following relationships for planar texturing:

$$PX_i = \pi/2\ \mathrm{Sin}(.5FY_iY) = \pi/2\ \mathrm{Sin}(FY_{i-1}Y) \text{ for } i > 1$$
$$(6)$$
$$PY_i = \pi/2\ \mathrm{Sin}(.5FX_iX) = \pi/2\ \mathrm{Sin}(FX_{i-1}X) \text{ for } i > 1$$

The phase shifts produce a controlled pseudo-random effect by shifting the X sine components as a function of Y and the Y components as a function of X.

To provide three-dimensional variations for texturing ellipsoids, the phase shifts are augmented by an added sine variation with Z:

$$PX_i' = PX_i + \pi\ \mathrm{Sin}(FX_i Z/2)$$
$$PY_i' = PY_i + \pi\ \mathrm{Sin}(FX_i Z/2) \qquad (7)$$

T_0 is a parameter controlling contrast of the texture pattern, and k is computed to produce a maximum value of 1 for T(X,Y,Z).

Antialiasing of the texture pattern is facilitated by the organization of the texturing function because, as each higher frequency in the series is computed, it can be tested against the spatial sampling frequency on the scene surface, and the series can be truncated before aliasing frequencies are added in.

The texturing function modulates the shading of a planar or ellipsoidal surface by the following equation:

$$I = (1-a)\{(1-t)[(1-s)I_d + sI_s] + tI_t\} + a \qquad (8)$$

where
- a is defined fraction of surface reflection due to ambient or scattered light,
- t is a defined fraction of texture shading
- s is a defined fraction of specular reflection
- I_d is the shading intensity due to diffuse or Lambertian reflection,
- I_s is the shading intensity due to specular reflection,
- I_t is the shading intensity contributed by the texturing function ($I_t = T(X,Y,Z)$),
- I is the combined surface shading intensity.

The values of I_d and I_s are computed in the standard way using the vector relations between surface normal, light vector, and eye ray [4].

We modulate the translucence of the sky plane by defining a threshold value for the texturing function below which we assign full translucence to the plane. The modulated translucence is given by the equation:

$$TR = 1 - (I_t - T_1)/D \qquad 0 \le TR \le 1 \tag{9}$$

where T_1 is the threshold value
D is a range of texturing function values across which translucence varies from 0 to 1
TR is the modulated translucence.

We modulate the translucence of ellipsoids in a similar manner, but vary the threshold value to increase translucence at the boundary of the ellipsoid. To do this, we use the equation of the limb curve, the elliptical projection of the silhouette of the ellipsoid on the image plane (x,z). This equation is written in image coordinates as

$$f(x,z) = a_1x^2 + a_2z^2 + a_3xz + a_4x + a_5z + a_6 = 0 \tag{10}$$

where z is the vertical image coordinate or scan line number
x is the horizontal image coordinate.

For points on the interior of the limb curve, corresponding to points on the surface of the ellipsoid, f(x,z) is non-zero, with a maximum value at the geometric center of the curve. If we divide f(x,z) by the maximum value we get a normalized limb curve function, g(x,z), which varies from 0 to 1 on the image of the ellipsoid. We can then modify equation (9) to raise the threshold as we approach the limb curve:

$$TR = 1 - (I_t - T_1 - (T_2 - T_1)\ (1-g(x,z)))/D \tag{11}$$

$$0 \le TR \le 1$$

where T_1 defines the threshold at the center of the limb curve
T_2 defines the threshold at the boundary of the limb curve.

2.1 Two-Dimensional Cloud Model

An efficient model of a cloud layer can be defined by a single textured plane in the sky (Eq (1)). We can place the plane at any altitude, A, and we can specify the solidity and density of the cloud layer by the texturing function translucence parameters T_1 and D (Eq (9)). We can define the spectral content of the cloud pattern by the texturing function parameters C_i, FX_i, FY_i, and T_0 (Eq (3)).

For example, we can model a high cirrus layer at an altitude of 10 km. We represent the characteristic long wispy tails of cirrus clouds by specifying FX_i to be double FY_i and using high values of T_1 and D to produce large regions of complete translucence fading gradually into opaque clouds (Fig. 1).

We can model a stratus cloud layer at a typical altitude of 2 km, by raising the texture function offset, T_0, to reduce both translucence and contrast in the intensity modulation. This produces a fuller cloud layer with less detail, characteristic of stratus clouds (Fig. 2).

Fig. 1 2-D Cirrus Cloud Layer

Fig. 2 2-D Stratus Cloud Layer

We can use the two-dimensional model to represent the bottom of a thick cumulus cloud formation. Figure 3 shows a view of an overcast sky modeled by a textured plane at 1 km. We make the clouds opaque by defining a very low value for T_1.

The textured plane can be used to simulate cloud dynamics by varying selected texturing function parameters with time. We can simulate cloud development by decreasing high values of T_1 and D. We can also move the entire texture pattern across the plane to simulate drifting [6].

The use of the two-dimensional model is limited because it has no vertical depth. For this reason it must be viewed at a distance, serving as

Fig. 3 2-D Cumulus Cloud Layer (Overcast Sky)

a backdrop for three-dimensional scenes. Another limitation is that the same texture pattern is applied across the entire plane, precluding the representation of different cloud formations in different parts of the sky. To complement the two-dimensional model and to allow arbitrary eye movement among the clouds, we need to provide a three-dimensional model.

2.2 Three-Dimensional Cloud Model

We have chosen the ellipsoid as the basic building block with which to model the primary three-dimensional structure of clouds. A single ellipsoid can be used to define an entire volume with only nine parameters, three specifying size and shape, three specifying position, and three specifying angular orientation. As in the two-dimensional model, we use the texturing function to simulate the secondary topographical detail by modulating surface shading intensity and translucence (Eq (8) and (11)). The texture model can be defined in a straightforward manner by specifying the frequencies and amplitudes of the function sine waves to produce a desired spectral content and by choosing the translucence thresholds to produce a desired cloud density. This approach results in a very compact data base because the same texture pattern can be used for any number of ellipsoids.

The elements of the three-dimensional model are demonstrated in Fig. 4. Figure 4a shows a textured ellipsoid, with the texture function modulating only surface shading intensity. Figure 4b shows the same model with modulation of translucence using a constant threshold across the image (Eq (9)). Figure 4c shows the final three-dimensional modulation of translucence which increases translucence near the boundary of the image ellipse (Eq (11)).

Observing real clouds, one can sometimes notice individual clouds that are surprisingly close to ellipsoidal in shape. In general, however, there is a tremendous variety of shapes that cannot be modeled faithfully by isolated ellipsoids. To account for this variety, our three-dimensional model includes the capability to link ellipsoids to create more complex shapes. In

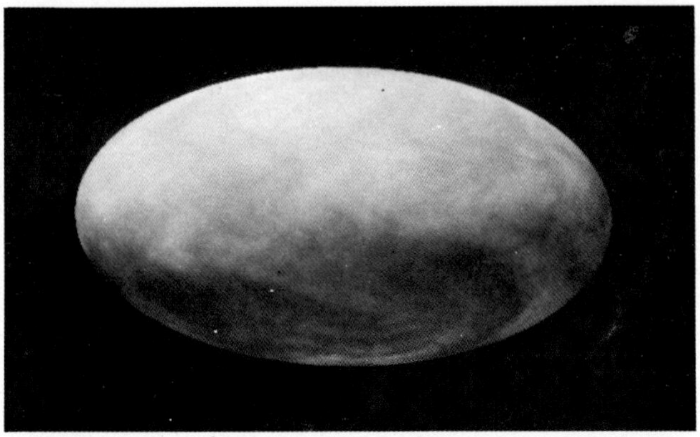

(a) Textured Ellipsoid

(b) Textured Ellipsoid with 2-D Translucence Threshold

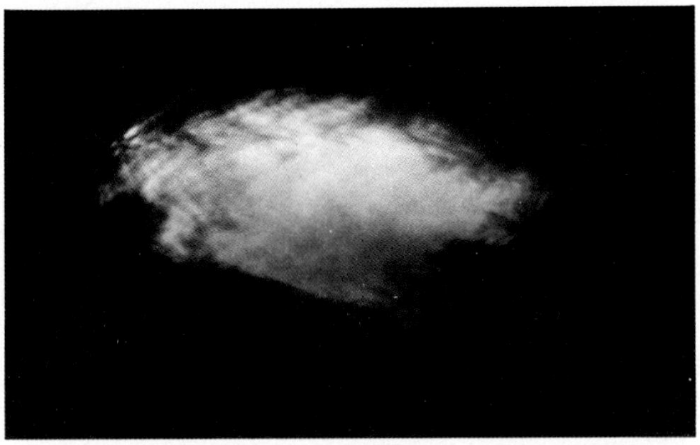

(c) Textured Ellipsoid with 3-D Translucence Threshold

Fig. 4 3-D Cumulus Cloud

our original approach to joining quadric surfaces, we chose to insert bounding planes at the junctures of the quadrics. Our strategy was to avoid the computation of fourth-order boundary curves produced by intersecting quadric surfaces [5]. This approach works well for solid objects, but tends to produce unnatural planar boundaries between highly translucent objects. To avoid these anomalies, we have included in our three-dimensional cloud model the capability to handle intersecting quadric surfaces without bounding planes. To do this we have extended our image generation algorithms to compute the visible points on the curve of intersection between two quadric surfaces. To minimize the added computation, we perform the computation on a scan line basis and start with an approximate depth sort used in the earlier algorithm. Using the computed quadric intersection points, we determine scan line regions in which surface priority is constant. We then reorder the surfaces from front to back within each scan line region. This provides an efficient means of rendering intersecting translucent surfaces. Figure 5 shows how this approach represents a typical cloud with a small number of ellipsoids.

Fig. 5 Complex Cloud Modeled by Linked Ellipsoids

2.2.1 Horizontal Cloud Formations

To model a wide range of horizontal cloud formations, we have developed scene modeling software that generates clusters of ellipsoids. For each cluster we define a template ellipsoid by specifying size and orientation parameters. We also define a horizontal elliptical boundary for the cluster, typical X and Y spacings, and the altitude of the cloud layer. The program replicates the template ellipsoid within the defined boundary at positions separated by the defined spacings. Size, position, and orientation parameters for each ellipsoid are altered by a prescribed amount of random variation. All ellipsoids in the cluster are assigned a common color and set of texture function parameters. We can model a specific class of cloud by choosing the shape of the ellipsoids in the cluster, the altitude of the cluster, and the texture function frequency and translucence parameters. For example, we use round ellipsoids and a high-contrast texture pattern for cumulus clouds, and we use shallow ellipsoids and a low-contrast texture pattern for stratus clouds (Fig. 6).

To facilitate modeling of complex cloud scenes, we extended the cluster software to generate macroclusters, or clusters of clusters. Each macrocluster is defined in the same way as the cluster, by a large horizontal region and grid spacing, a template ellipsoid, an altitude, a color, and a texture pattern. The macrocluster program generates the input data for the cluster program, adding random variations to each cluster. In this way, we can quickly generate a model for complex cloud formations covering large areas of the sky (Fig. 7).

(a) Cumulus Cloud Cluster

(b) Stratus Cloud Cluster

Fig. 6 Cloud Clusters

Fig. 7 Multiple Cumulus Cloud Clusters

2.2.2 Vertical Cloud Formations

We can model vertical development of clouds in several ways. We represent minor vertical development within cloud layers simply by increasing the size of the ellipsoids. By varying the ellipsoid size in a controlled manner, we can model natural variations in both vertical and horizontal cloud development (Fig. 8).

Fig. 8 Vertical Development Modeled by Ellipsoid Scaling

Major vertical development due to updrafts can be simulated by pushing the ellipsoids upward. To do this, we use an option included in our original cluster software. This option, designed to position trees on hills, allows us to define a set of "terrain" objects upon which subsequently generated objects will be placed. As each object is created, its (X,Y) position is tested against the (X,Y) region occupied by each previously defined terrain object. If a new object overlays a terrain object, its position is adjusted in altitude by adding the height of the terrain object at the value of (X,Y). We can therefore raise ellipsoids in a cluster arbitrarily by defining a dummy terrain object below them. This technique can be used to warp a cluster or to model a solid vertical formation using two clusters, one for the base and one for the cap (Fig. 9). This device has several advantages. First, it mimics nature because we simulate the phenomenon of vertical movement. Second, it models solid three-dimensional clusters with only exterior visible ellipsoids. Finally, it is computationally economical because quadric surfaces simplify the terrain object testing.

Fig. 9 Vertical Development Modeled by Terrain Following

2.3 Combined Cloud Model

To represent a variety of clouds in the sky at the same time, we can combine the two-dimensional and three-dimensional models. For example, we can use the two-dimensional model for a high layer of cirrus or alto-stratus clouds. In addition, we can include a pseudo-two-dimensional model composed of a few thin ellipsoids to represent isolated cloud layer regions (Fig 10). We can also use the ground plane as a two-dimensional cloud model representing a thick cloud layer viewed from above. Ellipsoids bounded by the ground plane can be added to provide three-dimensional clouds rising from the layer. This technique produces a complex scene very economically [3].

3. CONCLUSIONS

The cloud model described here, composed of a sky plane, ellipsoids, and a mathematical texturing function, allows economical visual simulation of a wide variety of complex cloud formations. The model is easy to construct, and image generation can be performed by small computers in a reasonable amount of time. Figures 10 and 11 were generated in 25 and 20 minutes, respectively, at 480 x 640 x 24-bit resolution using a Data General Eclipse S/250 16 bit minicomputer. This economy was achieved by approaching the problem of visual simulation from an aesthetic standpoint rather than attempting to model rigorously the mathematics of atmospheric physics. The aim here has been to

Fig. 10 Cloudscape Using Combined 2-D and 3-D Cloud Model

Fig. 11 Landscape Using Combined 2-D and 3-D Cloud Model

produce a visual impression of clouds as efficiently as possible. As a result, the model as it now stands might fall short of providing adequate simulation in applications where greater physical fidelity is required. However, we make no claim that we have developed the model to its full potential. On the contrary, we have taken only a first step in modeling the tremendous variety, complexity, and subtlety of cloud phenomenology. Nonetheless, we feel that the current model can be useful in many different applications including flight simulation, target recognition, meterology, entertainment, and art. Because the model provides such a wide range of control over scene geometry, shading, and translucence, it holds the potential for simulating infrared as well as visual images.

4. ACKNOWLEDGEMENT

One reviewer made several helpful suggestions which I hope I have implemented satisfactorily to clarify this paper.

5. REFERENCES

1. Blinn, J.F. Light reflection functions for simulation of clouds and dusty surfaces. Computer Graphics 16, 3 (Jul 1982), 21-29.

2. Gardner, G.Y. Computer-generated texturing to model real-world features. Proc 1st Interservice/Industry Training Equipment Conf, Orlando, FL (Nov 1979) 239-245.

3. Gardner, G.Y. Non-edge CIG. SIGGRAPH Video Review, Issue 11 (Oct 1983).

4. Gardner, G. Y. and Rulon, R.S. Producing high scene content with perspective validity. Proc 1984 IMAGE III Conf, Phoenix, AZ (May 1984), 79-94.

5. Gardner, G.Y. Simulation of natural scenes using textured quadric surfaces. Computer Graphics 18, 3 (Jul 1984), 11-20.

6. Gardner, G.Y. Beethoven's Sixth in CIG. SIGGRAPH Video Review, Issue 17 (Aug 1984).

7. Kajiya, J.T. and Von Herzen, B.P. Ray tracing volume densities, Computer Graphics 18, 3 (Jul 1984), 165-173.

8. Mason, B.J. The Physics of Clouds. Oxford University Press, London (1957).

9. Max, N. The simulation of natural phenomena panel. Computer Graphics 17, 3 (Jul 1983), 137-139.

10. Voss, R. Fourier synthesis of gaussian fractals: 1/f noises, landscapes, and flakes. State of the Art in Image Synthesis. Tutorial No. 10, SIGGRAPH '83 Conf, Detroit, MI (Jul 1983).

Modeling the Mighty Maple

Jules Bloomenthal
Computer Graphics Laboratory
New York Institute of Technology
Old Westbury, New York*

Abstract

A method is presented for representing botanical trees, given three-dimensional points and connections. Limbs are modeled as generalized cylinders whose axes are space curves that interpolate the points. A free-form surface connects branching limbs. "Blobby" techniques are used to model the tree trunk as a series of non-circular cross sections. Bark is simulated with a bump map digitized from real world bark; leaves are textures mapped onto simple surfaces.

CR Categories and Subject Descriptors: I.3.5 [**Computer Graphics**]: Computational Geometry and Object Modeling – *curve, surface, solid, and object representations.*

Keywords and Phrases: modeling, interpolation, space curve, spline, ramiform, blobby surface, generalized cylinder, texture map, bump map.

1. Introduction

Past efforts at computer generation of trees generally have focused on branching patterns [2, 7, 16, 21, 27, 28]; limbs and leaves were constructed from basic primitives [16, 21, 27] or ignored altogether by using mapping techniques [14]. The trees usually lacked detail when closely inspected.

The present work seeks to model trees with sufficient realism that they may be the subject of animation, rather than simple elements of the landscape. To accomplish this, the model should have a well-defined structure; beneath the bark the limb should be smooth; leaves should be properly attached to twigs. These requirements will be discussed in terms of a polygonal model, which is desired because of its generality. Bark and leaf detail are added using mapping techniques.

*Current address: Xerox PARC, Palo Alto, California.

Beyond being an aesthetic object to model, a tree provides a useful test of a graphics system. The need for smooth surfaces, the interesting topology at a branch point, and various mapping constraints all place demands upon the modeling process. The polygonal resolution of the model is given as view dependent, and this places a demand on the animation process.

2. The Tree Skeleton

The limbs of a tree may be specified simply as a list of three-dimensional points and a list of connections ("limbs") between those points. The lists accommodate an arbitrary topology ("branching pattern") subject to these conditions: all points must be connected, a point may have at most one incoming limb, and one and only one point has no incoming limb. This format serves equally well when procedurally generating a branching pattern or when measuring an existing one.

The branching pattern seen in Figure 1 was generated recursively. Parameters such as number of branches, branching angles, and length, radius, and taper of a branch were assigned stochastically from ranges of values that changed according to the developing geometry of the tree.

Any representation of the branching pattern is a "tree skeleton." The simplest is a drawing with straight lines, but the resulting appearance is unnatural (Figure 1, left). Trees are perhaps the strongest structures in living nature; each limb is a cantilever beam for which the bending moment and, hence, the deflection, increase smoothly towards the support point [12]. Any sudden change in direction of the limb would result in a discontinuity of the rate of change in the bending moment, introducing stress.

Continuity of direction at fixed points is a well-known property of the interpolating spline (Figure 1, right). The cubic spline, in particular, serves well as a tree skeleton because it has a continuous second derivative ("*C2* continuity"), which will be shown useful in constructing the limb surface.

Specifically, a limb consisting of n connections of $n+1$ data points will be interpolated by n spline segments. Not all cubic, interpolating splines exhibit *C2* continuity at the interpolated points; the popular Catmull-Rom, for example, is *C1* continuous at these points [3].

Rogers and Adams [24] provide a method for computing an interpolating spline that is *C2* continuous internally as well as at the data points. Their method maximizes curve smoothness by adjusting the parameterization of each segment according to the distance between data points. A tangent at each of the data points is computed.

Because the tree skeleton is defined by interpolated points, conventional control points are not used to manipulate the splines. Instead, each limb is represented by the coefficients of the cubic polynomials that define the spline. These coefficients are directly determined from the positional and tangential information at the data points [13].

Figure 1.
Data points interpolated by straight lines (left) and by splines (right).

3. The Limb Surface

Agin [1] defines a generalized cylinder as a space curve (a class of curves including the spline) and a cross sectional contour perpendicular to the curve. The surface of a tree limb, then, may be considered a generalized cylinder with a circular cross section ("disk") of varying radii (Figure 2). To polygonize the surface, a finite number (the "axial resolution") of cross sections are evaluated along the curve and connected together. Each cross section consists of a finite number (the "circumferential resolution") of points.

To prevent undesired twisting of consecutive disks, each one is oriented by two vectors, the "principal normal," **N**, and the "binormal," **B**. The principal normal is the unit length curvature vector, **K**, which Barsky gives [4] as:

$$\mathbf{K} = (\mathbf{T}\times\mathbf{A}\times\mathbf{T})/|\mathbf{T}|^4, \qquad (1a)$$

where **A** is the acceleration vector and **T** is the tangent vector. **A** and **T** are computed using conventional techniques [15], and **B** is simply **N**×**T**. **K** may also be evaluated as:

$$\mathbf{K} = (u\mathbf{A}-(\mathbf{A}\cdot\mathbf{T})\mathbf{T})\ /u^{3/2},\ \text{where } u = \mathbf{T}\cdot\mathbf{T}. \qquad (1b)$$

Figure 2.
Several spline segments interpolate the data points (asterisks) with *C2* continuity. A strobe captures a disk as it passes along the curve.

The vectors **T**, **N**, and **B** are known collectively as the "Frenet frame" [11]. Unfortunately, the Frenet frame cannot be computed at points where the acceleration is zero (such as at inflection points or along straight line segments). Various approximations, such as one presented by Shani [26], overcome this limitation.

An efficient means for computing a point **D** on the disk is to pre-compute a circle centered at the origin and, for any point **P** on the curve, transform the circle such that it is centered on **P** and lies in the plane defined by the principal normal and binormal. Thus,

$$\mathbf{D} = (\mathbf{N}_x x+\mathbf{B}_x y+\mathbf{P}_x,\ \mathbf{N}_y x+\mathbf{B}_y y+\mathbf{P}_y,\ \mathbf{N}_z x+\mathbf{B}_z y+\mathbf{P}_z), \quad (2)$$

where (x,y) is a point on the pre-computed circle. **P** is evaluated conventionally [15].

The Frenet frame and resulting polygonization are illustrated in Figure 3. Tangents, principal normals, and binormals are shown in black, green and red, respectively. The white dots represent the pre-computed circle. The axial and circumferential resolutions are 10 and 8, respectively.

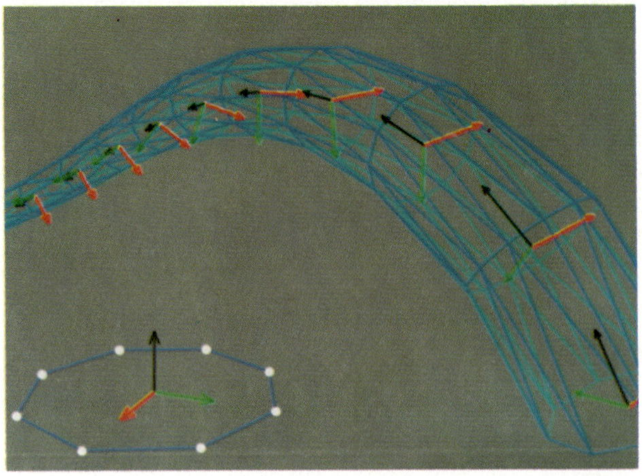

Figure 3.
The Frenet frame at parametrically equal distances along a curve.

4. Tension

The tension of a spline may be adjusted by scaling the tangent at an interpolated point [4, 17]. This is useful to stiffen part or all of the tree skeleton, or to increase the angularity of branching for smaller, non-supporting limbs.

Scaling the tangent, however, creates a discontinuity in the second derivative at the interpolated point. Barsky distinguishes between derivative and geometric continuities, the latter consisting of continuity in position, tangency, and *curvature*, not acceleration. Continuity of curvature (and, thus, of the Frenet frame) is maintained upon scaling tangents, provided:

$$\beta_1^2 A_{i-1}(1) + \beta_2 T_{i-1}(1) = A_i(0), \quad (3)$$

where β_1 and β_2 are beta parameters and i is an index to the interpolated points [4].

5. Branching

A "branch point" is the end of a limb that has two or more outgoing limbs. The outgoing limb of largest radius (or, if the radii are nearly equal, the outgoing limb that diverges least from the direction of the incoming limb) is considered "dominant." Initially, the incoming and dominant outgoing limbs are interpolated by a spline sequence that is *C2* continuous at the branch point. For each of the remaining, non-dominant outgoing limbs, an interpolating spline is begun at the branch point. Figure 4 depicts this ordering for a hypothetical tree.

Figure 4.
Order of creation of limbs (red, then orange, yellow, green, blue, and white).

As mentioned in Section 2, determining the *n* spline segments interpolating *n+1* data points requires the calculation of *n+1* tangents. The solution to this system of equations permits the first and last tangents to be set freely ("clamped") [24]. If the initial tangent of a non-dominant outgoing limb is clamped to that of the incoming limb, the smoothness from limb to limb is increased, which is appropriate for large limbs. If the magnitude of the tangent is reduced, the limb becomes less curved (Figure 5), which suits smaller limbs and twigs.

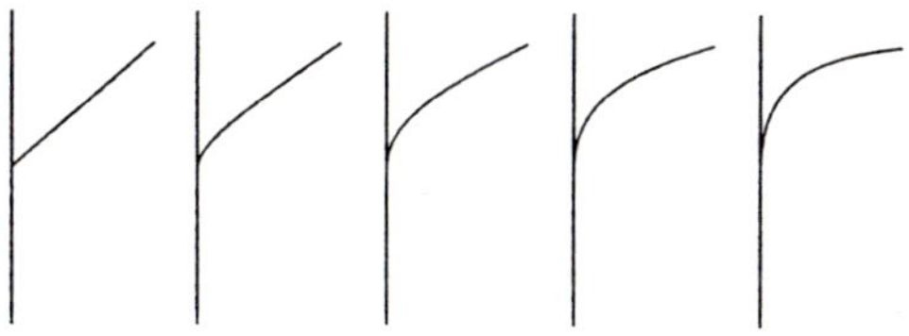

Figure 5.
The non-dominant outgoing limb with tension from 1 (left) to 0 (right).

Clamping the initial acceleration would over-constrain the system and so, as suggested by Equation 3, a discontinuity results in the principal normal, and is manifested as a twist about the tangent at the branch point. To maintain continuity of the Frenet frame, then, it is necessary to add a rotation to Equation 2, and to propagate this rotation through the tree.

6. The Ramiform

The surface at a point of bifurcation is described topologically as a triangular prism with 322 symmetry [18]. In computational geometry, such a form is significant for its branching, and so will be referred to as a "ramiform."

There are a number of ways to parameterize a ramiform such that its surface is smooth, without self-intersections and without gaps. Figures 6 and 7 illustrate one technique although others have been published recently [9, 22].

Referring to Figure 6, disks are created far enough along the outgoing limbs so as not to interpenetrate. A spline (shown in yellow), called the "saddle," may be constructed between the points of proximity of the disks, given the easily computed gradients at those points. The ramiform shape may be varied by changing the distances of the disks from the branch point as well as by scaling the tangents at the saddle endpoints.

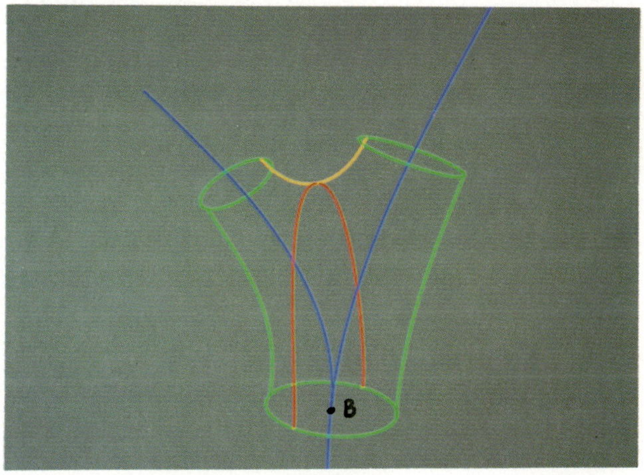

Figure 6.
Curve and surface continuity at the branch point **B**.

A two-segment interpolating spline (shown in red) connects opposite points on the lower disk to a point on the saddle that is farthest from the straight line segment (not shown) connecting the saddle endpoints. This point is determined readily by recursive subdivision of the saddle. Additional splines are constructed between the upper disks, passing through the two-segment spline, and between upper and lower disks, as shown in Figure 7. Points along these splines are connected to polygonize the ramiform.

Figure 7.
Ramiform and parameterization.

7. Resolution Issues

A tree tends to maximize its surface area to volume ratio. The limbs of a Norway maple, for example, occupy less than 20% of the convex volume that encloses the tree, as measured from a silhouette template [25]. This implies a large polygon to pixel ratio, especially for telephoto compositions; conversely, if the viewpoint is close to a limb, a large number of limbs will be off-screen. Thus, a method is desired for polygonizing limbs that varies the axial and circumferential resolutions according to the projection of the limb onto the screen and that culls off-screen limb sections.

Lane gives the maximum distance, M, that a straight line approximating a space curve will deviate from the curve as:

$$M = [\max|x^{(2)}(t)| + \max|y^{(2)}(t)| + \max|z^{(2)}(t)|]/[b-a]^2/8. \quad (4)$$

where a point on the curve is $(x(t),y(t),z(t))$, and $t \in (a,b)$ [19].

Thus, for each curve in the tree model, the acceleration vector is transformed to screen space and the axial resolution is determined using the above formula. After the transformation, the z term is dropped from the evaluation. Because acceleration of a cubic spline is linear, maximum absolute values need be evaluated for t only at a and b.

Circumferential resolution is made proportional to the projected size of a disk's radius. For extremely thin projected limbs, the model is rendered not as a polygonal solid but as a smoothly drawn curve.

Indexing polygonal resolution according to projected size (or volume) reduces the number of polygons generated, but requires the model be computed for any change in the camera to model relationship.

8. Verisimilar Bark

In 1978, Lance Williams digitized the surface of a plaster face [30] by x-raying the cast and using the digitized x-ray as a depth map. In the case of tree bark, a piece of actual bark was cast (Figure 8) and its x-ray was processed and used as a bump map (Figure 9)

Figure 8.
Tree bark and plaster cast.

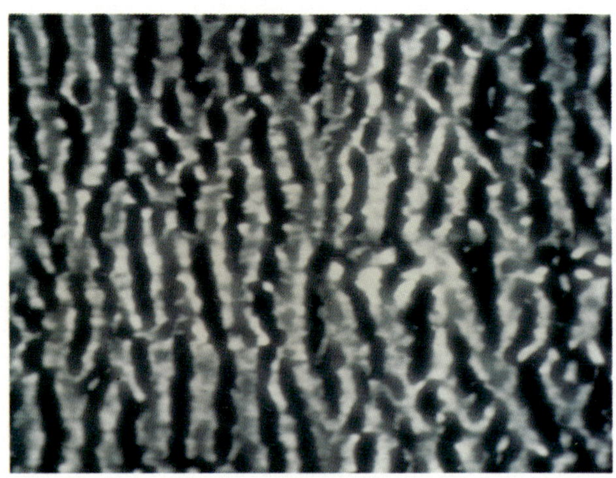

Figure 9.
Bump map for bark.

In order that the map seamlessly repeat around a limb, the top and bottom rows must be identical, as must be the left and right columns. This was accomplished by overlapping opposite edges of the map. Artifacts of this process were reduced by separating the map into several bandlimited images. For each separation, the merging width was adjusted according to the bandwidth, as suggested by Burt [8]. The resulting images were then summed together to produce the bump map in Figure 9.

The mapping itself must be a function of axial and circumferential distance along the surface of a limb, otherwise a tapered limb would exhibit an undesired compression of bark towards its narrow end. Accurate metrics exist for the generalized cylinders and for the curves shown on the ramiform (Figure 7); distances orthogonal to the curves shown on the ramiform are, however, approximated.

The mapping also must account for the progressive changes in bark depth and density as major limbs branch into minor limbs or twigs; discontinuities seem to occur at branch points of outgoing, non-dominant limbs.

The techniques of model creation are varied, ranging from procedural generation to real-world digitization. The two extremes have strengths and weaknesses, but digitization has often yielded superior realism. Regardless of the modeling method, the power of computer graphics remains in the manipulation of the models.

9. Trunk-like Surfaces

Roots of a tree generally branch below ground; above ground they merge with each other to form a shape not easily polygonized as a ramiform. Instead, planar "blobby" techniques inspired by Blinn [5] may be used to compute the surface [6]. The blobby cross section and curved profile give the resulting surface an asymmetric, organic appearance.

Figure 10 shows a series of planar contours around a tree skeleton. Each contour is an equipotential curve surrounding the points of intersection of the tree skeleton with the plane of the contour. The contours are evenly sampled and surfaces between adjacent planar curves are triangulated as described by Christiansen [10]. The shaded surface is displayed in Figure 11.

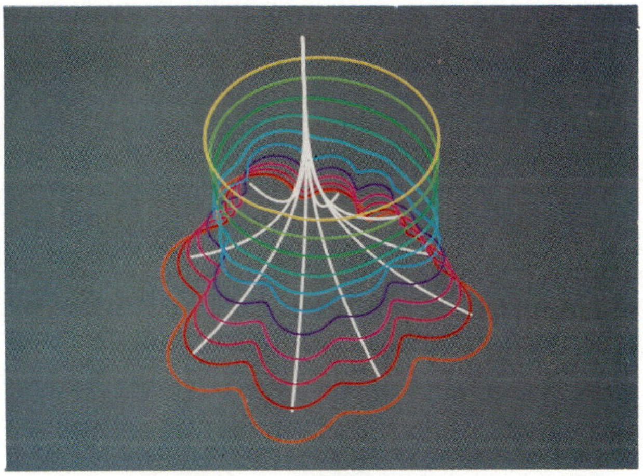

Figure 10.
Contours simulating the irregularity at the base of a tree.

Figure 11.
Trunk and ramiform with bark.

10. Leaves

A maple leaf was digitized from a photograph by a video camera; the veins were emphasized for dramatic effect, using a paint program. The resulting, non-black texture is mapped onto a three-polygon structure as shown in Figure 12. The structure is hinged along the dashed lines; the degree of hinging depends on the strength of a hypothetical wind as well as the extent to which the leaf faces the wind. The crease at the hinge is not visible if the structure is Phong shaded.

Figure 12.
Three-polygon leaf structure.

Figure 13 shows six leaf structures differently transformed to make a leaf "configuration." This configuration was measured from an actual maple twig and is one of two configurations used in the generation of Figures 15 and 16.

For each limb that does not exceed a given diameter and that has no outgoing limbs, a leaf configuration is chosen randomly, scaled randomly, and placed at the tip of the limb. The leaf configuration is oriented in the direction of the limb and rotated to an angle slightly below horizontal, conforming to observed maple leaves.

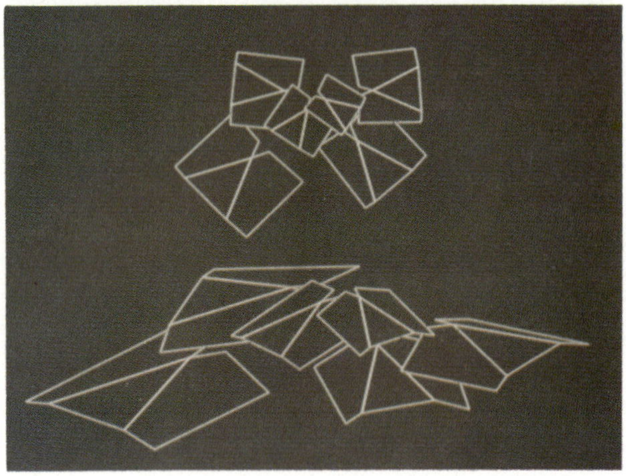

Figure 13.
Leaf configuration: plan (top) and perspective (bottom) views.

Three twigs with leaves are shown in Figure 14. The leaves that face away from the viewer are shaded with a lighter color to simulate the lighter underside of the maple leaf. The stems are rendered as unshaded curves defined by the twig tip and direction, and the leaf position and direction.

Figure 14.
A twig consisting of limb, stems, and leaves.

11. Conclusions

From the methods described, a complex tree model may be generated given sparse data. Features such as trunk blobbiness, ramiform shape, and leaf angles are parameterized and do not require explicit modeling.

The basic structure of the model is the branching generalized cylinder. This structure shows promise as a general body form allowing limbs to move without cracks developing between them. The analysis of the structure demonstrates the value of geometric continuity.

The use of screen projection to determine the polygonal resolution of a model suggests its use in determining the model *type* as well; for example, an extreme close-up could require the bark be modeled as a corrugated structure rather than as perturbations mapped onto a smooth surface.

Rendered images of the test tree are presented in Figures 15 and 16. Shadows were added by a z-buffer based post-rendering process [29].

Figure 15.
The Mighty Maple.

Figure 16.
Acer Graphics.

Trees exist in nature, and a logical progression from the present work is their portrayal in different settings and conditions. William Reeves has created some convincing and romantic images of forests [23]; but cracked limbs, shriveled leaves, knot-holes, buds, and snow or moss covered branches would be new elements in the development of realism in tree images.

Mandelbrot has suggested that emulation of nature is its celebration [20]. Insofar as emulation of nature requires its study, one is inclined to agree.

12. Acknowledgments

To Kevin Hunter for the stochastic three-dimensional clouds that are the background in Figures 15 and 16; to Dick Lundin for suggesting the pre-computed disk; to Val Kupris for casting the bark and to James McDonnell for x-raying the cast; to Lance Williams for transparent texture mapping and for "wrapping" the bark; to Pat Hanrahan and Paul Heckbert for many hours of consultation; to Ariel Shaw, Brian Tramontana, and Sasha Shamszad for photographic assistance; to Rick Beach and Subhana Menis for help with the manuscript; and to the "Ops" for unending patience and service.

13. References

1. Agin, G.J., "Representation and Description of Curved Objects," Memo AIM-173, Stanford Artificial Intelligence Report, October 1972.
2. Aono, M., and Kunii, T.L., "Botanical Tree Image Generation," IEEE Computer Graphics and Applications, Vol. 4, No. 5, 1982.
3. Barnhill, R.E., and Riesenfeld, R.F., *Computer Aided Geometric Design*, Academic Press, 1974.
4. Barsky, B.A., and Beatty, J.C., "Local Control of Bias and Tension in Beta-splines," ACM Transactions on Graphics, Vol. 2, No. 2, April 1983.
5. Blinn, J.F., "A Generalization of Algebraic Surface Drawing," ACM Transactions on Graphics, Vol. 1, No. 3, July 1982.
6. Bloomenthal, J., "A Representation for Botanical Trees using Density Distributions," Proceedings, International Conference on Engineering and Computer Graphics, Beijing, China, September 1984.
7. Brooks, J., et al., "An Extension of the Combinatorial Geometry Technique for Modeling Vegetation and Terrain Features," Technical Report for the Department of Defense, Catalog No. AD782883.
8. Burt, P.J., and Adelson, E.H., "The Laplacian Pyramid as a Compact Image Code," IEEE Transactions on Communications, COM-31, 1983.
9. Charrot, P., and Gregory, J.A., "A Pentagonal Surface Patch for CAGD," Computer Aided Geometric Design, Vol. 1, No. 1, July 1984.
10. Christiansen, H.N. and Sederberg, T.W., "Conversion of Complex Contour Line Definitions into Polygonal Element Mosaics," Computer Graphics, Vol. 12, No. 3, August 1978.
11. Faux, I.D., and Pratt, M.J., *Computational Geometry for Design and Manufacture*, John Wiley and Sons, 1979.
12. Fletcher, D.Q., *Mechanics of Materials*, CBS College Publishing, 1985.
13. Foley, J.D., and Van Dam, A., *Fundamentals of Interactive Computer Graphics*, Addison-Wesley Publishing Company, 1982.
14. Gardner, G., "Computer Generated Texturing to Model Real World Features," Proceedings, First Interservice Industry Training Equipment Conference, Orlando, Florida, November 1979.
15. Greville, T., *Theory and Applications of Spline Functions*, Academic Press, 1969.
16. Kawaguchi, Y., "A Morphological Study of the Form of Nature," Computer Graphics, Vol. 16, No. 3, July 1982.
17. Kochanek, D.H.U., and Bartels, R.H., "Interpolating Splines with Local Tension, Continuity and Bias Control," Computer Graphics, Vol. 18, No. 3, July 1984.
18. Lalvani, H., "Generative Morphology of Transforming Space Structure," Proceedings, Third International Conference on Space Structures, Surrey, UK, 1984.
19. Lane, J, "Curve and Surface Display Techniques," Siggraph Tutorial Notes, 1982.
20. Mandelbrot, B., *Fractals: Form, Chance, and Dimension*, W.H. Freeman and Company, San Francisco, 1977.
21. Marshall, R., Wilson, R., and Carlson, W., "Procedure Models for Generating Three-Dimensional Terrain," Computer Graphics, Vol. 14, No. 3, July 1980.
22. Nasri, A.H., "Polyhedral Subdivision Methods for Free-Form Surfaces," Doctoral Thesis, The School of Computing Studies and Accountancy, University of East Anglia, 1984.
23. Reeves, W.T., "Andre's Forest," Computer Graphics (back cover), Vol. 18, No. 3, July 1984.
24. Rogers, D., and Adams, J., *Mathematical Elements for Computer Graphics*, McGraw-Hill, New York, 1976.
25. Rogers, W.E., *Tree Flowers of Forest, Park and Street*, Dover Publications, New York, 1965.
26. Shani, U., and Ballard, D.H., "Splines as Embeddings for Generalized Cylinders," Computer Vision, Graphics, and Image Processing, Vol. 27, No. 2, August 1984.
27. Smith, A.R., "Plants, Fractals, and Formal Languages," Computer Graphics, Vol. 18, No. 3, July 1984.
28. Tomlinson, P.B., "Tree Architecture," American Scientist, Vol. 71, March 1983.
29. Williams, L.J., "Casting Curved Shadows on Curved Surfaces," Computer Graphics, Vol. 12, No. 3, August 1978.
30. Williams, L.J., private communication, 1981.

Approximate and Probabilistic Algorithms for Shading and Rendering Structured Particle Systems

William T. Reeves

Computer Research and Development,
Lucasfilm Ltd

Ricki Blau

Computer Science Division, Dept. of Electrical Engineering and Computer Science,
University of California, Berkeley

Abstract

Detail enhances the visual richness and realism of computer-generated images. Our stochastic modelling approach, called *particle systems*, builds complex pictures from sets of simple, volume-filling primitives. For example, structured particle systems have been used to generate trees and a grass-covered forest floor. Particle systems can produce so much irregular, three-dimensional detail that exact shading and visible surface calculations become infeasible. We describe approximate and probabilistic algorithms for shading and the visible surface problem. Because particle systems algorithms generate richly-detailed images, it is hard to detect any deviation from an exact rendering. Recent work in stochastic modelling also enables us to model complex motions with random variation, such as a field of grass blowing in the breeze. We analyze the performance of our current algorithms to understand the costs of our stochastic modelling approach.

CR Categories and Subject Descriptors: I.3.3 [**Computer Graphics**]: Picture/Image Generation - Display algorithms; I.3.5 [**Computer Graphics**]: Computational Geometry and Object Modelling - Curve, surface, solid, and object representations - Modelling packages; I.3.7 [**Computer Graphics**]: Three-Dimensional Graphics and Realism - Animation - Colour, shading, shadowing, and texture

General Terms: Design, Algorithms, Performance Analysis

Key Words: stochastic modelling, approximation

1. Introduction

Natural, as opposed to man-made, objects exhibit an immense variety of irregular shapes and random variation in their detail. To represent this variety in synthetic images, we would like to have models that are not entirely deterministic. The use of *stochastic* models has recently been advanced as an approach to creating naturalistic detail in computer-generated images [5]. The idea of "data amplification" is fundamental to stochastic modelling algorithms, as well as to other classes of algorithms described by Smith [13]. A simple data base specifies the general characteristics of the modelled object, and detail is generated algorithmically to describe the object fully. A complicated image can be generated from a small data base, and the amount of detail can vary with the displayed size of the object.

The best-known examples of stochastic modelling are the *fractal* algorithms of Fournier, Fussell, and Carpenter [5], inspired by the mathematics of Mandelbrot [9], and the particle systems described by Reeves [12]. Particle systems represent objects as clouds of primitive particles that occupy their volumes, rather than using more classical surface-based representations such as polygons, patches, and quadric surfaces. A particle system is not a static entity, as its particles can move and change form with the passage of time. The position, orientation, attributes, and dynamics of each particle are defined by a set of constrained stochastic processes.

Particle systems are important for three reasons. First, because a particle is much simpler than most graphical primitives, many more can be drawn in a given amount of computation time. Hence, a more complex and detailed image can be generated. Second, particle systems are both procedural and stochastic. By employing data amplification techniques, they require less human design time than conventional modelling methods. Third, particle systems can be used to model objects that change form over a period of time. In our experience, it is more difficult to represent complex dynamics of this form with surface-based modelling techniques.

This paper presents several new results in particle systems that were left as future research in our previous paper [12]. These results were used in the film *The Adventures of André and Wally B.* [7] to generate three-dimensional background images of a forest and of grass covering its floor. An example is shown in Figure 1.

Our new algorithms generate more sophisticated particle systems with greater internal structure. The strength of these stochastic modelling algorithms is their ability to transform a small set of simple constraints into a complete description of complex objects. The problem is that they create so much irregular, three-dimensional detail that exact visible surface and shading calculations become infeasible. Our solution is to exploit the visual complexity of the models by adopting approximate and probabilistic algorithms. The rich detail in the images tends to mask deviations from an exact rendering. We also present some recent work in stochastic modelling that enables us to model more complex motions, such as a field of grass blowing in the breeze. Finally, we analyze the performance of our current algorithms and discuss the potential gains of hardware support for rendering particle systems.

Several other researchers have modelled and rendered images of trees and vegetation. Brooks et. al. [3] at MAGI extended a combinatorial geometry system to model simple trees. Marshall et. al. [10] from Ohio State University used a

Figure 1. Forest Scene from *The Adventures of André and Wally B.*

procedural technique to generate polygonal models of trees. Both of these early efforts produced deterministic models of individual trees, whereas our algorithms create large groups of trees with stochastic variation.

More recently, Aono and Kunii [1] developed geometric models that are based on botanical descriptions of trees and that exhibit accurate branching structures. Their research emphasizes issues in modelling; our work is more strongly oriented towards creating complex, coloured images. Gardner [6] has simulated scenes of trees and terrain using textured quadric surfaces; his approach is more efficient than ours, but it creates objects that are less highly detailed. Smith [13] described a modelling technique called *graftals* that represents plants using Lindenmayer systems. Bloomenthal [2] has created remarkably realistic images of trees, based on finely-detailed surface-oriented representations. Both Smith and Bloomenthal emphasize the detailed structure of individual plants, whereas we take a more global view of a forest environment.

2. Structured Particle Systems

Particle systems were first used to model a wall of fire in the Genesis sequence from the film *Star Trek II: The Wrath of Khan* [11]. The fire is modelled as particles of light that move in three-space. Each particle system resembles a miniature volcano from which many particles explode upwards, eventually falling to the planet's surface due to the pull of gravity. A frame from this sequence, such as Figure 2, displays the trajectories of the visible particles during the time that the imaginary camera shutter is open to record the frame. The trajectories are approximated by a sequence of straight line segments, one per frame. Thus, a motion-blurred line is drawn to represent each particle.

Associated with each fire particle is a set of parameters that describe its position and characteristics: the location from which it erupted, its initial velocity, and attributes such as colour and size. At generation time, the parameters are assigned initial values, drawn from a random distribution. Each particle is generated and transformed through time independent of all other particles.

The particle systems that model natural phenomena such as trees and grass are more structured, and, consequently, the particles are not independent. Each tree is drawn as a set of line segments, and possibly small circles, that constitutes its branches and leaves. Many complex relationships exist among the particles representing the branches and leaves of a tree, as together they must form a cohesive three-dimensional object. The rest of this section describes new techniques and types of controls for generating *structured* particle systems.

2.1 Trees

The first step in modelling a forest scene is to populate the forest with individual trees, creating a tree data base that contains the location and type of each tree. The specifications in this pre-computed data base are subsequently used to generate and render the trees, frame-by-frame, during a second stage of the computation.

2.1.1 Creating the Forest

Sometimes the scene designer wishes to place each tree exactly, perhaps to simulate some real environment. The designer positioned the trees in Figure 3 with an interactive model editor to ensure that they fit into the scene with other, separately-computed elements.

When a vast number of trees are to be modelled, as in Figure 4, it is more practical to generate their locations procedurally with special-purpose programs. Our tree placement program requires four types of input: a grid size that controls the spacing between trees, a parameter that specifies the minimum distance between any pair of trees, one or more regions on the horizontal plane that will be filled with trees, and a terrain map that provides the elevation of points on the plane. The program creates at most one tree per grid point, generating random displacements independently in the x and y dimensions to offset the actual location of the tree from the given point. Should parts of the forest become more crowded than the minimum spacing parameter allows, grid points are left empty.

The layout of a landscape can be controlled even when the placement algorithm is stochastic. For example, texture maps can direct the program to leave the terrain bare where meadows, streams, or other open areas exist. An even more sophisticated placement algorithm could be based on empirical forestry models and consider factors such as elevation, water drainage, and sunlight to determine the density of growth.

Tree type selection is performed at the same time as tree placement. Each tree is assigned a type (e.g., maple, spruce, or aspen) either interactively or procedurally. The stochastic methods used for Figure 4 distribute the deciduous trees more densely in the valleys and evergreen trees more densely on the hills. The probability that a tree is evergreen increases with the elevation; we use a random number to choose among the possible tree types.

2.1.2 Generating a Tree

The particle systems program processes the trees in the data base serially; it generates a complete model for each tree and then renders the model. Starting with the main trunk, the algorithm constructs the tree by recursively generating subbranches. The data structure for the model is a tree in which each node describes a branch segment.

Before invoking the recursive branch generation procedure, the algorithm stochastically assigns a set of initial characteristics and dimensions. Some of these dimensions are illustrated in Figure 5.

The values for these parameters are randomly drawn from distributions associated with the tree's type. For example, the following equation determines the height of a tree:

$$Height = MeanHeight + Rand() \times DeltaHeight$$

where Rand() is a procedure returning a pseudo-random number uniformly distributed between -1.0 and +1.0. *MeanHeight* and *DeltaHeight* are specified for the tree type; they represent the mean height and the maximum difference from the mean. If the height is distributed uniformly between a and b, then *MeanHeight* is $\frac{a+b}{2}$, and *DeltaHeight* is $\frac{|b-a|}{2}$. In Figure 3, the deciduous trees have a *MeanHeight* of 60 and a *DeltaHeight* of 12; the evergreen trees also have a *MeanHeight* of 60, but a *DeltaHeight* of 16.

One parameter may depend on another. For example, the global *width* controls the breadth of the primary branches; this parameter is stochastically set to a fraction of the tree's height according to the equation:

$$Width = Height \times (MeanWidth + Rand() \times DeltaWidth)$$

MeanWidth is 0.6 for the deciduous trees, and 0.5 for the evergreens. *DeltaWidth* is 0.05 for the deciduous trees, and 0.25 for the evergreens.

Figure 3. André's Forest

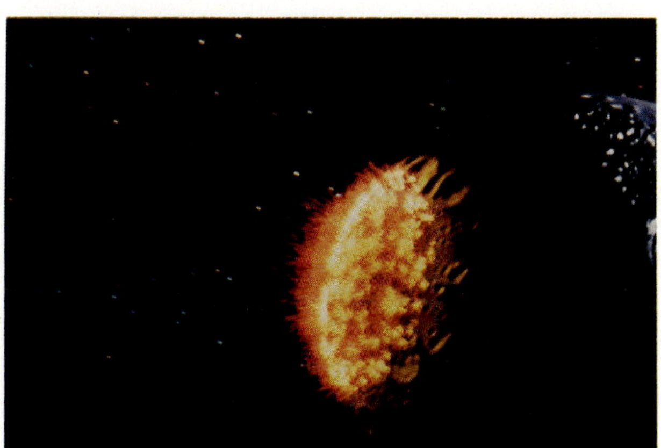

Figure 2. Frame from *Star Trek II: The Wrath of Khan*

Figure 4. Tree-covered Hills at Sunrise

The relationship between parameters need not be linear. For example, branches are tapered by decreasing the thickness as the distance *d* from the base of the branch increases, according to the equation:

$$thickness = thickness_b \times \sqrt{\frac{length - d}{length}}$$

where *length* is the total length of the branch and $thickness_b$ is the thickness at its base.

The height of the lowest branch is stochastically set to a fraction of the tree's height. The distance between two sub-branches is drawn from a distribution that depends on the tree type and the thickness of the parent branch. Another control indicates whether branches occur singly or in whorls.

The parameters of the branch length distribution depend on the dimensions of the tree, as illustrated in Figure 5. An approximate bounding volume for the tree is computed from its height and width; its shape varies with the tree type, conical for evergreens and elliptical for deciduous trees. For each branch, we select a *branching angle* from a distribution associated with the tree type. We next compute *MeanLength*, the distance to the surface of the bounding volume from the position where the branch meets the trunk. The actual length of any branch is taken from a distribution centered on *MeanLength*.

A recursive algorithm generates sub-branches. We sample a distribution to obtain the ratio between the diameters of the parent and each sub-branch. The sub-branch inherits many parameters from its parent, but some controls are adjusted to the dimensions of the child. For example, sub-branches are spaced more closely together as the branch thickness decreases. The recursion stops either when a branch reaches a minimum thickness or at a specified maximum depth of recursion.

Characteristically, aspen trees, such as in Figure 3, have forked branches, but our evergreens do not. For each species, we specify a probability that a branch forks. A parent-child relationship exists between a branch and its sub-branch, but two forks of a branch have a sibling relationship and share probability distributions.

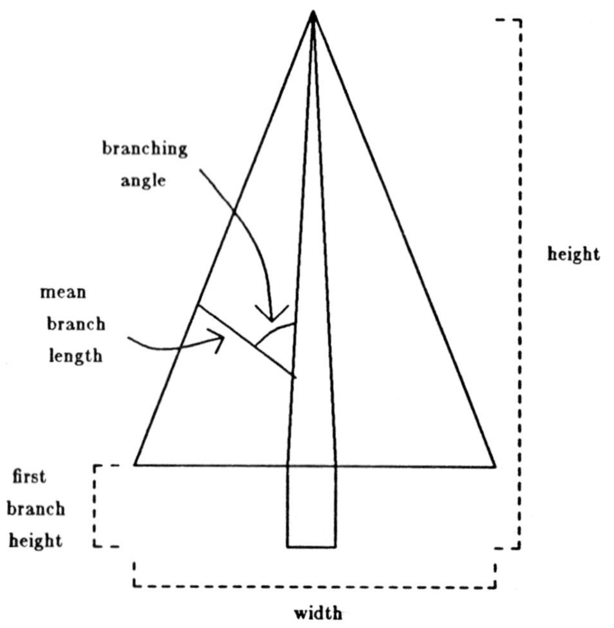

Figure 5. Dimensions Used in Tree Model

The colours in the image vary from tree to tree. The exact shades are offset by random amounts from mean values characteristic of the tree type. Two tables of colours are established for each tree, and the thickness of the branch determines which table is used. Colours for the trunk and main branches are taken from one table, and colours for the leaves from the other. Alternatively, one table may be used for old wood and the other for new.

The branch-generation algorithm produces trees with a regular structure, unlike real trees that have been affected by their environment and natural disasters. We simulate these effects by post-processing the three-dimensional description of the tree. Separate algorithms bend tree branches to simulate the effects of gravity, prevailing winds, and prevailing sunlight direction. Another algorithm randomly warps branches to simulate a form of catastrophe theory.

Finally leaves or needles are added to the branches that have no sub-branches. The stochastic parameters that control the placement and characteristics of leaves are: shape, orientation, spacing, density, colour, and location.

All of the random variables for the images in this paper were drawn from uniform distributions, as described above. In tuning the parameters, we concentrated more on visual results than on actual botanical data. Other, more accurate, distributions should be explored in the future.

Particle systems can be combined with elements computed using other techniques. For example, the tree trunks in Figure 3 were modelled as truncated, solid cones and rendered with conventional texture-mapping techniques.

Approximately 1.1 million particles compose the trees in Figure 3. Nearly sixty megabytes of binary data were generated from only twenty-one thousand bytes of input, resulting in a data amplification factor of over three thousand. The expansion factor is, naturally, less for scenes in which each object occupies only a small area of the screen. The input for the trees in Figure 4 was expanded by only a factor of four to generate fourteen megabytes of data; however, the input data base itself was generated procedurally from a much smaller specification.

2.2 Grass

The images of grass result from an extension of the work reported earlier by Reeves [12]. Clumps of grass are scattered randomly over the input terrain. A texture map, with a bird's-eye view of the terrain, optionally specifies the locations of bare spots or different types of grasses. Some stochastic parameters specify global parameters for an entire clump of grass: its position, orientation, area, density, and type.

Each clump contains many separate blades of grass. Both the structure of the clumps and the geometry of the individual blades are simpler than the models used for trees. Stochastic processes determine the number of blades within the clump and the characteristics for each blade: position, height, thickness, curvature, orientation, and colour. Short, straight-line particles approximate each blade's parabolic arc. Stochastic bends and kinks added to some blades of grass enhance the realism of the image. Simple flowers are created by adding yellow or blue particles to some blades of grass.

Eighteen thousand clumps of grass are visible in Figure 3. A total of 733,887 particles were drawn to render the grass.

3. Shading Models for Particle Systems

The fire particle systems require only simple shading calculations, because each particle is modelled as an independent light source[12]. Each fire particle is stochastically assigned an initial colour that changes over time according to a simple linear relationship that simulates cooling. The tree and grass particle systems reflect rather than emit light; they consequently require a more sophisticated shading model with ambient, diffuse, and specular shading components. For more realistic rendering, the shading algorithm also provides self-shadowing, external shadows, and coloured light sources.

A single tree may be composed of over one million independent particles. It would be a formidable task to shade each particle exactly, calculating whether it is in shadow and determining if it should be highlighted. In fact, unless the camera points directly at the sun from within the tree, it is almost impossible to tell whether or not any one leaf should be in shadow. Our solution is to use a probabilistic shading model for both the trees and the grass. For example, the particle's position and orientation determine the probability that it is in shadow. We calculate this probability and then use a random number to decide whether or not to render the particle as if it were in shadow.

3.1 Trees

Trees are self-shadowing, as branches and leaves of the tree shadow other parts of the same tree. In a forest, a tree is also shadowed externally by neighbouring trees. Our shading functions provide ambient, diffuse, and specular components and also approximate both forms of shadowing.

Highlights occur where the tree's branches or leaves are exposed directly to sunlight. This condition is most likely to exist close to the outer edge of the tree in the direction of the sun. Accordingly, the diffuse shading component for a particle varies with the distance into the tree from the light source, d_d, as shown in Figure 6. The diffuse component drops off exponentially as d_d increases according to the following equation:

$$D = e^{-\alpha d_d}$$

The parameter α controls the rate of the exponential dropoff. Random highlights are added by stochastically turning on a specular component whenever d_d is small and the cosine of the angle between the light direction and the branch direction is close to zero.

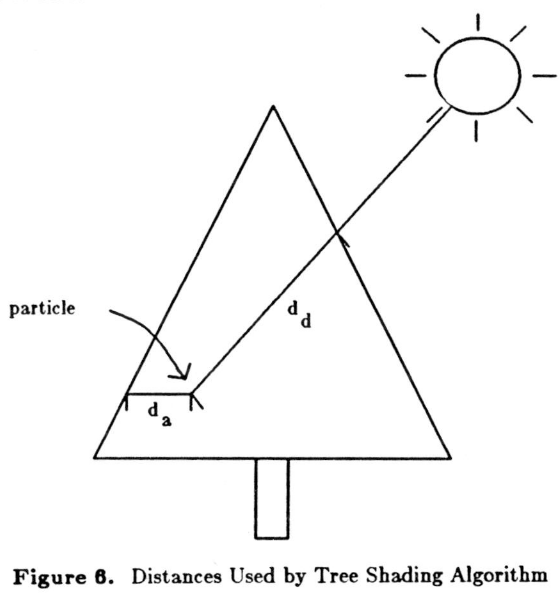

Figure 6. Distances Used by Tree Shading Algorithm

Self-shadowing is simulated primarily by controlling the ambient shading component. The ambient component for a particle drops off exponentially as the distance into the tree, d_a, increases. This distance, as shown in Figure 6, is independent of the position of the light source and represents the shortest distance from the particle to a point on the tree's bounding volume in a direction parallel to the ground. Another parameter, $A_{\min}$, sets a minimum for the ambient component and guarantees that there is some light even in the deepest interior of the tree. The ambient component equation is therefore:

$$A = \max(e^{-\beta d_a}, A_{\min})$$

A different problem is to add external shadows, those cast by other trees. Again, we use an approximation technique because exact computation of the shadows would be very expensive. The locations and heights of any trees positioned between a specified tree and the light source define a plane that skims the top of neighbouring trees and passes through the light source. An example is shown in Figure 7. Particles above this plane are in full sunlight, so the specular, diffuse, and ambient shading components all contribute to the shading calculation. The probability that sunlight reaches other parts of the tree decreases for particles located below the plane. If a particle is more than a specified distance below the plane, only the ambient shading component is used. For particles lying in between, a random number is selected to decide if the diffuse and specular components contribute to the shading.

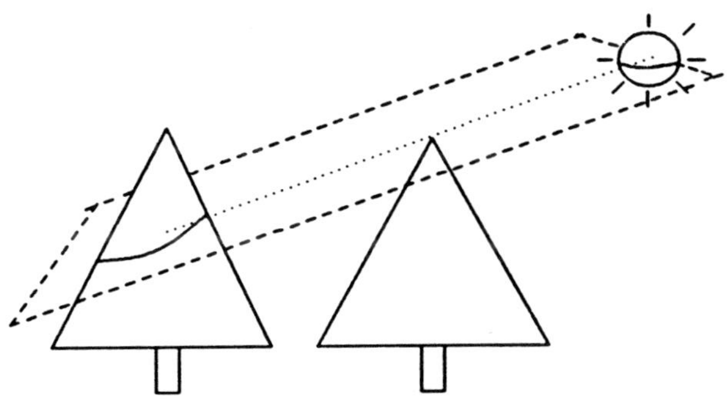

Figure 7. External Shadow Plane

To heighten the visual effect of the images in *André and Wally B.*, we used different colours for different types of light. A yellowish tinge to the diffuse and specular components produced an early morning sunrise warmth, and a bluish tinge to the ambient component of the light gave us a look inspired by the landscape artistry of Maxfield Parrish [8]. Figure 8 shows trees shaded with the techniques described in this section.

3.2 Grass

A similar stochastic algorithm shades the grasses. The contributions of both the diffuse and ambient components depend on the distance from the top of the clump of grass to the particle in question, decreasing exponentially as the depth increases. The difference between the two is that the diffuse component drops off much more quickly than the ambient component. As with trees, each lighting component can have a different colour.

The strongest visual effects are due to the shading function that casts tree shadows onto the grass. The principle idea behind our algorithm is a form of ray casting. We view the particle from the light source to see if it is visible through the trees. If the particle is not visible, it is in shadow. A simple and effective device for implementing this idea is the *shadow mask*. Our method is similar to a technique used by Lance Williams [15].

To create the shadow mask for a scene, we first compute an orthographic image of the trees from the direction of the light source. We then extract the silhouette information from this image and form a texture map. Before shading each particle of grass, we transform its position by this same orthographic transformation, effectively calculating a view of the particle from the light source. The calculated screen coordinates index into the shadow mask texture map to obtain a value that indicates how much the particle is in shadow. In the final colour computation, this value determines how much of the diffuse lighting component to use. If the particle is completely in shadow, only the ambient shading component is used. A single, pre-computed shadow mask is used for all frames in which the positions of the trees and of the light source remain constant. The shadow mask texture map in Figure 9 was used to shade the grass element in Figure 10.

The shadow mask technique effectively represents the shadows of trees on the grass because the trees are always between the grass and the sun. In general, the shadow mask technique works only if the objects casting the shadow are completely between the light source and the surface on which the shadow is cast. This limitation arises because the texture map that stores the shadow mask is only two-dimensional. Three-dimensional texture maps that store both depth and coverage information could solve this problem, but we have not explored this area.

4. Visible Surface Determination

Our previous research essentially ignored the visible surface problem with particle systems. The fires of *Star Trek II*, as shown in Figure 2, were composed of light-emitting particles. When several particles overlapped in a pixel, their colours were simply added together. With light-reflecting particles, such as those of the trees and grass, one particle can obscure another by being in front of it with respect to the selected camera position. We must now solve the visible surface problem.

The following sections describe two slightly different visible surface algorithms, one for the trees and one for the grass.

4.1 Trees

Consider a forest scene containing many trees. As we have seen, our stochastic generation algorithms usually attain a significant amount of data amplification. It is not feasible to generate particles for all trees in an image and then perform a traditional visible surface algorithm on them. Instead, we employ a painter's algorithm approach. We first sort all trees in the scene into a back-to-front order with respect to screen depth. Then, for each tree in turn, we generate a stochastic model, shade it, and render it into the image on top of any trees that have been previously rendered. As soon as a tree has been rendered, its data is discarded.

The accuracy of this back-to-front approach relies on the assumption that the bounding volumes of the trees do not intersect. While this assumption is inaccurate for forests in general, interesting images can be made with tree databases that conform to this restriction. The grass visible surface algorithm of the next section removes this non-intersecting restriction but is slightly more expensive.

Rendering each individual tree is not trivial either, as some branches of the tree obscure others. Within a tree we also apply a form of painter's algorithm that depends on a bucket sort. The bounding volume of the tree defines a set of buckets that are indexed by the eye space z distance of the particle — that is, by its depth into the scene. As a particle is generated, it is transformed into two-dimensional screen space and inserted into the bucket list corresponding to its average eye space z distance. After all particles have been generated, they are drawn in back-to-front bucket order on top of any particles that have already been rendered into the image. All particles are drawn as small, antialiased circles or short, antialiased straight line segments.

This bucket sort is another inexpensive but successful approximation. A completely accurate comparison sort of all the particles in a scene would require $O(n\log n)$ operations, where n is the number of particles. The approximate algorithm is linear in the number of particles, assuming that the trees have been sorted previously. Therefore, it requires only $O(m\log m + n)$ operations, where m, the number of trees, is much smaller than n. If we skipped the preliminary sort of the trees, a bucket sort of all particles could be accomplished with $O(n)$ operations, but the memory costs would be much greater. For our forest scenes, n typically ranges between 1.0 and 1.7 million. In contrast, m is usually less than 10,000, and, in close-up scenes such as Figure 11, it is only 195. We have never noticed any anomalies attributable to the bucket sort in any of our static or dynamic images. We commonly use about 2000 buckets. Even for a large tree, spanning fifty feet of depth, each bucket would cover a small area, about 0.3 inches. Since the images are so complex to start with, any imperfections are very difficult to detect as long as they are consistent from frame to frame.

4.2 Grass

We cannot create the appearance of a continuous carpet of grass without allowing clumps of grass to intersect. The visible surface algorithm for grass is more sophisticated than for trees because it permits intersecting clumps. The algorithm sorts the clumps of grass back-to-front and then calculates the bounding box of each clump in eye space. The clumps are generated in the back-to-front order, and the particles are entered into the bucket sort list. The difference is that the bucket list is not flushed and drawn at the end of each clump as it is at the end of each tree. Instead, only some of the buckets are drawn at the end of each clump. A bucket is drawn only if none of the bounding boxes from the remaining clumps overlaps it in eye-space z distance. Because the clumps are sorted, it is trivial to test for this condition.

Whenever the rear-most buckets are drawn, the range of the entire bucket list slides forward in eye-space z depth. Any undrawn particles remaining in the list may need to be reassigned to different buckets. This algorithm is more expensive than the non-intersecting tree algorithm because of two additional tasks – checking for overlapping buckets and reassigning particles when the range of the bucket list changes.

5. Complex Particle System Dynamics

The particle dynamics of the fires [11] were simple — each particle independently followed a parabolic trajectory. In the film *The Adventures of André and Wally B.*, the tree and grass elements were still. Since then, we have added realistic dynamics to depict a field of tall grasses blowing in the breeze. Stochastic models represent two phenomena, gusts of wind and the motion of wind-blown blades of grass.

The first step is to model wind. The scene designer specifies the terrain, a prevailing wind direction, and the average wind speed. A program generates wave fronts of particles that travel across the terrain. Each particle represents a small, localized gust of wind. The waves of particles display random variation, moving roughly parallel to the specified wind direction. New waves arrive at a rate that matches a specified wind gust frequency.

A *wind map* is a two-dimensional, top-down view of the terrain that specifies the wind intensity at discrete grid points. Letting the waves of particles move through time, we build a wind map for each frame of the animated sequence. The intensity of the wind at a particular location and time is determined by the number of wind gust particles close to the grid point.

Figure 8. Shaded Trees

Figure 9. Shadow Mask

Figure 10. Grass Element Shadowed by Shadow Mask

Figure 11. Close-up Forest Scene

Figure 12. Still from Film of Blowing Grass

Stochastic processes also model the reaction of the blade of grass as it is hit by a gust of wind. The simulated motion has the following key features:

- The blade bends around an axis that is perpendicular to the wind direction and passes through the blade's base.
- The amount of bending depends on the intensity of the gust of wind.
- The amount of bending increases with the distance from the ground, so that the blade is stiffest at its base.
- Over time and in the absence of other gusts, the blade returns to its original position following a damped sinusoidal motion called a ***bending function***.
- The effects of successive gusts of wind are additive. At each frame, a bending function is generated and remembered for subsequent frames. The effective bending function at a given frame is the sum of all active bending functions.

The use of a two-dimensional wind map limits the motion of the wind to a plane. However, the algorithm achieves a three-dimensional look by tying each blade of grass to the ground and varying the degree of bending over the length of the blade.

Stochastic processes add further variation to the motion. For example, all blades do not bend exactly perpendicular to the wind direction, and blades close together use slightly different wind gust intensities. A blade of grass is bent by transforming the particles that represent it, taking care to keep them connected.

We can experiment with stochastic wind functions and wind maps, watching the wind patterns flow in real time on our vector display system. After adjusting the controls interactively, we can re-compute the motion in a few minutes to inspect the results. A short animated film of blowing grass has been computed. Figure 12 is one frame from the film.

6. Performance of Particle Systems Algorithms

In order to characterize the performance of particle systems algorithms, we measured the execution of four programs that produced different types of stochastic elements. All programs were run under Berkeley 4.2 UNIX† on an essentially idle VAX 11/750 with floating point accelerator and 4Mb of memory. The programs were written in C, except for some assembly-language routines for mathematical functions and matrix manipulation. We computed the elements twice, once storing the images in the virtual memory of the user process, as reported in Table 1, and once using a frame buffer with microcode line-drawing routines (which we call an *enhanced* frame buffer). All images were computed at 512 by 512 resolution.

Execution profiling explains where the cpu time is spent in the four programs. Table 2 shows the distribution of the user cpu time among three major phases of computation, described below:

1. generate,
2. shade and render, and
3. draw particles

The unaccounted time was consumed by global initialization, argument parsing, and sorting the data base. We also omit the time spent drawing trunks on the Near Trees, because they were not modelled by particle systems.

6.1 Generate

The details of model generation depend on the type of object being modelled. For example, one-fifth of the tree generation time is spent in the sin and cos routines, computing branch vectors based on the angle a branch makes with the trunk or parent branch. Simpler stochastic processes are used to generate the Fire element.

Model generation uses random numbers extensively. The incremental pseudo-random number generator in our math library takes about twenty-seven minutes to compute the twenty million random numbers used for the trees in Figure 4. In contrast, inline code accessing a pre-computed table of a few hundred random numbers takes less than four minutes. The table-driven approach creates satisfactory visual diversity and can provide, at approximately equal cost, random numbers drawn from any type of distribution. The visual success of this optimization has been observed by others [5,13].

6.2 Shade and Render

The second phase performs shading and perspective calculations, clips particles, and sorts them into screen-depth buckets. Perspective and clipping routines typically take between five and ten percent of the program's total running time. Shading also consumes about five to ten percent of the compute time for the trees and grass. Less time was spent shading the Far Trees than the Near Trees because simpler lighting models were used and external shadows were omitted. The least amount of time was spent on the shade and render phase for the Fire element, because it has the simplest shading models and requires no visible-surface calculations.

Floating point matrix and mathematical library routines accounted for about one-fifth of the total user time. These routines are called during both of the first two phases, but not in the final phase which uses only screen coordinates. Additional floating point operations are performed by in-line code in procedures outside the math and matrix libraries. For example, we examined a procedure that accounts for one-third of the tree generation time. More than three-fourths of the instructions in its inner loop were floating point instructions.

	Far Trees *Figure 4*	Near Trees *Figure 3*	Grass *Figure 3*	Fires *Figure 2*
number of frames	1	1	1	11
user cpu time (hh:mm:ss)	5:31:18	10:27:27	4:44:31	52:50
memory (Mb)	4.95	10.17	--	5.04
lines drawn (1000's)	592	1067	416	268
lines per frame (1000's)	592	1067	416	24

TABLE 1. Overall measurements for particle systems programs

	without frame buffer				with enhanced frame buffer			
	Far Trees	Near Trees	Grass	Fires	Far Trees	Near Trees	Grass	Fires
generate	32.5	11.4	13.8	28.3	47.6	18.6	25.0	37.9
shade and render	25.1	28.4	32.3	23.6	30.3	45.1	57.6	30.1
draw particles	33.2	49.9	51.6	41.0	14.8	19.6	13.2	23.6
total	90.8	89.7	97.7	92.9	92.7	83.3	95.8	91.6

TABLE 2. Percent of user time spent in each phase of computation

† UNIX is a trademark of Bell Laboratories.

6.3 Draw Particles

The final phase takes as input the description of particle primitives in two-dimensional screen coordinates and draws the primitives into the frame buffer. Our enhanced frame buffers have microcode routines for drawing anti-aliased lines and circles. The host provides the x and y coordinates for line endpoints, the width of the line, and its colour; the frame buffer then determines which pixels to modify. When a virtual frame buffer is used, both line-drawing calculations and address computation are performed in software, and drawing particles is the most expensive phase of the computation. As Tables 2 and 3 show, the frame buffer successfully takes over much of this work, leaving the host cpu to spend most of its time generating, shading, and rendering the model. Furthermore, the real frame buffer provides physical memory for the entire image and reduces the operating system costs for virtual memory management.

	Without frame buffer	With enhanced frame buffer	ratio with / without
Far Trees	5:31:18	4:06:05	.74
Near Trees	10:27:27	6:13:52	.60
Grass	4:44:31	2:34:42	.54
Fire	52:50	41:28	.78

TABLE 3. User time with and without a real frame buffer

An important advantage of the virtual frame buffer is its ability to store data of an arbitrary precision. The particle systems algorithm builds up a picture by repeatedly adding very small amounts of colour to a pixel. Experience indicates that eight bits per primary colour, while sufficient for displaying a finished image, are inadequate for computing some images. A real frame buffer with twelve to sixteen bits per colour and functions for drawing anti-aliased particle primitives would provide valuable hardware support for rendering particle systems.

Table 2 shows that Near Trees consumed proportionally more particle drawing time than Far Trees. Because the Near Trees particles appear larger on the screen, the line drawing calculations for each particle take longer.

6.4 Summary

Notably, no single phase of the computation dominates. Theoretical results obtained by Fournier show that the cost to compute a stochastic parametric surface by a fractal subdivision algorithm is linear in the number of points to be displayed [5]. He argues that if the subdivision algorithm is implemented efficiently, the time required to generate the model should be less than the time to transform, shade, and display it. From our measurements, we similarly conclude that the cost of creating an image with particle systems is not specifically due to the expense of generating the stochastic model, but is more generally explained by the inherent need to process a great deal of complexity in all phases of image creation. Even when we offload most of the costs of drawing primitives to the frame buffer, more time is typically required to manage, draw, and render the model than to generate it.

It is difficult to compare our measurements with the costs of creating synthetic images using traditional models. Images as complex as our forest scenes have rarely been modelled without using stochastic, or other algorithmic, methods to generate detail. When they have, the modelling effort must typically be measured in human design time. The costs of shading, visible surface calculations, and rendering are also difficult to compare with previous work, because few other measurements are available. Crow [4] and Whitted and Weimer [14] have published some measurements for pictures using conventional models, but their images were much simpler than ours. An interesting area for future work is the measurement and performance analysis of more general-purpose modelling and rendering software. We are currently investigating this area.

7. Conclusions

We have demonstrated that particle systems are able to model complex and structured objects. Simple primitives, given a set of relationships that bind them into a cohesive whole, can be used to produce complex models with extensive and varied detail. These relationships must specify the constraints by which millions of particles are dependent on one another. Because our new particle systems are more structured and dependent, we have developed more sophisticated algorithms to model their dynamics.

Particle systems were first used to model an amorphous phenomenon, fire, and it seemed natural to use a volume-filling representation. The tree and grass images demonstrate that volume-filling representations, such as particle systems, can effectively model solid objects. Such objects are conventionally modelled by surface-based techniques or solid geometry.

Procedural modelling techniques can be used to create models with more detail than a human designer could ever specify, and stochastic approaches can provide a rich variety of detail. Unfortunately, it is infeasible to compute exact solutions to the visible surface and shading problems for the enormous amount of detail that we can generate. Our algorithms are based on the belief that exact solutions are not always necessary in scenes with great visual complexity. We described an approximate painter's algorithm for visible surface determination and introduced probabilistic approaches to shading. Shadow masks, implemented as texture maps, simplified the task of adding shadows to the image.

Performance analysis shows that the computation is distributed relatively evenly among the three major phases of our particle systems algorithms: model generation, shading and rendering, and particle drawing. In particular, the cost of generating complex, structured models does not dominate the computation, as one might expect. Instead, the expense arises from the need to process a vast amount of three-dimensional detail throughout all phases of the computation in order to create the visual richness that we desire.

8. Acknowledgements

We would like to thank the members of the Computer Graphics Project of Lucasfilm Ltd for forming a stimulating and enjoyable working environment. John Lasseter contributed significantly to the visual design of the forest scenes and provided welcome encouragement. Eben Ostby developed special compositing software for the forest backgrounds. The shading algorithms profited from our discussions with Rob Cook. The work of the second author was supported in part by a State of California Microelectronics fellowship.

9. Bibliography

[1] Aono, M. and T. L. Kunii, Botanical tree image generation, *IEEE Computer Graphics and Applications 4*, 5 (May 1984), 10-34.

[2] Bloomenthal, J., Modeling natural trees with space curves, *SIGGRAPH 85, Computer Graphics 19*, 3 (July 1985).

[3] Brooks, J., R. Murarka, D. Onuoha, F. Rahn and H. Steingurg, An extension of the combinatorial geometry technique for modeling vegetation and terrain features, Contract report 159 for USA Ballistic Research Laboratories, Mathematical Applications Group, Inc., June 1974.

[4] Crow, F. C., A more flexible image generation environment, *SIGGRAPH 82, Computer Graphics 16*, 3 (July 1982), 9-18.

[5] Fournier, A., D. Fussell and L. Carpenter, Computer rendering of stochastic models, *Comm. ACM 25*, 6 (June 1982), 371-384.

[6] Gardner, G. Y., Simulation of natural scenes using textured quadric surfaces, *SIGGRAPH 84, Computer Graphics 18*, 3 (July 1984), 11-20.

[7] Lucasfilm Ltd, *The Adventures of André and Wally B.*, (film), Aug. 1984.

[8] Ludwig, C., *Maxfield Parrish*, Watson-Guptill, New York, 1973.

[9] Mandelbrot, B. B., *Fractals: Form, chance and dimension*, Freeman, San Francisco, 1977.

[10] Marshall, R., R. Wilson and W. Carlson, Procedure models for generating three-dimensional terrain, *SIGGRAPH 80, Computer Graphics 14*, 3 (July 1980), 154-162.

[11] Paramount, Genesis Demo from *Star Trek II: The Wrath of Khan*, in *SIGGRAPH Video Review Number 11*, June 1982.

[12] Reeves, W. T., Particle systems—A technique for modelling a class of fuzzy objects, *SIGGRAPH 83, Computer Graphics 17*, 3 (July 1983), 359-376.

[13] Smith, A. R., Plants, fractals, and formal languages, *SIGGRAPH 84, Computer Graphics 18*, 3 (July 1984), 1-10.

[14] Whitted, T. and D. M. Weimer, A software testbed for the development of 3d raster graphics systems, *Transactions on Graphics 1*, 1 (Jan. 1982), 43-58.

[15] Williams, L., Casting curved shadows on curved surfaces, *SIGGRAPH 78, Computer Graphics 12*, 3 (Aug. 1978), 270-274.

Panels

Perspective - Computer Graphics in Europe and Japan

Chairs: Jose Encarnacao (Technische Hochschule Darmstadt)
Tosiyasu L. Kunii (University of Tokyo)

Moderator: Bertram Herzog (Herzog Associates, Inc.)

Panelists: Frank Lillehagen (Consultant)
Xavier Nicolas (Sogitek)
Yukari Shirota (University of Tokyo)
Wolfgang Strasser (Technische Hochschule Darmstadt)
Shunichiro Tsurumi (Hitachi Ltd.)
Takao Wachi (Osaka City University)

This panel will present noteworthy activities from Europe and Japan. The panelists will emphasize important and recent work from their respective regions. The topics will include general computer graphics, CAD/CAM and art.

Issues at the Interface: an Historical Trace of Prompting, Concurrency, Signification and Ease of Use

Chair: Robert M. Dunn (The Cadware Group, Ltd.)

Panelists:
Sara Bly (Xerox Office Systems)
Richard Guedj (SiGRID)
William J. Poduska (Apollo Computer, Inc.)
William Lasser (Metaphor Computer Systems)

Beginning with Sketchpad and continuing to Macintosh and beyond, designers and users of interactive graphics systems and applications have refined the nature of the working graphical interface between a person and a computer. The panel will trace the changing uses of graphical symbols and icons; address the evolution of concurrency in windows, menus and task activation; examine mechanisms for gaining attention and prompting for reactions; and focus on reducing visual, physical and psychological stress via improved screen design and applied principles of graphical presentation.

Sizing the Market: Where Do All Those Numbers Come From?

Chair: Carl Machover (Machover Associates Corporation)

Panelists:
Charles Foundyller (Daratech, Inc.)
Robert H. Katzive (Gnostic Concepts, Inc.)
Neil Kleinman (International Data Corporation)
Christopher M. Saleh (Data General Corporation)
Beth Tucker (Dataquest, Inc.)

Forecasters say that 6.2 billion dollars worth of industrial computer graphics hardware, software and services will be sold in 1985, that 2.6 billion dollars worth of CAD/CAM equipment was delivered in 1984 and that "hardcopy" will grow an average of 25 percent per year over the next five years. How do they know?

The panel includes market forecasters from industry and leading market research companies. They will discuss how such forecasts are made, how accurate they are, how good past forecasts have been and what the problems are in developing these forecasts.

Animated Computer Graphics in Television Broadcasting

Chairs: Christine Barton (National Broadcasting Company, Inc.)
Carl Rosendahl (Pacific Data Images)

Panelists: Robert Brandel (National Broadcasting Company, Inc.)
Larry Elin (MAGI)
Susan Rugtiv (Ketchum Advertising)
Douglas Towey (Columbia Broadcasting System, Inc.)

Issues involved in computer generated video animation will be addressed by the producers of the video and the clients who use the product. The producers of computer generated video include independent production houses and production departments within the television networks. The clients include advertising agencies and the news, sports and entertainment departments of the television networks themselves. Topics to be discussed include design control, equipment used and cost. Issues such as in-house production vs. contracted production and daily production schedules vs. longer term promotional projects will also be discussed.

Font Formats

Chair: Charles Bigelow (Stanford University)

Panelists: Philippe Coueignoux (Data Business Vision)
John Hobby (Stanford University)
Peter Karow (Karow-Rubow-Weber GmbH)
Vaughn Pratt (Stanford University and Sun Microsystems, Inc.)
Luis Trabb-Pardo (Imagen Corp.)
John Warnock (Adobe Systems, Inc.)

Methods of font representation for typography on display screens and printers such as Metafont, PostScript and Ikarus will be presented. Issues to be discussed include: the form of representation, transformation, data compaction, processing speed, software and hardware implementation, device independence, interchange standards, output legibility and aesthetics.

Aesthetics of Computer Graphics

Chair: Mihai Nadin (Rhode Island School of Design)

Panelists:
Charles Csuri (Cranston-Csuri Productions)
Frank Dietrich (Artist)
Thomas Linehan (Ohio State University)
Hiroshi Kawano (Metropolitan (Tokyo) College of Technology)

As graphics technology and software become more mature, it is critical to examine the aesthetics of computer generated images. Effective visual communication and artistic expression are dependent on aesthetic quality. Issues that emerge for artists, designers and computer scientists include: the formal attributes of images, aesthetic evaluation criteria and the desire to detect or implement aesthetic qualities. The panelists, having studied these and other issues, will present and debate their diverse viewpoints.

The Creation of New Kinds of Interactive Environments in Art, Education, and Entertainment

Chair: Stephen Wilson (San Francisco State University)

Panelists:
David Backer (Mirror Systems)
Myron Krueger (University of Connecticut)
Peter Richards (Exploratorium)
Sonia Sheridan (School of the Art Institute (Emeritus))
David Ucko (Chicago Museum of Science and Industry)

Artists and researchers are using the computer's interactive capabilities to develop innovative kinds of responsive settings. The gestures, sounds and other participant activities are used to control the flow of computer-mediated graphic, sound and kinetic events. Illustrated descriptions of several responsive settings will be presented. Panelists will discuss implications for changing traditionally passive art, education and museum settings.

Real-Time Simulation in the Real World

Chair: Zsuzsanna Molnar (Silicon Graphics, Inc.)

Panelists: Pieter Buning (NASA Ames Research Center)
Peter Doenges (Evans and Sutherland Computer Corporation)
Robert Langridge (University of California, San Franciso)
Tom Lasinski (NASA Ames Research Center)
Randy Smith (SRI International)

Flight simulation was the first well-known real-time simulation application using computer graphics. New computer architectures, combined with fast interactive graphics, extend the scope of simulation to encompass ever more realistic visual simulation as well as the modeling of objects and processes: computer prototyping. Panelists will discuss evolutionary trends, costs and effectiveness of real-time simulation citing examples from flight simulation, drug design, wind tunnel simulation, the testing of on-the-road car behavior and robotics.

Fundamental Algorithms: Retrospect and Prospect

Chair: Rae A. Earnshaw (George Washington Univ. and the Univ. of Leeds)

Panelists: James H. Clark (Stanford University and Silicon Graphics, Inc.)
A. Robin Forrest (University of East Anglia)
Robert D. Parslow (Brunel University)
David F. Rogers (U.S. Naval Academy)

Many advances and innovations have been made since the earliest line generation algorithm formulated by Bresenham in 1963. Extensions have been devised to allow the generation of arcs, conics and curves, and the exploitation of gray scale and color. Solutions to the aliasing problem have been devised; good quality pictures can now be produced on inexpensive displays. More recently, a study of program transformations has suggested new ways for the automatic generation of algorithms. Current progress will be reviewed and possible new developments and advances will be discussed.

Computer Graphics Technology

Chair: John Staudhammer (University of Florida)

Panelists:
Dean Bailey (Intel Corporation)
Steven Dines (Advanced Micro Devices)
Louis J. Doctor (Raster Technologies, Inc.)
Karl Guttag (Texas Instruments)
Jack L. Hancock (Wells Fargo Bank)
Klaus W. Lindenberg (Martin-Marietta Aerospace)
Edmund Y. Sun (Weitek Corporation)

The extremely rapid growth of computer graphics is due, in large measure, to the application of leading-edge technology devices. Initially, these devices were not inspired by graphics applications. However, the market has become so large that display oriented semi-conductor devices are becoming specialty product lines. In turn these devices are leading to different display hardware architectures which will profoundly influence emerging capabilities in computer graphics. The future will be shaped as much by these technical innovations as by the economic trends they engender. The panel will examine the forces behind these technological changes and estimate their influence on directions for the computer graphics industry.

Solid Modeling With Hardware

Chair: Pierre J. Malraison (GE-Calma)

Panelists:
Gershon Kedem (Duke University)
Greg Lee (Weitek Corporation)
Donald Meagher (Phoenix Data Systems)

This panel's focus is on special purpose hardware for solid modeling. Solid modeling concerns the definition, display, manipulation and analysis of objects stored as the complete, unambiguous representation of a bounded region of three-dimensional space. The three primary representation methods, constructive solid geometry, boundary representation and spatial enumeration, will be discussed. Recent developments in these representation methods and their hardware implementations will be described. The panel will conclude with a dialog with the audience to predict future developments.

NOTES

NOTES

Index

Abram, Greg ... 53
Ansaldi, Silvia ... 131
Austin, John D. ... 111
Badler, Norman I. ... 255
Blau, Ricki ... 313
Bloomenthal, Jules ... 305
Bouville, Christian ... 45
Brooks, Jr., Frederick P. ... 111
Buxton, William ... 215
Cardelli, Luca ... 199
Cohen, Michael F. ... 31
Demko, Stephen ... 271
Dempsey, Elizabeth P. ... 191
Dippé, Mark A. Z. ... 69
Duff, Tom ... 41
Eyles, John G. ... 111
Falcidieno, Bianca ... 131
Floriani, Leila De ... 131
Fuchs, Henry ... 111
Gardner, Geoffrey Y. ... 297
Girard, Michael ... 263
Goldfeather, Jack ... 111
Grant, Charles W. ... 79
Green, Mark ... 205
Greenberg, Donald P. ... 31
Greene, Richard ... 103
Hill, Ralph ... 215
Hirota, Katsuhiko ... 95
Hodges, Laurie ... 271
Hultquist, Jeff P. ... 111
Ikesaka, Morio ... 95
Inoue, Kouichi ... 95
Ishihata, Hiroaki ... 95
Ishii, Mitsuo ... 95
Kajiya, James T. ... 15
Kakimoto, Masanori ... 95
Lee, Mark E. ... 61
Lerner, Douglas M. ... 85
Lieberman, Henry ... 181
Maciejewski, Anthony A. ... 263
Max, Nelson L. ... 85
Middleditch, Alan E. ... 161
Nakamae, Eihachiro ... 23
Naylor, Bruce ... 271
Nelson, Greg ... 235
Nishita, Tomoyuki ... 23
Olsen, Jr., Dan R. ... 191
Pavlidis, Theo ... 225
Peachey, Darwyn R. ... 279
Perlin, Ken ... 287
Pike, Rob ... 199
Poulton, John ... 111
Pratt, Vaughan ... 151
Redner, Richard A. ... 61
Reeves, William T. ... 313
Rogge, Roy ... 191
Rowley, Peter ... 215
Samet, Hanan ... 121
Sato, Hiroyuki ... 95
Sato, Keiji ... 95
Sears, Kenneth H. ... 161
Shoemake, Ken ... 245
Spach, Susan ... 111
Steketee, Scott N. ... 255
Tamminen, Markku ... 121
Toth, Daniel L. ... 171
Uselton, Samuel P. ... 61
Van Wyk, Christopher J. ... 225
Westover, Lee ... 53
Whitted, Turner ... 53
Wold, Erling Henry ... 69
Yamaguchi, Fujio ... 141

Image Credits

PROCEEDINGS FRONT COVER

Erehwon
Michael Weliky
© University of California, Berkeley, CA, Graduate Group in Neurobiology.

TITLE PAGE

Space Station
Fowler/Donahue
© Boeing Aerospace Co.

PROCEEDINGS BACK COVER

1 **Fiero Test Drive**
Digital Scene Simulation[sm] by Digital Productions Los Angeles, CA, U.S.A.
© Copyright, 1985. All Rights Reserved.

2 **Seaside Cafe**
Adam. B. Chin
© Pacific Data Images.

3 **The Scene With Corkscrew**
Shoichi Kitaoka
© University of Utah, Computer Science Department.

4 **Quadric Clouds**
Geoffrey Y. Gardner,
© Grumman Corporation.

5 **Frontiers of Chaos**
H. O. Peitgen, P. H. Richter, D. Saope, M. Prufer, H. Jurgens,
© University of Bremen, Graphics Lab.

6 **Untitled**
Steve Martino
© Cranston/Csuri Productions.